W9-DAU-600

All About

MOTORSPORTS

The Race Fan
and Beginner's Complete Guide

Dave Taube

WINDMILL PUBLISHING

JAN -- 2002

ISBN: 0–9638358–0–7

Publisher's Cataloging in Publication Data:

Taube, David Allen.
    All about motorsports : the race fan and beginner's complete
guide / Dave Taube.
      p.   cm.
    Includes bibliographical references.
    ISBN 0–9638358–0–7

    1. Motorsports.   I. Title.

GV1019.2.T38 1996   796.72
                                       QBI96–30066

To order extra copies:

Windmill Publishing
Dept. BP
209 1/2 South Main St.
Swanton, Ohio 43558

_____ number of copies at $24.95 +
$3.00 shipping.
Do not send cash. Please send check,
cashier's check, or money order.
Credit cards accepted.
☐ MasterCard   ☐ Visa
Card number _____
Name on card _____
Expiration date _____

Ohio residents include 6% sales tax ($1.50)

Include your name and shipping address.
(Please print clearly)

Okay to copy this page for ordering purposes only.

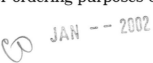

Contents

Acknowledgments

A very special thanks to the following individuals and/or racing companies for providing their assistance in the making of this book.

- Carolyn Nagel and Sharon Lewallen of Swanton, Ohio (for helping me on the computer)

- Dave Klockowski, advanced foreign car, 327 S. Reynolds Rd, Toledo, Ohio 43615 (419) 531-9988

- Mike Madden, manager, racing operations, TRV Motorsport, Inc, 300 N. Westwood, Toledo, Ohio 43607 (419) 535-5665 and 411 Doreman, Indianapolis, Indiana, 46202 (317) 639-0340

- Allen Tyler Motorsports, 67 Dixie Hwy, Rossford, Ohio 43460

- Bob Cicora, Cicora's Body Shop, 104 Church St, Swanton, Ohio 43558 (419) 826-0630

- Dale Wheating, Swanton, Ohio 43558

- Shane Yoder of J & G Industries, Toledo, Ohio

- A super special thanks to former Indy car driver Jerry Grant. (with just a tiny bit of luck, he would have won the 1972 Indianapolis 500) Jerry Grant, Cooper Automotive, 930 Roosevelt Pkwy, Suite 200, Chesterfield, Missouri 63017

High Speed Confusion

by Jerry Grant

The world of motorsports is unlike any athletic endeavor there is. Whether that is a statement condoning its existence or one of exaltation is left to individual interpretation.

The word "race" conjures up the idea of "speed", even outside the realm of sports. There's the race to the moon, that the U.S. won, to the race for the Whitehouse every four years. But for the purposes of athletic competition, racing isn't so much an act of rote speed as it is an act in relativity of speed.

Unlike the traditional ball-and-stick type of sports, there are many ways to race. Even though there are many levels of . . . say . . . football, basketball and baseball, (from pee-wee to the major leagues) there aren't many *types* in each of those sports, if any at all. That isn't a complaint, just a statement of fact. On the other hand, . . . racing not only takes place at many levels, but in several types. Even a non-motorized race event such as a college track meet has several kinds of racing contests. Add a motor, two, three or four wheels . . . all the different kinds of terrain they compete on, and what you have is a conglomeration of choices. Then with all those choices are the different classes within a specific type of racing. If that doesn't confuse a beginner trying to enter motorsports, the costs involved with this sport certainly will. Therein, admittedly, lies one of the biggest initial problems with motorsports. This is especially so with those considering this endeavor, if not the casual racing fan.

It does take money to race, and usually a lot of it when compared to the investment in other sports. If every racing prospect started racing at the level they wanted, everyone would be competing at the upper echelon, . . . such as Indy, Daytona, Monaco, Lemans, Baja and the AA/fuel dragsters of NHRA. But as Mick Jagger of the 'Rolling Stones' put it in one of his older songs . . . "you can't always get what you want". That's the reality of racing, just as in life itself. It's true for the big league racers also.

If we lived in a financially perfect world, all the money on earth couldn't buy a ride in one of those high-profile events, because you still need talent and experience to reach those levels. It's that way in all (professional) sports.

Unfortunately in racing, talent alone isn't always enough. Sometimes it's hard to know if one even has talent or not, which can be very frustrating. But it doesn't always have to be that way if a beginner is organized properly in learning this game. Racing's inherent lack of a learning hierarchy or a regimented system for moving up contributes to much of the confusion, . . . if not by a lack of knowledge then surely by the lack of finances for competitive racing equipment.

There are two areas of racing pretty much taken for granted by the average fan. First, in racing, you can compete to win or compete for its own sake. In other words, while it's extremely hard to win a race of any kind, the important thing is to be "out there" . . . as it's sometimes referred to in motorsports. The second point is most other sports require a more specific physical ability which all too many times is cut short by advancing age. Just when many people or athletes in this case, start to reach the zenith of their mental maturity, the body gives out. Racing doesn't have that problem. Many times race drivers continue to successfully compete well into their forties and sometimes their fifties, especially at the amateur levels. Make no misguided assumption about older drivers. These racers are "mixing it up" and sometimes even winning against the young-

Jerry Grant has won over 130 major races in his career. He was the first racer in the world to officially average over 200 mph in qualifications in a closed course, purpose-built racer. It was done at the Ontario 500 Indy race at the former Ontario Motor Speedway in Ontario, California. He has also driven in NASCAR events for Chrysler in 1967 and 1968 and won the world's manufacturing title for Ford with Dan Gurney at such courses as Daytona, Sebring and Lemans. He has also competed in the Indy 500 10 times almost winning it in 1972; but unfortunately was disqualified to 12th place because of a fueling infraction. He was battling eventual winner Mark Donahue with just a few laps to go. He had to pit, but was refueled from the wrong tank.

sters who sometimes have superior racing equipment. So therefore, money isn't always the sole ingredient for success. It certainly is a large factor. There is no doubt about that. Still, a successful racer needs talent, which can be more developed from experience in this sport than it can be from (untapped talent of) most other sports. While some people are born with more athletic ability than others, the less gifted athletes have a much better chance to develop skill from "scratch" through diligence and experience in racing, than . . . say . . . to hit a 95 mph fastball from a (major league) pitcher. This is one of the things that makes motorsports great. It doesn't necessarily pander to those born with a "silver spoon in their mouth", both talentwise nor financially.

Terry Grant

1 | What to expect from Motorsports

The decision to go racing isn't something you'll embark upon, hopefully, after blowing the doors off the star quarterback with his hot, new, expensive sports car. Remember it was only in your over active imagination. Sure, it was late Saturday night after the big football game and "Mr. Golden Arm" (as you call him) had a cheerleaders-all-over-him kind of game. Meanwhile . . . you were just sitting there on the bench itching to blindside the SOB from a 30 yard head-start. But . . . your fear of looking like an idiot overruled your sense of valor.

So after the usual pit-stop at the local hangout afterwards, you're ready to hop in your souped-up VW "Bug" and point it home. But . . . oh no . . . here comes "Mr. QB USA" in his shiny, female-filled Lamborghini Countach. Well, this kid's daddy is either filthy rich or he's takin' under-the-center . . . er . . . I mean TABLE payments from those UCLA alumnus. (that reads, **U**tterly **C**osmos-**L**ike **A**sseted)

Man . . . you just want to cram your fist down his throat. But before you can catch yourself, you blurt out across eons of empty beer cans and soda cups, "hey you . . . that's right, you . . . with all the babes hangin' on ya . . . your car's a pig!" Whoa . . . silence sets in. Will there be a brawl or is it just another trip out to thee old dragstrip later on. Well, the rest is history.

You knew that gosh-awful road better than anyone, afterall, you used it endlessly. Nevermind "Mr. QB" was smart enough to ignore you. You knew he had nothing to win and a lot to lose. Besides, he had to pay the babes their due of attention. Sheesh, the price one pays for popularity.

Okay, so "Joe Montana, Jr" goes on to further stardom . . . who cares . . . you're the next cross between "Big Daddy" Don Garlits, AJ Foyt and Richard Petty!

All kidding aside, let's hope you've put a little more thought into racing than just a passionate interlude with intimidation. The decision to race (or involve yourself as a mechanic or crew member, to somewhat of a lesser degree) needs to start with careful thought, burning desire and a strong belief in yourself. (not to mention money . . . that helps)

This author/racer certainly believes you must take that attitude. Why? That quarterback you thought you intimidated has talent, like it or not. Yes, he was born with some raw talent, (I said some "raw" talent) but he still had to work to develop it. Don't let his "fluff" (image) lead you down the wrong road.

REALITY CHECK

To race automobiles, or anything else, I do *not* believe for one second God-given talent automatically and necessarily wins races. Racing requires much more than just athletic ability. Do you think people like Al Unser Jr, Michael Andretti and Kyle Petty inherited a racing bug? They could just as easily been born to (poor) sharecroppers and they'd still win races.

Racing talent's educational (learned), mental, financial and yes, athletic, but it's not solely "pure" genetics which makes a great driver. Yes, they had advantages, but don't knock it, if you had that privilege you'd take full advantage of it also. You'd be pretty stupid not to. Those three racers were thoroughly schooled at an early age. Yes, they also had relatively good financial backing, but that's life sometimes. Everybody knows life's not fair anyway. At the risk of sounding like I'm preaching, the fact you can eat three meals a day should have you counting your blessings compared to many people in this world.

None-the-less, those three still had to go through the learning process with all its disappointments, letdowns and sometimes, tragedy. Being sons of famous racers guaranteed them absolutely nothing, except a better chance at developing a skill and/or a desire.

After you've committed yourself to racing, you'll experience guaranteed disappointments of all kinds. The main reason for that is inexperience. Murphy's law will rear its ugly head. (understatement) There's the mechanics or physics concerning this sport; the driver can be a problem; the weather; track conditions; family; politics and the biggie of biggies, lack of money. The list could be longer, but hopefully, you get the idea what I'm taking about.

Then there is this kind of silent situation which can be a problem with mostly young drivers. It's that ego! This problem can become magnified, but nowhere near as much as a lack of "raw" talent. But the truly committed type will never or seldom admit lack of talent to themselves or anyone else. Why? That ego? Could be. But don't take me the wrong way, who is saying that's bad? Still, the answers are complex and numerous. Since I'm not a psychologist I won't get into that area. All I know or need to know here is that racing, with its inherent problems, gets magnified to yourself (that ego) and others. (much to your embarrassment)

AS PLAIN AS THE NOSE ON YOUR FACE

As you get more experienced and older, you learn to cope with ego. Still, nothing helps you handle it better than the realiza-

tion of one important point. What is that point? Well, it's my belief racing is a sport which is simple, clear and concise. This certainly isn't obvious to you, the racer, but it usually is to others, like race fans, friends and family. (especially your spouse who is dead-set against racing because of its perceived dangers; I said "perceived"; more on that later) Also, it may even be obvious to your crew (but not always) and even racers you compete with.

Why is racing a clear and/or obvious appearing sport? It's not! It only looks that way to the man not involved. To the man shelling out his own blood, guts and money, it's very complicated indeed. But this same man knows it appears just the opposite (simple) to others. I came to realize this when a buddy asked me why I don't forget about a nagging racecar handling problem I once had for quite awhile and just buy a new (state of the art) suspension. Gee, wasn't that simple? Why didn't I think of that? Oh . . . I forgot . . . I'm on a teachers salary. (yes, occasionally, very occasionally, you just can't throw money at problems and expect them to be instantly solved; even in racing)

What's perceived in racing (it's easy if you're loaded, whether one's talented or not) and what's reality can be very misleading. So you understand, as I stated previously, in racing, everything seems simple and clear to most people except yourself. For example, when a racecar is dead on the track, it's dead; it's go or no go. Who or what's at fault in a situation like that doesn't matter . . . it's not going to win the race.

If things like that continue too often, the young or inexperienced racer loses confidence. That starts to wear on the ego because it appears as a lack of effort, ability, foresight, etc. You feel you have no one to blame but yourself. Well, . . . anyway, that's how you may feel others perceive you in that particular situation. Why? It's because you're "OUT THERE" as it's called in racing circles. It's Murphy's Law, 90% of racing luck is bad. Once you're out there, doing the actual hands-on job of driving the vehicle, you're relatively (and in appearance) on your own in the eyes of others.

MIND GAMES

Racing appears as a nonteam sport and your talent or lack thereof can present itself. When things go wrong as they do, and as fast as they can at times, there is nobody "to pick you up" immediately, like there is in team sports. You . . . the driver, the heart of it all, as you may initially feel, is what makes or breaks the "show".

Are you getting the idea racing is part head game? You ought to! Racing is very much a head game. Chances are, especially as a young and "raw" racer, you'll fail to understand or accept that even a great baseball player fails 7 of 10 times in the batters box. That same player can still make up for a bad day on defense. (or the second game of a doubleheader) Consider that same man can also have a poor game defensively. Does that mean his team will lose the game? Heck no, he has eight other players who can make up for his bad day.

In racing that doesn't happen, usually. When your machine decides to take a break or you take a break, (brain fade) or you're a victim of someone else's negligence, then forget about winning anything that day. Even if the problem is quickly solved the chances are greatly reduced to win or finish high in the final outcome. This is why those outside of racing feel this sport is clear, concise, cut and dry. The problems are obvious and therefore magnified to them, . . . but not to you! That, young man, (or rookie) can do a number on your head. Take heart. Don't shoulder all the bad things that can happen in racing on yourself, or on bad luck either. You must be patient. It's part of racing as much as injuries are to a multimillion dollar athlete.

PARALYSIS OF ANALYSIS

In racing, especially at the beginning when you're shelling out your own money, I doubt you'll lack effort. No way! That in itself can be a problem. I know that may sound contradictory to what I've said earlier, but trying too hard to figure out something that really wasn't there in the first place can cre-ate other bad situations. If you don't understand the problem I just mentioned, you undoubtedly will once you start this (sometimes confusing) sport.

The best example I can give you is when you have had a poor finish in a race. You just can't simply accept to yourself you've had a bad day, for whatever reason. It's something elses fault. (not necessarily someone else) You're tired, . . . poor racing equipment, (a popular excuse) a fight with the wife, etc.

Anyway, you might feel the handling of the racer wasn't right, therefore, you've made adjustments. The next time out on the track you find out, much to your chagrin, the racecar is handling worse then it did before. You may think you adjusted it incorrectly or not enough. Either way it's all wrong and now you're one, even more, confused individual. If only you knew you had no problem in the first place. That bad day you had could have been remedied by eight hours sleep, possibly.

Hang in there pal! If you have a brain you'll eventually figure things out. I hope I've eliminate some confusion. Meanwhile, what you do learn in these early stages of racing, with all that effort and money you spent, will not go wasted. If you're harboring any thoughts of giving it up, . . . don't just yet. Be patient. What you've learned in these crucial early stages is probably more than you think.

What do I consider as early stages or the crucial learning process? That depends on how much a person is able to commit themself to this sport. In other words, how much money can you afford to depart with? In my case, I could race only 2 or 3 weekends a year. That's not good at all. Now, after 14 years of racing, I'm beginning to understand this sport more clearly. (at least I think I am) I was lucky to learn anything at all at that pace. I didn't have much help. That's my fault.

THE LEARNING CURVE

A racer should try spending about 8 to 10 weekends a year racing. That's an average. You should bunch those weekends in a series of 2 or 3 groups; 3 weekends in a row in the spring; 3 weekends out of 4 in the summer; 4 weekends in a row during the fall, etc. This way, you'll retain what you learned in racing more efficiently. Too much time between races and you may find yourself learning over again. That relearning process slows everything down and eats up your money unnecessarily.

On the other hand, don't race too many weekends in a row. That'll tire you out, especially if you're short on help. More importantly, I doubt you'll be able to anyhow. Even the best race machines breakdown and need to be serviced and repaired. You can count on that! The weekends between races aren't just for your rest, but also for the attention your vehicle needs. I'm not exaggerating when I say for every hour of track time I spend in the racer, I spend another 30 hours under it. (probably closer to 40 hours) I tear the racer down completely, bolt for bolt, every 3 years, but then I like doing that.

Well anyhow, I'm getting a bit off course. I was talking a paragraph or two ago about how racing can be frustrating, ego-altering, confusing and every other negative known to man.

WHERE PREPARATION MEETS OPPORTUNITY

Now, here's another subject, . . . LUCK. Yes, I talked briefly about that earlier. There is such a thing as racing luck. But like I said before, most of it is bad, . . . like about 90% of it. I used to be a nonbeliever in luck or the lack thereof. I was taught through my football training that luck was something one created by hard work, . . . you know, . . . luck was where "preparation meets opportunity". Well, that may be the case with football, but it sure as heck isn't true in racing!

Unfortunately, bad luck is a part of racing, I'll get arguments on that, but you won't convince me otherwise. Don't get me wrong, poor luck wasn't any excuse for my slow start in this sport. Everyone, and I mean everyone will have bad luck. But when you don't prepare mentally for a race, or you compromise yourself by improperly prepping

your equipment, you're setting yourself up for a failure out on the track. That pal isn't bad luck at all, that's incompetence.

But, . . . that high quality bolt you properly installed and torqued to the recommended foot-pounds can still fail. That can send flying loose . . . say . . . a critical suspension component, bolting you and your machine off into the "bushes" at well over 100 mph . . . now that's bad luck.

So, . . . yes . . . there is bad luck. Yes, racing has much more than its share of it. It's an unfortunate part of this game. Take solace though, everybody has it. Some have more of it than others, but then, that's a relative matter. Take Mario Andretti for instance. I consider his luck poor. Some don't. Why? Some say he can have bad luck in a race, but afterwards he's still Mario Andretti. I understand the thinking, it's understandable, but misdirected. Has everything this man's done simply presented to him on a silver platter? Do you feel things were easy for him or any other racer when they first raced?

LUCK ISN'T BOUGHT

Mario should of won the Indy 500 at least 2 times more than he has. But he didn't and that's racing sometimes. I'm sure he knows poor luck is just as much a part of racing as the strike zone is to the batter in baseball. Of course, that doesn't mean he has to like it. Great driver or not, no true racer shrugs off a bad day or bad luck like yesterdays garbage.

Racers are competitive. Well known racers like the Andrettis', Unsers' and the Pettys' probably feel more pressure to win than most. Bad luck can only augment that. They're expected to win, especially with the big money and sophisticated teams behind them. So don't envy the big racing names in this sport. They know how racing luck is. They know one mistake by them or someone else, could send them off to that big pit stop in the sky. All the fame and fortune in the world can't make up for that indisputable fact.

Now that you know racing can have its share of poor luck, that doesn't mean you wait for it to happen or you accept it. Heck no. If you accept it, that only serves to slow down your learning progress more. If you accept poor luck (and by-the-way, you'll probably do that at the subconscious level only) you'll have no desire to improve. You may feel that you have to only maintain skill instead of seeking more. You may deny that's happening, but it ends up as such.

Remember, ideally, the only bad luck there is, is the type that's initiated by others. Bad luck initiated by you isn't bad luck, but rather incompetence. Take that school of thought and you'll be more successful (sooner) and you'll also learn to live better with yourself. (temper won't flare as badly when you do have problems that are not your fault)

What's a good way to avoid bad luck? One way is to get good help. Try not to be "the-jack-of-all-trades". It can drain you physically and more importantly, mentally. This is especially true when you're at the track. You're there to race, hopefully, nothing else.

Have your race machine properly prepped so as to avoid any more mechanical work than is necessary. (much more on that later on) I know this is hard. Finding somebody to do major volunteer mechanical work on site because they love racing is next to impossible. Things are no doubt going to happen that will require your immediate attention. If you're a financially poor racer, like 95% of us are, you'll have to do more than race that weekend.

THE SMALL THINGS PILE UP

Okay, so getting free skilled and experienced help is hard. Getting help to perform the maintenance and menial tasks isn't all that hard. Starting out, you may have to go without the help you need. Many times this is how some people want it to begin since it enhances the learning process. (also cuts down the time required to do that) That's fine for maybe the first 3 to 5 weekends. You'll then be very familiar with procedures and be able to pass that over to anyone you bring with you thereafter. I'm not just talking about race-related skills that need to be performed, but rather things that are nonrace related.

If you camp at the track overnight, you need someone to setup the tent, get firewood, etc. It's small tasks like that you have to do on your own otherwise. After carting around the track at high speeds all afternoon, you are going to find those small jobs not so small. That's especially so when the racecar needs unforeseen work.

Things can start to pile up on you and become overwhelming. An overworked racer can be ineffective and dangerous to compete with at any time.

So get help. If you can't find help, you're either not trying hard enough or you got a serious personality problem. It's out there! It's not hard to find. While there may not be a lot of skilled help around, there's a lot of the other kind.

A SLICE OF PIE

A lot of people love to be associated with racing. It's a pleasant diversion. (it's not all their time and effort and none of their money) So ask your kids, wife, girlfriend(s), associates, uncles, etc. I found out many times you need not ask. Some people volunteer their help. As a teacher, I've had to turn down help from students, yes, even from girls. (I like this women's liberation thing)

Caution, . . . don't take anymore help than what's necessary. It's not that "too many cooks spoil the soup", but rather too many people on the crew can have an overwhelming effect and be a distraction on your concentration. (especially those in it for the pure temporary novelty of it) You'll figure out you don't want your ability to maintain composure impeded by what looks like a chinese fire drill taking place around you.

Have you noticed a somewhat contradictory situation about the sport of motorracing. Probably not, but here it is anyway. Racing is both an individual and team sport. You want to be successful? Consider it a team sport. If you just want to be "out there" as they say, it's more of an individual sport. That's okay too. I'll cover more on that later.

Whether you consider racing a team sport

or not, make no mistake, if you want to be better at this, you'll need help. Therefore, racing is more of a team sport. Anyone who tells you otherwise has not won very many races, if any.

There are people in racing on their own who are good, very good. Still, you will find these types in less competitive classes of the amateur ranks. That's okay in those situations, but not for the more competitive classes in the amateur ranks, . . . and for god sakes, not in the pros. These individual type of drivers would probably not recommend you start racing on your own. Why? They didn't themselves. It's just that they got to know the sport so well, they knew exactly what to expect. (relatively speaking) They were better prepared and equipped to go on their own. They will have problems, but they know how to handle them. They know who, where and when to get the right kind of help. (on or off the track)

In amateur racing, there are many seasoned people who will be happy to help you. That's true of the individual types too, but sometimes they just won't have the time, because it's at such a premium to them.

DOWN THE YELLOW BRICK ROAD

The rest of this chapter is sort of a synopsis devoted to mostly those who don't understand the racers "mindset". It's also for those not sure if racing is the thing to get into at the moment. You guys already committed to racing (up to your neck) . . . well, . . . read along anyway. See if you agree with what I'm trying to say.

The racer, especially at the amateur level, can seem totally consumed by racing. Some have avoided things like marriage to do this. (I know, I'm one of them) These guys are not just weekend warriors, . . . to them racing is the "moral equivalent" of sex.

If "Joe Blow" thinks about sex on the average of once every 15 or 20 seconds, (or is it minutes) then some drivers apparently think of racing just as much, if not more.

Racing can get in your blood. It can (pleasantly) overtake you. Even if you're not suc-

cessful, you'll believe that will come. (that's the right attitude) The real racer does not just want to be "out there", he wants to be competitive.

This attitude is not only mentally necessary, but also important for the sake of safety. The guy that's just (so-called) "out there" to participate may not be quite as fast. That can be uneducational and dangerous.

The real racer knows he'll actually never stop learning. He knows racing can be devastating, tragic, and yet gratifying. Racing runs the gamut of "rollercoastering" emotions. Maybe that's why this sport is so personal. It's ego building and destructive; magnified at both the positive and negative sides; teeters on the brink of danger and tragedy . . . and yet somehow make these risks all worthwhile when that day of success finally comes.

For all your time, money, effort and anticipation, this game can sometimes be deceptive. When things look good, they can suddenly bite back! But you know, seasoned as you are, that the percentages should even themselves out. You'll almost feel guilty for having any good luck at all when it suddenly comes. But then . . . you remember all your bad luck you had. . . .

Remember that 25 cent bolt I mentioned earlier? You did everything right but it still failed you. Now you and your machine are suddenly careening out of control . . . no . . . check that . . . just the machine is out of control. You, seasoned as you are, are too busy to be scared. That's not because you're stupid, but because of your level of concentration for the moment. You had the presence of mind to keep your racer off the wall and out of others way.

Well, . . . at least you attempted that. But the laws of physics were against you. You hit the wall hard. You're not sure you're hurt, but you know your racer is. You're not mad about it, . . . you're downright sick. Heck, . . . you wouldn't feel so bad about it if it was you that got crunched. Instead, it is your precious machine! Shoot, the track insurance would have taken care of you . . . but insurance on your race car(?) . . . dream on pal! Ha, . . . now that's funny! (It's way too expensive . . . if you can find it; more on that later)

Do I sound like I'm a bit apathetic towards life and limb? Do I show no respect? No! I'm just making a point. Some racers' obsession will redirect itself only if only they're badly hurt.

TRIUMPH OR TRADGEDY

Until that happens, the young and inexperienced racers lust for speed must be tempered by some common sense. They must realize the need to pay attention to details, get help and accept the fact that racing doesn't always reward a great effort. (It'll never award no effort) But he'll hang in there tough.

Then success comes, . . . maybe too much. He may get overconfident. That won't last very long in racing. The old racer never lets that happen to him. But the young racer may again overextend those laws of physics and "put it" against the wall. But this time it may be for a different reason. He'll learn from that too, but quicker this time, since he sustained injuries. Nothing enhances learning like the threat of pain, injuries and yes, the threat of death. (sometimes, financial loss from a racing mishap doesn't slow down an aggressive driver)

As mentioned earlier, motorsports isn't only a wide range of emotions, but a quick change of those also. Example: one-half lap away from a big win and all of a sudden your powerplant decides to shut itself down. So, if that's not enough to "blank" you off, how about the same scenario, but this time another racers stupid move puts you in a situation that not only robbed you of a victory, but also destroyed your racecar, . . . and maybe you! What a shift of emotions. From a possible win to a tragedy.

LOOK BEFORE YOU LEAP

Aspiring racers, don't get in sport this until you understand what's involved. This isn't like most sports where you have a 50% chance to be on the winning team. Remember, there may be as many as 30 to 40 peo-ple striving to do what you are trying. Consider what your chances of winning are and doing that early in your career. It's almost zero. If you do win or succeed early, you're one of a very few to do that, . . . or you're talented, well-financed or have lousy competition to race against. Winning in the early stages is the exception, not the rule.

Once you've become relatively more seasoned, you will see that it'll still take more than money and talent to win. While you'll definitely need those things, you'll also need organization, determination, persistence and an undying belief in yourself. If you have those qualities, . . . that's good. But you still lack funds? Then you must compromise. If you compromise in order to compete, do it at the sacrifice of speed, never your safety.

A lack of money can be tolerated for only so long. You will need the ability to shell out the green stuff. It could be the hardest part of racing. If you're not swimming in the bucks, you better be "dang" good at performing your own money-saving tasks. (much more on this later)

Amongst other things, that won't be enough. You will also need expensive tools and equipment to perform those tasks. You may as well figure on having skilled work done, especially on the internal workings of your race engine. As you gain experience in racing, you should learn engine tuning and how to properly setup suspension and chassis handling.

Whether you are young or the mature man just starting out in racing, take heart. Yes, this is an expensive adventure, but don't let it scare you away.

COME PLAY WITH US

More people then ever are racing today. So, as much as we hear how racing is getting even more expensive, so is life in general. It is at the big league level, such as IndyCar, Formula One, NASCAR, NHRA and all the other pro levels that racing is skyrocketing almost out of control. (compared to club or amateur level) They'll survive though, despite all their fears. The prize money is also going up along with the availability of sponsorship packages.

If you're the mature person just discovering this sport, you have some wisdom and probably a better financial situation working for you. You'll probably realize you have the odds stacked against you of ever cracking the Indy or Daytona 500 lineups. Let's be honest with ourselves, who doesn't dream of that as racers?

That doesn't mean we shouldn't set (lofty) goals. Those goals needn't be specific. Maybe you want only to be successful (as perceived by you) or just enjoy this sport. It has its place. Others have discovered this. Paul Newman is a good example. He was in his 60's when he was doing well in racing. Sure, this man has good financial support, but like I said earlier, he still had to develop his skills.

The young person, 25, 26 years of age or younger, needs to approach racing a bit differently. This is assuming you're in the type of financial situation that's considered normal; not deep in debt, not financially stable either. I'm talking about the idea of making a living out of racing. Even if you can't attain that goal, you'll still enjoy racing.

This sport gets in your blood and usually stays there. There are plenty of incentives for the amateur too. National and Regional championships are there to win in just about all forms of motorsports. This also includes local and individual 'track' titles. (usually Late Model Stockcars, Dirt Motorcycles, Go-Karts, etc) Racers of all types and ages will soon find out there are many good competitors out there. Many are just as good as the pros. That is not an exaggeration! I know this. I have seen it myself, first hand.

As I said earlier, politics can play a part in this sport. The pros are good, no doubt about that, but they're also better at marketing themselves for the necessary (sponsorship) support. The fact that politics is involved in this sport isn't so much a reflection of racing, as much as it is on life itself. The fact is, this is neither good or bad, . . . but just a fact of life. It's just . . . there!

2 | The Commitments Involved

You found out in the first chapter racing requires a serious leap of faith. You need to believe in yourself. Really believe! Sitting down at the local drinking establishment and boring everybody with "I'm gonna go racing" rhetoric is easy. Going out there and doing it is another thing. So okay, AJ, it's time to quit talking, . . . and start doing.

Well, are you that rich and talented QB in college we saw in chapter one? Great! You've got racing already half-licked . . . somewhat. Finish college though, a graduate makes more of that green stuff. You will therefore have more to invest. (if "invest" is the right word to use)

Are you the bench-warmer with the VW? Great also! Keep it! We all know they're less expensive to own. Therefore, you'll have more to spend on racing. Are you single? Stay that way, . . . I did. I know that's easier said than done. Try it for as long as you can. (unless she's "rolling in it")

If your girl is starting to put on the pressure for marriage, have her read chapter one. If your mother is against racing too, have her do likewise, including this chapter. If both argue this is just too dangerous, tell them (in narrative form) about the myth of racing dangers. (you'll read about later in this book) Tell them you could walk out the front door today and get plummeted by a shower of meteorites. Tell 'em Highway 101 isn't as safe as the Daytona International Speedway is during the 500. They won't believe it, but at least you'll convey the idea of just how badly you want to race.

If your father is close by, chances are . . . he'll sway things your way. Shoot, he may just want to get involved himself. Oh, . . .

what the heck, . . . if you're 18 years old, your signature is good in most racing organizations anyway, if not all of them. Your ma and girl will still love you. (even if ma occasionally chastises you or your "betterhalf" gives you the silent treatment at times).

Okay, that aside for now, you know it is disagreeable out there . . . on the track itself, I mean. (we already know how disagreeable it is back home) Expect troubles. Also, anticipate such things as arriving at the track well prepared, only to end up a DNS or DNF. (**D**id **N**ot **S**tart, **D**id **N**ot **F**inish) It happens.

If you're ready to throw in the towel when things like that happen, you probably wasn't committed enough in the first place. Still, many racers blow off steam in this manner. They say "hell with it", break something and quit. Two days later they're right back at it. They really did want to "trash" it, but found out they love it too much after a one or two day cooling off period.

If you haven't rearranged your life for racing, it's all nonsense. (what many women seem to feel, if it's *THEIR* mate doing it; all those other racers are "brave") Your thinking, habits, demeanor, etc may change. You may not notice that, but your friends might. This isn't always bad, but just a circumstance.

SECOND GUESSING THYSELF

The actual driving of a racecar is only one phase of this sport. When things do go wrong, the truly committed racer will become more determined. He'll learn from both positive and negative experiences. Sometimes this change in thinking comes across as another negative to family members and friends. They may think . . . "gee . . . this guy is obsessed with the sport". This may be true, but it's not necessarily so. Things are probably just stacking up on you.

As that first race date approaches, the racer notices 'time' starts to intensify. Time funnels down. This is less evident to you and everyone else as you get more experience. But for the young racer, the pressure builds. All that time, money, effort, preparation, details, anticipation, and all the other things, start to close in. This could be when the racer realizes this sport can be selfish or self-encompassing. He or she may begin to understand their friends and loved-ones initial complaints.

The racer now second guesses everything they've done up to that point. But that's human nature, . . . the survival instinct. The experienced racer knows this isn't some necessary evil of racing, just those instincts. Be that as it may, you certainly can't stop now. Meanwhile, the time funnel narrows tighter and tighter. Weeks become days; days become hours; you arrive at the track, now hours become minutes; you are now in the racecar, ready to go; . . . you think, . . . "did I miss or overlook anything?" Minutes become seconds.

ACID TEST

The time has come. The command "start your engines" is made. The butterflies are there, making you impatient as hell. "Let's go" you scream to yourself. The time funnel now takes a 180 degree turn. The racecar is ready, you're ready, the other competitors are ready, why the heck isn't the grid marshall ready? Those seconds seem like hours. You're hot, doing a slow simmer inside a firesuit designed to protect you from fire. Seems like all it's doing is creating one.

At about the time you're ready to go crazy, you're finally led out to the track for a warm up lap or two. Now, things are a bit better, relatively. During the warm up, your nerves

may frazzle again. You finally get the green flag! (or light)

It is now down to hundredths and thousandths of a second. Nothing else matters now . . . money, women, the future, school, even life itself . . . you can't be thinking about it now. You haven't got a milli-second for that. (Your reacting, . . . not thinking) Your concentration level at this point is far more intense then any time you knew of, once you reached racing speed. If you can't concentrate now, get off the track and out of others way, you'd be a danger to yourself and everyone else.

If you get to this point, you'll learn or already know the kind of commitment and attention racing requires. This is even more so on a limited budget, which in racing, always seems to be the case. This is why I say, if you're truly committed, you'll probably need to get a second source of income.

There are two reasons for this. The first is obvious. The second income is to support your sport, hobby, habit . . . whatever you want to call it. (your wife may call it a habit) This is also where you could start to look selfish to others, again, especially if you're married with children.

NO MONEY TREE?

You now may be sacrificing time from the family. But to be successful, you need to do this. That can work for you. More on that later. It's seems unfair about racing, you have to have money. (and time) It doesn't seem right, but starting out in this sport, it makes sense. It's the only way!

Nobody is going to just hand over all the necessary funds you need right out of the clear blue sky. (or will they? More on that later) Now you may understand what I mean when I say racing is kind of selfish. It's a Mexican standoff between it and the family. But, of course, that's not true for some families or possibly for most families, for that matter.

As I suggested earlier, if you're single, try to stay that way as long as you can. If you can, make any mate coming at you in a gleaming white wedding gown understand one point, racing is a package deal that comes with you. I know that sounds a bit crude, but at least you're putting your chips on the table and surprising nobody.

Of course, this is a two-way street. The bride needs to make clear to her new "speed merchant" what she does and does not expect. (from racing) This is just good old fashion common sense. But, being a teacher, I've seen some pretty stupid things done over the years. (granted, it was by students) One can't take ignorance for granted, so therefore, it's necessary to mention these things.

People, including myself, need to be reminded they're quite capable of doing things they regret later on. It doesn't matter how old or mature we are. So, you married guys, about the worse thing you could do is take a great big unauthorized "killer" dip into the savings account. (for anything, much less for racing) Wouldn't that go over like a lead balloon? Here you come, . . . rolling into the driveway with a trailer full of racecar. Yes, racing's costly, but an ensuing divorce could be even more costly.

FAMILY TIES

There are racers who have quit racing because of family resistance. There probably could be a movie made on this theme. So don't be hasty! If you encounter resistance, you must adapt. Married racing prospects just starting out need to do so fairly slow. You must keep costs down as much as you can.

For now, you have to be the jack-of-all-trades, that is . . . if you're capable. You should have your (internal) engine work done by skilled labor though. (much more on that later) So, if you anticipate resistance from your wife, don't force-feed this on her. Approach this situation with "kid gloves". Talk to her. Start real slow. Work up to the idea of racing. Get her used to what you're thinking and what you'd like to do.

Women aren't stupid, they'll know what's up. So, . . . maybe they won't like what you're thinking, but they'll appreciate your respect for their feelings. This alone may win them

over, subconsciously that is. The wife may deny this to herself, and still to you also, but the costs and dangers still scare her.

The whole point is this, don't drop a bomb on her. Don't even tell her what you're going to do. Show her what you want to do. This process may take months, depending on your situation. Maybe a year . . . or only a few weeks. You have to judge your circumstances. You need to sell, sell, sell. Stress the positive points of your hobby. Avoid calling this racing at this time. If you have any kids, especially boys, they'll probably be on your side. No big surprise there. They may win-over their mother better then you could. Why? They may be willing to make sacrifices. They could also form a closer bond with their dad.

TELL IT LIKE IT IS

It's important to be honest. If you mislead or exaggerate, the only thing you've achieved is borrowed time. You could have an even nastier situation then you originally faced when you came up with this idea in the first place. Put your wife and family in a win-win situation. They need to know what to expect and that their lifestyle and standard of living won't suffer a bit. If anything, racing can enrich it. The travel, family togetherness, competition and the opportunity of meeting new people is beneficial.

Make no misjudgment, you'll find great people in this sport. They are stern and competitive on the track, but very helpful and concerned about their competitors off the track. It's truly an educational experience. This raises the responsibility level of the kids. Don't be surprised if your wife starts to see these benefits quicker than you thought. You just got to get over-the-hump, so to speak.

LOVE CHILD

I suppose some of the readers here may feel I'm using the word "kids" interchangeably with boys. Not true. Girls are included.

Don't underestimate them! They can get quite involved, as the boys. It's the 1990's pal, not the 1890's!

If your girls do bury themselves in your program, they might get involved for the right or wrong reasons. Either way, it is okay. Give them responsibility they can handle and feel important for. Same with the boys. They may find out there is more to being a teenager than football, basketball, baseball and females.

Of course, the crew you put together doesn't have to be family. But if you're young and single, a brother or sister may help. Still, it's a good chance they're too young or old to be the practical kind of help for your taste. Also, you may not want their help, . . . you know . . . that brother-sister love-hate thing.

Your father may be the exception. He could be the factor which determines how quickly you adjust and/or succeed. Otherwise, your friends or collection of recruits and volunteers can be of great help to you. But remember, it's free help, in a manner of speaking. You should treat them with respect and understand they're not the famous Wood Brothers pit crew team.

This (philosophy) sounds basic to anything in life, but it's not in racing. Believe me, racers get real cranky at the track sometimes. The pressure can really build up. Control it! You don't act towards your crew like you would family members. That's not saying you treat your family poorly, it's just a bit more of a touchier situation with friends, recruits, etc.

If you feel frustration approaching, get out of sight if you must vent it. Otherwise your crew may feel responsible and/or hurt. Your kids . . . well . . . they know you. They can handle a bit of misdirected anger from their dad, . . . if they understand you're just blowing off a little steam at yourself. Still, "cool it, pops".

LIFES AMENITIES

The better you organize yourself, the more you can take situations that do crop up in stride and get things corrected. Then you'll concentrate better. The crew will also. (organization begets concentration)

If your crew consists of volunteers, friends, etc, you need to provide for their meals and housing. They shouldn't have to spend a penny. I know that can be costly, that's why racers do a lot of camping. It's cheaper, fun and less time consuming then traveling to your room.

Some tracks aren't close to any towns, therefore, you're far from housing facilities. Most tracks allow overnight camping free of charge. Many have shower facilities and a few provide electricity.

I have also found out almost all tracks permit race organizers to throw a party after qualifications. (especially in SCCA events) There is plenty of food at these parties. That would certainly cut down the cost of feeding a crew.

THE BASIC STUFF

The engine building, chassis work, all the high tech stuff have been performed elsewhere. Your racer should arrive at the track ready to race. But things will happen. You'll need to be ready for those things, and so will your crew.

Whether the crew is your family, friends or whatever, they should know before they arrive at the track what maintenance they will be doing. That should be very clear and concise. Sometimes it may be necessary to show your unskilled help, like a daughter, exactly how to do a simple job.

Don't take some men for granted either. Judging by their skill or lack thereof, you'll know how to instruct each individual on your team. I'm talking about specific jobs and who does what.

When you have an unforeseen problem, you may try to remedy it yourself, or at least diagnose it. If you determined it can be repaired on-site and immediately, organize your help to repair it or assist you, depending on their skill. Remember, if the problem upsets you, don't take it out on anyone.

All your help should know basic things, like where all the tools are and how to use them. Never let anyone put tools back where they were not originally. If that happens, it gets some racers very ticked off. Then they have to screw around wasting time later on looking for them. Many times at the track, seconds are valuable. When a last second discovery is made, that problem sometimes needs immediate attention. You do not want to be wasting precious time looking for a tool that's not where it belongs. I know from experience that really aggravates me.

TROUBLEMAKERS

Your help needs to troubleshoot; look for potential problems. Example: is that oil line too close to an exhaust header? Good troubleshooters are a sign of a potentially good mechanic. Is your kid that way? Does he show an interest in tackling a complicated repair? Maybe he'd like to make it a career. More on that later.

No matter how much skill one may have, the really technical things will come natural to nobody. You have to train for that. So be careful, don't let anyone mess around with the inner workings of a raceshop built engine. (including yourself)

As far as that boy of yours is concerned, if he shows some skill, it may be in your best interest to get him training. Be careful though, young people can be fickle and lose interest fast. Wait until he's at least out of school.

Whatever the case, he and the rest of the crew should be aware of any problem incurred on the track. When you bring the racer in with its problem, they shouldn't have to be told things like: position the racecar for diagnosis and repair (put on jacks, etc); setup the tools they'll need; get adequate lighting; setup power sources; and cleaning the area on the racer of spewed oil or debris. (making the work area more accessible)

These things can be done while you're crawling out of the racer and firesuit and into a pair of coveralls. If you have a more mature (or older) crew, this stuff comes naturally. But not for your kids.

These things are simple, but very valuable. I know! I've been to many races as a

competitor, with no help. I can't overemphasize how these things can make a huge difference. It allows you to concentrate on what you need to do on the track. Overloading yourself doesn't help your driving.

With all these things going on in a race weekend, it's easy to understand how one small problem can throw a monkey wrench into the whole weekend.

That's why some racers get edgy and temperamental. Sometimes they anticipate problems that never present themselves. That makes them cranky too.

It wouldn't hurt you to make your helpers understand why you may get moody. This way, they won't take a problem personally. They'll understand the commitment required of them. Also, after experiencing a weekend of racing with you, your wife, or (skeptical) friends, whatever, may now begin to understand racing as not just a means of wasting time, money and effort, or getting (fatally) hurt. They'll see this is serious business to you, . . . not some passing fancy.

ON THE DARK SIDE

Speaking of injuries, as I mentioned in chapter one, anyone killed in motorsports, usually does so in a magnified manner. It's big news! One reason for that hasn't got anything to do with racing. It has more to do with sports in general.

In the USA, athletes are revered and/or looked up to. Although the big salaries may be changing some of that, young folks still admire them, especially the well known ones. Any well known athletes' death is big news. But in racing, as opposed to most sports, a racers premature death may be the result of participation. (in a race)

It's very rare to be killed while playing in other sports. On top of that, racing deaths happen in full view of a paying public. Furthermore, it's a good chance the accident has been recorded on film. (especially if it's a pro event) Then the recorded mishap may be played over and over again on television. All these factors serve to magnify the tragedy.

When was the last time you saw in person,

or on the TV news, a terrible highway accident? Furthermore, did you know who the fatalities were? People get killed everyday. Yes, that certainly is a tragedy and unfortunate. There are close to 50,000 deaths alone on the nations highways annually. But you don't see them. This sounds cold, . . . but yes, . . . they are statistics. We can't get paranoid about it and eliminate the automobile. You may say the automobile is necessary, racing isn't. That's true. But there are apparently many around who feel otherwise.

SAFER DANGERS

Because of that, racing is very popular worldwide. Still, the racing fraternity has had to get relatively paranoid about the dangers of this sports. Why? That should be obvious. Yes, the world would survive without this sport. We know that. So it has to be conducted in as safe of a manner as possible. Otherwise, it would be eliminated. We don't want that!

Because of the technology incorporated into today's racing cars, the rigid safety requirements and procedures, rules, advanced on-sight (and available) medical equipment, racing is not nearly as dangerous as it was. This is true even with the great speeds reached by today's higher profiled racecars.

When accidents do occur, it's amazing to see a driver walk away from an incident you thought sure they perished in. Racing deaths are becoming rare. The stats confirm this.

One last word about commitment. A young racing prospect should instinctively understand this: racing can be very dangerous with the wrong attitude; it requires lots of time, effort, especially with little money; you just can't quit it like a football or baseball participant. You have too much time, money and effort invested. If you want to excel, you have to practically change your lifestyle and thinking for this sport.

Expect the unexpected. Take this sport very seriously, whether you just want to be "out there mixing it up", or there to win. Either way, regardless of your reasons for doing this, there will be people racing that don't want you out there for the "joyride". Respect them and they'll respect you. They have too much involved to want it any other way.

DIAL 911

If you are at a race by yourself, or you have a problem that you and your crew can't solve, don't pack for home just yet. Ask for help from the other race teams. There's plenty of it out there in the pits and infield. If you're by yourself, this is even more important. By the way, it's much faster to go to the track public address system. I haven't seen a track that doesn't let you do that, yet. The chances of receiving help are darn right good.

Don't be afraid to ask not only for personal help, (labor, diagnosis) but for parts too. I've seen guys lend engines out. Granted, they weren't new, but it got somebody through the weekend. It is not as rare as I thought it would be when I started this sport. People can be downright generous in racing.

Racing may not always be fair, but it sure has a lot of people in it genuinely helpful to its rookies and hard luck participants. That competitor who wants to leave you in the dust on the track, is the same guy who'll bend over backwards to help you with your technical problems off the track. It has something to do with the fact that he's been in a similar situation earlier. He understands commitment!

You won't get this at the pro level, but that's understandable.

3 | The Classes

Ever since Adam and Eve (and all other creatures possessing legs) made their grand exit from the garden of eden, it seems we're fascinated with the idea of speed. We do it with ourselves, animals and machines; with high-level collegiate and Olympic track events to horse and dog racing. I don't know if we're taken by the pure speed or the competition itself. Doesn't matter. It's here to stay. We seem destined to line up anything with legs, wheels and wings. If that isn't enough, we race boats also.

WATCH OUT FOR INSECTS

When I was a young lad, with hormones coursing through my veins, about the only races I'd watch were the ones down at the beach. You know what I mean . . . the submarine races. Since I really didn't live near a beach, I eventually made it to a real race.

The first motor race I ever was witness to was the 1973 Indianapolis 500. After I was begrudgingly dragged to it, I fell in love with this sport. It hit me like a ton of bricks. Unfortunately, I never saw the race. I recall seeing about 7 or 8 pace laps and a start, which only lasted maybe 1 or 2000 feet.

There I was, inside turn one . . . I mean really inside turn one. Many of us jumped the retaining fence to get a closer look. Yesiree . . . the famous "snake pit" area. It's where one can stand in fascination watching people drunk out of their minds, doing some of the stupidest things you'll ever want to see. I heard about this, so I thought I'd check it out.

I figured that year was going to be a particularly interesting one. The streaking fad (idiots running around "buck" naked) was in full bloom . . . if you'll pardon the expression. Even some of the race drivers were walking down from the pits to sneak a peek. Anyway, forget that, I'm about 100 feet from the track waiting for the start. I think I was more busy watching the police. They had their hands full containing all us fence jumpers. I figured as soon as they spotted me, I'd be ready to "bolt" back where I belong. Well, they didn't spot me and about 60 or 70 others. What a view! It was great! Too great! As it turned out, I got the scare of my life.

I would have had the best view in turn one if it wasn't for all the others. I swear, everybody in front of me was 6'3", because I'm 6'2". I may as well been back inside the fence. Anyway, I'm straining for a view right down the front stretch of the track. Here they come! Man, do you know what 33 screaming Indy Cars sound like coming at you? It sounds like a zillion giant mosquitoes!

The closer they get, the harder it is to see them. Everybody's repositioning, tiptoed, girls climbing on their boyfriends shoulders . . . ah man . . . I'm losing my view. It didn't matter for long though! That sound suddenly subsides! People yell things like "gangway", "move", "Ole Jose" and what-have-you.

Everybody towards the front of me is sprinting for the fence, including this old lady. Before I have a chance to chuckle at all this, I see why everyone's making it fast towards the infield. Smoke, fire, tires and all kinds of metal debris is headed our way! Holy Toledo, it's a pile-up!

I quickly decided to head for safety. While doing that, one of the cars went past me. I think it was Salt Walther. He must of been doing over 100 mph from 60 feet away. It was scary, but not as much as the fact that when he was doing that, he and his racer was upside-down. (I think)

Well, I'm glad to say, Salt Walther and others recovered from their injuries. I didn't. No, I didn't get hurt, not physically . . . just financially. I was bitten by the bug, . . . and hard! I've been spending money on racing ever since. It has taken its toll on me financially, but I'd do it all over again.

TAKING THE PLUNGE

If I had the option to start racing all over again, I'd do things much differently. In the first place, I was slow getting started. There are two reasons for that; 1. I didn't know racing existed at the amateur (club) level. 2. I didn't think I had anywhere near enough money to go racing with.

Racing does cost money. Big-time racing cost big-time money. It also pays huge purses. It's all relative. Still, those purses hardly pay for the cost of this sport. There are many myths about racing. Some aren't far from the truth. Others have been exaggerated to the point of hurting it. Some of those myths did hold me back.

I was a junior in college when all this happened to me. If this took place earlier in my life, I would have skipped college. Racing influenced me that much.

Well, to continue my story about the '73 Indy 500 isn't so great now. What an array of situations I experienced. The first lap pile-up was cleaned up, only to have rain move in. Cancel the show for that day! Monday, Memorial Day, more of the same. Oh, . . . they got a few pace laps in . . . cancel Monday. Boy, was I upset and frustrated. I wasn't frustrated about the rain, entirely, but because I knew this was what I wanted to do. There was no doubt in my mind about it.

While studying to be a teacher and coach,

I wasn't sure that was what I wanted to do. I wasn't sure about anything. I was lost and confused about the future. Female problems didn't help things either. But when I attended this race, things changed. 180 degrees! Life had some direction now. I doubt anything will influence me so much and so fast, in such a positive manner.

But I was frustrated. How was I to get the big bucks for racing? How do I build a racer? I even thought I would need some political clout to race. How did I get that idea? I had no way of knowing then.

I also didn't know what to race or where. As naive as I was about this sport, I knew Indy Cars were way out of my league. I thought about Late Model StockCars because I thought they really were stock. (right from the factory) I also thought it was the only place I'd be allowed to start, if I was allowed. I was pretty confused, so was my friend, who seemed to show an interest in racing also.

We started attending local racing events at the Toledo (Ohio) Speedway. Afterwards, we'd go down to the pits to look at the cars more closely. Seems like everytime we'd go home afterwards, I'd say the same old thing to him, . . . like, "man, I'm tired of watching these guys . . . I'd rather be out there mixing it up with'em!" Looking back, I see I was asking for help to get started racing. But my pal was just as lost as I was. Still, for some reason, deep down, I was not as intrigued with stockcars as much as I was with formula racers.

Just as I discovered racing by luck, it wasn't until six more years later . . . a whole six years . . . I found out there was such a thing as formula racing at the club (amateur) and lower-cost level. Looking back, that also makes me sick. It was six years I could of used. Why couldn't fate be quicker?

When fate finally came, I found it at the Tampa, Florida airport of all places. I saw this magazine lying there exposing an ad about racing. I couldn't believe it! There was my answer. I now knew what to do. It seemed almost too simple. Once again, things changed for the better. Even at that time, I couldn't believe it took so long to discover this.

I was 27 years old. I now figured out Formula Vee's were the best class for me to start with. How I came about that is another story and unnecessary to elaborate on. That is because this time I didn't find out about it by chance. Now I knew who, what and where to go to find all the information I could. In my case, it was about formula racing.

I was almost 31 years old when I ran my first race. I had some pretty nasty financial woes to dig myself out of . . . I wasn't even married or I would of been even slower getting started. But I freed myself of that, saved up and purchased my first racer.

BETTER LATE THAN NEVER

Because of my late start getting it all together, it's one of the reasons I'm writing this. Others have written books on getting started also. I'm hoping this will be more detailed, for both the guy who wants to race or the race fan who just wants to further understand this complicated sport.

I guess I can take solace that I'm not the only one in the world to get started this late. Thank goodness, to race a car, boat, bike or whatever, takes more than just a young body. (relative to being 70 years old, that is) I'm sure there are quite a few people who would like to give racing a try. They probably think they have no opportunity or it's way too costly.

Some do know the opportunity is there, but don't have the slightest idea how to start. It's a mass of confusion to them too. I know! I hope to clear up some of that.

This book is also geared towards alleviating the confusion many racing spectators have. Chapter 3, by far the biggest chapter, is designed just as much for the race fan as it is for the racing participant. But you race fans should read this whole book. It'll help you understand this game. Therefore, you'll realize all those big-timers out there at Indy, Daytona, Baja or whatever, aren't there just because they were born with a silver spoon in their mouth.

You'll also look at a race much differently. No longer will you see this sport as some roman gladiator-styled spectacle. No longer will you see a bunch of vehicles going around in circles just as fast and unsafely as possible. You'll view a race as if you're inside the helmet of the driver. That makes it a whole lot more interesting!

THE NUTS AND BOLTS

In this chapter, I'll show you what choices you have in racing. This alone won't nor should help you make a decision based solely on its own merit. It will contribute to that, but there are many other factors to consider. You may know what type of racer you want to start with, but not what class. There is a difference. 'Type' of racing is things like: Autos, Bikes, Drag Racers, Off-Road, etc. 'Class' deals with levels (or costs) within these types of racing.

This book deals with 2 and 4 wheel racing. No hulls (boats) or wings. Racing airplanes, jets, whatever, is ungodly expensive. I don't even know if air races are sanctioned. It may be a military thing, I don't know. All I know is if you think auto racing is costly, try it in the air. End of that.

Now, about boats. I'm sure there are forms of racing on water that are affordable. That includes hydroplanes. The trouble is, I know little about boat racing. So, on that note, that's the end of that.

Oh, by-the-way, I'm also not listing the kind of racing that requires a good set of legs and lungs. For that, see a high school or college track coach. If you're anywhere near my age, see a doctor first.

Now, let's get down to the choices we have available to us.

There are two *forms* of motorsports:

I. OPEN WHEEL II. CLOSED WHEEL

I. OPEN WHEEL: They're just that. Tires not covered by fenders. To most people, whether a race vehicle has fenders or not, seems trivial. It is not. With fenders, race vehicles such as StockCars, won't be adversely effected by light incidental 'side by side' contact at racing speed.

If a wheel isn't covered, like a Formula car, those hot, sticky tires can contact or entangle other race vehicle tires. That can literally toss a vehicle in the air. When racing tires contact each other, they may bounce harmlessly away, entangle or ride over each other. That last situation is very bad. None of them is good, but I sure as heck would want to avoid that last one the most.

Mostly, tire contact results in bounce-away. But if they both come together square at the 'contact' or tread surface, one tire can ride over the other. Since the speed is high, the tire riding up to the top of the other will get harshly tossed, including the vehicle attached to it. Because of this situation, it will effect the way a driver races or how aggressively they do so. An aggressive style (bump & grind) of racing is much more prevalent in closed-wheel racing.

*Closed-Wheel examples: Late Models and Stockcars; some Modifieds; SportsRacers such as Can-Am & GT; some Off-Road cars; Improved Touring; Production Racers.

*Open-Wheel examples: Gran Prix (Formula One) & Indy (Champ) Cars; all Formula Racecars; Sprint Cars; Go-Karts; Midgets.

II. CLOSED WHEEL: After reading what Open Wheel race vehicles are, you don't have to be a mechanical engineer to figure out what Closed Wheel is. Still, don't take the word 'fender' for its generally accepted (street) meaning. What I really mean here is tires that are also covered & protected by bodywork, bars, in addition to fenders. Fenders are actually intended to stop a tire from throwing mud and debris; a situation more conducive to Off-Road and/or Motorcycle racing.

Open & Closed Wheel racing doesn't generally apply in Motorcycle and Drag racing. Drag racers have their own lane to run in. It is sometimes contained by walls. If they have tire contact with another racer, it's serious. They're way off course.

There are also two forms or kinds of racecourses:

I. OPEN II. CLOSED

I. OPEN COURSE: This is the kind of race area which does not meet back at some point over & over again or at a point where it started. A race may start at point A & finish at point B. That point B may be a few thousand feet or thousands of miles away.

In some cases, a race may be called Open Course, when in fact it's the opposite. That's just semantics. A race may end up at a point where it started, but the area is so large, it can't be confined or made practical for building or setting up of viewing areas and grandstands. That's usually the case with most off-road racing and some motorcycle and automobile events.

Drag racing is always Open Course. Road Rallies can end up where they got started, but they're considered 'Open'.

II. CLOSED COURSE: This is just the opposite. Most racing is on this kind of course. The area is confined for racing convenience in two ways: (1) the racer will always be close by for service, if needed, and (2) the racecourse itself will be consistent in configuration. Therefore, one can adopt a style particular to it. The driver will always know what's ahead, as far as turns, hills, slippery spots, etc are concerned. By-the-way, spectator viewing is much more easy.

THE BIG CHEESES

Before I start describing all the types (also called categories) and classes of racecars, now is the time to introduce you to a couple of the large, if not largest, race governing bodies in the world.

ACCUS—Automobile Competition Committee of the United States. This is the international governing body for the US. They are affiliated with the FIA. They help control racing events. They help determine times & locations; who runs and sanctions them; who may or may not participate (penalties); licensing procedures; a general policing of race sanctioning bodies, such as: NASCAR, USAC, CART, NHRA, IHRA and SCCA.

They help settle and mediate high level appeals & disputes.

FIA—Federation International de Automobile. This is the governing body for the whole world. Located in Paris, France, they control international auto events, such as Formula 1, Rally racing & World Endurance events.

They also have some control over any automotive racing events whose sanctioning body stages them across foreign borders. (such as when the Indy Cars race in Australia and Canada; and count on it, eventually South America, if not Europe; they have raced in England a time back)

FIM—Federation International de Motorcycle. Located in Geneva, Switzerland, they're the world governing body for motorcycles.

FISA—Federation International Du Sport Automobile. There is some confusion concerning these people and FIA. FISA is an 'arm' of FIA.

Their sanctioning controls are more specific. They help control international endurance sportscar races, such as the world famous '24 Hours Of Lemans' event.

INTERNATIONAL GROUPINGS

FIA groups all international racing of 4-wheel vehicles into 8 categories:

Group 1—Racing of nearly stock 4-seat production cars. Almost no modifications permitted.
Group 2—Racing of modified 4-seat special production touring cars.
Group 3—Racing of conventional stock 2-seat sports cars. Nearly no modifications allowed.
Group 4—Racing of special 2-seat sport cars. Extensive modifications.
Group 5—Racing of sportscars with 5 liter engines of high performance. Non-street cars.
Group 6—Racing of prototype, experimental sportscars. Built only for racing. Very few restrictions.
Group 7—Racing of 2-seat sportsracer type. Different then Group 4 because of few restrictions on engine size. (called Can-Am in US)
Group 8—Racing of single-seat, open-cockpit & no fenders. (Formula)

Most people in the US do not understand these groupings. But all 4-wheel, closed course racers fall somewhere within these groupings. Some racecars may be in a gray area . . . as far as what group they belong in. It's nothing to be confused about, for now. Besides, the FIA knows where they belong.

Your chances are small you'll ever need to deal with such organization as these. But, it's nice to know they're around.

CHANGING A TIGERS STRIPES?

When people get bitten by the racing bug, they generally know what type or kind of racer they want. Don't try to do them a favor by talking them into a different kind of racing. Like playing matchmaker in matters of love, you may end up the loser. Guide them if they ask, don't criticize their choice.

A potential racer has their reasons for choosing the type of racing they do. That same person may not be able to explain the choice theirself. But, it doesn't matter. Messing around with one of those personality, subconscious things is complicated enough. Don't take the chance of making things worse by sticking your two cents worth in.

What a person desires to race is one thing. What 'level', is another. There is a difference. A big difference! If a guy wants to drag race, don't tell 'em they're better off to race . . . say . . . motorcycles. Maybe they are, maybe they aren't. That's not the point. It's not your decision to make. What you can do, is help guide or direct a racing prospect to the proper level. (or class) Most of the time, that's determined by the financial situation, age and experience. This is what I'll try to be doing here in chapter 3, 4, 5 and 6, if not the whole book.

What class of racing one decides on would be easy to make, if money wasn't a factor. That's a big 'if' isn't it. Some classes are so close or identical, they appear the same, that is, to the average person and some inexperienced racers. Showroom Stock, Improved Touring and Production classes are good examples. Many of the classes within Drag Racing and Motorcycles appear a lot alike also. Ditto with Off-Road racers. Otherwise, the difference between a Pure Stock drag car and a Top Fuel (rail) dragster is as evident as that of an Indy Car and a Late Model Stockcar.

After reading chapter 3, 4 and 5, you should figure out the more mph (miles per hour) you want, the more money you will need to spend. If you have money, don't let that mislead you. You could start out in too high of a class. It slows your learning 'curve'. You may be "in over your head" and it can be dangerous!

If you're constantly getting your tail badly beat on the track, it's educational, but in a demoralizing and negative way. It's also boring, if racing can get to that point. Choose your class properly. Know the options. Read this. Ask experienced racers. Don't race blind.

AND HERE THEY ARE

The following 15 Categories or Types of racing are subcategorized further into classes. Each class is briefly or extensively described. You'll notice some of these classes are further broken down into what I call subdivisions or subclasses. (although in racing terms, they're still actually called classes)

Some classes are so simular, I have to subclass them to you for clarification purposes. These descriptions will vary and include some of the following: history; engine type/size; vehicle/chassis size and/or dimensions; power to weight ratio; tire make/size; fuel and many other factors pertinent to each class.

A.	Formula (33 classes)
B.	SportsCars-SportsRacers (10 classes)
C.I.	Production (4 classes)
C.II.	Showroom Stock (4 classes)
C.III.	Improved Touring (5 classes)
C.IV.	Grand Touring (8 classes)
D.	StockCar (15 classes)
E.	Sprint (6 classes)

F.	Drag (13 IHRA subcategories; 12 NHRA subcategories)
G.	Off-Road (3 Types)
H.	Endurance
I.	Rally (2 types)
J.	Solo (3 types)
K.	Motorbikes (12 classes)
L.	Racetrucks (Pick-ups; Semi's; Monster)

A. FORMULA RACE CARS (33 CLASSES)

These machines are built specifically for racing. (called purpose-built) They are low-slung, open-wheeled/open cockpit, one-seaters that are built mostly in England and Europe.

The first 14 classes listed are the ones raced in the US, amongst other places. They're chronologically ordered by their speed, sophistication and costs.

Even though the classes at the top are unbelievably high in costs and out of the reach of the average man, I include them for educational and comparative purposes. I've done this with all the racing categories, if it applies.

Starting with No. 15, the Aurora, are the classes raced outside the US. There are some exceptions, especially in the Vintage class. Some of these are headed for the US in the very near future. Matter-a-fact, Formula 3 looks like a reasonable bet to replace the now defunct Super Vee series. Formula Mazda is already racing here. It's just not greatly popular yet, but that may change soon.

Whether Go-Karts are really formula cars is debatable. They are open wheel and open cockpit, if you don't mind calling their seat a cockpit. Anyway, this category is where they undoubtedly best fit. I want to include them in this book because they're a very important part of the racing education process.

The Barber-Saab formula is raced here also, but it's fairly young and not nationally popular yet. But then, that may be only because they run professionally. (which means their numbers aren't quite there)

Here are the 33 formula classes which make up the first of 15 categories or types just mentioned above or on the previous page:

A. Formula 1. Formula One - F1 (Gran Prix)
A. Formula 2. Indy Cars - (Champ Car)
A. Formula 3. Indy Lights (and Indy Lights 'B')
A. Formula 4. American Indycar Series - (AIS) & AIS Light
A. Formula 5. Formula Atlantic - FA (Category 1 & 2)
A. Formula 6. Super Vee - SV (Formula Continental - FC)
A. Formula 7. Form. Ford 2000 - FF2000 (Formula Continental - FC)
A. Formula 8. Form. Ford 1600 - FF1600
A. Formula 9. Club Ford - CF
A. Formula 10. Formula Vee - FV
A. Formula 11. Formula 440 - F440 or 440
A. Formula 12. Enduro Go-Karts
A. Formula 13. Dirt Go-Karts
A. Formula 14. Sprint Go-Karts
A. Formula 15. Aurora
A. Formula 16. Formula Two - F2
A. Formula 17. Formula Three - F3
A. Formula 18. Formula 5000 - F5000
A. Formula 19. Spec Ford
A. Formula 20. Formula Mazda - FM
A. Formula 21. Formula Renault
A. Formula 22. Barber-Dodge Formula and Formula Russell
A. Formula 23. Formula 3000 - F3000
A. Formula 24. Formula Vauxhall-Lotus
A. Formula 25. Formula Forward
A. Formula 26. Formula First
A. Formula 27. Vintage Formula Vee
A. Formula 28. Formula Sabre
A. Formula 29. Vintage Ford
A. Formula 30. Vintage Formula Super Vee
A. Formula 31. Vintage Formula Atlantic
A. Formula 32. Formula Vauxhall Junior
A. Formula 33. Formula Europa Boxer

A.1. FORMULA ONE—There seems to be an on-going debate whether these racers are the most sophisticated and fastest in the world. There are those who say the Indy Car is. Well, it doesn't matter. It's unfair to both to compare them. It's like comparing apples and oranges.

If you just got to know, my opinion is F1 is more of a responsive, quicker accelerating and stopping, more complex, roadracing machine. But then, it's designed that way for roadcourses.

The Indy Car is built for brute speed. At least that used to be the case when they raced strictly on (high banked) ovals. Indy Cars are faster, but not quicker. With the Indy Car seeing more roadcourses these days, that may be changing. I still don't and never will believe Indy Cars belong on roadcourses. I thought it would hurt their appeal. I was wrong. I still think they're more appealing on high-speed ovals. I also thought the IndyCar fan would tire of roadcourse races by now. We will have to wait to see if that eventually happens.

The Indy people are marketing their sport very well. But, I'm starting to get off of my original subject here.

Formula 1 is built for world class racing on roadcourses for some of the best drivers in the world.

The engines they used varied from a Ferrari 3 liter (maximum size allowed as of the 1995 season) V-12 to a Renault 90 cubic

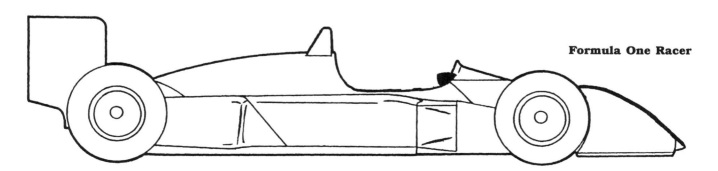

Formula One Racer

inch (ci) turbo. Turbochargers are now illegal in F1. From 1954 to 1961, many F1 engines were supercharged, (not turbocharged) using as little as 750 cubic centimeters, (cc's) to as large as 2500 cc's. The 'blown' engine (super or turbocharged) were banned in 1962, but reinstated again in 1966. Once again, they were disallowed starting in 1990.

The car must weigh at least 1285 lbs with the driver. (was 1145 minus driver before the '95 season) Max bodywork width and height: 86 & 56" respectively. Beyond the front and rear wheel centerline, it must narrow to 32 & 60 inches.

Max rear wing height/width: 36 & 44". Maximum fuel capacity: 66 gallons.

I could give you a ton more of these allowances, rules, etc . . . enough to fill a book, literally. All racecars have rules and regulations for constructing that particular type of machine. They are, in fact, a small book. That's not an exaggeration! As a driver, you don't have to know or memorize all that. The people building your engine and/or chassis had better know!

What do one of these Formula Ones cost? That's hard to figure. I'm not sure anyone knows exactly. That's because of the way they're built. There's quite a few fabricators and 'factory' teams involved with just one 'make'. (brand name)

With costs being relatively incidental, (I said "relatively") the costs get lost in the mire. Expense is seldom spared. Only the top stuff for F1. If you could buy one, I imagine you'd have to fork over a quarter million. That's just for the chassis, minus the engine. You are going to need a lot more than that to compete in F1. You will also need tons of spare parts, expensive maintenance equipment . . . it's almost prohibitive!

Unstable rules also contribute to F1's high costs. Some of it's politics, some of it's for the purposes of safely. 1995's rule changes certainly had something to do with the racing death of the talented Arton Senna. Sometimes changes are made solely to cut costs. A good example of that was the banning of the (over) $950.00 per gallon use of exotic blend fuel they consumed.

Get yourself eons of experience and talent. Then if politics don't screw things up for you along the way, you may have a chance to drive these beauties.

Since 1991, F1 has not made their yearly appearance in the US. So far, no event is scheduled for 1996. Look for that to change eventually, as soon as the large sanctioning bodies can get their politics straightened out. At one point, in 1982, 3 Formula 1 races were held in the US. They were held in Long Beach, California, Detroit, Michigan and Las Vegas, Nevada.

A.2. INDY (CHAMP) CAR—If you don't realize this is the premier formula racing series in America, then you must be living in a cave.

A brand new rolling chassis (pronounced "chassie") would set you back 225 to $400,000. That's just for starters. The formerly hot engine . . . the chevy . . . would cost another 90 to $150,000. Then start to get 100-dollar-billed & 500-dollar-billed to death. (not nickels & dimes) Race tires and wheels are around $5800/set. (4)

After a season of racing, qualifying, practice and testing, you'll have used up a couple of hundred tires easily, if not more. The wheel or tire rims are about $1,275 each! You'll need very skilled labor; feed and room them; a semi tractor-trailer transporter for all the other expensive equipment, besides the racers. If you wanted to race the entire 16, 17 event season, you'd also need a spare chassis or two for the roadcourse and a spare chassis or two for the ovals. You'll also need about 10 engines.

Like F1, it's a big-dollar operation. But unlike F1, there are ways to bring down the costs. Of course, you'll also dramatically lower your chances of being competitive, much less winning.

USAC and CART, despite their occasional differences, have done an admirable job of keeping costs from running too far away. They have banned such expensive computer-oriented devices as: ABS braking, the kind which prevent wheel lock in heavy braking situations; traction control; automatic steering correction; 'fly-by-wire' throttle; and 'active' suspension. Those are all expensive, artificially-enhanced systems which do help the racecar and driver, but relegates

Is this Indy car a Lola, March or a Penske. It doesn't matter to know now. It doesn't even matter to know what powers it or if the chassis is built for (high speed) ovals or for a roadcourse. What matters here is to recognize them. They are the largest in size of all formula machines and the most powerful of close course formula cars. A formula one racer is slightly more narrow bodied and shorter, which makes them more nimble, reactive and thus, more conducive to roadcourse racing.

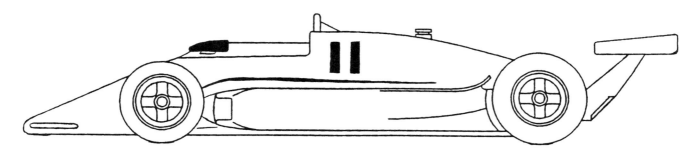

Compare the F1 and Indy car profiles. The F1 is only slightly smaller, but has a bulkier nose and larger rearwing sideplates. The Indy car is just a bit higher or taller over the mid-body section, but lately, the designers are lowering these areas to that of a F1 racer.

him or her back to nothing more than a "stuffed-shirted, robot". (ie, not a real driver)

Formula One has also banned most of that equipment. Use of exotic metals has been done away with also. FISA has gone as far as to even outlaw the use of radio communications between the driver on the course with their respective teams.

To run a top-line Indy team, one which is very competitive, will cost somewhere in the vicinity of 6 million dollars per season. It's astronomical, but still a bit less costly than F1. Need I bother you with more disheartening news?

The Indy racer is slightly larger in size to the F1. Its minimum weight is 1550 lbs. It's about 34 mph faster at top end than F1. (239 mph) Their engines are allowed to be turbocharged. That isn't necessarily the norm during the "big" event, ran in the month of May. The Indianapolis 500 is sanctioned by the US Auto Club. (USAC) It's still the largest single-day sporting event in the world.

USAC tries to encourage a diversified use of engines. Nonaspirated and/or stock-blocks engines (mass-production design for use in street legal autos for the general public) are allowed, but they're not overly successful. It keeps cost at a sane level, not to mention the speeds. Of course, die-hard Indy fans know last years (1994) race was the exception, due to Al Unsers win using a stockblock.

USAC's intention of containing costs and safety is admirable, but apparently many people felt otherwise. Out of a 2 or 3 year controversy came CART. (Championship Auto Racing Teams) They sanction all Indy-Car events except the Indy 500. That breakaway situation with USAC happened around 18 years ago. (1978)

Now a new situation has cropped up within the last couple of seasons. Indianapolis Motor Speedway president Tony George has announce the formation of a new Indy styled racing series. It's called the IRL, the Indy Racing League. In the racing world, much has been said and written about it; some of it not so kind. The current drivers and owners don't seem too enthused about it. But as of this printing, things seem to be coming to a head.

The idea of this new venue is to slow down the vehicles and contain the costs. Thus, this will even the playing field for a more competitive race. Hopefully, that makes for a safer sport for the driver. For the poorly financed driver, it's a better chance to be more competitive or at least get qualified for the race itself. This will also make it a better race for the fans to watch.

As of now, the plans are for this to start this year, in 1996. It will be primarily an oval series of eventually 12 or so events, including the Indy 500. (1996 will have only 5 races)

The Indy 500 version of the IRL controversy is where things get sticky. Mr. Georges' trump card, the Indy 500, was being considered as a closed event.

To participate at Indy, a team would would have to join the IRL. (or be invited to participate) Don't look for that to happen. That would invite more politics and maybe ruin the quality and tradition of the 500 itself. Of course, this is an oversimplified description of what was being considered. Many other scenarios were pondered about also. But as of now, CART has sanctioned their own race (US 500) for Michigan International Speedway at the very same time the Indy 500 takes place.

As of now, it appears as though the IRL engine/chassis rules will be the following: a 2.2 liter, twin-cam, V-8 configured engine with the turbocharger downsized from its current 2.94 inches at the inlet to 2.76. Still, a single cam, pushrod engine is being considered.

The aerodynamic packages on the chassis will be designed in such a manner as to slow the racecars down in the corners where most (nasty) accidents happen. (ie, smaller wings, bigger sidepods, less ground effects - if any at all, etc)

(For more interest in reading of this book, don't worry specifically about all the stats or figures for now. But you will need to understand them in a general sense, for comparative purposes. If you would like to familiarize yourself with racing terms, turn to the glossary in the back of this book)

Meanwhile, it looks as though CART will stay intact despite the formation of this new series. Some CART teams will probably adjust their rules so their participants can convert over inexpensively to IRL regulations for the Indy 500.

A.3. INDY LIGHTS—These are the former American Racing Series racecars. Their name was changed after the 1990 season. These started in '86 to help create a 'stepping stone' (trainer) for aspiring Indy drivers. They receive maximum exposure because they race at the same events as the Indy cars. Hence, this is a 'support' series racecar. Exception to that are all 500 mile races.

This is a 'spec' racer (see chapter 7 about spec racecars) with a sealed 4.2 liter, non-turbocharged, fuel-injected, Buick V-6 engine. (they are to convert to a 4 liter V-8 for 1997, probably a BMW) They generate 420 horsepower which can take them up to 180 mph. Maximum tire size is comparable to an Indy racer: 10 & 14.75" for front and rear. (in tread width)

The Indy Lights 'B' class use the old non-ground effects March 'Wildcat' chassis which must weigh at least 1325 lbs, minus a driver. But they have improved the main racers by going to the F3000-based Lola chassis in 1993. Both classes race concurrently. (a race within a race)

Maximum length, width, height: 170, 77 & 34". 'Spec' racetires are Firestone radials. (Firestones recent inception back into racing may be a sign of things to come. They've been out of racing about 20–25 years)

This basically is a scaled down Indy car, with wings and about 70% of the power. Unlike Indycars, they don't run on methanol. (wood alcohol)

Both IndyCar and Indy lights series are supported by Pittsburgh Plate and Glass. (PPG) In addition, Firestone adds more support to the Indy Lights.

A.4. AIS—This is the American IndyCar Series racecar. Because of the relatively short competitive life of an Indy Champ car, this series was created by former Indycar driver Bill Tempero to help extend their life. (this also created a market for owners of older Indycars to cash in on; instead of their cars collecting dust in someones garage)

Started in 1987, most of these are originally-built and older Indy (Champ) cars, but new cars are eligible also. Their power is scaled-down a bit and are dominated by normally-aspirated engines. Turbocharged engines are legal in this class. To those familiar with Formula 5000, these machines will somewhat reminded you of them. They're slightly slower than Indy lights and

Formula 5000, but that may be mostly due to the shorter, tighter racecourses they compete on.

The size or power of their engines determines allowable chassis minimum weight: 1350 lbs for a 275 ci V-6; 1450 lbs for a 311 ci V-8; 1550 lbs for a 355 ci V-8; 1750 lbs for a 390 ci V-8; 1850 lbs for a 410 ci V-8. The engines used mostly are Ford, Chevy, Pontiac, Buick and Cosworth.

Some drivers have been using sprint car motors. These low-end, high-output engines can generate upwards of 700 hp. That equates to speeds of around 170 mph . . . and can reach that in rather quick fashion. (you'll understand this more after you read about SprintCars in Category E of this chapter)

As of now, these racecars are required to use a 'spec' racetire of comparable size to Indy cars, in this case, Hoosiers. But Hoosier is having problems and may have to stop operation. This series can be a good training school for aspiring IndyCar drivers also.

This series consist of about 12 events on short or long roadcourse (or streets) in the western US. They race short ovals, but look for them to eventually compete on larger ones. As of 1992 they have also staged events in Mexico and Canada. So therefore, AIS has subtitled themselves as the International IndyCar Championship. They may schedule some future events in the caribbean.

They also sanction the AIS Light series consisting of former Indy Light and F3000 machines built between 1985 and 1992. They must use normally-aspirated V-6 engines.

Look for AIS to grow tremendously unless the new IndyCar Racing League (IRL) proposed by USAC can bring the high cost of Indy Car racing back down to earth.

A.5. FORMULA ATLANTIC—This racer is similar appearing to the Indy Light and AIS. It's an off-shoot of the old European Formula B and Formula Two racing machines. At the 1983 pro level, these were called Formula Mondaile.

Started in the US in 1974 as another 'trainer' for Indy drivers, these racers are still popular, but not quite like they were before. That's probably because of stiffer class competition from such classes as AIS and Indy Lights. (and FA costs have risen considerably)

They're powered by a 1600 cc, nonaspirated, in-line-4 (cylinder) fuel-injected Cosworth. Their highly modified 'crossflow' engine has 4 valves per cylinder. (produce 240 hp) Combine that with a minimum weight of 1050 lbs. and they'll reach speeds of about 165 mph. Some ground effects are allowed.

Their Yokohama 'spec' tire width is comparable to the Indy Light and AIS. (14.75 inches wide measure acrossed the tread) Maximum length, width and height: 39.4 inches, extended from front and rear wheel centerlines; 51.2; and 35.4 at the rear wing.

Until 1991, these ran separate pro series in the US called the Atlantic & Pacific divisions. These two combined with a Canadian series to form the 11 to 13-race series here in the US. Their races are 60 to 100 miles in length.

They also run at the SCCA amateur level. But they're slightly lighter at 930 lbs minimum weight and slower (top end at 145 mph) using a carburated induction system with a productioned-based 225 hp engine. This is the Category 2 (C-2) car at the pro level. Generally Category 2 is the pre-1993 built racer. (C-1 are the newer cars) FA is SCCA's most powerful amateur classed formula racer.

These high profile machines run as a support series at most non-500 mile IndyCar events and even occasionally at a Formula one race, which will be the case in 1995 at the Canadian Gran Prix.

Formula Atlantic, supported by Player's Ltd and Toyota, boasts the second highest purse payout in North America for formula racers. (IndyCars are first; Formula 1 isn't based in the US) A FA race winner can pocket $25,000 per race plus seasonal points and contingency awards and/or money at seasons end.

A.6. SUPER VEE—A moment of silence for these USAC-SCCA sanctioned machines . . . They've trained such drivers as Al Unser, Jr. and Michael Andretti.

SV started in 1971, but VW's pullout after the 1990 season spelled the end of these at the pro level. Those Ralt RT-5's probably won't collect cobwebs though. (a very popular 'make' that dominated this so much that it looked like a 'spec' class)

Some people want to keep this class of racer going, . . . and they'll probably succeed. Judging by the popularity it had, it'll probably be nipped and tucked here and there by some new rules and be givened a name. That is just exactly what happened last year, (1995) but not without some mild birthpangs.

Around the early 90's, both SCCA & USAC had their own separate ideas on how to revive this pro racer. Oldsmobile seemed receptive with both in using its 2 liter engine to power the RT-5 (and RT-4, a model from Ralt in the formula Atlantic class) to form a Formula 2000 class. That idea didn't seem to completely materialize. But SCCA's own replacement idea did. (F. Continental) Still, this wasn't fully supported by the manufacturing community either. The exception was Yokohama. They were the 'spec' tire used in this class.

USAC announced plans to convert SV to two divisions. (USAC F2000 & Hooters Cup) Those ideas worked, but now look to be temporary.

Now, started in the 1995 season, once again, SCCA and USAC has announced they will merge the two "off-shoot" Super Vee racers that I just elaborated on, into one machine for competition in a pro series called the 'US Formula Ford 2000 National Championship'. This will comprise about 10 races on both roadcourse and ovals.

Previously, what looked like another idea was SCCA's plan to bring the international Formula 3 series here to replace SV, starting with the 1992 season.

They felt this and maybe the other plans would help bridge the gap left by SV. (and maybe F. Atlantics small decline) They had planned to have a 15-16 race schedule on both roadcourses and ovals. They wanted to run in the same events as the Indycars do. (except 500 mile races)

If this panned out, they were hoping it would overtake F. Atlantic as SCCA's top formula class and make it the US's only true international series. (of US sanction) Some sponsorship was already worked out, but it looks as though the SCCA-USAC FF2000 merge will take presidence by these two organizations first, if not exclusively.

Meanwhile, the Super Vee was doing okay at the amateur level in the SCCA. It was named differently then, called *Formula Continental*. They were a bit slower also. Top end was about 145 mph. Of course, some were VW powered by the old unpopular 1600 cc horizontally-opposed, 4-cyl., air-cooled "Bug" engine. Mostly though, Ford stock-blocks of 1100 & 2000 cc were used, which was one reason why the Super Vee name was dropped for Formula Continental. Minimum chassis weight requirements for all 3 engines were: 882, 750 and 1150 pounds, respectively.

At the SCCA Super Vee pro level, (called 'Bosch-VW' SV series) SV's had the 1600 cc, nonaspirated, watercooled, Rabbit & Scirocco engines. They could approach an impressive 190 horsepower. (some question that) At first, they used the air-cooled 'Bug' engine. But that lasted only a few years.

Around 1974–75, USAC joined in with SCCA to create the 'Bosch VW Gold Cup' series for roadcourses and 'Mini-Indy' for the oval series. They merged to a one 11-race series in 1980. As you learned, it ended in 1990.

All SV tire widths were a bit more narrow, about two-thirds that of the Atlantic or Indy Light. Unlike Formula Continental, some ground effects were allowed. Both were allowed wings. The top speed for pro SV was around 163–168 mph. This was a very strong 'support' class for most Indycar events.

A.7. FORMULA FORD 2000—Sometimes this class is called SuperFord. They're pretty much the same racer of SCCA's FC and USAC's F2000 classes in the Super Vee section that I just covered. When Super Vee started to decline around the mid-80's, FF2000's were brought over from England to help fill the void. (FF2000, F2000, same thing)

Actually, FF2000 is a souped-up Formula Ford 1600. The FF1600 cc engine is replaced with 2000 cc power, by Ford, also.

Another major change, compared to FF1600, is these racers are allowed wings, but no ground effects. What helped this racer to get started in this country was its ability to be built from a FF1600 with a specially-prepared 'kit'. For those who did that, it kept cost contained. Therefore, no complete racecar purchase was necessary. (if you already had a FF1600)

A small number of people felt these two machines could easily be interchanged back and forth between FF1600 and FF2000. That failed miserably, but it wasn't the manufacturers intention anyway.

These racers are doing pretty well in the US. But still, their sanctioning series, what they're called and what they're allowed to do have been bandied around quite a bit the last 6 years. Things have stabilized the past year or two. They are still popular in Europe.

FF 2000 got started in England around 1975. The power is a stock-block SOHC, (Single OverHead Cam) 2-liter, (2000 cc) inline 4-cylinder Ford. The horsepower output is about 135.

As you learned previously in Formula Continental, their minimum weight must be at least 1150 lbs. They top out at 145 mph in amateur racing and almost 170 at the pro level. Racetire sizes are identical with SV. No turbocharging or supercharging of any SV or F2000 engines are allowed.

As you read in the Super Vee section, an 8-race SCCA sanctioned pro series called 'American Continental Championship' (ACC) was underway for these Formula Fords in 1992. (the Oldsmobile support didn't happen; but Olds did support the Sports 2000 racecars that you'll read about in Category B of this chapter)

You also read earlier USAC had started their own two division 10–12 race pro series two years earlier for these FF2000's. They also sanctioned a small 3-race series in cooperation with the Jim Russell racing school. It was called the 'USAC/Russell Triple Crown' series.

F2000's run a 'Canadian Automobile Sport Club' (CASC) sanctioned 9-race pro schedule called the 'Export A Inc F2000

The winner paces the course in a formula Ford 2000. Note the size of the chassis and racing slicks compared to an Indy car. It's smaller, but only by a few inches. It's underneath the bodies where all the difference in race cars are evident. Under slightly different rules, SCCA races these as formula continentals.

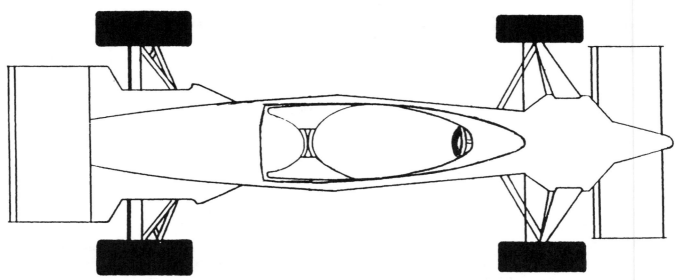

This is the profile of a FF2000. Drop the wings, then it would look like a FF1600. Most lower level formula racers do not have extensive sidepods. Put them in the illustration and it would look like the super vee. Add wider tires, with those sidepods and this would profile several high-speed formula racers. (Such as: an Indy car, formula 1, 2, 3, 3000, Indy Light, Aurora, AIS, Atlantic & F 5000)

This is a Formula Ford 1600. Note the CFF lettering? That indicates this Ford races in the 'Club' class, for older cars, although they are eligible for regular formula Ford competition, if so desired by the driver. FF 1600's are the second most numerous class of racer in the world, made evident by over 25 manufacturers, of which some of them are out of business. Remember, the only difference between the FF2000 & 1600 is the 1600 isn't allowed wings; uses a (Ford) engine (Cortina or Pinto 4 cylinder) 400 cc's smaller and therefore the entire machine must weigh 50 lbs lighter.

Series'. (formerly the Walter Wolf series) Of course, as you just learned, USAC & SCCA got together, like they did in the late SV class, to form the US FF2000 National Championship series for FF's in the US. They started racing in 1995.

A.8. FORMULA FORD 1600—These used to be the largest of all race classes in the US, if not the world. They are still very popular. But it seems like nothing affects them more than the economy. Of course, that's true in all racing, but apparently these are affected the most. Maybe that's because this is where racing begins to get expensive. (not to mention the classes I've just covered previously) Maybe it's their sheer numbers. I do not know. I know they're here to stay, bad economy or not. They are always in the top sec-

ond or third largest class in the SCCA. (hence, the USA)

Even though I'm not devoting as much space to the FF1600, it's not because they're unimportant. It is because they're similar to the FF2000. Lose the wings, take off 400 cc from the 2000 cc SuperFord engine, drop off 50 lbs for a 1100 lb. minimum weight, and you have the FF1600. Its tops out around 134–137 mph. The blocks are stock Cortina, Pinto and Fiesta Fords that produce 115 horsepower. The racetires are the same as the FF2000, FC and Super Vee.

There are a few pro series offered, but they're not very popular nationwide just yet. I assume one reason is a lack of further sponsor support from the Ford Motor Company.

This class of racing is available in the

This is a Formula Vee, the third most popular class of racer in the world. There are also many manufacturers of this machine, over 30, of which most are small, but still successful. This is a rare class because many amateur drivers have built & designed their own chassis. This volkswagon-based racer is easily recognized by its skinny, tall-looking race slicks, visible front shock-absorber mounting brackets and unusually high ground clearance. (for a formula car) Most FV's do not use sidepods, as do Indy cars and Formula Atlantics, to name a few. (The FFord 1600 & 2000 also have a tendency to avoid use of sidepods)

SCCA at both regional and national championship levels.

A.9. CLUB FORD—These are virtually the same class as the FF 1600. Same chassis & engine, etc. The only thing different is their age; they're older. That means their aerodynamic lines or body styles aren't very slippery or sleek. (some racers call them "dogs" down long high-speed straights) The cars are usually 6–7 years old and as old as 20, at times.

These racers compete at the same time (a race within a race) as the FF1600 in SCCA regional events. They are also allowed to compete as a regular FF1600 provided they adhere to FF1600 rules, but because of their outdated racing aerodynamics, they very rarely do well, much less win. They don't run in SCCA National events.

This class was created to keep older models in use and more accessible for those not financially able to race FF1600. They're a good stepping-stone trainer for FF1600 & 2000.

Other things are incorporated into this class to control any runaway costs. One example is the tires used are such to encourage longer wear, therefore cheaper costs. (they use street tires instead of racing slicks)

This class is serving its purpose well. Look for their continued growth, but not to the point of threatening the FF1600 or any classes below them, like Formula Vee & Formula 440.

This Club Ford racer is one of a very few regional-status classes that are eligible to compete for a national championship. Actually, these machines are one of 4 types of machines which race at the recently established ARRC event (American Road Race of Champions) near Atlanta, Georgia. Whether the ARRC is a true championship is up for debate. That's because this is an 'open' event. A racer doesn't have to be invited or earn points to run in this race.

The ARRC event was partially establish because the Road Atlanta racing facility lost host to the annual SCCA national championship held every October. It's now held at the Mid-Ohio Roadracing Complex.

The success of the IT (Improved Touring) Festival, another sort of unofficial national championship event, held in Topeka, Kansas around August also led to the formation of the ARRC. Whether the ARRC can match the popularity of the Valvoline sponsored SCCA National Championship 'Runoffs' is in my opinion, doubtful.

A.10. FORMULA VEE—An economical formula class to start racing in. This also used to be the most popular class in the world. It looks as if they'll always be right up there as the 1st, 2nd or 3rd most numerous racer around.

Their ease of maintenance and good availability of parts make them very cost effective. Some people claim FV's lack the learning 'curve' necessary to move up to more advanced racing. To that I say "hogwash". They base this on a lack of low rpm power and the swing-axle suspension. (with constant camber changes at the rear tires) Those who say that, don't understand how FV teaches racing.

There have been many big-name racers who started in FV. It is such an economic and highly competitive class, many FV racers are there to stay. They like it that much. Even though the parts availability is beginning to concern some for now, the costs are relatively low.

The rules are also stable. Rules stability may not sound like much to you now, but it's nice to have. Constantly changing rules are an aggravation and sometimes costly. It's done to improve competition and safety, but some people seem to get burned by it. But, that's hardly ever the case in FV.

This low maintenance racer has people trying to organize it at the professional level

with increasing success. Inaugurated in 1991, the 5–6 race schedule, called the 'Valvoline/Thalheimer Jewelers Pro Vee Series', hasn't had a complete nationwide following yet. It's looking more promising every year though.

VW's pullout of SV means FV factory help looks impossible. Despite that, Valvoline oil and Thalheimer's, a retail jeweler based in Naples, Florida, is lending support. But anyway, people who see any FV race knows the competition is very close and exciting. It's not unusual to see a 1 or 2 second difference in qualifying times by the top 10 or 15 racers.

"Vees" are powered by the VW air-cooled, normally-aspirated, 1200 cc, horizontally-opposed flat-4, "Bug" engine. It's maximum output is 60 hp. Their minimum weight is 1025 lbs with driver included. They can reach speeds around 110 mph. No wings or ground effects are allowed.

Their wheelbase must be within 83.5 & 81.5". Max overall length is 127". Max front & rear track is 51.4 & 49.8". (width between set of wheels/tires in front of racecar or the ones in back) The racetires are narrowly profiled and very distinguishable; no wider than 6.5".

One of things which makes this class so popular is that it incorporates many stock VW 'Bug' automobile components into its design. (read into that . . . cheaper costs) That includes, of all things, even some chassis parts, specifically, the front (steering) beam and suspension arms.

Other stock items on this racer (from the VW auto) is: the brake back plates, drums, cylinders and shoes; all wheel bearings; all wheels; steering box; engine case; removable cylinders, called "jugs"; crankshaft; distributor; oil and fuel pumps; carburation, to a degree; aftermarket racing pistons and rods may be used, but must retain stock size; and finally the stock transaxle case is also required, although the pinion gear must be reversed. Unlike the VW Bug street automobile, the FV racer has its engine in front of the transaxle. Usually, all transaxle gears are stock, except one, which is usually the third gear. The cylinder heads are allowed to be reworked only to a certain degree. (for better breathing and therefore better performance by the engine) Valves and valve trains and cams must remain stock.

This is not a 'spec' class. It doesn't have to be. Its costs are relatively low and stable. Therefore, even though it's a very highly competitive racer on the track, personal design, tricks or techniques may be used without driving up costs. Some drivers build their own FV racer. In addition, the more popular of the many brand-name chassis out there remain competitive for 15, even 20 years.

If this all sounds like overloaded technical jargon . . . it is . . . but absolutely nothing compared to what it could be. Like I stated earlier in this book, each class of racing has its own set of rules . . . enough to fill a small paperback book. That's just for the engine and drivetrain. The chassis rules is another book.

This is why it's unnecessary to know the technicalities, at least for now. The chassis, and especially the engine builders will know the rules. Still, as you get more familiar with this sport, it's then necessary to know the rules because you'll ultimately be responsible for them. You are the one who will be penalized if a technical rule is broken. (of course, you'll go back to the builder and ask why it happened, if it's the their fault. He better have a good explanation because he can't afford too many boo-boos like that . . . or he's out of business fast)

Why did I wait to gloss over these things here in the FV section? Because I could kill two birds with one stone so-to-speak. I can mention its existence and then tell you that with FV, you don't need all those marked up parts from a low volume, high dollar race parts distributor. You can scavenge them off of a VW 'Bug' at the junk yard. (although I have to admit that's getting very hard to do. That option is depleating itself fast, if not already completely gone)

But don't despair just yet. There are still plenty of VW specialty shops throughout the US, if not the world. They supply parts at what I think is still pretty reasonable costs. (in part, thanks to the 'Dune-Buggie' industry) On top of that, these parts are new, not necessarily reconditioned. (from a brand called 'Bugpack')

A.11. FORMULA 440—This is SCCA's youngest amateur formula class. Started around 1979 from scratch, they're similar in appearance to Go-Karts, but much more complex, covered with bodywork and larger in size.

Like Go-Karts, their limited suspension is very simple. Because of that, they have a hard time keeping their rubber firmly planted down in the turns and on bumpy tracks, which slows them down considerably. On the plus side, it keeps their costs down.

They're actually top-end faster on long straights than the Formula Vee, but usually slower in overall roadcourse racing. (depending on the track configuration and condition) Because of that and the fact they race at the same time with the FV in SCCA events, a lot of passing back and forth by these two competitors may occur.

Some FV drivers complain about that situation with F440. They say 440's slows them down. Maybe that's true, maybe not. I drive FV and find competition with F440 is nothing to lose sleep over.

Other classes in SCCA amateur racing have to share the track also. It helps keep costs down. If FV raced with FF, then the FF's would be held up a bit. So, perfect situations in SCCA club racing is almost economically impossible. 440's are better off racing with FV, than FV with FF.

440's are cost effective and provide for some very keen competition. They are still growing, but at a moderate rate. Predictions of their eventual demise years ago, hasn't even come close. In fact, their numbers were sufficient enough to warrent their SCCA National Championship status.

These racers were initially powered by a 2-cycle, 2-cylinder, air-cooled, Kawasaki snowmobile engine, which produces about 70 hp. Those engines are still used, but have been deemed a bit inferior despite their excellent history of reliability.

As of 1994 a new engine, the AMW, has proved itself a bit stronger. This 70-horse, two cylinder, 2-cycle, 497 cc engine uses 'reed' valving, but unlike the Kawasaki, it's watercooled. (generally meaning better low-rpm power)

Formula 440. Note the size of this racer. It's like a more sophisticated 'Enduro' go-kart, with even more bodywork. It is a bit more racer than an Enduro go-kart, with larger race slicks. But still considerably smaller than most other racing machine tires. That's a FV in the background. Like other classes in SCCA amateur racing, these two classes race together for their own separate points, championship, etc. Sometimes both class drivers complain about getting in each others way.

F440's can reach close to 120 mph. Their minimum weight is 700 lbs with the driver. No turbocharging, wings or ground effects are allowed. Wheelbase and track is about 80% the size of a FV.

They use a much shorter, but wider profiled racing tire. Yet, those tires are almost twice the size of its predecessor, the Go-Kart. Like Go-Karts, they're chain-driven.

A.12. ROADRACING (ENDURO) GO-KARTS—Yes, I do consider these a formula class. They look like a mini-SportsRacer, but fill most of the requirements of a formula racecar: open cockpit; (semi-)open wheels; purpose-built; low-slung; etc. So, think these are kids toys? I don't call racing on tracks such as Talladega & Road America, to name a few, at speeds up to 110 mph kids stuff.

As suspension-lacking Go-Karts go, these are a complex racer. They race for a National Championship in 17 classes. They range from a first-time novice with a stock 100 cc motor to the pro classed, duel-engine or motorcycle-powered 250 cc 'SuperKart'.

Yes, these do compete professionally. But the pro classes aren't quite as popular here as they are in Europe. The European pro classes such as Formula 'E' and Formula 'K' can be very sophisticated and expensive. They can get pretty complex at some levels on this side of the "pond" too, but not quite as numerous in comparison.

Despite that, what's considered the largest Go-Kart event in the world is the Elkhart

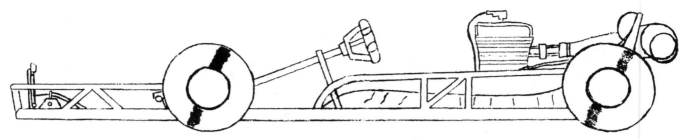

This is the Enduro kart without it's body work/number plate(s). Note how much longer it must be for stability at high speed. It's designed for the driver to sit (lay) flat for better aerodynamics. Therefore, the engine is sidemounted to allow for that.

Enduro Kart with bodywork

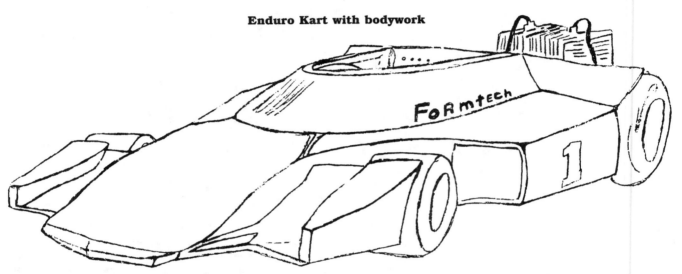

The sprint kart is usually shorter in size for better handling response. The driver sits up since aerodynamics doesn't come into play compared to this Enduro racer. The engine is sidemount. The dirt karts usually have their engines rearmounted.

Grand Prix. It's held every year (July) in Elkhart, Indiana. Purse payout is around $25,000, which is divided between top finishers in 12 classes. (so don't figure on making a living doing this; which can be said about a lot of classes in any racing) This event has been known to draw as many as 25 to 30,000 spectators.

These miniture rockets, generally, the 'Open' class, come loaded with some pretty expensive and strong components. An example would be a 6-speed gearbox. (instead of the normal centrifugal clutch) They're water-cooled and use a 125–250 cc motorcycle powered engine. Some of those same Kart engines are equipped with high-tech cams, titanium valves, coated pistons and even a special girdle to keep the heads from blowing off. They've also been known to legally use exotic racing fuels.

RoadRacing Go-Karts are somewhat aerodynamically designed, but are allowed no wings or ground effects. Minimum weights for the single & duel engined racers are 95 & 115 lbs. Wheelbase & track limits (width of the 2 sets of wheels) are set at 50 & 30". Overall length is limited to 80". The height limit is 26". There are no restrictions placed on overall width. Tires are purpose-built raceslicks.

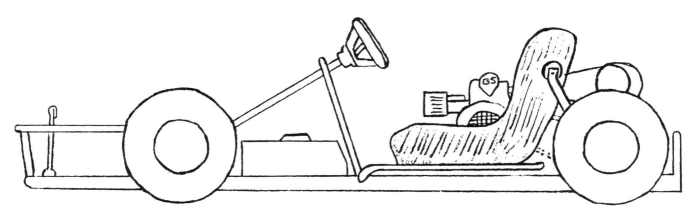

Enduro Kart of the future? Possibly . . . but for now this is more like those very high speed formula E & K Karts raced in Europe. (without the bodywork) This looks like a Dirt Kart also.

There have been many well known racers that started racing Go-Karts when they were youngsters. But don't let that discourage any of you older (or just plain old) folks from giving Go-Kart racing a try. The price is right and there's more older men and women doing this then you probably think. (you know that cute little saying . . . "the difference between men and boys . . . is the price of their toys" . . . doesn't apply in racing, . . . even at this "financial-friendly" level)

I'd like to mention an experimental Go-Kart racer, in Europe, which can reach close to 200 mph. That's right, a 200 mph Kart! Boy . . . you'd have to be on drugs to drive something as dangerous as that in a race. Trying that alone on a course is one thing . . . with a bunch of other "Kart-Missiles" is out of the question. Let me emphasize though, this is experimental. I've got to believe it'll remain that way.

I can't phantom a cost-effective, practical, and above all, a safe 200 mph 'Kart'. At that speed with no suspension, you better race on a glass smooth track or you'll flip the first time you hit a bump.

A racecar suspension isn't just for traction, but for safety too. At 200 mph, a small bump will be magnified. If there is no suspension to absorb the shock, it's absorbed by the tires. If they don't blow-up because of the sudden pressure put on them, which is already bad, then the shock transfers to the chassis. If that happens to only one side of the chassis, then that side will be thrown up

in the air and therefore flip the whole vehicle. So . . . look for this 200 mph go-kart idea to die quickly.

A.13. SPEEDWAY (DIRT) GO-KARTS— These are the newest and fastest growing Go-Karts. There are all kinds of classes with 2 and 4 cycle divisions throughout the US and the whole world. These racers range from the simple 5 horsepower "lawnmower" type for the very young and inexperienced, to the exotic versions used in the 'Open' class.

Most IKF and WKA sanctioned classes are determined by driver age, experience and the kind of engine they use.

The World Karting Association (WKA) 2-cycle division has National and Regional events. These are usually for the older drivers with stronger engines that compete in the 'Briggs and Stratton' sponsored, 12-class dirt series. Also, a 13-class series is available in separate Northern & Southern Divisions of the US.

Other series are available to race in also, with the other large Kart sanctioning body, the IKF. (International Kart Federation)

The 4-cycle racers run pretty much the same form of series even though they aren't quite as quick as the 2-cycle machines. (in most classes, not all)

In my opinion, this class and Quarter-Midgets (covered later) is where it would be the safest, most cost-effective and practical to start your youngster in 4-wheel racing.

These 2 and 4-cycle machines provide

Is this go-kart the 'Enduro', 'Sprint' or 'Speedway' (dirt) type? The 'enduro' kart is built for high speed, so it needs more bodywork to control aerodynamics. This racer doesn't have enough. The dirt go-kart can't benefit from the racing slicks pictured on this vehicle. It's a 'Sprint' go-kart. They race on short paved or dirt roadcourses of just a few laps and/or heats.

plenty of broadsliding and close action on a 1/10 to 1/5th mile dirt oval. From 50 cc to unlimited power, some Karts sport the wings, fairing and style of a sprint car racer. No ground-effects are permitted. (and would be impractical anyway in the slower classes)

Due to changing track surface conditions and various grooves formed during a race, the right tread-pattern tire is essential for proper 'bite'. To choose the correct tire requires some know-how and experience.

A youngster can begin racing these at no earlier age than 8, as far as sanctioned competition is concerned.

This level of Kart racing also offers a huge event down in Jacksonville, Florida during the Christmas/New year season. Sanctioned by the WKA, it's part of the 'WKA Briggs and Stratton National Dirt Series'. This event combined with the Enduro (RoadRacing) Karts at the Daytona International Speedway sort of forms Go-Kart's own racing version of NASCAR's Speedweeks. As many as 1000 or more racers are entered every year.

A.14. SPRINT GO-KARTS—At the start of this chapter, I said the first 14 formula classes would be listed in descending order of strength (not necessarily speed) and sophistication. This racer is the exception.

These are faster and perhaps more complex than the Speedway (Dirt) Kart. But, that may be only because of what they race on. Usually, they compete on longer paved courses of over 1/2 mile, but have been known to race on courses of 1/8 mile. They also run 2 and 4-cycle divisions. In turn, these are further subclassed by age, experience and power used.

The 2-cycles range from 80 to 135 cc's and can go as fast as 70 mph if there is enough road for acceleration. The 4-cycles range from an out-of-the-box stock 5 hp engine to an all-out highly modified version.

Also, like the 'Dirt' or 'Speedway' Karts, they compete at local, regional and national levels. Age limit is also eight.

This is the class, or more accurately, the type of Go-Kart which got it all going back in 1957.

Some people may start to confuse some Go-Karts as Quarter-Midgets. That will be cleared up later on in this chapter.

Maximum overall height and length is 26 & 72 inches. There are no limits placed on width. Wheelbase must be between 40 and 54 inches. The track (also called tread) must be at least 28″. Minimum dry weight (minus driver and fuel) is 85 lbs for a single-powered racer and 105 lbs for duel-powered machines.

Racings Lack of Early Exposure

I'd like to make a point about racing exposure. Many of you reading this information may be pleasantly surprised to find this sport is so involved or diversified. So, why didn't you know about this earlier? Probably for the same reason some people lack specific information on racing in general.

First of all, the sanctioning bodies themselves can't afford to spend large amounts of money on promoting their particular sport. It serves to drive up the costs of racing in general.

Another reason is the lack of news media coverage at the local level, especially in the amateur ranks. Heaven knows, even the big boys in the pros don't get all that much coverage compared to football, basketball, baseball and hockey. That's especially true from the large city newspapers and newsrooms.

They are more inclined to cover the 'ball & stick' kind of sports.

Cable TV is nowhere near as negligent. The cable network is steadily showing even more improvement, especially ESPN, ESPN2 and TNN. It's my contention that network TV was forced to reconsider its racing coverage due to its popularity on cable. So . . . they also have exposed more (pro) racing.

The high profile events like F1, NASCAR & CART get good exposure compared to amateur or club racing. Unfortunately, in a way, that serves to the casual observer or fan the myth that racing is financially way out of reach. That myth is slowly going away as racing improves its image and media coverage. (again, . . . thanks mostly to cable TV)

Another reason the public lacks racing exposure is because it can't be offered at the high school level. Reasons for that ought to be obvious. Money!

Some schools are already struggling to keep their main revenue-producing sport, football, alive. To have racing . . . ha . . . now that's funny. It's ungodly expensive and out of the question. (and where would all those high schools race at?) As a result, this hurts exposure to youngsters.

That's another reason older folks tend to discover racing at the age they do. Youngsters are too busy with the ball and stick type sports. Besides, they don't have time and especially the money to participate with anyway.

The first 14 formula classes I just covered are the ones raced here in the US, if not elsewhere. The rest covered are either not real numerous in the US, not raced here at all, they're experimental or about to come over here. Whatever the case, all of the following racers are not established in the US, but that could change. Descriptions will be brief.

A.15. AURORA—In the US, not all old Indy Cars any longer collect dust. They may go on to the AIS. (sort of a senior-car series, covered earlier) The Aurora does likewise for Formula 1. These cars start out here seldom older then 2 years. Formula 1 teams watch these drivers closely for prospective talent, much like Indy teams do for Indy Lights, AIS and other classes.

A.16. FORMULA TWO—This class no longer has the popularity it used to have, but they still race in England as a 'spec' series. They are required to use the Reynard-built chassis powered by the Cosworth engine.

Started twice in 1947 & '67 in Europe, it was one step away from F1. Now they're considered to be more of a stepping-stone trainer for the Formula 3000 racers.

These complex racers were powered by a 2000 cc BMW which were modified to produce 300 hp. They were a cut above our F. Atlantics and similar to our AIS and Indy lights of today. Generally, these have been replaced by the Formula 3000.

A.17. FORMULA THREE—Started 1950 in Europe, these lost popularity temporarily. Revamped in '75 and again in England in 1979, these are almost like our F. Atlantics.

Their engines are 400 cc larger, (2000) but restricted to 175 hp, compared to FA's 240 hp. Engine 'makes' are BMW, Alfa Romero, Toyota and Renault.

They were allowed wings. Their tires were comparable to FA. They appear to be losing popularity again in Europe, but going well in Britain under different rules.

This was the racer that officials thought would be introduced here in 1991 to replace the now defunct SV series. It still may happen, but for now, it seems to be put on a temporary hiatus by the recent inception of the USAC-SCCA sanctioned US Formula Ford Championship series.

A.18. FORMULA 5000—Not much to add about these big and loud racers. That's not because they weren't significant, but because I couldn't relatively say anything about them now that I haven't said about our F. Atlantics of today.

The F5000 is more complex and powerful though and probably more like todays Indy Light. Actually, they were close to the power and performance of the F1 back in the late 60's and early 70's, but a bit heavier. Some drivers claimed this made them easier to setup, drive and maintain than the F1 and many other complex racers.

These Gran Prix-styled cars (usually characterized by the high 'ram-air' intake scoop) were popular as a 8 to 14-race series in North America and as other series throughout the rest of the world. (even locations like South Africa) Places such as England and Australia were attempting to revive them.

This normally-aspirated, 5000 cc (mass-produced engine) racer was introduced in the US by the SCCA in 1968, but was renamed Formula A. (not as Formula Atlantic; don't confuse this with FA, although these racecars more or less evolved into them)

Their final year here was 1976. A few of them are surviving as a Vintage racer, even though there were plenty of these kinds of machines around. (you'll read plenty about Vintage racing in chapter 5)

In a way, F5000 really didn't fade away as much as it lived in another form. From an open-wheeled, single-seat formula racer, they were converted into a closed-wheeled, single-seat, sportsracer . . . namely, . . . the (also popular) SCCA Can-Am race machine of 1977 through 1986.

A.19. SPEC FORD—These are the FF1600's which compete under a very 'specified' set of rules and regulations. This helps to contain costs. Under this circumstance, more emphasis is placed on driver skill and away from racecar technology. This is further explained in chapter 7, section A. Meanwhile, these are gaining popularity in the US on the west coast.

'Spec' FF have an inherent tendency to be newer built machines than Club Ford. That's because CF's are a sort-of "senior-car" racer. That doesn't mean Spec Ford racecars can't be older, but rather, just harder and impractical for converting over to the Club Ford class.

This class looks like it may grow further the next few years since the 'spec' idea is gaining momentum.

A.20. FORMULA MAZDA—Another fairly new 'spec' racer in the US. Simular to FA, it's much closer to a Formula Continental. Actually, it has competed as a Formula Conti-

nental in SCCA racing, but only at the regional level. Now they have their own SCCA regional class, but still have not reached the sufficient numbers to be regrouped into national championship status. I look for that to change by 1999. Despite that, these machines have ran as an occasional 'support' race at NASCAR, IMSA and USAC pro events.

FM is SCCA's only 'spec' formula racer with no national status. Spec Fords, you read about earlier have neither regional or national status. They race for the sake of racing and nothing else, no points, regional or national championships. Look for that to eventually change.

Introduced to racing 1984, Mazda is a popular machine in Europe. It's gaining some in the US. Started in 1990, SCCA has completed the first 6 seasons with them professionally. They race separately in 11 SCCA regional events on the west coast which double as a (sort of, semi-) pro series. These races are the 'Star Formula Mazda Championships'. There are plans to bring this series further east to Mid-Ohio, Road America, Wisconsin and Watkins Glen, New York.

They're powered by 165–170 hp, 6600 rev-limited, Mazda rotary engine. It's proving to be very reliable. (won't blow or "grenade", as termed in racing circles) It's also very low-maintenance and relatively affordable for its class.

Its 95 inch wheelbase and 'Star' (make) chassis is designed with shear plates which cut down the costs of crash damage repairs. These are designed to safely tear away in such a manner as not to take other racecar components with them. This is important in such areas as the critical suspension-connecting points on a chassis. Once the chassis is damaged, repairs are very expensive, if not impossible. (this also enhances driver safety, by absorbing shock)

Front and rear track limits are 59 and 58 inches. Top speed of this winged racer approaches 155 mph. Minimum weight is 1330 including the driver. Spec racetire 'make' is Yokohama.

A.21. FORMULA RENAULT—A popular racer for around 20 years. They raced in

France and look like FF2000, but behave more like a SV because of its size and weight. This is also a 'spec' racer, but only by how it's powered. The chassis rules remain free. (free by design, not by dimensions required by rules)

This winged machine can reach 133 mph with its normally aspirated, 4-cylinder, 1721 cc Renault engine. Their Firestone 'spec' racetires are comparable in size to our FF2000 or SV.

A 12-event race series was also tested in England for this class.

A.22. BARBER-DODGE FORMULA, FORMULA RUSSELL—Even though these racers aren't placed in the "first 14" list for formula machines raced here, there is nothing foreign or unpopular about them. The reasons for their location here is because they're not formula classes unto themselves, but rather an extension of Formula Ford 2000/Formula Continental. These classes of racing have a more direct commercial emphasis.

SCCA controlled in 1995, B-D was sanctioned by IMSA, an organization traditionally Endurance/Sportscar oriented. B-D Formula is an extension of the Skip Barber school. Formerly supported by Saab, they supplied the 2 liter, 16 valve/4 cylinder, 225 hp engine from their 900 & 9000 series cars. Dodge now provides the engines. Zerex, the anti-freeze people, also provides support.

This 12-race, North American pro 'spec' series, started in 1986, called IMSA Zerex-Saab, is now renamed the 'Barber-Dodge' series.

Even though B-D Formula is simular behaving to FF2000/FC, its 'spec' tire (Goodyear) is wider and looks more like the ones on a Formula Atlantic.

Starting in the 1995 season, Barber-Dodge Formula will be powered by the 3.5 liter, V-6 Dodge engine, which produces about the same output as the Saab, but at more reasonable costs. It propels the 1300 lb Mondiale-manufactured winged chassis to around 160 mph. No ground effects are allowed.

Formula Russell is listed here too. Like the Barber-Dodge, this pro series is an extension of a racing school; namely the Jim Russell Racing Drivers School. FR is powered by the Mazda rotary engine (like Formula Mazda) which sits in a winged Hayashi-made chassis which is propelled to 150 mph.

This 'spec' classed racer competes in 2 west coast pro series sanctioned separately by SCCA & USAC. This racer is also eligible for SCCA regional-only competition as a Formula Continental.

A.23. FORMULA 3000—Raced in Europe & still popular in Japan, these are slightly scaled-down Formula One machines which were formerly overseen by FIA. In 1992, FIA ended the 9–11 event international race series due to increasing costs. They still race, but not internationally.

These are very sophisticated and use high-tech carbon-fiber monocoque chassis construction. Powered by a 3-liter (3000 cc) Cosworth DFV or a Honda V-8, there is a 9000 rpm limit on these engines.

Started in the mid 80's, it replaced Formula Two. These racers are just a step away, in class, from Formula One.

These expensive machines are not 'spec' classed, but the tires and racing fuel each machine uses must be. It's almost a carbon-copy of our Indy light.

F3000 may be racing in the US as early as 1997. There is some small talk that F3000 and our Indy Lights may form a series using one chassis. (partial 'spec' class) The idea is to incorporate the Indy Light into an international class. We'll see if that happens, because this is the kind of class the US woefully lacks. (especially since Formula One hasn't been making too many visits here lately)

A.24. FORMULA VAUXHALL LOTUS—Another new 'spec' class started in England and Europe around 1988. In fact, it's so new, not much is known about it in the US.

They're built by Reynard using a GM 2-liter, 4-cylinder, 16-valve engine that produces about 160 hp. These winged racers are classed like another version of our FF2000 or Formula Continental. They look amazingly like our now defunct Super Vee, especially at the front and rear wings.

Four 'open' wheels and an 'open' cockpit. That means this is a Formula racer. It has sidepods, wide racing slicks, front and rear wings and who knows what kind of power. Is it an Indy car? Too small for that. Is it a Formula 1, 2, 3, 3000, 5000, Indy Light or a Formula Atlantic? It's a Formula 3000, popular in Europe & Japan. Look closely at the driver's (head) size. A seasoned race fan would know this machines wheelbase (ie, size) is also too small to be a Formula one. This racer could easily pass as our Formula Atlantic. Many race cars look alike on the outside, but are different under the hood and/or bodywork.

Top speed hasn't been determined yet, but my educated estimate would be about 153 mph. Whether they can catch on in the US is doubtful for now, if that attempt is ever made. That's because we already have too many race machines identical to it. The only thing that'll make this class popular here is the bottom line . . . costs!

A.25. FORMULA FORWARD—Another new European 'spec' racer designed by a FF builder, Van Dieman. They're similar to a FF2000, but somewhat faster. They're powered by a fuel-injected, 2-liter, twin-cam Ford. Wings are allowed. 'Spec' racetire 'make' is Uniroyal.

There isn't very much information out on them here in the US, so whether this machine can make it over here or not is still anyones guess, if this racer makes that attempt.

This machine, developed around 1989, is almost a carbon-copy of the F.Vauxhall Lotus except it has a longer nose, but a smaller, more simply designed front wing.

A.26. FORMULA FIRST—This is another fairly new 'spec' racer, built by Van Dieman. This car is a bit more simple compared to our SCCA club (amateur) racer, the FF1600. It has a spaceframe chassis and no wings. It appears as a bulkier version of the FF1600. That's because its 1.6-liter (1600) engine is not mounted like nearly all formula racers are. It's transverse or sideways installed, much like todays front-wheel drive passenger cars. This racecar's Ford 'Escort' engine is (still) located back of the driver.

I'm not sure the thinking behind this, but I'd imagine it has something to do with cheaper costs, better handling characteristics (weight more evenly distributed from back to front) and less severe rearend damage in the event of an accident. Speaking of accidents, this racer has proven to develop some very close racing, . . . and at a reasonably low cost. That's the good news. The bad news is that it has also produced a high accident rate.

These started around 1987 outside the US, but really haven't been very popular.

Maybe they need more time. We will eventually see.

A.27. VINTAGE FORMULA VEE—This hasn't caught on either, but then most Vintage classes aren't designed to when compared to serious, competitive racing. (you'll know more about what I'm referring to after you finish reading chapter 5) I don't believe they'll ever become real popular. Not because of low numbers though. The reason is one of practicality. Unless any particular FV is a real relic, most remain very competitive for years as far as the chassis is concerned.

Bill Noble, a noted FV engine builder & racer, won an SCCA National Championship in a 15 year old racer. Does that indicate anything about FV? So why bother with a Vintage class? Are there some old chassis out and about that maybe couldn't win? I mean, they are extremely old! Could be the originally-built 'Beach' racers of the 60's aren't competitive? But then, everything's got to get (too) old eventually. This may hang on though. The long existence and popularity of Vee have those two factors working for this class.

A.28. FORMULA SABRE—This is USAC's relatively new 'spec' racer. It was introduced in early 1990, but it isn't racing in the US like originally planned. Instead, it currently competes in Japan.

It's similar to the Indy Light. It will be a complex machine with wings, but with no ground effects. They'll be powered by a normally-aspirated V-6 of US manufacture, probably Buick. Minimum weight is 1400 lbs with a 105 wheelbase.

If USAC is slow getting this established in the US, it's probably because of their desire to make them relatively cost effective. Right now, it looks as though they won't be racing here any time soon.

A.29. VINTAGE FORD—This class is growing fairly well in certain parts of the US. These are old FF 1600's that cannot compete with the new models.

Instead of racing slicks, they use a 'spec' radial street tire. The difference between this and Club Ford is that these are usually older and compete under regulations which are not as specific as Club Ford.

A.30. VINTAGE FORMULA SUPER VEE—This racer isn't exactly setting the world on fire. But then, like I stated earlier, it's not vintage racing's intention to overtake any regular classes in the first place.

Even older SV's used to be too sophisticated to retire to this class. They still could race in SCCA's F. Continental series. The ones which do race Vintage are mostly SV's of the 70's and maybe just a few from the early 80's.

Of course, now that SV has been eliminated, Vintage Super Vee cannot help but at least benefit a bit from that circumstance.

A.31. VINTAGE FORMULA ATLANTIC—This class is gaining popularity in parts of the US. Regular FA racers has been around for over 16, 17 years now and are getting stiff competition from a lot of new and/or upcoming classes. That and the fact early models are accumulating fast, won't hurt this class. Look for Vintage FA to grow a bit more.

A.32. FORMULA VAUXHALL JUNIOR—Started in 1991 as a 'spec' class, this is a European race vehicle simular to our FF1600. As our FF1600 is a slower, wingless version of the FF2000, so too is this class a slower, wingless version of the Formula Vauxhall Lotus covered earlier in category A.24.

The 'spec' tubeframe chassis is Van Diemen-made and powered by a Vauxhall (GM) 1.6 liter (1600 cc) sealed motor rated at 125 hp. But they're slightly quicker than our FF1600's. Their top-end speed is about 139-141 mph.

Like all nonvintage formula racers, they use racing slicks. In this class, they must be 'spec' racetires, supplied by Avon. (a foreign tire manufacturer)

A.33. FORMULA EUROPA BOXER—Finally, this is another European racer simular to our FF1600, except it's a bit more powerful and is allowed wings.

The 1.7 liter, (1700 cc) 16-valve/4-cylinder engine by Alfa Romero produces 145 hp for speeds up to around 147 mph.

The chassis is open to any manufacturer who wants to build them, but the engine (horizontally-opposed cylinders like the VW Bug) and raceslicks (Pirelli) are 'spec' classified.

This ends the first of 15 categories or types of race machines.

This first type, the 33 Formula racers, are among the higher numbered classes. (at least that's so for the purposes of this book) Other types high in numbers are the SportsCars and Drag racers of categories B and F. Category F on page 20 shows there are only 13 classes, but those 13 are each subclassed further. There are also many Motorcycle classes. You'll understand what I'm saying more clearly when you complete those sections.

The next type of racer covered are the SportsCars and the SportsRacers.

B. SPORTSCARS-SPORTSRACER (10 CLASSES)

Actually, this category of racecar is even larger than the Formula type. It's a very, very diversified category.

There are many kinds of sports cars: there are 2 and 4-seaters; big & small; hardtop and convertible; foreign and domestic. Racing SportsCars are: Endurance, such as FIA and IMSA (World Sports Cars); SCCA and internationally-classed Grand Touring (GT); Showroom Stock, (SS) which is a (true) StockCar, but . . . races on roadcourses, not ovals; sports cars which compete in events such as Rally and Solo contests; Improved Touring (IT); Production, sport cars that start out as street vehicles, but eventually are modified for competition; and of course purpose-built SportsCars and SportsRacers.

What's the difference between a purpose-built SportsCar and a purpose-built SportsRacer? Basically, it's their looks. SportsCars look exotically more street-legal and tend to have a 'closed' cockpit. (a roof) The 'open' cockpit SportsRacer doesn't look street-legal. (and as sexy as the SportsCar)

'Purpose-built' (nonstreet-legal, exotic looking) SportsCars (C.IV) were never intended for the street. They're built from the ground up for racing only. They are *not* the racers we're concerned with here for now. Even though they are listed here in category B, (including the other sportscars mentioned) each will be treated as their own separate category of racer later in this chapter.

For now, this category (B) covers only those machines raced on street or purpose-built roadcourses. For the most part, these race on the North American continent.

SportsRacers are sophisticated machines with enclosed bodywork over the entire chassis, including all four tires. As just stated, they're not fully enveloped. (no roof) Sometimes these machines are nothing more than a formula racer with bodywork adapted thereto. They may or may not use rear wings.

Some older Formula cars do get converted over to a SportsRacer, but usually that's not as simple of an operation as it appears.

With exception of some internationally-classed Endurance and GT racers, including a few pro Rally and Solo machines, all classes (or categories) below B.10. are vehicles originally designed (and sometimes used) for the street by the general public.

Some of these streetcars may be temporarily modified for racing, such as Showroom Stock and amateur Rally/Solo cars. Most Grand Touring, Production and Improved Touring cars tend to be permanently modified.

B. SportsCars	1. 'A' SportsRacer (ASR)
B. SportsCars	2. 'C' SportsRacer (CSR) (no such class as 'B' SportsRacer)
B. SportsCars	3. 'D' SportsRacer (DSR)
B. SportsCars	4. Sports 2000 (S2000)
B. SportsCars	5. SCCA 'Spec Racer' and 'Spec Racer' Ford
B. SportsCars	6. Shelby Can-Am (SCA)
B. SportsCars	7. Club Sports 2000 (CS2000)
B. SportsCars	8. Can-Am
B. SportsCars	9. Pro Sports 3000
B. SportsCars	10. MultiSports
B. SportsCars	(Production; see category C.I.)
B. SportsCars	(Showroom Stock; see category C.II.)
B. SportsCars	(Improved Touring; see category C.III.)
B. SportsCars	(Grand Touring; see category C.IV)
B. SportsCars	(Endurance; see category H.)
B. SportsCars	(Rally; see category I.)
B. SportsCars	(Solo; see category J.)

B.1. 'A' SPORTSRACER—This used to be the largest SportsCar class in SCCA, if not the North American continent. That's all changed.

These were open, (no roof) full-body, rear-winged, powerful 5000 cc racers which also commanded powerful bucks. That created severe problems. (like it always does) With it, their high-profile popularity took a beating (with the owners, not fans) much the same way the prestigious Can-Am racer did.

There are still a few around, but not many. They show up in small numbers at SCCA sanctioned Regional events. They lost their SCCA National and Pro status over 10–12 years ago. They may die out completely in a few years. That would be a shame. I understand there are some (non-Vintage) sanctioning bodies trying to bring these back. I hope they can.

They appear like a full-body Indy car, with a wider wing, but are not quite as fast and powerful. Most of these loud and raucous sounding race machines had the high-mounted ram-air intake scoop characteristic of the Formula 5000.

ASR are very similar to a Cam-Am racer. I do not know if this is true, but I heard through the grapevine these cars were fairly simple to convert over for Can-Am events. Makes sense to me, they are practically a Can-Am racer anyway.

These normally-aspirated, stockblock roadracers could reach speeds approaching 195 mph if given enough 'straight' to accelerate with.

They also used racing tires comparable in size to the Indy car.

B.2. 'C' SPORTSRACER—This is a smaller, slower version of an ASR. ('A' Sportsracer) The CSR can compare to a FF1600 in full-body fendering, but with a rear wing. The power comes from a 2 or 4-cycle engine.

Is this a Sport 2000 or a Club Sports 2000? It's a Sports 2000 racing in the club or amateur division of SCCA. Someday when this racer gets old, maybe it'll get relegated down to Club Sports 2000. Remember, club and vintage racing aren't the same. Club racing in the SCCA is with older vehicles still interested in being competitive. (without the higher costs) Vintage racing is more for show. (relatively speaking) Looks like this racer took a "ding" on the left front nose.

Two-cycles are limited to 850 cc and 4-cycles are limited to 1600 cc engine displacements. CSR's can reach about 145 mph.

This class is suffering a bit also, but still have SCCA National status. (by-the-way, that means they can race and accumulate points to qualify for participation in a national championship race at the end of the season)

B.3. 'D' SPORTSRACER—This is a very deverified class. In other words, there are many different designs of both chassis and engines. Some drivers have used high-powered, 150-horse motorcycle engines instead of the automotive type. Others have used snowmobile powerplants. Like a few Formula Vee race drivers, DSR competitors have also been known to build their own racing chassis from scratch.

This class is anything but a carbon-copy of CSR except in overall (rules) design. (full-body, unenveloped and rear winged) DSR's can be of 1 or 2-seat cockpit design. They are down-powered compared to the CSR. Like CSR, this class isn't quite as popular as before, but still has SCCA National status.

The 2-cycle engines are limited to 850 cc, (except multi-valve motorcycle engines; 1000cc) but the 4-strokers are allowed up to 1300 cc. These light and nimble racers are one of the better values in SportsCar racing. On a very short and tight roadcourse DSR's can record elapsed qualifying times approaching those of the much more powerful Formula Atlantics. They can reach speeds of about 120–125 mph.

B.4. SPORTS 2000—This racer, among others, is probably one reason why C and D Sportsracing has lost some of its luster. It's moving up in popularity at both SCCA pro and amateur levels, despite sponsorship problems.

S2000 gained SCCA National Club status in 1980. It is powered by a SOHC (Single OverHead Cam) 2-liter, 4-cylinder Ford pinto

This is the 'Spec Racer,' the largest racing class in the US. (if not the world) Except for paint color, the drivers cockpit and suspension adjustments, every racer here is an exact copy of the other. Very same construction, engine, chassis, trans, tires, etc. This sportsracer and all sportracers are similar to a formula racer, except their wheels are covered, for better aerodynamics. Still, sportracers are slower at top-end speed than a formula racer. Note the SCCA club racing decal on the right front fender? "Club" means this is an amateur class, not an older class, as Club Ford.

engine. The one or two-seat wide chassis must weigh at least 1280 lbs.

Put full body fendering, with no wings, on a FF2000 and you basically have a S2000. Couple the slippery aerodynamics and the 135 hp engine, with no ground effects, and you have a machine which can run about 150–155 mph.

At the pro level SCCA sanctions two series, the ACRL and NAPS.

The 'American City Racing League' is a west-coast oriented 6–8 race series. Three-driver teams representing a particular city (from as large as San Francisco, Ca to as small as San Jose, Ca) accumulate points towards a team and city championship.

These race machines feature pretty much the same engine-chassis rules as their SCCA club counterparts do. The only exception is that duel overhead cams (DOHC) are allowed instead of the original single overhead cams. (DOHC allow an engine to breath better, therefore it performs better)

The 'North American Pro Series' (formerly 'Olds Pro') is a bit more popular. It's an east-coast oriented 9–11 race series using more powerful S2000's.

There are 2 divisions of racers in the NAPS series. The 'A' racers, sometimes called Super Sports 2000, uses the 2300 cc Oldmobile Quad 4 (16 valves/4 cylinders) and the Ford Cosworth YAC engines. These engines can push the NAPS 'A' racer to 160 mph. The 'B' classed are pretty much the same vehicle used in ACRL and the amateur level of SCCA.

As of the 1994 season, these sponsorless series may find a company to support the purses offered at these events. If or when they do, count on the series name(s) to change. (title or name changes happen a bit more in slower classed pro racing)

B.5. SCCA 'SPEC RACER'/'SPEC RACER' FORD—Here it is, the largest (SCCA) class in the US. Introduced in the early 80's, it captured SCCA national status in 1985. They provided a low cost, low maintenance alternative for people who wanted to race, but weren't prepared to empty their wallets or sell a few of their kids.

As of 1993, there was one 'Spec Racer' *racecar.* (as opposed to several 'spec' *classes* already covered; don't confuse the difference) Now there are two.

The original class, SCCA 'Spec Racer' (formerly Sports Renault) uses a transverse-mounted, stock, SOHC 1.7-liter, 4-cylinder, 90 hp Renault engine. Its minimum weight is 1580 lbs.

This racecar is one of a few, if not only, which is designed and built by a race sanctioning organization. (SCCA)

The latest version, called 'Spec Racer' Ford, uses a 4-cylinder, 1.9 liter, fuel-injected, ford engine which has a little more power output than the SCCA spec-racer. It races a 6-7 event pro schedule called the 'Spec Racer Pro Series' that started in 1994. I anticipate this series 'name' won't last. With its popularity, corporate help and a new series name could soon arrive. Meanwhile, 'Spec Racer' Ford has SCCA national championship status, like its cousin the SCCA 'Spec Racer'. Both race together 'as a race within a race' at the club level.

These machines have a locked-in design and a sealed engine (ie, tamper-proof) which puts emphasis on driver ability rather than vehicle technology. The 'spec' tire used is the much longer lasting (shaved) Bridgestone street radial. (no racing slicks; that helps keeps tire costs down through longevity)

Because 'Spec Racers' are still gaining popularity, they have excellent resale value. These racers are indeed quite a success story. You can read more about them and the 'spec' racing concept in chapter 7, section A. (these also haven't exactly helped the CSR and DSR classes of racing either)

B.6. SHELBY CAN-AM—This is another new 'spec' class that was introduced near the late 80's. It was an experimental class. They seem to be gaining popularity (initially) fast. In 1991 they earned SCCA national status.

This is more complex, faster and expen-

sive machine than the 'Spec-Racer', but with the same relative cost-effective ideals. The first Can-Am racers has been gone for years. This is an attempt to bring them back at a cheaper level.

The engine is a normally-aspirated, 3.3-liter, V-6 which delivers 255 hp at 6800 rpm's and about 155 mph to the chassis. This engine is designed to last longer between rebuilds. The 'spec' racetire brand is Goodyear.

This is not a fully enclosed SportsRacer at the front end, but rather semi-closed. That means the front and rear portions of the front (steering) wheels are closed, but the top portion of them is exposed or unprotected. This helps improve the drivers visibility. The rear tires are completely enclosed, including the outside portion of the wheels. The only way you're going to see them during competition is to be *under* them. (not a good situation, I might add)

This 105 inch wheelbase, nonground effects racer also has a large rear wing that extends the entire width of the body, which is 77.5". Overall length is 168.5 inches. Maximum height is limited to 41". Minimum weight must be at least 1820 lbs with a full load of fuel.

Their popularity continues to grow. The 8-9 event 'Dodge/Shelby Pro Series' was inaugurated in 1992. The race vehicle here is called SHELBY SPEC RACER. This is the only SportsCar category machine that occasionally races on ovals. I also look for the engine rules to eventually change to a stronger version as this series gets older and more established.

At the printing of this book, the latest on the "rumor mill" has Dodge opting for a 450 hp engine, refining some body lines (aerodynamics) and changing the name of the racecars to SHELBY 'SUPER SPEC RACER'.

These racing machines, like just about all slower classed pro racing cars, race as part of a support series. (ie, one of many shorter races of various classes before the main feature or race is held)

Shelby Spec Racers have supported such events as IndyCar, NASCAR Winston Cup, IMSA GTP and SCCA Trans-Am races.

B.7. CLUB SPORTS 2000—This class may of started a bit ahead of its time, but the possibilities are still there. What Formula Ford is to Club Ford, S2000 is to this CS2000. This class is for older S2000 racers, but usually and more specifically, they're pre-1985 models with the older outboard suspensions.

Remember, S2000 is only 14–15 years old, so give CS2000 time to get itself established further.

This is one of the few club classes that can race for a so-called unofficial national championship at the recently established (1994) American Road Race of Champions. It's held at Road Atlanta, Georgia during the fall.

(note—don't confuse club racing with club-classed cars. Club racing is another term used for amateur racing, especially in the SCCA. Club-classed cars are older (designed) vehicles which are too impractical to upgrade for more competitive purposes. It would cost too much money. They very seldom win in their original class, so they race with others of the same (older) class. It's a sort-of 'B' class. Therefore, CS2000 machines race with each other in the same event at the same time with the S2000's, while S2000's race each other)

B.8. CAN-AM—This used to be a very prestigious SCCA-sanctioned pro class in the US and Canada. (Can-Am stands for Canadian-American Challenge Cup; also the name of the series) These were a big, strong 560 hp racer with a 305–350 ci (cubic inch), push-rod, nonaspirated, fuel-injected, V-8 engine. They were almost like an Indy car with full-body coachwork. (but 'open' cockpit)

What they really were was a purpose-built vehicle for high-speed roadracing. They were conceived, at least in part, to help alleviate the North American continents lack of Formula One events. These machines looked like an 'A' SportsRacer (ASR) or a Formula 5000 with full bodywork, but it had more power and a different aerodynamics package than F5000.

Some Can-Am racers had an earlier and more primitive form of a ground-effects pack-

age. Most had the high intake air-scoops (for their induction system) characteristic of the ASR's and F5000. Others were more easily distinguishable by their higher than normal rear wing. It was located more directly over the top up of the (rear) wheels than normal. But FIA ruled them illegal in 1969.

Most rear wings on practically all winged racecars are placed lower and behind the rear wheels at the trailing edge of the bodywork. Not so with these. Therefore, the wings received cleaner (less disturbed) air flow to better do their job.

Minimum weight was 1650 lbs. Top speed was around 195 mph, but given enough straight they could top out over 200 mph.

This class started in 1965. It was temporarily halted for a few years in the mid-70's to be replaced by F5000. Then Can-Am was reinstated again with further rule changes. In 1982, the world-classed Group C endurance sportscars became eligible also. (you'll know about Group C later)

This is an old Can-Am race. These powerful racers priced themselves right out of existence. These also could be the A sportsracer, which also fell on hard times. Notice how sportsracers have built-in sidepods for enhanced aerodynamics? Sidepods also serve to house radiators, batteries and other accessories including ground effects packages. They also serve to better protect a driver in side impacts. Note the large engine air-intake scoops? Formula 5000 racers used simular devices. Most classes of racing rule against them. They help ram more air into an engine for better power output; a sort of natural turbocharger. (but they also hurt aerodynamics)

The high cost of running these without adequate financial help from the manufacturers hurt them. After flourishing several years, they began to suffer increasing costs in the 70's that wasn't justified by the crowds they drew. (or in this case, didn't draw) It finally deceased in 1986, after it looked as though it was going to be bailed out by Dallas, Texas millionaire Donald Walker.

There was also a 2-liter class for these machines which ran in conjunction with the higher powered racers.

B.9. PRO SPORTS 3000—This is a 'spec' classed SportsRacer raced in England. Started over there in 1992, this basically looks like nothing more than a reincarnation of our NAPS (class 'A') Super Sports 2000 race machine.

PS3000 are powered by a 3.0-liter, 24 valve, Ford-Cosworth V6 which is 700 cc and two cylinders larger than are (pro) versions. It produces about 300 hp.

This racer can top out at around 168 mph.

B.10. MULTISPORTS—Introduced 1989 in Europe, this 'spec' class would match up close to our 'C' SportsRacer. This two-seat wide cockpit racer incorporates a transversely-mounted, 4-cylinder, normally-aspirated, 1.6 liter Ford powerplant which can approach a top end of 135–140 mph.

'Spec' tire make is Uniroyal. (race slicks are illegal)

This ends the category on SportsCars.

Take note, these first two types of race machines, the Formula and SportsCars, (SportsRacers) race only on paved surfaces. Those surfaces may either be purpose-built for racing (roadcourses) or street circuits.

The only exception are a small portion of the formula racers already covered and the Shelby Can-Am. No, I don't mean those racers compete on dirt or clay, but rather the shape of those paved surfaces. Indy, Indy Light, AIS, Super Vee, Go-Karts and Shelby Can-Am also race on a high-speed or short oval, in addition to roadcourses.

Speaking of racers competing on ovals, there has been talk of bringing the Formula

One race machines over here for the Indianapolis 500. The 500 would be part of the F1 race schedule which would count for points towards a World Championship. Actually, from 1950 thru 1960, the Indy 500 did count for points towards a Formula One world championship. But few F1 drivers took advantage of it. (probably due partly to scheduling conflicts; Indy is a month long event) But some well-known drivers did occasionally compete, like Jackie Stewart, Graham Hill and Jim Clark. I don't think this will happen now, especially due to the recently formed Indy Racing League. (IRL)

Another option bandied around was to build a roadcourse within the infield of the Indianapolis Motor Speedway. By using that and part of the regular track, a F1 event could be held sometime during the month of May. It could be just before or after one of the two Indy 500 qualifying weekends.

Mind you, it's just talk for now. I'll believe those things will happen when I see it. Then if it does, I still won't believe it'll last. There is just too much politics that'll eventually get in the way. The main reason politics enters these kinds of things is because of the bottom line, . . . MONEY.

The next 4 categories, C.I. thru C.IV., race only on paved roadcourses, mostly in the SCCA and IMSA.

C.I. PRODUCTION CAR RACERS (4 CLASSES)

C.I. Production 1. 'E' Production - EP
C.I. Production 2. 'F' Production - FP
C.I. Production 3. 'G' Production - GP
C.I. Production 4. 'H' Production - HP

This is the type of racing in which the classes therein confuse many people. That includes even some of those who race in this category.

Every year each of these classes is subject to reclassification. The reason is to keep the competition as equal as possible. This is partly necessary because of the automotive industries' tendency to make yearly model changes. Such changes may be: performance packages and availability; standard equipment; and adding or eliminating models. So essentially, the following cars mentioned below are classed according to their performance potential or 'power-to-weight ratio'. The SCCA makes these determinations in the US. (and probably with help from the automakers.)

These are older, mass-produced sportscars. They're originally built street-legal for use by the general public. The cars in this kind of racing tend to be foreign-built and small in size, yet sometimes still street-legal after race modification.

Some modifications are permitted to increase performance and safety. Such things would be removing passenger seats, radios, . . . any dead weigh which would not contribute towards better vehicle performance. A rollbar must be installed and some glass must be replaced by the shatterproof kind. (or plexiglass) In most cases a fuel cell must replace the gas tank. This aids in the prevention of fire in case of an accident. Serious Production racers use racing slicks comparable in size to the originally designed tires for their car. Others will use a shaved radial.

A 'spec' carburetor is installed, using a variety of jetting. The proper gear-ratio should be installed in the rearend for competitive purposes. No race-prepared turbo or superchargers are allowed.

Though not immediately necessary, some competitors install fully-prepared race engines which are not necessarily faster, but more reliable. (won't blow) Others put in better transmissions, trick clutches, distributorless ignitions, fiberglass fenders, new gauges, wiring, etc.

Generally, these cars are 'open' (convertibles) and are originally designed to accommodate two people at a time. That is somewhat starting to change though. More hardtops (closed) are trickling into Production racing. One reason is because the SCCA is encouraging some of their IMPROVED TOURING (category C.III.) competitors to convert their car to this class. The "softtops" are getting even older and dying out through attrition. They are not being replaced. The

automotive industries tendency has been to cease their production.

Production car racing is sanctioned by the SCCA and have both regional and national status. There are no professional series for these cars in its truest form. Yes, there are pro series with race vehicles close to these stockcar-like machines, (in SCCA and IMSA; they will be discussed later) but there isn't a specific Production pro series for this class.

Production racecars compete on roadcourses of usually 1.5 to 4.0 miles in length in the US and Canada.

Typical 'makes' are: Alfa Romero, Austin-Healey, BMW, Datsun, Dodge, Elva, Fiat, Ford, Honda, Lotus, Mazda, MG, Morgan, Opel, Porsche, Renault, Saab, Subaru, Sunbeam, Toyota, Triumph, Volvo and VW.

Since these 4 classes are mostly determined by judgement, the differences between them seems outwardly vague. But, it only seems that way for now. The only thing I need now to describe these 4 classes is their performance grade, which is their overall quickness, speed and maneuverability.

C.I. 1. 'E' PRODUCTION—At 132 mph, this is the fastest Production class.

Make and model examples: BMW 2002; Ford Capri and Pinto with 2000 cc power like those in the FF2000 and S2000 racecars; Mazda Miata; Toyota MR2; VW Golf, Rabbit and Scirocco with 1715/1780 cc engines simular to those used in Super Vee, minus the high-tech and expensive modifications.

There are many more examples I could list, but it would be pointless and impractical to mention them all here and now.

C.I. 2. 'F' PRODUCTION—Top speed: 123 mph.

Examples: Datson PL510; Dodge Colt FWD (front wheel drive) 1600 cc engine; Ford Escort and Fiesta with 1600 cc engine like that of the FF1600; Honda Si, Civic and CRX with 1500 cc engines; Toyota Corolla; VW Rabbit and Scirocco with 1600 cc power.

C.I. 3. 'G' PRODUCTION—Top speed: 115 mph.

Examples: Mazda GLC (front wheel drive);

Datsun B210; Renault Alliance and R5 LeCar; Subaru GL Coupe; VW Rabbit and Scirocco with the 1457/1471 cc engine.

C.I. 4. 'H' PRODUCTION—Top speed: 109 mph.

Examples: Honda Civic with 1237 cc's; Mazda GLC with 1300 cc's (FWD); Datsun 1200; Opel GT with 1100 cc's; Toyota Starlet.

This ends category C.I. You may be wondering why there is 4 categories for the letter 'C'. I could of lettered them separately, but I didn't want to. I wanted to keep 'Production', 'Showroom Stock', 'Improved Touring' and 'Grand Touring' categories related to each other because . . . that's what they are . . . related to each other. Except for the exotic GTP's in category C.IV., these racecars are modeled, at least in appearance, after small and mid-ranged mass-produced automobiles available for sale to the general public.

Of course the same thing could be said of most StockCars too, at quick glance. But StockCars are larger in numbers then C.I thru IV categories put together. Besides, these cars aren't really stock, which you'll understand clearly after reading category D. But mainly, StockCars race on oval-configured tracks.

C.II. SHOWROOM STOCK (4 CLASSES)

C.II. Showroom Stock 1. Showroom Stock 'GT' - SSGT

C.II. Showroom Stock 2. Showroom Stock 'A' - SSA

C.II. Showroom Stock 3. Showroom Stock 'B' - SSB

C.II. Showroom Stock 4. Showroom Stock 'C' - SSC

These are the "true" Stockcars. They're mass-produced sports and GT cars built specifically for street-use by the general public. (don't confuse "factory-named" GT here with GT racers; I'll explain GT racers in Category C.IV.)

Opposite of Production cars, these tend to be much newer, larger (sedan type) and stronger automobiles. No complex performance modifications are permitted. Roll cages must be installed along with other safety equipment.

There cars are mostly SCCA-sanctioned at the amateur level. The ones which compete in Nationals can't be over 4 years old. The Regional event machines can't be over 6 years old. In addition to running the 15–20 lap club races, they are also an occasional Endurance racer. More specifically, all SS cars are eligible for SCCA's 24 hour race called the 'Longest Day of Nelson'. It's held each year at the Nelson Ledges race coarse near Warren, Ohio.

All club SS's race on shaved street radials, including most pro classes.

These machines also compete professionally in SCCA and IMSA events.

SCCA has a very popular pro series in SS called 'World Challenge'. It has made quite a few changes over the years making it look unstable. Usually class instability happens when a class is trying to survive extinction. Not in this case though. It's just the opposite. The fields are getting too full. So, the racecars were classed further into 3 divisions.

But it wasn't that way for another SCCA SS pro series. The 9-race 'Rabbit/Bilstein Cup', for (almost) stock VW Rabbits, passed away a few years ago, or . . . it merged into the 'World Challenge'-classed 'Super Production' division. It depends on who you talk to as to what happened. All I know is Volkswagon's sponsorship pullout in Super Vee racing sure didn't help this class.

Pretty much the same thing happened in IMSA. Their two marque-type (particular car make and model) classes, 'Renault/Falcon Cup' and 'Alliance Cup' went the same route their 'RS' series did. (lack of factory support) 'RS' was a Champion Spark Plug-sponsored series for slightly stronger cars.

As of this printing, IMSA's Firestone-sponsored 'Firehawk Endurance Championship' series for SS cars may see financial trouble down the road. Firestone's recent inception back to Indy Car racing prompted them to drop their support. But there are plans for this series to continue in 1995.

Some pro SS races are more enduranced-oriented than others. If you know anything about racing, you'll realize that club SS and pro SS machines aren't precisely the same. But basically, in name, style and configuration, they're close.

C.II. 1. SHOWROOM STOCK 'GT—These cars are the strongest of the SCCA-sanctioned (club) SS class. They must be no older than 1 year and in current manufacturing production. (available for sale to the general public; as in all SS classes) Example of cars raced here are: Camero Z-28, Ford Mustang, Pontiac Trans-Am, Nissan 300ZX Turbo, Mazda RX-7 Turbo, Chevy Corvette and Toyota Supra Turbo.

These race cars can reach about 150 or so mph if given enough straight-line track.

Two SCCA pro series were offered for these cars. It's became popular thanks to good factory support. First, in 1985, was the start of SCCA's 8-race series called the 'Escort Endurance Championship'. Those races ranged from 3 to 24 hours in duration.

Second, the 10-race 'Corvette Challenge' series started in 1988. It was renamed 'World Challenge' a few years later. The change became necessary when foreign-built, high-performance cars became eligible. The length of the races in this class were shorter then the 'Escort Endurance Championship'.

Eventually, the 'Escort Endurance Championship' class merged into 'World Challenge' to form one 8-race series. (with A, B, C and D divisions; D was eventually dropped) Example of cars that ran 'World Challenge' A-division, called the 'Sports Car' class : (besides the Corvette ZR-1) Mazda RX-7 Turbo, Mustang Cobra, Lotus Esprit Turbo, Nissan 300 ZX Turbo, BMW 540i, Camero and Porsche 911 and 944 Turbo. This class now runs as a stand-alone (no races within a race) race for 1 hour in duration. (reduced from 3 hours; no long endurance races anymore)

The slower B and C divisions race together in a 1-hour event separate from division A, called 'Touring' and 'Super Production' respectively. They fit better in the SS classes coming up next.

IMSA sanctioned a 11–12 race schedule of endurance events for Showroom Stock cars called the 'Firestone Firehawk Endurance Championship'. (now renamed 'Street Stock Endurance Championship') It's broken into 4 divisions. The strongest of the 4, 'Grand Sports', closely match SCCA's SSGT club racer. Example of these racers are: Trans-Am, Firebird, Camero and Camero IROC-Z, Porsche 944 and S2 and BMW.

The other three divisions, 'Sports', 'Touring' and 'Subcompact' best fit in the SS classes coming up.

IMSA also sanctions a SS-oriented 10–11 race series which best fits in SSGT, but actually it's much more superior than SSGT. It's the Bridgestone Potenza (sponsored) 'Supercar Series' inaugurated in 1991. These are minimumly-prepared exotic sports cars and coupes such as Dodge Stealth, Ferrari Testarossa, Chevy Corvette, Nissan 300ZX, Mitsubishi 3000GT, Lotus Esprit Turbo, Acura NSX and Porsche 911 Turbo, to name a few.

These 'Supercar' series vehicles are all performance rated and minimum-weight adjusted to even the competition. Required 'spec' tires are the shaved Potenza RE71 made by Bridgestone. (hence the series name)

About half of the races are 100 kilometers (about 62 miles) and the other half last exactly 30 minutes.

C.II. 2. SHOWROOM STOCK 'A'—These are slower versions of SSGT racers. SCCA National competitors can't be over 4 years old. Regional cars can't be over 6. Example of makes and models are: Pontiac Sunbird Turbo, Alfa Romeo GTV-6, BMW 325e, Toyota Supra, Ford Thunderbird, Mitsubishi Starion, Mazda RX-7, Camero, Porsche, Honda, Eagle, Nissan and Oldsmobile.

These race cars can reach a top speed of about 135 mph.

As far as SCCA pro series racing is concerned, these cars are a sort-of go-between; too slow for SCCA's 'World Challenge' (A) division or 'Sports Car' class and too strong for the C division, called 'Super Production'. SSA's best fit in the B division, formerly called the 'North American Touring Car Championship', now called 'Touring Car'.

Because of minute rule differences between club and pro SS racing, some bleeding from the two bordering classes, SSGT and SSB, may occur. But generally, SSA racercars are almost equivalent to pro SCCA 'Touring' racers.

In IMSA pro SS racing, SSA best matches the 'Street Stock Endurance Championship' 'Sports' or B division. (not to be confused with the stronger '*Grand* Sports' division)

C.II. 3. SHOWROOM STOCK 'B'—These are even slower versions of SCCA club SS racers. In SCCA they can't be over 4 and 6 years old for National and Regional events. Examples are: Chevy Cavalier, Acura Integra, Peugeot 505 Turbo, VW Scirocco, Honda CRX Si, Toyota MR2 and Corolla, Nissan Pulsar.

These cars can reach a top end speed of around 120–125 mph.

SSB's are basically eligible at the pro level in SCCA's 'World Challenge'-classed, 'Super Production' or C division.

SSB is closest to IMSA's 'Street Stock Endurance Championship' 'Touring' division racer.

C.II. 4. SHOWROOM STOCK 'C'—These are the slowest of SCCA's club SS class. A few of these might be eligible for a pro series such as SCCA's 'World Challenge' classed 'Super Production' or C division, but are more suited to IMSA's fourth 'Street Stock Endurance Championship', the D division called 'Subcompact'.

In SCCA club events, these cars also cannot be over 4 and 6 years old to compete in National and Regional events.

Examples of Showroom Stock 'C' cars are: Volkswagon Golf GTI, Honda Civic Si, Ford Escort, Isuzu Impulse, Nissan Sentra and Mazda 323.

These cars can top out in the vicinity of 100–110 mph.

This ends category C.II. You've read about 4 different types or categories of race cars. Now there is two more 'C' categories left, plus the other nine *Types* of race vehicles. "On James" . . . .

Are these converted street cars from SCCA 'production,' 'showroom stock,' 'improved touring' or 'grand touring' categories? They are too old & small for Grand touring (GT) but they could be any of the first 3 to the untrained eye. These are 'showroom stock' category, class B cars. (at least the #47 car is) Mixed in the background are probably 'A', 'C' and maybe SS GT cars. Note the tires? They help cushion any impacts to the wall behind them.

C.III. IMPROVED TOURING (5 CLASSES)

C.III. Improved Touring 1.   Improved Touring 'A' - ITA

C.III. Improved Touring 2.   Improved Touring 'B' - ITB

C.III. Improved Touring 3.   Improved Touring 'C' - ITC

C.III. Improved Touring 4.   Improved Touring 'S' - ITS

C.III. Improved Touring 5.   American Sedan - AS

These are older Showroom Stock cars with some minor performance modification permitted. No supercharging and turbocharging permitted. Unlike the SS category, automatic transmissions are not permitted in IT. As in just about all closed-course racing, no station wagons can compete either.

After the Showroom Stock cars outlive their original eligibility, they don't necessarily get relegated back to the street, they can race here in IT. But if they're turbocharged, that unit must be removed from the engine. An exception would be the strongest SS class, SSGT. They are almost always too strong to legally race any IT class, turbocharged or not.

Like SS, Improved Touring classes are performance-potential rated. These also race on street radials. But, IT race only SCCA regional events. (no national status)

There are no pro racing series for this category of racecar. A possible exception to that would be the American Sedan classed racer and the '24-hours of Nelson' event held every June near Warren, Ohio. SCCA-sanctioned Improved Touring and Showroom Stock cars are the only classes allowed in this endurance event.

C.III. 1. IMPROVED TOURING 'A'—About 95 models are approved for SCCA club competition in 1996. These can change yearly. (as in all IT classes)

Examples: 1971–76 Alfa Romeo Spider, Mazda RX 2, 3 & 4, 5 Chevy models like Corvair and Monza, 5 Mustangs, Mercury Capri, 2 Porsche 914's, etc. Most are powered by a 6-cylinder, 1.7 to 2.8 liter engine.

Top speed is around 112 mph.

C.III. 2. IMPROVED TOURING 'B'—Slower speeds, but more models to choose from. Around 205 cars are approved for SCCA club competition.

Examples: Alfa Romeo GTV, 4 BMW's from 1968-83, Chevy 4-cyl Monza, 2-liter Datsun S10 II from 1978–81, VW Scirocco and Rabbits, Capris, Colts, Horizons, Celica, Saabs, Bobcars, Fiats and Dodge Omni.

Top speed is about 105 mph.

C.III. 3. IMPROVED TOURING 'C'—130 cars are approved for competition.

Examples: six combination Datsun 1200 series to S10, Honda Civics, Renault Alliance, VW Beatle & Super Beatle, Escort, Fiat 124's, Colts, Chevette and Pulsar. This is the slowest of the Improved Touring category.

Top speed is almost 95 mph.

C.III. 4. IMPROVED TOURING 'S'—In just about all categories I'm covering in this book, the classes are ordered from fastest to slowest. That's true here in the IT section, except now. ITS is the fastest of this category.

Thirty eight cars are approved for competition: 4 Datsuns 240Z to 280ZX, Mazda RX-7, Porsche 914 & 924, Triumph TR-8, Jensen-Healy 1973-76, etc.

Top speed is about 120 mph.

C.III. 5. AMERICAN SEDAN—There is some minor debate whether this racecar is an Improved Touring or Showroom Stock category machine. My opinion is it's more of a Showroom Stock car, at least in appearance. But I'll leave that debate to others.

Since this is listed as an Improved Touring machine, I should tell you it doesn't look like one because this car tends to look newer compared to most IT racers. This racer is even faster than what some believe to be the final and fastest IT car, the ITS. They can reach a top-end of around 130-140 mph.

As implied by its class title these are limit to American-made sedans in relatively stock form such as the Chevy Camero, Ford Mustang, Mercury Capri and Pontiac Firebird.

Like IT cars some suspension modifications are allowed. Unlike some Showroom

Stock racecars, no automatic transmissions, turbocharging or fuel-injection is allowed.

Even though I mentioned there is no pro class racing for IT cars, this racer is the exception. It can be relatively easy to convert this machine to a pro-class eligible machine in SCCA's 'World Challenge' (class B) 'Touring' division. This is the another reason why I feel it's a SS category racer.

American Sedan is a fairly new SCCA amateur class which was underway in 1993 as a regional class only. But as of 1995 this class has growth sufficiently enough to gain national status.

This ends category C.III. This next category of racecar is much more involved and complicated. So if you need to go to the "cooler" to grab a "brewski", do it now. Me? . . . naaaaa, . . . I don't want one!

C.IV. GRAND TOURING (8 CLASSES)

C.IV. Grand Touring   1. Grand Touring '1' - GT1
C.IV. Grand Touring   2. Grand Touring '2' - GT2
C.IV. Grand Touring   3. Grand Touring '3' - GT3
C.IV. Grand Touring   4. Grand Touring '4' - GT4
C.IV. Grand Touring   5. Grand Touring '5' - GT5
                               *FIA/FISA/BPR GT (International class Super-Car)
C.IV. Grand Touring   6. Trans-American - Trans-Am
C.IV. Grand Touring 7A. Grand Touring 'Prototype' - GTP
C.IV. Grand Touring 7B. Grand Touring 'World Sports Car' - WSC
C.IV. Grand Touring 7C. Grand Touring 'Experimental' - GTX
C.IV. Grand Touring 7D. Grand Touring Prototype 'Light' - GTP Light
C.IV. Grand Touring 8A. Grand Touring 'Supreme' - GTS (now GTS-1)
C.IV. Grand Touring 8B. Grand Touring 'Over' - GTO (now GTS-1)
C.IV. Grand Touring 8C. Grand Touring 'Under' - GTU (now GTS-2)

The first six classes are for the more newer mass-produced sport sedans. (sedan; a full body, two-door, hardtop, 2 full-seat, 4 passenger automobile) These are modestly to highly modified for racing. They're SCCA-sanctioned at both national and regional amateur levels, except Trans-Am, which is an exclusive SCCA pro classed racer. SCCA also sanctions a 2-division (East and West) NASPORT series for GT3 and GT4. (more on them in a bit)

These first six classes look like a smaller version of NASCAR's Grand National race machines, but are still fairly restricted in comparison.

Even though these are 'stock' in appearance, the big difference between GT and StockCars is *what* they're designed to race on. StockCars mostly compete on ovals. GT's race on road/streetcourses.

Like Showroom Stock and Production cars, GT's are suppose to look stock, but that's where the similarities end. GT's are usually highly modified specifically for racing underneath their stock-silhouette styled exteriors. This is especially so at the pro level. The club GT cars tend to be modified from street production cars rather than built from scratch. The high level GT's have a purpose-built tube-frame chassis and are performance-equalized by allowing those with smaller engines to compete at a lighter weight within their particular class.

SCCA GT classes 1–5 are generally predetermined by power-to-weight ratios. (they're listed first in this category)

Trans-Am is almost a carbon-copy of GT1 but a hair stronger and usually more sophisticated.

Most racers listed in 7, which have now been eliminated, were purpose-built, stronger and sophisticated sports prototypes. The street cars that GTP somewhat emulated were generally not (if at all) mass-produced in great numbers to the middle-classed general public. (you need to be a "ka-zillionaire" to buy one of those street-legal Porches, Jaguars, etc)

GTP's were fully-enclosed, closed-cockpit, exotic styled, low-slung (body) machines closely patterned after those sexy, expensive sports cars. But they were built and designed from the ground up for high speed roadcourse and Endurance racing. I like to call the GTP racer a crossed-hybrid of a powerful Stock and Formula racer.

The GTO/GTU, since reshuffled to GTS 1 and 2 classes, listed number eight here, are different from the prototypes. These are more production-based. Translation; more volume in numbers available to the general public and not as expensive. But these were still high-performance racers, not necessarily built from the ground up in their earlier years, but at least highly modified for racing then. As of late, they operated as more of a production-model silhouette, but under that exterior skin they were kind of an less expensive version of a prototype.

The first 6 listed GT classes in this category are not the overly expensive, exotic, high-speed, internationally-classed machines raced at LeMans, Daytona and Sebring. Those high-profile types are to be covered later in this category. (numbers 7 and 8)

Understand, in this category, the classes don't necessarily get slower as they're ordered downward on the list. (the slowest vehicles are the GT5 and the former GTU) This is done to keep particular groups of racers properly ordered within the sanctioning bodies they compete in.

C.IV. 1. GRAND TOURING 'ONE'—Don't confuse this with the new IMSA GTS-1 class coming up later.

GT1 is about as close to Trans-Am as it can get. They compete at the SCCA regional and national levels. Paul Newman, the actor, won 4 national championships in this class. These are the strongest of SCCA's GT club racers.

Example of cars raced here are: Oldsmobile Cutless, Corvette, Camero, which is a popular model in GT1, Ford Mustang, Pontiac Trans-Am and Fiero V-6, Porsche 911, 924 and 944 Turbo, Toyota Supra and the Nissan 300ZX Turbo.

Obviously, turbocharging is permitted if it's standard equipment on that vehicle/model. As in stockcar racing, the GT vehicle must be as stock appearing as possible while retaining the manufacturers original (stock) dimensions, such as the wheelbase, track, etc. GT1's must also use only components (engine, transmission, etc) matching manufacturers original 'make' and model. In other words, no cross-breeding of one 'make' component to another 'make' vehicle. (this is true of all 5 of SCCA's GT classes, not to mention just about all 'stock-silhouette type racecars)

GT1's do not use racing slicks. They use either bias-plied or radial type tires. (GT2 thru GT5 must also use the same kind of tire)

This racecar can reach speeds of about 160 mph.

C.IV. 2. GRAND TOURING 'TWO'—This class is a bit slower than GT1. You'll notice that some of the same modeled cars that run here, also run in GT1. Obviously, they use smaller engines, or ones which do not use a turbo, or they have a heavier chassis. (remember, GT1 thru GT5 are power-to-weight performance rated; and also, don't confuse GT2 with IMSA's new GTS-2 class)

Examples: Alfa Romeo GT, Mazda RX-7, Lotus Elan, Sunbeam Tiger, Toyota Celica, Porsche 911, 914/6, 944 and 944S, Pontiac Fiero, Nissan 280Z and 300ZX.

Top speeds are around 151 mph.

C.IV. 3. GRAND TOURING 'THREE'—This is probably SCCA's most competitive GT class. (the most number of vehicle-make race winners)

Make and model examples which compete in this class are: BMW 302i and 316, Chevrolet Yenko, Ford Capri and Pinto, Chrysler Daytona, Acura Integra, Honda CRX Si and Prelude, Porsche 911, 914S and 914/6, Mazda RX-7, RX-2 and RX-3, Nissan 200SX and 240SX, Toyota Paseo and Corolla, VW Scirocco, Mazda RX-2 and 3.

These racers reach about a top end of 145 mph.

There is a pro SCCA series specifically for GT3's called the 'National Sedan Sport Championship'. (NASPORT) It's a growing venue with an Eastern and Western half US schedule of 7 races each. Most of these races are held in conjunction with SCCA National club events.

C.IV. 4. GRAND TOURING 'FOUR'—Typical cars running in this class are: Ford

This is a GT racer which competes in SCCA. It's newer and slightly larger. Does it race GT categories 1, 2, 3, 4 or 5? In this case, 3. Look closely to the left lower corner of the number 23 on the vehicles right side. See the GT-3? The GT cars are street vehicles allowed more modifications, as evident by the enlarged fenders to accommodate wide race tires. Actually, GT race cars never see much street use. The modifications are too extensive internally, and all the "creature-comforts" have been eliminated within them.

Cortina, Nissan 510, Sentra and Pulsar, Honda CRX and Civic, Datsun B210, Fiat 124 and 131, Mazda GLC, Saab Sonett, Toyota Corolla and Tercel, VW Rabbit, Opel GT and the Chrysler Colt.

Top end speed is right around 129 mph.

GT4's also have their own SCCA pro series. Like the GT3's, they have their own separate class in both the NASPORT East and West divisions. In the East series, they are called 'GT Lite'. They also run about 7 races yearly.

C.IV. 5. GRAND TOURING 'FIVE'—These are the slowest of the GT racers in SCCA racing. The top speeds are right around 124 mph.

Examples of these racecars are: Alfa Romeo Giula, Austin Mini-Cooper, Fortech Mini, Honda Civic, Mazda GLC, Nissan Sentra 1200 and 210, Toyota 1200 and Starlet, Renault 5 and VW Beatle.

If you have any knowledge of street cars, you'll unavoidably notice that these racecars get smaller in wheelbase and overall size as they move down in class.

This concludes all the SCCA-based club GT racecars. (not pro)

*(FIA/FISA/BPR GT (International class SuperCar)—Before I get into the North American pro level GT's, a paragraph or two is in order for pro-level, internationally classed GT cars. (sometimes called SuperCar(s))

These racecars certainly do not get much attention in this country. One reason is because they don't compete here enough. (which is being addressed by IMSA's Bridgestone/Potenza Supercar series) None the less, they do exist. The loss of the internationally FIA-sanctioned World Sports Car Championship will help this SuperCar class. Eventually they're bound to be eligible to race at the large 12 and 24 hour races of Sebring, LeMans and Daytona.

The FIA-sanctioned international-classed GT's are actually more 'Showroom Stock' styled machines, but . . . here's the catch. Most street-legal based racing cars sanctioned for racing have to meet a minimal production-run for their particular make/model on a yearly basis. You've read such terms as 'mass-produced' in this book. What number constitutes mass-production? Well . . . let me put it this way. In the US, in order for street-legal cars to be built and sold to the public for profit, certain safety standards must be met and built into the vehicles. That applies only if there are 500 or more of those vehicles built yearly. (that number may of changed, but you see my point) The point is, the US government feels the magic number of 500 or more is mass-production relative to the automotive industry. What that number is to any particular sanctioning body to qualify a certain class in racing, whether it be 5 or 5 million, is a matter for their own convenience. (with probably a lot of input from the manufacturer)

So, . . . all the mass-produced, production-looking racecars you've read about, or will read about later, are patterned after production runs of a particular street-model which number into the thousands, if not the tens of thousands. That's not necessarily so with these internationally classed street-legal racecars. (in this particular case, the GT SuperCar)

This is one reason why IMSA and other sanctioning bodies, in all kinds of racing, have to occasionally change or reshuffle particular classes within their jurisdictions. (and sometimes they do that a lot) Their classes need to reflect to a point what the manufacturers are building. Otherwise those manufacturers will not help support racing since it wouldn't help in the marketing of their product.

Some racecar classes require a production run of as little as 25 copies per year. If you immediately think, "mercy . . . they must be gosh-awful expensive vehicles" . . . you would certainly be right 99% of the time! (taking into account that some kit or replicar-manufactured vehicles aren't all that high priced)

The US is one of the richest countries in the world. Even its average citizens and race fans can't identify with those kind of 'high-browed' numbers. That's another reason internationally classed racing isn't all that popular, especially in the US. Be that as it may, FIA-sanctioned GT competition still has its place within the racing confines of the well-financed stalwarts of speed. (did that sound politically correct enough for you high-dollar efficieonados? . . . and . . . did I spell that right?)

So, . . . while these internationally-classed cars may actually be a 'Showroom Stock' class, they're called GT. It's only semantics in the same way some StockCar classes aren't anything close to true stock. These cars are also much more expensive vehicles. So much so that maybe even a $200,000 paid US president couldn't comfortably afford one. (it'd give'em that politically incorrect, high-browed, nose-in-the-air, snobby, snooty, stuffy, I'm-better-than-you, elitist image anyway)

International GT racing generally provides for two classes of competition: GT Class 1 and GT Class 2. There are other international levels, but it's not necessary to cover the few others in a domestic-oriented publication such as this.

Class 1 car/models require a minimum production run of 25 per year, such as Bugatti, Jaguar, Lotus, Mclaren, Porsche, Ferrari and Venturri.

Class 2 isn't much different. Their production-run numbers must meet at least 200 copies per year.

Both classes of cars may either be open (convertible) or closed cockpit. (hardtop in automotive vernacular) Turbocharged or not, 2 and 4-wheel drives are all eligible as long as they are 2-door, 4-seat cars fully legal on public roads. But all that computer-enhanced telemetry, such as ABS, automatic throttle, suspension-control and 4-wheel steering systems have to be eliminated.

Engines of any production-run size may be used and are to burn only nonexotic mixes of fuel. They must be catalytic converter equipped and meet strict sound decimal standards. Each vehicle is equipped with an air-restrictor device inside its induction system to control power output. Class 1 cars get a smaller restrictor, (or larger intake manifold) therefore more air, meaning more power. (kind of like those used in NASCAR Winston-Cup Grand National events on high-speed tracks) The target horsepower output for each class is 500–550 for class 1 and 300–350 for class 2.

Two and 4-wheel drive cars must weigh at least 2425 and 2755 lbs respectively.

Some of these cars are so fast and powerful, they actually have to be broken-down or detuned to meet racing standards. Amongst other things, now you know one of the reasons why low-production models from such makes as Ferrari and Porsche are so expensive. Some stock production models can reach well over 200 mph. The fastest stock production car ever built was the Mclaren F1 GTR, clocked at 241 mph.

International GT 1 and 2 won't be doing that. They'll be toping out at around 190 and 170 mph respectively.

A relatively new sanctioning body based in Paris, France is organizing international GT racing also. They're called the BPR. They are three men, Jurgen Barth, Patrick Peter and Stefane Ratel whose last-names (and initials) comprise its name. In 1994 they sanctioned about 8 events, most if not all 4 hours in duration. What got my attention was the fact that one of those events was held in China. Very few races of any kind have ever been staged over there. If they can pull that off, they certainly could be a new and rising promoter on the horizon. 15 events were scheduled for the 1995 season.

C.IV. 6. TRANS-AM—This is an old high-profile SCCA pro class which popularized the previously rejected mix of sedan-styled autos competing on roadcourses. Started in 1966, these cars are somewhat like a more "nimble" version of NASCAR's Winston Cup Grand National racer, with probably a bit less power. But that may be only because of what they race on. Most roadcourses aren't built for overall top-end speed like ovals are. Still, if Trans-Am raced on ovals such as Daytona and Talladega, I doubt very much if they could keep up with a Grand National StockCar. On the other hand, I doubt a GN StockCar could be competitive with one of these Trans-Am racers on a roadcourse, especially a tight one. Either way, Trans-Am became so popular, NASCAR tried to start a series of their own.

Trans-Ams were originally production-based in the 60's. Now they are more highly modified cars with a purpose-built chassis of tubeframe type built from scratch. Their bodywork copies popular mass-produced sport sedans of mostly domestic origin, but do include foreign models. Like most stock-appearing racecars, these do not have wings. They do incorporate a rather long 6–7 inch high spoiler across the top trailing edge of their bodywork much like those on the NASCAR GN racecars.

Unlike some forms of popular pro racing, more emphasis is placed towards a handicap system which balances competition by matching horsepower with car weight. A common power-to-weight ratio is a 2600 lb minimum-weight car with a 311 maximum cubic inch engine.

These cars tend to be just a bit smaller than the NASCAR Grand National machines. Matter-a-fact, after thinking about it, these racers are much more like NASCAR's Busch-sponsored Grand National StockCars rather than the 'Winston Cup' racers.

This class continues to remain popular and enjoys good factory support. (especially since front-drive cars such as Beretta are allowed to convert to rear-wheel drive) Trans-Am continues to receive sponsor support from Proctor & Gamble.

Legendary racers such as Mark Donahue, (leads winners list at 29 victories) Dan Gurney, Al Hobert and David Pearson have competed in this class and won. Peter Gregg, Bob Tullius, Willy T. Ribbs, Greg Pickett all have several wins. Paul Newman has won 2 of his own and even comedian Dick Smothers has a win. (no laughing matter) Chevrolet still leads as the most frequent visitor to victory circle. Foreign builders such as Porsche follows closely behind in the overall manufacturers chase.

A season consists of around 14 races in virtually every region of the US. The race length is usually around 100 miles. These have supported race weekends with Indy

This is a Camero which races in the SCCA pro division, . . . specifically, it is a Trans-Am. It's basically a stockcar, purpose-built for racing road courses, but on a higher, faster and more sophisticated level then GT-1, SS GT and late model short track stockcars. This car could pass in appearance to many NASCAR, ARCA and ASA sanctioned stockcars; although NASCAR Winston Cup Grand National stockcars are a bit larger and more powerful. You won't see a late model short track stockcar looking this unblemished after a season of racing. They get side-swiped and banged around quite extensively on those tight 1/2 mile ovals.

cars and are occasionally the main feature themselves.

Some of popular Trans-Am machines of the 90's is the Ford Mustang, Chevy Camero and Corvette, Pontiac Trans-Am, Chevy Beretta, Olds Cutlass Supreme, Porsche 944 and Nissan 300ZX, to name a few.

The maximum wheelbase allowed is 116 inches. They do not use street radials, but rather racing slicks of a maximum 15 inches in width.

Top end speed of these machines is around 170 mph.

Even though the rules in this class of racer have good stability, changes have been make to keep their costs in line. An example is the doing away of expensive carbon-fiber interiors. They're rev-limiting engines to 8500 rpm's and cutting down the amount of time a team is allowed to test their vehicles during the off-season. (that last one has been implemented a lot lately in other forms of high-dollar racing, such as F1 and Indy cars.

C.IV. 7A. GRAND TOURING 'PROTOTYPE' —These were the highly exotic, most sophisticated GT racing sports cars in the world. Foreign-born and conceived in 1953, they were used as an international marketing tool for the car manufacturers. They were also a compliment, or competitor, to Formula One, depending on who you talk to. While enjoying a few long stints of good factory support and fan popularity, this class of racing always seemed fraught with political in-fighting, sky-rocketing costs and a misguided perception as a third-rate venue by the world sports media. This situation helped spawn into existence, in 1969, the US version of a sports prototype racing body, . . . called the 'International MotorSport Association'. (IMSA) With financial help from tobacco magnate R.J. Reynolds, which supported GTP's since 1972, the new 'Camel GT' series was born. (officially in 1971)

Finally, after a few last-gasp efforts to revive these, they were officially declared ineligible with IMSA after the '94 season and by FIA/FISA on the international level in 1992. The only place prototypes may probably race now is in Europe's most popular racing event, the '24 Hours of LeMans'. What the Indianapolis 500 is to Indy cars, the '24 hours of LeMans' is to GTP's and other simular classes. Because of that, don't be too surprised if another attempt is made by a newly formed sanctioning body, either FISA/FIA or anyone with megabucks, to pull these true prototypes out of the grave.

A transformation did developed in 1993, but not in its purest form. IMSA replaced their GTP series racer with a more cost-effective, production-based replacement called 'World Sports Car'. (also a previous FISA prototype series title if the word 'Championship' was added, forming WSCC) This new racer will be covered in a few moments.

Meanwhile, the IMSA GTP racer could reach speeds of 200 mph. These low-slung, two-seat wide cockpit, single seaters had completely enclosed bodywork at all of the wheels, including the cockpit. This purpose-built racer incorporated some ground-effects into their strong carbon-fiber and aluminum honeycomb chassis. This machine was built to the same kind of standards, care and expense of Formula One and Indy race cars. These racecars were a bit safer due to their somewhat wider, longer size and enclosed cockpit.

Just before GTP's demise, their engines could be turbocharged if a 3-liter or smaller engine displacement was used. (recently changed from 3.5 liters) Some teams used V-6 to V-12 configuration, single or twin turbo, air or water-cooled engines. There was much diversity in this class of racing, especially in the earlier years. Rule changes narrowed that diversity down a bit through time.

IMSA GTP machines which were not turbocharged used engines all the way up to 6.0 liter displacement. (sometimes 7-liters, under special FISA-international circumstances) They were also allotted lighter minimum weights. IMSA's "sliding scale" minimum weight rule helped to keep competition close while individual manufacturing incentives were kept intact.

Turbocharged or not, minimum-weights were set between 1625–2250 lbs. Whatever that power-to-weight ratio was, an adjustment to that ratio was made if an engine

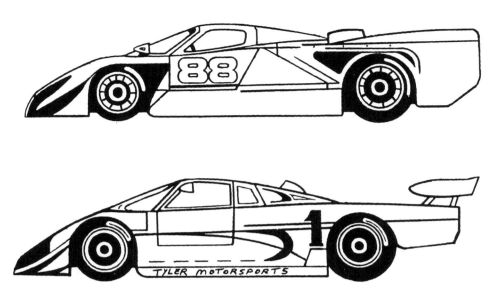

Not much difference in size between the GTP & the GTP light. The big difference is power. Number 88 is the full size GTP racer. These racecars have been replaced, due to their high costs, by the World Sports Car division of IMSA.

used four values per cylinder and/or Group C characteristics.

Group C prototypes are pretty much the European version of our GTP's. They had a different aerodynamics package, turbo and fuel consumption requirements and minimum-weight rules.

IMSA GTP's competed on various road-courses and temporary street circuits. Their 15–16 race schedule included a 24-hour event. (SunBank-sponsored '24 Hours of Daytona'; now supported by Rolex) They also ran a 12-hour event. (Sebring) The other races were much shorter. About half of them were determined by kilometer distance. (around 300-500 km's) They competed in all kinds of wet or dry weather conditions. That meant they used racing slicks in dry conditions and treaded racing tires in wet weather.

In addition to the drivers championship, there was also a manufacturers point race for a championship. (which is also true in most Showroom Stock and GT categories)

GTP's weren't just popular here in thee good 'O US of A. The original GTP's, started in Europe, were eventually recommissioned

in part as Group C racers. They competed in a 9–12 event series throughout the world, but mostly in Europe. They were basically built with the same specifications as our GTP's as far as their looks were concerned. This was also a very diversified series. There were numerous body aerodynamic, wing and ground-effects packages, turbo and non-turbo engine sizes and configurations. But they did tend to be more expensive than our GTP's.

But, . . . GTP's are now officially history. Whether 'prototypes' ever make a comeback again can only be determined by the passage of time.

Okay, . . . so much for that. Usher out the old, . . . and in with the new. Enter the WSC racer. (concentrate now; this is where the reading gets complicated; 7B,C thru 8 A,B,C)

C.IV. 7B. WORLD SPORTS CARS—In 1992 IMSA announced this class of racer would replace the Camel-sponsored GTP (Camel GT) as their featured series. Other than the obvious cost-effective goals this was also designed, in part, to help give this style of racing back to the private race teams, those not heavily supported by a manufacturer.

From a great distance the difference between a GTP and WSC racecar isn't too obvious. The exception to that is the WSC's have an open cockpit. That prompts me to test you. With the WSP's cockpit not enclosed, what class (or more specifically, what category) is this racecar? Hint: one-half of the name is already in the WSC title. Answer; SportsRacer! But . . . it's unofficially a GT SportsRacer in this case because it costs "mucho pesos". 'World Sports Car' is a more commercially oriented name for what's actually a GT-styled SportsRacer.

Let's take this little test a step further. What class of SportsRacer, or now what's commercially called 'World Sports Car', do you think this class can easily evolve into? Answer; Can-Am! Think about it. Aren't these WSC cars looking like the old SCCA-sanctioned Can-Am racer of the 60's, 70's and 80's? Well . . . they're looking that way, . . . but WSC's are more expensive and complex. Of course, a Can-Am name could be slapped on these racecars and that would make them Can-Am, albeit, certainly a different version.

To the untrained eye, WSC's might be mistakened for a slightly more street-legal looking GTP. That includes the rear wings. But things aren't always as they look. Under the body lurks a different animal. The ground-effects package has been eliminated. In other words, these are flat-bottomed machines. Their overall size limit of 183 inches is smaller than the GTP, even the GTP Light.

Minimum weights of 1600 to 2000 lbs are determined by horsepower output of their 5.0 liter V-6 and V-8, normally-aspirated, production-based engines. That engine size will vary according to the number of valves allowed per cylinder. That's 2 valves/cylinder for engines up to 5 liters; 4 valves for those up to 4 liters; and appropriate sizes for the 3 and 5 valve per cylinder engines.

Turbocharged WSC's will be allowed to compete in the 12 and 24-events sanctioned by IMSA, but they will not be eligible to collect points for the Exxon WSC championship. These turbo-equipped WSC machines are called LeMans-styled WSC's.

More than likely, they'll be the racers eligible for competition in the new and upcoming internationally-sanctioned World Championship series supposedly starting in 1996. As of now, they're eligible to run at LeMans, as implied by their name.

Because IMSA WSC class of racing is so new, you can count on adjustments being made by IMSA down the road. This isn't politics in my view, but rather a learning process which hopefully will even the competitive field. But you can also bet those changes will ruffle some feathers along the way. (I call those kinds of early situations "racing birthpangs")

Already, one ugly situation has developed within the ranks. IMSA has expressed a desire to place rev-limits on the engines. This was designed to keep engines reliable and cost-contained. Others will tell you it was to keep Ferrari manufacturing contained. (Ferrari dominated the inaugural 1994 racing season with their $950,000 model, the '333 SPs'. This is cheaper racing? Generally, WSC racers cost about 200–$230.000; that's expensive enough)

Anyway, for 1995, all multi-valve engines (3 or more per cylinder) are rev-limited to 8,500 rpm's. Otherwise, two valve/cylinder is limited to 10,500 revs.

The race series, now fully supported by Exxon petroleum, will still include the same basic schedule as the former GTP series. That includes the 24 and 12-hour races of Daytona and Sebring. The other 10 or so events are slated for 2 hours each except for the 3-hour Watkins Glen and 4-hour Brainard events.

On the international scene, WSC's or their equivalent, are attempting a new mini-series earmarked for 1996. FIA and ACO, the organizers of the world famous '24 Hours of LeMans', hope to have in this 4 or 5 event tour the "big three" endurance events known worldwide: LeMans, Daytona and Sebring.

WSC racers should be able to top out at around 188 mph.

C.IV. 7C. GRAND TOURING 'EXPERIMENTAL'—These machines were basically the same racer as the Porsche 935 which was popular at Monza (24 hours of LeMans) in the '70's. They were a sort of silhouette-ancestor to the GTP.

GTX had various experimental innovations incorporated into them for the purposes of a 'Formula Libre' kind of competition. (Libre means free from regulations; Formula means the style of rule itself, not necessarily the type of racecar)

This class was subject to points earned towards a national championship with FIA and IMSA-sanctioned racing. GTX's have been out of existence for quite a few years now.

C.IV. 7D. GRAND TOURING PROTOTYPE 'LIGHT'—These are the lighter and less powerful version of the GTP. They were eliminated right along with GTP.

The 'Light' was also a true prototype and was constructed to the same basic regulations as the GTP. This class also incorporated the 'sliding scale' rule of its own version. Their minimum weights were between 1550 to 1850 lbs, varying at an average of about 200 lbs lighter than their big brother the GTP. Turbocharging was not permitted and eligible engines could not exceed 3-liters in displacement size.

These machines raced the same schedule as the GTP and competed with them as a "race within a race" for their own class and points towards a national championship. The manufacturers also had their own championship chase. Even though they raced with the GTP, they have never beat them overall for a first place finish. But they have finished as high as in the top five.

Like the GTP, these used both racing slicks and treaded racing tires if it was wet. Also like GTP, the Lights had no wheelbase limits, but overall length, width and height couldn't exceed 189, 79 and 39.5 inches. So these racers were even longer than IMSA's new WSC machines. Rear wings on the GT Lights were limited to the widest part of the coachwork between the axles and no higher than the top of the cockpit body.

Maximum wheel and tire widths were limited to 16 inches. Wheel diameter was also 16 inches. There were no ground clearance rules, but also no skirts were permitted to improve ground effects.

This machine could top out near 176 mph.

Even though there is no such class as WSC Light replacing GTP Light, at least in 'name', IMSA was sanctioning a production or stock silhouette-based, 3-division pro venue named the 'Exxon Supreme GT Series'. Evolved out of the old 2-division GTO/GTU classes, this new GT series was increased to three by adding a GTS division and changing or reshuffling the GTO/GTU rules. The 3 divisions were Grand Touring 'Supreme'- GTS, Grand Touring 'Over'- GTO and Grand Touring 'Under'- GTU.

Did you notice I was using words in that last paragraph in the past-tense? That's because those new GTS/GTO/GTU classes have been reshuffled again! It's now GTS-Class 1 and GTS-Class 2 as of the 1995 season. It can get confusing. You'll need to concentrate amongst all these IMSA's class changes the last few years.

One of the reasons I mention GTS here in the GTP Light section is because of what may be a misleading situation cropping up between upstarts GTS and WSC. Even though GTS isn't quite as quick and powerful as the WSC, they have been beating some WSC's in the 12 and-24 hour races. This was especially so in the 1994 Daytona 24 hour event when a (then) GTS racer (not GTS-1) placed first overall. It beat superior classes! That's not supposed to happen to a stronger-classed vehicle like the WSC machine. (an never will, regularly) But remember, 12 and 24-hour Endurance events measure equipment reliability in addition to speed and driver skill. These confusing race results, especially to race beginners, simply won't continue in the long haul. WSC will get over their initial teething problems.

Another reason I present this circumstance is because the GTS could end up being renamed and/or retooled into a WSC 'Light' class sometime down the road. Time will tell.

C.IV. 8A. GRAND TOURING 'SUPREME'— (now GTS-1) As I previously just mentioned, GTS was the result of some IMSA class reshuffling when the 'prototypes' were eliminated. The former GTO class was rechristened to here, the GTS and then eventually to GTS-1. GTO was IMSA's closest race machine to the SCCA Trans-Am racer.

GTO's were mass-produced, foreign and domestic appearing sedans, with minimal body modifications, with the idea to look as stock appearing as possible.

The engines in GTO were 'over' 3.0 liters in displacement, but not over 6.0 liters. Turbocharged engines couldn't be over 3.0 liters. The car engine, drivetrain and body/chassis had to meet as standard equipment as provided for sale for that model to the general public. Minimum weights were between 1800-2250 for normally-aspirated racers and 2500-2700 for the forced-air units. These weights varied on a sliding-scale formula based on an engines horsepower output to help even the competition.

But as you've read, that all was changed. GTO's were reclassed to GTS before the 1994 season. GTS was still stock appearing, but they were then a more purpose-built, semi-prototype, tube-framed chassis-designed race machine compared to GTO. Like GTO, GTS's looked a lot like SCCA's Trans-Am racer.

GTS had to be two-wheel drive cars and still production-based at the drivetrain like GTO. GTS weren't powered much differently than GTO. Turbocharged machines had to be 2 to 3.0 liters in engine displacement. The atmospheric types (nonturbocharged) could be over 3.0 liters. Minimum weights were still the sliding-scale type set between 2400 to 2700 lbs which was close to the original minimum-weights of the GTO.

Both GTO and GTS machines used an unusually wide racing slick as stock-appearing racecar standards go. Many of these racecars had their rear-wheel quarter-panels extended and/or wheels-wells enlarged to accommodate these wider race tires. The tires were not to be over 16 inches measured across the tread.

GTS machines turned out to be quite a competitor. Almost too competitive. As you read earlier, in their first year of 12 and 24 hours events, it proved itself more reliable than the stronger WSC racer.

Example of GTS cars running in this class

is about the same as the old GTO class. They are: Cougar XR7, Nissan 300ZX, Camero (V-8 engine), Mazda RX-7, Ferrari F-40LM, Corvette and Capri's.

Like the former GTO and GTU racecars, you must of figured out by now GTS competed with the WSC's as a 'race within a race' for their own class competition, points towards a national title and purse. (money) Like most GT classes, GTS also included a race for the 'Manufacturers' title.

The GTS's have been reshuffled again for the 1995 season. Instead of GTS being the first of the former 3-divisioned 'Exxon (sponsored) Supreme GT' series, it is now the first of a 2-division series with the same title. GTS is now GTS Class 1. (GTS-1)

The latest GTO's which evolved to GTS for 1994, and covered here in this section, (C.IV. 8A) now merges with the old GTO class of pre-1994 (just below and coming up next) to form the GTS Class 1 racer. Confusing? Maybe a bit now, but it'll eventually become more clear as you read on.

Both GTS-1 and the other GTS class, eventually coming up, called GTS-2, have a simple but separate set of chassis rules for each class. One is for the purpose-built tubeframe-chassis vehicle, which must use only a normally-aspirated engine. The other set is for the more production-based unibody racing machine. The unibody racer is allowed to be turbocharged.

GTS-1 and GTS-2's run the same 12–13 event schedule as WSC's because they all compete together on the same track at the same time.

By the way, this is what I call multiclass racing. It's most prevalent in all amateur and some pro classes of SCCA, most of IMSA's classes, which are all pro level, off-road racing and finally the motorcycle classes.

C.IV. 8B. GRAND TOURING OVER 3.0 LITERS—(now, also GTS Class 1) This class, with the GTU, was originally the main supporting series for the GTP events. This particular racer was limited by 3.0 to 6.0-liter engines which were allowed to be turbocharged.

Eligible vehicles were mass-produced foreign and domestic models that allowed some minimal body modifications. The class dominating racers were the Chevy V-8 powered Camero and Corvette, twin-turbo Nissan Z, Ferrari F-40LM, Porsche 911, Mazda RX-7's, (both V-8 and 4-cylinder engines) Capris and the turbo Cougars.

IMSA's former class of 'All American Challenge' (ACC) racers, which competed within the old GTO class, as a class within a class, became GTO when the GTO's moved to GTS. (and eventually GTS-1) ACC's racers were formerly restricted only to mass-produced, American-made cars with V-6 and V-8 engines. These ACC racers were allowed an engine-to-weight ratio of 9 lbs chassis weight for every cubic-inch of engine displacement. (with all ACC's weighing at least 2500 lbs)

So to repeat, the ACC class was regrouped to GTO as part of the fairly new 3-division (GTS/GTO/GTU) Exxon-sponsored 'Grand Touring Supreme' series. ACC's move to GTO made them the second and most powerful machine of those 3-divisions. The engine of this new GTO division racer was about the same as the original GTO, but were increased to 6.5 liters instead of the latters old 6.0 liter restriction.

Now as of the 1995 season, the original GTO which has gone to GTS, now evolves to the new designation of GTS-Class 1. The old GTO class, made up mostly of the ACC racers, would also best fit into this GTS-1 class too, at least in most cases. The rest, or borderlines, could be retooled to GTS Class 2.

IMSA also had a long-running international-sedan type series started in 1969. Recently eliminated, it was called the 'LuK Clutch Challenge' series. These mid-sized sports cars had to be specifically-recognized, volume-produced vehicles from the worlds leading manufacturers. Chassis modifications were permitted, but engines, drive-trains and bodies had to remain stock.

This class of machine was designed more for affordable racing. It never participated in endurance events, but more as a support series for IMSA's shorter-distant races. (shorter or sprint-styled races)

Even though the 'LuK Clutch Challenge'

racers were eliminated, the race machines haven't been left out in the cold, so-to-speak. They would probably best and most efficiently be converted over to the new GTS Class 2 racer.

C.IV. 8C. GRAND TOURING 'UNDER' 3.0 LITERS—(now basically GTS Class-2) Obviously, the main difference between the former GTU/GTO classes was the engine size. As implied in the class title, the engines here in GTU were 'under' 3 liters in size. But unlike GTO, no turbocharging was allowed. Otherwise, except for speed, GTU was pretty much the same as GTO.

Example racers include: Mazda RX-6 and 7, Porsche 911 (flat six), Nissan 240SX, Pontiac Fiero and Dodge Daytona.

Tire widths were limited to 13.5 inches, a little smaller than the original GTO, and the wheel diameter was the same as GTO at 16 inches maximum.

Unlike GTO, GTU wasn't reclassed so much the last few years by IMSA. The rules within GTU changed, but not as drastically and not as much compared to the others. Therefore it wasn't as confusing to the race fans since GTU's title didn't change much either.

Basically, GTU goes to GTS Class 2. GTS-2 is an image of GTS-1, but it's smaller, lighter and down-powered under the hood in comparison.

An educated estimate is GTS-2's will reach top-end speeds of 168 mph. The GTS-1 should reach about 183 mph. But remember, all the speed in the world doesn't amount to a hill of beans if that engine blows itself up. So, reliability is important in all racing, but much more in endurance events. This is especially so at Daytona, Sebring and LeMans.

This ends the entire C category of race-cars. Categories A, B and the four C categories totals 6. There are now 9 categories of race machines left to cover in this chapter. But in actuality you're about 40% of the way through this chapter.

D. STOCKCARS (15 CLASSES)

D. StockCars 1. Grand National (Grand Sport)
D. StockCars 2. Baby Grand
D. StockCars 3. Late Models
D. StockCars 4. Pro Stock Late Models
D. StockCars 5. Sportsman
D. StockCars 6. Grand Touring (mostly covered in category C.IV.)
D. StockCars 7. Improved Touring (mostly covered in category C.III.)
D. StockCars 8. Showroom Stock (mostly covered in category C.II.)
D. StockCars 9. Production (mostly covered in category C.I.)
D. StockCars 10. SuperStock
D. StockCars 11. Mini-Stock (LEGENDS)
D. StockCars 12. Figure 8 Cars
D. StockCars 13. Modified
D. StockCars 14. Mini-Modified
D. StockCars 15. SuperModified (Mini-Super Modified)

If you haven't figured out by now the difference between a StockCar in 'name' and a real stock car, then this category should complete their comparisons. A real stock car is what you drive around on the streets and go to work in. StockCar as relative to racing is one of the biggest misnomers you'll come across in sports. Still, in racing, many StockCars are more stock than others. Does that make sense to you? It should by now, especially since you've read all about the machines listed in Category C of this book. If not, hang tough and as you read on it'll become more apparent.

The largest misuser of this word are the folks up in the high-profile professional ranks. But it's for purely innocent reasons. This word StockCar benefits racing, fan appeal and the manufacturers. It's a natural marketing theme that draws attention to StockCars by identifying the love Americans have for (their) cars with the racetrack. This is important because it draws advertisers, which means racing sponsorship. Translated: MONEY. (and you know we need that to play this game)

Looking furthest down the list of StockCars ordered above, it becomes obvious a Modified StockCar is more a confliction in terms than a misnomer. When you think

about it, all race vehicles are modified. So therefore, it's important to distinguish between the literal and figurative terms used in this chapter, if not the entire book. Then all the classes in this chapter become more clear.

D.1. GRAND NATIONAL—(Winston Cup) This isn't a class unto itself as much as it's the major league of American-built, full-sized vehicle style of stock car racing long supported by the tobacco company RJ Reynolds.

Started in 1948, this is a racing series sanctioned through NASCAR. (National Association of Stock Car Automobile Racing) The US Auto Club (USAC) also had their own version, but it wasn't anywhere near as popular as NASCAR. (and it wasn't called Grand National). It eventually was dropped.

Two other sanctioning bodies race this same basic automobile under their own regulations and class name. Whether these are actually Grand National cars is a matter of interpretation. The ASA (American Speed Association) and ARCA (Automobile Racing Club of America) are the two organizations with these larger-styled stockcars. ARCA has some (former) NASCAR affiliations. These associations hold an occasional race on a superspeedway. (paved, banked, oval track over 1.5 miles) On these large superspeedways, I would consider ARCA and ASA racecars Grand National vehicles, albeit underpowered compared to the NASCAR machine, which tends to race more of their events on large ovals. More appropriately, and especially on short tracks, ASA and ARCA racers are closer to Baby Grand classed racer.

Grand National (GN) is actually a more commercially-oriented name coined by NASCAR. GN probably should be more appropriately labeled as a GRAND STOCK class. But I will use the 'Grand National' moniker here because this title is better known by the racing public.

The GN rules and regulations instituted by NASCAR for the Winston Cup series not only sets the standard for superspeedway StockCars, but for some of the short-track oriented stockcars too. That's especially so for the short-track stockcars which occasionally race on superspeedways. Afterall, NASCAR Winston Cup GN racecars compete on short-tracks also. So don't confused NASCAR's 'Winston Cup' Grand National with 'Busch' Grand National. Both are termed GN StockCars by NASCAR, especially the Busch racers, but actually they're two slightly different classes. For the purposes of this publication GN is superspeedway oriented, Baby Grand, coming up next, is more short-track oriented.

NASCAR requires their Winston Cup racers to be as stock-appearing as possible. The car and model must appear to be of American 'make' and no more than 4 years old. The car must also be a hardtop sedan. No station wagons or front and 4-wheel drive cars are allowed. Modifications may be made to the body or coachwork for safety reasons. An example are the retractable roof flaps designed to create downforce keeping an out-of-control and/or laterally moving vehicle planted on the ground, and thus, from rolling over. The wheelwells may have the cut-away or enlarged look to enhance quicker tire change and prevent tire rubbing on the bodywork. (since the race tires are larger than stock street types originally designed for it)

Engine blocks must be of the same manufacturer as the car model. They are to be internal combustion type (no rotary engines) and normally aspirated. (no turbo or supercharging) These reciprocating-piston engines are to burn automotive grade fuel. Engine components (parts) must originate from the manufacturers stock production castings or forgings. They may be subsequently refined, modified or improved with further machining under strict specifications.

Engines cannot be altered by their original number of cylinders, bearings, cams or spark plugs locations. The type of valve actuations (how long each valve stays open, allowing more fuel to enter combustion chamber) and their numbers per cylinder, along with the combustion chamber cannot be altered.

Carburetion cannot be laterally located on the engine and is limited to one 4-barrel type with air filter attached. No air-scoop ram induction is permitted.

Piston bore (cylinder size) and stroke (piston movement up and down) alterations is permitted so long as engines don't exceed 358 cubic inches. This is where racing mechanics can extract extra power out of an engines originally designed parameters, by changing the engines compression ratio.

Wheelbase is between 110 to 115 inches. Minimum weight is 3400 lbs. All cars must clear the ground by 3 1/2 inches. Roof tops must be over 50 inches off the ground. Wheels must be of identical size at all 4 corners; 10 inches wide, 15-inch diameter. Tire width or cross section cannot exceed 13.75 inches.

No wings or ground effects are permitted. Spoilers located at the top trailing edge of the bodywork is permitted. No automatic transmissions are allowed. Fuel capacity is limited to 22 gallons.

After reading all that you may ask yourself, "Gee, compared to all those other race cars I've read about, these guys can't do anything to their machines!" Wrong! They do plenty. A lot is in the area of safety. The engines may look stock and sound stock, according to my description, but remember, these are literally larger in size. Their tube-frame chassis, which is purpose-built, can safely handle these larger, heavier engine blocks, unlike, say, a Formula car. So, . . . these engines already have more stock horsepower to begin with. Then their cylinders may be bored to a larger size and/or other ways may be implemented to increase their horsepower.

Watching the way these guys bump and grind each other at round 195 mph on the superspeedways, they need all the protection they can get. After looking under the roof of one of these cars, you'll immediately see there is nothing stock about them. Tubes of steel (roll cage) completely surrounds the driver. This cage also serves to stiffen the chassis for better handling characteristics. That's nice to have at such high speeds. You'll notice a lot of straight clean sheet metal (usually aluminum) instead of curvy, soft carpeting you'd find in your street car. Without going into unnecessary detail, that sheet metal is there for a reason, and must comply to strict NASCAR specifications.

To run a full season in NASCAR's Winston Cup Grand National StockCar series requires a grueling effort. 29–31 races from about 300 to 600 miles in length, spread over about 9 months doesn't leave much time for fishing, especially for the crew!

The race tracks NASCAR GN's run on are ovals varying in length from 1/2 to 2.6 miles. Initially, almost all races were held in the southeast US. That's changing fast due to its popularity. Now NASCAR makes stops further up north at Michigan International Speedway, Dover, Delaware, New Hampshire, Pocono, Pa, Watkins Glen, NY, which by-the-way is the only nonoval roadcourse they run on and of course their new hotspot, the Indianapolis Motor Speedway.

NASCAR GN's used to take an occasional trip out to Riverside, CA but that track is out of service and torn down. That's been replaced by Sonoma, Ca. They do run in the desert at Phoenix International. Otherwise, NASCAR stays home in the southeast two-thirds of the time where they draw a very good following.

This class of racing, in my opinion, is the most tightly contested professional racing in the world. They put all the other highly-visible pro racing organizations to shame. Where else would you see as many as 25 to 40% of the racers on the same lap at the finish with the winner. Any one of 20 to 25 drivers could win a race and do so by fractions of a second. Even the racecars a lap or 2 down may of only ended up there due to some unfortunate break or accident. Lord knows it wasn't because of inferior equipment.

Many times the season championship isn't decided until the final 1 or 2 races of the year. Because of these situations, NASCAR has proven beyond any doubt that given a choice between the high-technology (therefore, high dollars) racing, such as F1, GTP and Indy Cars, and tight competition, such as this series, most racing fans are prone to choose the tight competition.

While high-technology racing has its place and can be exciting, in the long run, it'll never replace what makes racing fans really want, . . . close, fast and fair competition.

This is why these GN StockCars are doing so well. I heard a stockcar fan say, "The cars aren't the stars, it's the racers who drive them." So true! This is one of the reasons 'spec' racing is gaining popularity in the US and the rest of the world. It gives racing back to the drivers, not the manufacturers.

The most popular GN car 'make' and models are: Buick Regal, Chevy Lumina, Ford Thunderbird, Mercury Cougar, Oldsmobile Cutless and Pontiac Gran Prix.

These machines can reach a top-end speed of 200 mph on the superspeedways and around 145–155 on a half-mile or so track.

D.2. BABY GRAND—Baby Grand is a class hardly heard of. That's because it's titled under many different banners. Examples are: LATE MODELS, PRO STOCK, SPORTSMAN, LATE MODEL SPORTSMAN, GRAND SUPERCARS, SUPERCARS, GRAND LIGHT, LIGHT, etc.

'Baby Grand' is a generic name first used by NASCAR, but now used more exclusively for the purposes of this book. Baby Grands were slightly smaller stockcars raced in NASCAR's former Late Model Sportsman division. They were a sort of AAA farm affiliate of the Winston Cup series, now called 'Busch' Grand National. (or 'Busch' Light) Even though NASCAR used to refer these as Late Model Sportsman class, they're are not the kind of slower Late Model and Sportsman racer covered later in this category. NASCAR Baby Grands racers are a bit more complex, but like all professionally based racecars, their actual numbers are nowhere near those of the slower more locally-based Late Models and Sportsman racecars.

Baby Grand racecars are for all intents and purposes the same pattern-built machine the Winston Cup racers are. They are just a bit smaller and 100 lbs lighter than the Winston Cup racers. (3300 lbs minimum weight) Powered by V-6's limited to 274 ci, these machines are now permitted a 358 ci V-8 for the 1995 season. Yes, these are the same sized engine as their faster counterpart, the Winston Cup racer, but the horsepower output is still lower mostly due to a different cylinder-compression ratio. (9:1)

These cars aren't quite as popular as the Winston Cup racers, but Busch beer support is steadily changing that for the better. Generally, they compete on short and long tracks in a bit more geographically diverse locations of the US compared to Winston Cup cars. About 50% of their schedule is a support race for Winston Cup events.

As far as other sanctioning bodies are concerned, some of their racecars look like Baby Grands, but that's generally where the similarities end.

IMSA sanctioned a series of races, but it's now deceased. It was the 'Luk Clutch Challenge' for international sedans. Obviously, unlike Winston and Busch Grand National series, foreign autos were eligible. (Luk Clutch is a German Co. which sponsored this series) Also, IMSA's former Firehawk series (now Street Stock) Grand Sports racer are somewhat a cousin to Baby Grand racecars, but like the LuK Challenge racer, they are built and designed for roadcourses. This would also be the case for the IMSA GTS-1 cars, although they could be a bit overqualified.

SCCA's Corvette Challenge and Trans-Am racers fits in very closely here also. But they're designed to turn left and right with lower power ranges, (better vehicle acceleration) like all roadcourse racers.

The IROC racecars would be a bit overqualified because of a higher power to weight ratio. (meaning: a Winston Cup GN class of engine, but packaged in a Baby Grand sized model; formerly Camero, now Dodge Daytona)

As mentioned earlier, the ASA & ARCA sanctioned Stockcars are closely matched, if not a bit more powerful than the Baby Grands. ARCA's chassis is the same basic 3400 lbs, 110 inch wheelbase as the Winston Cup versions. They are generally powered by a 350 ci V-8.

ASA racers used to be about the same machines ARCA raced. Now they are more 'spec' styled and slightly smaller with a 105 inch wheelbase, 2800 lbs minimum weight and powered by a V-6. ARCA and especially ASA machines, would probably not be quite fast enough to consistently win at the Winston Cup GN level on superspeedways. They can compete with Baby Grands. But they can still top-out at around 180–190 mph on superspeedways, even though these two organizations run all but one or two of their races on short-tracks.

The NASCAR 'Busch' GN cars (Baby Grands) are smaller, sports car sized racers. Popular examples are: Dodge Daytona, Chevy Camero and Ford Mustang. They top-out at about 130–135 mph on short tracks and 185 in testing on such high-speed tracks as Talladega and Daytona. (with the new V-8 engine)

D.3. LATE MODELS—This is a slower, short-track class of stockcar that isn't necessarily purpose-built for racing from the start. In other words, a particular vehicle may literally have been a street car when it was new. That isn't usually the case but sometimes it is.

The difference between these and the Grand National stockcars is substantial in degree of sophistication. None the less, these are serious race machines. These race in smaller regionally or locally based pro sanctioning organizations. The rules and regulations for these racers are oriented towards short track (mostly 1/2 mile) paved, medium-banked ovals. Sometimes they run on dirt tracks. In addition to the organizations rules, many times these racers will also have to conform to a particular tracks rules. But that is usually a minor adjustment.

A fact that would go unnoticed by the average race fan is that if you could tear away a Late Models sheet metal or body panels, you would notice a chassis design balanced heavier on the drivers side. Because all stockcars are naturally heavier at the front end than the back, their engine locations may be placed back towards the driver further than normal. But Late Models are also sometimes offset laterally. They're built to be heavier on the left or drivers side than the right or passenger side. This is accomplished by offsetting the engine, drive train and other component to that side. This improves handling on those tight high-speed tracks where turning one way, usually left, is the norm. Most GN and Baby Grand cars aren't allowed to offset laterally.

These racers also use racing slicks of anywhere from 8-16 inches maximum width, depending on local rules. In power only, these could compare to an SCCA sanctioned GT2 or Improved Touring 'S' class. But otherwise, it's like comparing apples to oranges as far as their design is concerned. None the less, they have there own niche in racing and fill it well. I like to call these cars "Saturday night specials" because they usually are the main feature race at a local track. Their races are usually around 30 to 50 laps. Many times these same cars run a couple of heat races preceding the 'Main Feature' event.

Some typical and popular models at this level is the Camero, Trans-Am and Dodge Daytona. Most of these models are of American manufacture and are powered by a normally-aspirated 350 ci V-8. Nowadays, depending on local or regional track rules, the tendency is to go to smaller fuel injected, V-6 engines.

Depending on the size and conditions of the track, these can top off at speeds of around 125 on those short straightaways. So, these are powerful racers. Their minimum weight requirements are usually around 2500–2800 lbs with wheelbase at 108–110 inches. That's about the size of Baby Grand cars.

One unmistakable characteristic about these cars is that they tend to show wear and tear on their side body panels as the season nears its end. Tight racing and tight budgets are the cause of that, especially if the car isn't financially supported. (no name/paintings/decals to keep visible and clean for a sponsor)

D.4. PRO-STOCK LATE MODEL—These are not necessarily more powerful than Late Model cars. They are pro-based, purpose-built for racing and, of course, cleaner, less beat-up versions of the Late models covered above.

They're sanctioned by larger national/regional organizations which schedule longer events of anywhere from 50 to 300 or so

laps, usually but not always on short 1/2–5/8 mile paved ovals.

These are distinguished from Baby Grand because they are not quite as complex and powerful. Occasionally they race on dirt (or clay) in smaller, less diverse locations of the US and Canada.

Some of these larger pro-based organizations are: 'All-Pro Sanctioning Body'. It includes about 22 races in 7 or 8 states. Some of those events are on dirt tracks; NASCAR also sanctions the 19–20 event 'Slim Jim All Pro' series; The 'National Dirt Racing Association' (NDRA) holds about 15 races on half-mile dirt tracks in the southern mountain areas of the US. Some races are on mile-long tracks; the 'American-Canadian Tour' (ACT) series is northeast based; and the Southern All Star Super Late Model Dirt series, which features about 23–27 races in the deep south.

These machines top out at around 120–130 mph on the short tracks.

D.5. SPORTSMAN—This is another class that flies under several titles.

Examples are: HOBBY STOCK, STREET STOCK, CADET, BOMBER, AMATEUR, HOBO, NOVICE, JALOPY, RUNABOUT and even KAMIKASI and SUICIDE divisions. (who said race people don't have a sense of humor)

This is an amateur class that's usually a level well below the Late Models. I say "usually" because it's a relative thing. Some tracks and/or local race organizations Sportsman division cars are stronger than their Late Models. But in most cases, it's just the opposite. A good example would be NASCAR's old Sportsman division. The level of competition there compared to the local tracks level is like the difference between night and day. So when I speak of the Sportsman level of racing, I'm talking a level below a particular organizations 'main', 'featured' or 'top' class.

What are Sportsman stockcars? They're actually a less sophisticated Late Model with a lower horsepower, relatively stock, 6-cylinder engine and smaller race tires. In most Sportsman divisions, racing tires are not permitted. They must use shaved street radials, and in some cases, bias-ply (non-radials) only.

(note—95% of the time, one can pretty much count on the fact that if any class of racer is allowed to use racing slicks, the racer was purpose-built for racing. Those not permitted race slicks are (former) street cars converted over for racing. So some, but not all, Sportsman racecars were formerly street legal)

This class usually doesn't compete for cash purses. So in essence, it's amateur racing that helps support an evening of race events before the 'feature'. This can also be quite interesting to watch since the drivers are relatively inexperienced. They're usually young and that means sometimes they get a little warm under the collar. (hot tempered) This combination also leaves the sides of these vehicles even more tore up than the Late Models. I guess it's easier to do some bumping and grinding at slower speeds. Either that or the drivers are more brave. (translated: wild and crazy)

These cars can reach top-ends approaching 100 mph. So its nothing to take lightly. Sometimes they race on tracks which aren't paved and even shorter than the usual 1/2 mile or so. In that case they might reach 70–75 mph. But boy, do they do some serious banging around with each other. So much so, in fact, the cars start to look like roll cages with 4 wheels and a motor. When it gets to that point, the race promoters encourage the drivers to get their panels replaced.

You might also understand why these cars have a harder time getting higher level sponsorship. A sponsor is very image-conscience. Why would they put their name on an outwardly beat up vehicle? Besides that, their name may literally be knocked off the car or distorted. Also, these cars don't race but locally. That means a nationally-sized company would not want to confine or funnel their market to one very small area.

This is generally amateur racing, so the costs are relatively low. (I said "relatively") That and the fact racers can't get large sponsorship anyway only means this class will always remain at its current entertaining level. Besides, a racer has to start and/or

learn the race game somewhere. Some guys consciensely(?) refuse to leave this class. Afterall, the costs are lower, . . . and let's not forget, all racing, no matter what level, is still a ton of fun.

D.6. GRAND TOURING—For many people, including myself, about the only difference between GT (not GTP) and StockCars is what shape of racetrack they compete on. Grand Touring is a form of stockcar racing. StockCars race on ovals of .1 to 2.6 miles in length. Usually they race in a counter-clockwise direction. The short tracks aren't always paved.

GT cars usually race roadcourses or street circuits of around 1 to 4 miles in the clockwise direction. That's about it. They look the same, but are designed and setup differently for what they race on. For more details refer back to Category C.IV. (if you can't recall the details on GT racing)

D.7. IMPROVED TOURING—This is also StockCar racing, albeit, not in its traditional form. Essentially, IT is in the same boat with GT relative to StockCars.

IT racing is slower and less sophisticated than GT, and they compete only on paved roadcourses in the clockwise direction. That's about it. (for more details on IT racing refer back to Category C.III.

D.8. SHOWROOM STOCK—This ought to be obvious just by name alone. All these racers' are is newer (not necessarily faster) versions of Improved Touring racers. Otherwise, when comparing them with stockcar racing, they're no different than GT and IT.

You can refresh your memory on SS cars in Category C.II.

D.9. PRODUCTION—These are StockCars too. These cars are the same as SS, IT and GT machines relative to StockCars. If you need to read back about the Production racer, go to Category C.I.

D.10. SUPERSTOCK—Alternate racing semantics refer to these as DIRT TRACK STOCKCARS. Obviously that's because they compete almost exclusively on oval dirt tracks of mainly 1/5 to 5/8 miles in length.

As far as the vehicle itself, it isn't designed all that much different than the Late Model racer underneath their outer skin. Speaking of outer skin, at first sight, these racers are instantly more boxier looking. Their bodywork isn't the factory-stamped, curvy, aerodynamic kind. It's more of the straight sheet-metal type that's attached around the cage and chassis in such a way for quick and easy repair. Sometimes these racers have elongated bodywork built-in at the rear portion of the chassis which serves as a wing. These powerful racers negotiate sidewinding turns simular to that of the dirt-track Sprint cars. Unlike Sprint cars, Super-Stock do more side-by-side banging with each other. So therefore the straight, clean bodywork is easier to replace.

Other than that and the suspensions design for dirt surfaces, their engines, drive trains and roll cages are built from the ground up with the same basic size, dimensions, weight and power ratio of the Late Model.

Like the Late Model a typical SuperStock is around 108–110 inches in wheelbase, powered by a 350 ci normally-aspirated V-8 and limited to about 2200 minimum weight. But there are several minor variation based on local track rules. It's certainly not unusual to see fuel-injected V-6's.

On a half-mile dirt track these cars aren't quite as quick as the Late Model. That's because dirt is inherently harder for any racecar to grip. They can get up to 100 mph and beyond.

This is a short track oval racer which may be called one of several classes of stockcar at the hundreds of local track locations. This straight-sheetmetal model is more than likely called a 'super' late model stockcar because it competes on dirt or clay. 'Late models' tend to be cleaner looking because they race on asphalt or cement, which eliminates sidewinding turns and all that bumping and grinding. Late models are not necessarily stronger powered than super late models, but they usually have the stock appearing body paneling, which in many cases is the Camero or Dodge Daytona. This racer could also appear as a sportsman. It's all semantics within most local associations, but generally, the sportsman class is for beginners using lighter-powered, older and generally more beaten up cars which used to be street legal. Late models (super or otherwise) are purpose-built for racing short 1/2 mile ovals of dirt or asphalt. This car was definitely purpose-built for racing.

D.11. MINI-STOCK—This is another local-type racing class. Subject to various rules at many tracks and/or organizations, these racers are not much different from SCCA's Showroom Stock 'C' roadracer. They are both domestic and foreign racecars usually modified from former street versions of: VW's old Bug and Karman Ghia, Scirrocco, Rabbit; other foreign models such as Opel GT, Mazda GLC, Toyota Corolla, Renault Alliance; domestics models such as Ford Escort and the old Pintos, Chrysler Colt and the old Chevy Chevettes.

Mini-Stocks are usually modified street-legal cars under 95 inches in wheelbase that are converted over for racing. Some are purpose-built machines. More on them later. A few safety modifications such as roll bars, fuel-cells and some suspension tightening is not only allowed, but more importantly, it's necessary. That's because the ovals they race on are very seldom longer than a (paved or dirt) quarter-mile. They're usually a tight course of about one-fifth to one-tenth mile in length. They're located in the infield portion of a half-mile track, usually incorporating part of the main tracks front straight as part of the smaller courses main straight.

Sometimes they'll use racing slicks. Some tracks don't allow them for this class. It depends on how sophisticated they are and if there is purse money involved, which generally isn't the situation. Whatever the case, these cars are an excellent support event racecar.

The Mini-Stock has been built under different names, raced under different rules, in different locations, and definitely under anonymous national exposure. That's changing pretty quick thanks to a newly created class. A purpose-built Mini-Stock is making those in the short-track racing fraternity sit up and take notice.

These new Mini-Stocks are 'spec' racers called 'LEGENDS'. Started in 1992, their series grew from 14 races in 3 states to 475 events across the US, parts of Canada and Mexico by the conclusion of the 1994 campaign. That's incredible growth.

Legend Series racers are full-body, fiberglass-fendered, 5/8-scale replicar versions of the 1937 Ford-Chevy Coupes and Flat-back Sedans. (1940 Ford Coupe also) Built by the well-known Allison Brothers Race Cars and sold thru 600 Racing, Inc, these machines are sanctioned by Spec Car. All vehicles are precisely identical in terms of design. Only the fiberglass skin is different according to the model they emulate. These models offer no aerodynamics advantage over one another. Even all component are of the same brand if manufactured outside of Allison Racing. (like Simpson restraining and safety equipment, Carrera shocks, Wagner brakes, AC Delco battery, etc)

This front-engine, rear-wheel drive racer is powered by a stock 125 hp Yamaha FJ 1200 cc motorcycle engine. The wheelbase is 73 inches with the weight limited to 1150 lbs. Their overall length, width, height is 126, 60 and 46 inches respectively. They use unshaved 13 inch diameter Goodyear radial street tires which are 7 inches wide. These tires can last an entire season.

LEGEND cars compete mostly on paved ovals of about 1/5 to 1/4 mile in length. But they are becoming so popular, because of their relatively low costs and maintenance, races are even scheduled for competition in hill climbs, drag events, ice racing, solo and roadcourse racing. Legends racecars also help support events in SCCA roadcourse racing, monster trucks and tractor pulls.

Many Legends races will take place indoors during winter months at such places as the Astrodome, RCA Dome, Silverdome, Superdome and the Georgia Dome in Atlanta.

There are four amateur divisions, competing for National/Regional/Local points, which are determined by age and experience: Pro, for experienced pros only; Semi-Pro, experienced pros who have been out of racing 8 or more years; Charger, designed for beginners; and Masters, for drivers over 40 in age.

Once again, this is 'spec' racing at its purest. Look for this classes continued growth, although it cannot possibly continue at its present rate. There are also quite a few cable TV packages in the works for this kind of racing.

D.12. FIGURE-8 CARS—Some tracks have a figure-eight shaped racecourse which the

Mini-stocks race on. That's right . . . a race-course with an intersection! Sounds crazy? It is, but it's for purely entertainment purposes and it's not as dangerous as it sounds.

Obviously, the cars that run on this kind of course are bigger than Mini-Stocks and are not sophisticated but built like tanks. It's a "thrill & spill" event that a lot of non-purest/young race fans seem to enjoy. The drivers take this very seriously though. They seem to relish a win more than they do coming out of these races in one piece. Although that's an exaggeration it's not too far from the truth. The fans seem to sense this also which adds to these racers popularity at certain local tracks.

Actually, these are called 'Figure-8 Cars'. These racecars are not the subcompact vehicles mentioned above, but rather more in the mid-size range, such as a Chevy Nova or Camero. If they were full-sized vehicles they would absorb shock better but also would be less nimble. The figure-8 course is seldom over a few hundred yards long, so they don't have a chance to built up dangerous speeds at the intersection.

For what should become relatively obvious by now is these drivers don't fool with race tires and high-technology. They just beef everything up on the chassis and especially on the roll cage. Their engines are usually in-line six configured because they're the ones least likely to be damaged from a front quarter-panel side collision. Their radiators are recessed in for collision protection and also further enhanced with heavy-duty nerf-bar styled bumpers at the front and rear. (usually none on the sides; the sides are heavily protected by roll cages)

Even though these racers are usually based locally, they have run in nationally sanctioned events for a national championship.

D.13. MODIFIED—At first glance it's hard where to categorize this kind of racecar. About all Modifieds look like a narrowed-body stockcar minus the wheel fenders with chopped down roofs simular to some Drag racecars. Most Modifieds to not install any kind of glass. Some people think these look more like an oversized, lower slung and

wider version of a Sprint racer. They do act like them because they have powerful low rpm engine torque. (good acceleration)

These are classified as StockCars. (another misnomer) This is because of the kind of tracks they run on. They run on both dirt and paved ovals of 1/2 to 5/8 mile and sometimes on 1/5 and 1 mile tracks. Most Modified events are not long in duration. They're considered a hard dash or sprint styled racer. The races may be 20 to 35 laps. On the other hand they have been known to run a more enduranced-styled race of 50 to 100 laps or more. It all depends on who sanctions these racers and what general region of the US they're in.

These racers are most popular in the midwest and northeast US, but occasionally can be seen in Florida during SpeedWeeks prior to the Daytona 500, in the Raleigh-Durham, NC area and on the west coast. Such organizations as the International Motor Contest Association (IMCA), Yankee, SK Modifieds, Modified Racing Association, Southern NY Racing Association (SNYRA), Northeast Auto Racing Association, DIRT, NASCAR and USAC have sanctioned these.

A typical Modified weighs about 2500 lbs, is wheelbased between 100–110 inches with a V-8, 350-400 ci, normally-aspirated engine of 500 horsepower. That means with that kind of power the engine is fairly well modified also. Some of the few large organizers like NASCAR for example (which sanctions their 'Featherlite Tour Series') require 6.8 lbs of chassis weight for each cubic inch of engine displacement. That chassis has to weigh at least 2438 lbs. So like Sprint Cars these vehicles have high power-to-weight ratios even though they're heavier than them.

Like the Late Model and Sportsman stockcars, these racecars may vary both in small and large ways. But one thing all Modifieds have in common is that their sanctioning bodies require the engines be located in front of the driver. That power has to be transmitted to the rear wheels. (no front-wheel drives)

Other than the major requirements just mentioned, there are as numerous things done to these racers as there are ideas conjured for racing in general. Some Modifieds have a formula racecar style of rear wing and some use the kind of large wing seen on the 'World Of Outlaw' sanctioned Sprint cars. That is, they put them right on the roof.

The Modified racecars center of gravity is relatively low like a Formula machine, yet between the wheels, the drivers area and body, which incorporates a roll cage, is a sort-of quasi-stockcar with side-mounted nerf bars. Sometimes this stockcar body which is barely off the ground in the first place, has its roof lowered below its normal position for better aerodynamics and a lower center of gravity. Like some of the Late Models these cars are sometimes allowed to off-set their engines and drivetrain towards the inside of the track. This is the cars driver-side, since they race in the counter-clock-wise direction. Some also set the engine back close to the driver to achieve better vehicle fore and aft balance. Sometimes the drivers themselves are located further back to facilitate this.

Because Modifieds may be offset both laterally and linearly, they can take advantage of that with as wide racing slicks in front as well as on back. Most of these racers are limited to 13 inch wide slicks. (if they're not on dirt, which they usually are not) On most front-powered racing vehicles, using too large of a racing slick on the front would give it too much grip. This would cause the lighter rear end to become unstable or loose in high-speed turns. (this is not a problem with rear engine vehicles such as formula racers) But these highly modified vehicles try to achieve that perfect front-rear balance to increase their traction, therefore speed, in the turns.

Some Late Model Stockcar sanctioning bodies at the local level also allow the engine to be set back like these Modifieds.

Maybe you understand now why these vehicles are called what they are. Not only are some of the modifications obvious to the average race fan after a close inspection, but they're also obvious to the fans from a distance. These are Modified because unlike StockCars and silhouette-styled stockcars, these vehicles definitely *look* much more modified. These are a different kind of race

vehicle that not very many people have seen raced.

These may be mostly StockCars in style and name, but remember, with all their power and speed they can't be bumping and grinding around out there on the track. That's because these are powerful open-wheeled vehicles racing on a congested track. Therefore, this is a bit more of a dangerous form of competition. That changes a drivers strategy.

Top-end speeds are diversified because of the various kinds of tracks they run on. Under ideal conditions on a 5/8 mile paved oval they can reach about 133–138 mph. But more importantly they can reach that very quickly because of their low-end engine torque coming out of a turn. (high hp output while at low rpm's, much like a Sprint Car)

D.14. MINI-MODIFIED—There are also Mini-Modifieds. They're basically the same concept, but a smaller wheelbased racer with a complicated power-to-weight ratio of one lb of chassis weight per cubic centimeter engine size. Some of these racecars have the larger air-cooled VW Bug engine. Others are using 4 and 6-cylinder watercooled types.

These are nothing more than a less powerful version of the regular Modified. Depending on where they're racing and with what sanctioning body, they may either compete as a race within a race with the Modifieds or as a stand-alone racer prior to the running of the Modifieds. Therefore like most lower powered racecars these are support machines.

Under ideal track conditions they can top out at around 102 mph.

D.15. SUPERMODIFIED (MINI-SUPER-MODIFIED)—Simply put, a more powerful and slightly different designed version of a regular Modified. Sometimes one organizations Modified and anothers SuperModified are for all intents and purposes the same car. It's only a matter of semantics.

Most other times the SuperModifieds are the machines with the big wide wings located in the back and up higher than their SprintCar-styled roll cage. They use about 3 inch wider racing slicks than the Modifieds

(16" max) and generate almost 350 more horsepower. (850 hp) The typical V-8 engine displacement is 425 to 470 cubic inches. The Mini-SuperModified isn't much different than the SuperModified. It just uses the V-6 engine. Both may be fuel-injected and sometimes they are supercharged. Like most powerful short track racecars, these are not turbocharged though. (that's because a turbo works much more practically with long-sustained, high-rpm engine output; superchargers deliver their power more quickly and at lower rpm's) Some organizations may allow SuperModifieds to burn higher rated fuel like alcohol.

Some SuperModifieds are so radical, their engine is offset directly to the drivers left and between the two driver-side wheels outside of the chassis. This really makes the racer inside-heavy for those super fast left turns. The tracks these race on are usually a little longer than a half-mile. They're closer to 5/8 mile, although they occasionally run the mile at Phoenix International in Arizona.

These frightfully powerful machines are not heavier than Modifieds, but rather 700 lbs lighter at 1800 lbs. Like the SprintCar, Modifieds and SuperModifieds have to be push-started. This saves the weight of starters, batteries, magnetoes, transmissions, etc. You'll learn more in the upcoming SprintCar category why this is necessary. You'll also understand better after reading about SprintCars why Modifieds are simular to SprintCars, even though they look somewhat like StockCars.

SuperModifieds are considered by many in the racing fraternity as the most quickest accelerating closed-course (circle-track) racecar in the world. These race only on paved courses.

SuperModifieds can reach almost 170 on the Phoenix 1-mile and 145–155 mph on the short-course straights. That's cookin'! They reach that top-end in cat-like, DragCar-style fashion.

Modified and SuperModified classes seem to be hanging on. These cars never were as popular throughout the US as other forms of racing. But they are surviving well in the northeast and New England states. I don't think their intent was ever to become a large

class af racing because of the wide array of rules and regulations at each particular track and/or region. When they do put on a show, it's something different to watch.

The US Auto Club usually puts on only one race a year in one of these classes, and they're one of the larger sanctioning bodies in the US. Of course they only put on one Indy Car event per year also. (but as you read earlier that's about to change in 1996) It just so happens that one race is the largest one day sporting event in the world, the Indy 500.

Besides USAC's lone event at Phoenix, other sanctioning bodies are the 'International SuperModified Association' (ISMA), Western SuperModified Racing Association (WSMRA-which now sanctions the Phoenix event) and the 'New England SuperModified Racing Association'. (NESMRA) These can also be seen sometimes during SpeedWeeks prior to NASCAR's opening race, the Daytona 500.

Modifieds and SuperModifieds should continue as the relatively stable class they've been through the years. They've hung on this long, there's no reason to believe they can't continue. This class doesn't seem so burdened with politics and major rule changes that other classes experience.

This concludes category D. You have completed 7 of the 15 categories as listed on page 20 in this chapter. Next is category E, the Sprint Roadsters.

E. SPRINT ROADSTERS (6 CLASSES)

E. Sprint Roadster 1. Super SprintCar
E. Sprint Roadster 2. SprintCar
E. Sprint Roadster 3. Mini/Micro SprintCar
E. Sprint Roadster 4. Midgets (Modified, Half and Micro-Midgets)
E. Sprint Roadster 5. Three-Quarter Midget
E. Sprint Roadster 6. Quarter Midget

SprintCar racing started, or maybe more appropriately evolved, in the 30's. It depends on who one listens to. More on that later. For now don't let the word roadster used in the category title throw you. Most fans don't consider these machines that. They believe real roadsters are the old ragtop two-seaters in the early days of the automobile. They think of the early Indy racecars before the rear engine machines came into being as roadsters also. Again, it's just semantics for now. But back in the 30's, there just wasn't all that much difference between an Indy Car or Roadster and a Sprint racer, at least in looks.

I call them a form of roadster because they're open cockpit, open-wheel and mainly because their power comes from in front of the driver. That used to be the case with the older Indy racers up until around the early and mid 60's. All the racecars in this category except the Quarter-Midgets have their engines in front of the drivers with a bit higher than normal chassis to ground clearance. Most of the racecars here are purpose-built with high power-to-weight ratios that compete on dirt, clay or asphalt ovals of usually 1/20 to about a mile in length. This category has a very stable set of rules. (Seldom any major changes) One of the major changes made years ago was the installation of a roll cage. (I think it was mandatory in 1971) There were too many deaths taking place. That had to stop immediately.

E.1. SUPER SPRINTCAR—These are not necessarily a more powerful version of the SprintCar but they are a slightly larger version. USAC used to run a series with these racecars when they were called DIRT CHAMPIONSHIP cars. They still run this series under a different banner called the Silver Crown series. They race only about 9 to 10 times per year on tracks of one mile or so on dirt. They used to run occasionally on paved tracks but not anymore. They can reach speeds of around 140–50 mph. It depends on the track. Their races are usually longer in duration compared to regular SprintCars, about 100 miles. Since they compete on longer tracks they do reach higher speeds than the SprintCars simply because they have more room to accelerate.

As race cars go, there isn't a whole lot of restriction on engines. Their limit is set at 355 cubic inches with no turbocharging.

Wheelbase maximum is 96 inches with total coachwork not to exceed 15 ft. Minimum dry weight (excluding all the fluids and driver) must be at least 1428 lbs. Some drivers use a 316 ci engine of V-6 configuration. The minimum weight for the car using that engine is set at 1350 pounds. So therefore, USAC does use a sliding scale type of formula for determining power-to-weight ratios for these machines. I believe USAC is the only sanctioning body for these machines. There are not very many events held for these cars but they do seem to have a following good enough to maintain their existence.

For those of you not familiar with what a SprintCar is, (or in this case, a SuperSprint, which is only an enlarged version of a Sprint car) they are single-seat, front-powered vehicles with a higher than usual ground clearance. A steel tubular roll cage surrounds the driver in an exaggerated and extended fashion above the coachwork. This is necessary because the drivers themselves have their head and shoulders located above the line of the coachwork. You'll understand the reasons why the drivers have to sit up higher as you read on.

The coachwork hugs in on the driver, engine compartment and drive train much in the way as some formula cars. In other words, the suspension is extended out or exposed. These use wide racing slicks on paved roads, when they do occasionally run on them and treaded racetires on unpaved tracks. These tires are almost, if not, the same width the Indy racecars use.

Speaking of Indy cars, some of the engines used in the SprintCars are strong enough to power an Indy Car to over 200 mph. It has been tried by some of the poorer Indy teams in the past. While they can get the Indy Champ car shooting along at fairly high speeds, they will not win the pole position because their power range doesn't reach high enough rpms. You may ask "why not use a higher geared transmission to compensate for the lower rpm's?" There isn't a trans strong enough to handle those kinds of torque loads. A higher geared trans is a weaker trans. Lord knows the strong ones used nowadays occasionally break. Also, those teams using SprintCar engines in an IndyCar discovered those engines aren't reliable enough for long distance events anyway. But the engine did get them in the show, so-to-speak.

Anyway, these Sprint engines can put out as much as 700 hp. But they are built more for low-end torque than high-rpm horsepower. The reason is because the tracks Sprints races are conducted on are most of the time short. The straights are even shorter. SprintCars need to accelerate very quickly. That and the races themselves are not long. That's why these are called "Sprint" races. They are short and fast races of usually 30 to 50 laps on a 1/2 mile oval. So top-end horsepower on a short track can't be achieved nor is it necessary. Picking up those low-end rpm's out of a turn quickly to higher rpm's on the short straights is what matters in this kind of racing.

This low-end, high torque output coupled with a blocked radiator from dirt track debris sometimes creates engine overheating problems. Also, since these racecars are traveling sideways (slingshotting) in the turns on the dirt tracks they do not receive a clean or direct flow of air through the radiator. An alcohol-based fuel helps alleviate this problem because it burns cooler. This is also a safer fuel because it has a lower flash point and is less likely to ignite outside of the fuel tanks in the case of a nasty accident, which these racers are known to get into.

Quick tight racing with those big exposed racing treads or slicks and that sort-of funny L-shaped configuration can create spectacular accidents that keep only those with the most courage racing these vehicles.

E.2. SPRINTCARS—Again, these are smaller than the SuperSprints by about a foot in overall length. The big difference between these and the SuperSprints is the shorter length of the track they run on. SprintCars run on both paved and dirt tracks of usually no longer than 5/8 of a mile. The tracks may be banked or flat. Their chassis minimum weight is lighter and engine size is larger, even though their class name doesn't imply that. Some sanctioning

bodies used the word SuperSprint as a more commercially oriented name. Their Super-Sprint is nothing more than a Sprint racer with a different title.

Whatever the case, Sprint racing is very popular, especially in the mid-west and parts of California. One reason is because it hasn't changed much throughout the years. It's truly one of the forms of high-powered racing still left to driver ability. It's not unindated by costly technology which usually leads to who can outspend the other. Former Formula One great Jackie Stewart called SprintCar racing one of the last great spectacles in motorsports.

These guys are known to run a very heavy schedule. I'm not talking about one particular sanctioning body but rather the race drivers themselves. Since their travel is not too long, (confined mostly to the mid-west) they may race as many as 3 to 5 separate events per week. It depends on logistics and scheduling. Yes, even an occasional race is held on a weeknight. (like Thursdaynight Thunder on ESPN during the summer)

This isn't amateur racing by a long shot. These guys have a little harder time getting good sponsorship because of their inherently smaller coachwork and limited geographical diversity. This makes it harder to display a sponsors name. Besides, these racers get their coachwork pretty muddy which made it hard to display those names and insignias if they're racing on dirt. There may be clear and dry weather conditions, but sometimes the tracks are watered-down to keep the dust in check. Any dust hampering a drivers vision is something a racer doesn't need. Anyway, many of these guys will run as heavy of a schedule as possible. They like it . . . they're not laughing all the way to the bank, but it's a (part-time) living.

Yes, these Sprint racers are smaller than the SuperSprints, but that wasn't my main point when I was comparing the two. I was talking about their power-band or similar power-to-weight ratios. SprintCars are more powerful than SuperSprints but not as top-end fast because they race shorter courses. Anyway, the SprintCars minimum weight is generally 425 lbs lighter than the Super-Sprint. (at 1000 lbs, dry, minus driver) But

This is a sprint car with the large 'world of outlaws' style wing on it's roll cage. It looks like this has been doing it on dirt, judging by the kind of tires. Some sanctioning bodies don't allow wings, especially on asphalt tracks. These are very powerful, purpose-built machines designed for small, tight ovals.

USAC's Sprint cars are minimally allowed around 1225 lbs and their engines are more powerful. They're limited to 410 ci's. Most SprintCar engines in other organizations, such as SCRA (Southern California Racing Asso), Northern Auto Racing Club (NARC) and the United Racing Club (URC) may be limited to a stock SOHC (Single OverHead Cam) 355 ci engine.

Some sanctioning bodies don't even have restrictions on engine size and chassis weights. That's because in SprintCar racing the laws of physics do a better job of controlling this form of speed than the man-made ones. This is especially so in the case of SprintCar racing on dirt tracks. The man-made restrictions come more into play on the paved surfaces. On dirt, traction isn't as prevalent. An underweight SprintCar would be too unstable and fidgety, therefore slow, no matter how much power it has. The tires would slip and slid way too much. The power is not transferred properly to the ground.

On the other side of the coin, an over-weight chassis would be simply out of the question, like in any form of racing. Actually, depending on how well the engine puts power down to the ground, the ideal weight for these machines is around 15–1600 lbs. So many organizations let the driver determine their own restrictions on dirt tracks. Not so on paved surfaces!

Most of these racecars use a Chevy V-8, but others are used including a V-6 by Buick. The wheelbase is also shorter at 84 to 90 inches compared to the SS's 96 inch maximum. Their maximum coachwork length is a foot shorter at 14 foot. Maximum overall width which includes the tires is 78″.

Most wheel rim diameters are set at 15 inches with a maximum width of 10 and 14 or 15 inches on the front and back respectively. USAC allows a larger 17 inch rear tire width. Many times, the rear tires are offset to facilitate high acceleration in the turns. This is done by using a larger (in circumference, not width) race tire on the outside of the rear axle coupled with a smaller one in width and/or circumference on the inside of that same rear axle. (inside as relative to a vehicle during a turn, in this case a left one)

Some SprintCar suspensions are also off-set to the left. (since they race counter-clockwise) In other words, their left side sus-pensions doesn't protrude out as much as the right sides do. This keeps the racecar heavier on its inside (tires) in those high-speed left turns. This prevents those tires and the chassis they're attached to from lift-ing up and rolling over. Another way of de-scribing this is to say the longer right side suspensions acts as a stronger lever com-pared to the opposite side to keep that left or driver side rubber down on the ground. Some organizations allow this offsetting of tires and suspensions, some don't.

USAC, WoO (World of Outlaws) and the CRA (California Racing Association) are three of the bigger sanctioning bodies for this kind of racing, although there are oth-ers as mentioned just a few sentences back. By the way, WoO allows the use of those big wings on top of the cage. Sometimes these are called Super SprintCars. USAC allows those big wings on special occasions.

Another characteristic about these cars is that in most cases you can see the drivers whole upper body, but you can't see where he does his gear shifting at. These racecars don't have gears to shift! Before a race, a gear is matched to the track and its condi-tion and then is installed. That's usually done in the rear axle housing. Experience and some expertise is required on how to properly accomplish that. This means the SprintCar engine must pull the race vehicle through various speeds during a race with no gear changing. That means adequate power must be available through low and high ranges of rpm's. Those rpm's may range from 3000 to 7500 on the SprintCar engine.

These low-end, high-torque engines can get the low rpm's up quickly coming out of those turns. Matter of fact, it does this so well that many drivers would find it almost impossible to take their hands off the steer-ing wheel to shift gears. These racecars are a "handful" indeed and requires extraordinary

concentration to keep them going where you want them to. There is no time or chance to shift gears even if that option existed. If shifting was possible, I doubt if there would be a transmission, clutch or pressure plate which could handle the workload anyway. It would eventually begin to slip and burn up. This is a common problem for high power-to-weight racecars like F1 and Indy Cars. Because SprintCars (along with the Modi-fieds) are amongst the strongest power-to-weight circle track racers in the world, they would have this clutch-burning or slipping problem all the time. Because of this they eliminated the transmission, clutch and other accessories. (along with the weight)

SuperSprints usually do have a clutch and a on-board starter. But then they race one mile courses under less hectic condi-tions. Longer straights means faster top-end speeds so they must change gears to prevent overrevving the engine. But on SprintCars the driveshaft connects the rear axle directly to the engine. There is no transmission and clutch. This is also why these machines have to be push-started. Once the engine is turn-ing over so are the wheels. This also elimi-nates the need for a starter, battery and other accessories. This lightens the racecar and therefore makes it quicker. It also make them more fidgety and harder to control even if they didn't have all that power. But that's what makes a SprintCar what it is.

The reason why these machines can't seat the driver down to the ground closer, and therefore lower the cars center of gravity, is because of where the driveshaft has to be lo-cated. This shaft has to transmit tremen-dous loads of power, even more than the Su-perSprint. It has to be straight, extremely solid to be super-strong and it has to be con-tained for the safety of the driver. No con-stant-velocity joints here, they wouldn't last. The driver sits right over this driveshaft. If it lets go it could literally tear him up. (a hous-ing unit under the drivers seat or around the driveshaft prevents this possibility) This is a situation that could not only endanger dri-vers but also those around them. So these drivelines must be true-straight and strong. They have to run through an area that aligns with the ring-pinion gear in the rear axle housing and the engine.

The rear axle housing that helps to support the rear tires has to be straight and strong too. No independent suspension on these machines. That requires CV joints, . . . again, . . . they wouldn't hold up under constant SprintCar acceleration either. With those large 15 inch diameter tire rims, the axle housing is lifted off the ground more than most 'exposed-suspension' racecars. With it, everything else including the driveshaft has to rise to stay properly aligned to handle those tremendous torque-loads. This includes the driver. In other words, he has to get over, higher and out of the way of that driveshaft which he's literally straddling above. (unless he wants to get his keester, not to mention some other REALLY important body parts "buffed, polished and sanded" extremely well)

When the old Indy car drivers wanted to alleviate this problem in the earlier days of racing, when they looked like cageless SprintCars, the only way to do it was to put the engine in back of the driver. That opened a whole new plethora of ideas not necessary to explain here now.

But what if an engine was put in back on a Sprint racer? Number 1, a ton of new problems and engineering dynamics would present themselves that's not conducive to SprintCar racing. (but it is to Formula Car racing) Number 2, it would no longer be a SprintCar anyway.

Now, you may be thinking, why not shorten the wheel rim diameter to lower the SprintCar closer to the ground? Well, that is essentially what some people do. But that creates a ton of other problems too. They can be solved thought. But then you end up with a vehicle that's not a Sprint racer but rather something less than a Sprint racer. They end up with a race vehicle called a Midget. That's what I will be covering soon. Now, maybe you understand why SprintCars are Sprint-Cars and why their drivers have to sit high off the ground.

A SprintCar race is also conducted in a different way compared to most racing events. Before the main feature of a Sprint race is underway, several heat races, semi-features and consolation races are conducted to determine the final starting positions. How this is conducted depends on the number of entrants at that event. Most sanctioning bodies use the the same formula to determine how those heats, semis and consolation races are conducted. This not only makes for accurate qualifying for the drivers, but also gives those experiencing temporary mechanical problems a chance to recover from them. This also makes for better competition and more of it for the drivers. It's more action for the fans to view.

Speaking of views, here's a little racing tidbit about SprintCars. Most Sprint sanctioning bodies do not allow the use of rear view mirrors. Why? Mostly for two reasons. Number one, the organizations to not want their drivers to know what's behind them for fear of purposely creating blocking situations. This is extremely unsafe with these relatively unstable and powerful open-wheeled machines. This lets the driver concentrate on his own task and not worry about who is behind him. Instead they'll worry about who is ahead of their race machine and therefore aggressively work to reach them. In other words, this encourages offensive driving instead of the defensive type. The former kind of driving is safer and more pleasurable for the driver.

The second reason is because usually the drivers don't have time to stare into them anyway. They're too busy with controlling their own vehicle. Like I stated earlier, these are a handful to control. Concentration is a must, especially for the less experienced. So mirrors can only create a form of racing paranoia and/or a break in driver concentration.

A night of SprintCar racing pretty much fills up most of the evening activities. Because of that, this form of racing doesn't always require support races from other forms of motorsports. When other races are on the evenings ticket, they're usually Midget, Three-Quarter Midget and even sometimes Late Model Stockcars.

Under ideal conditions on a 5/8 mile paved oval a SprintCar can top out at around 130 mph. On dirt, they're about 10 to 15 mph slower. But take into consideration this is a more dangerous form of speed than say a Late Model doing the same speed on the same track.

E.3. MINI/MICRO SPRINT—This is a relatively new phenomenon in SprintCar racing that not many fans are familiar with. The reason why is because they really are familiar with this class of SprintCars, they just don't know it.

There really isn't much to cover here because this class or classes is nothing more than a different name put on SprintCars or Midgets by different sanctioning bodies. That's okay though! These racers will have different rules compared to the vast majority of Sprint machines in this category. But basically, as far as their chassis, engine and overall designs are concern, they are bonafide Sprint and/or Midget race cars. I don't believe anyone ever questioned that, they just haven't been too familiar with it.

Their minimum weights, overall length and engine sizes vary amongst some larger or more regionally-based organizations, but not by much. That's because SprintCars and Midget racing regulations are pretty stable, as I mentioned earlier. But again, the almighty 'dollar', and how to save more of them is at the heart of why even stable classes of racing must make adjustments and/or changes to better reflect todays financial situation. (the more things change, the more they stay the same)

On one hand, one organizations Mini-Sprint is nothing more or less that anothers version of a Midget. On the other hand, two different class titles from two organizations may exist for virtually the same vehicle. The Micro Sprint and Quarter-Midget Cars may be identical right down to the last bolt, but just named differently by two or more organizations. Still a Micro-SprintCar's name implies something smaller than an ordinary Sprint or Midget racer. To some organizations that could be simular to a sophisticated Go-Kart, or the Micro could be something between a Go-Kart or Midget or Three-Quarter Midget. It all boils down to semantics and minor differences between the racecars.

This same situation continues with the Midgets coming up next. There are Modified Midgets, Half-Midgets and Micro-Midgets. They are all basically descendants of the Midget. A rule change here . . . a tolerance there . . . as stated several times before, it's just mostly semantics.

E.4. MIDGETS—These are purpose-built racers that are pretty much a scaled-down SprintCar. Their construction is patterned after Sprints, but the courses they compete on are shorter, less banked ovals of usually a tenth to 1/2 mile. These courses have been setup in such indoor facilities as the Pontiac Silverdome, north of Detroit, Michigan and the Convention Center in Ft. Wayne, Indiana during the winter months.

USAC is still one of the major sanctioning bodies for these cars and is doing a pretty good job of handling them judging by their increased popularity. They do most of their racing on dirt tracks, and have even occasionally competed on tracks as long as a mile. But that's seldom and obviously not indoors. Speaking of indoors, more arena's they've raced in are the Rosemont Horizon NW of Chicago, Illinois, and the RCA dome in Indianapolis, Indiana. You can bet they'll eventually race in most of the domes.

USAC offers two series of (30-45 event) race schedules called the (Jolly Rancher) Western States series and (Jolly Rancher) National Midget series. The races vary in length, depending on the size of the track. If they are running indoors (which is roughly 5 times per year) they're on a 1/10 to 1/5th mile track. They run about 100 laps, otherwise on the longer 1/4-1/2 (and sometimes longer) tracks, they lap it 30-40 times. Some Midget races which are special events can go as long as 100 laps on a 1/2 mile course.

Other sanctioning bodies in Midget racing is the United Auto Racing Association (UARA), the CRA which also sanctions the SprintCars, the American Racing Drivers Club (ARDC), the United Racing Club (URC) and the American Midget Racing Association. (AMRA)

Sometimes the race field (number of participates) can get very bunched up. 25 racers on a track as short as 1/6 mile have been known to occur. This same race can go 100

This is a smaller version of a sprint car called a midget. It's an older model but that doesn't affect its competitive edge. The only thing they need is a good driver and a quick engine. That looks like a VW Flat-4, horizontally oppose 'bug' engine. This one races on a hard surface, since it has slicks installed.

laps. I pity the poor people who have to keep track of them while they're racing! I suppose they have computers to help in that chore.

Like the SprintCar, this is a strong racer which can literally twist their left-front racing slick or tire right off the surface while accelerating out of a (left) turn. Also like the SprintCar, these are the same vehicles you see going through a dirt track turn almost completely sideways. That isn't showing off at all. It's necessary to keep the speeds up. If you want to win, you have to master it. It isn't all that hard once you learn it. Like anything else you do long enough, you get used to it and good at it.

These race cars do not generally offset their chassis and tires. Their minimum weight and wheelbase length is right around 1000 lbs without the driver and 66–76 inches. In some cases, that is the same minimum weight as the Sprint racer when compared to various organizations. Wheel rim width can't be more than 8 inches at all corners and 13 inches in diameter.

Engines, of aluminum or iron construction, do vary widely between 5 basic types:

1. 4-cycle, Duel OverHead Cam (DOHC) with water-cooled, four cylinder (in-line) engine which is limited to 127 cubic inches.
2. Modified stock, push rod, V-4 or in-line-4, 2 valves/cylinder and limited to 157 cubic inches.
3. Modified stock, push rod, 4-in-line with a limit of four valves per cylinder. They can't go over 148 cubic inches.
4. Stock production Single OverHead Cam, (SOHC) water-cooled 6-cylinder with 4 valves per cylinder and limited to 143 cu. inches.
5. Stock production, air-cooled, push rod with 2 valves per cylinder are limited to 140 ci. (Mostly, these are the VW air-cooled "Bug" engines; these seem to be the most popular with Midget drivers)

These powerful little race machines also need push starting because they lack onboard starters simular to SprintCars. As previously mentioned, they are really nothing more than scaled-down SprintCars with smaller wheel diameters, a shorter chassis and smaller engine. Putting a full size SprintCar engine in one of these would serve no

purpose because that extra power couldn't be put efficiently down to the ground on the shorter tracks they compete on. The heavier block would also make these machines bog down or handle poorly in the corners, not to mention put an undue strain on the suspension, making them more dangerous than necessary. The laws of physics would work against these racecars in such a scenario as that.

In ideal conditions on a 1/2 mile dirt oval, they can reach a top end of about 90 mph. But understand, top-end speed isn't necessarily what this kind of racing is about. It's more about driving ability in cramped, crowded and low-traction conditions. (then vehicle handling and speed) This is true of Sprints and SuperSprints also.

E.5. THREE-QUARTER MIDGET—This racecar's sophistication can vary widely depending on who the sanctioning body controlling them is. The US Auto Club's and the American Three-Quarter Midget Racing Association (ATQMRA) versions are serious ones indeed amongst others. Although nowhere near as old as their Midget series (got started in late 40's) these run 30–35 races per year on mostly dirt tracks of a quarter mile or less. Like the Midgets, they also have been known to race indoors during the winter.

They're configured like a Midget, but obviously smaller and lighter. These small race machines are purpose-built with a relatively sophisticated suspension system. Their wheel rim is about the same as a Midgets but the wheelbase measures around 6 inches shorter than the Midget. They're mostly powered by in-line-4 motorcycle engines, which like the Sprint and Midgets, can not be turbocharged. Their minimum weight is limited to 750 lbs minus the driver. Like all USAC sanctioned racing, these also race for cash purses.

Other locally-based organizations run 3/4 Midget races also. But when the race machines of those and nationally-based types are compared to each other, it's pretty obvious the other organizations racer is closer to being a Quarter-Midget. So it's probably a matter of definition. (semantics)

The sophisticated version of this racer has the drivers almost sitting on a line above the engine; not on top of it, but just above and close behind, because of its smaller wheelbase or size.

For those of you curious about the speeds of these vehicles, it really doesn't matter. They constantly accelerate and decelerate for a position. They hardly ever 'redline' themselves. (reach maximum or dangerous rpm's for their particular engine) But if you want to know anyway, it's almost 70 mph under ideal conditions.

E.6. QUARTER-MIDGET—This is an even smaller and much less sophisticated version of a Three-Quarter Midget. Matter-of-fact, what they could be considered is a complex form of a Go-Kart. Some of these are confused as Go-Karts because almost all of them are rear-engine powered. That power may be a modified lawnmower engine.

The difference between these and the Karts is their engine power, suspension, bodywork and driver-protection capacities. The Quarter-Midget is a purpose-built racer that is set up to turn left on short 1/20 to 1/4 mile paved or dirt tracks. They can get to about 40 mph. Their suspension is a form of coil-over and torsion arm type. It isn't too complex because it isn't necessary as much at 40 mph. None the less, it's much better than a Go-Karts, which is for all theoretical purposes . . . nonexistent.

They do need the coachwork to protect the racer from flying debris, dirt, etc. The coachwork resembles the larger Sprint and Midget racers. Some high speed Karts have coachwork to help streamline the vehicle, but coachwork on a Quarter-Midget is not necessary, aerodynamically speaking.

The Quarter-Midget is not configured much in the way a Midget is underneath the bodywork. It's more like a Go-Kart. Their coachwork is much physically higher constructed than a Go-Kart along with the driver protection area, which is a roll cage very much like the Sprint and Midget machines.

The weight of the entire racer without the driver and fluids is around 160 lbs. Wheelbase: 36–40 inches. The engines are not as sophisticated and powerful as the Go-Kart.

They use 7 to 8 cubic inches of engine displacement which puts out about anywhere from 3 to 4 horses in the slower classes to 15 hp in the fastest classes.

There are 10 levels which compete regionally and nationally for championships. There are 2 each of the following classes: Novice; Stock; Stock Modified; B Modified; and AA. The first three use a single-barrel carburetor with 3 to 4 hp capacities. The last two have more power, around 15 horses. Like the Go-Karts there racers are chain driven. They do use a racing slick of 6 inches in width that must fit on an 8 inch diameter wheel rim when they race on paved surfaces.

These little racecars, sanctioned by QMA, (Quarter-Midgets of America) have sported a perfect record when it comes to safety. There has never been a fatality in this form of racing, or even a life threatening injury. Accidents . . . yes, but nothing that a good bone surgeon couldn't correct. That's pretty darn excellent when you consider this form of racing has its roots dated back to almost a half century.

This is a quarter midget. Not a very complex machine, but then it's not necessary for the speeds they attain. They're practically a sprint go-kart, but race mostly on 1/10 mile paved ovals using less powerful motors. Their engines are located in back. Obviously, these are built for children.

These racecars are usually driven by pre-teen youngsters at least 5 years of age. Once they turn 16 that's it as far as their careers in Quarter-Midgets go. (that is if they can still fit in them as a 15 year old) They also compete at locally sanctioned tracks. Some of these racecars (and Go-Karts) is where many of todays racers got their start, including the big name competitors.

This concludes Category E. (Sprint Roadsters) Remember categories A thru L in this chapter, describing all the different kinds of racing vehicles, does not mean these racecars are categorized out in the real world as such.

For instance, in Category E that I just completed on Sprint Roadsters, . . . SprintCars are NOT a category E racer or styled racer. There is no such thing as a Category E racecar in name. Category A thru L is used strictly for organizational purposes in this publication. Don't go out and say . . . "man, I'm going to go Category A racing!" (or whatever letter you used) No one including veteran race drivers will know what on earth you're talking about! What you mean to say is . . . "man, I'm going Formula Car racing!" Matter-a-fact, just say you're going racing! What kind it is doesn't matter to your mother, wife or girlfriend. They'll already be blowing a fuse about it as soon as you mention those three little words. They are: a. I'm; b. going; (and) c. racing. And for god sakes DON'T smile when you say that! Otherwise they'll think you're joking!

F. DRAG RACING CARS

F. Drag Racing Cars	Et.	Elapsed Time Handicap Drag Racing (Brackets)

(IHRA Professional classes)

F. Drag Racing Cars	1.	Top Fuel Dragster - TF (or AA Fuel, Rail Dragster)
F. Drag Racing Cars	2.	Nitro Funny Car - NFC or AA/FC (AA Funny Car) *
F. Drag Racing Cars	3.	Pro Stock - Pro
F. Drag Racing Cars	4.	Alcohol Funny Car - AFC or BB/FC
F. Drag Racing Cars	5.	Pro Modified -P/M

(IHRA Amateur classes)

F. Drag Racing Cars	6.	Top Sportsman -T/S
F. Drag Racing Cars	7.	Factory Modified-F/M*
F. Drag Racing Cars	8.	Modified Eliminator
F. Drag Racing Cars	8A.	Dragsters -/D
F. Drag Racing Cars	8B.	Econo Altered Funny Car -/EA
F. Drag Racing Cars	8C.	Econorail Dragster -/ED
F. Drag Racing Cars	8D.	Altereds & Roadsters -/A and /SR
F. Drag Racing Cars	8E.	Modified Compacts -/C
F. Drag Racing Cars	8F.	Modified -/M
F. Drag Racing Cars	8G.	Econo Modified -/EM
F. Drag Racing Cars	9.	Quick Rod - (8.90 Bracket Racer)
F. Drag Racing Cars	10.	Super Rod - (9.90 Bracket Racer)
F. Drag Racing Cars	11.	Hot Rod - (10.90 Bracket Racer)
F. Drag Racing Cars	12.	Super Stock (A thru E)
F. Drag Racing Cars	12A.	SuperStock/Production -SS/P
F. Drag Racing Cars	12B.	Super Stock -SS/
F. Drag Racing Cars	12C.	MX -/X
F. Drag Racing Cars	12D.	Modified Stock -/MS
F. Drag Racing Cars	12E.	SuperStock/GT - SS/GT
F. Drag Racing Cars	13A.	Stock -/S
F. Drag Racing Cars	13B.	Pure Stock -/PS

This kind of racing deals in straight-line, quarter-mile quickness. It's over with in seconds. Sometimes the distance is only 1/8th mile.

Drag racing started in Southern California around the late 30's on an informal basis. In the early 50's associations began to form. (NHRA, IHRA, etc)

Momentum built in the mid-50's to the point where drag racing is today. Now, there are several different types and classes of drag vehicles in those organizations, NHRA alone has around 220 classes . . . so many as to completely confuse the average non-racing layman. Hopefully, some of this confusion will be laid to rest in this chapter. Meanwhile, I'd like to explain the format or procedures used to score drag racing.

First of all, for those not familiar with this

---

*Classes that have been eliminated.

sport, drag racing starts with two vehicles racing each other from a standing start. The racers are lined up side to side with each other and then signaled when to start by a series of lights called a Christmas Tree. The racecars may be signaled to start simultaneously or in time-staggered intervals called handicapping. The Christmas Tree is a system of 3 (or sometimes 5) amber lights and one green one for each of the (2) lanes. These lights display themselves as a visual countdown for each driver. They illuminate downward in 4/10ths or 1/2 of a second intervals, depending on the class of racecars competing, until the green light at the bottom is indicated.

In the Pro Start system of starting a race, 3 amber lights illuminate simultaneously, 4/10ths of a second later the green light comes on. The vehicles are lined up side by side or what's called in drag racing vernacular, a heads-up start. In a Pro start, there is no handicapping at the starting line.

Ideally, competitors required to use the nonpro-type of start try to time themselves somewhere between the last amber and the green light, depending on how far away they are from the starting line. How far they are from that starting line is called 'Staging.' In some classes of drag racing the staging (how a vehicle is positioned) near the starting line is controlled by regulations. Therefore 'Deep-Staging' is the practice of rolling a vehicle as far into the starting line, or more appropriately the light beam on the Christmas tree, as possible without fouling or going over that line. If they foul, a red light positioned below the green will illuminate. Whatever the case, techniques used in staging is a practiced skill that's a big factor in determining who wins or loses. So, while brute power can win races, a vehicles ability to quickly start and overcome the physical law of static inertia (getting out of the hole or starting from a standstill) is still dependent on driver ability.

The first one across the finish line a quarter-mile away without fouling at the start line, or taking off too early, wins the battle, not necessarily the war. In other words, they won part of the war, so to speak. It's like out-scoring your opponent in the first quarter of a football game, . . . it means something but

it's not recorded as a complete victory. Depending on the class of racers, if a competitor fouls while lining up or staging, they may either be immediately disqualified or they can back-up their machine and reposition themselves correctly. In any case, fouling at the start of the race itself means the other car racing with the one which fouled is the automatic winner. (unless they both fouled; the one who fouled by the least margin of time, in other words, the one who took off earlier is then the loser; in some classes or organizations, both drivers would be disqualified)

The loser is eliminated from (class) competition and the winner goes on to further competition. This continues until only one competitor for that particular class is left and an overall winner is decided. This tournament style of drag race scoring is called Eliminator.

Before all this happens, in most classes but not all, each vehicle goes through a series of runs to qualify and determine an ET (Elapsed Time) for the day. This is the time any particular vehicle took to travel that 1/4 mile before the eliminating series begins. Then those elapsed times determine where, how, with whom and if a particular racecar will be positioned or paired, in what is usually a 16 car Eliminator series. An example is a 16-step or position latter very simular, if not exactly like that of the NCAA basketball tournament. The 16th seed car, or in this case the 16th fastest vehicle is paired in the first round with the fastest qualifier, the 15th fastest with the 2nd fastest, etc. The idea is to pair the fastest with the slowest as early as possible to create the closest matches in the final rounds.

Sometimes this series may include 32 cars or even as many as 64 vehicles. This qualifying is similar to seeding each vehicle.

Here's a little tidbit for drag racing fans. When a car is running the quarter-mile, be it racing or qualifying, two separate performances of a vehicle is is monitored. The Elapsed Time is the seconds measured in the thousandths it takes to cover the quarter-mile distance . . . The other is the top-end speed.

Drag race drivers don't generally care

about the top-end speeds any more than a circle track racer, such as those in IndyCars, cares about a races overall length in time. It all relative to them. If a drag racer "snails" across the finish line first, that's all that matters. If an Indy drivers average speed for a race (not qualifying) he won was a lowly 77.557 mph, . . . so be it. He doesn't care! (that winners share of the purse is still very green and the trophy still gleams beautifully) Still, there are situations in drag racing where top-end speeds do count for something during a race. One is to attain record-breaking barriers. Another is to collect more seasonal points towards a national championship. Bottom line . . . that usually means more purse-money won at the end of a season.

BUT . . . top-end speeds are always important to the fans in drag racing. They want to know what it is! So . . . you do what the fans want. Why? Where would any kind of racing be without them, especially at the pro level? Hence, the top speeds of drag racers are recorded near the finish line by the breaking of two additional light beams. (the start line also has this electronic beam, which when broken by a race car starts the ET recording) These beams at the finish line are relatively close together, 66 feet, so the time it takes a vehicle to break one and then the other at well over 200 mph could match the blinking of an eye. But thanks to the wonderful world of electronics, the time occupied in the breaking of those beams can be converted instantly to mph.

This recording of speed became even more important when Top Fuel and Funny Cars began approaching an incredible 300 mph. This barrier has since been attained several times. The fastest was a "mind-numbing" 314 mph! That's unbelievable, but true. To me, that's the equal of a 240 mph average race qualifying time for an Indy Car at Indianapolis during the month of May. (yes, an Indy Car can without a doubt do that right now, . . . but . . . remember, . . . they couldn't do that easily, if at all, within the current rules)

F. ET. ELAPSED TIME HANDICAP DRAG RACING—In addition to elimination style of

format between the various classes, there is also a categorized form of racing offered by many (local) tracks. It is called 'Elapsed Time' Handicap racing. This is where many drag racing novices begin and where around 70 to 80% of all drag racing competitors are. Most of the cars raced here are street-legal. Each of the tracks keeps a system of points all season in four Elapsed Time Brackets of cars and a separate bracket for motorcycles. The top finisher(s) at the seasons end are sent to the World Finals by the track.

In this kind of drag competition, usually called 'Bracket Racing,' any two machines of various performance potentials may race on a potentially equal basis. The anticipated elapsed time for each are compared, with the slower one receiving a head start. This staggered timing is performed by the Christmas Tree at the beginning of a race. It's equal to the difference of the two 'dial-in' times of the two racers. This means any two cars can be paired in a race. The loser is done for the race event while the winner continues on in an eliminator-style of series for their bracket. (the 4 IHRA & NHRA brackets will be covered shortly)

Here's an example. Racer 1 has been timed in three qualifying runs in the quarter-mile of 15.070, 15.050 and 15.090 seconds. The driver of that vehicle feels that a Dial-In of 15.06 is the most accurate or appropriate time for him and his machine. (times are usually shown in hundreths here) How he determined that is through experience and weather (barometric pressure, temperature, humidity) conditions for the day. There's more to it but that isn't important for now. The dial-in time must be within the highest and lowest times in those three runs. Likewise, a driver of racecar 2 records 17.870, 17.901 and 17.940 seconds with his or her runs on the same track the same day. Car 2 decides a dial-in of 17.89 is their most accurate time. The difference in dial-in times between the two (17.89 minus 15.06 = 2.83) is 2.83 seconds.

When the two are lined up and staged for racing at the line and christmas tree, racecar 2 will get a 2.83 second headstart over car 1. Car 2 had longer times. That means that vehicle is slower than car 1 in covering the quarter-mile. Of course, baring any foul starts or other infractions, then the first to the finish line wins.

What if there is a tie at the finish line? In that case there is a tie-breaker. It's determined by what's called 'Reaction Time.' This happens at the starting line. Both lanes are timed by the tree independently of each other. Timing of a racecar does not start until that (nonfouled) vehicle(s) begins to move acrossed the infrared light beam at the start line. Whoever of the two had the shortest reaction time means they were the quickest to start, therefore, they win that tiebreaker and that particular pairing or race. This is one of the reasons I stated earlier why starting well is so important. The measurement of reaction time is actually between the last amber light and when the race vehicle broke the light beam on the starting line. This is why I stated earlier the reason drivers try to take off near the last amber. They learn to anticipate the green. They start moving towards the line, which is only inches away if they stage themselves shallow. Of course, if they hit the line before the green, they foul. Staging lights on the tree helps them position their machines. (if they're right on the line, they're Deep-staged)

This isn't the end of it though. What if a driver does a faster Elapsed Time in the race than they did in the qualifying times to determine their dial-in? This situation is called a 'Break-Out.' It's also grounds for disqualification. If both drivers break-out, or in other words run ET's under their dial-in times, the win goes to the driver who breaks-out the least.

This puts a premium on consistent times and prevents drivers from sandbagging. Sandbagging in drag racing is like sandbagging in anything else. It's the practice of deliberately withholding best performance in the early stages of an event to gain an (unfair) advantage later.

If a driver should both foul at the starting line and break-out, the foul is considered worse of the two. You may ask, "what's the point of continuing a drag race between two cars if one of them fouls at the start?" Well there isn't, but, the one driver who fouls at the line doesn't know if the other did also, so

he or she should continue racing. Suppose both foul equally and one of them also break-out? If they both fouled equally in time, then the winner is the one who didn't break-out. If both foul at the start, but one still fouled worse than the other then only the red light of the driver which took off earlier will illuminate. The worse thing a driver could do is to run out of their lane. That supercedes all other infractions, because it could mean the coming together and colliding of two machines down the dragstrip at high speeds.

This is a form of (handicap) racing which seeks to measure the driver skill, not just the equipment he's driving.

NHRA sanctions four street-automotive categories in ET handicap racing. One advanced category for nonstreet-type autos and two classes for motorcycles. If a vehicle dials-in between the following times, they're designated as such:

ET of 6.30 to 7.49—Advanced category for turbo and supercharged, alcohol and nitrous burning Dragsters, Funny Car, Altered and factory experimental cars.
ET of 7.50 to 10.99 seconds—Super Pro category
ET of 11.00 to 11.99 seconds—Pro category
ET of 12.00 to 13.99 seconds—Sportsman category
ET of 14.00 seconds and over—Street category
ET of 7.49 seconds or faster—ET motorcycle
ET of 7.50 to 10.99 seconds—Sportsman motorcycle

The first two street-type categories are not really pro classes in the literal sense of the word. There are also eighth-mile equivalent times for each of these categories, but I won't get into that in this book. It's not complicated anyhow. Some smaller tracks just don't have the room for a quarter-mile strip plus the room it takes for the race machines to stop. So they they use a formula to equate to quarter-mile averages. Also, they may use different names/divisions for their ET Bracket categories, such as Heavy, Trophy, Jr Dragster, Trophy Modified, Motorcycle, Womens classes, High School classes, Open, etc.

IHRA has just slightly 4 different times and categories for street-cars and one for motorcycles.

ET of 0.00 to 9.99 seconds - Top ET
ET of 10.00 to 11.49 seconds - Modified ET
ET of 11.50 to 13.49 seconds - Super ET
ET of 13.50 and slower seconds - Street ET

As in most racing there are two levels and it's no different in drag racing.

First, there are the professionals. The pros have 5 basic subcategories in IHRA (International Hot Rod Association) racing as listed on page 86. NHRA sanctioned pro racing has only three subcategories, not counting the motorcycle subcategory. These two larger drag racing organizations differ a bit in their class groupings amongst themselves and other drag racing series, but basically they are close to the same.

Second is the IHRA amateurs which have 8 subcategories that further break down into subdivisions or classes. That ends up with well over a hundred classes. Some of them are so similar that the only real difference is some small piece of equipment on the racing machine. But when most races are won in the thousandths of seconds, those small pieces of equipment could be the difference between consistently winning or losing.

Generally, the differences described in each of the following classes will be limited to larger and of more obvious type in nature.

Examples are: type of fuel used; engine size, in cubic inches or power to weight ratio; number of engines on a racer. Yes, some racers use two engines at the same time on the same car; turbo or supercharging, and what one can or cannot do to that engine; body style or aerodynamics; transmissions; minimum or maximum weights; wheelbases and kinds of tires.

There are dozens of other things, rules, regulations and whatever which isn't necessary for me to cover in drag racing. (like in previous categories of this chapter) Covering these following things now would be putting the cart before the horse. But to give you an idea what could be covered, here is an example: added ballast weight rules; battery and electrical systems; braking systems; clutches and drivelines; engine locations; exhaust systems; fuel pump and fuel delivery systems; flywheel shielding specs; paint; parachute requirements; ground clearance; harmonic balancers; hood scoops; liquid cooling systems; seat and seat belts; floor specs; rollcage; driver location; rearend axle requirements; steering; starters; suspension types and their locations; windshield and glass; traction devices; fenders; window nets; general appearance and lettering; protective clothing and helmets; firewalls and equipment removal. That doesn't cover it all, but it gives you an idea how involved drag racing and racing in general is.

There are even provisions in both IHRA and NHRA drag racing for jet-powered ground racers. But those are more for exhibitional purposes than anything else. It is not necessary to cover this kind of dragster anymore than there is to cover jet-powered air racing in this book.

Motorcycle Drag racing will be covered in Category K on Motorbikes later on.

There is also Off-Road Drag racers, more specifically named Sand Rails. They will also be briefly discussed later in this chapter.

Yes, even the Big Trucks, not necessarily the Monster Trucks, do some drag racing. That's covered a little bit in Category L, RaceTrucks.

IHRA Subcategories 1 through 5; Professional Classes

None of these pro subcategories breakdown into further divisions or classes. So, in essence, these are stand-alone divisions or classes. But don't get the word stand-alone class confused with a stand-alone event. A stand-alone event is an event like the Indy 500. Only one class of race machine is participating at that event. It's one of the very few stand-alone events held in the world.

On the other hand, these pro dragsters aren't stand-alone event racers even though they race separately in their own class, but they do participate amongst other classes at the same event, just not at the same time.

F.1. TOP FUEL (AA or RAIL DRAGSTER)— These are the big-time, major league, numero uno dragsters sometimes nicknamed Diggers or Slingshots. They are the fastest, quickest race sanctioned, reciprocating piston-powered vehicles on earth. If they haven't done it yet, (which they have) it's just a matter of time before they reach the 300 mph barrier. They normally top out around 285-295 mph. Of course, mph is layman terms. What the driver is really interested in is shortening their elapsed time.

These are purpose-built, open-wheeled machines (being open-wheeled isn't all that important since these racecars do not normally bump each other) which are long, narrow and low slung, but not low-slung as a formula car. Their wheelbase must be at least a minimum of 180 inches. Their nitromethane burning "powerplant" is for the most part unrestricted. But they must be of the piston-type and no more than 500 ci's.

Most Rail and Funny Car Dragsters (covered next) are not self-starting. Like Indy cars, a remote starter is usually placed or injected somewhere on an engines flywheel or crankshaft which subsequently turns them over for starting.

Top fuel race machines supercharge their engines instead of turbocharging. Supercharging is a much quicker reacting power enhancer than turbocharging for getting out of the hole. (starting from a standstill) No electronic controlled fuel injection systems are allowed. The engines are capable of producing 5000 hp. (although many claim 3500 to 4000 is more accurate)

You may notice after closely observing one of these machines that they do not use a radiator. That's because they don't run long enough to seriously overheat the engines. Besides, believe it or not, the engines are torn down after almost every run. Then they are inspected, parts are replaced if necessary, reworked or polished and put back together. Many parts of these engines, including the engine block, are made of lighter aluminum metals. This increases the power-to-weight ratio, therefore, their quickness.

As Top Fuelers became stronger, it was necessary to lower their center of gravity to stabilize them more at increasing speeds. To start with, the driver had to be lowered closer to the ground. Since the engine was in front of the driver in earlier days, they had to place the cockpit fairly high over the driveshaft in much the same fashion as a Sprint car. That meant the driver couldn't be lowered pass that driveshaft in redesigning. If so, the driveshaft strength would have to be sacrificed by the installation of constant-velocity joint(s). That kind of sacrifice was out of the question. So, to solve that, the drivers cockpit and engine locations were redesigned completely.

Ultimately, the cockpit and engine locations were flip-flopped. That made them both more easy to lower towards the ground since the shaft was no longer under the cockpit. This not only stabilized the machines, it also made them safer for the drivers. When a front-engine rail dragster blew up, many times the poor driver would "eat" flames and engine debris. That was bad enough! It was also generally hard for the driver to see pass or over the engine itself under driving conditions. That's not a good situation at over 290 mph or at any speed. Anyway, the front-located cockpit made for a better, safer and faster racer for the driver and fans.

These racecars also use wings, the rear one being higher (Max. height. 90 inches) to catch a smoother flow of air and aid in vehicle dynamics. Front wheel diameter is limited to at least 13 inches or more. Most of these machines use narrow treaded tires on the front end since there isn't much weight there. (NHRA Top Fuelers are allowed smaller wheels)

Rear wheels and rims are open to whatever the race driver chooses, but they always use racing slicks of automotive type. Now don't be confused about the type of racetires some amateur and all the pro classes use here. You'll notice later in higher levels of drag racing, which allow race slicks, they are called 'automotive type.' That means automotive in the sense of air-filled or pneumatic type. Otherwise some pro racers would be allowed the use of a solid type rubber compound, or non-pneumatic tires. That's nothing but hard or soft rubber throughout the entire tire carcass, right down to the rim.

This is an AA/fuel dragster. They are the most powerful racer in the world. Although top speed is around 290, the 300 mph mark was finally achieved by a Kenny Bernstein vehicle. But, to drag racers, what's really important is the 'elapsed time' that's taken to cover a quarter-mile run. Notice how long they're built. When you start as quick as they do, you want a long wheelbase to prevent the vehicle from nosing up hard and flipping backwards. These engines run such a short time they don't require a cooling system, and obviously, only a small fuel tank is needed.

The rims themselves would be much taller in diameter to accommodate what would be shorter profiled tires, otherwise a normal sized nonpneumatic tire-rim combination would be too heavy with all that extra rubber. So, . . . the automotive type tires here are not the treaded types like those used on street-legal cars.

There are other racetire differences too. The construction between them on most pro dragsters, as opposed to those on a closed-course race car which must negotiate turns, is like the difference between day and night.

The sidewalls of a drag race tire is very thin and flexible. That becomes even more evident during acceleration. The tread is about a quarter of an inch thick. The sidewalls are only a mere tenth of an inch. That enables it to flex or sag on the ground. This provides a larger tire footprint on the ground for increased traction even though the rest of the tire narrows during acceleration. The tire looks short on air pressure when it's just sitting there bolted on a racecar. They actually are low on air compared to other race-

tires, but that's done purposely. That's one reason why drag cars with these larger footprints don't usually slide sideways easily when they're out of control. They grip the ground too well. It rolls the entire racecar over sideways. Also, the sidewalls on the tires in front of the slide could collapse or buckle, therefore tilting the car into the slide. That enhances shifting lateral forces and the center of gravity, which makes the chances of a nasty rollover even more likely.

So, as a competitor applies power to those tires, the down and forward force wrinkles the sides, flattens or shortens them, and therefore puts more rubber on the track. This phenomenon also makes the vehicle a different animal to control. Fortunately, drag cars aren't suppose to make high-speed turns forcing those sidewalls to crunch down towards the rims. That's why these tires can be used. On the other hand, at any speed, the relatively unstable behavior of them can cause a machine to drift out of their racing lane. A good and experienced driver controls or prevents that.

Also, high speed machines such as Top Fuelers and Funny Cars are 'live axle' equipped in the rearend. That means a solid, one-piece, wheel to wheel axle turns them simultaneously. That aids in straight-line performance, not to mention traction. Still, just the slightest jerk in vehicle side loads, even from sidewinds, can trigger dangerous drifting. At over 280 mph, that'll get a drivers attention fast.

So, going down a drag strip, essentially getting shot out of a cannon, at well over 280 mph while still controlling certain laws of physics and vehicle dynamics isn't as easy as some of those drivers make it look. It takes practiced skill and nerves of steel.

Top Fuel Dragsters use specially made transmissions called Lencos. They are a form of automatic with a primitive clutch and release mechanism used at the end of a run. Top Fuelers usually use two range trans. Funny Cars go with 3 and Pro Stocks have a 4 range transmission. Whatever the case, these clutch-type transmissions do not have a neutral gear while the clutch is en-gaged. That and the fact that they're changed by a button or lever, which air-shifts them, means a gear cannot be missed during acceleration.

Another device holds pressure firmly to the gear and/or pressure clutch plate to keep them from slipping during a run. Even more than the Sprint car, this clutch has to hold a tremendous amount of torque. Therefore, this device is recommended but not required.

Duel parachutes are required in the aid of stopping in all pro classes. (and in many amateur classes too)

F.2. NITRO FUNNY CAR—There was nothing funny about these nitromethane-burning speed merchants. They were close-wheeled, relatively current production-looking vehicles which were pretty much a shorter version of front-engine mounted rail dragsters, with a body attached thereto.

Their body was usually just a large one-piece fiberglass shell which resembled a somewhat smaller and/or narrower version

This funny car racer is either an alcohol or nitro methane burner. Basically, these are like a shorter AA/fuel Dragster with a one-piece fiberglass shell bolted on its frame. But there is a big difference; the engine is located in front of the driver, who is seated very close to the rear slicks and up higher off the ground in order to clear himself of the drive train components.

of an automotive model of usually American make. It flipped up off the racer to allow driver entry.

They had basically the same engine rules as the Top Fuel machines do. With these racers, the engine was located in front of the driver. That meant the driver center of gravity was higher off the ground. Couple that with the obvious larger amount of space which had to cut through the air at high speeds compared to the Rail Dragster, then you'll understand why this racer was just a bit slower than the Top-Fuelers, even though it used the same engine. But they weren't much slower! They could go around 280–90 mph, but usually topped-out more often at 270–280 mph. They were the second fastest racer around. Funny Cars also have broken the 300 mph barrier.

No wings were allowed, but they used spoilers incorporated into the body for safety purposes. Their wheelbase was to be between 100 to 125 inches compared to the Rail Dragsters 180 inch minimum. The rear tire tread could not be outside the normal unaltered body line and fenders. Windshields were not only mandatory, but necessary to aid in vehicle aerodynamics.

The body regulations were extensive, but I'll simplify them a bit here for purposes of this book. The body (shell) was to be of coupe or sedan type which was mass-produced and available to the general public. (preferably of American manufacture) Minimum body width was 63 inches. Length was limited to no more than a 40 inch overhang past the front axle and 54 inches past the back axle.

Like the AA Fuel Dragsters, there was no minimum weight rule. (NHRA dragsters have weight rules) IHRA Top Fuel and Funny Cars were both self-starting race machines. (self-starts was formerly not a regulation)

Sometimes this Funny Car racer was called a DOUBLE A FUNNY CAR. (AA/FC) It did not have to burn nitromethane fuel, although most did. As for the IHRA, this class was eliminated around 1992 because participation was lagging. Also, track insurance companies didn't like the idea of nitromethane anywhere close to the drivers or spectators. This is also getting to be the situation with NHRA events.

F.3. PRO STOCK—Take away those big air-intake hood scoops and these are the drag vehicles that look like NASCAR Grand National StockCars. Obviously, they are stock looking, but they're about as stock as that term is used or abused in racing. This class is limited to US manufactured engines, drivetrains, chassis and bodies.

The engines are a maximum of 500 cubic inches for vehicle weight of 2350 to 2649 lbs and a minimum 501 ci's for vehicles over 2650 lbs, including drivers in both cases. No super or turbocharging is permitted. Fuel must be unaltered gasoline in this racer. Carburetion is limited to any two 4-barrel type (duel-quads) of an American 'make.' Internal engine modifications are permitted, but no fuel injectors are allowed. Top speeds approach 190–195 mph.

Drivetrains cannot be altered except for vehicles originally designed as front-wheel drive. This gets complicated and isn't necessary to explain.

Transmissions must be a maximum of 5 forward speeds and remain in stock location. Clutchless units are allowed. Rearends must be stock, but are allowed to be of full-floating type. (see glossary for what this is)

Chassis frame may be replaced by a reinforced one as long as a fully automotive tube-suspension system is used. Floors may be replaced but still must appear stock. Wheelbase must be at least 100 inches.

Body silhouette-models must be no more than 5 years old in style as originally factory produced for either a coupe or sedan. These are not actually produced on an assembly line, but with a few exceptions, they must appear that way. No trucks, early models or sportscars are permitted here like they are in the IHRA Pro Modified division. Original steel body paneling is required, except for front hoods which may incorporate an air scoop of no higher than 13 inches off the original surface. Doors must be functional. (open and close) Glass may be replaced by plexiform glass and permanently shut or affixed on the doors. Fiberglass doors are permitted to lighten this vehicle.

These racers use rear slicks and may use treaded tires on the front. Roll cages must be installed and the driver must operate this racer from its original factory-stock seat position. With some exceptions, wheelbase must be stock and at least 100 inches in length.

F.4. ALCOHOL FUNNY CAR—To the eye these look like a Nitro Funny car. They are a bit slower even though their engines are 50 ci's larger than their 500 cubic inch counterpart, the Nitro Funny Car.

How these machines can be modified is more restrictive. For example, they are not allowed to use turbo or supercharged engines and can't have more than two valves per cylinder. Actually, they can supercharge but they can't use the 'screw' type supercharger which performs better than the fan or roots type.

Transmission rules are more open compared to the Nitro's. Aftermarket planetary units are limited to 3 speeds. (see glossary for the definition of what a planetary transmission is)

Alkys, as they're sometimes called, are also a bit lighter compared to the Nitro Funny Car, with a minimum weight requirement of 2000 lbs. Obviously the fuel they burn is alcohol based, which is usually methane, not nitromethane.

Minimum wheelbase is the same as a Nitro at 100 to 125 inches. Otherwise these two dragsters are pretty much the same. But the Alcys top out usually around 20 to 30 mph slower than the Nitro's.

F.5. PRO MODIFIED—These are similar to the Pro Stocks, but they are a bit quicker and their body styles may be more early-model designed. Some models emulate pickup trucks and sportscars.

The engines are subject to many modifications. 710 cubic inches was the limit on carburated engines and 526 ci's for those supercharged. But now they may use engines over 800 ci's depending on whether they supercharge or use nitrous oxide. No more than 2 valves per cylinder and no hemi engines are allowed if supercharging is used. (hemi—meaning hemispherical or rounded engine-cylinder heads; increases compression and therefore power)

Turbochargers were allowed on only 4 and 6-cylinder engines, but that has since changed. Racers not using superchargers may use a certain mix of nitrous oxide in their fuel, a mix not allowed in most other pro drag racing classes.

Their minimum weights can vary from 2300 to 2600 lbs according to the kind of engine they use. They're usually longer than the Pro Stock versions, but not all the time. (103 to 115 inch wheelbase)

The suspension and chassis rules are basically the same as the Pro Stock. Top speeds can reach 210–220 mph.

IHRA Subcategories 6 through 13; Amateur Classes

Some of these amateur subcategories breakdown into divisions and further into classes. Some do not.

F.6. TOP SPORTSMAN—This is a minimum dial-in ET type class of 8.49 seconds in the quarter-mile which uses the handicap system for starting a race as explained previously. Different race machines such as full-bodied cars, Altereds, such as roadsters, Funny Car styled bodies with Top Fuel length chassis are competing here. Any kind of frame is generally acceptable.

All racecars require a full roll cage. Parachutes are required on vehicles that run over 150 mph. Transmissions rules are mostly open (no restrictions) along with the rearend and drivetrain. Carburetion rules are also open. Racers must be self-starting. Fuel permitted may be alcohol-based and full bodied racers may use a nitrous oxide mix. No nitromethane is permitted. There are no limits on size of engines in cubic inches, except dragsters (long rail-frames) which must use a small block. (350 cubic inches and under) Also, the dragsters are the only racers allowed to super or turbocharge their engines.

Top speeds are around 170 to 185 mph.

Wheelbase on full bodied racers must be at least 90 inches, otherwise they may be altered. Front-engine dragsters must be at least 185 inches and 200 for the rear-engine versions. Altereds and/or Roadsters can't exceed 130 inches.

Minimum weights vary widely by type of racer, engine size, fuel, etc. This class draws racers of other classes together as a sort-of "melting pot" of amateur drag racing.

F.7. FACTORY MODIFIED—This class was for 1980 or later American built, mass-production models that were made available to the general public. Unlike the Top Sportsman class, this was restricted to two-door passenger models. No wagons or trucks were allowed. Front-wheeled vehicles could be converted to rear-wheel drive. Wheelbases had to be stock distance if originally over 105 inches with some exceptions on front-wheel drives.

Transmissions were open with a maximum 5 forward speeds and a reverse gear. As required in all classes up to this point, parachutes are mandatory. These burned fuel minus any additives and nitrous oxide. Also, as in all classes so far described, the racing slicks must not protruded outside the normal contours of the wheel quarterpanels or wells.

The engines varied widely. Many internal modifications were permitted but they had to be a small-block V-6 or V-8 of internal combustion, reciprocating type. Cubic inches allowed for any particular racer would depend on the vehicles weight. For every 8 lbs of vehicle weight, 1 cubic inch of engine displacement was permitted. (driver weight included)

There were some weight minimums. Automatic transmission equipped racers had to weigh at least 2100 and 1800 for V-8's and V-6's respectively. Stick shifts had to weigh at least 2150 and 1850 for V-8's and V-6's. Top speeds were right around 170–185 mph.

Roll cages were mandatory and the driver had to be positioned as originally designed by the auto manufacture.

This is another class that has since been eliminated by the IHRA.

F.8. MODIFIED ELIMINATOR—This is a 7 division subcategory in which each division breaks down further into classes. Most racecars here are purpose-built strictly for drag racing, but some may serve as duel-purpose vehicles. (street or passenger cars)

Bodies, engines, drivetrains and chassis may be altered as described for each division, class or both. All racers must be self-starting. As implied by the division title, these racers are modified in several areas.

They cannot race in street-stock type ET brackets because they would be too quick in most cases. Some of these can compete in the special IHRA bracket designed for them as previously covered. NHRA doesn't have that. Anyway, the machines here compete in an eliminator series. (the following 7 divisions are F.8. A thru F.8. G)

F.8. A. DRAGSTERS—There are 7 classes, A thru G, in this division. In all 7 classes, wheelbase must at least be 180 inches. These are the long rail type machines very simular to the Top Fuel dragsters. But these are down-powered versions. The engines must use straight gasoline and be any cubic inch size as long as it's the piston type. Any engine location and modification is permitted as long as it is not supercharged and limited to two valves per cylinder.

The seven dragster classes here are determined by cubic-inch/weight ratios. The lightest class requires at least 3.30 lbs for each cubic inch of engine displacement. The heaviest class (G) requires 8.40 lbs for each ci for opposed 4-cylinder engines. (opposed means a flat type configuration such as a VW "Bug" engine; it's formally called a horizontally-opposed four cylinder)

Top speeds vary between 180 and 210 mph.

F.8. B. ECONO ALTERED AND FUNNY CAR—As implied, these racecars are of Funny Car or Altered type with some minor body shape alterations. These are a form of rail dragsters with a one-piece fiberglass shell in designed of an American made coupe, sedan or sedan delivery. (station wagon)

Wheelbase must be 100 to 130 inches. Some body lengthening and shortening is allowed to accommodate for that. Some lowering (chopping) of roofs is permitted. (better aerodynamics) Drivers may be located anywhere between the engine and rear axle.

There are many amateur categories in drag racing which break into a ton of classes. This racer here is in the altered category. It's definitely altered alright. Look at the driver seated in it. It's not that he is a giant, but rather the car is small. See that strong frame below the engine? A weak frame would twist under a full load of engine torque. They need to be strong. That's the supercharger sticking out the front hood. It's powered by the engine crankshaft (for quicker response) rather than the engine exhaust, which you can see protruding out the side(s).

Transmissions are limited to automotive production automatics which may be strengthened or beefed-up. Suspensions are open or optional.

Five classes exist for these nonsupercharged, gas burning racecars. They're determined by a vehicle weight/cubic inch ratio formula similar to the previous class just mentioned. The 5 class weights start at 5.00 lbs for each cubic inch of engine displacement and end at 7.50 pounds, depending on engine heads and structure. (V-8, V-6, etc)

These machines top out at varying speeds of 155–195 mph.

F.8. C. ECONORAIL DRAGSTERS—This class is almost identical to the Modified Eliminator Dragsters just covered in category 8.A. They have the same number of classes (7) but have slightly lighter overall weight-to-cubic-inch ratios.

Minimum wheelbase is identical to the dragsters for rear engine models. Unlike Modified Eliminator Dragsters, a front-engine dragster is permitted with a minimum 125 inch wheelbase.

Econorail Dragster classes A, B and C allow any ci size engine and internal modifications, but must use only one automotive production carburetor of any 4-barrel size. Classes D, E and F engines are limited to 4 and 6 cylinders. Here, rotary type engines are permitted. Class G have rules similar to the first 3 classes but no hemi engines are allowed.

Like Modified Eliminator Dragsters, these burn gasoline and allow no supercharging. Top speeds are about 160 to 190 mph.

F.8. D. ALTEREDS AND ROADSTERS—In this class, racecars are very diverse with even more engine, body and chassis modifications. The rule book here reads as long as a War and Peace-sized book. (that's exaggerated a bit)

Basically, these are the radical looking pre-1930's cars or trucks of American 'make' with oversized wheelwells to accommodate larger tires. The Roadster bodies may be channeled, (narrowed) but not chopped.

(that's the front part of roof cut and angled down (to a smaller windshield) for better wind resistance) Altered racecars can both channel and chop their bodies. Both machines usually are chassis-cleared higher off the ground in the back, compared to the front, mostly due to large tires. These cars do look mean!

The open top racer (by production design) are the Roadsters, which may also be sportscars and trucks. In this entire division, all wheelbases are 90 to 125 inches. They are powered by piston engines which do not have to match manufacture model and year as originally offered. Obviously, if these fairly early models where limited to their original engines, they wouldn't stand a chance to be competitive. Any number of carbs and fuel injection systems are optional. Transmissions are also optional.

Thirteen Altered classes determined by weight/cubic inch ratios are permitted without supercharging, except the first two which may be super or turbocharged. There are only two (which are nonsupercharged) Roadster classes. In all 15 classes, fiberglass-body replica's are okay.

The first 7 Altered classes may use race slicks. Top speeds: 110–160 mph.

F.8. E. MODIFIED COMPACTS—These cars are factory-built and mass produced passenger vehicles with originally equipped engines that are street legal. No small sportscars and pick-ups are allowed.

Automobile bodies must remain fully stock dimensionally with the kind of materials originally used. (with a few exceptions, such as hoods and fenders) No removal of materials and equipment for lightening of vehicles is allowed. No relocation of engine and drivetrain is permitted.

Transmissions must be stock stickshift or automatic. Street gasoline is the only type of fuel allowed.

Modified Compacts are allowed to remove the exhaust system and replace it with headers and a straight pipe. (headers are specifically-designed small pipes used for exhaust systems which fit a specific set of engine heads for better spent-fuel escape and therefore, horsepower) Certain types of turbo-

chargers may be used, if stock. Roll bar (not cage) must be installed. (roll bars are relatively easy to remove since these are street cars) Bumpers may be removed. No parachute is required.

There are 7 classes in this division all determined by a weight-per-cubic-inch formula. Class A is the lightest starting at 15 lbs/ci. Class D is the heaviest starting at 19.50 lbs. The other last 3 classes, E,F,G, provide in their power-to-weight formula the number of cylinders permitted. In all classes any carburetion or fuel injection is allowed. (with some class G restrictions) Classes A - D wheelbases cannot exceed 101 inches and the rest are limited to 105 inches.

These racers top-out anywhere from 105 to 160 mph.

F.8. F. MODIFIED—This class is basically the same as the Modified Compacts. The big differences are that these have lighter weight ratios, starting 7.50 and ending at 10.50.

This division also has 7 classes, but unlike Modified Compacts, these must be of American manufacture. They also can't remove bumpers. Sportscars and pick-ups are permitted as long as they meet minimum weight and wheelbase requirements starting at 2650 lbs with driver and 90 inches.

There is a large diversity in engine sizes, number of engine cylinders and model years. Some of the racecars are pre-1960. No Modified bodies can be altered or drooped. (chopped with the high rearend ground clearance)

Modifieds may use racing slicks. Modified Compacts can use only aftermarket slicks or automotive tires suitable for street use. In both classes, rims must be stock size and at least 13 inches in diameter.

No fuel injection is allowed in Modified.

They top-out at around 145 to 165 mph.

F.8. G. ECONO MODIFIED—There are 7 classes here. The weight ratios start at 7.50 lbs in class A to 13.50 in G. They are even closer to Modified than Modified is to Modified Compacts. In this class no convertibles are allowed.

Engines may be modified more but their 'make' must match with manufacturers body-model. This matching isn't required as far as standard equipment for that year and model is concerned. Engine and carburation must remain stock and in stock location, but unlike the Modifieds, they must use a stock radiator.

The gasoline must be of the kind offered to the general public. Modifieds and Modified Compacts are allowed to add some oxygen-bearing or octane additives to increase horsepower.

There are no restrictions on tire size and type if they don't protrude outside their wheelwell fenders. The top speeds are 135 to 155 mph.

F.9. QUICK ROD—Now I'm back to a subcategory. This class is just about a replica of the subcategory Top Sportsman, (F.6) with rail dragsters, full-bodied cars, Funny cars, but no Altered or Roadsters. About the only thing different is the slightly slower speeds. A big difference is the way they race.

These are ET Bracket cars that have to run (at least) in the 8.90 quarter-mile standard. Anything faster (8.89 seconds or less) has to race elsewhere. (usually)

The difference between Quick Rod and Top Sportsman ET is the time bracket or standard required (bottom line, speed) and the type of ET system used. (ET verses Dialed-In ET; Dial-In ET in the Sportsman category requires the driver to use their lowest time from their qualifying runs and then they may lower that more by 1/10th second)

Top speeds: 150–170 mph.

F.10. SUPER ROD—This is also a ET bracket class which requires a 9.90 standard in the 1/4 mile run. The racecars must be of full-body type or Roadster. No Altereds, Funny Cars or Dragsters.

Any internal combustion engine with or without supercharging, fuel injection is legal. They may use alcohol and gasoline, but generally not mixed with nitrous oxide. Wheelbase may be altered but must be 90 to 125 inches.

No racing slicks are allowed. Tires used must be suitable for street use. As in about all classes of drag racing, no wire wheels are allowed. (wire wheel rims)

These cars have to remain as stock appearing as possible, but don't necessarily have to be street legal.

Top speeds are around 125–140 mph.

F.11. HOT ROD—These are just about a duplicate of the Super Rods, but even more stock appearing. Like Super Rods, doors must be operational. In this class, roadsters are also permitted. With rules being almost identical, about the only difference is the number of carbs allowed, which is free in numbers in Hot Rod.

This is a slower ET Bracket racer with a standard time of 10.90 in the quarter mile.

The top speeds are around 115–130 mph.

F.12. SUPERSTOCK—This is a subcategory in drag racing of 5 divisions. What sets these apart from others in drag racing is the "split" in allowances. In other words, one subcategory not listed here in F.12., like the Funny Cars for instance, are pretty open or liberal with both the chassis-body and engine regulations. (as relative to street-legal automobiles) Another subcategory like the drag racing Stock, is very conservative with both chassis-body and engine rules.

This subcategory has a split personality. It's conservative with the chassis-body rules, but yet liberal on what's allowed concerning the engines.

Most drag racing cars or any other forms of racing for that matter is split, but this subcategory carries it a bit further than most. As you'll see in subcategory 13, (which is next; Stock) those racecars are regulated in a more consistent fashion. They have both conservative chassis-body and engine rules. That won't be so here.

F.12. A. SUPERSTOCK/PRODUCTION—This first of 5 divisions, the SS/Production, has 10 classes of which each class is further subclassed between vehicles using an automatic or manual transmission. (10 classes; 20 subclasses)

As with many drag racing cars, these classes are based upon wt/ci ratios. They start at 7.0 lbs vehicle weight for every ci of engine displacement for Class A-SS/Production down to 9 other classes, finishing with

Class J-SS/Production which starts at a wt/ci minimum of 13.00 lbs.

NOTE - Before I forget, I'd like to explain how drag racing cars are numbered.

Let's say a particular racing number on the side of a J-classed race vehicle was . . . oh, . . . any number, let's say 78. I'm using the J class in the SS/Production (SS/P) division that I'm now covering. Here's what the number-letters on the side on that machine with an automatic-equipped transmission would be. (and show) It would be 78 SS/JPA, . . . not 78 SS/PJA. (P & J should not be flip-flopped) Other divisions outside of SS/P, may have their number-lettering designations in just a slightly different order.

Anyway, 78 is the cars number for identification purposes to both fans and race officials. The number 78 may be assigned by the racing body or the driver as long as two racers in the same class don't have the same number at the same event. The SS letters mean this racecar is in the SuperStock subcategory. (or for the average joe, he'd probably substitute the word "subcategory" that I use, for another term, like the word class or division, etc. I call it a "subcategory" to keep semantics in this book consistent)

The J means this car is in class J, of the SS/P subcategory, (or division) which means it must have 13 or more pounds of weight for each cubic inch of engine displacement. (again, in other subcategories, that sub-classed-designated letter, in this case J, could be located one space off to the right, like I just shown above. So don't be confused by that. These different orders are necessary to prevent duplicate number-lettering designations between classes with simular titles.

The P is a common letter in this particular subdivision. It stands for the Production portion of SS/P. The A means the car uses an automatic transmission. If the racecar used a manual transmission, there would be no designation for it. (in most cases) Then that vehicles' number would be 78 SS/JP.

The reason why I'm explaining how these numbers work is to show that in all drag racing, these numbers aren't just put on a vehicle for the heck of it. They have a definite meaning to any spectator familiar with them

and more importantly to the officials overseeing an entire race event. Don't try to learn all these class designations now, if ever. It's not really necessary. Just know the designations for your class or the ones your interested in. The others will eventually seep into your memory as you get familiar with racing.

These class designations are listed with all the class titles at the beginning of the drag racing category of this chapter.

Well, I'm sidetracking myself a bit. The SS/P body must be of American 'make,' including wagons, pick-ups and convertibles. Basically, there is no altering of any kind to the chassis-body.

The engines are open to internal modifications, including some port and polishing to the heads. (in doing that, it means an engine breaths better or takes in more air and therefore performs better) Engine cylinders may be bored out to larger size by .070 inch but must maintain stock in piston-stroke. (up and down piston-distance movement) A standard production carburetor of US make may be internally modified. Any size cam and compression ratio is generally okay.

Any passenger car transmission is permissible up to four forward gears. Any gear that will fit in that stock transmission case is allowed. The clutch type automatic is not allowed. Rear axles rules are open.

Any kind of tire may be used as long as it fits safely within the stock wheelwells. Gasoline only, no additives of any kind. Supercharging is permitted.

Top speeds vary from about 125 to 140 mph.

F.12. B. SUPER STOCK—These 16 classes (32 subclasses) aren't much different to the SS/Production. These are a bit faster in some lighter-weight ratio classes and slower in others. That's because the weight ratios are more diverse, from 6.0 to 17.0 lbs/ci. Unlike SS/P, the cars in this division may be foreign made and more sportscar oriented. Still, they must be factory-produced and showroom-available. (meaning available for sale as new and now to the general public) Of course, no body altering of most kind. The wheelwells may be trimmed somewhat since these are generally smaller vehicles. Internal modifications are also allowed deep in the wheelwell-fenders to accommodate for tires which may be as wide as 14 1/2 inches and 33 inches in diameter, as measured through the complete tire, not just the rim.

The engine modifications are similar to the SS/P except this 16 class division (each further subclassed by manual/automatics) must use the same make and year engine originally installed. Special equipment such as superchargers not factory installed would be prohibited. Otherwise like SS/P, it's okay. No crossbreeding of parts. (chevy engines get only chevy parts, etc)

Top speeds are more diverse, 120 to 145 mph. In comparison, these cars are a bit newer, sportier and faster than most of their SS/P counterparts. But not by much.

F.12. C. MX—No, this is not an intercontinental ballistic missile. (older folks will understand that joke) This is a small 3 class division with 8.50, 11.0 and 12.0 lbs or more weight/ci ratios for nonsupercharged 4 and 6 cylinder coupes, sedans and sportscars.

There are many engine modifications allowed in this division. Internal modifications are about the same as Super Stock and SS/P. In MX though, location of the engine from original stock may be altered, (controlled by a percentage formula) but not by too much. Mixing of vehicle year, make and model is optional in this class.

Transmissions are limited to 5 forward speeds and must remain in a stock location relative to where the engine is. The exception to that are the rear engine cars like VW. These types of cars must use an identical make of engine to the model and be in stock position.

All 3 classes require the use of unaltered gasoline, like all classes in this entire SS subcategory. By the way, all 6 cylinder cars must weigh at least 1700 lbs and 4 "bangers" must weigh a minimum of 1200. (both w/driver)

There is some slight roof chopping modifications allowed on the coupes and sedans, but windshield must retain original angle.

Top speeds are around 125 to 145 mph.

F.12. D. MODIFIED STOCK—These are the most stock of this SS subcategory. These cars are reserved for those no older than about 10 years. They must be of US make, 2 door sedan or passenger vehicles with a 100 inch or over wheelbase. Absolutely no body altering except at the wheelwells. (same exception as in Super Stock)

Engines must retain the same make as the model and remain stock. Displacement is unlimited in the first of the 3 classes. In classes B and C, the ci's are limited to 366 in original-production. (front-wheel drives may be converted over to rear-drive with a minimum wheelbase of 96 inches)

Class A minimum weight is 3350 with an 8.50 pounds per cubic displacement. Stock hemi engines are allowed. Class B and C minimum weights are both 3000 lbs. Class B wt/ci is 9.50 to 10.49 for wedge or canted valve engines. Class C weight ratios are 10.50 or more. These Wedge, Hemi and Canted valve engines is partly what makes this almost stock class Modified. (see glossary in back for those type engine definitions) But those modifications are factory-standard and installed. None of these classes are allowed to supercharge.

Top speed is around 125–140 mph.

F.12. E. SUPERSTOCK/GT—There are 13 classes starting with a 8.50 to 8.99 lb/ci displacement for the first (A) to 14.00 or more in the 13th class, which is M.

This is reserved for cars also not older than 10 years and of US manufacture. They must be two-door sedans or convertibles with any production V-8. This is an extended version of the engines rules in the Super Stock category. That is, the engines must match models in make but their year of production is optional. In addition to the wt/ci ratios, all these cars are performance rated for proper classification. It's these ratings and the fact that all engines are V-8's is what mostly separates this from Super Stocks described in subcategory F.12.B.

Of course, this is also an even stronger class than the SuperStock/Production subcategory. (F.12.A) When I say this is a stronger class, I'm talking in general terms. Some stronger SS and SS/P cars may be faster than the weaker SS/GT cars, but that's only in very few classes. The strongest SS/GT classes are stronger than the strongest SS and SS/P classes.

Top speeds are around 125–145 mph.

There is also a separate (14th) class in SS/GT for front-wheel drive vehicles that have been converted to rear-wheel drive.

F.13. A. STOCK—I said The Modified Stocks were the most stock for the SS category. This is the 2nd most stock category for the entire drag racing category.

There are 62 classes of which 56 are reserved for American-made sportscars. (Class AA, A thru Z, AF thru FF; further subclassed by type of transmission used, manual or automatic) In other words, about half these classes are separated only by the use of an automatic or manual transmission.

In addition to make and model performance ratings, these racers must basically adhere to original factory wt/ci ratios. Actual weight may be adjusted to under 75 or over 150 lbs of that original weight to accommodate a specific class.

The classes start with AA, 7.00 to 7.99 lbs/ci ratios. Then class A thru Z, (except there is no class S) and then AF thru FF. Class FF has the heaviest weight ratio with a 27.50 lbs or heavier/cubic inch engine displacement.

The engines in all these classes must be of the same year and make of the model used. Only factory-standard equipment permissible. Any use of superchargers is prohibited. Some overboring of cylinders is okay along with engine balancing. (for smoother performance: engine less likely to work against itself) There is no lightening, porting and polishing of engine parts. A carburetion system must be correct year, make and model for engine used. No internal modifications here either. No body altering of any kind is allowed. (other than the paint) All chassis-frames are to remain stock.

Tires are limited to the street-types of 12 inches wide and racing slicks a maximum of 9 inches wide. Classes AF thru FF can use only street tires.

Transmissions must be stock but may be beefed-up for added strength. As in many drag racing classes, traction bars are allowed to prevent rearend leaf spring suspension systems from overbuckling and/or breaking under heavy torque pressure. Wheelbase must remain stock.

As you can see, not a whole lot of altering is allowed in this class. That's why it's called what it is.

Top speeds can vary from around 95 to 135 mph.

F.13. B. PURE STOCK—Like the Stocks just covered, and some other drag classes, these Pure Stocks are also street-legal cars. This is obviously the most unaltered and unmodified racer in drag racing. Absolutely no modifications are permitted for added performance, but it is allowed for the purposes of safety.

Like the Stocks, they burn gasoline with no additives. But unlike them, they cannot use racing slicks. There are untold number of classes in this subcategory.

Top speeds vary from 80 to 125 mph, generally.

(NHRA Professional classes)

F. Drag Racing Cars	1.	Top Fuel-TF
F. Drag Racing Cars	2.	Funny Car -FC
F. Drag Racing Cars	3.	Pro Stock-PRO
F. Drag Racing Cars	4.	Pro Stock Motorcycle-PRO (see category K)

(NHRA Amateur classes)

F. Drag Racing Cars	5.	Top Alcohol Dragster-TAD
F. Drag Racing Cars	6.	Top Alcohol Funny Car-TAFC
F. Drag Racing Cars	7.	Competition Eliminator
F. Drag Racing Cars	7A.	Gas Dragsters -/D
F. Drag Racing Cars	7B.	Econo Dragsters -/ED
F. Drag Racing Cars	7C.	Altered and Street Roadsters -/A & /SR
F. Drag Racing Cars	7D.	Econo Altered and Funny Car -/EA
F. Drag Racing Cars	7E.	Super Modified -/SM
F. Drag Racing Cars	8.	SuperStock Eliminator
F. Drag Racing Cars	8A.	Super Stock -/SS
F. Drag Racing Cars	8B.	Super Stock/GT -GT/
F. Drag Racing Cars	8C.	Super Stock/Modified Stock -SS/S
F. Drag Racing Cars	8D.	Super Stock/Modified-SS/M

F. Drag Racing Cars 8E. Super Stock/MX - SS/X

F. Drag Racing Cars 8F. Super Stock/Modified Compact -SS/C

F. Drag Racing Cars 9. Stock Eliminator

F. Drag Racing Cars 9A. Stock Cars-/S

F. Drag Racing Cars 9B. Stock Trucks-T/S

F. Drag Racing Cars 10. Super Comp -S/C

F. Drag Racing Cars 11. Super Gas-S/G

F. Drag Racing Cars 12. Super Street-S/ST

F. Drag Racing Cars ET Handicap Drag Racing Brackets

F. Drag Racing Cars Junior Drag Racing League

Even though I just covered IHRA classes, NHRA is a larger sanctioning body in drag racing. Matter-a-fact, it's one of the largest sanctioning bodies in all of racing, if not the largest. At this printing, it currently is the largest in the world.

To show the difference of the classes from those in IHRA, I would like to cover them briefly. (although I'll probably get long-winded with some) I'll try not to be too specific in most cases, because admittedly, it would become a bit redundant and long-winded for the purposes of this book.

Mostly, the idea here is to show how the NHRA classes are arranged, rather then how they are regulated within the organization. But, I'm not making any promises. I purposely left out some information in the IHRA classes so they could be covered here in NHRA.

NHRA Subcategories 1 through 4; Professional Classes

There are four pro subcategories or divisions. These divisions do not breakdown further into classes. They compete in 18-19 major events held throughout the US for the national championship. (the IHRA pro schedule is usually around 10 to 12 national events)

F.1. TOP FUEL—These are pretty much the same as the IHRA versions. But unlike them, they must have a minimum weight of at least 2000 lbs with the driver included at the end of a run. (and without most of their fuel)

F.2. FUNNY CAR—Simply put, this machine is a form of Top Fuel racer, but with a one-piece silhouette-styled body. That body must somewhat emulate a 2-door coupe or sedan, usually, but not always of American manufacture. Funny cars have a shorter wheelbase than the Top Fuelers, at 100 to 125 inches. Their minimum weigh is heavier though, at 2275 lbs, including driver, but minus fuel.

All Top Fuel and Funny Cars in both organizations must use automotive type racing tires that are actually slicks as previously explained on pages 91 and 92. They are to be a maximum of 18 inches wide and 118 inches in circumference. The tires are specially-made for these two types of classes, including the Pro Stocks coming up next.

F.3. PRO STOCK—These are the NASCAR-looking 2-door coupe or sedan machines that cannot be any older than 5 years. They have the large engine ram-air scoops. Maximum engine ci's is also 500, but they must burn only automotive grade fuel. They must weigh at least 2350 lbs with the driver. With some allowable alterations, their wheelbase must exceed 99 inches.

Tires must be the automotive-type slicks and must fit inside the stock wheelwells. The tires also have to clear the inside of the fenders by 3 inches.

IHRA and NHRA Pro Stockers are about the same.

F.4. PRO STOCK BIKE—(covered in category K)

NHRA Subcategories 5 through 12; Amateur Classes

In here are eight subcategories or divisions. The first two subcategories are considered more as Pro-Sportsman. Some of these subcategories breakdown further into divisions and classes. The amateurs compete both nationally and regionally in 7 geographical areas of the entire US, consisting of about 60 total race events annually. The IHRA has a similar setup.

F.5. TOP ALCOHOL DRAGSTER—Don't confuse these with Top Fuel Dragsters. Top Fuelers burn the much more potent nitromethane. Obviously, this class burns alcohol-based fuel.

Actually, nitromethane, like diesel, is an even slower burning fuel than alcohol and other fuels. How can a slower burning fuel be stronger? Simply put, nitromethane releases oxygen as it burns. That's where you'll hear the term 'oxygen-bearing fuel' come from. That means while it creates its own oxygen during the burn process, it therefore has more of it to burn. Nitromethane pushes the piston in an engine all the way down to its stroke for maximum power. Most other fuels run out of air before they can do that. Unspent fuel gets wasted and blown out the exhaust system. So while it's slower burning, it burns in its entirety. Matter a fact, it's still burning fuel as it's blown out of the exhaust pipes. Couple that with this type of race machines shorter exhaust system and you should understand why the flames are prancing out the exhaust pipes like they are on Top Fuelers. (but not necessarily with gas-powered rail dragsters) This is why nitromethane-burning dragsters are called Top Fuel, . . . they burn the top stuff!

Nitromethane is also pretty expensive. It costs around 35 to 40 bucks a gallon. The pro dragsters burn about 7 to 9 gallons per quarter-mile run. Why doesn't everyone including the general public use nitromethane? Well, even if it came cheap, you wouldn't want to use it in your street car. It's poisonous and also very corrosive to most metals. Even those who use it in racing don't usually do so at its full strength. It's mixed with methane. After a race or run, the fuel system in a racer has to be flushed to prevent it from deteriorating metal away.

For you befuddled "mechanical engineers" out there, diesel fuel is also slow burning. The engines it burns in are much slower rpm units with longer piston-strokes. The cylinders in these engines have a better chance to pack in more oxygen and use higher compression ratios, even minus a turbocharger.

Well, despite all that, all kind of internal engine combinations are used with Top Alcohol Dragsters. Some of these use two engines. Some are supercharged, others are allowed the use of different fuels, including nitrous oxide (not nitromethane) or methanol. Yes, nitrous oxide is basically the same stuff your dentist uses to eliminate pain or to put you into outer space with.

Minimum weight is determined by several combinations, but are usually between 1450 and 1550 lbs. The lightest vehicles are 1.8 lbs of weight per cubic engine displacement through 9 other (called) weight breaks, the heaviest at a 4.40 lbs/ci. These dragsters may have a shorter wheelbase at 150 inches compared to Top Fuelers, but have the same maximum at 300 inches.

These usually top-out at around 245–255 mph.

F.6. TOP ALCOHOL FUNNY CAR—These are about an exact replica of the Pro versions, but they burn alcohol or methanol. (wood alcohol) They are allowed a larger sized engine in cubic inches, but only produce in the neighborhood of 2000 horsepower compared to the nitro-burners 3500-5000 range. (565 ci engine maximum, compared to Top Fuel's 500 ci's) They may even be lighter than their counterpart at 1800 lbs minimum but have to weigh at least 4.10 lbs/ci engine displacement. Still, they're not always as quick as the Top Alcohol Dragster, but can get consistently in the 230–250 mph range.

F.7. COMPETITION ELIMINATOR—There are 5 divisions (A thru E) in this subcategory of drag racing. This is a fast amateur division with speeds ranging from 160 to 190 mph. The first is:

F.7. A.–GAS DRAGSTER—There are 7 classes of Top Fuel-styled or rail type racecars. A thru G, are determined by weight/engine size ratios. The lightest starts at 3.40 lbs/ci to the last which is 8.40 lbs/ci in size. All engines, except class F in some cases, must use only two valves per cylinder. Each racer is allow one piston-type engine and the use of gasoline only.

Rear tire rules are open, to automotive type tread or slicks in most of these Competition Eliminator divisions.

F.7. B.–ECONO DRAGSTER—Here there is 6 classes (A thru F) of gasoline only, non-supercharged, single-engine, rail-type dragsters. The lightest weight ratio starts in class A at 3.40 lbs/ci and must be at least 1350 lbs. Class F is 6.25 wt ratio and may be as light as 950 lbs total minimum weight.

These are relatively more economical to race, thus they're titled as such.

F.7. C.–ALTERED & STREET ROADSTERS—These are 15 StockCar-looking classes, AA, AAT, BB, BBT, A thru K, in the Altered division which are indexed by not only weight/engine ratios, but also type of pumps, (super or turbochargers) number of engine cylinders and number of valves for each of those cylinders. Their wheelbase must measure between 90 and 125 inches. Their single, piston-type engine must burn gasoline grade fuel only.

The Altereds are called such because of what's done to their bodies, or more specifically to their roofs. Some roofs are chopped down to enhance aerodynamics. Their quarterpanels or wheelwells may also be enlarged to accommodate the use of larger-than-normal tires. This is the class where you'll find 1/2 ton pick-up trucks, Rancheros and El Caminos racing also.

These may be stockcar-appearing racing cars, but that doesn't mean they're late or of recent manufacture make.

The Street Roadsters which are the pre-1937 unaltered body styles, are divided into 4 classes, A thru D. No supercharging here. Determined by weight ratios and type of transmission, (automatic or manual) all classes here are limited to one 4-barrel type carburetor of various sizes according to their class. Wheelbase must be at least 90 inches and remain in stock manufacture position.

There is also the regular Roadsters which do not have to adhere to pre-1937 body requirements.

Tires are to be automotive type tread or slicks.

F.7. D.–ECONO ALTERED & FUNNY CAR —Here there are 5 classes (A thru E) for non-supercharged, gas burning, single engine machines which also may be of the older and more radical-looking type, but not all the time. These also have the chopped roofs and the enlarged wheelwells. This is also where you may see some 1/2 ton pick-ups, Rancheros or El Caminos competing at.

But, all the machines here must use automatic transmissions. These aren't too much different than the regular Altereds. They have heavier weight ratios, which in this case means they're slower and more economical to race.

Both Econo Altered and Funny Cars have a maximum of 125 inch wheelbases, but a minimum base of 90 and 100 inches for the Altered and Funny Cars respectively.

F.7. E.–SUPER MODIFIED—There are 6 classes, A thru F, for nonsupercharged 2-door or hardtop passenger, gas burning vehicles which are a 1967 model year or later. Minimum wheelbase must be at least 96 inches. No crossbreeding of engines is allowed. They must match with manufacturers body make and year. These racecars tend to be larger. The smallest weight ratio starts at 8.50 lbs/ci in class A to a 11.50 ratio in class F.

These are called Modified because several internal alterations to the engine is allowed. Some external ones are permitted also. One example is the use of duel four-barrel carburation instead of the usual one unit 4-barrel.

Rear tires must be the treaded-automotive type and not to exceed 14 1/2 inches wide when new and 15 1/2 inches after use, regardless of wear.

F.8. SUPER STOCK ELIMINATOR—Now I'm back to another subcategory with divisions. There are six divisions here, (A thru F) breaking further down to 80 classes of racecars. Just about all of these classes do not allow super or turbocharging. Top-end speeds in this division are around 115–140 mph for the slower classes to 145–150 for the faster machines. The first is:

F.8. A. SUPER STOCK—This is a Stock-Car-appearing division reserved for 18 classes (A thru P, SS/X & SS/XA) for foreign, domestics and sportscars. The cars in these classes are all performance-rated by the NHRA since they're all so simular. What additionally separates these are their minimum weight/cubic inch engine ratios. The lightest, starting with class A, must have at least 6.00 lbs of vehicle weight per cubic inch of engine displacement. The heaviest, class P, starts at the 17.00 lb weight ratio.

Each classed model must have at least a total of 50 units built and available to the general public to be eligible for competition. So this would exclude prototypes automobiles. These are not Stock (as opposed to Superstock here) because some relatively minor performance-enhancing modifications are allowed, such as: overboring of engine cylinders of .070 (70/1000th, not quite 1/10 of an inch); replacement of pistons; minor rear axle and suspension relocation; widening of rear wheelwells for larger tires, which can not be slicks; minor adding or subtracting of car weight; and the installation of no more that 5-inch high ram-air engine hood scoops.

Unlike many pro-classed and Modified/Eliminators (IHRA category 8.A. thru G.) and NHRA category 8.A thru F, just about all sportsman or amateur-classed vehicles require their drivers to operate from the stock automobile-seat position.

Before I forget, I need to clear up something. Amateur drag racers, (or any kind of racer) in most cases, do not have to worry about qualifying to enter an eliminator series. That's because everyone in amateur racing must be given a chance to compete. Otherwise this would discourage beginners. So drag racing at the amateur level gives everyone a chance to do so by using handicap starts. But don't confuse this with Bracket Racing. Bracket Racing is mostly for amateur using street-legal cars. Drag competition cars are built to certain specifications for a particular class. If they must qualify, then fail to do so, that would definitely discourage them from continuing. Bracket racers would also think twice about building or buying their own specifically-classed race vehicles for future use. Who wants to invest big bucks and time on a drag car if a competitor isn't sure they can qual-

ify it in an eliminator series of drag races? So, unlike the pros, all amateurs are given the chance to compete.

F.8. B. SUPER STOCK/GT—These are very close to, but slightly larger or heavier versions of Super Stocks just covered. There are 13 classes for manual-transmission cars and 13 more for automatic-equipped machines. (classes A thru M; and A thru M followed by the letter 'A', meaning automatic trans)

These cars must be no older than 15 years from factory production. They can use only V-8 configured engines for their particular model as originally offered from the factory. But they can use a different year-produced engine.

All classes must weigh at least 2670 lbs with driver. Weight/engine ratios start at 8.00 lbs in class A to 14.00 lbs in class M.

No racing slicks are allowed.

F.8. C. SUPER STOCK/MODIFIED STOCK —There are only three classes here of 8.50, 9.50 and 10.50 minimum weight/cubic inch ratios. Cars must be no older than the 1967 production-year with at least 500 unit built per year and available to the public.

Not much can be altered in the body, wheelbase, which must be at least 97 inches, drivetrain and even the engine to a certain point. Still, some engine head porting and oversizing of valves is permitted.

No race slicks are allowed.

F.8. D. SUPER STOCK/MODIFIED—The Super Stock/Modified Stock class title just covered sounds like a confliction in terms doesn't it? Not so here! There is more freedom to alter equipment here, but it's not obvious even to the veteran driver unless they read the rule book carefully. Still, this is a quicker class than the the SS/Modified Stock. That's mostly due to the carburation rules. SS/Modifieds can use two 4-barrel carbs. (sometimes called "duel-quads")

There are 7 classes, A thru G, with weight ratios starting at 7.50 for class A to 12.50 for class F. Class G is a 10.50 ratio with different engine rules.

Race slicks are allowed, which must fit

within the fenders. Inner wheelwells may be altered though, to accommodate larger slicks.

F.8. E. SUPER STOCK/MX—Here is 4 classes (A, B, C) for nonsupercharged cars with minimum weights of 1200 lbs for 4-cylinder and 1700 lbs for 6-cylinder engines. There is a fourth class (D) for a 15.00 lb/ci machine with a super or twin-turbocharged powerplant.

Wheelbases are stock but must be at least 90 inches. The exception is those vehicles in MX which use a cars original nonsupercharged engine. So some engine relocation and/or crossbreeding is allow here. (crossbreeding example: a chevy engine in a ford car, or visa-versa, etc)

This is another class where some chopping of the body for aerodynamic purposes is permitted, in this case the roof.

Aftermarket race slicks are allowed, but can't extend more than 2/3 of that width outside the cars original-designed body fenders.

F.8. F. SUPER STOCK/MODIFIED COMPACT—This has 6 classes (A thru F) for street-legal, originally equipped (car) engines, which may include the rotary type. This is a diverse division which allow several minor internal engine modifications in classes A, B and C. Classes D and E are more stock in comparison, but still have several engine modifications.

The first 5 classes are for larger cars with starting minimum weight ratios of 15.00 to 18.00 lbs. Class F is a smaller, 165 ci, 4-cylinder racer with a minimum wt of 2400 and 2550 lbs for automatic and manual transmissions respectively.

All wheelbases must remain stock. No racing slicks are allowed. Tire width may extend 2 inches outside the cars original fender line.

F.9. STOCK ELIMINATOR—This is an 80 class NHRA (2) division subcategory for stock cars and trucks, based on ET handicap starts.

F.9. A. STOCK CARS—There are 60 classes here for 1960 or newer model-year, factory-production vehicles which are performance-rated by the NHRA. The cars in this class must meet production numbers exceeding 500 units per year and also be available to the general public.

These classes are split between manual and automatic transmissions. In addition to performance rating, the lowest vehicle minimum weight/engine ratios are 8.00 in class A to the heaviest in class HF at 27.50 lbs. (class designations are A thru W, minus the letter S, for a total of 22 classes and AF thru HF for 8 more, totaling 30 class for types using a manual trans; double that number to 60, including racers using the automatic type of transmission)

Very few alterations to anything is permitted. Straight gasoline must be used and street tires with full tread patterns must not exceed 12 inches in width. As an alternative, 9-inch wide slicks may be used with certain restrictions.

Top-end speeds vary widely from about 80 to 130 mph.

F.9. B. STOCK TRUCKS—These are limited to 20 classes of 1/2-ton trucks that are no older than the 1980 production year. There are 10 classes, A thru J, for manual trans and 10 more for automatics that are A thru J also, but followed by the letter or designation 'A'.

Obviously, like the class title implies, not mush altering is allowed, although some ground-effects packages and bed covers may be used. Tailgates must be up. This is an important aerodynamics rule. Drivers of these vehicles would probably like to see that rule eliminated because closed gates create a lot of wind drag. The bed covers help eliminate that.

F.10. SUPER COMP—This is a single class subcategory for Dragsters, Funny Cars and factory-experimental cars which run in the 8.90 second or slower bracket. Anything faster than that means they cannot race this class. This also helps discourage overequipping a vehicle and helps keep the costs in check.

Any piston-type engine, with or without super or turbochargers, depending on the fuel used, is permitted. Some cars in this class use natural gas, propane and even diesel. No nitrous oxide is allowed.

Minimum weights are 1350 lbs with driver except with 4 and 6-cylinder cars, which must be at least 1000 lbs. Wheelbase must be at least 90 inches. Tire are basically open to driver choice.

Top-end speeds can be around 140 to 153 mph, with some reaching an occasional 160.

F.11. SUPER GAS—This is another single class subcategory which runs in the 9.90 second or slower bracket. Patterned like Super Comp, anything quicker than 9 & 9/10ths seconds in the quarter-mile means they have to race in another class.

This class is for full-bodied coupe or sedan-type cars, which allow some body chopping and/or altering. Pick-ups, Vans, Roadsters, Sports Cars, and Panel Trucks are also allowed. Open-wheeled Altereds, Dragsters Funny Cars and Motorcycles are not allowed.

These have the same basic engine, fuel rules as Super Comp, but are heavier, with a minimum 2100 lbs weight with driver, except 4-cylinder vehicles which must weigh at least 1200 lbs. Wheelbase must measure between 90 and 125 inches in most of these classes.

This class of racer is allowed the use of racing slicks.

Top-end speeds vary from generally around 120 to 140 mph.

F.12. SUPER STREET—This is the final single-class bracket machine which competes in the 10.90 or slower time standard or bracket. Almost an exact replica of the Super Gas class, these machines are heavier. Minimum weights are 2800 lbs for 8-cylinder engines, 2000 for 6-cylinders and 1200 for 4-cylinder or rotary powered vehicles.

This is the only class in NHRA which does not compete nationally. They only run in regional events. They top-out at around 80-120 mph.

F.–NHRA ET HANDICAP DRAG RACING BRACKETS—(this is covered on pages 88-90), NHRA format is about identical to IHRA.

F.–(NHRA) JUNIOR DRAG RACING LEAGUE—The NHRA conducts this drag racing program for kids 8 years of age and older. Parents, don't panic just yet. Matter-a-fact, don't panic at all. This is an extremely scaled-down version which is both safe and economical. It's designed to create an opportunity for the youngsters to race with their peers in near-replica, 225 lb minimum-weight, 90 to 150 inch wheelbased dragsters like the pros drive. (in looks)

The competition is structured to be ran in Elapsed Time brackets on a dial-your-own or preset format which incorporates the break-out rules. These rules or formats will sometimes vary between tracks.

There are 3 classes: 1. Minor; for ages 8 and 9 with ET's of 12.90 or slower. 2. Major; age 10 or older with no ET limits and a dial-your-own basis with break-outs simular to the Minor class. 3. Open; also age 10 and over with Pro Starts and no break-out rules.

All three classes race on a eight-mile strip. The engines are restricted to one per car, nonsuper or turbocharged, any sized carburetor, a 5 horsepower Briggs & Stratton 'make' engine which must be unaltered and 'as cast' condition at the block. Some porting, polishing of stock or aftermarket heads and deck-machining is okay. Oversized cams and valves are also permitted as long as they remain in stock position.

Open class engines are restricted to a maximum bore or cylinder size (width) of 2.6680 inches and a stroke (up and down movement) of 2.4430. Gas, alcohol or gasohol is okay, but the use of nitromethane and nitrous oxide is strictly prohibited.

Like Go-Karts, these vehicles are chain or belt-driven. One centrifical, dry-type clutch (like those used on most Go-Karts) are used. No gear-type transmissions are permitted.

Rear tires must be of pneumatic (air inflated) type with a minimum 18 inches in diameter and 7 1/2 inches wide.

It is not mandatory for these youngsters to wear firesuits but they must wear full-sleeve shirts and trousers which are abrasion-resistant, including gloves. They also must wear a neck collar or donut to help prevent whiplash injuries from accidents or rollovers.

Is this a rail dragster or an off-road vehicle? In fact, it's both. This "sand digger" is just one class of many off-road and local racing organizations in the US and the world. Note the paddled rear tires? They literally dig in the ground to enhance traction. Also there are races in the mud called "mud boggs." Usually these are off-road, closed-course, non--drag events held in specially prepared or watered terrain. (If not provided for though natural causes by mother nature) Those race machines resemble the dune-buggy type off-road class, ATVs or super 1600's in the SCORE/HDRA series. These locally and sometimes privately sanctioned events are much shorter in duration and sometimes use a much shorter course.

They also must incorporate a 5-point, 1 1/2 inch wide driver and arm-restraint system like those used in all of racing.

NOTE—A 5-point driver-restraint series of belts (or system) are those with 5 half-belts (each at least 1 1/2 inches wide, but usually 2 1/2 to 3 inches in width) which are bolted in strategic locations near the drivers seat, shoulders and groin areas. Of those 5 belts, 2 wrap over each shoulder, two around each hip or the waist area and one between the legs and up lightly against the crotch. (to prevent diving under those belts in a frontal impact) They all come together and lock near the drivers belly-button. They are all length-adjustable for proper tightness. These belts keep the driver securely planted in the seat during accidents and high speed turns. This system also helps all race drivers to more accurately read the behavior or handling characteristics of the racecar at high speeds. ("driving by the seat of your pants" isn't just a cute little saying. The more firmly a driver is planted in that seat, the more accurately they can read what's happening at the racecars chassis)

Well, back to the Jr racers. These competitors must also wear a full-face helmet or an open-faced one with goggles. The helmets aren't just any cheap "5 and 10 cent variety store" type either. They must be bonafied Snell standard 80 to 95 rated quality.

I paid $350.00 for a Simpson Super Bandit helmet with the ventilation system. Not cheap, but then look what goes into it! (yeah, . . . yeah, . . . I know, . . . some of my pals would say the same thing, and then ask "why'd ya buy it?" Well, . . . I've been called a few things in my life, but no one ever called me cheap when it came to protecting "thee ol hairy, sphere-shaped computer" planted on top of my shoulders)

Lastly, like all racers, these youngsters must use arm-restraint belts. These are also strategically located to prevent an unconscience driver's arms from flailing outside the confines of the cockpit during accidents and rollovers. This helps prevent broken, crushed and/or lacerated arms and hands.

This is very fast growing program. It has some pretty good incentives too. Among them is a college fund. This program is conducted at the regional level with points accrued from a drivers home region towards an invitation to the national championship. The 500 or so competitors who reach the national championship round automatically receive $200.00 towards college. "Big deal" you say? The national champ receives a cool $5000.00. The runner-up gets $2000.00, semi-finalist gets $1000.00, quarter-finalist gets $500.00 and eighth-finalist receive $300.00. A national 'team championship' is worth $10,000.00, which is to be divided equally among the team members. (held in a noninterest bearing trust fund towards the college of their choice) That's nothing to take lightly!

This program has a bi-monthly magazine called the 'Jr. Drag Racer'.

This concludes Category F on Drag racing vehicles. Coming up next are the Off-Road racers of Category G. As you look further into the various categories, you'll notice some race machines fit into more than one category. No, those are not errors. For instants, Categories K & L, Motorbikes and RaceTrucks, can also be a part of Gategory G, Off-Road or Gategory H, Endurance. This is, at least in part, what makes some categories what they are, a mixture of other categories.

G. OFF-ROAD RACERS

I STADIUM RACERS

G. Off-Road	IA.	Grand National Sport Trucks (now called Thunder Trucks)
G. Off-Road	IB.	Ultra Stock
G. Off-Road	IC.	Super1600
G. Off-Road	ID.	Superlites
G. Off-Road	IE.	4 Wheel All-Terrain Vehicles
G. Off-Road	IF.	Ultracross 250 CC Motorcycles
G. Off-Road	IG.	Unlimited Single Seaters (No longer raced)

II & III CLOSED SHORT/OPEN LONG DISTANCE

G. Off-Road II & III	A.	Class 1 (Buggy)
G. Off-Road II & III	B.	Class 2 (Buggy)
G. Off-Road II & III	C.	Class 1-2/1600 (Buggy)
G. Off-Road II & III	D.	Class 3 (Truck)
G. Off-Road II & III	E.	Class 4 (Truck)
G. Off-Road II & III	F.	Class 5 (Baja)
G. Off-Road II & III	G.	Class 5/1600 (Baja)
G. Off-Road II & III	H.	Class 6 (Sedan)
G. Off-Road II & III	I.	Class 7 (Truck)
G. Off-Road II & III	J.	Class 7-S (Truck)
G. Off-Road II & III	K.	Class 7/4x4 (Truck)
G. Off-Road II & III	L.	Class 8 (Truck)
G. Off-Road II & III	M.	Class 9 (Buggy)
G. Off-Road II & III	N.	Class 10 (Buggy)
G. Off-Road II & III	O.	Class 11 (VW Sedan-Baja)
G. Off-Road II & III	P.	Mini-Mag (Sedan)
G. Off-Road II & III	Q.	Class 20 (Motorcycle)
G. Off-Road II & III	R.	Class 21 (Motorcycle)
G. Off-Road II & III	S.	Class 22 (Motorcycle)
G. Off-Road II & III	T.	Class 24 (ATV)
G. Off-Road II & III	U.	Class 25 (ATV)
G. Off-Road II & III	V.	Class 30 (Motorcycle)
G. Off-Road II & III	W.	Class 34 (Buggy)
G. Off-Road II & III	X.	Class 40 (Motorcycle)
G. Off-Road II & III	Y.	Class 50 (Motorcycle)
G. Off-Road II & III		SCORE International Trophy Truck Series

There are three subcategories or types of off-road racing in the United States. They are:

(I) Short Course Enclosed, (Stadium Racing)
(II) Closed Short Distance
(III) Open Long Distance (Desert)

I. STADIUM RACING is sanctioned by MTEG. (Mickey Thompson Entertainment Group) This kind of racing is relatively new. It was founded in 1979 by the late racing innovator and numerous record-holder, Mickey Thompson. It was one of the fastest growing sports in the US, but has curtailed a bit. There is plans of taking this sport into other countries. Meanwhile, going into the 90's, there were 7 classes of competition offered (now 6) in a 10-event series called the Off-Road Championship Gran Prix. Also, MTEG features AMA (American Motorcyclist Association) sanctioned stadium motorcycle racing called the Camel Supercross Series. Plans also call for the development of a stadium-style dirt drag race series. Other classes or support events are also being considered.

Initially, most of the races were held in Southern California's larger football stadiums such as the Rose Bowl, Jack Murphy Stadium and the LA Coliseum. These events have also moved eastward to such places like Denver's Mile-High Stadium, the Houston Astrodome, the RCA Dome in Indianapolis, the Superdome in New Orleans, the Pontiac Silverdome and northward to the Kingdome in Seattle. Each stadium is setup to emulate its own rough hilly baja-type dirt course. No two courses are setup in the exact same way.

Stadium racing was partially conceived to make off-road racing more accessible to spectators and television. (TNN & ESPN) It made it a more marketable commodity for the support groups. This has increased its popularity, but its also increased sanctioning and setup costs. Because of that, race fields will have to be high in numbers, not to mention the spectator base, for continued future support. Only time will tell if this venue can continue.

To prepare the stadiums for this kind of competition takes about 3 days and 110 to $130,000. The fields themselves are not tore up, but protected. Around 700 truckloads (12-13,000 tons) of dust-free, clay-based dirt is hauled in.

II. CLOSED SHORT DISTANCE off-road racing is a longer and more open-spaced version of the nonstadium type. It uses a course setup for a mile to a mile and a half.

These courses are usually setup within an oval racetracks infield area. The 24–25 classes of 2 and 4-wheeled racers that participate in the long-distance desert races also race this class, but with a more limited schedule.

This particular form of racing is suffering a bit from a lack of finances, but those in the administration of off-road racing feel it will eventually stage a comeback. Meanwhile, going into the 90's, scheduling is very limited. Of the 10 or so Desert Racing Series events, (to be covered next) only two races of this short-distance variety will be held. On top of that, these 2 races will not count for points towards a season championship. This form of off-road racing is sanctioned by SCORE. (Southern California Off-Road Enterprises) They merged with HDRA (High-Desert Racing Association) in 1985 to form SCORE/HDRA. (now called Short Course Off-Road Enterprises)

III. OPEN LONG COURSE racing is the actual desert races we hear of where some of the participants are more well known in other forms of racing. Names like Rick Mears from Indy Car racing pops into my mind. This is where he got established. Rick's brother, Roger, is well established in this kind of racing. Ivan 'the Ironman' Stewart, Walker Evans has been around a while too. Parnelli Jones also did this a while back.

This kind of racing got started about 1967 and is sanctioned by HDRA, which is now SCORE/HDRA. Other sanctioning bodies such as SODA sanctions these events also. Several locally-based organizations, including those in other forms of racing, sanction Desert racing.

The largest off-road organization is SCORE/HDRA. They usually have about a 10 race series (8 are these long distance Desert races; 2 are short-course) which features the prestigious BAJA 1000 (the longest event) which draw drivers from all over the world. Other events are around 250 to 500 miles in length. Whatever the distance, it is racing through some of the murderous desert and forest terrain you'll ever want to compete in.

This form of racing is against the clock because obviously not everyone can possibly start at the same time. There are several 'races within races' because there are several classes. Fields range from about 175 to 200 racing vehicles. Several 'checkpoints' insure the drivers stay on course and are accounted for. About 40 to 50% of the field can figure on not finishing because of vehicle breakdowns. This is also a class which will see several age groups in addition to an unusually high number of women.

The following 7 Stadium racing classes will be briefly described. There isn't much point in getting too detailed when there are only 7 different classed vehicles. The Superlites and Super 1600 do look a bit alike, but they will be properly distinguished to avoid any confusion. The last class, Unlimited Single-Seaters was eliminated, even though it's still described in this section.

G.I. A–G Short Course Enclosed (Stadium Racers)

G.I. A. GRAND NATIONAL SPORT TRUCKS—(now called the THUNDER TRUCK series) This is the main class for Stadiums racers. They're open to both foreign and domestic trucks with a maximum 3000 cc engines. (3.00 liters) Plans for the future involve a new 'spec' truck class called 'Thunder & Lightning'.

Thunder Trucks are modified but limited to 6 cylinder engines. These purpose-built pick-up styled trucks are not allowed super or turbocharging. Wheelbase must be measured between 101 and 119.5 inches for those marketed as mini or mid-sized production two-wheel drives. The truck models used must be in full production of at least 5000 units per year and available for sale to the general public. There can be no alterations to the body with some minor exceptions at the wheelwells. (suspensions are subject to more movement because of the very rough terrain they race on; therefore they need more room to keep the metal inside those wheelwells from tearing up the tires)

The suspensions cannot be 'computer-active', (artificially-enhanced smoothness) but can be beefed-up. They can be either manually or mechanically adjustable. Those suspension rules are optional at both the front and the back.

Even though the courses are very short, these powerful vehicles can quickly accelerate to over 100 mph. But that's not what makes them necessarily a winner. These trucks have to be agile like a cat and as tough as a bull. The driver of these vehicles have to be pretty tough too. They also have to possess enough talent to keep these machines on their wheels while trying to win.

Some of the main or popular makes represented are: Chevy, Ford, Toyota, Jeep, Dodge, Mazda, Mitsubishi and Nissan. Generally, the events itinerary for these machines are a couple of heat races of around eight to ten laps and a feature of about twelve laps.

The tires are limited to a width of 10.2 inches for DOT (Dept of Transportation) approved types for light trucks. Engines may be set back according to specific guidelines to help balance the vehicle. No crossbreeding of engine and model manufacture is allowed. Roll cages are mandatory. Transmissions rules are open. Weight must be at least 2550 lbs.

The only kind of fuel permitted is straight unaltered gasoline as made readily available on the streets to the public.

G.I. B. ULTRA STOCK—These are the sleek, somewhat stockcar looking, all-terrain sport racers. They are by far the most automotive looking of these seven classes.

Started in 1985, these racecars utilize a body replica of no older than 3 years for coupe, sedan or GT style production. In addition, these must also be two-wheel front or rear drives and made in at least 5000 units/yr and offered for sale to the public. The word "replica" used just a few sentences back is not loosely used. Actually, most of the racer bodies emulate a certain make and model enough to be recognizable to the race fans. This also keeps the factories interested, which helps financial support. Anyway, these incorporate a narrowed-down, sleek-looking stockcar, while at the same time retaining the wild and frenzied capacity of a true off-road racer. The name of this class is enough alone to justify its physical appearance. Ultra is a term meaning "beyond or ahead of its time". These are stock appearing, but a bit more futuristic looking. (one could say the word stock is even more abused than it usually is in racing)

This racer has pretty much the same kind of regulations the GN Sport Trucks do. Engine modifications are very similar but must be limited to uncharged types of 2500 cc or 152.5 ci, gasoline burning, 6 cylinder types. Like the trucks, fuel injection is permitted.

Body, chassis, suspension and roll cage rules are also very much alike. The minimum wheelbase is shorter at 94 to 106 inches and minimum weight is lighter at 1850 lbs. Tire rules are identical. Unlike the trucks 67 inch maximum allowable track (wheelbase width) the Ultra Stocks are limited to 74 inches.

G.I. C. SUPER 1600—These are the light and very agile single seat off-road machines which could best be described as MTEG's answer to formula racing. The fastest of the current 6 classes, these are engineered more specifically for toughness. It's not all that unusual to see one do a complete rollover back on its wheels and keep right on going. One reason for that is they're not required to carry very much unnecessary equipment like the Ultra Stock and Sport Trucks are.

They have no doors, stock bumpers,

This is the super 1600 racing here in a MTEG stadium event. This style of off-road vehicle is popular in SCORE/HDRA desert events, such as the famous Baja 1000 and in many local off-road organizations. These aren't essentially "dune buggies" to most off-road enthusiasts, but they're close. (That 'semantics' thing again). Many local clubs don't require paneling on their sides, top, and hood areas. Thus, they're usually classed as dune buggies. Many dune buggies are strictly 'recreational vehicles.'

dashboards, fenders, heavy flooring, etc. They are essentially a roll cage with wheels and an engine. That's oversimplifying it a bit, but that's for educational purposes. Like the previous two classes, suspensions and transmissions are optional but must have an operational reverse gear. Engines are limited to normally-aspirated, 1650 cc, piston-types with no fuel injection. No more than 4 valves per cylinder is permitted. A maximum of two carbs for air-cooled engines and only one for the water-cooled types are permitted.

These baja-types are almost identical to those raced in the desert events held by SCORE/HDRA. These also have a sheet metal or fiberglass paneling around the entire cage to help ward off flying mud or debris. The tire rules are identical to the Trucks and Ultra Stocks. Minimum weight is 1300 lbs.

These rear-engine racers also compete in the same format as the Sport Trucks do. After qualifying they run a couple of races before the feature. Understand, each car doesn't run two heats. The entire race field is split in what is usually two groups. Then a designated number of front finishers from each group goes on to the feature race for their class. This is done because there is usually too many racecars entered to race at once. This same format is used with the classes that have large fields. The feature race is usually 20 cars from the top 10 of each heat. Speed is irrelative, but they can go 125–30 mph.

G. I. D. SUPERLITE—These were originally known as Odyssey when this class was introduced in 1984. They appear much like the Super 1600, but are scaled down in size

These are in the same situation at the MTEG super 1600s. They're racing in a stadium event, but are also very popular at the local level and in some high level pro desert races. These are superlites in the picture, but some local organization may call them 4 wheel ATVs. They are obviously smaller than the ultra stocks, super 1600s or Baja type vehicles.

and power. Actually, they're a larger version of a rollcaged, 4-wheeled ATV, with sort of the SprintCar look. Sizewise, their wheelbase is limited to 65 1/2 inches. Minimum dry weight is 475 lbs, quite a bit lighter than the Super 1600's 1300 lbs.

Their 360 cc engines are limited to the single-cylinder, normally-aspirated types with a maximum 4 values/cylinder. They are open to some minor modifications. No crankcase induction is allowed. (that's pretty much the kind of carburetion used in small 2-cycle engines)

These racers are belt-driven with centrifugal clutches similar to those on Go-Karts and small 3, 4-wheel ATV's. A roll cage is not only mandatory, but quite necessary since, like the Ultra Stock and Super 1600's, it is part of the chassis. (or at least acts in that manner)

Tire sizes are smaller then the Ultras and Supers, at about 13 inches diameter, but are a bit wider. No paddle-type or studded tires are allowed.

These 2-stroke powered machines seem to be the favorite with women and kids. Top speeds are almost 100 mph.

G. I. E. 4 WHEEL ALL TERRAIN VEHICLE —These are ridden, not driven. If you can't understand what's meant by that, you will in a few seconds. They are sort of a hybrid of the Superlites but even smaller and less powerful.

These vehicles are susceptible to what seems as exaggerated driving techniques. But it's necessary to maintain a competitive edge. They are driven hard into corners at high speed and turned with a slingshot-style much in the same manner as dirt SprintCars. The slightest dirtmounds can throw them into the air surprisingly high. It's necessary the rider be in excellent physical shape. They are forced to use their arms and legs as one of the shock absorptions systems and must constantly shift their weights to keep from flipping over. That wouldn't be a good situation because these machines do not have roll cages or bars. This is what I meant by "ridden". The rider has literally more physical impact on vehicle dynamics or behavior.

The minimum weight must be 330 lbs,

dry. (minus fuel and rider) Engine rules are practically the same as the Superlite, but smaller at 250 cc's. Tire sizes are also identical. Suspensions are free, but like all MTEG classes, they cannot be computer enhanced. Transmissions or gearboxes are also open.

These machines get good factory support from Honda, Suzuki, Yamaha and Kawasaki. They can reach about 70-80 mph on the stadium courses, although they are capable of going faster under different conditions.

The 3-Wheel ATV's were eliminated from competition in 1986, mostly because they were outlawed in this country, which hurt their factory support.

G. I. F. ULTRACROSS 250 CC MOTORCY-CLES—This is a drastic change in vehicle type, from four to two wheels. Started in 1987, this is the youngest class, which also has good factory support. Obviously by the name, the engines are limited to single-cylinder, normally-aspirated 250 cc's with a limit of 4 values minus crankcase induction.

Like all the MTEG classes, the internal engine modifications are limited to strengthening, polishing, porting, balancing, cam profile and change of pistons.

These motorcycles must be chain-driven.

Unlike all the other classes, the suspension must remain relatively stock, but measure 50 to 60 inches at the wheelbase. Minimum weight must be at least 216 lbs, dry. Tires cannot incorporate metal studs, be shaved or grooved. They have to be production types that are available to all competitors. Minimum wheel diameter is 17 inches with a maximum of 5 inches in width. (spoke-type wheels are okay) They must retain stock fenders.

These vehicles are known for their "air time" because they launch off bumps and hills that are a bit more steep. That's because these machines race in the opposite direction from the five previous classes. The dirt mounds are inclined more steeply on the side they race from.

These motorcycles also run in heat races before the feature race starts. This class is by far and away the one that will have the most passing of racers back and forth in a (MTEG) nights racing program.

G.I. G. UNLIMITED SINGLE SEAT—This used to be the oldest and most recognizable racecar in the MTEG division of classes. The engines were limited to whatever the drivers wanted to use. But costs was the final nail that drove them into the proverbial casket. (in 1986)

Usually, the engines in these were around 2100 cc and much more costlier, not worth it when the Super 1600's was almost its equal. That's because that added horsepower was unusable on the short course. (power could not be properly transferred to a dirt surface efficiently) Hybrids of these do race in the Desert Series.

G.II/III. A–Y Closed Short Distance/ Open Long Distance (Desert)

These are the SCORE/HDRA classes. (Southern California Off-Road Enterprises and High Desert Racing Association) They will be very briefly described. This is done not because of the number of classes or that I feel they don't warrant it, but because of the nature of the races. Even though this is off-road racing, this is also a form of Endurance competition, especially when such events as the Baja 1000 can tear up 30 to 60% of the vehicles.

Off-road racing calls for rugged, well conditioned drivers that can withstand the constant thrashing about, even in the smaller 250 mile events. Relatively speaking, getting into all the numerous regulations wouldn't be practical. Reliability of the equipment is more pertinent. A driver needs reliability to win any form of race, but obviously it's more of a factor on 1000 miles of bumpy and treacherous terrain, than on a nice smooth road.

Speed is necessary to win also, but an entrant must finish the race with an intact racing machine and a competitor who can take the beating. All the (engine) specifications and allowances in the world will not mean a thing unless those two criteria are first met.

In addition to all this information I just gave you about off-road racing, please be informed that this form of racing isn't just sanctioned by SCORE/HDRA. There are numerous organizations and sanctioning bodies locally throughout the US. For the list of them and their addresses, see the back of this book under the section of 'sanctioning bodies'. There, you'll find these associations are not just located in the southwest part of this country.

Speaking of this country, you'll also find this sport isn't just confined to the US. The "Indy 500" of off-road racing in this country, the Baja 1000, actually takes place in Mexico. There are other huge and well known off-road racing events in other parts of the world. Generally, they're Rally type events. None the less, they are, at least partially, off-road races. A big one is the Paris to Dakar race. It's considered one of the most dangerous events in the world. It's about a 8000 mile trek down France and into Northern Africa. It consumes about 19 days, with less than a third of the entrants finishing.

Speaking of International, you can bet this kind of racing is conducted under the watchful eyes of FIA/FISA. (the International race-control body in all racing)

As I stated earlier, I'm going to keep the following SCORE/HDRA class descriptions very brief and confined to the ones which are race-sanctioned in this country. There are different classes of off-road racing in other lands, but they're not much different than what we have here in the US.

G.II/III. A. CLASS 1—These are the 'Unlimited Single-Seat' race cars which closely resemble the MTEG Ultra Stocks, or a quasi-bodied dune buggy. They do not have any wheel fenders and are slightly more narrowed at the body and/or chassis. They're rear-engine powered, with open or 'unlimited' regulations, by a VW or Porsche. These are generally the fastest of the buggies.

G.II/III. B. CLASS 2—The 'Unlimited Two-Seat' class is a bit wider at the body, but just about a carbon copy of the Class 1 machine, and even more like the Ultra Stock. This class is right up there as the 3rd or 4th most numerous class participating in desert racing.

G.II/III. C. CLASS 1-2/1600—This class is a fairly accurate copy of Class 2, except it is a machine limited to 1600 cc's of engine displacement.

These also look like a narrowed version of an Ultra Stock with no fenders, but behave more like a MTEG Super 1600 racer. This class was the most numerous (or popular) in Desert racing as this sport went into the 90's. Classes 1, 2 and 1–2/1600 are all two-wheel drive race machines.

G.II/III. D. CLASS 3—This is the first of six pick-up-utility styled race machines. It's a short wheelbased 4-wheel drive vehicle such as the Ford Bronco. (the wheelbase cannot be over 108 inches)

G.II/III. E. CLASS 4—This is the 2nd of 6 pick-up trucks. It's a 4x4 truck-styled racer much like the Class 3 except it must have a wheelbase over 108 inches. (all pick-up and utility styled trucks must be closed-fendered or wheeled)

G.II/III. F. CLASS 5—This class is a more radical-looking 'Unlimited Baja Bug' type racer. (Baja is pronounced "Ba-Ha") Basically, it's nothing but a roll cage with VW Bug-styled paneling and small token fenders. (almost open wheel) This is the first of three Baja type racecars and definitely the most modified looking.

These are the fastest of the three Baja racers.

G.II/III. G. CLASS 5/1600—This racer is a more stock version of the Baja Bug class just covered. It's fenders are a bit more pronounced, the wheelbase and track widths are shorter and its power is limited in size to 1600 cc's. (most are original VW Bug manufactured bodies)

G.II/III. H. CLASS 6—This class is the only production sedan in SCORE/HDRA sanctioned racing. It's not really a passenger type street car as we would think of in the terms of luxury, but it's a vehicle such as the Jeep Comanche. It is not one of the highly entered racers.

G.II/III. I. CLASS 7—This is the 3rd of six truck racers. This racer is classed as a mini or mid-sized pick-up, but they're still larger than Class 3 and 4 trucks. These are also more modified two-wheel drives.

G.II/III. J. CLASS 7-S—This 4th truck racer is the same sized machine as the class 7 just covered. The only difference is that it is more stock. It is one of the more heavily entered trucks in desert racing.

G.II/III. K. CLASS 7/4x4—The 5th truck class, this is the same mini or mid-sized racing truck as Class 7-S, except they are 4-wheel drives. This makes a big difference in tough terrain, but they're still relatively stock like Class 7-S.

G.II/III. L. CLASS 8—This is the last of the truck racers. They are the only full sized pick-up in SCORE/HDRA racing. They are two-wheel racers that are the most heavily entered of the desert trucks. They can also be the most expensive of the trucks.

Is this a local organizations version of a Baja buggie, Ultra Stock or a dune buggie? Take your pick what you would class it as. What you would need to know is what's under that body paneling to properly determine that. It's got nice paneling; wheelbase looks long enough . . . must be a super 1600 in stadium racing, . . . probably a class 1–2/1600 or a class 9 in SCORE/HDRA desert racing.

G.II/III. M. CLASS 9—These are the short wheelbase buggies of 1 or 2 seat size that are similar to Class 1, 2 and 3, but the wheelbase must not be over 100 inches. These vehicles are very popular and sometimes make up the second largest entered class in all of desert racing.

G.II/III. N. CLASS 10—This is another very popular racer. It's practically a carbon-copy of Class 9, but it's allowed a longer wheelbase. The power is also a bit down in comparison but it's still basically a roll cage with body paneling attached, like in Classes 1, 2, 1-2/1600 and to some extent Class 5.

Compared to those classes this racer is more modified. But power can be no more than 1650 cc's. Like all the Buggy types, this one does not require front and rear bumpers.

G.II/III. O. CLASS 11—This is the 3rd and last of the so-called Baja racers. They're the stock production VW sedans (Bugs) that have been converted over for desert racing. There is not much done to its fenders,

bumpers and body. This racers looks very much unaltered.

The other two Baja type racers are Classes 5 and 5/1600. They are VW based too. It's what makes them Baja racers. Don't get Baja and Buggies confused. Buggies are not necessarily VW chassis based, although they may be VW powered. (the 6 Buggie classes are 1, 2, 1-2/1600, 9, 10 and 34)

G.II/III. P. MINI-MAG—This is a class limited to Mini-Mag racers built specifically by Chenowth. There is not a whole lot of information out on these. Apparently, there are not too many raced either. None the less, these are down-sized production-sedan appearing racers.

If you recall, I claimed class 6 was the only sedan racer in desert racing. I'll stick by that. The Mini-Mag is not production as related with general availability to the public. But they do look something like the Sidekick, Samurai and Tracker automobile models.

Here's a roll cage with a VW engine and 4 wheels attached. It's a local organizations dune buggie. Add some paneling, a rule here or there . . . and you've got an off-road machine eligible for many other events, both big, little, desert, mud boggs and stadium competition.

G.II/III. Q CLASS 20—This is the 1st of 6 motorcycle classes. Basically, the main rule for this 2 wheeler is that they be no more than 125 cc in engine displacement. This class is also the first of three motorcycle classes which are determined by engine size. The other 3 are determined by the riders age. Of the 3 classes determined by size, this seems to be be least popular based on number of total entries and final desert point standings.

G.II/III. R. CLASS 21—This is the 2nd of six motorcycle classes. The basic requirement for these are they must be 126 to 250 cc's in engine size.

G.II/III. S. CLASS 22—This is the 'open' motorcycle class. It's by far and away the most popular in numbers. (at least in desert racing) The engines must be at least 251 cc's in size.

It seems this class is widely diversified in schools of thought. The heavy bikes such as those over 500 cc or so, would be competitively hurt by the lack of maneuverability, yet the lighter ones, around 251 and 350 may be down on power. The compromise seems to be best near 350 to 500 cc's. (although I may get arguments on that) Power from an engine of 750 to 1000 cc's would probably be impossible to transfer efficiently to the ground. (not to mention handling it in the rough terrain is enough to tire anyone in 250 miles, much less 1000 miles)

G.II/III. T. CLASS 24—These are the mass produced ATV's. (All Terrain Vehicles) Even though they are mass produced, to survive an off-road desert race, they have to be substantially strengthened.

This is the 1st of 2 ATV classes. The main regulation for this particular class is that they be under 251 cc's in engine size.

G.II/III. U. CLASS 25—This is the other ATV class. The frames are just a hair larger, if at all. They must be over 250 cc's in engine size. Unlike the open class in motorcycles, this class isn't quite so open. They cannot go over 600 cc's in engine size.

G.II/III. V. CLASS 30—This is the 4th of 6 motorcycle classes. But this is the first of 3 classes that is determined by the riders age. In this case, it's an open class for riders 30 years of age and over.

G.II/III. W. CLASS 34—This is the final 4-wheeled class. These race machines are closely related to the MTEG Superlites and can be considered as a buggie. (a sometimes fenderless, 4-wheeled roll cage usually accompanied with body paneling in desert racing)

This machine looks somewhat like a modified SprintCar except the engine is located in back. It may be best described as a very large ATV with a roll cage.

This single-seater is not allowed more than 360 cc's of engine size.

G.II/III. X. CLASS 40—This is the 5th of 6 motorcycle classes and the 2nd of 3 determined by the riders age. To race this open class, the rider must be forty years of age or over.

G.II/III. Y. CLASS 50—This is the final motorcycle class. It's not the most popular class for what should be obvious reasons. None the less, there are hardy souls who can handle this. As some of those myths about old age get "blown out of the water" and desert racing continues, look for this class, which requires an age of fifty or over, to grow larger in numbers. (that should also be true for classes thirty and forty)

G.II/III. SCORE INTERNATIONAL TROPHY TRUCK SERIES—All the classes mentioned in divisions II/III race at the same time on the same course. Other than the Baha 1000, a typical 2, 3, 400 mile desert event is ran in huge loops of around 100 miles each. They don't take off all at once, but rather in staggered-starts. Maybe a more accurate statement would be they race the same course the same day. Whatever the case, there's as many 'races within races' as there are classes. An overall winner is also determined.

An inherent problem with off-road events such as these are the physical restrictions in viewing them. Being out in the desert watching a race isn't like sitting on row one at Indianapolis. Televising was difficult also, mostly due to the long, obstructed distances. That's to say nothing of corporate-support packages. Manufacturers felt off-road racing didn't provide an adequate means to promote their products. Teams found them few and far between when compared to the more spectator-friendly confines of oval-track and roadcourse racing. Thus, the one big problem with off-road racing was the lack of both physical, TV and media exposure.

MTEG stadium racing was suppose to eliminate some of these problems. But the setup costs in preparing the race courses isn't currently justified by the turnout of spectators. Racing fields themselves (number of competitors) are also dwindling due to the costs of remaining competitive. SCORE/HDRA has their own answer, it's a much larger form of Stadium racing, but without the stadium and the setup costs.

SCORE/HRDA is attempting a new format on shorter, more confined desert courses for the more highly financed teams. The races would be cut down (except the Baja 1000 & 500) to about half of their original distance. New rules would made such things as pit-stops necessary. This would help television, which is the main motivating factor in creating this class. (they started their 7-event schedule in 1994) On-site spectator viewing will be somewhat improved, but it still won't be a panacea for Off-Road racing. That's because it'll always be difficult for people to reach these remote events. Hopefully, TV will help bring it to them. In turn, this should improve exposure and sponsorship potential.

The idea is for a one-truck class, one event winner, with an overall drivers and manufacturers championship decided by season-long points accumulation. Each race would be one day prior to the traditional off-road schedule held for baja bugs, buggies, sedans and truck classes opting not to race Trophy Truck.

This form of racing merely separates the few big boys with good financial support and horsepower from those who don't. (it's believed there would be only about 12 to 15 teams rich enough to participate) It'll help poorer teams by leveling the competition at traditional off-road races. It makes for slightly safer conditions for all involved by sparsing out the fields and creating less speed differentials between high and low financed machines.

On the other hand, some vehicles, regardless of finances, are as much as 75 mph faster than others. That's a lot, but even worse are the dusty conditions which a passing car encounters when they lap these slower vehicles. Dusty conditions won't change in off-road racing, but under more equally matched fields, an oncoming racer will be better able to judge a competitor's progress before they pass in physically confined areas of the desert. Still, the traditional off-road races won't be thin down much, if at all. The fairer competition may encourage more participation.

Trophy Truck regulation will be relatively nonrestrictive. A typical engine may be as large as a highly modified 700 hp, 8.0-liter, V-10. It can be moved back from it stock location to achieve more vehicle balance.

A tube-frame chassis can replace the stock one and also incorporate unlimited suspension travel. Most off-road race trucks are limited to a specific amount of movement in inches for vertical wheel travel. The Trophy Truck suspension systems may be equipped with sophisticated, nitrogen-cooling, multi-mounted, monotube gas shocks with large variable-rate coil-over springs.

An ideal weight would be in the vicinity of 4500 to 5500 lbs. A typical transmission would probably be a manually controlled 3-range, beefed-up, automatic.

These vehicles can top out at 130 mph. That's scary on uncertain terrain.

H. ENDURANCE RACING

H. Endurance Racing 1. FIA/FISA Sports Prototype (Category C.IV, 7A) FIA/FISA/IMSA World Sports Car (C.IV, 7B)

H. Endurance Racing	2. FIA/FISA Sports Car IMSA GTS-1 & 2 (Category C.IV, 8A,8B,8C)
H. Endurance Racing	3. FIA/FISA Supercars (Category C.IV, p, 56, 57, 58)
H. Endurance Racing	(Off-Road; see Category G)*
H. Endurance Racing	(Rally; see Category I)*
H. Endurance Racing	(Motorbikes see Categories K and G)*
H. Endurance Racing	(Race Trucks see Category G)*

Endurance isn't so much a kind (style) of racing as much as it is a form (type) of racing. These events are measured in length by a predetermined time schedule as opposed to the usual predetermined distance. (kilometers or miles)

There are different kinds of Endurance racing and different types of vehicles that race in them. Most of them we have already covered in other categories, especially the ones on GT and Off-Road racing. Motorcycles also participate in Endurance events.

For the benefit of those that do not have a basic understanding of racing, don't confuse this with Rally racing. (or more appropriately, Rallying) Rallying is not really a 'speed' event. Some question if it's racing at all. I'll tackle that issue towards the end of this chapter in category I, which is next. Anyway, Rallying is a form of an automobile event that requires precision and timely driving techniques, not necessarily high speed. Endurance racing is usually a high speed event which can last as long as 24, 12, 6 and as short as 2 hours.

Another thing about Endurance racing needs to be addressed. The word Endurance is used in a sort of relative fashion that might confuse the average layman. Many drivers, officials or whatever, may consider a race as either an endurance or sprint-styled competition. Here's an example of what I'm saying.

Indy drivers used to have what they considered a sprint-styled race or an endurance-styled one. If you asked them, they'd generally tell you the Indy and Michi-

gan 500 races are more of the endurance-style, including the former 3rd 500 leg of the triple crown series. (which hasn't existed in about the last 12 years)

Indy cars also raced what they unofficially called sprint races. No, they weren't with SprintCars, but Indy Cars running short races of 100 to 125 miles on high-speed ovals, which would usually require only one pit stop. I can remember back in the 70's and early 80's an Indy race event called the Michigan Twin 200. Amongst another race at that event were two Indy car races of 100 miles each. When compared with 500 miles, a 100 mile race could be called a sprint race since it was short and fast. It's all relative.

Today the Indy cars don't have any of these sprint-styled races on the large ovals. They still race on ovals but they're the shorter ones like Milwaukee, Phoenix, Nazareth, Pa and New Hampshire. The short-distance oval races today tend to be longer at around 170-200 miles, which would require several pit-stops. So these are not what could be loosely called "sprint-styled" races of the past.

Other race sanctioning bodies or organizations have the very same situation with semantics. Their drivers consider the race schedule with ideas of what style or kind each one is. It's all a matter of wording. It shouldn't be confused with the actual form or type of racing offered by a sanctioning body.

Endurance racing is as much a Category here in chapter 3 as Formula, StockCar, Production or SportsCars is. Don't confuse endurance STYLE with endurance TYPE Also remember, Endurance type races stop or end in a predetermined time span. (24 hours, 12 hours, 6 hours, etc) Endurance style is just an informal use for relative distances of races.

SCORE/HDRA's Baja 1000 is an endurance styled race, that's obvious. But it's still off-road racing, for obvious reasons. Its length is determined by distance. (even though each racecar's separate time to complete the event is recorded) On the opposite end of the spectrum, Endurance races that last only 2 hours aren't as long as other

---

*endurance styled, not Endurance Type.

types of nonendurance races. Therefore, Endurance doesn't necessarily mean long.

In Endurance type racing categorized here, there are two large sanctioning bodies which concerns this country. The first and smaller one is based right here in the US, IMSA. The other is the worldwide race sanctioning organization, the FIA. (Federation International de Automobile) Another body is referred to as FISA. (Federation International du Sport Automobile) Actually FIA controls most racing throughout the world and FISA is the body that's more SportsCars oriented for Endurance racing.

Basically, IMSA's Endurance schedule is comprised mostly of the shorter events, but they do have two long races of 12 and 24 hours. The 24 hour race is held at the Daytona International Speedway and isn't counted towards the World Championship for SportsCars and Group C-Prototypes. (Prototypes are the styled sport racer that look like IMSA's former GTP class)

Most FIA/FISA Endurance races are held outside the US. Most are in Europe, such as Lemans and Paul Ricard in France, Monza in Italy, Nurburgring in Germany, Jerez in Spain and The Spa in Belgium. Other sites are South America, Silverstone and Brans-Hatch in England, Suzuka and Autopolis in Japan, Mexico City, Montreal, and the US locations of Daytona, Sebring, Fla and Watkins Glen, NY.

Endurance races are conducted in pretty much the same way SCCA amateur events are, but on a much larger scale. With Prototypes, Sports Cars and the other classes, there's isn't enough time to race them separately. So they run together as 'races within a race'. (IMSA's racing classes, off-road, motorcycles and others do this also; it's nothing unusual) It's the only way to run 12 and 24 hour races with several classes.

H.1. FIA/FISA/IMSA SPORTS PROTOTYPE / WORLD SPORTS CAR—One type of FIA/FISA International car raced is the 750 and 900 kilo (which is the Group C racer) Sports Prototypes. The 750 kilo Prototype used a normally-aspirated 3.5 liter engine, as some Group C racers. As of 1991, rules will discourage their turbocharging, except

at Lemans. An sample of the 'makes' are Jaguar, Nissan, Porsche and Mercedes. But as you learned earlier in category C.IV. on Grand Touring Cars, the Prototypes have pretty much priced themselves out of existence. They still may compete at a few international events such as Lemans, but they're pretty much being replaced by the World Sports Cars, especially here in the US, by IMSA.

H.2. FIA/FISA SPORTSCARS & IMSA GTS-1 & 2—These are the basic machines for Endurance racing. They resemble mass-produced street sport cars. There are a few mass-produced classes, but here, just about all sport cars are purpose-built for Endurance racing. The bodies may be 1-piece fiberglass shells that only resembles a specific model or the more stock versions with highly modified wheelwells to allow use of wider than normal racing slicks. The one-piece racers look pretty much like the old IMSA GTO/GTU/AAC race machines. The Sports Cars that are more stock appearing, with or without oversized fenders, have many rules and organizations to race under.

H.3. FIA/FISA SUPERCARS—The other type of Endurance racer is the SuperCars. These are the exotic, street-legal, expensive sport cars that are so sophisticated that they actually have to be detuned to slow them down for racing. I'm referring to such made as Porsche. Ferrari, Lamborgini and Masserati. These are the same vehicles covered in Category C.IV. on pages 56, 57 and 58.

(SCCA also holds a few endurance events of their own. One race I can think of is the 24 hours of Nelson ledges)

All these racers have their own separate points race to the worlds championship, both for the drivers and the manufacturers. But the ones held in the US (Sebring & Daytona) are currently not counting for points since they're not FISA sanctioned. There may be some logical explanation for that . . . but to be sure . . . it boils down to politics. It's a dirty word to me and should be to race fans. Let's hope the powers can settle their differences. If that happens soon, there is talk of an FISA-sanctioned Endurance event in Hawaii. I'll believe that when it happens. Meanwhile, I don't understand why they want it in Hawaii, instead of the mainland. The mainland has much easier access.

One more thing about Endurance racing that may not be apparent to the novice fan. If you think about it, it would be almost impossible to have drivers race an entire 12 or 24-hour race exclusively. Driving an automobile on an interstate highway for 24 hours is tough enough, even with all its quieter and smoother riding amenities. To expect a driver to run as fast as 190 mph for that long isn't only stupid but you may as well sign their death certificate.

Most teams have three drivers for each race vehicle that participates in a 24 hour race. The 12 hour events still usually require three drivers, even though they're half the time. The drivers do not race in thirds (8 hours at a time in 24-hour races) but in shifts of about 2 hours. That in itself is tiring enough, as it is in any kind of high speed racing.

I. RALLY

I. Rally Competition 1. Road Rally (amateur class)
I. Rally Competition 2. Pro Rally (US & Internationally based)

I.1. ROAD RALLY—This is the type of amateur autosport competition that got SCCA started way back in 1944. Some people do not consider this racing. But most do, including myself, because it involves automobiles in competition, albeit not at high speeds.

In Road Rallies, you're competing with and against time. Rallying could best be described as competition with coordinates and timing. These contests are held on public roads any time of the day with the normal traffic (which is not involved) and within legal speed limits and laws.

At this level of rally competition, drivers use their stock, everyday automobile which is not specifically built for racing or high speed competition. Inside their car may be instrumentation specifically designed for Rallying, but nothing that directly enhances performance of the vehicle. This instrumentation aids in the drivers ability to perform. Most of the time the driving competitor has a co-driver to help them, sometimes referred to as a navigator.

What happens in Rally competition is each driver receives identical directions to a specific location just before their individual start, which is in staggered intervals one at a time for each car. The instruction are in written form. It directs the competitors over a planned route and/or course. Both driver and co-driver do not know ahead of time where they are going, not until they receive these directions. Even then, by looking at the directions, the destination may not be evident. They have to follow and figure them out along the way. The directions must be followed closely because tricks may be disguised in them to make the event challenging.

In addition, competitors are expected to be at certain points via the instructions within timespans called 'checkpoints.' This insures against cheating and allows the drivers to pace themselves. It also informs them of posted speed limits, what to be aware of and how they're progressing. In the end, the car that comes closest (not quickest) and most accurately in the time expected at the finish line wins.

In some Rally events, cars may be judged or scored accumulatively on how accurately they complete these certain designated checkpoints. It is then these checkpoints are called 'Special Stages'. It's like several mini or sub races within a race. The winner is the one who collected points and/or reaches the finish most accurately.

Rally events can be very simple to downright complicated. They're based on a competitors ability to follow instructions, stay on schedule without breaking any speed limits or laws and being considerate of other road users not involved in the event. The length can be only a few minutes (a bit under an hour) to as long as across the entire country. (days) Most last a morning and/or afternoon at the SCCA level. (the prominent sanctioning body for US Rallies)

SCCA Road Rallies are conducted in Classes E, (Equipped) U (Unequipped) and S (Stock) at the national, divisional and regional levels.

When they are held, local, state and county police are informed well in advance. There are around 500 Rallies sanctioned by SCCA alone each year at various levels of competition. Points are also awarded in the 3 classes to determine annual winners and lifetime standings.

I.2. PRO RALLY—In (SCCA & ARA, American Rally Association) Pro Rally, the competition is much more like all-out racing, but it's still against the clock. It's similar to off-road racing. The format may be the same as regular Road Rally, but are illegal to run on public highways. These races can last from 12 to 16 hours and traverse several hundred miles. With that kind of space needed, these are usually held in fairly isolated areas in all regions of this country.

They compete in a 9 to 12 event pro series of generally 200 to 450 miles in length. It was supported by car manufacturer Subaru, but now is supported by tire producer Michelin. Like Road Rallies, the courses are kept secret right up to when the event takes place. Unlike Road Rallies, the cars are highly modified compact production autos specifically prepared for this form of racing.

These vehicles compete at both the national and divisional levels in 6 classes: 1 Open, 2 Production GT, 3 Production, 4 Group A, 5 Group 2 and 6 RallyTrucks. An 'Overall' winner is also determined. So in essence, each class races for their class and an overall title.

There is also a separate points chase for the co-drivers in each of these 6 classes and for the 'Overall' competition. This kind of racing also has manufacturers vying for a seasonal points championship, including the tire makers.

Pro Rallying can be almost as punishing as off-road, but the terrain tends to be more gravel and dirt road oriented, with an occasional paved surface. Off-road racing tends to be the nonroad, miscellaneous-surface type with more gorge-like apparitions suited to ATV's and 4 wheel drives. But don't take that as necessarily "the gospel". There are plenty of Pro Rally drivers who would take exception to what I say . . . and they just may be right. One reason is Rally events also take place in severe winter conditions. Also, the competitors cannot practice, since the course is not revealed until the contest is started. Unlike desert off-road racing, obstacles like huge trees, steep river inclines, limited sight, night (dark) conditions, mountains, with any combination thereof makes this sport a bit more dangerous than desert off-road. I guess if any of the drivers agree with my opinion comparing how difficult these two forms of racing are, would depend on which of the two they participate in.

While Pro Rally can also be grueling timewise, the terrain isn't quite so rugged when put in light of relative speed between the two forms of racing. Off-road desert racers have the chance to "mash the accelerator" more. But still, like desert racing, Rally competition can prematurely "knock out" half the field of race vehicles before it's over. Those fields can average somewhere between 50 to 80 racecars. Either form of competition in these two endeavors of off-road competition is no "cakewalk through the tulips".

Some Pro Rally events are more established and well known to the racing fraternity worldwide than to the general public. In addition to the Paris-to-Dakar event held across the "pond" is an event the Unser family of Indy racing fame seem to dominant here in the states. (13 wins by Bobby Unser and at least 2 by his son Robby) The event I'm speaking of is the Pikes Peak Hill Climb in Colorado Springs, Colorado.

This is one of the nations oldest racing events. Matter of fact, I'm pretty sure that the Indianapolis 500 is the only other race that is older. This 'climb' is a form of Solo event which is held on a gravel road of 12.42 miles with 156 turns going up about 4700 feet in sea level. It already starts at 9400 feet. Because of that, competitors can expect any kind of weather conditions on the way up. Even though it's July, they've been known to run into snow. So far the best time in this event is 10:47.27 minutes by Ari Vatanen in 1986.

The main class of these hillclimb racers is the Open Wheel. The slower classes in descending order is the following: Stock Car, Truck E, Open, Truck F and Production. The Open/Unlimited class has been eliminated.

Eight or nine World Rallies are sanctioned annually at the international level by the FIA. An example of these racers are those classed in Group A and the Group B Supercars. They are compact-sized, specially-prepared production automobiles limited to 300 hp and a 4-wheel drivetrain equipped with special electronic gadgetry. That type of drivetrain splits torque between the front and rear axles for better handling characteristics.

Most of these international events are held in European countries and a few down under in Australia/New Zealand. The fields can be as high in numbers as 300. None are currently held here in the US.

J. SOLO RACING

J. Solo Racing 1. Solo I (Trials & Hillclimb versions)
J. Solo Racing 2. Solo II (Slaloms)
J. Solo Racing 3. Pro Solo (Autocross)

Solo racing is conducted in two forms. One is for all-out speed against the clock on race tracks. The other is a form of nonspeed event which places more premium on precision driving at full throttle on extremely tight courses. Even though many do, these races don't necessarily occur on race tracks, roadcourses or ovals. Many events are setup on large parking lots at shopping malls, airports, abandoned roads, hillsides and stadium complexes.

A course may be setup, usually using orange colored pylons in either an open or closed-course fashion at about one-eighth to a mile or so in length. Other courses may be the purposely-constructed 1, 2 or 2 1/2 mile ovals and roadcourses. But most Solos are designed for lower speeds by incorporating tight turns and very short straights. One (race) vehicle runs the course as quickly and

accurately as possible. Cars race one vehicle at a time or as pairs, depending on the type of event. Time used up in completing a run is kept and recorded. Obviously, the lowest time wins if the vehicle stayed on proper course and did not hit or touch any markers. In that situation, the driver is either assessed a penalty or disqualified. A penalty is usually in the form of time added to the initial lap recording.

Most vehicles run one lap (closed course) but some events may allow more. It depends on the time available to the event, the number of cars and the size of the course.

If the course isn't closed (open) then it's called a 'run'. Either way, depending on the event, each vehicle in each class is allotted a specific number of runs or laps. Times may be 'averaged' or 'accumulated' with the possibility of a 'throw out'. (driver may disqualify their poorest time for the day)

This kind of racing has an inherent kind of safety and concentration factor unlike wheel-to-wheel, bumper-to-bumper racing on ovals and roadcourses. Drivers do not have to worry about accidents caused by others while they are racing. Although group racing always requires strict concentration, it cannot be "blind" concentration. Drivers have to be aware of race vehicles near or around them. They need to expect the unexpected.

In Solo racing, this isn't so. One is out there alone. They can afford to be blatantly aggressive. Their vehicle is not only safe from other cars, but usually of close-by retaining walls. The courses are also marked to allow plenty of runoff space if control is lost. That allows even more aggressiveness because of reduced chances of injury to the car and thee "Ol bod".

Solo racing is seeing increasingly more women participation. Most Solo racing is SCCA sanctioned. Currently, they are trying to develop a handicap system for women to increase more of their participation.

J.1. SOLO I—This is the all-out speed version of Solo racing. Various classes racing here are generally the same as those in SCCA club (amateur) events. This includes Production, GT, Showroom Stock, IT and even the Formula classes. Solo I classes are generally not mass-produced street-legal automobiles. (except Showroom Stock) Street-legal cars mostly race Solo II. The drivers in Solo II are NOT required to hold a competition license or even wear a protective fire suit. (helmets are required) In Solo I that's not the case. The drivers need a racing license, firesuits and other safety equipment, such as removable rollbars. This is because they're usually racing on roadracing circuits (trials version) or up a hill like Pikes Peak. (hillclimb version) That means speeds are much faster and relatively more dangerous.

As stated earlier, the racecars in this class are all race-prepared. I suppose one could say Solo I is almost like race qualifying similar to NASCAR and IndyCar events. In May, the Indy cars spend 4 days doing this. But Solo I is a one day event. The qualifying-like event itself "IS" the race.

Solo I racing competes at the SCCA National level about 35 to 45 times per year. In addition to hillclimbs and racing circuits, they've also been known to occasionally compete on street circuits. Solo I racing is prevalent out west and down south. An event at seasons end determines a National Champion.

The racers may use race slicks. (since the course is usually long and hard enough (asphalt) to adequately build up heat for proper grip)

J.2. SOLO II—This class is much more popular than Solo I. That's probably because of the lower cost of racing at this level. A driver doesn't need a racing license, firesuit or a race car that's prepared like a rocket. But it is still a form of all-out racing. Solo II racing involves a much tighter racecourse. The courses are designed with several hairpin-type turns and short straights. The maximum speed for an inexperienced racer could be only around 50 mph. The more challenged-designed courses allow greater speed. So this is not the type of nonspeed event characteristic of Rallying.

Technically, this is a speed event, but precision maneuvering is important. The old adage 'the shortest distance between two points is a straight line' certainly applies here. You can't run straight in Solo II, but driving too hard will put you out of that shortest possible distance and therefore increase your time. Skidding sideways, spinning tires, under or overbraking, under or oversteering . . . they all serve as inefficient driving and therefore will lengthen the time it takes to complete a run. So, the idea is to reach the finish line as quickly as possible. To do that on such a tight, twisty road configuration means properly operating the correct (racing) line and efficiently putting power to the ground.

The slightest inapparent loss of control can put a vehicle as much as a second off the pace. That's an eternity when events are won and lost by thousandths of a second.

Solo II isn't only played on stable surfaces like asphalt and concrete. They also take place in open fields and in the winter on frozen lakes. On ice, you dane-well better be finessed, patient and precise if you want to win.

Even though Solo racing is serious stuff, these slalom-type events are a blast to compete in. Over 90 are held yearly in this country at the National and Divisional levels, (12–15 major events each) which culminates in a National Championship round usually located in Salina, Kansas every September. Several hundred are regionally/locally conducted which may compete under a slightly different format and/or organization, but are still generally overseen under the watchful banner of the SCCA.

There are 4 separate classes for men and women in Solo II. (what SCCA calls Categories)

a. STOCK—This class is broken down into 9 subclasses. The first is the Superstock class, then the rest from A to H. The autos here have each make and model rated for performance potential.

Some random examples are: Class Superstock, Dodge Viper; Class A, Porsche 911 and Lotus Elan; Class B, Corvette; Class C, Mazda RX-7; Class D, Porsche 944; Class E, VW Golf GT1 and Toyota Corolla GT-5; Class F, Chevy Camero Z-28 and Ford Mustang; Class G, BMW 325, Dodge Shadow and

Honda Civic; Class H, Pontiac Sunbird and Toyota Celica.

b. STREET PREPARED—This class allows a certain amount of change to wheels, tires and suspension. These tend to be older cars like the Stock class. There are 5 subclasses, ranging from A to E.

c. PREPARED—This class is for older and/or former production type roadracing cars. There are 6 subclasses. Engine modifications are allowed on a very limited basis.

d. MODIFIED—This class is for former Formula, SportsRacers and SportsCars, of which there's 5 subclasses. (A thru E)

People competing here usually don't start in Solo racing. That's because their racecar aged or the old body can no longer compete in side-by-side competition characteristic of high-speed, closed-course racing.

But that's not always the case either. Some of these machines are borrowed or a driver just plainly gives themselves additional competition by entering their closed-course machines in Solo events. The man lending/renting out his race machine knows it's an unlikely occurrence it'll be destroyed in an accident. They also need not use their strongest, high-dollar engine.

J.3. PRO SOLO—Money isn't the only thing here that separates this type of Solo from the other two. Pro Solo incorporates a drag race type of start with two competitors on mirror-image courses. Once the paired vehicles make there first turn, they go in opposite directions and away from each other. They continue on in with the same number of turns and distance and usually meet back at a common point at the finish line. They are still racing against the clock, in a manner of speaking, but the format is a bit different.

The categories and classes are just about the same as the Solo II subcategory. The STOCK class has 6 subclasses instead of 9. (they use numbers here; Classes 1-6) STREET PREPARED is also 2 classes smaller than the Solo II version. (3 Pro Solo classes) PREPARED and MODIFIED have 2 classes each. (Solo II Prepared and Modified has 6 and 5 classes)

There is some consolidating of these classes to facilitate a handicapping system. This is another thing that's different at the pro level. Handicapping allows for an 'Overall' winner for all classes or the entire event. This 'Overall' winner is awarded points towards a national championship. Separate Overall titles are offered for men and women. All the separate classes also offer a National Championship, which is also run at Salina, Kansas in September.

In addition to the handicapping system used for determining an Overall Champion, another handicap system is used to determine individual races within these classes. But this system isn't incorporated until the final top three finishers in each class is determined. Then these three are matched using time penalties to equalize them. Those drag race type starts are staggered at different fractions of time. This puts a premium on driver skill and not so much on the vehicle. All 3 finishers go head to head in a round-robin fashion to determine the final class winner for that class and for the day.

Pro Solo hasn't been around very long. It started in 1984. Total prize money is approaching 2.5 million. That's a good indication the manufacturers are supporting it well. There is about 10 or so events like this held per year. Each event averages about 140 to as many as 170 racers.

These pro events are more fairly dispersed throughout the United States.

K. MOTORBIKES (12 CLASSES)

K. Motorbikes	1.	Non-Speed Competition
K. Motorbikes	1A.	Enduros (open course)
K. Motorbikes	1B.	Closed Course Enduros
K. Motorbikes	1C.	Reliability Trails Enduros
K. Motorbikes	1D.	Observed Trail
K. Motorbikes	1E.	Scottish Trail
K. Motorbikes	1F.	Rally
K. Motorbikes	2.	Hillclimbs
K. Motorbikes	3.	Drag Racing
K. Motorbikes	4.	Ice Racing
K. Motorbikes	5.	Dirt Racing
K. Motorbikes	5A.	Motocross/Supercross
K. Motorbikes	5B.	Scrambles Racing
K. Motorbikes	5C.	Hare Scrambles
K. Motorbikes	5D.	DTX (Tourist Trophy)

K. Motorbikes	5E.	Hare & Hound Racing
K. Motorbikes	6.	Desert Racing
K. Motorbikes	7.	Oval Dirt Track Racing
K. Motorbikes	7A.	Speedway Racing
K. Motorbikes	7B.	1/2 Mile Dirt
K. Motorbikes	7C.	DTX (Tourist Trophy)
K. Motorbikes	7D.	Ice Racing
K. Motorbikes	8.	Sidecar (HackCar)
K. Motorbikes	9.	4-Wheel ATV
K. Motorbikes	10.	Roadracing
K. Motorbikes	11.	Endurance
K. Motorbikes	12.	Grand Prix
K. Motorbikes	*	Youth Classes; a 4–8 years old, b 7–11 years old, c 12–15 years old

This category of racing isn't necessarily two-wheeled. If that was so, I would title this Motorcycles instead of Motorbikes. There are 3 & 4-wheeled vehicles in here. They are few in numbers, but worth taking time for.

Like off-road racing, which most motorcycles racing is considered, there are many locally-sanctioned clubs in the US and worldwide. Rules do not vary widely but procedures may. Specifications for each class will not be greatly detailed here. There's a reason for that. It's not necessarily important what they race with as much as what they race on.

What's done to improve motorbikes for racing through modification is limited compared to 4-wheel race machines. This is especially so with vehicle handling and dynamics. The center of gravity can be lowered on a bike and it can be made more aerodynamic. The high-speed roadracing bikes can experience the same automotive phenomenon of 'pushing' (understeer) and 'looseness' (oversteer) but it's not quite as complicated with 2-wheelers. This isn't quite the case with engines. There are always modification that can be applied to an engine to make it stronger in any kind of racing. With 2-wheelers, what's done isn't quite as relevant. A particular class of bike, especially a dirt racer, can have all the engine strength in the world, but if it can't efficiently put it to the ground it doesn't make any difference how powerful it is.

For those who can't comprehend what I'm saying, let me explain it another way. Two motorbikes are racing up a relatively steep, curvy and gravely road. They're both traveling the same speed. One bike is racing smoothly without overspinning the drive tire. The other racer is all over the place and digging hard in the dirt, . . . generally not handling smooth. It's not because he's an inferior rider in this example, but because he has more power than he can use and he's trying hard to take advantage of it. But it's doing him no good. The law of physics won't allow the vehicle movement he wants.

Sometimes if an engine is modified, the added power can be offset by the extra weight required for the modification. Usually that will not happen, but it's possible with lighter vehicles. Because of that it's not necessary to be overly detailed with racebike specifications. What's more important is what kind of terrain being raced on or how the rider handles the vehicle. You're going to see that not all motorbike events are high speed or even any speed at all.

Despite inefficient power-to-ground transfer with most dirt bikes, that isn't the situation with all motorbike classes. There are awesomely fast 2-wheelers out there racing on paved, high-speed ovals and roadcourses. You better know what you're doing if you park your "keester" on one of them. What's done to their engines is quite sophisticated. (and very expensive) Like all racing, these expenses need to be kept at a minimum, otherwise the competitors would . . . shall I say, "feed on themselves". They'd be forced to spend more and more money for faster equipment in order to remain competitive. The speeds would continue to rise, . . . and so would the costs. Racing would end up as a measure of nerve and wallet thickness . . . not necessarily skill.

Some of the major sanctioning bodies for motorcycle and/or motorbikes are: AMA, (American Motorcyclist Association) WERA, (Western/Eastern Roadracers Association) DRA, (Desert Racing Association) and those covered in Off-Road (SCORE/ HDRA, MTEG) and not covered in Drag racing. (NHRA, IHRA, IDBA) There are other bike sanctioning bodies that are more regionally and locally oriented. (Just refer back to the 'Race Sanctioning Bodies and Associations' in the appendix)

K.1. NONSPEED COMPETITION (A–F)

K.1. A. ENDUROS—This is a non-speed, open-course type of event similar to an SCCA Rally. But to put it quite mildly, this does not take place on public roads. They're held on trails, wooded areas, dirt roads, abandoned paved roads and sometimes in areas where there are no roads.

The idea is to maintain a designated average speed on a route without getting ahead or behind in time or schedule. Like a Road Rally, a route sheet of instructions is given each competitor before the event. There is also 'checkpoints' in Enduros which may or may not be known by the participants. The kinds of Enduros vary a bit. The type of course themselves can also be desert-like, forest-like or downright mudholes, so to speak.

The time of Enduros is normally a couple of hours, a whole afternoon or longer. They cannot be over 24 hours. Events close to 24 hours require a specified number of 'rest stops' at around 1/2 hour each. Refueling stops are required every 40 miles.

The AMA is the largest sanctioning body for this kind of event. They have riders classed as AA, (most skilled) A and B, according to an accumulated points-earned system. Points are usually determined according to a rider finish in a previous number of events.

There are different types of engines in the various AMA Enduros classes, including those classes determined by rider age. (30, 40 and 50 yr old and over; and womens classes also) The motorcycle engines range in size thru 7 classes starting at 86-100 cc's to over 500 cc's, including the Unlimited class using a 4-stroke engine. There is also a class for the '3-wheel Sidecar' motorbikes. They are allowed the use of any size engine.

Enduros run nationally, regionally and locally for points towards a Regional and/or a National Championship.

K.1. B. CLOSED-COURSE ENDURO—This is a type of Enduro where the only difference is the kind of course they compete on. The rules are identical to open-course

Enduros just covered. Closed Enduros compete on courses 3 or more miles in length. The finish and starting points are the same place. The competition must traverse the course two or more times. Like open Enduros, the courses are very seldom paved roads, but they are generally shorter in duration.

Checkpoints must be at least one mile apart.

K.1. C. RELIABILITY TRAIL ENDURO— This is another form of Enduro. There are two basic types according to how they're scored at the checkpoints.

One is scored by the normal time and distance recordings. These are also much longer, sometimes 1, 2 and 3 days. These multi-day events are also qualifying events for the ISDE. (International Six-Day Enduro) The best from the US, according to how they perform during these multi-day events, go on to this world-classed event. It's usually held in Europe.

The other type of Enduro is how they're unaccumutively scored. It's important to arrive at an Enduro 'checkpoint' exactly as expected. (not early or late, called 'zeroing out') In Reliability Trail Enduro you're not penalized again for the same minutes early or late at the next 'checkpoint'. In other words, scoring is done from checkpoint to checkpoint rather than the entire run.

There are also "special tests" in RT Enduros, in what's usually a Motocross section. That adds more diverse scoring and helps eliminate ties.

This type of Enduro is indeed a hard event to find. There are not too many held in the US. There are only about 6 Reliability Enduros held yearly.

Since these AMA sanctioned events require such a large area of land to compete on, they are usually held out in the mid to far west where civilization isn't so concentrated.

K.1. D. OBSERVED TRAIL—This is the kind of competition that's most different of these Enduro subcategories. This is still a nonspeed event. Some people do not consider this a form of Enduro. They may be right. This is the slowest of the nonspeed events. The other classes are at least speed events of some form. Still, OT events fits best here in this subcategory.

Even though an Enduro doesn't necessarily reward the fastest rider, the idea is to still maintain some designated speed average. But in Observed Trail events, speed means nothing. The challenge is to negotiate a number of difficult obstacles (mud, logs, very rocky terrain, water, hills or any combination) and natural terrain without putting down a foot. The rider can even stop and study or walk through the obstacle or section before an attempt is made. Once the attempt is started, the rider can't stop or touch their feet to the ground without being penalized. A point system is used to grade the rider for such things as dabs, (foot touches to the ground) failures, sections not attempted, etc. The scoring is done and kept tracked by individual scorers at each designated area. In the end, the rider with fewest points wins.

These events are also not real abundant. There still is a series of around 6 to 8 events held in the US and partially sanctioned by AMA. This culminates in a National Championship. On the international level is the 14–15 event World Championship. Most of these are held in Europe, Scandinavian nations and the North American continent.

Obviously, the motorbikes used in this kind of competition needs to be as light as possible so they remain nimble. (usually trailbikes) Because of this, classes aren't determined by equipment size, but rather by age groups and ability levels. Most clubs classify riders as Novice, Amateur, Expert or Master according to a system of points earned over time.

There are other forms of motorbike events that almost border as entertainment, but these are still a form of Reliability Trail competition. Such events are: Secret Mileage Run, (a distance covered by a rider in which they must estimate the exact mileage covered at the end) Map Run, (tests a riders map-reading skills) Economy Run, (tests a riders ability to get good fuel mileage) Field Meet, (tests ability to handle motorbike on difficult man-made obstacles) Observation

runs, (test riders vision skills) Duel-Sport Run, (test riders driving ability on different kinds of surfaces) Snow Run, (events run on snow) Timed Road Run, (same as Enduro except routes are not marked) Treasure Hunt, (test riders navigational and mental skills) Poker Run (a 30 mile run with 5 checkpoints) Bingo Run, (similar to the Poker Run) Trash Run, (riders collecting most roadside trash, most weight is the winner) Scavenger Hunt, (also tests riders vision and timing skills) and a Lime Run, (test riders ability to drive consistently and follow directions)

These are generally sanctioned by the AMA, with all types of vehicles including Trikes (3-wheel motorcycle) and Sidecars. These classes may include Passenger, Solo and Buddy divisions.

K.1. E. SCOTTISH TRAIL—This is a nonspeed event which combines Enduro and Observed Trail biking. Some of the course is negotiated with relative ease while other sections are very difficult. The checkpoints are individually timed, not combined and averaged as in regular Enduro. This allows a rider to take their time in the Observed Trail portion of the event without being penalized later for the 'timing' portion of the competition.

Scoring is calculated by adding/subtracting points at checkpoints and dabs in the Observed sections of the course. Usually 2 types of courses are used, an open-course of about 20 miles and a closed-course, less than 3 miles.

K.1. F. RALLY—Motorcycles have been known to participate in automobile Rally events. The rules for them is pretty much the same as it is for the 4-wheelers. (See Category I)

K.2. HILLCLIMBS—This used to be one of the most popular forms of motorbike competition in the US. (if not the world) It has suffered lately, but not enough to be eliminated. They're a series of uphill trails traversed against time at various distances. They're conducted either by a series of matched races where competitors are eliminated, such as in Drag racing, or by the best total performance after all competitors have attempted the course.

The start is on level land. The hills in these events may be any gradient. Hillclimbs scored by time tended to be less steep. Otherwise, those races determined by distance have very steep gradients. The rider goes until he can no longer keep his speed, and therefore, balance. As soon as one of the feet touch the ground, the distance traveled by that rider is determined.

The largest sanctioning body for the 2-wheel Hillclimbs vehicles is the AMA. If you recall earlier, there is also a hillclimb for the 4-wheel vehicles. The best known one is the Pikes Peak Hillclimb formerly sanctioned by the US Auto Club. (USAC) Auto hillclimbs are always determined by time and not distance.

Most motorbike organizations have Sportsman and Open divisions encompassing about 7 classes determined by engine size. (86 to 750 cc's; Open is sizes over 750 cc) An 8th class is for riders over a certain age, usually 40.

The AMA still sanctions a 7–8 event National Championship Hillclimb series in the eastern half of the United States.

K.3. DRAG RACING—The International Hot Rod Association have a motorcycle division at both the Pro and Sportsman levels. The Pro Level bikes are practically rockets with wheels, especially the 'Funny Bikes.'

There are 4 IHRA Pro divisions: Funny Bike/Top Fuel, Top Fuel/Harley, Pro Competition and Pro Stock.

The Funny Bike/Top Fuel division may use nitromethane, unlimited size, single, supercharged engines. There are 3 classes. One class varies by engine cc size and they're all classed by the number of valves per cylinder and type of fuel they use. The classes includes Funny Bike/Blown or Funny Bike/Normally Aspirated, with wheelbases limited to 72 inches.

A second division, the Top Fuel/Harley is limited to the Harvey Davidson make, which is also a nitromethane burner.

The third division is the 9-classed Pro Competition which is a single or double-powered racer based on engine size, fuel and vehicle weights.

The 4th IHRA pro division is the single-classed Pro Stock. These are the most stock appearing of the 4 IHRA divisions. These racers cannot be fuel injected and they must burn straight gasoline. Specific weight regulations are contingent by the number of valves per cylinder for either 2 or 4-stroke engines.

The NHRA has only one major class of pro dragbikes. They title them as Pro Stock, which is simular to the IHRA's version. Generally, the NHRA Pro Stocks are more popular than IHRA's version. This is partly due to the lack of 2-wheeled drag classes in NHRA. NHRA tends to be more pro-oriented than IHRA. NHRA dragbikes are 2 inches shorter in wheelbase (70 inch maximum) They are not allowed to use nitromethane or nitrus oxide. These can reach almost 180 mph.

The IHRA Sportsman Eliminator division has 5 classes: 1 Top Gas, 2 Super Comp, 3 Pro Gas, 4 Super Gas and 5 Super Modified. (Super Modified sometimes may be reclassified as Super Eliminator) All these classes are determined basically by their 'standard times' at both the 1/8th and 1/4th mile distances. Top Gas is the quickest. They must complete the quarter-mile in under 8.21 seconds to qualify there. The other classes must run under 8.61, 9.21, 9.91 and 10.51 seconds respectively.

The IHRA also offers a sportsman level class in Top Bike, Modified and Street Stock in addition to the ET Bracket drag bikes.

Another drag racing body which concentrates solely on 2-wheeled drag racing is the IDBA. (International Drag Bike Association) They do not receive much media exposure, but none the less, they are a bonafiee organization. Their classes basically match those of the IHRA and the AMA.

The AMA sanctions bike drag racing, but generally as an affiliate, seldom solely. This organization structures their drag events in 3 divisions: Dragster, Modified Stock and Stock Divisions. They're broken into 15 classes.

The AMA Dragsters are nonstreet-legal machines in 5 classes (A thru E) starting at 86 cc's in class E to the open class A for any size engine over 900 cc's. The Modifieds are 5 street-legal classes with the same engine sizes of the Dragsters, but are more limited by rules. Their engines may be somewhat modified. The Stock division also has 5 classes identical to the Dragster and Modifieds in engine sizes, but obviously they are the most stock and limited by rules. Unlike most pro dragbikes, AMA rules prohibits both the use of exotic fuels and racetire slicks. (except slicks in the Dragster Division)

A few bikes have more than one engine and can total 3500 cc's. These and the other Dragster bikes can approach 195 mph. The rpm's can reach 13,000, producing 240 horsepower. But more importantly, this can be achieved very quickly, . . . enough that the sheer thrust of these machine can tear the riders grip off the handle bars . . . and tax the neck muscles trying to keep the head positioned where it belongs.

The g-forces can flip a dragbike back over its rear end if wheelie bars aren't attached. (wheelie bars are mounted rearward on drag vehicles of all types to artificially lengthen them and therefore keep front tires in ground contact)

One more point about dragbikes in general. Most use flat-profiled racing slicks about 6-8 inches wide. The faster dragsters and opened class machines use slicks almost as wide as those used on smaller 4-wheel drag cars. It's a wonder, with all that grip and power, riders don't get thrown off more often. These bikes can do a 600-700 foot wheelie down the track at well over 100 mph. That's while under the most acceleration. Some of the strongest dragbikes, specifically the IHRA FunnyBike/Top fuelers can reach 195 mph.

Major sanctioning bodies may schedule, in part or whole, an 8 or 9-event national drag series separate from their regular program. (NHRA, IHRA) Others, such as Dragbike USA, IDBA and AMRA (American Motorcycle Racing Association) schedule their normal 11 to 13 events annually.

K.4. ICE RACING—Ice racing is usually an oval form of short track competition, (covered later in K.7. A & B) but as the name im-

plies, these are mostly setup on small lakes and ponds which are not only frozen, but for safety reasons, they're also shallow. (these lakes and ponds are numerous in states west of Lake Michigan, like Minnesota and Wisconsin)

There are two forms or types of ice racing, Studded & NonStudded. (tires) The Non-Studded type race 5 classes and use only rubber (tires) on their wheels. Three of those 5 classes are the SideCar vehicles, so these riders do not have to worry about slipping off on their sides. The other two classes are the regular two-wheelers. Two-wheel riders balance themselves by dragging a foot on the inside portion of a turn, as practiced in Dirt Oval (Speedway) competition.

The stud-mounted machines run 13 classes. The first 9 are for two-wheeled bikes powered by engines starting at 1–85 cc to the open class racer starting at 501 cc's. The first 2 classes are for age groups 7–11 and 12–15. Class 10 is 40 plus. The last 3, Classes 11, 12 and 13 are for SideCars.

Concerning the studs, how far out, where and at what angle they may be mounted is subject to specific rules. (limited to 3/16th inch protrusion, of specific style) They may be only screwed in from the outside, not from the inside out.

Obviously, these events are limited to when and where they can compete. Still, the AMA sanctions a National championship for this type of competition.

K.5. Dirt Racing (A through E)

K.5. A. MOTOCROSS/SUPERCROSS—This is one of the newer types of motorbike racing compared to others. It's also very popular. It started about 1960 and actually evolved from European-type Scrambles events.

The courses are closed-type with mostly irregular and ungraded natural terrain. The hills may be of various size and gradients. (practically small mounds) They may include small jumps and tight turns on a track of about a half to 1 1/2 miles in length. Most types of motorcycle racing do not actively require a minimum width of tracks, but Motocross tracks requires no less than 20 feet.

The starts must be free of hills, sharp turns or anything that would interfere with a long-distant view. That's because all race vehicles begin the event lined up even at the starting line. It's one reason the track must be of maximum width. This helps prevent them from over-funneling into each other at the races start. The races are ran in heats (or Motos) of certain predetermined time or laps. Points are earned during heats. The rider accumulating the most is the (class) winner. Sometimes these heat races are used to determine the starters for a feature race, if there is such an event for that day.

There are 3 skill levels for Motocross riders, Group A, B, C. Group A, Experts, race in 6 classes. The first 3 are determined by engine size, 86–125 cc, 126–250 cc's and the 'open' class. (251 cc and over) The other three are Plus 25, (in age) Senior (30 & over) and SuperSenior. (40 & over) The age classes may use any size engine over 86 cc's.

Group B, Novice, have the same classes, but add a 7th one for women.

Group C is mostly for beginners. It has only 3 classes which are exactly as the first two groups in engine size.

These events can be the most strenuous and grueling in two-wheeled racing. Because of that, the classes determined by age are usually limited to a session no longer than 10-20 minutes. The heats for the other classes last a bit longer or take more laps, whatever the case.

There are some regionally-oriented sanctioning bodies throughout the US, but the main one is still the AMA. They offer a system for earning points towards a National Championship in each class. (12 event series) There is also a World Championship series for 125, 250 and 500 cc powered race machines. Each of the series have a schedule of 12 to 13 races. Only two or three are held on this continent. The rest are held in Europe and the Scandinavian countries.

AMA sanctions a form of Motocross held

This could be one of a dozen types of off-road bikes. Note the comparative light weight (size) and thin construction compared to the bigger roadracing cycle. This makes them nimble. You can see the wheels have plenty of room to bounce-travel and the frame clearance is well off the ground, as in all off-road racers.

within stadiums for 125/250 and 125/500 cc racebikes. It's SUPERCROSS. This was a smaller scheduled series of around six races annually, but it's increased lately in both the number of events and rider participation. The CMA (Canada Motorcyclist Association) has only 2 of these type events, usually near Montreal and Toronto. Mickey Thompsons MTEG Stadium Motorcycle class is also a form of supercross. AMA's Camel-sponsored Supercross series is very popular, especially with young folks.

Supercross tends to encourage youth participation. AMA offers 3 classes for 4–8, 7–11 and 12–15 year olds. The classes are further determined by wheel size, (not wheelbase, but it must be stock size) and engine cc displacement. (the youth start very young in Hillclimbs events also)

Supercross events are held in large arenas such as the Pontiac Silverdome (during winter) and the LA Memorial Coloseum. With this type of motocross, the courses can't always include both left and right turns. That's because the middle of the (football) field cannot be tore up to allow more room, unless it's been protected by additional amounts of dirt. That requires much more time and money. (the time is a huge factor during the football season, the arenas can't always be set up overnight) The 1 1/2 mile maximum can't always be met either. That qualifies these events closer to Scrambles, which is next.

K.5. B. SCRAMBLES RACING—You must have an impression by now Scrambles is a form of Motocross. The difference between the two is the following: First, the courses in Motocross are unpaved and usually the open-course type on natural terrain at various lengths. In Scrambles racing, the course is specially prepared, although they are still not paved. This is why Stadium Motocross (currently called Supercross) is actually Scrambles racing.

The second difference is the distance and/or length. Scrambles are not time limited. These events race a specific number of laps, possible only on closed-courses. Scrambles courses must be 1/4 to 2 miles in length. That requirement can be met in most

football stadiums. (since running tracks around them are usually one-quarter mile; so the length criteria is met) Like Motocross, Scramble courses must be at least 20 feet wide with hills, jumps, left and right turns and some natural terrain in events held outside an arena.

Scrambles is designed to test rider skill. Motocross is more endurance oriented, although it is still largely designed to test rider skill also.

The classes are different than motocross, but not by much. In AMA Scrambles, Class 1 starts with engine size between 86 to 125 cc's. This continues to Class 7, which is 'open' to 501 cc's and over. Class 8 and 9 are for the Sidecar motorbikes and 10, 11 is for age groups 30, 40 and over, respectively.

K.5. C. HARE SCRAMBLES—This is yet another form of Motocross. It is simular to Scrambles because it's closed-course. But it is more like Motocross since it's conducted on natural terrain with a specific number of laps or at a specific limit in time, usually 2 or 3 hours. Hare Scramble courses can be as long as 40 miles in length. So this kind of racing tests a riders endurance and skill. Unlike Motocross and Scrambles, these events tend to be a bit more speed oriented, which in turn, makes this also a form of desert racing, although they don't necessarily get into those conditions. In a few cases, the tires in this type of racing may be studded as those in ice racing.

The 10 classes are very similar to Moto and Scrambles except there are no Sidecars. There is a class for women and 3 classes for 30, 40 and 50 year olds. The last class is 'open' for four-stroke engines.

The AMA sanctions an 8 to 12-event series for a National Championship which is decided by the accumulation of points throughout the series.

K.5 D. DTX (Tourist Trophy)—This is both a form of Motocross and Oval Dirt Racing. It's covered more specifically in Category K.7.C.

K.5 E. HARE & HOUND RACING—This is

actually a Motorcycle version of Desert Racing. See Category K.6, which is next.

K.6. DESERT RACING—This is more popularly known as HARE AND HOUND RACING at the motorcycle level. But instead, it's an open-course form of Hare Scrambles. Like Hare Scrambles, it's also over 40 miles in length and without any of the man-make, prepared terrain. Like Enduro, there are checkpoints, but they are only used to insure against cheating. (prevent rider short-cuts) The winner's determined by finishing order, not a time standard.

AMA and DRA (Desert Racing Association) sanctioned events are shorter in duration compared to SCORE/HDRA off-road motorcycle races. Even though this is shorter, open-course racing, some of these events may be ran in large loops of at least 30 miles two or more times. Events can be well over 100 miles, but seldom longer than 1/2 or a full day.

AMA sanctions a 5 or 6 national-event series in the SW desert areas. (why this is called Desert Racing) The most famous of these is the annual Barstow (Ca) to Las Vegas race held on the Thanksgiving Day weekend. More of these events are locally-based throughout the US.

The 10 classes are identical to those of Hare Scrambles, but numbered differently in the age and womens classes.

K.7. Oval Dirt Track Racing (A through D)

K.7. A. SPEEDWAY RACING—This is also called Short Track Racing. In either case, the race surface is a flat dirt or clay oval of not quite 1/2 mile in length. (maximum 2250 ft.)

The bikes racing this class are light and powerful with emphasis on power sliding. This is the same kind of sidewinding or broadsliding action seen in the corners of SprintCar events that are raced on dirt tracks. Also like SprintCars, these bikes have to be push started. This eliminates multi-speed transmissions, starters, batteries, etc., and makes the vehicles even more

lighter than normal. They match a gear to the track as practiced with SprintCars.

For all intents and purposes, this is a SprintCar-styled class of motorcycle racing. A nights racing program consists of heats, semis and the main feature. Sometimes there are solo-styled qualifying races before the heats to determine starting positions. Otherwise a lottery system is used to position riders at the start of the heats. Where qualifiers, heat or semi-main finishers are positioned for the feature depends on the number of participants entered.

Like Motocross, this is a very popular form of racing. When the rider powers into a corner, they have to drag their inside foot to maintain balance and speed. (it's usually the left foot since they race counter-clockwise)

Speedway racers mostly compete in 3 classes sanctioned by the AMA: Class 1, 1-250 cc sized engines; Class 2, 251-350 cc; Class 3, 351 to 500 cc.

K.7. B. 1/2 MILE DIRT—This is Speedway racing, but it's slightly different. The difference is the track may or may not be banked, but it is always longer. Not by much though. The distance must be between 2250 feet (the maximum for Short Track) and no longer than 2640 ft. (exactly 1/2 mile) Otherwise, everything else is identical including the classifications.

K.7. C. DIRT TRACK MOTOCROSS (DTX)—DTX almost run the same surface track as the Speedway and 1/2 Mile Dirt classes. But this is a sort-of-combination Short Track and Motocross. It's mostly Short Oval Track racing with a hill, a small jump or a dogleg (right) turn on one of the straights.

Some people consider this more as Motocross. That's probably true. It depends on what kind of track it is and how it's prepared. If a situation presents itself where one can't interpret exactly the kind of racing this is, then the best thing to call this is what some clubs title them, TOURIST TROPHY SCRAMBLES.

The bikes racing this class are definitely the type designed for motocross, not the sprint types. In other words, motocross-designed bikes are built strong at the suspension to take the beating from jumps. Speedway bikes emphasize more engine power with minimum vertical suspension travel.

The AMA and others generally sanction 4 or 5 classes. They are determined by engine sizes ranging from 85 to 500 cc. But the rules in this class are oriented towards Short Dirt Track racing.

K.7. D. ICE RACING—This is also oval racing, but it's obviously not on dirt. It's covered specifically in Category K.4.

K.8. SIDECAR—Some organizations call this HACKCAR RACING. In addition to the Sidecars classed in AMA RoadRacing, Ice Racing, Enduro and Scrambles, there are Sidecars for the Short Track also.

For those who do not know exactly what a sidecar is, it's a one or two-wheeled, somewhat flat, bullet-shaped, one-seat vehicle attached to the side of a motorcycle. This vehicle is relatively light and powered only by the motorcycle. The distance between the cycle and sidecar wheel(s) is 30 to 45 inches.

In racing sidecars, the seat is usually situated in such a manner that the rider sits like they would on another motorcycle. This allows the sidecar rider to shift their weight and aid in vehicle race handling characteristics.

In Short Track SideCar racing there are two classes. Class A is limited to a 650 cc overhead cam engine or a 750 cc twin vertical-pushrod type and any 2-cycles of single or double cylinder. Class B is open to anything over 650 cc's.

This is not the safest or best kind of cycleracing to started at. The racing is much harder than it looks. Because two riders are in the one vehicle, to put it simply, it takes some basic understanding of dynamics, skill and coordination to win in any kind of sidecar competition. The course they race may be dirt, paved, bumpy, hilly or any combination thereof. Speeds may be moderate to very fast.

Regardless, the rider in the sidecar does most of the work. They use their body weight to keep the racer on all wheels for faster turning speeds. You have to be in excellent shape to move around on these vehicles.

Sometimes the sidecar rider (nicknamed a Monkey) will actually move back and forth on the bike and sidecar behind the operator. Both riders must stay aerodynamically low.

Some organizations besides the AMA offer Amateur, Semi-Pro and Pro classes. They may be further skill-grouped as Novice, Junior or Experts. The ACU (Auto-Cycle Union) is a British-based organization sanctioning several forms of racing, including these Sidecars. If you look hard enough, some organizations offer this at the Mini-Bike level for the youngsters.

K.9. 4-WHEEL ATV—Yes, the AMA does offer classes for these kinds of vehicles. Other organizations do also, like SCORE/HDRA and MTEG which was already covered earlier in this chapter.

The AMA version of the ATV is pretty much a carbon-copy of the others. What they race on isn't all that different either. These also race cross-country style in the deserts and in the Stadium Motocross of AMA in addition to Scrambles, Short Dirt Track and even Ice events. These do not (or could not) compete in Observed Trail events. Those vehicles must be two-wheel types since balancing of the machine is required. In ATV Ice racing, the tires are allowed to be metal studded. Sometimes AMA ATV classes may not be offered at many meets and events. The reasoning varies, but I would say the biggest reason is because of legal and/or insurance problems. Most track owners or promoters can't get insurance for them or they feel they're too dangerous. (they tend to rollover easy; they have no roll bars) Sometimes, there is no time for them on a racing nights docket.

Classes within different organizations will vary. Generally they tend to be divided mostly by age, but also by engine size, experience and sex.

The AMA recognizes two age-group Youth Classes: 6 to 11 yr olds and 12 to 15. Each class has a Stock and Modified division.

There are six Amateur classes for 16 yr olds and over. They have four 200 cc maximum-powered divisions further classed by engine type and rider experience. Another two divisions are for 251–500cc powered machines.

There is a class for women, (0–250cc engines) and 3 additional ones for 30, 40 and 50 years and over. The 3 mens classes are limited to 500 cc engines.

K.10. ROADRACING—This is where motorcycle racing can get expensive and very fast like drag bikes, especially compared to dirt and off-road bike classes. Understand, that's not to say this form of racing is superior to lower expense racing. Some people equate the more money spent in racing, the more it's superior to less expensive classes. That's not true between the various CATEGORIES (or TYPES) of racing, but it may be the case within those categories. Then again, the classes within these categories are mainly separated by speed potential. To reach those higher speed levels, you definitely need more money, not necessarily more skill. One needs a skill in nonspeed motorcycle events, such as Reliability Trail or Observed events, as well as speed events like RoadRacing. So please be advised, this is the more glamorous or higher profiled type of motorcycle racing, but not necessarily better. That's for you, the fans, to decide individually and privately.

There are a few regional and local sanctioning bodies which sanction Roadracing events. (AFM, OMRRA, ARRA AND MRA to name a few; see Sanctioning Bodies in back) The two big ones in this country is the AMA and WERA. As you know by now, AMA is a

This is a high-speed roadracing motorcycle. As you can see, it's much more powerful and a lot heavier than all the other competition motorcycles. They do not have to be quite so light and nimble on paved, smooth, high speed, 2 to 2 1/2 mile road courses. These are built for 'brute' speed and require nerves of steel while coupled with common sense. (Not to mention . . . talent) Note, they use racing slicks also. A rider needs to use his body in different ways with all kinds of motorcycle racing. But with high speed events, he'd better know what he'd doing.

very diversified organization. WERA isn't that, but very oriented towards road sprint and endurance racing. Both these organizations and FIM (Federation International Motorcyclist) control US events. FIM partially controls most international motorcycle events in other countries.

The AMA offers roadracing at both the amateur and professional levels. The amateur level is the Championship Cup Series (AMA/CCS) which has about 20 classes of street-type motorbikes. The 2 and 4-stroke engines range from 50 cc to the most powerful bikes that are 751 cc's and higher. These classes come from 4 basic divisions:

- Showroom Stock Production–generally stock street-legal machines with six classes from class 1 of 50–80 cc's to class 6, 751 cc's and over.

- Modified Production–less stock, but still street-legal with six classes almost identical to Showroom Stock Production.

- Grand Prix–fastest and most modified and possibly street-legal racers with 5 classes simular to SS and MP, but split between 2 and 4-stroke engines.

- Vintage–bikes at least 20 years old in 3 classes: 86–250 cc, 251–500 and over 501 cc's.

There's also a 90-event regional schedule of roadraces held throughout the US called the AMA Sprint Series. Add the Suzuki sponsored National (Cup) series with AMA, WERA and other bodies, then the number of events increases to around 200 per year.

The AMA professional level of Roadracing is the Superbike, Pro Twin and the National Supersport series. These 3 classes race about 9 times per year at the same date and track, but not concurrently.

WERA's amateur and pro classes are a bit different in name only. Their three Pro classed racers are called Formula USA, Two and Three.

Just as the SCCA holds a National Championship every year to determine a champion from each (automobile) class, WERA and AMA do the same for motorcycles. This is an event for competitors who accumulated the most points at Nationally sanctioned

amateur races. Points earned are determined by finishing positions at those events. Those in the top 25–30 rung of seasonally accumulated points go to the Championship round. (one race for each class)

The professional classed racers earn the National Championship through total points earned at the end of the seasons race series. (in the same manner Indy Champ and NASCAR drivers do)

The tracks that these powerful motorbikes race on are the very same ones the SCCA, CART, NASCAR and IMSA compete on. This includes tracks such as Daytona, Talladega, Road America, Blackhawk, Brainerd, Moraso and at least another two dozen sites. You'll notice some tracks are ovals. Regardless, these races are not run on the entire oval. What some race fans don't know is within the infield area of these ovals is another race track. These are roads consisting of left and right unbanked turns. Motorbike races may take place on both the roadcourse and part of the oval, which is incorporated as one racetrack.

At some tracks, the roadcourse crosses outside the confines of the oval. (as is the case at Michigan International Speedway) If this is the kind of track used for a race, obviously, both tracks cannot be used entirely at the same time. To do that would require an intersection, which is crazy in any kind of high-speed racing. So the roadcourse only is used. Most roadcourse bike racing organizations require both left and right turns. The track must be at least 1 mile in total length. Tracks with a straight over 1/2 mile are usually avoided. At some race sites, public roads are used in part or whole.

Most amateur roadraces are around 30 miles in length. These are not very long compared to endurance events. It's why AMA calls one of their roadracing schedules a "Sprint Series". (not Sprint Races) Some sanctioning bodies have Grand Prix roadraces. This kind of racing is the combination of paved and dirt race surfaces. (don't confuse Grand Prix TYPE or STYLE classes with Grand Prix EVENTS) Sometimes this term is used to advertise bike and auto events. It's important not to confuse the way it's used, otherwise you may think you're seeing a

Grand Prix styled bike race when in fact, you're not. Grand Prix racing is mostly a commercialized term to promote world-classed roadraces of any kind.

The Pro races are much longer in duration than the amateur races. One example is the very old and well established Daytona 200. (mile) This is also one of the faster tracks on the pro bike series. Matter-of-fact, the speeds are so high, a chicane was put in at the back straight to help force lowering of speeds. Some racers have been clocked up to 180 mph in that area. Average speeds for these kinds of races can be well over 100 mph. But then in the case of Daytona, a large portion of the track used in that event is the oval. That's not much slowing down for any tight turns, so the averages will be up slightly. The speeds reached at such street circuits as Miami is nothing to take for granted either.

Whatever level of Motorbike Roadracing, one thing is for sure, you better know what you are doing. Unlike auto racing, you haven't got the benefits of a roll cage in accidents. Get plenty of experience at the slower levels of roadracing. You can bet the sanctioning bodies wouldn't have it any other way. They'll start you at a level that's safe and hopefully suited to your satisfaction and their judgement. For that reason the amateur levels are further broken down not by just class, but also by safety levels. (Expert, Junior & Novice)

Like most sports, racing is another sport you cannot jump into at the so-called "Major League" level and expect to survive, much less win. This is even more true in motorbike racing. The reason for that is the nature of this kind of racing. It's two wheels, not four. It makes a big difference. Because of that a premium is placed much more on driver skill, not just big money and superior equipment. (not always true in some forms of motorsports)

A novice or rookie starting immediately into higher levels of roadracing isn't going to realistically happen. Even the skilled rider realizes the "point of no return" on a high-speed two-wheeler. All the skill and best technology in the world wouldn't do a rider any good if he goes beyond the bounds of common sense. Being too rambunctious in this kind of racing is only a bad situation waiting for a "Murphys law result". Technology (the best equipment) is a factor in bike racing, but it still cannot replace a talented rider like it can in comparison with a 4-wheeled racecar. That's what makes bike roadracing great. It's still "state of the art", not "state of the bank account."

These high profiled, pro-classed race machines have reached slightly over 200 mph on rare occasions. They can top out in the 170–185 mph range.

K.11. ENDURANCE—I cannot say anything concerning bike Endurance racing that I haven't already said basically about Roadracing. Obviously, the big difference is in the length of the races.

WERA has a National Endurance Series of around 15 events per year. Most races are 6 hours. Two races are 24 hours. (Nelson Ledges & Willow Springs) AMA has shorter Endurance events that are usually scheduled with a Professional and/or Championship (amateur) Cup race weekend. With both clubs, the classes vary a bit, but they're patterned basically the same.

For WERA, bikes are categorized in 3 basic divisions: Production, Superbike and Formula/Grand Prix. Each has 3 or 4 classes, ranging in cc engine size of 250 to 'Unlimited'. This is the most prestigious of the endurance series for motorbikes in the US. AMA's isn't quite as prestigious, but it's still big. AMA is a big and more diversified sanctioning body. It cannot solely concentrate its efforts on just endurance racing. WERA is smaller and less diversified. But it's still the largest organization based solely on Motorcycle Roadracing. That's why their endurance series are bigger, or more accurately, more focused.

The biggest and most prestigious of them all is the World Championship Grand Prix Series and the World Superbike Championship sanctioned mostly by FIM. Most of those races are held in Europe, with one or two each in the US.

Anybody who thinks Endurance racing is hard and tiresome on 4 wheels will appreciate how tough it is on two. They race in the rain too, just like the cars do, unless it gets too heavy. Obviously, the long (24 hr.) events need more than one rider. At the AMA events, they're much shorter and usually only one rider is needed. Actually, with AMA, it's a matter of semantics when comparing endurance roadracing to their sprint series. That's not the situation with WERA.

K.12. GRAND PRIX—I will not elaborate much here, because this kind of racing has already been indirectly covered. This style of racing is a combination of bike events already described, with the exception of Hillclimbs and non-speed styled contests. This could be the quickest and most accurate way for a beginner to determine what class to race.

Grand Prix racing is a closed-course event that is characterized by both natural and man-made terrain, including paved roads. The racer will experience a drag race type start, high-speed roadracing, muddy conditions such as those found with Motocross, dirt roads, water splashes . . . and possibly conditions which are desert or forest-like, all in just one of several laps. Races are about 100 miles.

These competitors have to be a "jack of all trades". The motocross bikers seem to be the ones who win this type of event the most. Many contestants slow down significantly when driving off-road.

The scoring of such events is complicated. The use of a computer is required to keep track of individual times and final overall results. As many as 500 racers are released at intervals of 10 to 20 vehicles. Shortest time to cover the coarse wins, barring any penalties, which must be added or subtracted to the competitors overall score. Not too many will complete the course without incurring some type of infraction.

Rules regarding modifications and classes are complex because no one vehicle would have a distinct advantage on the entire course.

* YOUTH CLASSES—The AMA offers the following eight classes for youths 4 to 15 years old in nonhigh speed events. (they all must be accompanied by an authorized adult or legal guardian) The rules for this

level of racing are basically the same as in higher level amateur competition. These age groups compete usually at 'Youth Meets' only. But some run at the National level in conjunction with a regular amateur event weekend. Rarely, Youth Meets take place in conjunction with Pro weekends.

Class 1, Stock Minicycle, maximum 55 cc power, ages 4–8; Class 2, Stock Minicycle, maximum 65 cc, age 7–11; Class 3, maximum 85 cc for Stock Bikes, ages 7–11; Class 4, maximum 85 cc for Modified Bikes, age 7–11; Class 5, maximum 85 cc, Stock Bike, age 12–15; Class 6, maximum 85 cc, Modified, age 12–15; Classes 7 and 8, ages 6–11 and 12–15, for Hillclimb races only.

All these classes have specific rules concerning wheelbase, wheel size and overall length. Most of the 4 to 11 yr old classes are not street-legal machines. Very little internal engine modifications are permitted, if at all.

This ends Category K on Motorbikes. One more category is left.

L. RACETRUCKS (3 TYPES)

L. Racetracks 1. Pick-Up Trucks
L. Racetracks 2. Semi Trucks
L. Racetracks 3. Monster Trucks

L.1. PICK-UP TRUCKS—There is not much history when it comes to RaceTrucks. It's a relatively young form of motorsports, but it's growing very fast. I don't know why the sudden interest in this the past few years hasn't developed much earlier. Pick-up trucks are certainly popular with Americans in all walks of life. My opinion is corporate America didn't realize this until now.

The SCCA started a series for this type of vehicle in 1987, called the 'Coors RaceTruck Challenge'. (then changed support and series title to the 'TruckGuard/Shellzone Challenge') The ALL-PRO Racing Association, a sanctioning body for shorttrack stockcar competition, also ran a series for racetrucks. But both series has since died out. None the less, the rules for trucks varied, depending on the type of racing and the sanctioning body. I already discussed MTEG Stadium racers earlier in Category G (Thunder Trucks) and truck classes in SCORE/HDRA Desert events. But the All-Pro and SCCA versions was one of the first to race on paved surfaces.

The SCCA Truck racers were limited to a short wheelbased, rear-drive, manually-controlled transmission with a 2.4 liter 4-cylinder engine. The engine could only be modified by internal balancing, but there seemed to be many gray areas left to rules interpretation. Some suspension modifications were okay, but all mounting points for those suspensions had to remain in stock position. Racing slicks were not allowed, but any soft compound-type tires used for qualifying had to be used in the race. That meant the tires didn't last long enough. The rims were limited to seven inches in width and 15 inches in diameter. Any bodywork modifications was limited to a front spoiler and the rear bumper. Roll cages were mandatory along with a racing seat and a 15 gallon fuel cell installed in the truckbed.

This racer wasn't quite as fast as the MTEG and SCORE/HDRA trucks. They could top out at around 110 mph, almost the same speed of stock nonrace trucks available to the general public. These vehicles were somewhat lowered to improve their aerodynamics and handling.

They never did quite reach the big league level, even though they occasionally help support IndyCar events. One reason was probably because of hesitation by potential sponsors. But I would say the biggest reason still involves the age-old problem of competitive-fairness. The richer factory-support teams outspent the privateers. The sanctioning bodies attempted to level the fields by changing the rules. The factory-teams could no longer take advantage of their resources and then they were unhappy. It was a "catch 22" for all involved. Once the factory teams lost direct support, they were back to step one. The factories then moved from direct support to the contingency type. (that's purse payouts to the winner and usually other top finishers) But that's didn't always make business sense if their make of vehicle failed to win.

It looks as though all that's changing for the better now. I expect sponsor and factory participation to improve even more then it already has so far. "We can thank the SCCA and All-Pro for buying us the bowling ball, . . . and it looks like we can thank NASCAR for rolling the strike". The jury still isn't quite out on them just yet, but the future looks pretty good.

Back around 1994 the desert truck racers got together with NASCAR to form a truck racing series on paved surfaces. Even though this idea had been brewing in the works for several years, many problems forced the sanctioning bodies and corporate sponsors to take a conservative approach. But lessons learned from previous attempts helped pave the way.

After a few exhibitional races were staged in 1994, a full 20–25 event race schedule is drawn up for 1996. It will be called the (NASCAR-sanctioned) SuperTruck series. The series will get support from Sears Craftsman brand tools and TV coverage from TNN, ESPN, CBS and ABC. This is just what the desert racers were looking for since their budgets in the desert figure to be unchanged on the paved surfaces. This venue is much more accessible to fans and TV cameras, which means maximum exposure for sponsors to hawk their products.

These races will be held on short ovals and a few roadcourses throughout the US. The largest oval track will be Homestead in Florida. There is the possibility of racing these on the superspeedways in the future, but it's also a concern how well they'll cut safely through air at well over 120 mph.

The typical truck racer will be a 3400 lb, full-sized pick-up such as the stock Ford F-series, Dodge Ram and Chevy C/Ks. They will ride on a Winston Cup-styled chassis. The bed is slightly shortened to accommodate the chassis and the ground clearance is much lower than the stock version, 4 inches. A 45 degree, 6-inch spoiler will mount on the beds rear section.

Under the hood will be a Winston Cup-styled Ford, Chevy or Dodge 358 ci V-8 with a 9.5:1 compression ratio and two valves per cylinder. These engines should produce about 640 horsepower. The Winston Cup racecars produce around 710 horses, so the trucks will not be too far off the pace. What makes this interesting is NASCAR will probably drop the compression ratios for their automobile series in 1996 to match those of the trucks.

Regardless of engine rules, the trucks will never attain superspeedway performance of the sleeker automotive-type racers. This should be obvious because of the trucks inherent aerodynamics disadvantage. The trucks are a few inches longer than the WC racers, that's good, but are also 9 inches taller. It's a good chance a low pressure area will create dangerous lift right behind the cab as the air flowing over it is suddenly washed down to the front portion of the bed. That'll make these lighter and unstable at excessive speeds. There is talk of installing a type of wing to alleviate that, but for now, on the short tracks, that's not a problem. Personally, human nature being what it is, I'm willing to bet the farm Supertrucks will find their way to the superspeedways. But it's at least a few years away. Either way, I'm also betting truck racing is here to stay.

L.2. SEMI TRUCKS—This is a subcategory in racing which seems to be faring well in Europe. This type of racing, the big Peterbilts, Kenworths, etc started in the US in 1979. But it has not caught on here like it has in Europe. Probably the main reason for that wasn't necessarily the lack of fan and corporate support, but rather, a venue with which to race them on.

The first race was held at the Atlanta superspeedway on a more or less experimental basis. Enthusiasm for this endeavor was so high that a series was started the next year. But it was eventually discovered that these heavy 14,000 lb vehicles were tearing up the racing surfaces. No track owner was willing to make that sacrifice, even if the grandstands were filled at all truck events. It is expensive enough to repave any flat surface, but race tracks with banked turns required the added expense of special equipment and procedures. So the big trucks took to the dirt. But the sport still isn't faring well in the US.

In Europe, especially France, Italy and Great Britain, they are doing a little better. Even the Russians are getting into the act.

The European championship is sanctioned under the banner of the ETRO. (European Truck Racing Organization) Included in that 7–10 event series is a 24-hour race held every other year at the famous Lemans circuit. It's a mixture of all-out racing, economy driving and various other truck-related subcontests such as tire changing. (changing a truck tire isn't the same as those on a stock car)

Even though the big semi-trucks are more popular across the ocean, they are holding on in the US. A big problem is they are not receiving overwhelming support from the manufacturers. That's a problem of inheritance, not fan support.

In order for manufacturing to support this kind of racing, it has to invest in such a manner of self-support to justify the cause. Sponsors don't get into racing just to be "nice guys". In other words, they have to promote their products. The problem is their products are not generally sold with insatiable demands from the public, but mostly to other businesses. The average fan cannot identify or find use for a brand new $90,000 International, Mack or other make of over-the-road truck any more than you and I can for buying the Apollo 13 space capsule. (unless you have money to blow on frivolous adventures; and how many of us have that?) This lack of manufacturing support also has a domino effect on other forms of exposures, . . . namely television. No television means the word doesn't get distributed as widely as the producers would like.

The Semi's are divided in basically two ways, the 450 and 300 classes. The 450 class is limited to that number in horsepower. It is the more expensive of the two. It involves using state of art equipment. The 300 class is likewise limited to 300 horsepower. In either class, a limited amount of modification is permitted on the engine, especially at the turbocharger and fuel pump.

The trucks must be in standard condition and remain in factory-stock specification. A rollcage is installed in the cab along with specially prepared racing seats and a 4 or 5-point driver restraint harness system.

The tires do not have to be stock size, but rather lower profiled types maintaining a minimum of 5 millimeters tread thickness. Because of the vehicles heavy weight, the use of racing slicks would be out of the question. They couldn't hold together under such heavy loads. They would blow due to high heat build up while rolling at speed. There are tires specially prepared for these machines. The big racetrucks do not necessarily use shaved-down type tires. Whatever the case, they do not last long. So there is great tire expense with Semi Truck racing. The tires will last only 12 to 16 laps on paved roads.

A big problem with this kind of racing is overheated brakedrums. Because of that, special brake liners are permitted with custom-made cooling ducts. It doesn't completely solve overheating, so sometimes a system of cooled water is sprayed onto the drums. This also creates problems. Cool water hitting overheated drums can cause cracking due to sudden shock in temperature range.

The suspensions are relatively stock but may incorporate better quality shock absorbers, springs, shackles and kingpins. The drivetrain must remain stock, with exception of the rear axle gear, which may be fitted with any higher ratio available.

These machines can reach speeds exceeding 115 mph.

L.3. MONSTER TRUCKS—This is a relatively new form of racing. Some folks do not consider this racing as much as a form of entertainment. It may of started out that way, but it's changed throughout the last 7 or 8 years.

These 10,000 lb vehicles are stock-bodied 4x4 pick-up trucks with immensely over-sized wheels, tires and a specially designed suspension system composed of oversized coilover springs and shock absorbers. The tires may be 10 feet tall and weigh several hundred lbs. The chassis is of tubeframe construction housing a large supercharged 550–600 ci, 1600 hp engine. Most engines are mounted mid-range or in the bed of the pick-up styled racer.

The drivers of these vehicles take a tremendous pounding due to the nature of this sport. But that isn't the half of it. Since they're seated several feet off ground, any movement or shock placed at the suspension gets violently magnified up to the driver. The drivers may be 14 to 15 feet off the ground and sometimes even more. That may not sound like much if you take it for granted, but remember, you're in a moving vehicle. If you were to hop in one of these things, you would quickly understand what I'm talking about. Then when you started moving it would get your attention fast. On top of that, when you start moving over obstacles and it gets downright frightening.

The drivers are whipped to and fro from any direction including up and down. But all the while, they must sustain control over a continuous array of impediments such as junk cars, small hills or sets of mounds, mud bogs or any combination thereof.

In the earlier days of this sport, most of the events were confined to tractor-type pulls, jumps and mud races. Today, the MTRA (Monster Truck Racing Association) sanctions events over the entire US. Monster Trucks are also popular throughout the world. One race may include a combination of Solo and short drag-style starts into a 250-300 foot oval strategically marked with such obstacles as a series of junk cars and small mounds.

Other races are the drag type. The racer uses a christmas-tree style start down a straight to a jump with a specific-gradient ramp. Hopefully this racer will land simultaneously on all four tires. Failure to accomplish that usually means the driver ends up on their side.

A typical nights racing may include 24 entrants. First are the qualifying rounds of competition to determine who and with whom a truck competes along side with, in a final 8 or 16-vehicle eliminator-styled series. The paired trucks may race together with the loser eliminated. At some events, each one in the entire field may run the course solo-style with the shortest time declared the winner. Either way the loser of these events aren't necessarily done for the night. They can still move on to events such as the mud competition later on in the program.

A system of points for each vehicle is accumulated and recorded during the season to determine a national champion.

This completes all the major categories, divisions, classes and most subclasses of race vehicles. You certainly discovered there is a ton of them. If that isn't confusing enough, there are a few numbers of locally-based race vehicles such as Sand Rail and Truck Dragsters, Off-Road 4x4's and ATV's, Motorcycle and homebuilt contraptions raced in the US not covered directly in this book.

Couple that with all the classes raced throughout the world and you would probably have to be hauled into a mental facility strapped in a 'straight jacket' trying to make sense of it all. I hope you realize by now how complicated this sport is. But it certainly doesn't stop here. The costs involved are even more enigmatic. After reading about the costs, you won't have to be forcibly hauled into the mental ward, . . . you'll walk into it voluntarily. It's like that old comical song of the sixties which puts it so indearingly . . . "they're coming to take me away, ho ho, ha ha, hee hee, to the funny farm where life is beautiful all the time and I'll be happy to see all those nice young men in their clean white coats, . . . they're coming to take me away . . . to the happy home with flowers and trees and chirping birds and basket weavers sitting there smiling and twiddling their thumbs . . ." Well, . . . you 'oldies' fans know what I'm babbling on about.

4 | The Cost of Racing

If a person asked a race competitor what it cost to race, they'd either get a long look or the answer . . . "expensive". There's about 6.5 billion people in this world. Since racing is such an international sport, let's say one million of them race something on 2, 3 or 4 wheels. If you asked for a specific dollar figure from each of these racers, you'd get one million different answers. (and still many bewildered looks) Asking the cost of racing is like asking parents the costs of raising a child from conception to departure from the nest. It's very, very hard to put a dollar figure on racing, if not impossible, but it's worth a try. I can't do this with pinpoint accuracy, but I'll come as close to reality as possible.

There's a word I'll use that'll help put some sanity into this endeavor:

FACTORS (I. Controlled and II. Uncontrolled)

Many things determine the cost of racing. It's necessary to breakdown, separate and explain these factors to accomplish some order. These factors are categorized as 'controlled' or 'uncontrolled' for the purposes of this book. How they're utilized is determined mostly by the drivers in club racing and the owners at the pro level. Some controlled factors come into play according to general racing goals: future professional aspirations, time, desire, finances, etc. Some uncontrolled factors are: racing mishaps, age, weather, rule changes, marital status, (if the race bug bit you after marriage) etc.

Before these are explained, something needs to be made abundantly clear concerning those students who mix college and racing.

I'll assume for purposes here you're the 18 to 22 year old high school graduate or college student. You high schoolers may have plans for college. If your plans include that, start it and finish. I can't emphasize that too much. Believe me, I'll repeat it more than once. Meanwhile, if you're the collegian hung up on racing, you're better off resisting it for now also. As a student, . . . you can study and get familiar with racing for now. Go to a stockcar, sprint or drag race, whatever you prefer. Check out motocross, dirt or roadracing motorcycles. But don't get directly involved as a driver just yet. As mentioned before, you should know what type racing you prefer, so just stick with only studying that for now.

Racing is like college. It's initially very time consuming and requires concentrated effort. Combining both fulltime college and racing is very hard. Doing both will eventually cause one or both to suffer. That may still apply even if you're financially set. If you're blessed financially, doing both can still tax your time, if not your personal sanity. You can always race later. That's one of the great things about racing, it's not completely youth oriented. Most athletes can physically handle racing long after their football, basketball or track days are numbered. It's not unusual to see 50 year olds racing at both pro and club levels. So time is on your side.

Some financially blessed students can't resist racing, so they confine it to the summer months when vacationing. As far as I'm concerned that's okay. Those types are more than likely getting plenty of support. But be careful! Don't mislead yourself if you experience some success. It's like a student that gets a summer job which paid very well or they liked too much. They quit school to pursue it further. That may be a short-term advantage, but too many times it's a long-term disadvantage that manifests itself later, when it's too late to easily correct. So avoid a decision to quit school for racing. A little racing success now doesn't guarantee any down the road. Besides, the people you race against early in your career may not be a good gauge of your skill. That's because of a financial advantage you may have. (superior equipment) Don't let it portray a false sense of accomplishment.

Some forms of racing while in school is okay. Motorcycle racing (not all) isn't so draining or time consuming. Go-Karts are likewise because they are relatively low maintenance racers. All high-dollar racing requires commitment. So, for those struggling through school, stick with it. No racing except to occasionally watch and/or study it. Going into it before or, worse yet, during school could more than likely be a mistake. It's hard enough for those collegians who can afford a few races in the summer, much less for those who can't.

For those few collegians who are racing successfully, they're probably doing so in rented machinery. (better yet, "borrowed", if they have a racing daddy) Owning your own racer is the main reason why you shouldn't race while in school. It's even more time consuming than renting your equipment. Another reason is simple . . . money. College students may spent more of it in racing than they should. Remember what I said earlier. This sport can get in your blood. You could end up dipping into thee ol college piggy bank. By the way, if you go to college and graduate, it means there's a better chance you'll make more money. Therefore, that means a better chance later to race successfully.

It sounds a bit unfair that racing requires money, but that's the way it is . . . that's life. Hey, this isn't quantum physics, . . . what I'm suggesting to you is none other than plain old fashion common sense. So . . . okay, . . . some students are luckier than others. That's the breaks sometimes. No one claims life is fair.

Luck can perpetuate itself in racing through other ways too. It helps weed out those who only thought they wanted to race. It tests loyalty. It's one of the reasons why there isn't many 'undesirables' in this sport. Even though you may have money to race with, it doesn't mean you have the natural skill. To acquire skill in this sport, you work for it, nobody is born with it. (as compared to those with natural foot speed, size and muscular coordination needed for football, basketball, baseball, etc) Racing has its characters, but it's mostly circumstances due to an individuals frustration. Racing can be awfully frustrating. That may occasionally be vented off the track, but seldom on it. Anyone purposely creating dangerous situations in this sport will find themselves on the outside looking in very fast.

Now, . . . to the factors this volume lists concerning costs of racing. When I use the word 'costs', I don't always and necessarily mean financially, at least in the direct and literal sense. I may also mean such other things as time, sacrifice, support accessories, etc. In the end, these things eventually cost money also.

These factors are listed as 'controlled' (how a competitor treats this sport) and 'uncontrolled'. (unplanned circumstances effecting a racers budget) In addition to costs, is information I believe you should know if for no other reason than to understand why things are as they are.

I. CONTROLLED FACTORS (1 THRU 15)

1. Class of Racing; 2. Level of Racing; 3. Marital Status; 4. Chassis (Closed-course, Drag, Off-Road, ATV, Motorcycle); 5. Engines; 6. Maintenance; 7. Wheels & Tires; 8. Travel/Lodging; 9. Race Fuel; 10. Transport Equipment; 11. Crew; 12. Time; 13. Facilities; 14. Financial Responsibility; 15. Accessories.

I.1. CLASS OF RACING—The type of racing a prospect shows interest in, such as motorcycle, off-road, drag, formula or whatever, is usually something adopted through a process of exposure, osmosis or whatever. But more important is the level or class chosen in that particular type. As covered in Chapter 2, the type of racing a person likes is a psychological thing. To start out in racing, the key is to choose the right class financially and competitively. This isn't as confusing as it seems once you understand your options.

Remember two important points: (1) Speed costs money. The more speed you want, the more it will cost, including possibly something other than money. It may not be obvious now, but racing those speedy little roadracing Go-Karts, for example, will not necessarily be cheaper than some sophisticated, but slower formula racers. Why? For one, that slower formula car has a safer suspension system. Another is it envelopes drivers for better protection in accidents.

(2) My first point was more speed may cost more than just money. The second point is, speed can be increased at lower costs if the danger element is increased. The price for higher speed is expensive enough financially. Can you sacrifice an arm here or a leg there? Nobody can. I know that question sounds crude, but it's asked to make a point. It's not a knock on Go-Karts, but at any speed they are not as safe as some supposedly faster racecars. That's because Karts lack an adequate suspension, among other things. Fortunately, competitors adjust their driving techniques with them. That's what makes Karts what they are. But many people, like your mother for instance, they may not see that. All racing is dangerous to them.

Racing safety isn't necessarily sacrificed at higher speeds, but rather, how one races. The point is, sophisticated racing costs more. It's not always brute speed that runs up costs or danger. So understand your class, costs and safety. Don't necessarily let safety factors influence your class choice. (I don't think anybody does anyway) Let your finances and experience determine that. (which at this point, you probably do not have any racing experience) Don't let loved ones influence your class level because of

perceived safety standards. I know you'll stick with your 'type' of racing religiously, but class yourself so you can proceed progressively and smoothly through the learning process. Don't start yourself too high too early. Many racers can run a higher class financially, but they are uncompetitive. It can be depressing when a person finishes a race successfully, but still gets their doors blown off, so-to-speak.

It can also be unnecessarily dangerous. If you're not at least competitive while learning to race, then of course, it means you're too slow for the time being. That means you could be a dangerous "backmarker" to many of the front runners. Remember, many times in racing, it's not the overall speed of the race machine that creates danger, it's differences in speed with their competition on the track.

So the bottom line 9 times out of 10 is this: starting out in too high of a racing class can simply slow up the learning process; sometimes dramatically runs up the costs and create unnecessary danger.

The point is to figure out your best level financially, competitively and practically. The wrong choice is also wasted time. You have to do some research to make the right determination. This isn't as tough appearing right now, especially for level-headed, mature, ego-suppressed adults. (sorry kids) Trust your instincts. After seeing the choice of classes within your type of racing, you should have a pretty good idea where to start. It's not nuclear physics here. It's simply sounder judgement when all the options are known. So, find what those options are. You'll know more of what's available when you finish reading this book. You'll be more susceptible and open to choices.

I.2. LEVEL OF RACING—The distinction here isn't between pro and amateur levels, but rather how serious some take this sport. There are amateurs who take racing so seriously that they're willing to sacrifice a more comfortable life style. They would love to turn pro but lack money (sponsorship) to reach that level. Of course, there are some other factors, but many racers do whatever possible to support this habit.

The average Joe (nonracer) does not always understand how this gets into the blood. They find some of the motivations and/or sacrifices for racing financially wasteful and dangerous. The real racer won't. It's part of their personality. Some people are in this game for less obvious reasons. What that exactly is may never be known. Even some serious racers may find the reasons enigmatic. Whatever, most want to be "out there" running as hard as they can. It could be the thrill of competition, ego-gratification or the danger of participation. It's not as crazy as it sounds.

In many ways, the motivation to race isn't any different than it is to participate in any sport. Why play football and risk a serious injury? Racers are like golfers. Some are obsessed with the sport. To any kind of professional athlete, this obsession with any sport makes perfect sense. This makes sense to the general public also. That's obvious, because of the money involved. But unless you're playing any sport without the motivation for winning and turning pro . . . what's the point, . . . what's the point? What's the point of doing anything if there isn't money involved? Bad attitude! That's about as greedy and a self-centered train of thought as one can get. In the most basic and primitive way, why does anybody do anything? For love! Of course, what that love's directed to may be many things. (and I'm not touching that with a ten foot pole)

I.3. MARITAL STATUS—This subject is covered more in Chapter 2. It'll be covered somewhat in the 'uncontrolled factors' section also.

For our purposes, we're still assuming you're that 18 year old just graduated from high school. Whether you go to college or not, as far as marital status is concerned is irrelevant for the moment. Even though most 18 year olds are single, you shouldn't have to shove a gun in their face forcing their understanding of marriage and it's responsibility. With raising kids, or not, one has to make marriage work. A good marriage won't make you a better racer. A bad one certainly won't help your racing.

The point is, assuming you're not married, engaged or too serious with any female, it

would be all too easy to say . . . "stay that way." That would be self-centered on my part. There are all kinds of reasons for human companionship. Without getting into reasons for staying single, one thing is clear . . . it's a lot cheaper! Use tact and timing if you have your eye on a particular person and the other on racing. Be straight forward and clear up front with them. That way there will be no surprises in this matter later on.

In the case of females, most will accept racing as long as it appears not to be "your mistress". I said "appears". If it is your "mistress", stay single or take acting lessons. You'll need them! Put yourself in the opposite role. How would you like to be taken for granted as a result of some obsessive behavior? It's degrading from someone you care for. There are a few racers with that tendency. I've seen that helpless look women get when they're with them at a racing event. That's especially so if the racer is just off the track and irritated. Women generally will sacrifice more than men to keep a relationship running smoothly. Even so, learn to sell your racing ambitions in a positive manner. Talk to your partner. Get them involved. If they want to help, that's good. In the interest of finances (not ruining something) be sure your spouse knows what they're doing. If they don't, be patient. They want to help because you are you, not because they're necessarily a good samaritan. (like racing, it's an emotional thing)

So what's this have to do with the cost of racing? If you can't figure that out then consider this. For an 18 year old, generally you're not starting at what's the top of the ladder in life. Money comes hard enough for those in the work market for years, much less for recent graduates. With that and the overpriced entertainment venue of today, (called dating) that person you're dating could become quite an expense. I know that sounds cheap now, but it's stated to make a point. A decent night on the town costs 60 to 100 dollars. That's not exaggerating. Do that three or four weekends a month and it'll hurt. It won't break you like racing can, but it'll cut deep into any race budget you have. (or any budget for that matter)

A big way to cut dating costs is to treat the

race weekends like a date. Sounds crazy? Maybe yes, maybe no. I'm not going into the moral issues of it. If you have to go out of town with your girlfriend over the weekend to race, you will have to judge your date, her parents and what they'll think of that idea. You can bet those parents will be judging you. This is something I'm sure you'll know how to handle or avoid. Obviously, the more established you are with your girlfriend's parents, the easier it is. If you can pull it off, taking her out of town over the weekend, you've "killed two birds with one stone"! (you've raced and dated) If you can't, then you'll have to make sacrifices . . . racing or your girlfriend.

It's not like your girlfriend is a mechanic, but her presence is helpful. I've seen guys race by themselves often, including myself. They are their own crew, sponsor, mechanic, manager and whatever. They're single and don't date much because it cuts into their time and the budget. A racer can save quite a bit of money that way, but sometimes racing by yourself causes unnecessary pressure. It can detract from the concentration needed to compete consistently. Saving money by sacrificing help may be overfocusing. It can have a self-defeating effect. It's always good to have any kind of help in addition to the company. I've found anyone, especially those of the opposite sex, has a distinct calming effect on racers besieged with problems at the race track. (I think it's something to do with not wanting to look like an idiot if you are upset at circumstances)

I.4. CHASSIS—We're getting closer to the nuts and bolts of racing costs. Things are becoming more specific. In the area of more focused dollar-costs for a chassis and engine, (and accessories covered later) are quotes that still are going to be relatively vague. That's unavoidable. The factor discussed in this particular case, the racing chassis, (a racer minus engine and wheels) are further subcategorized into the various forms of racing. (Formula, Off-Road, etc)

There are mediating circumstances which determine what to offer a prospective seller for a race car chassis. See Chapter 7 where it says "Don't Buy Problems". That's infor-

mation on what kind of chassis not to buy. Also, discussing chassis in this section is almost tantamount to meaning the whole race vehicle. The chassis, . . . vehicle, they're almost the same thing. Usually though, a chassis refers to racer minus the engine. Anyway, you may find a chassis for relatively a "song and dance" if the seller wants out of racing. If he is moving up or down in class, you just may find the opposite, since there's no urgency to sell quickly. Whatever the situation, read the chapter on 'Buying vs Renting'.

What about specific prices? They will vary widely. They have to. The circumstances a used race vehicle is sold under determines its price. (not always value) That's mostly due to nonnegotiable new racecar prices. Racecars depreciate very quickly. But that's more prevalent in big money racing, like Formula One and IndyCars. The club race machines hold their value a bit longer. The pro racing technology changes for the better so quickly, after one season high profile racecars are obsolete. It's the main reasons why many teams purchase a brand new rolling chassis every year. If they don't, they lose a competitive edge. (Al Unser's 4th Indy win was an exception; He won in a racer over a year old)

Despite technical advances, it's a shame to mothball a one year old Indy car to the garage. So something was done. The AIS (the American Indy Car Series) was created to extend their life, (other than use as a back-up car) while at the same time providing an excellent trainer for future Indy car drivers.

In the less costlier ranks of racing, older race chassis tend to remain competitive longer. It's not because they are necessarily built better, but because the new chassis sales market is small. The competition is driver oriented, (supposedly) as opposed to manufacturer-oriented. In other words, money availability at the amateur level dictates that the race car chassis last longer. Without that, all amateur racing would suffer or price itself out of existence.

So, . . . the following figures coming up are as close to normal as practical for the purposes here. You may pay less or pay more. Remember, because of a lack in market for racing chassis or cars by the buying public, not often will you be forced to pay for what a race car is actually worth. Keep that in mind, before you're shocked at the prices you're about to see.

The chassis prices listed below are without wheels, tires, spare parts and engines, unless stated so otherwise.

Closed Course Vehicles

- INDY CAR CHASSIS: Brand new, no tires, wheels nor engine; about $400,000. A high-financed, one driver team will have one oval-course chassis and another one for back-up including chassis accessories for roadcourse setups.
- INDY CAR CHASSIS: For a 2 year old racer in AIS; (American Indy Car Series) 10 to $30,000.
- INDY CAR: ARS, (American Racing Series) an Indy Spec Racer. New; about 75 to $125,000. Used; 40 to $60,000. (now called Indy Light)
- FORMULA ONE: Hard to narrow down because there are so many fabricators involved. An educated guess for a chassis is 400 to $650,000.
- FORMULA ATLANTICS: Used; 15 to $25,000. (Formerly Formula Two) New; 48 to $57,000. (most of these high profile racers up to here aren't bought, they're rented; but any racer can be rented; more on that later)
- SUPER VEE: Used; 8 to $28,000. A wide discrepancy for 2 reasons. There where many uncompetitive models left over after the Ralt was built. (it dominated the pro class) Also, because SV was raced at the club level, they were not quite as fast, due to the rules, as the pro versions. New; (No longer built) around $40,000.
- FORMULA FORD 1600: New; 18 to $22,000. Used; 4 to $12,000. Lots of 'makes' in this class. A large bearing on price is the cars age and reputation.
- FORMULA FORD 2000: New; 27 to 29,000. Used; 6 to $20,000, depending greatly on the 'makes' competitive reputation.
- VINTAGE FORMULA FORD: The older competitive Fords range at 6, 7 and $8000. Others are as low as 15 to $2,500.
- FORMULA VEE: New kits are around $5000. You supply the stock VW parts, which may be another 500 to $800 minus engine. Used VW parts are less expensive and in many cases can be bought from junk yards or taken off certain VW Bugs. Rolling Chassis; (With VW parts in-

stalled and ready for an engine) 8500 to $12,000. Used; 3500 to $6000. You may do better but it'll be an older chassis. These racers really last. A 15 year old chassis won the FV National Championship a couple years ago. Many times the used price includes an engine.
- FORMULA 440: New; (with engines) 8 to $9,500. (without engines) around 75 to $8,500. Used; 2 to $4,000 and as much as 35 to $8,500 for 1 or 2 year olds. This is a class, like Formula Vee, that's recently come out with several new 'makes'.
- FORMULA SABRE: A new foreign spec class. (Japan) Real hard to find used ones yet. New; (Race ready) 75 to $80,000.
- FORMULA MAZDA: New; around $32,500. Used; (Not many around because this class is relatively new) 26 to $29,000. They hold their value very well.
- 'A' SPORTSRACERS: This class is almost dead. No new ones are built. Used; 7 to $30,000 from bad to good copies.
- 'C' SPORTSRACERS: New; Approximately $25,000. Used; 5 to $15,000.
- 'D' SPORTSRACERS: New; Approximately $20,000. Used; 3 to $18,000. Both "C" & "D" used racers are with engines and race-ready.
- SPORTS 2000: New; 27 to $35,000. Used; 10 to $23,000. A popular class. Don't expect to find many cheap Sports 2000 racers.
- SPEC RACER (FORMERLY SPORTS RENAULT): Very popular. New kits $12,000. Used; Not cheap, these have excellent resale value, around 10 to $12,000.
- SHELBY CAN-AM: New; $35,000. Used; So new the used chassis are not plentiful. 28 to $31,000.
- E, F, G & H PRODUCTION: New; Not applicable since these are not purpose-built racers. These are converted street cars. Used; generally around 4 to $8,500. You may find them a bit cheaper or much more expensive. All these are usually sold with a race ready engine and spares.
- SHOWROOM STOCK GT: New; These are newer high performance street Cameros, Corvettes Mustangs and such. They aren't usually resold because they can be used for other purposes. They're street-legal and seldom resold as racers. If for sale, you'll pay around 9 to $15,000 if they're not dinged up.
- SHOWROOM STOCK A, B & C: New; Not applicable also. Used; Generally around 3000 to $8,500 with engines.

- IMPROVED TOURING: New; Not applicable. Used; these are actually older Showroom Stock racers, 2500 to $5,500 with engine.
- GRAND TOURING (GT) (SCCA SANCTIONED): New; N/A. These cars are usually converted new cars to specialized racers by private race builders. Used; 7500 to $15,500 for GT1 and GT2 of better quality. 5500 to $9,500 for GT3, GT4 and GT5.
- GT (IMSA SANCTIONED) GTO, GTX, GTU and TRANS-AM: New; 30 to $75,000. Used; 12 to $35,000. The GTX and Group 'C' can reach a price tag of $250,000 in the World Endurance Series category. (these are now defunct and re-classed)
- GTP & GTP LIGHT: new; In line with Indy car racing, $250,000. Used; $150,000.
- WORLD SPORTS CAR: New; Also in line with IndyCar costs. (but the new Ferrari is $750,000) Most of these are supposed to be about $175,000, new.
- ENDURO GO-KARTS: New; Complete, ready to race: Approximately 30 to $3,800. Used; 1500 to $3,500. (completely race ready).
- SPRINT GO-KARTS: New; (complete, race ready) 2200 to $3,000. Used; (complete, race ready) 800 to $2,000.
- FKE FORMULA GO-KART: Not well established here in the US. Their costs are in line with Enduro Karts, but on an experimental basis. This class was testing an auto body design in Europe.
- DIRT GO-KARTS: New; (race ready) 100 to $1,500. Used; (race ready) 100 to $750.
- GRAND NATIONAL STOCK CAR: New; (race ready) 75 to $110,000. Used; N/A, These are seldom sold as used for racing. Their bodies (actually Body Panels) don't last a few races much less a full season. The cage and chassis may be used as long as it's competitively possible.
- BABY GRAND STOCK CARS: New; (race ready) 20 to $30,000. Used; (race ready) 10 to $20,000.
- LATE MODELS: New; (race ready) 21 to $25,000. Used; (race ready) 5 to $15,000.
- SPORTSMAN LATE MODEL: New; (race ready) You won't find many new ones of this kind of racer. There are many beginners here. Eventually they sell their old racers to move up in class. A new one is about $10,000. Used; 3 to $7,000.
- MODIFIED & SUPERMODIFIEDS: Some can be quite expensive. While others are pretty moderate. Race ready, the good ones are 30 to $50,000.

- DIRT CHAMPIONSHIP: New; 18 to $20,000. With engine, add 20 to $22,000.
- SPRINT CAR: New; 30 to $35,000 w/engine. A good used rolling chassis, 15 to $20,000. Rolling chassis hold value.
- 3/4 MIDGET: New; $20,000. (race ready) Used; 5 to $15,000. (race ready)
- QUARTER MIDGET: New; 12 to $1,500 w/engine. Used; 700 to $1,000 w/engine.
- MIDGET: New; $30,000 w/engine. A good used one; 18 to $25,000.

Drag Race Vehicles

These are the hardest to estimate. Quotes are for new vehicles only. Some engines are hard to receive in a packaged deal.

- TOP FUEL/FUNNY CAR: These 2 types of dragsters are major-league expensive. They are right up there in price where it's useless to discuss. To campaign one of these for a year is about 2 million.
- PRO STOCK AND MODIFIED DRAG RACERS: Chassis; 20 to $25,000.
- FACTORY MODIFIED: New; (race ready) 55 to $65,000.
- TOP SPORTSMAN: New; (race ready) 65 to $75,000.
- MODIFIED SPORTSMAN: There are about 7 subclasses from dragsters to econo-modified. It's hard to figure, but all 7 classes will average about $40,000. For a race ready vehicle, dragsters are higher at $50,000 to Econos, $30,000.
- QUICK ROD SPORTSMAN: New; (race ready) 18 to $23,000.
- SUPER ROD SPORTSMAN: New; (race ready) 13 to $17,000.
- HOT ROD SPORTSMAN: New; (race ready) 8 to $12,000.
- SUPER STOCK SPORTSMAN: 4 subdivisions with numerous street-legal subclasses. A very wide range depending on manufacturer that are generally available publicly. Add list price plus 3 to $4,000 for competitive racing upgrades.
- STOCK & PURE STOCK SPORTSMAN DIVISIONS: Numerous subclasses. Same as Super-Stock, except add list price of your car plus $2,000 for race add-ons.
- BRACKET RACERS: (this is a scoring type of drag racer open to many classes) This is where many racers in drag racing start. This puts more emphasize on driver ability, not sophisticated machinery. The cost for this type of racing is hard to figure. It varies, but a few people

"in-the-know" say it's 15 to $3,500 to get started. They emphasize it's a vague figure because of different types of race machines participating in brackets. Most times, no race add-ons are necessary.

Off Road Vehicles

- THUNDER TRUCKS (MTEG): New; Not cheap at all. 155 to $200,000 race ready.
- ULTRA STOCK: New; Approximately $45,000, race ready.
- SUPER 1600: New; 30 to $60,000 w/engine. Good resale value.
- SUPERLITES: New; Approximately $10,000, but can get up to 14, $15,000.
- DESERT RACERS (11 classes) MINI-MAG or SCORE/HDRA (12 classes): The Class 1 Buggy vehicle can cost about $45,000 for a competitive race-ready racer. After that, with few exceptions, new racers start at about $25,000 to 10,000 down in class. Used vehicles depreciate relatively quick. A good used vehicle is hard to find. But remember, you usually get what you pay for. At times, some vehicles with proven performance command as much as $35,000. Take the six SCORE/HDRA motorcycle groups away and the 19 remaining classes will narrow to 3 basic vehicles: 1. VW Bugs; 2. (mid to full-sized pick-up) Trucks; and 3. (purpose-built dune) Buggy types. Even though each of these vehicles are relatively similar in their respective class, there are some extremes in used vehicle prices due to their age. VW bugs: Used; 18 to $4,600. Trucks: Used; 7,000 to $25,000. Buggies: Used; 2,200 to $10,500. Class 1 buggies are more pricey.

All off-road racecars take a tremendous beating. Good used equipment is expensive and hard to find. But after a year or two, prices start to fall dramatically. Look at the chassis and suspension very closely. Remember, the chassis are more prone to hidden damage. It may not look broke or cracked, but these machines can suffer metal fatigue due to the severe nature of competition. (but then, this can be the case with all racers, including those that have plowed into a wall and were repaired) In all higher levels of racing, this is always carefully checked. But that doesn't mean it's the case in club racing.

ATV, Motorcycle Racers

- SCORE/HDRA MOTORCYCLES, CLASSES 20, 21, 22: New; Class 20, 125 cc, $3,200, Class 21, 250 cc, $3500, Open Class (22) $4,400. Used; (For all 3) 10 to $1,400, 12 to $2,000 and 15 to $3,100, respectively, for fair to average equipment.
- ATV RACERS: (MTEG & SCORE/HDRA SANCTIONED) New; 3 to $6,000. Used; 25, 45 to $5,000 for a decent racer.
- DIRT TRACK SPEEDWAY: Used; 125 to 500 cc, 800 to $3,000.
- ENDURO & MOTOCROSS BIKE: Used; 1 to $3,000.
- RELIABILITY TRAIL-HILLCLIMBS: Used; 400 to $2,000.
- DESERT RACER (HARE): Used; 2000 to $3,500.
- SPRINT, ROADRACING, ENDURANCE: New; (50 to 750 cc and open) $1,500 to $12,000, and 15 to $20,000 in the Open class.
- PRODUCTION-SUPERBIKES-FORMULA, FIM, World Class Competitors: New; 25 to $40,000. Used; This is too high of a class for used ones sold cheaply, if they're resold at all. 10 to $15,000. These world-class cycles command high finances. A one-rider team finances can approach 1.9 to 2.1 million dollars per season.

What you just read indicates a ballpark figure for a (race-ready) chassis. Most people are under the impression race machines are the most expensive portion of racing. That's true for some less expensive classes, but not many. It depends on your style of racing, support equipment and other factors.

Here's an example of what I spent to start myself in racing. I've raced Formula Vee's for 14 years. I remember pretty accurately what the costs were. I paid exactly $2,500 for a well taken care of used rolling chassis. Then it was $500 for a relatively competitive engine, but actually, one that was more reliable. (for racing at the regional level) That engine probably would not of been strong enough to race competitively at the national level. (you'll know what regional, national racing is later)

The approximate start-up costs for my first race totaled $4,510. That was $3,000 for a 5 or 6 year old 'Lynx B' Formula Vee. (including engine) $350 for 4 brand new M&H race tires; $250 for a used race suit, flameproof underwear, helmet and shoes, (a steal); $400 for 2 race schools, (entry fees, travel, lodging, etc); $225 chassis rebuilding costs and paint; $60 for membership and licensing costs; 1st race entry fee, travel costs, $225. (IRP, Indianapolis, June 1981)

Understand, $4,510 put me into my first race. Start up costs are always high with racing. (like in business) Mine wasn't. I could have spent close to twice that amount. But, I didn't have to spend money on support equipment, garaging and things like that. Today, I can still race for about $165 per weekend. That's not bad for Formula Vee. Still, that doesn't include the long range costs such as an engine rebuild, tires or the chemical treatment for them and miscellaneous bills for other necessities like bearings, brake pads and fluid, oil, fuel, filters, batteries, tools, trailer licensing, etc. Then, if I take an unplanned exertion off the track, the costs really start to mount. About $125 of that $165 quote was the entry fee for most SCCA race weekends. Other then start-up costs for some Go-Kart classes and Formula 440's, that's about as inexpensive as Formula racing gets. Go-Karts, Motocross and most Motorcycle classes can do better, . . . much better.

Remember, this is amateur racing and usually no cash purses are offered. Costs are not offset by any (large) cash purses anyway. That's true even for most professional racing, including the winner of the Indy 500. The first place share of money for that event is worth well over 1.5 million dollars, plus well over another million for endorsements. Myth: cash purses do not help defray entire racing costs. Not even close! Actually, if anything, it drives up competition and therefore, the costs. In some amateur racing, there are clubs holding pro races in the popular classes, like FV and FF 2000. But the purses are not large enough to unreasonably force up competitive costs for the sake of the money alone.

What are some things many 'club' (amateur) racers can do to help cut costs? Well, it's not real rocket science stuff. For example, I do things with my racing tires and fuel that you'll read about later. But by the same token, some of the things I do may cost me some competitive edge. You'll know more

specifically why that is, before you finish this chapter.

I.5. ENGINES—Engines do not necessarily have to be the most important part of a race machine. A good example is in motorcycle Trail and Motocross events and Off-Road or Endurance racing. Engines like those need not be tweaked to gain every ounce of energy possible. Although it's important, the main job of an engine like that is to allow the chassis, driver or rider to do their job. Let me put it this way, an engine can be the most powerful one built, but if it blows apart at any point in an event, that power doesn't mean a thing.

Many people believe an engine must be the strongest to win a race. There's validity in that thinking, but it's not always true. In the wrong hands, (driver, builder or poorly setup chassis) an engine can lose its efficiency and reliability. A race vehicle has to handle well. If the chassis can't transfer power to the ground properly, it's wasted. On the other hand, a race car that's expertly setup is worthless without an engine to properly power it.

What are the costs involved with a good race engine? Plenty! That's not an exact science any more than buying your first used racecar is. But for a point of reference, I'll take a crack at it. Later on, I'll elaborate on what's involved with maintaining them. Meanwhile, common sense dictates not to overrev them, ignore or bust'em up in mishaps. Keep them tuned, well oiled, (myself and most drivers change oil after every weekend of racing) properly cooled and clean. Do that and you won't have to keep rebuilding or buying new ones constantly.

Fortunately in amateur racing, engines last much longer. Not necessarily because they're better, but because they're smaller, lower revved and less powerful versions of the high horsepower, high-dollar juggernauts characteristic in the professional ranks. It's important how long they last at the amateur level because essentially, many forms of club racing survives off it. When they fail it's frustrating. When they blow and ruin the block, it's devastating to the $25,000 a year salary of the 9 to 5 "average joe".

- INDY CAR, TOP FUEL, FUNNY DRAGSTER, FORMULA ONE, WSC, GTP: An Indy car engine generally costs 100 to $125,000, brand new. Does that serve to discourage you? It ought to. Top-fuelers and nitro methane Funny Cars need to have their engines torn down after every run. Those runs are around 5 or 6 seconds. The Indy car engine is torn down after every race. Remember the teams at these levels have several engines. Formula One, Endurance and Road Racing motorcycles also get torn down and rebuilt after every race. That's true for GTP and Grand National Stock Cars also. These teams are running for big money. It means competition will be at its highest. It requires superior equipment and power. Even a lose of a few horsepower isn't tolerated at these levels. Therefore, the engines are kept at the peak of their performance. Costs are impractical to discuss, but rebuilds can range from 5000 to $20,000.
- SUPER VEE, FORMULA ATLANTIC: These engines are suppose to last 3, 4 or 5 race weekends. That figure, I feel, should be more like 2 or 3 weekends. (if not less) It's about $6,000 for a rebuild. Pro Super Vee (series now defunct) requires a teardown after every race.
- FORMULA FORD 2000 AND 1600, SPORTS-RACERS: Hopefully, an engine can last 7 to 10 weekends before they show a significant loss of power. But now that the 2000's are starting to race professionally, that 7 to 10 race reliability will probably go down extensively. They will likely tear them down after every race. Rebuilds are 4,000 to $4,500.00 for a good one, but can be as low as $1,000. An occasional problem with these engines is in the crankshaft. They had a history of cracking under long-term strain, but it looks as though that may of been solved.
- FORMULA VEE, FORMULA 440, PRODUCTION and IMPROVED TOURING: All these engines can last 12 to 16 races weekends and sometimes more. Rebuilds are around 600 to $1,500 for FV's. Some well known and reputable FV engine builders can command up to $3,400 for a rebuild and $4,500 for a new one. Formula 440's costs are about 1/2 to 2/3 of FV's. Production and IT racers are sometimes never rebuilt from the ground up. But they can run into the hundreds easily if a driver "drops one all over the track".
- SHOWROOM STOCK: Usually they never are rebuilt either. But that has nothing to do with a lack of care, but rather the practicality of it. These are street-legal racers. Competition racers in these classes are performance-rated. Building a stronger engine only means they would have to move up in class, where that stronger engine would gain no competitive edge. Like many classes, these engines need only be reliable.
- SPRINT CARS: A complete rebuild would be around $6,000.
- MIDGETS, 3/4, 1/4: Some 3/4's can last an entire season. Rebuilds are $5,000 for the top Midget competitors and about $1,000 for the lower competitors. Quarter-midget engines do not need relatively much attention. Rebuilds are very inexpensive sometimes as low as $25 and as high as $150.
- LATE MODEL STOCKCARS: Rebuilds are 7 to $8,000 depending on how competitive a driver can afford to be.
- SPORTSMAN STOCKCARS: These guys avoid rebuilt as long as possible. When they finally have to get one, it's about 2 to $3,000.
- ENDURO AND SPRINT GO-KARTS: These are very high revving engines. Some RPM's reach an unbelievable 16,000. (an Indy engines maximum RPM is around 14,000. The laws of physics subject those larger sized ones to blow at anything over that) The Enduro and Sprint engines can last as much as 10 to 15 hours at those revolutions. Six to 8 hours would be normal. New engines are about 5 to $1,500. The lower level of Go-Karts, such as dirt types, seem to last forever. But some rebuilds are high as 6 to $700 in the lower level. 50 to $150 is normal.
- PRO STOCK DRAG CARS: These pro category engines don't have to be rebuilt over and over again like Rail and Funny Car engines do. When they are, it's about 5 to $10,000.
- FACTORY MODIFIED, TOP SPORTSMAN, MODIFIED SPORTSMAN: Even though these are amateur levels, the costs are more like pro level. Drivers generally hope an engine lasts an entire season, but it's not usually the case. One or two rebuilds per season is the norm. For rebuilds, 3 to $10,000.
- QUICK, SUPER AND HOT ROD DRAG DIVISIONS: Engines can last one to two seasons. 1 to $4,000 per rebuild.
- SUPERSTOCK, STOCK DRAG DIVISIONS: Hopefully, they never need a rebuild . . . but it happens. When an engine gets tired, the machine may be moved to bracket racing to facilitate the lost power. Rebuilts are 5 to $1,500.
- OFF-ROAD TRUCKS: Some of these are $200,000 vehicles in the MTEG series, others are the Desert racers. Engine rebuilds aren't

as frequent as one would expect for machines of that price. That's because of the relatively low top-end RPM's and work load required and the nature of their sport. Remember, I said "relatively". Still, power is important. Rebuilds can be 5 to $10,000.

- OFF-ROAD ULTRASTOCK, ULTRALITE: These vary widely. MTEG sanction racers command about 3 to $5,000 once or twice a year. SCORE/HDRA vehicles, depending on class and competitive desire of driver, get torn down and rebuilt after every race. Some last a year. Some hardly last at all.
- SUPERBIKES, FORMULA BIKES, PRODUCTION: (high speed sprint & endurance) Rebuilds are after every race, usually. They can range from $2,000 for the Production to $10,000 for the high-revving international racers.
- DIRT BIKES, DESERT BIKES, ENDUROS: Some teardowns are necessary two or three times a season for the desert types. Many get away with an engine lasting one or two seasons. Rebuilds are 5 to $1,200. Dirt bike engines are less expensive in most cases.
- RELIABILITY & OBSERVED TRAIL: Hopefully, these hardly ever need rebuilding because high-speed engines aren't needed. Production engines are all that's necessary. Rebuilds are approximately 1 to $300.
- MOTOCROSS: May need rebuilding once or twice yearly at top level, 4 to $1,000.

The cost of rebuilding race engines is vague at best. Those figures just quoted are not carved in stone. Inflation, among other things, will effect rebuilding prices. In all but the high levels of racing, the figures quoted are purposely on the high side. That was done for a reason. If you could rebuild a race engine by yourself, the costs are cut close to a third to maybe one-half. But rebuilding a race engine and doing so at the minute tolerances and high standards, using so-called tricks-of-the-trade, is usually another matter.

What you can do and what you believe you can do is likely two different things. If you're good enough to rebuild your own race engine the right way, you ought to consider doing it for a living. It's good money. Otherwise, most racers should have their engines rebuilt by a competent, reliable, reputable pro, . . . especially racers in amateur level who can afford it. Find out who the good ones are. The veteran racers will know. Ask them. They're pretty honest with those kinds of things, but make sure they aren't affiliated with a machine shop themselves. You want an objective reply, not one advertising their own business. Most amateur race drivers simply can't afford the best engine work. But always get honest engine work. Don't pay for work not needed. Learn to recognize what area of an engine needs to be rebuilt. If the compression rings around the piston are worn, crank bearings used up, to name a few things, then the engine needs those replaced, but not if the block is cracked, it's then ruined. You'll need an entire overhaul. A cracked block is usually the result of an accident. Sometimes a block cracks if the crankshaft or a connecting rod fractures. Those fast moving parts usually ruin anything in their way.

At high speed, an engine can blow or fracture a connecting rod. As a result, the crankshaft may suddenly lock up due to a rod wedging below the cylinder. Aside from the block cracking or tearing apart, a sudden shock to the drive train could damage a gear or the transmission housing. These nasty situations are sometimes figured into the quotes given in this chapter. But not all quotes are worse-case scenarios. If an engine only needs to be blueprinted, the costs quotes generally could be cut 40 to 50%. (blueprinting is tearing down an engine, checking internal components and replacing only what's needed; always replacing rings and bearings, no matter how good they look; the components are meticulously reassembled, balanced, with all tolerances and clearances fitted to the highest degree)

A properly trained mechanic can assemble a car engine. But remember, a good race mechanic knows how to do that using tolerances measured in the thousandths of an inch or more. This is necessary with race engines because of the heavy jobs they're expected to perform. These engine must be loose enough to avoid power-robbing friction, yet allow free-flow of lubricants. On the other hand, the internal workings need to be tight enough to avoid destructive centrifugal lashing forces. Couple all that with thermal dynamics (expansion and contraction of metal) and you should have a relatively fair idea how complicated race engines are. It takes expensive equipment and specific skills to assemble a high performance engine. Therefore, the costs are higher compared to rebuilding the family car's powerplant. It only needs to pull you to a maximum of 75 mph. (legally, that is) Remember, nobody can have both a powerful and reliable race engine, relatively speaking, without paying big, big bucks for it. Ask the builders, drivers and car owners in the pro ranks, they know all about it.

I.6. MAINTENANCE—Maintenance is essentially cheap insurance against premature breakdowns. Don't cut corners on it. The best way to avoid costly and unnecessary engine/chassis problems is to follow a strict maintenance regiment.

(a through j)

a. KEEP THE OIL CLEAN—Change it after every weekend of racing. Use only race or synthetic oils. Synthetic oil producers claim changing their oil as often isn't necessary. Those oils do stand up better to heat, but they get just as dirty. So, they should be changed like regular race oil. In addition to dirty oil, one also does not need air in the oil. Air in your oil takes the form of foam. Foam can hurt the oil viscosity and circulation. Artificial oil will combat against that. A quart of synthetic oil ranges from 5 to $7.00 per quart. (compared to $1.40 for racing oil) In the long run, synthetic oil is cheaper. (and much better)

Try to reclaim your used oil by cleaning it instead of throwing it away. Oil doesn't wear out, it just gets dirty. (especially when it's used like it is in racing) Personally, I haven't tried this yet, but it's my intention to do so.

What I read was to boil 4 gallons of it at a time. Then add 1 pint of liquid silicate of soda and stir it for 10 minutes. Let the oil settle until it's clear, about 12 to 24 hours. That may vary. Siphon the clear oil off the top. It's important not to tilt or jar the container. It could stir the old sediments lying at the bottom. I didn't read this, but I'd avoid mixing different brands, types and grades together. That way the product retains its originally designed characteristics.

b. KEEP ALL FILTERS CLEAN—Every oil change should be accompanied by a new (racing) filter. I don't recommend stock passenger car filters. It's possible that high oil pressure from a cold running race engine could suck the filtering element out of it's original position inside the canister. Some guys only change the filter every other time. I don't recommend that even for a regular car, much less an expensive race engine.

Air filters—Use the sponge type, not the paper filament kind. Sponge types can be cleaned and reused. It saves dollars. I think oil-soaked sponge filters are superior in cleansing ability. Some feel they restrict airflow to the engines induction system. Some guys don't even oil-soak them. That seems to work out fine. Others feel the 'oil-soaks' flow restriction can be remedied by using a much larger size. Also, a proper location, using a ram-air effect without hurting vehicle aerodynamics can help. Whatever the case, I don't trust paper-filaments in racing applications.

c. CHECK SPARK PLUGS AFTER EVERY WEEKEND—Learn how to read a plug. It'll tell you what's going on inside your engine. Keep them clean and very accurately gapped. Look for corrosion, breakage and discoloring. A good race engine spark plug can cost as much as $15, but they will not foul or miss.

Contact the manufacturers for a chart explaining how to read them.

d. KEEP THE VALVE LASH PROPERLY ADJUSTED—Unlike passenger engines, racing engine valve tabbets should be as close to the valve stem as possible; actually touching, even when the valve is closed. You should be able to rotate the push rod in the valves closed position with one finger. Proper lash allows maximum entry of fuel and air. If lash is too close, the valve will not shut enough, meaning a loss of cylinder compression. (and power) Also, the valve may overheat and fracture, because the transfer of heat from the valve head to the valve seat can't be conducted away. (no contact to the cooler valve seat)

e. CHECK ALL WIRING—Keep them securely harnessed from heat, mechanical friction and properly hooked up to nonslip, wire-secured terminals.

Make sure the sparkplug wires snap on securely and are accompanied by a tight plug jacket. The screw-on types are best because they can't slip or vibrate off.

f. CHECK ALL (SUSPENSION) CONNECTIONS—There are several kinds, sizes, threads and metals for connecting nuts, washers and bolts. Torque them properly with a snap-type torque wrench. A nut not properly tighten enough is a hazard. But they can be overtighten also. Most hardware stores have charts displaying proper foot-pounds a specific bolt-nut assembly should be turned to.

One loose nut or a stripped thread on your suspension could send you and your expensive racer into the bushes. (and maybe you to the hospital)

g. CHECK WHEEL BEARINGS—A worn or loose wheel bearing becomes dangerously obvious to the driver at high speeds. These 10 to $25 "rollers" are not expensive compared to losing control of an expensive racecar. Make sure they're fully packed with the proper grease. Don't overtighten them to the wheel spindal. Doing that will cause them to prematurely ware, build up heat and won't allow the wheels to roll freely like they're intended to. This is a fairly delicate chore, but you don't need an engineering degree to do it. The wheel nut can almost be tightened with your hand. A Lock Shim will keep that spinal nut from turning once the proper tightness is completed.

Here's a little food for thought. Think what life would be like without bearings of any kind. They keep wheels, automotive engines and all kinds of mechanical devices from burning up due to friction. (it would take only seconds for that to happen) That even includes such items as computers, phonographs, . . . anything with electrical motors . . . if it rolls, more than likely it'll need a bearing. Without them, we may as well be living back in the 19th century.

h. HEIM JOINTS—These are ball type joints which move or rotate in all directions. It's kind of like your elbow, but the range of motion is much more pronounced. They wear out fast, especially if they're bearing heavy loads, like those on a racecar suspension. Worn (loose) heims on the steering and suspension make themselves dangerously obvious at high speed. They're 15 to $45 apiece, depending on their size and type. Most lighter weight vehicles can get away with using 10 to $15 ones. Even then, they're not cheap.

i. SETTING THE SUSPENSION—You should learn this. Doing so will help you understand this sport much better. It's a science. It can be a complicated and confusing learning process with 4-wheeled racers. You don't really learn it . . . you understand it. Matter-of-fact, at any particular track, figuring out what the best or proper setup requires patience, if not understanding. Some drivers will guide you. They can't really teach you since there are so many individual techniques. Ask them what they're trying. They're sometimes busy trying various setups themselves. This will save you money in the long haul.

Hiring a service to setup your car is expensive, but they do know what they're doing. Still, you may not know what to tell them. If they ask how you want your racer suspension setup . . . what'll you tell them? In that case you tell 'em to set it up neutral, if that's possible. Remember, no two tracks are the same. Not any one particular setup is going to be perfect for each turn. Setting up a suspension perfect for each turn is virtually impossible. (unless you have the megabucks for a computer-operated suspension, called 'active suspension'; they're illegal anyway, even in Formula One and IndyCar) So what do you do? You need to know what is best for you. You do that through experience, but please, get someone to guide you along so you know what to look for.

You need to realize if your racecar is handling loose, . . . pushing . . . or handling perfectly neutral. Many drivers don't want a neutral handling racer. Have you ever been in a properly setup chassis at 100 to 170 mph? You have to experience this to know what I'm talking about. Words can't adequately describe it. How a street car handles at 65 mph is absolutely nothing compared to a 120 mph racer. Besides, automobiles are heavier and more predicable. Push'em up to 120 mph and watch how the wind toss'em around. Do that on ice, . . . I'm sure you will want to stop at a rest area and empty the contents of your colon after that experience. But in a lighter, quick reacting race car, you have to experience it to understand. Nothing beats experience. That's not just some cute little anachronism.

Learn it gradually and safely, but not on your own, if you can help it. Be sure you're getting experienced help. A pro school (Chapter 8) is one way to learn this early, but some are geared towards driving techniques only. The sanctioning body school might be helpful, but they're more geared towards safety. (that's not a knock, safety is very important) The key at the sanctioning body school is to have the right instructor, which is pretty much left to luck. There are also some good books explaining vehicle handling. (see appendix) Either way, some instruction is better than none. That's also true of experience. That's why you must fill each sanctioning clubs schooling requirements. It keeps safety up and costs down. Impromptu visits off the racecourse can be very expensive and sometimes real hard on the bones.

j. INSTRUMENTS—All racecars have instruments to help forewarn problems. That's not always enough. They're not conducive to quick reading while you're at speed in long sweeping turns, checking the mirrors, reading handling feedback, avoiding others, etc. In the long straights you can glance at the panel for readings, but not easily in heavy traffic. In curves, a quick drop of oil pressure, due to forces pushing the oil away from the oil pick-up, even for a split second can hurt your engine. A loud buzzer or a 'dummy' light will quickly expose the problem. A driver can save an engine from damage and expense if they're quickly warned of impending trouble.

Some have their instruments setup to shut down the engine if oil pressure drops or temperatures rise too high. It's like an engine governor and insurance against overextention. It's a good idea to enhance your instruments by using these forewarning devices. It's cheap insurance.

I.7. WHEELS & TIRES—Always check wheels for cracks and deterioration. They take tremendous side loads when cornering at high speeds. If one breaks, it could send your car flipping violently. A situation like that is much worse than losing a tire at speed. It rarely happens, but check them closely anyway.

When a tire loses air, blows or an engine starts going sour, the driver usually receives a warning. That warning may be spongy handling or a sudden vibration. It may be only a one or two second warning. Sometimes that's all that's needed to slowdown safely. If a wheel goes, usually no warning is apparent.

How a wheel falls apart is significant. Half a wheel rotating at high speed can flip or throw a racecar violently out of control. Even wheel failure on a 'straight' may force the chassis to drag unpredictably. That means it's possible a racer behind you will not get the chance to react or read what direction you'll head. Tire-failure spins are a bit more predictable. How does a driver behind you know which direction to turn to avoid your predicament? It's hard to explain. I've had racers spin in front of me many times. Somehow it's obvious where to go without thinking. I guess it is a "learned instinct", so to speak.

Race tires are expensive. It's possible in some classes to spend more on them than anything else. They cost about $300 each in Indy car racing. They may last only 100 miles. But that's the high end in professional racing. Dirt and Desert racers do not wear tires like others do on asphalt. They use up or ruin them in other ways. The Formula classes, Dragsters, Sprints, StockCars and Roadracing Motorcycles go through them fast. The amount of weight, heat and lateral forces imposed on them regulates their durability. 50,000 mile passenger car tires are used for Showroom racers and other classes. They are shaved down at the tread to improve handling and grip. Racetires (or slicks) are purpose-built for greater adhesion. They're not only useless, but dangerous on wet surfaces. That's because their smooth surface can't channel water away quickly enough from between it and the surface they roll on. They partially ride over enough water to slightly lose contact with the road. (called hydroplaning)

Most race fans do not realize these tires lose their usefulness through heat cycles and high heat build-up. They then lose their ability to stick. (on race surfaces) As anyone knows, tires are made primarily of rubber. Racetire rubber is much more pliable or softer than passenger car tires. These Slicks (or racetires) are also made much thinner to avoid too much heat build-up. Too much heat hurts a tires ability to stick. Heat hardens them. In some racing classes, heat-cycles are what determines a tire's life. (not heat build-up) After a tire is heated, then cooled after competition, that's one heat cycle. Some race tires lose their optimum stick after three cycles.

In the case of high-speed racing, such as Indy Cars, the heat alone breaks tires down, not heat cycles. At this point, smaller pieces of rubber can be literally worn and thrown off. This is especially so in turns where tire scrub is prevalent. It's a reason "marbles" (loose rubber) collect there. This loose material isn't safe to race on at high speed. That loose rubber just isn't as sticky lying there on the track like it would be on a tire carcass. One reason is because that rubber isn't warm. It's cold, hard and relatively slippery, . . . that's because those little pieces act as ball-bearings. (why they're called "marbles")

A racer needs to warm a tire to make it work right. But not too much. Certain race tires are designed to run best at certain temperatures. Manufacturers custom-build them to reach optimum performance in certain types of racing. These differences are compounds, amongst other things. Compound can be best described as softness of the rubber within a tire. Coming off a race and thoroughly warmed, you can dig your fingernail in and literally pull out a chunk of

rubber. It's that soft and pliable with some compounds. When that rubber cools down it sort of crystallizes. The next time out it's a little harder and not quite as sticky, . . . they get to be more like a passenger tire. That hardness is okay for 60 to 70 mph driving, but not for racing, . . . or at least racing others competitively using new and softer slicks. Some passenger tires can handle high straight-line speeds. It is in the curves where race tires outperform them.

In some classes, race tires are banned to keep costs down. Street tires treads can be shaved down or down to smooth. That puts more of the tire surface against the track. Contrary to what most people believe, a bald passenger tire (minus exposed interior cords) has superior grip compared to the treaded type . . . but only on a dry, clean, hard surface. As you should know by now, passenger car tires also last much longer. That's because they're designed with harder compound rubber and for much slower speeds on street-legal autos. (they don't create, and therefore, collect too much heat)

Some racers say there isn't a thing which can extend the short life of a racetire. You have to buy new ones. The debate continues. I don't buy new slicks very often. That doesn't mean you shouldn't. Some racers, like myself, combat tire hardening by using a specially-made tire softener. (in my case, it's called Formula V tire traction treatment) It's believed this commercially-made product extends racetire life. Obviously, some guys don't believe it. It probably depends on what forces are imposed on the tire. Softeners will not extend race tire life to that of a 50,000 mile passenger car radial. Not even close! But these chemical softeners are supposed to extend the normal use of a race slick. That means added cycles. Sometimes it's hard to get that extended wear if you race on a tight course. For example, with my Formula Vee racer, one M&H, Goodyear or Bridgestone slick is 90 to $105 apiece. They normally last at the optimum peak of 3 or 4 cycles. I can get 3 to 4 more extra cycles if I treat them with the chemical softener. Then they start to harden.

Some drivers buy one weekend old race tires right at the track. They're not always hard to locate. Tires offered by richer competitors go for 25 to $30 each right after a race. Make sure the tires were recently bought, right there at the track. Immediately treat them chemically. At 30 to $35 per gallon, it saves the price of 1 or 2 sets of racing tires. Not bad, although to be honest, nothing sticks better than a brand new racetire.

I almost quit using chemical tire softeners. But one time I won a pole position on a set of 3-year-old racetires. By racing standards, 3-year old raceslicks are not only old, they're fossils. What was I doing running on racetires that old? Being cheap . . . but that's beside the point. I was running during a practice/qualifying session. Then I had an electrical problem. I came 1200 miles to Florida only to find that out? Needless to say, it was upsetting to discover that then. To vent displeasure, I got rather aggressive, to put it mildly. I was at the point where I didn't care if I smashed my racer into a wall or not. I was downright furious. That intensity won myself the pole and a big surprise. I was the fast qualifier on ancient racetires. Among other things, the chemical softener had to be partly responsible for that. So I'm still using the softeners, despite what others say against them. It wasn't a slow racing field either. It was a nationally sanctioned race with the defending FV national champion right next to me. Bottom line: I believe these chemical treatments can save 50 to 60 percent in tire costs. They don't make you faster by themselves, but they do seem to postpone the tire hardening process for a while.

Still, nothing beats new tires for optimum grip. Opponents say chemical treatments do soften rubber. But softness isn't enough to make an old tire sticky. In a way, it's hard to argue with that. But what's better to race on if you can't afford new ones? Old hard tires or old soft tires? Take the soft ones every time. Some clubs ban chemical softeners. The higher levels of racing can't afford tire softeners. The big money dictates they go with the best at all times.

Some other thoughts on saving money with new tires is to avoid them during schools and your first 3, 4 or 5 race weekends. Progress through the "learning curve"

at your pace. Learn safety, procedure . . . the rudiments of racing. Save the new tires when you've determined you're ready. Once you race with new ones, you'll be surprised how your racer sticks to the track. It's almost like you need to relearn racing. But that new learning process will be under more familiar, predictable and comfortable circumstances. You may need to readjust the suspension too. Something poorly financed drivers with new racetires do when they (occasionally) buy them, is to use them only in qualifications of a race event. If they don't qualify well, they go back to older (chemically treated) tires and save the new ones when their chance of winning increases at other races.

I.8. TRAVEL/LODGING—Some ways to save on lodging is not to use them. That's easy for a single person with no family. You can race where camping in the infield is allowed. Rent an air-conditioned room the night before a race (not the event) if the weather is miserably hot. When doing that you can find good rooms below $28. They're still around, but you have to look farther in remote areas, where some tracks are located. I avoid smoldering summer heat by racing in the winter, (Florida) spring and fall.

The family man's best tool is the recreational vehicle. With the way they are today, it's like a house on wheels. Whatever you are, single or the family man, it's important to be well rested for a race. That means cooling down at night during those "dog-days" of summer. If you don't get that, hopping into a two-layered firesuit and helmet won't help you concentrate on racing. A full weekend of that, especially in an enclosed race machine, (like Formula or StockCars) can make you a physical wreck. It won't hurt to avoid fancy $70 rooms. The only thing necessary is a clean bed, shower and, mainly, air conditioning.

Some race organizations have agreements with cooperating motel/hotel chains near a racetrack to offer racers reduced rates. Make early reservations. If this is not the case, smaller, private, nonfranchised establishments are always less expensive. Matter-of-fact, 75 percent of the time they're not half as expensive as a large franchised motel's reduced-rate package. Two exceptions are such franchises as Motel 6 and Econo Lodge. These are good rooms for only $25.50 in some places. (as of May, 1995)

As far as traveling costs are concerned, it's best staying close to home. Sometimes, if you want to race much, that's hard to do with certain classes. In addition to lodging, automotive fuel is worth cutting down too. The best way to do that is shop around interchange exits on state and interstate highways. In some states, that works the opposite as far as cheaper costs are concerned.

I.9. RACE FUEL—For the teams at the upper levels of racing, the fuel is limited to one type. Some drag cars use nitromethane. The Indy cars use methanol. (it's a wood alcohol) Sprint cars burn alcohol.

Most race machines burn regular racing fuel. At the track, you can expect to pay a minimum of $3.60 per gallon. Off the track you get it for about a dollar cheaper. Some Go-Karts use gasoline mixed with ether and/or nitromethane. Where do they get nitromethane? Many times it's an ingredient in model airplane fuel. Just go to a hobby or toy store and pick up a $6.00 pint. Expensive? Yes! Illegal in most racing? Yes! I used a pint in my tank. It does pep up the engine. It's also easy to detect. It'll make your exhaust smell sweet.

Some save on race fuel by using aviation fuel. It's rated between 100 to 130 octane. Look at it this way. If it's good enough for aircraft, it's good enough for most race machines. It's $2.10 to $2.30 per gallon. You can only get it at an airport. It is also a cooler burning fuel for air-cooled engines like Formula Vees and 440's, Karts and Motorcycles. It's hard to tell any difference between racing and aircraft fuel for me. The biggest difference is the price.

For certain motorcycle classes which are not high speed events, racing fuel isn't necessary. Regular gasoline will do. Everyone has an idea on the price of street fuel. But, here's a shocker! What does a gallon of fuel cost for Formula One racers? An unbelievable $950. I know, . . . it's an exotic blend, with several chemical ingredients mixed in for both strong horsepower and good

mileage, but that's outrageous. The F1 racer could go the entire distance without refueling. Apparently officials in F1 felt the same way about those costs. As of the 1993 season, that fuel was banned.

I. 10. TRANSPORT EQUIPMENT—It's not much of a problem transporting Midgets, Go-Karts, Motorcycles and some smaller Formula cars. But towing a full size stock car, drag vehicle, especially a Rail dragster, requires a 30 to 40 foot trailer. Equipment like that can cost 15 to $20,000 or more, depending on that vehicle's amenities. Also, what will you pull it with? The family car? It's possible, but usually, anything your family vehicle pulls that large can only enhance it's premature death. This is especially true for a compact and underpowered car. It's also just plain dangerous.

A car should never pull an additional 75 percent of its own weight without a beefed up suspension. It can still handle poorly even if the trailers weight is properly distributed. What is saved using improper tow vehicles will eventually be offset by a damaged automobile suspension and drivetrain. Most importantly, it's dangerous. If you don't believe it, you may find out the hard way. It's difficult and disconcerting wobbling all over the road. If it's windy and wet, it's that more unstable on the trailer and overbearing on the tow vehicle.

If your racer isn't over 1000 lbs, you can build your own trailer. You can use an intermediate sized car with no special suspension and transmission-cooler equipment. I built my own trailer. I received all my materials very cheaply. Otherwise, you're better off buying a good used trailer with a load capacity of 2500 to 3000 lbs. Price range can be as low as $300. A more accurate figure would be 5 to $1,000. Figure 1000 lbs weight for the trailer, 1000 lbs for the racer and no more than another 1000 lbs for accessories. My Cameros owner manual allows 3800 lbs pulling weight before I need special equipment. In my particular situation, the loaded trailer weighs a total of 2950 lbs. I built it wide (illegal over 8') and low to the ground for aerodynamic stability. That means it doesn't toss my car's rearend around. It also means easier and safer unloading of the racer.

Make sure you have about 50 to 75 lbs of trailer tongue weight loaded on the cars hitch. Use a ball and hitch type connection. Those allow turning and twisting without connection slop. It's important your trailer has a spring suspension. Many self-builders don't install them on their trailers. They let the tires absorb any road shock. Too heavy of a shock at 60 mph can blow a tire. On a wet road it can throw the car and trailer out of control. You're also sending unnecessary shock to your race vehicle suspension, unless you have the racer blocked and locked to the trailer floor. Either way, unsprung trailer vibration can loosen what's holding that racecar to the trailer, no matter how well it's anchored. An unsprung, heavy and vibrating trailer is an accident waiting to happen. So, spring-suspend your trailer.

Be sure you have shock absorbers (properly) mounted. A specialist will guide you on how to do that. A spring suspension without shock absorbers will sway the trailer back and forth for a while if you run into anything from small bumps to gusty winds. That's also dangerous. The trailer-tongue throws lateral strain on your cars rear tire grip. Speaking of tires, make sure they have suitable load capacity. A 3000 lb trailer should have 2 tires with 1800 lb capacity each. Not too many passenger tires have a weight capacity past 1800 lbs. Consider a two axle trailer if your total trailer weight approaches 3600 lbs. After you have started a trip, stop after about 25 to 30 miles. Check your hitch, safety chains, (required by law) race vehicle anchors or attachments and the tires. Lay a hand on the sidewall. In very hot weather, after about 15 minutes of travel, you should be able to comfortably keep a hand on it. If not, they're overheating. Check the air pressure. If the pressure is okay, then you're overloaded or have a defective tire. As I mentioned earlier, you probably need another axle in that situation.

One more situation to avoid is an uncovered trailer. Obviously, you need to protect the racer from elements such as weather. You also need to discourage gawkers, mostly the ones doing any driving. A few tend to stare at race cars too long and forget they're still behind the wheel. It's flattering having people admire your racer at first, but it gets old fast and sometimes creates unwanted traffic congestion around you, especially on an interstate highway.

I.11. CREW—It's hard to consistently win without them. They allow a driver to concentrate. A driver shouldn't have to worry about racing problems. Sometimes having a crew is a trade-off . . . or is it! If you're a middle income family man, getting general help isn't too much of a problem like it may be for the single 18 year old. But getting good (free) technical help is. (more on that later) But consider, you're not running the 24 hours of Lemans. At club level racing, one good-to-above-average individual is all you really need. There are exceptions. Each club event race lasts just a few minutes to three-quarters of an hour. Planned pit-stops aren't required. So you don't need a 4 to 5-man pit crew. Any pit stop during a club race means you have some kind of a problem anyway. You're not going to win the race and probably not even finish close to the top. It's not a disaster. There's no large purse usually involved. There is always the next race. The sun will rise the next day.

One good, relatively technical individual takes a load off your mind, even if you don't need one. Coming in after a race with mechanical or technical problems can be a burden. If a driver knows there's someone to help, it's less overwhelming. It has a calming effect on him or her. Several times racers come in from a race with problems. They have to park immediately and determine the time it'll take to correct them, if that's possible before the next session. Even if there's no problem(s), routine maintenance has to be performed anyway.

A good crew member, many times, is less expensive than none at all. If a driver acts as there own mechanic, crew member or whatever else, they may overburden themselves. That can rob a driver of his cool and concentration, . . . and therefore from the main goal, . . . to win. Good help can prevent overlooked, underestimated and improperly performed tasks. The driver can better focus on winning . . . not problems. Racing in itself is draining enough without having everything amplified. Therefore the driver gets "more bang for their buck."

Speaking of bucks, many racers camp at the race site and bring their own food, to save a few pesos. It saves lodging costs too. So, . . . any added costs of that extra individual is priceless when put in light of their help. But, if your trip to a race involves some overnight stays in a room, the price differences between a 2-bed room might be $10.00 if you have that extra person. Big deal. Restaurants costs will be twice as much, but if anyone can afford racing, no matter how poor they claim to be, they can afford doubling the grocery bill. The bottom line is this: One good crew member, who really loves racing, or just loves to be involved, is an asset that saves you money and your sanity in the long run. Believe me, I know that first hand. Just their mere presence keeps a driver much more competitively focused. Look at the big picture, without one, you might save 10 or 20 percent of your total weekend costs, but you will not compete as well.

I.12. TIME—How does time effect a racing budget? The answer isn't complicated, but rather, just a matter of common sense. The time a racer has is determined by their job, marital status, children, the will to race and money.

If you have limited time to race, it's probably because of your job. Time consuming jobs, fortunately, tend to pay better. More on that later. Meanwhile, some jobs are time controllable, especially if you're in your own business. But, it may be another trade-off. Most businesses are either hard to start or they start slowly. If your business is doing well, time is enhanced. On the other hand, working as a long-distance truck driver, pilot or anything which keeps you away for days or weeks, only puts you behind the 8-ball. Self-sufficient club racers need that time. For many amateur competitors, every hour of tracktime requires at least another 10 to 20 hours of maintenance. (in the long haul) Time consuming jobs can hurt that unless you offset it by hiring a race service.

If you're married, time may also be at a premium. (not to mention your budget) How bad do you want to race? If you're like some, they avoid marriage, dating . . . whatever it takes. If you "discovered" racing after marriage, I'd advise you to use careful judgement about what you race. Remember your family responsibilities come first. (read Chapter 2 again) Start in a class you can afford. Take another look at the chassis section in this chapter. Start-up costs can be 200 or 300% of your initial chassis costs. That's only if you have time to do your own maintenance. Otherwise it will be more. That includes some luck. (no race damage, etc) If time isn't on your side, try renting a racer. (see Chapter 7)

Renting may also help you more accurately decide what level to race. Making a wrong decision there is a costly and time consuming mistake. But race the type of machine you like and not what someone suggests. If your time is short due to family considerations, especially with one that's not interested in racing, then wait until the kids are raised. Meanwhile, consider helping another competitor in your type of racing. That'll facilitate your learning process. I know that can be a problem finding one. Try going through channels. If you're successful, learning the sport this way will be an invaluable experience.

Don't worry about racing at an older age. People have started racing at 40 to 45, even 50 years old. It's not as unusual to see that as you may believe. There's even those in their late 60's competing. They're not just "out there" either pal, they're even occasionally winning. So, . . . waiting won't hurt you if you keep yourself fit. It'll allow you time to save money too. As established before, it gives you more time to learn this sport. That can save you some yen also. Racing can be complicated looking and intimidating for a new competitor. That's probably more so for an older one. That can be avoided with this "hands-on" experience.

The obvious problem with racing is the expense. Even worse is its start-up or initial costs. Pile on top of that any mistakes as a result of inexperience can make the learning process that more frustrating and discouraging. (if not dangerous) Things like that have served to drive some out of this sport. The main reason for that may be due to impatience. Not enough time was used to properly prepare things. Racing may be a team sport, but it can be played individually, although not with any consistently long-term success. It's not like football where a coach determines if you're ready. In club racing, you make that decision. Too many times, it's not an objective one. Most of the time that's due to impatience and an underestimation of this sport.

I.13. FACILITIES—If you're single and live in an apartment complex, you've got a problem. You need a garage, a shed . . . some form of climate control shelter. You'll need electricity and lights. That rules out many rent-a-storage facilities. You might have your own gas-powered generator but will you be permitted to run that noisy equipment there? If all those things are available or allowed, you still have to live fairly close. Even if the storage facility has lighting, chances are for your purposes it will be inadequate. Heating may be nonexistent and the hours anyone is permitted there may be limited. More than once, racers burn "midnight oil" preparing their machines for racing.

Also, the space in and around those facilities just isn't enough. You would need a good sized bench. You could skip having a workbench, but what if it's raining and the floor is wet? I doubt space-rent people will allow anyone to setup shop at their facilities anyway. You need to think of these things in advance. If you're a family man or own your own home, especially with a garage, you can take all this for granted. Otherwise, how do you avoid that expense?

In my situation, I was lucky. My dad lets me use his garage. Many fathers will do that for their sons. Just make sure he completely understands what's involved. He'll probably like the idea of you being back around home anyway. My father was very good about letting me use his garage. Matter-of-fact, he let me double the size of it. I cut a door in the back wall, leveled the ground and poured three cubic yards of concrete. It was only a two day job. There was already a shed connected to the back. I just beefed it up a bit

and added insulation. It was all done for $480 in 1981. That's pretty inexpensive!

You may not be so lucky. But then everyone's lucky in some way. It's so obvious at times, it's taken for granted. Anyhow, I had no electrical outlets in that back portion of the garage. So, I simply strung in lead cords and was careful not to overload any circuits. I had access to my dads one horsepower grinder, a table saw and a sufficiently sized drill press. They've come in handy. With facilities like that (especially rent free) I built my own custom-made race trailer. It could have easily cost me $2,500 if I had it built. It started when I was offered a good drop axle in exchange for cleaning up a scrap pile. As it turned out, that scrap wasn't so junky, so I built a strong, good-looking race trailer with that material. (one persons junk is another's gold) I was fortunate in that respect.

What about those who do not have facilities? Well, if you want to race bad enough you will compromise. If you have to, rent a storage facility if for no other reason than security. I would hate the idea of leaving an expensive race car stored on a trailer, parked all winter on your apartment complex parking lot. That's crazy. Even if your racer was secure under those conditions, it's subjected to elements of humidity and other weather conditions, even if it's tightly covered. Race tires will be subject to temperature extremes; unprotected metal starts to rust, batteries die and bushings deteriorate, etc. You should remove tires and batteries anyway. It's just not a good idea to race without proper facilities, if you're doing so without some pro race-service help.

Here's a last resort suggestion for poorly financed racers. Have you exhausted all options? Do you still have your own home, but no garage? The least you have to do is store your racer. Never mind for now how you're going to maintain it. Other than paying rent for storage, you can erect a large, fully enclosed tent and literally back your trailer into it. It's not as crazy as it sounds.

If your trailer isn't much longer than 15 feet, and higher than 4 to 6 feet, you can buy big enough tents. Then use boards to reinforce the tent floor against the ground with the trailer weight. Reinforce the top. Heavy snow could collapse it. Install a small kerosene heater. You don't need it toasty warm in there, but at least above freezing. If you want to keep the temperature up around 70 degrees, that will help drive out humidity. But it'll also severely drive up fuel consumption, unless your can tightly insulate the tent lining. It's a good idea to do that anyway. It helps eliminate humidity. Remove all racing fuel from the racer and tent. You don't want it going up in flames. Check it daily. Keep this setup within sight of your house. If you have a fully enclosed, weather-tight trailer, you can do the same thing. Matter-a-fact, this is what you should have in the first place. If you need a trailer, which you'll more than likely need, a fully enclosed one is the only kind to have if you have no garaging facilities. Remove the trailers hitch and tires for security.

I.14. FINANCIAL RESPONSIBILITY—What's in question is how serious you are about racing. This affects how you treat it financially, regardless whether you're rich, poor, single or married. Some guys treat racing more seriously than others. Racing gets in the blood. It's addictive. The more you do it, especially with some early success, the more you want to continue. But you will need to make sacrifices. Still, not all the money, talent and sacrifices in racing guarantees winning. There are too many circumstances. Most of them are bad.

Murphy's Law certainly is a prominent factor in racing. But for everything which goes wrong, you can't always throw money at it. While the love of money may be the root of all evil, it's not a panacea to all problems either. That's true in life . . . and it's true in racing. Don't misunderstand, it's nice to have money, but you can't always buy solutions. I can hear it now, many racers are probably thinking, . . . "is this guy crazy? If only I had the money . . . I'd blow their doors off!" Sorry, anyone can talk, so that doesn't always wash.

Put an X amount of race drivers on an even level with machinery. Now . . . what determines who wins? It's mostly talent. But, if nothing but god-given talent won any kind of sporting event, then certainly sports would be much more predictable. If sports was too predictable, then why have it? You can't buy victories anymore than a major league baseball owner can buy a pennant. That's what I mean by being level headed. Keep your perspective. Don't get obsessed with it. You may frustrate and self-defeat yourself, and worse, maybe others.

You don't want to hurt anyone. Any sacrifices must be paid solely by you, not your wife or children. If you're married, racing shouldn't have anything but positive effects on them. Maintain your family's normal standard of living. Don't let it hurt them like alcoholism can, for example. Discuss with your partner what's involved. Don't pull any surprises, . . . like for example, on the bank account. Nothing, short of cheating on her, beats attacking the savings account for that special engine which "puts you in the racing Hall of Fame." I hear divorces are pretty expensive. I hear they can be emotionally exhausting too.

If you're going to treat racing like an obsession, it's good advise to give this sport a second thought. Otherwise, you better postpone any thoughts of marriage. If you want loved ones to understand racing, . . . show them, that means more than just explaining things. But that doesn't always work with those who have not experienced the feeling of racing. It's like describing a new color to the blind. You have to get involved first. Then explain things. If your family likes racing and wants to help, then you can become more involved with it.

I.15. ACCESSORIES—Now it's down to odds and ends, nuts and bolts, tools and support equipment. No matter how well prepared a racecar is, some unexpected situations will manifest themselves at the track or at home. Unless you hire a race service to maintain your racer, which is rare in club racing, you'll need tools and support accessories. Anybody with an ounce of foresight understands that. You will not necessarily need power tools, but you will need the basics: wrenches, sockets, screwdrivers, etc. It's not unusual for the racer to possess a one or two thousand dollar tool inventory.

The following are accessories you should have if you plan to race your own machine.

Of course anyone with a brain knows you'll need the basic hand tools. That goes without saying. But with that inventory, it's important to have them organized in a tool box. A good one will have a couple of fold-out shelves with drawers, grips, clips and individual compartments. The fairly good sized portable one is a couple of hundred bucks . . . and worth it. They keep tools (and your head) organized. It gets aggravating looking for a particular tool you know is lying within your reach. Many times drivers get upset looking for them. It's irritating wasting precious time when there's a limited amount of it at the track. This happens to drivers racing alone and discovering an "11th hour" situation.

At a racing event, 90% of the time, maintenance isn't performed on a clean, hard cement surface. It's usually outside on grass. They get caught up with a task, put a tool down and lose track of it. That's bad enough on cement, much less grass. It's not hard to lose small tools. Looking for them is aggravating when you're pressed for time or already upset at circumstances. So, get a well organized tool box. Lay it on a tarp if you're working on grass. A tarp will prevent small tools, such as sockets, from being obscured in grass or dug into loose or sandy dirt. (and therefore lost)

A portable generator is nice to have. All racing facilities have electricity. But it's seldom available anywhere outside the pits or garaging areas. A good one is going to cost about 5 to $700 for a 1 to 3 horsepower, two-outlet unit. Considering size and how noisy they can be, you're probably better off with a Honda brand name. I find they're quieter and easy to carry. But for beginning racers, hold off on them. Generators are more convenient than necessary.

The only reason you would need electricity is to charge your racecar battery. Not all race vehicles are self-charging. Alternators take up precious space, absorb horsepower and add unnecessary weight, especially on formula racers. On the other hand, if you're going to be using power tools or electrical lighting, then they're nice to have. If you have to use 'power' tools for an emergency

repair at the track, how prepared were you in the first place? Still, if you've brought family, you need all the convenience you can muster. Many race drivers like camping at race events, but only conveniently. (called "roughing it smoothly") Chapter two explained how kids can help with racing. But at too young an age, they can be just the opposite. So at night some electric power is almost a necessity. (to power that electrical babysitter called a TV) Of course, all of this is predicated you don't have a recreational vehicle. Most of them have their own generating system.

Another item you should have at the track is a floor jack and stands. A good quality 1000 lb capacity floorjack can set you back 80 to $120. What about stands? You can build your own stands more inexpensively and safely. Some of those store-bought stands on the market shouldn't be trusted any further than they can be thrown. A jack gets your racer partially off the ground. But you should never trust a jack to keep a vehicle up if you're going to crawl underneath it. The same goes with some of those cheap stands I see in department stores. You can build four solid wood blocks to put underneath the tires or axles to safely lift a racecar off the ground. Make them wide-based, at least 15 inches long and wide. Do not build them too tall (8 or 9 inches high) so lateral forces can flip them off base. Knocking a suspended vehicle off a poorly based set of supports is a lot easier on a grassy, unstable surface. Doing that on top of anyone underneath it will definitely spoil things, to say the least.

Most racers need a battery charger. There is a way to crimp on that though. I've used battery cables and my auto to charge a race battery. But I only needed 5 to 7 minutes charging time. Idling your street vehicle to charge another battery for over 10 minutes is not a good idea. First, your savings by avoiding a charger unit are eventually offset by fuel consumption. Second, idling a car engine that long can overhead its cylinder valves. Third, long idling may cause incomplete combustion. Unspent fuel could collect in combustion chambers and drain into your oil, diluting it. If your battery needs long and constant charges at the race track, a $35 charger and a walk to the garage or pits for juice to power it isn't much to sacrifice, particularly if an expensive automobile engine is at stake.

Most race teams have large compressed-air tanks. You don't need them that badly. A six dollar bicycle tire pump serves the purpose for any size race tire. They're just a bit slower, that's all. They also take up much less space.

Other equipment you need at the race track are special setup measuring devices. When you're familiar with racing, you should learn how to setup your car. That requires some special tools that hardware outlets don't stock. They are not complicated devices. An example are measuring tools used to check front wheel toe-in, camber, bump steer, heights, alignments, etc. It's hard to explain, but after seeing them, you would understand their relative simplicity. They're expensive because the volume for them is low. You can build them yourself. The key is to use strong materials. What's involved is an exact measurement of heights, distances and angles. So anything that's flimsy, like (roller) tape measures, may not measure those distances precisely. An example is checking axle squareness and alignments. When checking at increments of 1/16 to 1/32 of an inch, tape measures may slightly bow due to gravity, effecting accuracy. You may need two people and a steady hand. It just doesn't do the job easy. It's also awkward recording measurements underneath a vehicle. But you can take accurate ones with a tool using strong, light materials, like a one-inch aluminum square tubing. Your devices may not look nice, like the chrome-plated ones sold at race shops, but they'll be just as accurate and much less costly.

If you become more established financially, there are things you'll want more than what you'll need. Such equipment are welders, drill presses, milling and metal lathes. That equipment is not practical enough and too expensive for small home operations. I have access to a drill press, table saw and grinder only because they were my fathers. With those conveniences

and a power bandsaw I bought at an auction, building a race trailer, I mentioned earlier, was cheap. I wouldn't recommend buying all that just to build your own trailer. Even with good power equipment bought cheap at an auction, you'll still need the material to work with. You're usually better off buying a good used trailer.

As mentioned earlier in this chapter, if you do not have access to building facilities, look for an enclosed, back-door, walk-in type racecar hauler. They can be expensive, even when sold used. You could easily fork out $2,000 for a good 15 foot one. Be sure you have the right strength of towing vehicle to handle it. When empty, larger trailers can weigh a couple thousand pounds. When loaded, it means that figure may triple. No ordinary car will pull that without incurring some inconspicuous damage. The best vehicle to have is a one or two ton, V-8 powered, or diesel pick-up truck. By-the-way, a small pick-up is great for Go-Karts and some motorcycle racers. I've even seen racers haul formula cars with custom made beds fitted to their pick-ups. A little imagination goes a long way. If you have a pick-up, you could put a bed cap on it and store your tools and accessories in there. Then you can buy a much smaller and lighter trailer. (unless you've got a large stockcar or drag machine)

One accessory you may want to consider is an air compressor. No, . . . not the portable type, they take too much room. Some people incorporate the power unit on a generator to turn a small pump. They use hosing to move compressed air to an out-of-the-way tank. That tank size varies, depending on where it's located on your trailer. You'll realize compressed air is a versatile asset. You can use it to power air tools, inflate tires, for cleaning, clearing, washing and painting. (although painting is something you would orginarily do at home)

Another nice thing to have at the track, is something other than your trailer for sheltering yourself, tools and the racer from the elements. A sturdy folding-type canopy is practical for shielding out inclement weather, including a glaring sun. Use some imagination by building your own, it saves money. Good ones cost 1 to $800, depending on their size. Build a big one with 1/2 to 3/4 inch piping or round/square tubing. Big tarps go for as low as $50. But don't make them a project. They should be designed for quick and easy setup. Make sure it can stand up to high winds. (sure, . . . you can rent garages at some tracks, but they can be 150 to $200 per weekend)

It's also convenient to bolt a small rotary bench-vise somewhere on the trailer. It's handy, sometimes necessary and inexpensive.

II. UNCONTROLLED FACTORS (1 THRU 6)

1. Accidents; 2. Weather; 3. Rule Changes/ Format/Classes; 4. Marital Status; 5. Prize/ Purse Money; 6. Age/Attitude.

II.1. ACCIDENTS—This can be a big factor in racing. It's the one thing your love ones worry about most. This phenomenon is also what some people claims to bring in the spectators. (that's more myth than anything else)

Racing isn't as dangerous as people think, especially at the club level. It does happen, albeit, less dramatically. But for a professional race driver, they can expect around four serious accidents during a long career. Pro racers have money and careers at stake. They've paid their dues. They still put their time into racing, if not for testing and races, then for their sponsors. There is pressure on them, but it's probably more self-inflicted than anything. Pro racing is a great life and profession. They do not want to lose it.

Pro racers generally do not own or work on their own race machines. That's especially so in professional ranks like Formula 1, NHRA, Indy, NASCAR, and High Speed Motorcycle racing. With all these circumstances, these guys (and women) have more reason to stick their neck out on the chopping block. (take more risks) How they survive those nasty looking mishaps isn't as mysterious as it looks. A large number of people witness such incidents. With TV coverage being as widespread as it is, (and instant replay) people, not real race fans, develop an overamplified negative perception of the sport. Yet, while that's an innocently misguided ramification, these mishaps are usually fascinating to everyone in a human-nature, morbid sort of way.

Is it a mystery trying to figure out how most racers survived horrendous accidents? Not at all. Race cars today, especially the blinding fast ones, are built to break apart on impact in a particular manner. Safety is engineered into them. If that wasn't so, they'd be even more aerodynamically slippery and faster. Drivers are quite aware of these safety features. They also realize fire isn't as threatening as it used to be. It used to be racecars were nothing more than a 4-wheeled firebomb. Not so anymore. No racer wants accidents. But then nobody wants war either, but it still happens. On the opposite end of the spectrum, some feel all these safety innovations affords the driver just that much more aggressiveness. That's doubtful! The drivers know planting a race machine firmly into a wall or sticking a front end into someone's cockpit at any speed guarantees no immunity from the "grim reaper".

In club or amateur racing, fatal accidents are extremely rare. One reason is because less is at stake. Another is most racing facilities themselves are safer. There is usually more runoff space. That's the area between the track and a retaining wall. Those walls are sometimes cushioned with a symmetrically-locked wall of old tires. These do a great job of absorbing shock. Have you noticed them at some of the IndyCar road-course events? Why aren't all tracks protected like that, especially the ovals? It's due to space or a lack thereof. An example is the Indianapolis Motor Speedway. An outside retaining wall encircles it with absolutely no runoff space. Lining that wall with tires for cushioning only serves to tighten the track. That's dangerous. Hitting those tires at over 200 mph will also scatter them, no matter how tightly they are bound. It's not a good situation for others to be dodging scattered and airborne debris that large at 200 mph speeds. On the other hand, why they're not lined on the inside retaining walls where there is more room is a bit mysterious.

With a few racetracks, the course design

has been outstripped by the speed of todays racecars. Again, nowhere is that more evident then the Indianapolis Motor Speedway. This (first) US supertrack had no way of anticipating 234 mph race machines when it was built early this century. To redesign it would be a monumental task. Financially, it's almost an impossible task. Besides, to do that would be toying with its unique configuration and tradition. Sometime back, there was an article written in a popular sports magazine about the speedway. There was some consideration about completely redesigning the entire facility. As I read it, even as an naive teenager, I knew that would be a huge undertaking. It was hard to believe then, (about 20 to 25 years ago) and it still is now. If it does happen, it won't be in my lifetime.

Another reason why amateur racing is safer hasn't everything to do with the nature of speed, but rather priorities. I explained how pro drivers have more at stake. But that's not financially. In their own way, they do have more a stake. That has to do competitively with winning. The pressure to win is there if they want to continue racing, especially for the pros not winning races.

Amateurs also have a lot a stake. It has to do with finances, time, and the will to race professionally. Amateurs put as much time and effort in as the pros, if not more. Sometimes politics get in the way. While politics has its ugly presence in racing, it cannot always be avoided. But talent and hard work both play a role in getting to the top. Amateurs know that and race off it. It's their dream. Take that away and you take away their hopes and maybe even the will to race. It's like taking away a young athletes goal of reaching . . . for example, the Superbowl, the World Series or whatever. Whether it's big or small, . . . if you take that away, you take away their essence. (kinda like life)

In amateur racing, the risks are not quite there like they are at the pro level. Yes, amateur race speeds are slower, but safety may only be a perceived phenomenon. Some say the "safety net" in club racing is offset by inexperienced competitors. But, can you not get hurt at 130 mph as badly as 230 mph? Unfortunately, you can. You can get hurt in

a race car at 30 mph no matter how much protective technology is designed in. It's the nature of the accidents which kill, not necessarily the mishaps themselves.

One time in a race at Blackhawk Farms, (near Beloit, Illinois) I saw a Formula Vee roll sideways several times in front of me. The car got up on top of a retaining wall and continued to roll wildly. In a situation like that, there is nothing for the roll bar to grab on to. (no ground) The driver's neck could have been broken or crushed if the car had rolled closer to the back portion of the cockpit. That driver was extremely lucky, even though the racecar was destroyed.

Everyday millions of us hop out on the highway with all the drunks, insomniacs, drug addicts, idiots and those talking on a telephone at 70 mph. If you're aware enough to avoid them, that doesn't mean you won't plow into a nice sturdy bridge abutment yourself. How about those telephone poles that jump out in front of you after discovering that patch of 'black ice'. It happens every day to the tune of thousands per year, yet some feel racing is dangerous. If it is, then it is. Let's go ahead and make both racing and highway travel illegal. They both have killed. This is an attitude many racers, if not consciously, then at least subconsciously, have carried with themselves. It's not extra baggage or anything like that, but rather, a sort-of deintimidating factor they use to justify the risks. I've come to that conclusion several times myself.

I've seen racers survive nasty mishaps, yet they were so upset with others and mostly themselves, they could have "spit nails". I was amazed they weren't happy avoiding physical injury. Instead, they threw a fit. Now I know why.

I heavily damaged the front end of my racer once. There were no injuries. But if so, the guy I was involved with could have been hurting. I was very quickly heading towards an out of control racer in such a matter as to "T-bone'em". (at around 100 mph) It could have been avoided. I purposely failed to slow for his spinout. I knew it might cost me a second place finish to slowdown, so I kept it floored. I intended to follow his sideway-sliding car right on around. Unfortunately, he didn't end up sliding in a normally predictable manner like he started to. Near the end of his slide, he rolled backward up a slightly banked and high-speed dog-leg turn, right square in front of me at full speed. My steering reaction was enough to avoid plowing him hard thru his cockpit. But my reaction wasn't quite enough to avoid him completely. I was so close, there wasn't even a chance to brake. My front end caught his right rear suspension and engine squarely at about 95 mph. My racecar became a temporary aircraft. His racer was a mess. Mine wasn't too bad. We both walked away.

I was upset at myself and plain sick about the damage. Looking back now I'm thinking I could have messed him up badly, not to mention myself. Instead, at the scene . . . all I could think of was . . . "Taube . . . you idiot." I was also thinking . . . "Gee . . . hurt me . . . just don't hurt my racer!" Well, is that a screwed up attitude? To the nonracer, . . . yes, . . . to most racers, . . . no. They have an understanding what's involved in racing and its commitments. They believe it's a sane sport. They do take precautions. They do watch out for each other. Sometimes it's themselves they ignore in favor of their precious car, . . . not to mention their time and money. This appearance feeds "ammunition" to the racing critics.

There isn't much to explain about accidents financially. It can be very devastating to the amateur. Some accidents have forced racers out of the sport, others have only been set back. I never heard of a racer quitting after an accident because they were afraid. It just doesn't happen. They usually come back more determined then ever. That's not stupidity, . . . it's a love of racing.

How drivers handle racing-accident costs depends on their attitude and preparation. To put it in a sort-of oversimplificated way, just figure on them happening. The key is to avoid the heavy ones. They are rare. If there is a trick to avoiding a heavy mishap, I believe the key is to be aware of traffic. That's not rocket science stuff. But in many speed events you have to literally watch way out in front of yourself. With some exceptions in motorcycles and drag racing, the machines right beside you, or close in front and back,

generally can't decelerate quickly enough to build-up dangerous speed differentials. (ie, they can't contact you hard) But touching tires via open-wheel racing in just the right manner can send someone flipping wildly. That isn't fun.

Chassis and engines can survive some pretty nasty accidents. The body and suspension can't. Be prepared for that, but not necessarily at the track. Hauling spares for accidents like that can be impractical. That's 'if' you can repair your damage quickly. Anyway, your real danger is way out in front.

They say with IndyCar speeds being as they are, the best thing to do is head right for an out-of-control vehicle. By the time you get to that vehicle, it will have moved out of the way. But most racing isn't the speed of Indy cars.

First, flagmen at the track will help forewarn you. Sometimes though, that's not quick enough. The first thing you trust is your instincts. Get on the brakes only on the race surface . . . not in the runoff or grassy areas. That'll send you sideways, spinning, possibly all over the place, and won't slow the car down quick enough to make a big difference in most cases. When you squeeze the brakes on a race surface, don't necessarily slam on them so abruptly that they lock up. I know that's easier said than done. But consider, with racing, you're wide awake and watching for mishaps. They shouldn't sneak up on you. Whether you lock brakes on asphalt or grass, one thing's for sure, YOU CANNOT STEER LOCKED WHEELS! (that's why ABS brakes were developed)

If you're close to a vehicle which loses control, I'm going to suggest you try to pass it as closely as reasonable. Sound crazy? Not really. The idea is threefold. First, staying relatively close, while braking fairly hard under control, sometimes keeps speed differentials between the two vehicles closely matched and crash damage to a minimum if there is contact. Don't lock them wheels! There's no turning that way and believe it or not, it doesn't slow you down that much quicker. A locked tire at speed develops a tremendous hot-spot instantly. Some friction efficiency is lost between the rubber and road under that kind of heat. (and 'flat-spots' your tires, even if you pass safely by; now you have an imperfectly round tire and a whole lot of vibration) Try to avoid a runoff area if you were close to the original mishap. It's a good chance the original victim(s) of that mishap will end up in the grassy areas anyway. If it's possible, it's even more important to avoid runoffs in turns. In turns, runoff areas abruptly end with walls, cushioned or not. That's not as scary as other racers having no choice but to possibly use 'YOU' as that same wall. In any case, you should be able to understand racecars can't stop or turn quickly in slippery runoff areas.

Second, passing close leaves room for those guys behind you to maneuver and avoid you also. They will likely need those runoff areas, but since they are further back, they have more time to slowdown and safely steer in them. This is why you should know what's behind you while racing, otherwise they can hit you hard avoiding the original car which lost control.

Third, when a vehicle gets loose, it's pretty easy to predict where it'll initially head. But that can be some very short reading. Sometimes, all you can do is to point your machine slightly to the falling-away side and slam the heck out of the "binders", if you instinctively know turning will do you no good. If you panic, much less panic early, it's a very good chance you'll unnecessarily put yourself out of control and into a wall. If that happens, try to keep it there. Bouncing back into traffic can be fatal. At least a wall is predictable, it's not moving, it's smooth and many times it's cushioned. Having another vehicle "T-bone" you or sticking a part of their suspension through your cockpit is obviously a dire situation.

By-the-way, drivers are insured in racing. Even though that's of little consequence for the moment, it's nice to know. Maybe your racecar can't get immediate surgery, but the driver will. Count on that. You can be a skilled, fast, conscientious racer, but a few times you can't anticipate mishaps. Racing can be a trade-off. For all your efforts, it can be devastating. But as much as you're supposed to realize that, don't you dare think about it "out there at speed". The only thing to fear is fear itself. I know that's a cliche,

but take this message for what it's worth. If you find yourself in constant fear during a race, you do not belong in racing. Even if you're good. It's at least my theory you can't be a good, fearful racer. It just doesn't work. If you experience this while at speed, then your concentration isn't where it should be. Real racers haven't got the time to be afraid. That doesn't mean they're stupid, heartless or disrespect life. Not at all! In fact it's the opposite. They're lovers of life. You'll find out why in Chapter 6.

II.2. WEATHER—This factor is something that effects an entire race event or schedule, the driver, the race machines power, how it handles and also the racing surface itself. How this effects the driver is not an uncontrollable factor. The drivers know they must prepare for hot conditions by keeping themselves in shape and taking advantage of those expensive new 'cool suits'. So, it's an issue I'll cover very little of in this section of the book.

Weather conditions are taken for granted by those not directly involved with racing. Everyone knows rainouts occur. That is straight forward stuff. But it stops only high-speed events which use racing slicks. There are racetires made to run in wet conditions, but not racing slicks. All events like NASCAR and oval races sanctioned by CART do not use wet racing tires. The reason is because of the overall high speeds they reach, especially in the turns.

Racetires built for rain have to be grooved to channel away water. That means, unlike racing slicks, the tire carcass must be thicker to make room for designing in a tread pattern. The compound must be somewhat harder so that pattern can be strong and more stable. But high speed raintire characteristics aren't always conducive to 200 mph speeds. They can reach high speeds as made obvious by Formula One, but their performance in turns will never compare to race slicks in dry conditions. F1 racers have to slow down in curves anyway. They don't have brutal turning speeds seen in IndyCar and NASCAR oval races.

There are other reasons some organizations avoid wet weather racing, but prevention of accidents is the main one. As you now understand, Indy cars and F1 do race in wet roadcourse conditions. The speeds are not continuously high like those of a super-speedway oval. Only a deluge and lightning stops roadcourse events. But then, the same thing can be said for a football game.

Most amateur events are not called off because of inclement weather. Some Off-Road races seem to prosper in it. Aside from these conditions, is an underlying situation not so obvious to some race fans. That's heat and humidity. These conditions mostly effect high speed oval events. The tire traction at the Indy 500, Michigan 500 and several NASCAR superspeedway races is affected. The race engine must overcome heat and humidity, not to mention the driver.

Humidity is the water (vapor) content of air. Not only does it affect a driver's respiration, but the engines ability to breath. Ever notice how your auto performs stronger when the air is dry? (and colder too, more on that later) Dry air burns more explosively and efficiently in an engine. Water never has and never will burn. It hinders the burning of fuel and therefore, engine performance.

Heat also hinders an engines performance. Not internal heat! An engine must have warm temperatures to protect against metal fatigue and friction. (and proper circulation of lubricants) What is meant by metal fatigue? Drop a cold egg into boiling water. The sudden temperature change can shock that egg's molecular structure and crack it. That's also true with glass and other brittle materials. It sorta works the same way with metal. Sudden temperature shock can weaken or crack it. That's why it's not a good idea to gun any cold engine, especially in the winter. For one thing, the oil isn't completely circulated. The sudden hot temperatures produced by friction of unlubricated parts and spent fuel can shock and crack a frozen cylinder wall, or a piston. That hairline fracture is nothing but trouble. You will lose compression. Fuel and radiator coolant eventually seeps into the oil, affecting its lubricating properties and hurting the engine. Or it could be a faster process. There's nothing as damaging, other than a broken crank or rod, like a disintegrated cylinder. It could

separate at the crack and lock-up an engine, while you're rolling along at high speeds. So, it's important to properly warm an engine, just don't let it get too warm.

Heat of another form greatly affects a racing engine. Heated air is also lighter air. In any engine, more air is burnt than fuel. Ever try to hold your breath? You can't do that very long can you! It's likewise with an engine. The more air an engine breaths in, the more of it to burn. Cold air is heavier air. Heavier air has more volume. With identical engines, one burning cool air will out-perform one that's not. Don't be confused. Warm air ignites more completely if it's dry, but unlike cool air, there isn't as much of it to combust.

As just stated, heated air affects ignition of fuel. Liquid fuel cannot burn. Say what? It's true. Only fuel vapors burn, not the liquid. Liquid fuel is more volatile under warmer conditions. (evaporates faster) A carburetion system is designed to speed up that process so the fuel can be quickly burned. If cool air enters the induction system of an engine, the fuel cannot remain vaporized long without condensing back, . . . that is, . . . if it gets condensed efficiently in the first place. In any case, condensed fuel is liquid fuel. Liquid fuel passing through an engine (actually in the form of tiny droplets or mist) cannot burn and therefore, is unused and wasted.

It takes fractions of a second for that mix of air and fuel to travel from your carburetor to the pistons. So, relatively speaking, this warm and cool air situation is a trade-off. Cool air is both advantageous and harmful. That trade-off is the separation between most racing engines and the one in your automobile. Race car drivers don't care much about miles-per-gallon. (all high-speed sanctioning bodies do; it keeps speeds safely down) Horsepower is what drivers want. So, ideal conditions for race engines is cool, dry air. More air, more horsepower. But cool air means some fuel is not burning efficiently. The colder, the more wasted. It's condensing back to liquid between the carburetor and cylinders. But racing (induction) systems are more sophisticated concerning these cool conditions. (it's also why fuel injection creates better performance in all engines; fuel is vaporized much closer and separately to each cylinder)

For your family car, cool and dry temperatures would be the ideal too. Especially with fuel-injected versions. But, that engine isn't turning god-awful rpm's like race engines do. Therefore, with race engines, even those with efficient induction systems, that exploding fuel is not only ideally pushing a piston to the bottom of its stroke, but it's still burning as the exhaust valve opens. Nowhere is that more evident then watching a Top-Fuel Dragster running at night. That's burning fuel coming out of their exhaust pipes. (now you know what they mean by "keeping those candles lit") Unavoidably, that's also wasted energy. But nothing can be done about it without incurring other trade-offs.

This is a trade-off your auto can avoid at 55 mph. Most combusted fuel isn't wasted by superhigh rpm's. It takes a lot of fuel and air to torque a racing crankshaft to higher-than-normal rpm's. To double an engines horsepower does not simply mean to double its intake of fuel and air. The laws of thermal dynamics doesn't work that way. It's has more to do with the laws of diminishing returns. But, . . . still, . . . warm air vaporizes more efficiently. It means your personal car can makes up for the lack of air by vaporizing and burning all its fuel efficiently at comparatively slow speeds. The racing carburetor or fuel injector can vaporize fuel efficiently in cool or hot weather. But as stated, race induction systems are much more sophisticated and, of course, expensive. So, the bottom line is this: race engines like cool dry air; your car likes cool dry air too, but survives warm conditions efficiently with lower rpm's. (I take for granted you know fuel expands when burned. It's what creates force to push down a piston)

In the case of all engines, a device which increases air intake for their induction systems is something I've mentioned frequently in chapter three. They are super and turbochargers. These are literally pumps which force additional air into an engine. As I said earlier, all engines burn more air than fuel. (thank goodness air is free) I could claim these devices make up for warm (or light) air

conditions, which they actually do, but they work that much better in the cool. These "blowers" pack air at more than normal atmospheric pressure created by a descending piston in the combustion chamber. That means the more air is compressed, with no additional fuel, the more wallop the spark plug sets off. These turbos enhance more horsepower than any degree of cold and dry air conditions could do on there own.

That is how heat and humidity effects race engine performance. What it does to the driver is covered in Chapter 6. There is another element heat effects. That would be the racing surface itself. Many people do not understand when race drivers complain how slippery a track is. Some immediately think "ice". Obviously, they know that's not really the situation, so they're confused, when in fact the track is dry as a bone.

A track can lose grip several ways. The obvious ways everybody understands. But on a warm, dry track, . . . it can be slippery? It sure can. It'll never happen on the interstate highway, but it can on the racetrack. It can also get slippery on those seldom-used, one-lane, tar and stone backroads of the countryside. Huh? What on earth is this guy talking about? Simple. Those backroads serve as an exaggerated example, in part, to what happens on an asphalt racetrack.

Ever notice the tar bleeding or rising above the stone on those scorching hot days? It's a fairly thick layer of goo you wouldn't want to run fast over. Nobody purposely does, but it's not because drivers fear they'll lose control of their car. It has more to do with preventing tar and stone from being thrown into their wheelwells or on the vehicles quarterpanels. To a less exaggerated degree, these slippery conditions occur on asphalt, but it's not as obvious. It'll get very noticeable on a hot high-speed racing surface to a racer. Oils, not tar, seep up from asphalt, but not in the quantity tar does on those old stone and tar backroads.

This situation usually isn't a huge factor in most racing. But it creates considerable impact on high-speed tracks, especially on ovals where corner speeds are faster. At the Indy time trials, especially on 'pole day', is where this gets the most attention. Unbelievable as it sounds, a 5 or 10 degree fluctuation in surface temperature has a big impact on how well tires grip the track. It can be the difference in winning the 'pole position' or qualifying 10th. It's another reason drivers like to wait for the late afternoon to attempt qualification. That big star in the sky is lower and the track's a bit cooler due to less penetrating sunlight.

Of course, clouds play a big factor also. An overcast day is ideal. A slight breeze makes conditions even more ideal. But winds over 10-15 mph may effect how racemachines cut aerodynamically through it. You may think drivers complaining about winds, heat, whatever, are nitpicking crybabies. Absolutely false! At such tremendous speeds, the window of opportunity closes to a narrow gap. Things are magnified beyond what's obvious to an uneducated race fan.

A 230 mph Indy car is definitely "pushing the envelope". The faster they go, the more narrow a race track becomes. Which is to say, at those speeds many things become apparent to a driver, especially the ability to turn. The drivers might also complain the track's dirty because of loose rubber from other competitors. These so called "marbles" may not be on the racing line where most racers are, but they certainly narrow that line. That decreases a drivers margin of error. If a driver drifts a bit off that line in the turns . . . they could lose valuable traction . . . thus parking their racer into a wall.

As stated a few sentences back, drivers complain of track grip. That's when oils are taking away its adhesion . . . by literally from lubricants lost via blown engines, (those spills are well cleaned by track personnel) or more than likely by the oil ingredient present in asphalt. That thin layer of asphalt oil bakes to a slightly unstable consistency on the surface. Yes, . . . bakes! Those surface temperatures can reach well over 120 degrees. Check out any asphalt road on a hot stagnant day. Better yet, close all your car windows, vents, . . . leave it exposed in the sun a few hours, then go sit down on those leather seats. You'll get the message. Heat like that can melt things, . . . like road oils and tars.

A track may be called narrow. The drivers

mean speeds are high. It may be called crowded, that's too many slow cars, called "backmarkers". It may be too green. That means there is no rubber residue in the racing line which helps the tracks grip. Don't confuse rubber residue with marbles. Residue is the dark colored film on the racing line of the track. This is especially evident in the corners where greater tire-scrubbing forces are created. When enough racecars travel a specific line, they leave a thin and soft layer of rubber. This rubber isn't as saturated with specific oils like asphalt. Heat doesn't effect it as much. A race-tire will grip this rubber-enhanced asphalt even tighter than without it.

People hear race drivers describe these track conditions as such. Unless it's pouring rain, the average joe just stands there in amazement wondering what the heck these guys are talking about. Racers complain all these things are slowing them. But their biggest complaint may be the luck involved when race teams draw a better time for qualifying. Nothing can be done about that. Only one driver qualifies at a time. At least there's no politics involved. Overall, they're really not complaining per se, just stating facts. These situations are legitimate, they're just not obvious to neophytes. Like all good drivers, they adjust to track dynamics, although the racecar handling can go only as well as those laws of dynamics permit under these circumstances.

On the opposite end of the spectrum are the off-road racers. They don't have to worry about these things. It's the same conditions for everybody. I can't speak for the drivers, but as a spectator, I'd rather watch them wallowing in the mud. It's a show alright, but I understand most drivers and motorcycle riders would rather choke in the dust and heat. There's more tire grip in bone dry, albeit, sandy and loose terrain conditions.

Meanwhile, how does weather effect racing costs? Directly it doesn't! But it effects how you approach racing, which in turn, determines costs. Simply put, some amateurs will not race in wet, slippery conditions. It takes away any competitive edge they might have. It's also not worth the risk to equipment.

Speaking of risk, have you noticed not too much is mentioned about life and limb in this chapter? That's for a reason. Life and limb is at risk in all racing. Most drivers and many people feel life in general is a big risk anyway. Personally, there are times I feel safer in a racecar than driving through Chicago or New York. But anyway, this subject will be covered later on in this book.

Before I move on, there is one more thing I would like to mention about heat and how it directly effects the drivers. Some racers avoid summer racing. I know I do. The heat on drivers in full racesuits is draining. Some air-cool engines such as Formula Vees, 440's, Go-Karts and motorcycles can be effected also. All engines must be properly warm to perform reliably, but too much heat will hurt them by breaking down the oils. Keeping oil at its proper temperature in scorching summer heat isn't impossible, but keeping yourself properly cool might be. This is especially true for the older folks, no matter how well in shape they are. You may not think this is a big deal now sitting there in your air-conditioned room reading this, but you'll likely change your attitude quickly once you meet up with these circumstances. If summer is the most convenient time for you to race, go to a race shop and inquire about those new 'cool suits'. They are expensive. Personally, I don't know much about them because they're a relatively new item on the race market. I think the "jury is still out" whether they work very well. I'm still waiting for their prices to level off. I don't know if they'll ever come drastically down in price since it isn't exactly a high-volume product.

II.3. RULE CHANGES—Rule changes do not effect racing at most amateur levels in an immediate fashion. Changes are made for the good of the sport. Many spectators, teams and drivers will question that, especially at the pro level. But that's because of money. Regardless of what they say, changes are made in the interest of safety, containing costs and leveling the competition. If this wasn't true, I guarantee you would be seeing 260-70 mph speeds at Indianapolis and Michigan by now. A few better-financed teams would dominate the sport and bore most people to death. Remember, most fans like those terrific speeds, but not while compromising fair and tightly close competition.

When changes are made in the name of safety, especially at the pro level, it's usually designed to slow down the cars. This sometimes makes teams, specifically IndyCar teams, feel the technology they utilized was wasted, including the money spent. These teams or individuals feel targeted. A few spectators aren't thrilled about anything slowing down the cars also. At the amateur level, rule changes seldom are controversial. There are two basic reasons for that.

First, in a sense, club racers do not have a sounding board via the news press like professionals have. Whether that's necessarily good or bad depends on who you talk to. The second reason is most changes do not immediately effect racing costs greatly. Amateur race purses are practically nonexistent. Club racing survives smoothly on its own merits because money doesn't cloud issues. Rule changes are also oriented towards detecting cheaters. Rule breakers are regretfully harder to police at this level. That's because of the larger number of competitors as opposed to a smaller number of scruteneers to police them.

Rule changes made in the interest of tighter competition also irritates some better financed teams. Tighter competition never seems to work out ideally at the pro level anyway. Matter-of-fact, it seems to discourage new manufacturers from entering the sport. A case in point is IndyCar racing. Some factory-support teams wishing to enter have to share their engine with other teams. It gets complicated, but basically the idea is to prevent high-dollar teams from developing and hoarding superior equipment. This current rule is already being bandied around at CART and may be thrown out by this printing.

Rule changes at the pro level always seems to compromise competition in the eyes of the drivers. Making these changes is like being the president. You can't satisfy everyone. In a way, rule changes could be listed in the 'controlled factors' that was covered earlier in this chapter. But these decisions are never made at the individual level. Sanctioning bodies may be composed of drivers, car owners and team members appointed to oversee or study a proposed change.

At the amateur level, usually the largest rule changes are about the classes themselves. There are specific requirements in many organizations about the number of competitors required for a particular class. If those numbers don't meet national level requirements over an allotted time period, the class is eliminated. Those still competing in an eliminated class must move to another if they so choose. It may seem that specific class would have to spend money to meet requirements for a new one. That's not always so. That class is only eliminated in the sense it can't compete for points and a national championship. They still may race their class as either regionally or locally, although they won't usually have many people to race against. This is one of the reasons why there are several small and specialized clubs in all forms of motorsports.

Some organizations have a dozen or so regionally popular classes scattered throughout the US. These few classes may be small, but they are popular in specific areas. An ex-aggerated example would be motorcycle ice racers in Florida. You won't see them competing down there very much. In other cases, these clubs or classes downgrade themselves or evolve in the interest of limiting costs. They may also cater to the formation of a new or experimental class of race vehicle. Keeping these clubs small keeps the administrative costs in line.

II.4. MARITAL STATUS—This factor is categorized as both controlled (number I.3, earlier in this chapter) and here in the uncontrolled section. Previously, marital status was targeted primarily to the young man or anyone single and racing. But in this section, it's treated for those who have become interested in this sport while already married. (with a bigger expense, . . . kids)

One of the unique things about racing is people discover it at all ages. Still, there isn't much which can be said about it here then what's already been stated in the first two chapters. But for a quick overview, you are going to quickly realize two undisputed facts about racing. One, it's much more than going about in a machine as fast as you can. Two, it takes money. If you play this game right, you won't have to mortgage the house, sell a kid or do both.

There are several reasons to race. A person may race because of the old adage, "a need for speed", or for ego-gratification, competition, living on the edge or just the need to be "out there". Whatever, don't make a decision about racing until you've educated yourself enough to eliminate disastrous mistakes.

Admittedly, reading this book is a start, but it's not a panacea to an end. Even if books in general could achieve that, it would still take more than one book to explain this sport in detail. You still have to take off your reading glasses, get out in the world of racing and see what's going on. It wouldn't hurt to get your hands dirty also. Matter-of-fact, it's the best way.

There is nothing like experience, nor will there ever be. Before you spend one penny on racing (excluding race tickets) get involved. There are so many ways to do that in this sport, that it's actually one of the contributing factors in its reputation. What's that reputation? Well, among all its perceived dangers and costs, is an underlying state of confusion. That would be, . . . how do you enter this sport and, once in it, how do you move up and when? This last statement alone perpetuates some questions. Why is there necessarily a need to "move up"? Do you have to start at the bottom, or what you perceive as the bottom? It's a philosophical question I guess. But unlike "ball and stick" sports, you don't have to start at some particular level, work up and graduate.

Whether that's good or bad depends on many factors. But one thing is for sure, diving head first into racing is like high-diving into a small lake. It may look safe, but how do you know what's underneath or how shallow the water is? It's a good idea for a single or married man (or lady) to spend a year checking all options. Racing is less costly that way. If you determined racing is too costly for the time being, then you won't be accused of shirking family responsibilities. The only exceptions to that would be the type of racing which won't break the bank immediately or in the long run. Some of those exceptions would be a few Motocross and Motorcycle classes, Quarter Midgets (for the kids only) and Go-Karts. Given the chance, those can get expensive also, but not relative to other types and classes of racing.

II.5. PRIZE/PURSE MONEY—To call money won in a race as "prize" or "purse" is nothing but semantics. Calling it prize money isn't saying much considering the funds it took to pursue it, especially at the club level.

Occasionally amateur races do offer purses. When they do, it's nothing to open a swiss bank account over. The same thing can be said about most professional levels. There are not too many people making a living directly off of racing purses. A hugh portion, if not all, gets pumped back into race expenses. There are rare exceptions, but not many. Sponsorship foots most of the bills, if not to the drivers, (who therefore pass it on to the team) then directly to the team itself. The purse payout for a particular race, if there is one, doesn't always determine if the event is amateur or professional. But the amounts do. Some amateur events may offer $500 to win, $250 for second, $125 for third and another $1000 or so for positions 4 through 11 or 12. By pro standards that's laughable.

Professionals would have a tough time surviving a $500 purse for even a last place finish. This isn't to say amateurs are inferior as competitors. That's silly! Would you call Olympians inferior athletes? They are (supposedly) amateurs! On the other hand, no matter what amateurs say in any sport, racing included, they don't want to remain that way. After all, if you'll do something you love for the fun, sport, or whatever, why wouldn't you do it for money, if an opportunity presented itself? The key words are "if opportunity presented itself".

There are many talented amateur drivers out there in racing. Some should be professional drivers. That's not to say the pro drivers today are just lucky, know the right people or have their noses up "Daddy Warbucks" rearend. Some people steadfastly believe that, but it's a "snap" conclusion made out of frustration rather then reality. Whatever the case, those who feel that way are just going to have to accept it, whether they like it or not. There's more than one way to skin a cat. (the means justifies the end) But most pros have paid their dues.

One problem with professional racing, like any sport, is that it has to compete with other sports financially. There is only so much time, money and market out there in the big, bad world. Professional sports has limits imposed on the number of teams and the individual athletes on those teams. Racing competes with other professional sports for the entertainment dollar. Couple that with the competition for time which pro and amateurs vie for. What I'm saying is that some racing is having one heck of a time just filling their fields. Certainly that's because of a lack of money, not the lack of interest. Sponsors out in the marketplace also have limited funds. Sometimes they do not understand how racing can promote what they're selling. Whatever it is, only so much money is available to race with. That's why there are many good racers not doing it professionally. Maybe they haven't been discovered or their talents are camouflaged by inferior equipment. Whatever the reason they'll always be there. But think about it, it happens in football, basketball, baseball and hockey. Players are cut. They've come so close to making it they could taste it. At least the opportunity was there. But with racing . . . well, the carrot sometimes is dangled out in front of a driver . . . a hundred miles away. In other words, the opportunity wasn't lost . . . it was never presented in the first place. It's one of the things frustrating about this sport.

Looking on the bright side, racing in general and at all levels has done a better and more intense job of selling itself to the public. A good portion of that credit goes to cable TV, specialize race publications (newspapers, magazine) and even to a certain extent, network TV. Whether network TV's interest is genuine, a purely financial decision or a fascination with the blinding speeds of todays racecars and it's personalities, doesn't matter. In the end it helps all racing receive positive exposure, while at the same time, debunking some myths which have festered within it.

In addition to money race teams receive through sponsorship, a small portion of their budget comes from prize money. We always hear the huge purse distributed at the Indy 500. The last place finisher can probably be guaranteed $85,000 in 1996. First place? Probably 1.4 to 1.8 million. (including much more because of endorsements) But that is the exception rather than the rule. Even a highly competitive IndyCar team couldn't survive costs on their winnings alone. In 1996, a competitive season of 17 races will cost about 6.5 million dollars.

At the lower levels of racing, purses are sometimes put up by the drivers, local sponsors and wealthy individuals. (rarely) These are usually private events closed to spectators for insurance saving purposes by the track and sanctioning organizations. There are many more private race events held than people realize. The SCCA sanctions at least a couple hundred of them a year. They don't get too private though. Teams are allowed 4 or 5 free individual entrants and some additional ones who pay 5 to $15. There are as many as four or five hundred teams entered in the big ones.

As I'll discuss in Chapter 10, purses serve a purpose to amateur racing not understood or even known by some racers themselves. Entering races with purses, no matter how small, means the driver can claim this pastime as more than a hobby. It's a bit complicated and yet oversimplified here, but the bottom line is racing can be written off on taxes if it's done right.

One more thing, no matter what level, class or type of racing involved, there is the cost of entry fees. For many amateur events, you can count on those fees to be 15 to $165. Most are closer to $140. At the pro level, the entry fee varies widely. For local circle track racing, the fees may be zero to $100. ("zero" if your presence brings in the fans) National pro events are closer to $500. The Indianapolis 500 is "who knows". It may be nonexistent or unquotable. I understand it used to be $20,000 for the Indy 500 with 'consideration of entry' or 'special membership' or whatever. I guess it wasn't really an entry fee as much as it was a test of commitment to race. Sheesh! How much commitment does a person need? To have an Indy car ready to go in the first place is quite a financial undertaking. That's how I was thinking at first. On second thought, to know USAC's reasoning makes this understandable. What used to happen was some people were entering relatively old or outdated Indy cars that were legal, but strictly "a prayer on 4 wheels". If they didn't qualify for the race, at least they got some (sponsorship) exposure on pole day. Tricky! Very tricky! But it was also taking away valuable track time and diluting sponsorship dollars to those who were there and genuinely committed to racing.

II.6. AGE/ATTITUDE—There's nothing you can do about age. There is something you can do about aging. This isn't going to be a lecture on fitness. Fitness is important in racing, sports and life in general. Anyone who doesn't know that really ought to get out in the real world more. What's meant by age in this case is a conglomeration of experience, perspective and attitude.

For the most part, older people have that going for them. You don't learn these things overnight in racing or from any sport. Realize only general circumstances are in order here. What's older is always relative. The 30 to 40 year old person will generally use a more cognitive decision-making process than the 18 year old. The 18 year old may tend to make decisions based on less thought and more instinct. They tend to be less patient and prone to mistakes. This doesn't make them hasty, but rather, young individuals who have less experience to fall back on. The point is it's not who is more intelligent, but rather, who's more battle-harden in life. So, because of that, older people initially have more going for them. Their decisions are based on prudence, patience, experience, caution and, yes, a more established financial base. Too bad those things can't be bought cheaply by an 18 year old itching to get out there and blow everybody's doors off.

5 | Vintage and Competitive Racing

Taking into account what's been written so far may conflict with what's about to be said. As you read further you'll notice, as in life, there are exceptions. It's not that I take a rules-were-made-to-be-broken attitude, . . . no, not at all, rather, it's better to be in the game and lose than not to play at all. It's like the old adage, it's better to have loved and lost than not to have loved at all.

You should be aware racing is established better as a team sport. As a racer, you may not fully except that. It's 'you' out there racing your competitors, not the car, not the team! That's a subconscious attitude. You never admit or say that to anyone, including yourself. You may feel the 'driver' wins races . . . the racecar loses them. Of course, we all know accidents are caused by the other guy. Spinouts, unplanned excursions, break-downs, . . . that's just rotten luck, . . . fate, whatever. Certainly it's not negligence, fool-ishness or brain-fade. Sometimes, there's a need to rid race-hardened veterans of that philosophy.

RUN FROM SCHOOL

That mentality does have its place, but not in vintage racing. The driver must tone down. Behavior modification isn't suggested, . . . it's demanded. Why? Before I answer that, an understanding must be met. In most major US sports, they can be radically divided into two levels. The amateurs and professionals. The professional level isn't something we conscientiously decide to compete at. The will to compete profession-ally is worked and strived for. We don't get up one morning and decide to play sports professionally. Anyone knows that. All true athletes strive to play professionally. Even more for those competing at the college level. Yes, college football and basketball players are amateurs too. Of course, that's up for heated debate. Let's leave that to be argued by others.

We are taught directly and indirectly to win. Our coaches, parents, society and envi-ronment dictates this. They must not just participate, but win. Win at all costs! An undying American attitude somewhat dimin-ished during the Vietnam war. Trying for only the moment isn't enough! Everyone with an ounce of pride can do their best. That's not enough! If everyone just tries their best, eventually the laws of diminishing re-turns sets in. This is not theory . . . it's fact. This isn't just human nature . . . it's reality. Someone has to win and someone (or the rest) has to lose. Otherwise, what's the sense of keeping score . . . or even playing the game in the first place. Would the people of this country (or any country) want its mili-tary and leadership to possess anything less than this attitude? I hope not. If we felt that way during World War II, the Japanese would have overrun us. To try your best is one thing, that's easy in the short run. To sacrifice something, working hard over the long run to win or to be the best is some-thing else. Not everyone is willing to work long and hard to win. In other words, talking and doing are two different things. One is easier than the other.

There it is, the ideal american sporting (and war) philosophy. This certainly holds true for athletes in automobile racing. Don't tell me race drivers aren't athletes. I'll tell you why they are later.

THROW IN THE MONKEY WRENCH

Now . . . get this . . . understand this . . . after all that was just explained, throw it out the window. Confused? Hang in there! This applies only to Vintage racing. It's a phenomenon a bit hard to understand in an already tough world of competitive racing. But it has its place. To understand competitive racing helps you understand the vintage version. We broke down sports to specific levels. Let's take this a step further, . . . breaking down racing.

In football, basketball, tennis or whatever, the mathematical changes of winning a specific game is 50 percent. This is true with both individual and team sports. Not so with racing. I know this contributes to the frustration experience in racing. The changes of winning a particular race may be low as 2 to 3 percent. Even from an unseasoned spectators view, the Indianapolis 500 has thirty-two losers. Notice I said "unseasoned". That is an exaggerated example, but I believe you understand my point. Take our win-at-all-costs attitude, mix that with racing's inherently low chances of winning and . . . waa-laa . . . there you have it . . . one tough and frustrating venue. That's not the worst of it. All the preparation, will and desire sometimes can't overcome circumstances. It's called bad luck. What's my point? Well . . . one is vintage racing circumvents frustration.

DEFRESHER COURSE

Go back to the beginning of this chapter and read it again. It describes athletic and racing attitudes and philosophy. As mentioned earlier, one can toss a portion of that philosophy out the window in describing vintage racing. Why on earth would one want to do that? Actually, as far as I'm concerned, there is a couple reasons for that. One, we're

not fighting a war here, and two, you will understand as you continue reading.

Racing requires a good, tough mental attitude and discipline. It can be very, very frustrating though. Vintage racing isn't as tough. But it does take stern discipline. The vintage driver needs to reject the inclination to battle natural instincts. In other words, maintain a different type of control. That can be very tough to resist, especially for an experienced racer. This isn't necessarily because it's hard to teach an old dog new tricks, it's more like getting a doctorate degree to dig a ditch. To the veteran racer, what's the point if you can't run hard. Here's where I explain why racing is a mental sport. All sports are mental. Some more than others. I can think of two sports more mental than the rest. Auto racing and high diving. When those olympic-styled high-divers start twisting, turning and going through all those gyrations through freefall, it amazes me. What keeps those athletes from doing a big 'belly flop' into the water? It's instinct and practice. They cannot think of what they're doing. That would slow them down. I have watched and participated in many races. What a driver does in the heat of a race isn't shear thinking, it's reaction!

Thinking is done during a caution or slow-down in an event, if there is any. Most athletics allow themselves time for thinking. In baseball you step out of the batters box. In football you go to the huddle. You don't get too many breaks in racing. Whether Off-Road, Motocross, Endurance racing or whatever, the breaks you're lucky to get are used for thinking, . . . not rest. Racing is constant reaction. Drivers react by the seat of their pants to limits of race vehicle dynamics. Other factors they react to are track conditions, weather and what other competitors do. The driver's brain is like a computer. It's the best one any race machine could have. If a racer starts thinking, especially in an overt manner, they will slow down. Slowing down won't win races and can be dangerous. It's like entering an interstate in LA at 20 mph. You'll be seen by most drivers but someone is liable to misjudge where you're at. (half asleep)

Most race drivers tend to 'see' ahead in

their mind than where they physically are. They need to read the situation way ahead of themselves. A slow racer may not be seen quick enough. Why is 'thinking' bad for racing? It requires deduction, comparisons, etc. It requires time. Thinking slows racers. Reaction requires speed . . . computer-like speed. It's important for maximum performance. It also prevents accidents. It's the one tool drivers need on a race vehicle to maximize its speed. Without it, a competitors move, a bump or a gust of wind could send a racecar out of control.

LIKE A FINE WINE

We know racing is a tough mental discipline. But vintage racing requires a different discipline. The attitude is different. It requires deviation from our natural instinct. It's human nature to floor the accelerator pedal on a race car. But, self-preservation for the sake of the racecar itself is now in order in vintage racing. (self-preservation for the driver . . . that's always true) Now the 'car' is the center of the show. Look in the dictionary under 'vintage'. One of the definitions is "an exceptionally fine wine from the crop of a good year." Good racecars get old. That doesn't mean they should age. In the spirit of a fine wine they should be preserved and nurtured. It's what vintage racing is, a fast-moving car show.

Some race machines aren't as old as they are technologically outdated. Some machines are just plain old, but charming and nostalgic all the same. They are raced in their original specifications. Modifications are out. Vintage racing seems out of reality for competitive drivers. They want to "mix it up" with other racers, fight the course itself or fight the clock. But think about it, drivers, like racecars, age also. That's not to say young drivers avoid vintage racing. Most do. But not all. Young racers just aren't frustrated enough yet. An attitude of less competition, more show and a lot of fun prevails. What vintage racing is all about is love of the older racecars. That combines with a practical sense, to put a carshow to speed. Regular carshows are for automotive lovers, not necessarily racecar lovers.

MOTHER NATURE TAKES OVER

Vintage racing began around 1934 in England. After WWII, its popularity moved to the US. The British took vintage racing very seriously. That was due to the fact they held more events compared to us. But we began to change that. Our vintage events went way up in numbers and size. Then it got very serious. Too serious! Modern race machines were introduced. To make a long story short, these vintage events became too fast and competitive. Then came the first grumbling from within. (and sanctioning bodies have been under constant internal scrutiny ever since) As a result, the US sanctioning club for vintage racing disbanded. What reformed was the Sports Car Club of America. (SCCA) This used to be the largest club or sanctioning body in the world. I believe the National Hot Rod Association (NHRA) is now the largest. Still, the SCCA is very prominent and strong today. Some years back, ideas were contemplated they would take control of Indy racing. Obviously, that didn't happen!

Around the early 50's, racing became deadly serious. That's not a play on words. It was a problem. Some of racing's deadly reputation was spawned in the 50's. Again, in 1959, more disenchanted racers felt some ideals in competitive racing were waning. They formed the first true vintage race club in the US. (VSCCA) That's up for debate, but unnecessary for argument here. The vintage clubs didn't stop with the VSCCA. Other groups formed through the 60's and 70's. This wasn't so much because of internal club problems, but because vintage racing grew even more in popularity. The clubs themselves stayed relatively small which created demographic problems. There were many of these clubs who held only a limited number of events. That wasn't bad, but in some ways, very good. The events became better organized and larger in individual size. But some conflicts persisted. Though some vintage clubs have formed from internal strife, others have disbanded to never reform. There are well over 30 Vintage Racing Organizations (VRO's) in North America. Over 100 major events are held yearly.

Although VRO's have a different policy and attitude compared to normal or competition racing, they do not lack for professionalism. Their philosophy is oriented at restoration, preservation, showmanship, spirit, sport, fun and recreation. That doesn't mean they lack for racing, but rather, for avoiding an "ugly spectacle". These race machines are considered charming works of art. The drivers don't want them banged around. Many members of VRO's are very fussy about their racecars. Some think nothing of re-doing a paint job any more than changing the oil. This helps instill in the drivers their incentive in maintaining that vintage spirit. You should understand by now why overzealous driving upsets vintage competitors.

DECISIONS DECISIONS

To a certain extent, this cautious circumstance exists at competitive amateur levels of racing. But it's more mechanically and financially oriented. (to survive in racing) It may cost the racer that competitive edge, but at least he'll be around for the next race. You may want to weigh this factor in your decision to race. Do you want to be "out there" racing? (as I mentioned in Chapter 2) That's okay in competitive racing . . . but you still must make an honest attempt to be fast. (as somewhat opposed in vintage racing) If you don't race hard, you put yourself and others in unsafe conditions. Slower is unsafe? You bet! Large speed differentials in any race is always (relatively) dangerous.

In vintage racing being 'out there' is 95 percent of the game. Finishing the race intact is the other 5 percent. You may not believe this is for you. It's still worth consideration. This sport certainly is subject to less surprises. Read on and think about it. Do you like working on your car's looks . . . or performance? The time you spend initially prepping and/or restoring any racer requires patience. Don't be surprised if your ratio of preparation to actual 'at speed' time in the cockpit can be as high as 30 to 1. That's not an exaggeration for the $30,000 a year man. If you're well-to-do, you will probably have your prep work done. Vintage racers like doing their own work, rich or not. That's not always the case with competitive racer, especially at the pro level.

Another factor to consider about vintage racing is safety. Even though racing of any kind is inherently dangerous, so is driving on the interstate highway. But the vintage safety record is very good. Consider, the built-in safety technology isn't always present in the older vintage race cars. They can also be quite an undertaking to handle. Given those conditions, it makes the vintage safety record look all that much better. Competitive racing also is much safer compared to the 60's, 70's and especially before and during the 50's. Racing itself is mostly responsible for that improvement. Aside from safer technology of the machines themselves and the driving gear wore by the drivers, it's also due to faster, better and 'on-site' medical services.

THE ACID TEST

All race drivers need to be physically fit. Not so much to avoid fatigue on the track, although that's important, but for other competitors out there with you. Vintage drivers tend to be older. Hence, they have more physical limitations. Going out to race with heart problems, for example, doesn't serve anybody. Most clubs require a yearly examination, some every two years. It varies between clubs. Like racing in general, eyes, reflexes and muscles need to be fit. No, you don't have to be Charles Atlas but you need to avoid fatigue.

Remember, the idea behind vintage racing is, among other things, showmanship and having fun. The top goal isn't to win, but to finish. That includes not only the car, but the driver too. As in competitive racing, vintage drivers must be properly attired. That means fireproof underwear, suits and gloves. Shoes must be of proper materials and quality . . . like the helmets. These things are inspected prior to an event. Your race machine will require an inspection before an event also.

To avoid surprises at all levels of racing, have a checklist you can systematically run through. Do this a week or so beforehand. If you find a problem that needs attention, you'll have time to correct it. Don't do what I've done a couple of times. I found stress cracks on the chassis the day before leaving for a race weekend. I corrected the problem but lost time in the process. Then I drove most of the night to a race to make up for what I lost. But it made me a zombie (for all intents and purposes) the rest of the event. It didn't make me a very effective racer. Matter-of-fact, it made me a danger to myself and others. Lack of sleep makes one very grumpy, especially with all the things that can go wrong. Even the little things were irritating. It was an effort to not just throw something in frustration. I didn't like myself. It'll never happen again. Get the sleep or don't race . . . it's simple as that.

Have the racer ready to go one weekend in advance. Have no doubts in your mind the race car is ready. A clear mind concentrates much better. If you're wondering during the heat of a race if your racer was completely checked out, you're already in trouble. Even if you're not in danger you can not drive your best. It's like I stated before, thinking slows a racer. Anyway, I'm getting a bit ahead of myself. As mentioned earlier, your vehicle, race apparel and gear will be inspected prior to an event. The technical inspector will have their own checklist to run through. They can be very thorough in their work or very fast. They cannot be both. It depends how much time they have. If they are thorough, they'll ask you questions. Be cooperative. This person is not out to spoil your race weekend, but to insure you're around afterwards. If the inspection is done in rather quick fashion, remember, you know your race car better than anyone. If you know somethings not right, it can still escape the most thorough inspection. You're cheating yourself by not correcting it now. Worst of all, you may be cheating others. Having a racecar fall apart or fail at high speed isn't fun.

WHERE RUBBER AND ASPHALT MEET

Inspection is over. You passed. Now it's track time. Don't get too rambunctious. Learn the track. Find less dangerous areas with more run-off room. In those areas you can take more risk to gain speed. But first things first.

Now it's time for a 'rolling' inspection. Once you're out on the track for practice, check your racers handling characteristics. Does it feel a little mushy? (even on a dry track?) It's more than likely the tires are not up to temperature yet. While you're waiting for that to occur, check your brakes. Always do this first. Move the steering left and right to check response. This also helps warm up the tires more quickly. Now check your mirrors. Will you know what's back of you and at what distance? This is very important and has to be learned. It's not as easy as it seems. Race drivers can't spend much time staring in the mirrors. On the other hand, it's important to use them. Next, check the instruments. Are they working? They can be subject to severe vibration and fail. They can warn you of potential problems. Make sure they are located for quick easy reading. Instruments operating at normal readouts should have the arrows within them pointing straight up. That's why they look improperly rotated when mounted on the panel. It's not sloppy workmanship. They're placed in that manner for quick reference by the driver.

Check your clutch and transmission linkage. Missing a gear (because linkage is sloppy) from low to high acceleration out of a corner can have your competition slamming you in the rear. Now that you've done that, some time has passed. Temperatures in your engine and tires should be up more. Recheck your handling and brakes. If all is well, you're ready. That doesn't mean to start racing now. Always check the flag signals from the flagman. Then if your signal is green, you can speed up and start practicing. Of course, if you're on the track for the race itself, the 'pace' vehicle will line up the racecars. All these things are pretty elementary, but not to the beginner.

I remember my first race. I was so preoccupied with myself (scared) I forgot to strap my helmet down. A safety official caught it. He 'black-flagged" me into the pit area and buckled my helmet tight. How he saw it was amazing. But he did. (they probably look for those kind of things with beginners) Another thing to do is not only make sure you're buckled in to your racecar, but buckled tight. The tighter you're buckled in, the better vehicle feedback you'll receive. Driving by the seat-of-your-pants isn't just a cute saying. It's what a driver uses with his brain to determine how the racecar is handling. (at high speed) Once you have done these on-track checks, get down to business.

When qualifying for a race, what I do is get behind a specific race driver who is "track educated" (knows the course) and has a reputation for being fast. I follow him. You'll learn the shortest way around the course, if you can keep up. If you can't, wait, . . . then follow someone who may pass you. Following someone who is very fast isn't a good idea even if you can keep up. Know the track first then try following fast drivers. Knowing the track means about two or three weekends or events on it, not just a few laps. Don't be blinded by pride. Use good judgement. Know your limits. Don't be intimidated by faster vehicles. It may be the car is faster, not the driver. Even if a driver is better, accept it. Strive to improve yourself through practice, experience and diligence. Improving yourself to avoid shame isn't the way to learn. It's self defeating in the long run and will only lead to unnecessary pressure and frustration.

On the flip side of the coin, many drivers literally separate themselves from others. They feel they'll gain the maximum speed by battling the track alone and free from incidental interference. That's certainly okay! Whatever you prefer is what you should do. But try both ways to learn which way is best for you.

Remember, you should realize qualifying for most amateur races doesn't involve the solo-type procedure like at Indy. All the racers in your class (and usually a few other simular classes) are on the track running as hard as possible. A particular driver can have a zillion bad lap-times and one great one. That great one will be recorded as the official time for the machine. If it's the best of the other drivers' best times, you'll start the race in your class in the front. 99% of the time, you do not have to worry about qualifying so poorly that you won't be allowed a starting position in the race. This isn't pro racing where race fields are limited to a specific number of vehicles.

In learning to race vintage style, everything is about the same. What's the big difference? Don't try to make a dangerous pass, especially in a corner. This is true for practice, qualifying or the race itself. Pass in the 'straights' on a racecourse. Make sure it's a clean pass. Do not slam-the-door on someone. (that's cutting in too abruptly and certainly too soon) All racers should check their mirrors when possible, but not while turning a corner. Don't be overly concerned if someone is behind you. It's still mostly the responsibility of the passing car to do that safely. Maintain your line of speed but don't unnecessarily block a faster driver. You'll know they are much faster than you by how quickly they moved up from a distance. What many drivers about to be passed do is point to the side they want to be overtaken on. It doesn't mean you have to concede your position, but it lets the driver in back know you're aware of him.

SANCTIONING BODY SCHOOLS

Like schools for competitive racing, there are options available for vintage school requirements. Basically, these schools are identical. What gets you a competitive license will get you a vintage license also. One method of licensing is to attend a (vintage or competitive) sanctioning body school. Many sanctioning bodies in all types of racing hold their own schools. They are more safety and fundamentally oriented. Some are held in conjunction with a private racing event. (private race events are not open to spectator viewing) Like competitive (or club) schools, many vintage schools require two separate weekends of instruction. On the other hand, some require one of their schools and a professional one. (see chapter 8). Whatever the case, do some research.

Don't just make an arbitrary decision based on what you find first or what's cheaper. The sanctioning body school will cost you anywhere from 50 to $150 for entry fees. That is for two days of learning basics. These schools can be great or good. It depends on your instructor. The professional schools run from 3 to 5 intense days of fundamentals. They teach safety, maintenance, and of course, the quick way around a course. Their facilities and equipment are very good, if not excellent. These can cost 900 to $3,000. Some are higher. But, you get what you pay for. Unlike club or sanctioning body schools, pro schools provide the race cars. That's what drives their costs up. So actually, I think you're much better off going through a professional school. This is especially so with 4-wheel racing vehicles. That's not to say motorbike schools are poor. It's just that some racing bikes aren't expensive as cars for your first sanctioning body school. Consider the risk you're taking at your first school with a race car you just bought. This is not the time or way to find out racing isn't for you. I could go on, but you'll know more about professional schools in chapter 8.

OVALS AND ROADCOURSES

Racing took roots on the streets of Europe and Great Britain. Racing on the streets created logistic and safety problems. The safety problem magnified as the competition became more fierce and faster. Also, containing a paying audience was pretty much impossible in those days. If the costs of racing on the downtown streets wasn't scary enough, the mishaps were. With rising speed, much needed run-off area (needed to slow down an out-of-control vehicle) became a premium. The carnage was on. The city streets had to go. Street racing then became prevalent in the countryside. Barricading out nonpaying spectators was easier, in addition to protecting life and limb. (of both driver and spectators alike) Still, because these events were held on public property, not all problems were solved. Much cooperation within a community was needed to hold these events. Still, not all spectators paid for their view.

In the United States, this problem was handled differently. While 'streetcourses' were around then (and still are today) the 'roadcourses' (purpose-built, specifically for racing) came into more prominence. But not like the almighty oval! Oval race tracks was the way to go! The racing was faster, more confined for better and easier viewing and most of all, easier to promote to a paying audience. All types and sizes were constructed in the US: quarter-mile, 1/2 mile, 1 mile and an occasional superspeedway.

The first superspeedway was the Indianapolis Motor Speedway. (not a true oval in todays sense of the word) Most of these ovals were flat surfaces of dirt and clay. While all these changes took place in the US, vintage racing was beginning to get squeezed out. That wasn't quite so true in England. All those ovals didn't quite fill the bill for vintage racing. The romance, nostalgia and beauty of these events did not blend well with the cold man-made confines of a dirt covered oval. But as more paved, purpose-built roadcourses were built, vintage racing started to grow. None-the-less, some vintage racing occurs on the ovals. But ovals are more designed for Stockcars, Sprintcars, Midgets, Formula and in some cases, the Jalopies. Don't let that word jalopy conjure up ideas of old dilapidated junk. Usually those cars are over 25 years of age, more like antiques. Good for viewing, not always good for racing. Sports-Cars, Formula, Production, Motorcycles, Prototypes and GT's are usually raced on paved roadcourses.

CHOOSING A VINTAGE

Have you decided to race vintage? Which class do you race? Finish this chapter, then read chapter 2 again. No . . . on second thought, don't do that. This is a no-thinker. You probably already know what and how you want to race. If that's not your particular case, don't despair. You're lost alright, but there's a pleasant cure. This is like being forced to marry any one of a number of Miss Americas. (of your choice) Tough choice isn't it? Time will eventually lead you to what you want, . . . or more importantly, what you don't want. You'll probably want to race several vintage type machines. That's possible, but very expensive. Find out the costs, maintenance, . . . read this book all the way through. Do your research. Then go with what your personal taste, goals and finances allow.

Some people say the best deals on vintage racers are ones not advertised. They say find vintage car leads by talking to antique dealers, automotive historians, garage dealers located near race tracks and relatives of well-known older drivers. To me that's a long shot, especially for a particular type or 'make' of vintage car. Some excellent cars may be found in back of someone's barn or buried under a pile of car parts in a garage. Still it'll be nothing more than sheer luck to find something in that manner. The thing to do is check in the appendix of this book. This will direct you to the proper cars. When you see all those classified ads of vintage cars, don't get lost on which particular one to purchase. Don't buy 'sight unseen'. Get leads on choices you've eliminated or narrowed down to. It's a very good chance vintage race club drivers, members or officials in that particular area will know about a machine you have your eye on. Contact them if it's financially worth it. The first person you talk to may not know anything about it, but may know someone who does. If all fails, you'll have to talk to the person selling it. I don't always feel I get an objective view from those who stand to gain financially as a result. Give yourself plenty of time to research the buy. Then check it out. I hope you don't have to travel far. It works against anyone if the seller knows you came from a long distance.

VINTAGE RACE CLASSES

The few vintage cars described in Chapter 3 generally are broken down more specifically by rules. The ones described in this chapter race under a larger classification, in most cases, but not all. A case in point would be the Formula Ford. This race class is identical in both vintage and competitive sanctioning bodies. That's not usually the situation in most classes. It can become confusing, at times, to a casual observer, but it's nothing to be intimidated by. After further study you'll realize it takes only minor mechanical adjustments to race a particular vehicle between two different vintage clubs.

Most vintage sanctioning bodies divide all race vehicles into six major groups: (this may not be precise, but it'll give you an overview what to expect)

Group A - Pre World War II

Group B - Vintage I 1946-59
    Class 1 - Production cars under 2 liters
    Class 2 - Production cars over 2 liters
    Class 3 - SportsRacers under 2 liters
    Class 4 - SportsRacers over 2 liters

Group C - Vintage II 1960-1963
    Class 1 - Production cars under 2 liters
    Class 2 - Production cars over 2 liters
    Class 3 - SportsRacers under 2 liters
    Class 4 - SportsRacers over 2 liters

Group D - All Monoposto cars through 1969
(These are open-wheel single seaters with aluminum or fiberglass bodies on tube frames for formula types)
    Class 1 - Front engine Formula Junior
    Class 2 - Rear engine Formula Junior (Early)
    Class 3 - Rear engine Formula Junior (Late)
    Class 4 - Formula Vee & Formula III 500 cc
    Class 5 - Formula I & II
    Class 6 - Formula Ford

Group E - Historic I 1960-1973
    Class 1 - Production cars under 2 liters
    Class 2 - Production cars 2 to 3 liters
    Class 3 - Production cars 3 to 5 liters
    Class 4 - Production cars over 5 liters

Group F - Historic II 1960-1973
    Class 1 - Prototype race cars under 2 liters
    Class 2 - Prototype race cars 2 to 3 liters
    Class 3 - Prototype race cars 3 to 5 liters
    Class 4 - Prototype race cars over 5 liters

While the classes remain relatively stable, the years which qualify a group is constantly updated. This is usually done annually. Remember, vintage cars aren't purpose-built from the ground up for this type of racing. You don't build them, you restore them.

VINTAGE RACING ORGANIZATIONS (VRO'S)

Before getting into VRO's, it's important to understand their philosophies are pretty much identical. Because of that and their growth, including diverse locations throughout the US, the Vintage Motorsports Council (VMC) was formed. (in 1988) The VMC is represented by members of various clubs. (VRO's) Among other things, they formed a general-national policy on vintage racing. They also prevent and solve common problems. It gives all VRO's a voice amongst each other. This organization keeps all VRO's informed about specific drivers and their status. (for the purpose of a driver crossing lines, racing in more than one VRO)

The 13/13 rule the VMC enforces is for safety. If a driver is involved in a racing accident, an investigation is conducted. A decision is based on racecar preparation and driving etiquette. If a driver is suspended from a particular race, they are placed on automatic probation for 13 months. Another infraction within that time incurs a 13 month suspension. Why 13 months instead of 1 year? This is done so a driver can't regain eligibility at the same event he was suspended from a year previously. This may not seem like such a big deal, but consider some events are very big and popular. With low numbers of vintage events compared to normal racing, the penalty is worse than what it appears.

To explain clearly, say a driver was booted out of the Indy 500. Indy isn't vintage racing and they don't have any such 13/13 rule. (penalties are handled individually) If they did, a penalized driver would not regain eligibility until 2 years later. Ouch! . . . that really smarts for many people. This 13/13 rule helps enforce proper behavior at vintage events. The rule can best be followed by what vintage competitors unofficially call the 7/10 rule. That describes a relative speed and/or effort practiced. That's 70 percent effort, but 100 percent car preparation. Racecar negligence will get you tossed out of competition also.

The first place vintage inspectors check are tires, wheels, brakes and suspension. Keep them fit! I can personally point out through experience that competitive racing is about 19/20 at the club (amateur) level, if such a rule existed. (which doesn't) The only reason it's not 10/10 like professional racing is because tearing up or overextending race cars is expensive. Amateur racers do not have the luxury of much financial help. But understand, if this racer is still in the competition to win toward the end of a particular race, throw any 19/20 rule or simular philosophy out the window. It doesn't apply. They want to win! Period!

For a list of major VRO's, check the Appendix. You'll also find vintage race schools, race tracks and magazine/books specifically for vintage racing. You can write each VRO for specific information on schedules, schools, racing classifications, rules and licensing. Don't assume you have to be a driver to join these clubs. As in all racing, these clubs are constantly seeking volunteers for help. They may need some clerical help, but mostly they want help to score, flag and direct races. They need safety and medical personnel also. But, you must be a member. Drop them a line.

6 | Women Racers, Fans and Athletes

A. ARE RACE DRIVERS ATHLETES?
B. THE RACE FAN MYTH
C. WATCHING A RACE

For whatever reasons women exist in todays world, one indisputable fact is established, they are no longer the perpetual "baby-machines" of yesterdays old male-dominated school of thought. It's not that I'm necessarily pro female, but rather sympathetic to their needs. That doesn't include any female's physiological, psychological or ego-driven need to prove themselves equal or superior. To debate that would take another book. That book could be ten feet thick and still nothing would change. Men and women will think what they want to. Stereotypes, malignment, mistrust, whatever, will never fade from the minds of people. You can't change the stripes on a tiger. Besides, what's the point if you could. Seems women have always yearned to equalize themselves by male standards. They don't want to prove anything to men as much as to themselves.

It's said, if one is told something enough times, it's perceived as the truth. I suppose that can be said about advertising and politics. Just keep pounding a message over and over and over until the truth is perceived, taken for granted or literally taken for the truth. Therefore, many women have grown up in a society believing through constant negative input, their role in life is dictated by their own limitations. Those limitations may span a very wide spectrum. It may be physical, emotional, psychological, intellectual, physiological or a thousand other things. The point is that's all changing very quickly. It doesn't matter if women themselves dis-

covered they're not limited. It doesn't matter if they just got up one morning and decided, "The hell with men, I'm tired of pandering to them". It doesn't matter what anybody thinks of women, or in this case, women and athletics. These attitudes are changing, whether any individual man or even some women themselves like it or not.

"ME TARZAN"

Most people realize men are, literally, physically stronger than women. I do not think most women would deny it. The women who would, do a great disservice to themselves. They, in fact, perpetuate negative attitudes, myths and misunderstandings towards themselves. Therefore, the entire issue of women is further clouded. In today's highly technological, easier lifestyle, strength doesn't play the role it used to. It's still important and necessary, but it's by far, not the only thing required to survive, . . . bring home the bacon, . . . make the world turn or a requirement to compete in athletics.

Strength more than anything, is one thing which has served to malign the female. It's the one aspect which makes itself not only obvious, but it's easier to measure and prove. The "Me Tarzan" mentality doesn't mean a male is also superior to women in everything else. This is where too many assumptions are made. So, with that and the advent of a "push-button" society, those assumptions are disproved by women fed up with that train of thought. No longer is male dominance necessary.

Up until about the middle of this century man functioned literally by "body". In previous times, therefore, strength was an obvious necessity. Many, if not most men recognize that. The problem is too many still won't admit strength doesn't play the role it used to. The men which do, don't necessarily concede dominance in the literal sense of the word. Therefore, the battle of the sexes continues.

As if women don't have enough resistances blending in with society, the battle to compete on the athletic field is magnified. Not so much with women against women, but females with males. In the minds of true male-driven, male dominant, ego-perpetuated men around the athletic world, no sport has taken a "hit" like automobile racing. As if racing wasn't already being questioned as a true sport, the inception of women didn't help its reputation with the nonracing, nonathletic general public. Of course, that's especially true with men.

The women may have had another world opened up to them. I'm not necessarily speaking of Janet Guthrie, Shirley Muldowney or Lynn St James, but they're certainly a good reference point to start from. Women began making inroads in racing years before Janet Guthrie ran in the '77 Indy 500. Nowhere is that more so then the Sports Car Club of America. (SCCA) Many women are racing Formula, SportCars, GT and Production classes. Several others are trying in smaller associations. That includes Late Model StockCars, Motorcycles, Off-Road and Drag racing. Matter-of-fact, there has already been one woman to win a world championship in motorsports. While few have won any races at all, this lady has done that enough to win the whole thing. (a national championship)

The Lady with the Pink Race Car

Shirley Muldowney didn't accomplish this feat in a lower class either. It was done in drag racing's top class, the Top Fuel dragsters. (in 1977) When you think about it, what she accomplished far outweighs what any woman has done athletically. Let me emphasize the words "any woman"! She has staved off fiery mishaps and discriminations to not only succeed as a woman athlete, but one among a sport overwhelmingly dominated by men. She was not an overnight flash-in-the-pan. Her racing career has spanned well over thirty years. Her racing accomplishments are unrivaled in (drag) racing, not necessarily because she's obviously a female, but rather, because she won the world championship 3 times.

To race competitively in Top Fuel is quite an accomplishment in itself. But there is more to be said about this than just being "out there"! When she won her first event, it proved without a doubt Shirley Muldowney belonged. Then there was the world championship. No matter how much men howled about the help she received, winning the world championship cannot be a fluke, especially since she has done it three times.

Nobody, probably including Shirley herself, believes women are superior athletes any more than they believe men are. But . . . don't confuse 'superior' with 'strength'. Men athletes are physically stronger. Just take a look at the NFL, college and high school gridiron rosters and no one can deny what's obvious. Racing also takes strength. But it's a different type, just as there's different types of speed. One can be quick, but not fast, and vice versa. Being quick, fast, strong, large and smart certainly are great attributes for an athlete, but it doesn't guarantee success. There are other factors to consider, such as attitude, desire, etc. The strength required to block a 300 pound lineman isn't the same kind of strength required to maintain control while essentially getting shot out of a cannon. (What it's like in the quicker throngs of drag car racing)

Janet Guthrie

Consider the different type of athletic ability Janet Guthrie must possess. Shirley Muldowney's athletic skills do not require stamina like that of Janet Guthrie. I do not doubt if Ms Muldowney needed it for a 500 mile drag race from New York to Chicago, she wouldn't hesitate to muster it. Of course, that is exaggerated, but hopefully, you see the point. Ms Guthrie was indeed in the right place at the right time when she was offered a ride at Indy. Many complaints here was that the opportunity was a publicity stunt. But Janet Guthrie wasn't born with a drivers wheel in her hand. She had worked her way through the ranks to gain racing recognition long before the Indy opportunity presented itself. (via car owner Rolla Vollstedt) Matter-of-fact, she already raced in some Indy and NASCAR events previous to her '77 Indy race. She was also NASCAR's first woman driver in the Winston Cup series. So she was no public stunt like many thought. Even though she failed to qualify at Indy in 1976, she came back in 1977 to qualify for the race. But as racing can be at times, her equipment failed after 27 laps of the race. Undeterred, she was back again in '78 to finish in the top 10. Like Shirley Muldowney, she quieted the critics who felt women didn't have the physical or mental attributes to handle a 200+ mph race machine.

Looking Back

The cases of Shirley Muldowney and Janet Guthrie received quite a bit of attention. Janet Guthrie's was much more subject to the aura of the Indy 500 while Shirley Muldowney's was spread out over time. But there have been many others. They haven't been necessarily at the top of their racing career, if it's considered a career at all. Previous to Janet Guthrie, was the first woman ever to compete in an Indy car event. Her name is Arlene Hiss. (wife of former Indy driver Mike Hiss) She participated at the Phoenix race in March of '76. In Europe, a lady named Lella Lombardi was entering Formula One races. Last, but not least, there is Lynn St James. There's a lady whom I thought showed more mental discipline during that cold weather fiasco at Indy in 1991, than many of her supposedly well-

seasoned competitors. It seemed fascinating many drivers were sticking their cars in the wall simply because they failed to properly warm their tires. Lynn St James wasn't as quick as many of those drivers, but that wasn't what was keeping her off the wall. It was patience and self discipline.

Despite these high profile cases of women racers, they're still rather the exception than the rule. But it's a start if not in the racing consensus than at least for women themselves. For every Janet, Shirley or Lynn, there are at least another couple of hundred in the SCCA alone playing the race game. Most of them compete at the solo and rally levels. Women are increasing in numbers at the off-road level, including the motorcycle organizations.

The problems women like Janet Guthrie, Shirley Muldowney and Lynn St James encountered early in their careers or at Indy didn't stem only from their gender. That's what many drivers would have us believe. But rising up with the strenuous process of what constitutes a driver as a seasoned racer isn't an exact science. Many drivers at both the amateur and especially professional levels started their race careers with much less apprenticeship, reputation and experience. Somehow, they found a way to slip through the cracks of the system to short-circuit it. Whether this is fair or not isn't the point.

What constitutes an established racers preconceived notion of what's fair probably has more to do with what only seems fair for their purpose. Some men for instance, have run the Indy 500 with considerable less racing experience and savvy than Janet Guthrie and Lynn St James. Some were considered seasoned at speed itself, but lacking in the right kind of it. Yet, a couple or so of these men won the 500. Looking back it's hard to believe today that drivers like Mark Donahue, Graham Hill and Jim Clark were considered at best, suspicious. Their successes were a source of uneasiness to traditionalists who felt doubts were cast at what it took to handle an Indy car. Yet, I can personally name 'lesser knowns' early in their careers who had no business being in the race. Why their presence escaped scrutiny is beyond the casual observers view. As one Indy driver admitted, drivers coming to Indy with less than acceptable eligibility were unfairly judged for reasons other then what mattered on the race track.

'Eligibility' was a code word for 'acceptability'. I suppose racing reflects life in the manner of prejudice. Yet in fairness, it's always easy to look back and make judgements ourselves on matters which are not fully understood. Yet, there was a situation a few years back which demonstrated the racing fraternities knack for exposing themselves. A seasoned Trans-Am racer lacking Formula experience entered the Indy 500. Despite the fact Wally T. Ribbs is a black man, nobody, other than maybe Mr. Ribbs himself, questioned his credentials. I don't believe Mr Ribb's really thought he couldn't handle an Indy car. His honesty was refreshing, but at the same time, it may have been a subconscious move to redirect any potential heat or controversy away from himself. Not a bad idea. But then, on the other hand, it may have been unnecessary. Too many of the preconceived ideas of what it takes to race at Indy had already been shattered.

Speaking of what it takes to drive at Indy, among many things is athletic ability. While some race drivers and many fans question what it takes to reach that pinnacle, the general public questions what it takes to be a race car driver in the first place.

A. ARE RACE DRIVERS ATHLETES?

The argument concerning race drivers and whether they are real athletes has somewhat died down with the late generation of fans. This is especially so with the higher speeds of today. Everybody knows what looks easy isn't always so. After all, if something is easy, . . . is it worthwhile? This is a fact of life. This also fuels the idea that anyone can drive a racecar. In fact, most people could. After all, they can handle their street cars with ease. Of course, that's a ridiculous notion, but that's how some think. It isn't that they're not very smart, but rather, in every-

day life they get a 'taste' of racing. It's called a drivers license and it's the closest thing to 'sport' many nonathletes come to. But they're not generally the people questioning racers. Mostly, it's former athletes from other sports who are. They feel racing is nothing more than a 'staged political event' put on wheels. If that isn't bad enough, this is augmented by the members of second and third generation 'name' drivers moving up in racing rather quickly. They cry nepotism. It's a situation which doesn't seem to bother too many drivers. They know they have nobody to answer to in a helpless circumstance like that. I guess it goes hand in hand with some general public's distorted views that racing in itself has no significance.

Some will always feel racing is a contemptible futility which leads to nowhere but waste. Even in war, death and destruction serves a productive function towards a goal or ideal. They consider racing a misappropriation of time, energy, effort and money. Of course, most of those ideas are, thankfully, disappearing through human attrition. If you understand the original purpose of sports, you'll know it developed out of a need for survival. Athletics was used to keep idle warriors mentally and physically prepared. So, . . . some of these older and former athletes don't see any connection between racing and survival, or more explicitly, with war. Then they saw their views cemented even more by an equally unsympathetic news media. The sports segments of TV news broadcasts told us much about racing in this country by telling us nothing at all. Any race news which managed to hit the airwaves was in the form of tragedies. Case in point are the bungled starts at Indy or the deaths which took place there.

In the mid-50's, before a session of Congress, there was an impassioned plea to ban racing in this country. It bore out of, admittedly, too many deaths. Only a few weeks earlier at the 24 hours of Lemans, over 80 spectators were killed when a driver lost control of his racer and got airborne. It was the worst race tragedy to ever happen. The situation in the 1955 Indy race saw previous two time winner Bill Vukovich perish while leading the race. The news media was highly critical of those events and rightly so. But the focus was put on the sport itself instead of the circumstances. But racing has survived. Even though the speeds at the upper levels are increasing, the safety technology has not only kept up, but easily surpassed it. Race cars are built to fall apart yet internally stay intact upon impact. Therefore, impact energy is more safely diffused. Fires are practically nonexistent upon impact and the tracks are better designed.

The Human Touch

Still today, there are a few casual race observers who question a racers athletic ability. While safety and speed technology has made its presence known in racing, it doesn't remove the driver off the hotseat. This same technology rewards the car and dumps the driver from "the pan into the fire". This reveals itself most obviously on high speed ovals. The problem is separating the performance of the driver from the racecar. The confusion is based on the average "Joe fan's" premise that a drivers right foot determines speed. It's true, a bad driver can't get the most out of a good car, but a good one can get the most out of a bad car. Still, a bad car most likely will not win.

While at speed it's universally agreed there's only so much which can be done with an ill-behaving race machine. On the other hand, a good driver can hopefully communicate a quick cure from his help. This takes an understanding of some laws of motion. That isn't an easy task. There are many variables involved. Correcting one problem may create another. Of course, if this situation happens in a short race at the club level, it's a dead issue. The problem need only be corrected prior to the next race. It comes down in situations like that as a matter of driver intelligence. Not too many question a racers intelligence, . . . sanity . . . maybe, but not intelligence.

Speaking of sanity . . . even though I toy with that word, it shouldn't be taken literally. Race drivers do not have a death wish. It's true there is a mystery to the idea an individual could perish in a race mishap. That is definitely not shared by the race driver. They don't race to live on the edge or bandy with death. On the contrary, they don't want or believe they can get killed. Yet, this tough-mindedness doesn't serve against them, but rather acts as a safety buffer. It enhances the concentration a race driver so importantly needs. Even in most life threatening situations, they are unbelievably relaxed. They are emotionally detached, not because they don't care, but because it distracts from their immediate task. Emotion is an enemy of concentration.

Racers must be emotionally stable or detached to fight off its distractive effects. Ever notice the difference emotionally between a racer and, say, a football player before competition? It's like the comparison between night and day. The football player appears ready to do battle, to put it mildly. The racer looks ready to sleep. It's not an accident. Racers must introvert themselves or risk losing control. Any anger is postponed to the races end. That, unfortunately, sometimes makes for interesting news coverage or viewing from the stands.

Even though racecar drivers are mostly conservative, introverted and emotionally distant, it doesn't mean they can't occasionally vent their frustration via another's driver head. Race drivers are very self-reliant and dominant. They go hand in hand in racing and when it's lost, it's irritating to them. While those two traits aren't conducive to a blissful marriage, they certainly are in racing. Once a race is started, a driver is never more on his own to any degree when compared to other competitors in any sport. If there is an exception, I can only think of the long distance marathon runner. But those runners are not subject to other's mistakes or put in life threatening situations.

Race car drivers test above average in abstract thinking. They are much healthier psychologically. They are not the sensationalists many from the old school of thought believe they are. The only stimulist they're addicted to is that of man and machine. They love a challenge. The very top drivers compete best under stress. They do realize racing has inherent dangers. It's another reason they must maintain emotional control. It encourages them to keep danger to its lowest level by not taking unnecessary risks. Thus, they are cautious men as only the relative meaning of that word can be taken.

May the Force be with You

Most drivers do not use their bodies in the same kinetic manner as 'ball and stick' athletes do. The obvious exceptions are motorcycle riders, motocross and to some extent go-kart and midget racers. Still, many drivers were very good athletes in high school and college. As can be expected, racers have excellent vision and good reaction. They can anticipate special situations. As a result, they acquire knowledge and make decisions more quickly. It's worth stating again about driver intelligence. They are among the smartest athletes in all sports. Many top racing drivers have tested IQ's with those of the smartest people in the world. Regardless of all those attributes, racers are not always judged as athletes as much as they are actors. The reason for that is understandable but misguided.

Drivers do not actively impose physical forces on someone or something else. A football player, more specifically a lineman, blocks another man or tries to avoid a block. Wrestlers attempt to pin their opponent. The baseball batter hits the ball. The list goes on and on. These athletes have one thing in common, they do the imposing. They apply the forces. But in racing, like no other sport, these forces are applied to a static and defenseless driver.

Even though these forces aren't always obvious, it isn't only because the drivers themselves are 90 percent hidden from view. A more exaggerated and much more obvious example are motorcycle riders, off-road racers and to some extent midget and sprint racers. They can expect to be buffeted, pummeled and just plain thrown around for anywhere from a few minutes to 3 to 4 hours. Road racers such as stockcar and formula drivers will be treated in the same manner but in a less restrictive, less obvious manner. Drag racers face tremendous front loads. All these racers will fight G-forces, in-

ertia, sideloads or centrifugal forces. At the top levels of racing, they must handle such forces as accelerating from 0 to 300 mph in 5 or 6 seconds, handle a 215 to 230 mph turn, yet concentrate with unparalleled conviction.

Some drivers can expect to lose 5 percent weight from an already lean body. They sustain these forces, concentration and handle stresses with an incredibly high heart rate of 170 to 190 beats per minute. All the while, doing a slow-fry with cockpit temperatures reaching 135 to 150 degrees. (while wearing a convention denying, fireproof suit and underwear) At rest, drivers have low heart rates, blood pressure and a lower cholesterol count. When is the last time you saw an accomplished race driver who was fat, out-of-shape and just plain uptight? Not to often, if at all. Even a race event of a few minutes can knock the life out of a driver. Out of shape drivers not only fiss out quickly, but are dangerous to all concerned. Imagine racing hundreds of miles over hot scorching sand in those long distance off-road races. How about those blinding speeds motorcycle roadracers reach! What's more disconcerting then getting tossed, kicked, bucked off your seat in motocross racing. The drag racers unequalled experiences of, for all intents and purposes, getting shot out of a gun. All these circumstances require a hard work ethic and diligence to master.

Like any other athlete, race drivers aren't born, they're developed. They aren't anywhere close to the cretins, machismo charlatans, thrill-seeking, death-defying robots "stuffed-into-a-machine-sofely-for-the-purposes-of-entertaining-the-masses" some feel they are.

B. THE RACE FAN MYTH

As you well know by now, there are many types of racing. Within those types are even more levels, or in this case, classes. Each has its own set of rules. Without getting into the complexities of them, generally race machines are governed by engine size, vehicle weight, dimensions and what they literally race on. There are a zillion other rules laid down but not necessary for the fan to know. In some areas, designers have a free choice. This is where the manufacturers put their own theory, experiments, design and testing to use. Hopefully, this in theory is where automobile racing helps improve automobiles for the general public. Today, with speed at many levels increasing, the emphasis is towards safety.

Many question how racing in general improves street automobiles. But their quality has improved despite their increasing complexity. It seems today it is all one can do just to reach a spark plug in those engine compartments. But other factors and amenities designed into cars have contributed to their complex nature. They may be harder and costlier to service, but the service itself is relatively less frequent. Opponents argue racing technology does nothing for the public other than entertain. They rationalize it's tantamount to running a horse at top speed into a wall to test horseflesh. These people are not seeing the big picture. Without getting into something not intended here, racing is responsible, in whole or part, for much improved automotive dynamics, safety, efficiency and design. On the other hand, nobody in racing claims this was its sole intention.

As mentioned previously, racing was questioned as a sport. That's because it failed in the war-like philosophy of many to have any significance. If that's the case, of which it's not, if it hasn't prepared man, it sure has improved his machinery. We may categorize critics of racing to those who thought putting a man on the moon was a waste of resources. Only the sequels which benefit man long after the critics have left this world will see those improvements the most, if they're not taken for granted.

"Death Wish" . . . Brought to You by . . . The Race Drivers

Stadiums, theaters, movie houses are built on the idea of congregating the masses to entertain. TV entertains also. But "being there" as the saying goes today is more than just a cute little acronym of words. It's meant literally for what it's worth. There is no comparison to seeing an event on the screen or tube than experiencing it in person. You have to be there to feel the excitement.

Racing certainly is no exception. It may be too much of an exception. Over the years, race fans, like drivers and the sport itself, have been unfairly maligned by the media. It is true, some fans get involved for the wrong reasons. That would be the small segment who never feel they paid a fair admission for a ticket until they've seen a racer maimed or killed. But that may be only what it appears to be. While the media's view may in part be understandable, it's more than likely confused with the mystery, curiosity and finality of death itself, which draws the spectators. The fans revel in the 'idea' of death, but not death itself. They admire a person who can accept the fact they could be killed racing. You can bet your bottom dollar they don't share this same morbid feeling for race drivers they personally know. I read in a book once about what former Indy car driver, Sam Posey said concerning the race fan. He may have been talking more specifically of the Indy 500 race fan, but I feel it runs the gamut of motorracing spectators. Here's what he said.

"I think in this century, men are confronted with machines, and they're not used to machines. They don't really understand what machines are all about. It's obvious that mankind's future is very closely linked to machinery. Also, technical people depend on it for everything they do."

"So, when man drives a racing car, he is having a confrontation with a machine. He is trying to push a machine to do something his will asks for. The machine is not capable of doing everything the driver wants of it, or we would be lapping the Indianapolis Motor Speedway at 2000 mph. So, basically, the spectator comes to see man confronting his machine and is curious to see what's going to happen."

"The next point is: people have always been interested in death. Death is the one thing that binds us all together. We're all going to die, and you wonder how you're going to do it. Will it be graceful? Will it be sudden? Will it be painful? What will it be? I think when people come to the race track they know they may see someone die. It's intensely interesting to them how it will happen. But I think when the fans do see someone die they are terribly shocked and extremely depressed. They wish they had not been there. I think what the spectator wants to see is the crash! They want to see the action! They want to see the car splitting apart! The more flames the better. The more wheels that zip off into orbit the better. But the fans want the driver to jump out alive and wave to the crowd, because that's the moment of the greatest thrill. That's when man has conquered his machine. The machine has bitten back, but the man jumps out laughing and therefore, the spectators dream of immortality is confirmed."

On the Dark Side

When this author read what Mr. Posey's analysis was of the race fan, it struck a nerve with me. I've witnessed many racing accidents in person, both as a spectator and as a competitor. Every time I see one, I feel shame for myself. Not necessarily for the moment, but for the first time I witnessed a race mishap. I thought I wanted to see someone die that warm Indianapolis day in 1973. Even though all the victims of that pile-up at the beginning survived, it was, nonetheless, an ugly, unforgettable spectacle. From then on, racing suddenly became a serious sport and not something contrived for sadistic purposes. I suddenly realized racing wasn't a circus, because I was disgusted with myself and my thoughts.

Looking back, I realize what was wanted and what was perceived as wanted were contrasting. It's like traveling about in your car and wondering inconspicuously upon an ugly accident scene. One part of you wants to witness it and the other wants to be a million miles away. The darker side of you wants to unravel the mystery of that particular situation, and, yet, at the same time restore order. Yet the intellectual side of us knows through experience that what is done is done. All the wishing and hoping in the world won't reverse what happened. So therefore, we want

to be removed from a hopeless situation. But the less curious and more informed race fan knows racers are taking certain risks every time they buckle in. Like the racer, they don't see this sport as some roman holiday at the coliseum. It's what it's meant to be. A contest of talent, control, speed, endurance and will. Not a sideshow, not a test of an individuals preparation for other ulterior endeavors, (survival and/or war) and certainly not an automotive testing ground for the various manufacturers.

These types of fans want to see pure competition in its more uninterrupted form. Matter-of-fact, at times, these kind of fans feel a bit inconvenienced at any kind of delay in a race. It doesn't matter if it's weather related, a caution period to clean up minor debris or a nasty pile up which injures several drivers. Although that sounds cold, it really isn't anything personal. It's like a football game with much at stake, but continues getting delayed every few minutes because of an injury. It does detract from it and gets a bit irritating, but it's certainly nothing personal.

C. WATCHING A RACE

Going to a race for the first time or for the 100th time can be equally confusing. Watching is one thing, following it is another. If that isn't bad enough for the fan, think how the driver feels. Sometimes they have no idea where they're located within a race. They may not know if they're a lap down or a few hundred yards from the lead. Does that sound crazy? Of course it does, but of course it really isn't. There's actually quite a simple explanation for it. Eyesight reads in straight lines. Light travels in straight lines. Sound can turn a corner. Understand? 95 percent of sporting events are confined to an arena where everyone, including the athletes can see one another. Other than very closely confined racing of Go-Karts, Midgets, some Off-Road and Motocross levels, the confines of most racing are spread way out. Unless you, the spectator, have a good elevated seat, you won't see the whole arena, or in this case, the track.

Certainly down on the track, neither will the racer. At the professional and upper amateur levels, teams can keep their racer posted by radio as to where they're positioned. Strategy can be more accurately used in longer races. But that's usually not the case in lower levels of racing. As long as a racer knows they haven't been lapped, they know their chances are fairly good to win. But they don't usually know how good. A tight 1 or 2 mile course has several turns and no long straights. A racer may not be able to keep visual track of the leaders. He may subconsciously lose the competitive motivation to keep it floored and take a risk or two, here and there. I call it the "A J Foyt Syndrome". If you can't win a race, why bother! That's an oversimplification but it boils down to risking the equipment for a win or points towards a championship, but not for anything less. That attitude has its own merit, especially at the amateur level. On the otherside, it's not too popular with never-say-die, never give-up advocates of tradiional, yankee-trained ball and stick athletics. An answer to them is they don't have the big bucks invested in their "uniforms", (racecars) not to mention their "bods."

Keeping Track of Confusion

Many athletic fans, not necessarily race fans, complain some drivers are literally hidden away in the cockpits. Certainly the motorcycle and especially motocross advocates have a distinct advantage here. Even midget and sprint car drivers are more exposed for the spectators to watch. Watching those guys get bounced around while working their hands with cat-like quickness certainly explains what was alluded to earlier, they're athletes, not robots. But the men racing in vehicles which limit their physical appearance don't apologize for it. The same people who lodge these complaints don't expect apologies any more than they'd expect Michael Andretti to drive his Indy racer sitting atop the wing.

Many men feel a driver's obscurity contributes to the mystery which entails the battle between man and machine. On the other hand, women see that phenomenon, coupled with their perceived, albeit innocent sexual perception of the "unknown", as highly mysterious also. They both wonder, who are these series of waxlike models hidden under their helmets within the sleek, provocative confines of a rocket, seemingly laughing at the danger.

Be that as it may, to follow a race can be confusing. It's not like watching other sports because racing is so nonregimental and lacks in strategy to the untrained, superficial eye of an individual. It's a fancy way of saying that all they see are vehicles going in circles and nowhere, as fast as they can. They pass by quickly and it's not always easy to spot the leader. It's where many people lose track of the sport, when in fact, they never gave it a chance. The key to understanding a particular race is to understand racing itself. To truly like this sport and to follow the progress of it, you must do some inner studying of it. How many times have you seen a mother who couldn't care less about football suddenly take an interest when her "boy" is playing. She may have been initially against the idea but took an honest liking to it once her fears were handled. It's the same way with racing. The casual fan will never understand this sport. They attended because of its atmosphere of intrigue and mystery.

The Vehicles

To really take interest in a race, you must get to know the vehicles. You don't have to be a mechanical engineer. It would be nice to understand their very basic workings. To understand them bolt to bolt wouldn't be anymore necessary than knowing the inner working of say . . . a hockey player. You obviously know why some race vehicles have two wheels and most have four. What isn't so obvious is why those particular wheels are located as they are. For instance, Off-Road racing cars have their wheels placed below the chassis. What we're really talking about is suspension. The cars are built high to allow for suspension travel. It absorbs tremendous shock and keeps the vehicle from bottoming out.

Most other race cars are built low to the

ground for stability, better aerodynamics and therefore, higher speeds. The Formula racer is built the lowest. Its bottom is almost dragging on the race surface and they would, if the friction didn't slow them. Matter-of-fact, many times the sparks you see flying from underneath the Formula One cars are from mounts so placed to keep the vehicle floor from grounding. In that manner, with the relative limited amount of space available for suspension travel, they can be setup for a softer and safer ride. Without the mounts the vehicle would be subject to floor damage. Therefore, the suspension would have to be tightened and/or raised. That means less tire grip and therefore lower speeds in the curves.

There is much more to that than what was just explained. To any fan who knows what the 'instantaneous center of rotation' is would sufficiently impress many racers. Some racecar drivers may have it meticulously explained and demonstrated, . . . with a (Formula) racecar suspension used to enhance it right in front of their face . . . and they still may not understand it. It's admittedly tough to understand. But it's an example just how complicated a race machines suspension geometry is. (not to mention racecars in general) All these things must coordinate with the complicated workings of tires, shock absorbers, vehicle balance, etc, to the race machines design. If you understand why tires aren't used just for rolling, then you'll appreciate what's involved.

In addition, special skills are needed to setup that car, with all its sophistication, for the weather conditions of that day, type of racetrack, its condition and the drivers preferred handling techniques. Figuring that out is just as hard as getting that extra 1 or 2 horsepower to put a machine over the top. For the mechanic or engineer, it's a sport all in itself. The average fan doesn't have to know all these things, but it certainly enhances the will to watch a race.

The Driver

Another way to understand this sport is to know the driver. No, you don't have to date

him. Just know who he or she is. This is something you can educate yourself better with a couple of ways. The best way to do this is obviously to visit the paddock. That's okay for smaller races. You'll pay a pretty dollar for that privilege at pro events. But even so, you're not going to figure out a driver any more than you will the meaning of life. But at least you'll understand he's a human being stuffed inside that firesuit.

Most amateur races are short in duration. Even some professional one's are short, such as Midget and Sprints. There isn't much left to strategy other than stomping the accelerator to the floor and keeping out of trouble. But there is always the technique of finding the right line on the straights and in the curves. It is a trial and error factor that good drivers must deal with against the course itself and the competitors sharing it. Given equal race cars, the more talented driver will do their overtaking of the other in the corners. Otherwise, a smart driver with superior powered equipment will play it safer by passing in the straights. Passing on a short tight course requires more driver talent than necessarily superior equipment. That's why many avid race fans feel short track racers are better than the so-called 'name' drivers. But the fact is many of those 'name' drivers started on the short tracks. They may have lost some temporary edge on the short courses, but given time, they'd prove themselves quite competitive, if not winners. Short track drivers don't just hop in faster machines and win. That's been proven extensively by the lack of rookie winners at Formula One, NASCAR, Indy Car, IMSA and NHRA.

A driving technique to watch for is how a racer uses braking. If he has slower equipment, making up for it is accomplished by traveling faster and deeper into a turn. The exit out of the turn will be slower, but hopefully a pass was made, a block is applied, and the racer is on their way. Figuring out various driver techniques at any level of racing isn't easy.

Another way to learn about them is through driver profiles provided by the sanctioning body or the track. Admittedly, it's usually not detailed and only filled with past accomplishments. Newspapers are a good source, but unfortunately, that's not the case in amateur racing. Pro racing doesn't get much daily newspaper 'ink' much less the classes below it.

Learning drivers is best done by repetition. It's not necessary to know the driver intimately, just their technique. Many race fans keep track of races by using a lap chart. But they are so time consuming they actually take away from the race itself. Matter-of-fact, they're so time consuming, there's no point even being at the race. The best thing is to get to a point where the whole track is visible. Sometimes that's hard and it can be expensive at high profile, big league events. Drag racing is the exception. In any race, it's a good idea to bring a radio and binoculars. It may not be on radio at the local scene, in which case an announcer may help you out. (that is if you can hear them amid all the noise)

Also, learn the flag and light signals. The light signals work in much the same way normal traffic signals operate. The red and green signals mean obviously stop and go, respectively. The yellow doesn't necessarily mean to slow down, but rather, to not pass anyone, because there's a problem on the track. Of course, the speeds are slowed down anyway.

The bottom line is to learn this sport intimately. It's like anything else. Once you understand what's going on both in front and behind the scenes, it's more fun to watch. There are plenty of books on racing at libraries. There are also plenty of national and regional racing publications for either an overview of this sport or the ones geared to a specific type of racing. You'll probably be very surprised how much more interesting it is to watch a race if you see it as something besides a bunch of cars going around in circles like a chinese fire drill. (see the appendix in back for a list of these publications)

7 | Buying vs. Renting; The 'Spec' Idea

A. THE 'SPEC' RACECAR
B. RENTING A RIDE
C. BUYING RACE MACHINES (NEW)
D. BUYING RACE MACHINES (USED)

A. THE 'SPEC' RACECAR

After reading Chapter 4, you may be completely turned off at the cost of racing. Before you decide to throw caution to the wind anyway, there are other options. It's assumed at this point you know the type of racing you like. You also know what class to start at. Hopefully, you're not going to start in too high of one. I refer to 'what' you'll race as opposed to what you 'think' is affordable.

Have you thought about renting a racecar? Before you say "no way", consider what's at stake. Are you mechanically inclined? Do you have time to devote to this sport? If the answer to both of those questions is yes, then you may be better off buying your own racecar. Then again, you may not. The big determining factor is usually money. If you don't have the money to just run out and purchase a racer, then you may have to borrow it. That could be a problem.

No matter how good your credit may be, it's usually not good enough to get a bank loan for a racecar, especially for a younger person. Most banks simply will not lend money on a racecar, regardless of collateral. There are some which will, but you'll probably take a while tracking them down. The younger you are, the more the odds are stacked against you. That could be a blessing.

Buying your first racer too early may be a waste of money, anyway. But a young, well informed racing enthusiast might be better off owning his own racer in the long run. He has to be sure he knows what he wants and what the costs involve. This is probably something he's planned for years. He knows his options and probably had unlimited access to help or advice. It's a good chance his racing knowledge is a result of family ties to the sport. But what about the youngster just out of high school, college or an older family man? Finding out the costs of racing can be one expensive proposition at any level for these types of prospects. That's because they may start too early, at the wrong level or without proper help. Most of this can be avoided by renting a racecar.

For many drivers, a less expensive start is at a professional race school. That will help you decide what kind of car you want to race. Of course, going to a school doesn't insure you'll have any more mechanical ability or time then before you started. Afterall, even the best schools are only five days and most of them have only a basic three day course. More on that in the next chapter.

Right now, we are concerned about a couple of situations relatively new to racing, the 'specification' (SPEC) concept. One has to do with "evening-up the competition". The other has to do with essentially containing the costs. In other words, racing competitively without breaking the bank, so to speak.

Squaring the Competition

This form of racing, designed to test drivers and not the manufacturers equipment, is called 'spec' racing. (specification) This lends itself to the idea of equalizing racing vehicles.

It's an idea that racing should be contested between individuals, not machines. Talent should win races, not money. It's relatively new to US racing. (started catching on in the early 80's). It's been going on in Europe and is one of the reasons some drivers go there to train. While racing has high financial stakes, the idea of 'spec' racing is also to level the playing field, if not to at least lower the costs.

A universal problem in racing, which involves manufacturers, is the costs. Each manufacturer strives to produce a better machine. That means the costs are pushed up. Not necessarily because a new racecar is more expensive, which it probably is because of inflation alone, but because it makes early models obsolete. Thus, a team or person is forced to buy the latest and best model to remain competitive. This isn't a knock on racing manufacturers. Nobody denies their necessity to the sport. Their representation draws on itself in fan appeal, creativity, technology and, unfortunately, costs also.

'Spec' racing was initially aimed at the lower classes in amateur racing. That has changed somewhat with the advent of such pro classes as the 'American Racing Series'. (ARS) This is a form of Indy car racing. The whole idea in this particular class (now called 'Indy Lights') was to judge potential Indy car prospects more accurately while they trained. The costs aren't necessarily low in this class, but the race machines are virtually identical. Only the paint job and the number is different.

A classic example of a new 'spec' racing class was inaugurated in 1984 by the Sports Car Club of America. (SCCA) Formerly called Sports Renault, it's a SportsRacer type of race machine, which is an open cockpit and closed-wheeled racer. (don't confuse the name with the European Formula Renault, raced and made in France) Today this race machine is called the Spec Racer. They are all built identically. All materials, engineering, product names are the same on these sportsracers. They must use a specific race engine and brand name tire. (including that tire's identical style and design) You can purchase or rent these race machines. Either way, you're not competitively disadvantaged. For a brief description of them, look back in the 'sportscar' section of Chapter 3.

These racers have proved to be a huge success. It is now SCCA's largest class, surpassing Formula Ford and Formula Vee. That makes them one of the largest classes in the world. Both engine and chassis have a locked-in design. The engines are sealed to prevent any tampering. The racing tires used are Bridgestones (Potenza RE71R0) street radials, which may be shaved to a prescribed depth. The manufacturers are few and they have absolutely no say as to how they're built. This racecar must conform to exact specifications, materials, design, . . . everything is identically built and put together. The only area of modification allowed is the driver cockpit. That is to provide adjustment to driver size and preferred comfort. The engines in these racers are unique. They are the only engines built by a sanctioning body. (SCCA) Although, obviously, a race shop builds them, in essence, they are actually workers for the SCCA. They have no incentive to "fudge" on a particular engines specifications to gain horsepower. Matter-of-fact, the people building these engines have no way of knowing who will purchase them or who the engine already belongs to.

Although all these racecars are identical, another area left open to driver preference is chassis tuned up. (or setup) All drivers obviously don't race the same way. Their styles are different and therefore they'll want their machine setup in a specific way. Don't confuse 'setup' with 'custom-built'. All race vehicle suspensions, with exception of most Go-Karts, have adjustment for such things as ride height, wheel camber, toe-in, caster, shock absorber ride adjustment and other built-in features. Because of this, a driver may custom-set his racer for a little push (car wants to go straight, relatively speaking, in the turns) or to be a bit loose (back end tends to 'fishtail' out of a turn) or ideally to be neutral.

Whatever a driver desires in a setup, there isn't any secret which will give them a faster handling advantage over other racers. What Spec racing does is remove the major variables. (like 'trick' engines, suspensions and aerodynamics) It lowers costs, (until you plow one into a wall) lowers and simplifies maintenance and mainly provides drivers equal competition within itself. Hopefully, driver talent will be the main factor in winning a race. That isn't always how things end up, but in the long run, the theory behind 'spec' racing works. The "cream will come to the top", or at least much closer up than what it would have otherwise.

Rent-A-Spec

Do you buy or rent 'any' racecar is not the question here. What's also not presented is whether to buy or rent any 'other' class of 'Spec' racer. Make the distinction. The SCCA 'Spec Racer' is a class of sportscar racing just like Indy cars are a class of formula racing. What's in question here isn't to buy or rent . . . for example, . . . an Indy 'Light' racer, (which is also a 'Spec' race machine) but rather, a 'Spec Racer' racecar. Many people confuse these types of 'spec' categories. (a 'Spec' racer or machine as opposed to 'Spec Racer' class in SCCA; formerly named Sports Renault). I hope that's a bit more clear. 'Spec Racer' competition at SCCA sanctioned events is one of the best ways to find out whether a driver has talent or not, . . . especially for the money not spent. You might avoid buying one at least for the time being if you're new to racing. Rent one to test yourself with.

What does it cost to rent a 'Spec Racer'? It depends on how many races you contract for; how far the race service providing the car must travel; if you provide your own tires, safety suit and gear; if the race event is a pro event; (which I'm sure will eventually be available at this level) or if it's a national, regional or a sanctioning body school event. Shop around at the race services providing these kinds of racers. (see appendix in back

of book) You can expect to pay between 8 to $1600 per race weekend. If you provide your own street tires (must be Bridgestones) then knock off about 250 to $300. Most rental services require you pay the entry to an event, which is usually 125 to $175. About half these services provide firesuits. You just arrive and drive. They maintain the car and set it up to your liking, if you, in fact, know what setup you like. To insure against any stupidity, most, if not all, of these services require a 2 to $3000 crash damage deposit or bond. It's refundable if no damage is incurred or partially so, relative to damage. Some deposits are only $1000. If the weekend of racing involves 2 races (double events) the costs will increase 20 to 40 percent. If you rent for an entire season (6 or more races) you can generally deduct 8 to $1,500 or maybe even more. The more you rent the less expensive it's supposed to get. I say "supposed" because there is always the reality of wrecking the equipment.

Buying a 'Spec Racer'

There are 'Spec Racer' rental services who simply won't rent their equipment to anyone with insufficient experience. You can understand their thinking. Racecars are expensive enough without tearing them up. But the inexperienced racer can buy one. They are not cheap. A new 'kit' can cost $15,000. A race-ready machine is $19,000. (don't forget to figure in inflation depending on how old this book is since its last update) If you want to buy used, you may pay as much as $13,000. That's not a real good deal, but you're not buying used in this instance to save money. You'll do that while racing these.

Remember, the maintenance on these is relatively low. (provided you keep 'em off the wall) Another great thing about them is their resale value. As you saw when you bought a used one, their value remains high by most racing standards. That's because there is nothing they competitively lack, since they're all identical. An engine may be used-up or tired, but they haven't any special secrets engineered into them in the first place. They're more reliable too, and therefore, subject to less maintenance and costs for a longer 'competitive' life. When it's time to overhaul one, the costs aren't high.

Changing the Game?

It looks as though 'Spec' racing is an idea here to stay. Like anything else in a capitalist society, it boils down to money. For racing to survive far into the future, it cannot continue at its present rate. It's becoming way too costly, especially at the higher-profiled, professional ranks. More 'Spec' classes will immerge in the future. But it will have to be done at a slow pace. To do otherwise will leave many racecars instantly obsolete . . . a 'white elephant', (overly expensive and a useless possession) otherwise, 'Spec' racing would be defeating the very purpose it exists for.

This is not to say competitive, manufacturer-backed racing will completely cease to exist. That won't happen either. High speed, competitive racing is needed for the sponsors who can back it, industry who reaps technological benefits from it and people who follow it. This doesn't mean 'Spec' racing is inferior, but rather, a bit more "user friendly", cost efficient and a bit more fair, if not more consistent. But, this also doesn't mean it can't be expensive.

The ARS or Indy Light IndyCar is a 'Spec' racing machine also. There's nothing cheap about it. The 4.2 liter Buick engine, amongst other engines, can propel them up to 180 mph. To reach those kinds of speeds takes money. But at least one team isn't outspending another to "buy" a win or a championship.

Some people still feel championships can be bought. They can't be bought with any guarantees, but I know for sure, Spec racing wins can't be bought in any way, shape or form. This helps stabilize racing, makes it more predictable and brings it to where it's supposed to be . . . back to the drivers.

'Spec' racing should not be confused with 'rules changing'. An example I use is, once again, the Indy cars. You may wonder why I use the Indy cars so much as an example. There are two reasons for that: 1; they are the racecars even the casual, nonrace fan

can identify with, and 2; they are also the machines most subject to yearly changes. Thank goodness the kind of changes taking place yearly in Indycars do not take place in 95 percent of racing. If that was so, racing would have priced itself out of existence a long time ago.

Every year IndyCars get faster and faster, not the drivers, . . . not the track! Why? Because it's considered by some people to be the main technological idea behind racing in modern times. The sanctioning body (in this case USAC or CART) makes rule changes to slow them down. But technology finds a way to offset that. The drivers, manufacturers and some fans want that technological edge. They want to go as fast as the laws of physics will allow them. But rule changes must be made to equalize competition also. That'll prevent the sport from boring itself into obscurity. (too much domination by heavily financed teams) Then you have no racing at all in its true sense.

The technology is nice to have, but not everyone can afford it. The race fans, officials, owners and drivers have to realize that eventually the technology will reach a saturation point. For example, even speed of light can't reach over 186,000/second. Eventually, this will be the situation in racing. Bobby Unser was right when he thought Indy cars could reach 300 mph. They'd be doing 260, 270 right now if their technology wasn't controlled. They formerly used 1000 horsepower engines. Their ground-effects packages have been reduced along with the size of their wings. For years now, those 1000 "horses" have been lowered to around 750. Yet today they are faster. (They're not necessarily 'top-end' faster, but faster in the turns; better overall lap time)

This high technology is nice, but useless and dangerous in the wrong hands. Good drivers need to be properly trained to handle it. Well financed teams at amateur levels may train a driver for faster racing, but is that driver the best available from a particular 'pool' of available talent? Who knows? A good driver in the best machine doesn't mean he is better than another driver in an inferior car. How is talent determined? Many times it's not. There is no way of determining that in an efficient, practical manner. But 'Spec' racing can help simplify this problem and none too soon. The Indy car speeds are probably going to reach 240 mph by the year 2000. (unless the newly formed Indy Racing League can controll that) They'll need the very best drivers to handle them. Meanwhile, through the ranks of 'spec' competition, drivers can be more quickly discovered and therefore properly trained. Right now this situation in racing is more theory than fact. I suspect money will always be a factor as to how a driver survives or fails in the IndyCar race game. Still, the 'spec' racer is a step in the right direction.

One more thing about spec racing; this will force some drivers to understand the intricate workings of a racecar and their handling characteristics. Some drivers don't understand this completely. They can feel the difference between a good or bad handling machine, but they still don't know how to correct it or communicate it to a mechanic who can correct it. A big reason for this is because of different tracks, track conditions and types of racecar suspensions. The variables are endless. With a spec machine, a bit more consistency is possible. The variables are more simplified to adjust to track and current weather conditions. This makes for more clear driver understanding of vehicle dynamics.

B. RENTING A RIDE

The advantage of renting any kind of racecar is the time left open to what really matters to a driver. That is to race distraction-free. That's something not always possible if a driver owns their own racecar. If they're renting, they can more efficiently use their athletic ability and concentrate better. Racing requires more than just money, talent or the ability to just point a racer straight ahead. It requires some strength and endurance too.

Articles have been written about the characteristics of race drivers. Some 'ball and stick' type athletes question the racers athletic ability. I can answer them quickly and

clearly. I've participated in high school football, basketball, baseball and some college football. Take my word for it, you need to be in shape and possess athletic ability for sports like those and for racing too.

In addition to all the physiological requirements of these sports, racing also includes a psychological fact unmatched elsewhere. That is, one mistake could send a racer to an early grave. Not too pleasant of a thought. The race driver has these things to contend with while driving. If he owns his own machine, its destruction is another set of circumstances to contend with. Racing is like being both a competitor and coach. Renting a racecar can sometimes offset some of these distractions. It allows better concentration for the driver.

On the negative side, renting takes a good chunk of money. How much money depends on how often you race and at what level. The levels covered in here concern amateur and pro automobile racing. Not too many drag vehicles, off-road and motorcycles are rented. For the sake of accuracy, I'll stay with 'closed-course' race machines. There's some negotiable options which can save money, time and effort when renting.

Some dealers are more flexible in this area than others. You may provide your own race tires, firesuit, gear and maybe even racing fuel. If you get to know the race service personnel very well, they may even allow you to transport and maintain the car for a particular event by yourself. (or with reduced help) You'll have to be well established to do that. If you get that involved, you may as well purchase your own race vehicle, especially if you plan to race eight or more weekends a year.

Damage Control

Isn't it amazing racing has all these variables both on and off the track? Now to concentrate on a specific situation with renting. The kind prevalent with the "arrive and drive" situations. (as opposed to owning a machine and hiring a service to care for it) Renting a car can be similar to owning one. Who pays if a driver plows one into a wall or blows up an engine. The driver will always bare some responsibility, but it's a matter of how much.

If you ruin your own machine, it's a big loss. (I'm assuming the driver escaped unhurt) Ruin someone elses racecar and you might be a bit better off financially. It depends on prior agreements in writing. You may be out 2 or $3000 in damage deposit or bond you paid previously. You may possibly bare the cost of the entire racer. You need to be very sure and understand clearly what's in writing about who pays what in a racing accident. Leave nothing to individual interpretation. The damage portion of an agreement should be free of tricky and/or vague wording. The people owning this service will insist on that too, if they're not some fly-by-night outfit. (very rare in racing)

Insuring (Damage)?

You might be asking yourself, "Can I get racing insurance?" Yes and no. Yes, on yourself . . . on the race machine your renting, . . . no! Track insurance at most events insures hospital costs to drivers. But what about off the track? It depends. There are some policies on disability. You can get your own racecar insurance for its storage and transportation. But once that racer rolls onto the track, that's where the 99 percent of policies end. If you can get it insured cheaply while on the track, that would certainly be news to me and many other drivers too. Even if one can get a race machine insured while racing, the premiums would be too high for practical purposes. So you may as well forget any idea of insuring a car you rent. (or own too) Just figure on being responsible for damage. Maybe not all of it, but at least 2 or $3000, or whatever the contract calls for.

Some race rental services have lower rates. That may be offset by higher damage deposit. Others may waive any responsibility for accidents caused by equipment failure. That can be a touchy area. The parties need to know what constitutes an equipment failure. If a race car loses control on a straight portion of a track under dry, ideal conditions and nobody close by was involved, then it's a good

chance it was equipment failure. One thing's for sure, an accident caused neither by mechanical or driver error, but rather, by another driver, still falls on the person renting the machine. It's the risks of renting racecars.

Racing always is relatively risky. Some pro level race organizations or services require on-track car insurance, but they're rare. It'll be high, but it's either that or they don't race. Personally, the only people I understand to insure racecars on the track is the Lloyds of London group and K and K Insurance out of Fort Wayne, Indiana. The costs are so prohibitive, there's no sense in obtaining a policy. The premiums alone could purchase a new racer in just a couple or three years, if not less.

A rough estimate to insure a brand new $27,000 Formula Ford would be about 2 to $4,000 per weekend. That's at the pro level. (Formula Fords do race at the pro level in the Canadian series, Walter Wolf and the recently formed Formula Ford Championship series) Insuring your own race machine or one you rent just isn't practical. For that kind of insurance premium cost you're better off to use it as a deposit towards any rental damage incurred. At least with no damage the race service reimburses back your deposit. With an insurance outfit you can kiss it goodbye forever.

The Green Stuff

Does renting sound expensive? Yes, if you're not exactly Howard Hughes. No, if you don't know what you want in racing. One weekend of renting a racecar can clear up many things instantly. Of course, being inexperienced may disqualify you from renting higher speed equipment. That would include race classes which reach well over 110 mph. It means anything more sophisticated than a Formula Vee could be hard to rent. If you're under 18 years old, the best place to start is at the Go-Kart level. With the exception of some low speed motorcycle classes, it's the only place juveniles can start. Some organizations allow 16 year olds to race with official parent approval, but the cost will discourage 99 percent of them from doing that.

What are some of the costs in renting a racecar? It varies widely within several parameters. A tired old stockcar may go for 2 to $800 a weekend, to an uncompetitive Indycar ride for $100,000. These are ballpark figures for one race weekend and strictly on an "arrive and drive" basis. After you see these, remember, developing a formula for predetermining a set price is practically impossible for our purposes here. But, the following should give you an idea what you're up against financially.

Formula 440	4 to $900
Formula Vee	5 to $1,100
'Spec Racer'	8 to $1,600
Formula Ford 1600	15 to $3,000
Formula Ford 2000	28 to $3,500
Sports 2000	41 to $4,800
Formula Atlantic	13 to $17,000
Trans-Am	20 to $30,000
Indy Light	25 to $35,000
Indy Car	$100,000

Actually, a $100,000 price tag on an Indy ride is almost a joke. It's an uncompetitive ride (rental) found under extremely ideal driver conditions. Some insiders claim a rock bottom deal can get as low as $30,000. That would have to be under conditions characterized as . . . maybe, . . . once in a lifetime. For a race service to offer a deal like that, it would have to be out of options. On the other side of the coin, a normal circumstance would require a well seasoned, proven winner to rent a competitive 'ride' at $250,000 per race. A good shot at winning the Indianapolis 500 would cost about $1,000,000. However, a full seasons competition cost 6.2 to 6.9 million. An average back-of-the-pack drive is 500 to $750,000 per season. In Formula One, a top ride would run 2.5 to 4.0 million per race. Of course, these are ungodly figures taken care of by high-dollar sponsorship programs.

There is one more very important note worth mentioning. I don't care how much money you have, it will not be enough unless you can handle these sophisticated machines. For example: Mike Andretti and a few others had trouble obtaining a license a few years back for the US Grand Prix in De-troit. (Granted, it was political BS) It also wasn't easy getting his F1 ride for 1994. With those kind of odds, that eliminates just buying a ride. It's big money, but it's also big talent. Even if a race service allowed a questionable or unproven talent an opportunity to drive its race machine, it doesn't mean the sanctioning body will. Other drivers will also have a 'say' whether a driver is ready or not. (through the licensing procedures).

Looking out for Number One

There are eight general situations to look for in a rental service and how they affect the costs. Forget about the high profile professional levels for now. It's not pertinent for our purposes here.

1. What kind of cost packages are offered or how are they broke down. Example: can you use your own tires, racesuit; how far will the service travel; do costs vary according to a particular 'make' or 'model' of a race machine or its reputation and/or history. (not to be confused with higher level race machines)

2. Does the race service require references? Is your history of tearing up equipment poor? They may ask for references from a sanctioning body. At most pro levels, you may have an easier time financially than you will securing personal references. This is especially so for a good, but young driver. The more you race and keep equipment intact, the better off you'll be. A good or poor reputation can precede a driver nine times out of ten. Many drivers hesitate giving out any kind of reference, good or poor, for psychological reasons, among other things.

3. What are the competitive levels offered by a race service? If the same car is offered at both pro and club racing, it could be good or bad. The pro prospect may not like the idea of renting cars used by amateurs. Of course, that's high-brow thinking. But it's a plus for the club drivers to know the equipment he races is competitive enough to race in the pros. Personally, I wouldn't trust these kinds of practices. It sort of puts the idea of getting what you pay for in jeopardy, especially for the pro competitors. This never happens at the high profile levels of racing.

4. What are their damage deposits (or bonds) and/or insurance requirements, if any. This one is a biggie.

5. If prize money is offered at an event, how is it divided between the service and the driver? Obviously, this is mostly a professional race situation, but some amateur or club races do offer what I call a "token" purse.

6. Do they have vehicles available for practice only? Some services use noncompetitive or older racecars to break in some drivers. This practice keeps the competition racecars more fresh, and younger drivers more seasoned.

7. Get references on the race service. Just as a race service may check you out, you should do likewise. Get a general overview by asking other drivers, professional school and sanctioning body personnel. Asking other rental companies about their competition isn't objective. An exception to that may be those who rent different classes of racers, or are too geographically separated to be a competitive threat.

8. Engine deposits. Sometimes the chassis damage package is hard between pro drivers and rental teams to agree upon. Most amateurs won't even be given an option on damage assessments. They take the rental companies requirements or walk. But requirements on the engine deposits, if a rental service has one, are usually less stringent. This is because the engine can be protected. It may be accomplished with a rev limiter or a governor. Some services equip the engine with a tachometer which records the highest RPM reached during a session. Either way, if an engine fails or blows, who's responsible is a bit more predictable. Make sure the engine agreements are clearly understood. Personally, I wouldn't rent from services requiring money for an engine deposit.

C. BUYING A RACE CAR (NEW)

Three situations should determine whether one purchases a brand new racecar. The first and most important one is the financial status. The second is how often you race and the third is one's experience in racing.

If your financial situation is at the point where you wake up every morning wondering where your next meal is coming from, then you're reading the wrong book. At the opposite end, if you're lighting your cigars with twenty dollar bills, then obviously money isn't a problem. That doesn't mean you'll be successful. What it does mean is you can afford some mistakes. Whether you had sufficient racing capital to begin with isn't what this publication is about. But avoiding costly decisions and mistakes of what money you do have, is. So for purposes of this chapter, it's assumed you're a racer in the upper to lower middle class income bracket. This addresses the first reason why a person 'could' purchase a brand new race machine. The 'how' of it is another situation.

The second reason a driver may be better off with a new racer is how often they race. Another way of putting this would be how serious one is about this sport. Assuming one is in not only to compete, but to win, then one goal, at least, should be to race professionally. That means you need top equipment. It also means racing much more often. Fifteen to eighteen weekends per year is needed to properly train and season a potentially talented driver. For the person which honestly judges themselves within this category, a new racer may be the way to go. Remember, a race machine is a very perishable commodity, especially at the upper amateur and professional levels. They lose value fast.

Sometimes a race machine is obsolete after only 3 or 4 seasons. This is no disaster for those racing 4 or 5 weekends a year. But it's not good for those trying to keep their racers updated and competitive. Therefore, they need new equipment, not necessarily because it's new and fresh, but more importantly, because it's of latest technology. But remember, the latest technology doesn't guarantee success, but it does enhance the chances of success.

Look at the Big Picture

If an extremely serious driver puts together the cost of training at a (pro) school or through the school of 'hard knocks', (accidents) with the cost of support equipment, tools, travel and other expenses, something becomes clear. The cost for that rolling chassis wasn't quite so high after all. It fades to an unexpected smaller percentage than you thought it would be. You find long term costs are much higher than the racing chassis itself. (minus engine) So purchasing a late design or updated racer every few years may be in the best competitive and financial interests of a driver. Outdated, constantly broken down race machines can be expensive. (and more importantly, cost wins) A 2 or 3 year old race machine can resell at a good price, offsetting costs in the long run.

For those driving purpose-built racers, (designed and built for specific racing purposes only) the best way to determine a top 'make' and 'model' is by its record. The numbers and popularity alone isn't always an accurate parameter for determining it. Its how well it's doing in the win column among several different drivers. For the truly involved race driver, determining the best 'make' of racecar is usually obvious at both pro and amateur levels. In addition to that, the manufacturer of these machines are also well represented by promotion, dealers, driver opinion or word of mouth and the racing media.

What about nonpurpose-built race machines? (street legal vehicles) These vehicles have to go through some extensive modifications. (except showroom stock racers) So for all intents and purposes, they may be bought new, but it's relatively impractical financially. They have to be somewhat torn down anyway. Why equip or modifying a new car, when doing likewise to a used vehicle, serves equal purpose, but at lower initial costs.

A nice feature of nonpurpose-built race machines, is a manufacturer hasn't got some terrible, inherited or designed advantage over another of the same class. The racing of these types of vehicles is more predicated indirectly at the speed potential each 'make' and 'model' is determined to have. The costs are predictable because of limited design parameters originally intended for these machines. (and the general public) A nonpurpose-built racing vehicle's efficiency is inherently low. There's not much to change to make them faster. Therefore, the costs are

kept sane by racing standards. Changing engine size and power doesn't give them an advantage, it just moves them into a different 'category' or class. This is a less precise, sorta less intended form of 'Spec' racing. Also, nonpurpose-built vehicles, including used purpose-built racers, have one thing in common over a new purpose-built machine, the prices are negotiable, especially for lower class vehicles. You won't find this to be true when ordering a brand new racer. The price is set, either you can afford it or you can't. There is no gray area. If there is some doubt whether you can afford to buy new, interpret it as meaning it's unaffordable. It's sorta like . . . "if you have to ask" . . . .

That's a slight exaggeration, but it's stated to make a point. You can try to negotiate a new racecar price. There is nothing to lose, but it's like beating a dead horse. The low market for racecars demand prices which must be met. Don't be too surprised to discover a new racer, same model, slightly lower in cost a year later. Why is that? It's a sorting and testing process. A completely new, yet unproven model demands higher costs to develop initially. If the machine proves itself as a worthy racer, then the manufacturer can increase the numbers in production. But unlike any new product available to the public, don't expect drastic price drops for new racecars with increased production. A good sales year for many racecar builders may be only 10, 15 orders. Not exactly "Big 3" sales figures. So they can't increase profits by doing large volume production. That is because racecars are low volume sellers. Not too "doggone" many people have a racer parted in their garage.

D. BUYING A RACE CAR (USED)

The veteran driver which purchases a new racer does so without much complication. They know what to look for and what they want. But for the beginner and veteran, this process of figuring out the best used machine isn't quite so simple. For instants: where and when does one shop; what do you look for; what's a fair price; what's the conditions a vehicle was purchased under; and are there plenty of spare parts available. Many other small variables determine how good or bad a deal may be.

The veteran racer will handle themself efficiently in this situation compared to the beginner. That's why it's strongly advised a beginner purchase a racer with help from someone familiar with this sport. For educational purposes here, let's say a beginner decides to go racing with no prior experience. The only thing they know about this sport is what was watched on TV, observed in person or read in a book. It's a start, but a far cry from what's necessary to make an educated decision. Without help from anyone other than a person you're buying from, a purchase could be a disastrous waste of time, effort and money. Never purchase a race machine solely on what a seller says. They may be sincere, but even so, their motives may still be subconsciously clouded. It's human nature to be self-objective, whether a determined effort is made to avoid it or not. None-the-less, since people can't read minds, there are questions which must be asked. The first one to ask is . . .

Why are They Selling?

An answer will be one of three general replies. 1. They wish to move up or down in class or to another type of racing; 2. They wish to get completely out of racing; or 3. They don't like the car.

If a reply is the last one, I would think you're dealing with an extremely honest person. Find out why they don't like the machine. If they reply "it's a dog", you have a really honest person. You can also bet this person isn't motivated by money. They don't have to be that brutally honest. On the other hand, you don't necessarily have to do any reading between the lines either. Just take their answer for what it's worth . . . the race machine is, in fact, a "dog".

But a person that honest may be underselling himself. His idea and your idea of what a "dog" is may be two different things. After all, he may have money and wants the best. You're not necessarily to that point yet. Sometimes racers sell machines because

they think they can do better with superior models. This is something a buying prospect needs to realize with this type of seller.

What about the buyer dealing with the individual who just wants to change their class of racing? Of the three types of sellers, the hardest deals are potentially right here. Oftentimes, the seller has no motive to sell at a fairly low price. That's because the urgency wasn't there in the first place. They continue to race the vehicle, with essentially a 'for sale' sign attached to it. This race driver takes the attitude that 'anything' he has is for sale. It just has to have the right price before he'll allow that to happen. While the best prices aren't always negotiated in these types of situations, most of the time some very reliable and competitive race machines are purchased in this manner.

The best seller to negotiate with is still the one looking to get out fast. For whatever specific reason it is, one things for sure, the seller knows an idle race machine doesn't gain value sitting around in the garage. Many times these sellers are anxious to sell, if for no other reason than to open up some space it takes up in the garage. If they're an older driver retiring from the sport, the urgency isn't quite there, but you're still bound to command a cheaper price eventually. The younger and despondent seller may hold out for a higher price, but their lack of patience is on your side. Whatever situation a purchase is made under, like any other large purchase made, it's important to find out how motivated the seller is.

Time Hurts Us All

The best time of the year to purchase a race car is in November and December. It's not always the entire winter or when it's considered the off-season in a particular geographical region. The idea is to catch a potential seller fresh off the preceding race season. Many times, the seller will want to sell early in the off season and then decide in time, it's not what they really wanted to do. Whatever the case, there is never a time of year when race machines aren't on the market. The best way to find what's available is simply to check racing magazines and newspapers. There is more than enough to choose from in any class. (see appendix for the publications available)

A situation that someone may find tracking down buys through classified ads is what's called "market testing". I have found a few times some sellers aren't as interested in selling than they are checking out what the market value for their race machine is. They ask an inflated or greatly reduced price to check buyer response. If they ask a reduced price, they usually have a racer which is bent up or old. Either way, these people are interested in selling, but they're not going to compromise themselves. This is not to say you're going to get a bad deal, it just means you're not going to receive the best possible deal. You have to remember, as a potential racecar buyer, the idea of saving money isn't the same as holding out or negotiating for a once-in-a-lifetime steal. It's not like racing is a necessity of life. (some would take exception to that; . . . come to think of it, . . . I take exception to that . . . "how dare me!!!") So offer a price you want, but don't belabor it. If a seller isn't even considering any kind of negotiation, it's because he knows what the fair market value is or just doesn't want to compromise.

After a while of looking, the buyer will notice one or two year old race machines are sold in this manner. The reason is very simple. For example, a brand new $25,000 Formula Ford, or any new racer, depreciates extremely quick as soon as it's raced. Unlike a passenger car, which may depreciate 10 percent immediately after its first mile, a race vehicle may depreciate 25 to 50 percent. That's a lot, and you should understand sellers won't cut a depreciated price like that any further than they have to. After one year, that $25,000 racer may only command an $8,000 price tag. So when it appears a seller is too rigid, they're not just testing the market as much as they're attempting to cut their losses.

Out With the New

For the reasons you just read, finding that 'steal' for anything less than a 3 year old

racer will be very hard, if not impossible. But how this effects a beginner competitively isn't as obvious in the lower amateur classes. What's considered a "lower" amateur level class? None are, in the true sense of the word, but a good rule of thumb is this: any race vehicle which cost more than $25,000 brand new and race ready will lose value quickly. That eliminates go-karts, motocross vehicles, some motorcycles, just a few formula classes, one half of the production classes and just a few drag vehicles. An exception to this rule might be midgets and sprint racers.

Any used racing machine that's at least 8 years old is suspect. That's old, but it doesn't mean it can't be competitive. That depends on what class it races in, how it was maintained, if it was kept incident free and if that particular 'model' has an excellent reputation or hasn't become consensusly obsolete. Remember, the racer which cannot become obsolete by design is a 'Spec' racing vehicle, as covered earlier in this chapter. Still, other race vehicles can last as long as 20 years. (like some Formula Vees) I'm not necessarily referring to vintage machines. Vintage machines have their place in racing, but their existence hasn't helped keep prices down in many cases. That is neither good or bad, but rather a situation depending on whether one is a buyer or a seller.

The very best circumstances to purchase a race machine isn't obvious to a beginning racer. Many deals are negotiated at track sites by people adept at very good timing. Sometimes offers are bounced around and discussed at "bench racing" get-togethers. ("bench racing" . . . drivers who informally congregate at race tracks, race garages, etc, . . . for among other things, bragging, complaining or to swap what is usually exaggerated racing stories; usually with a beer in their hand and too many already consumed)

One thing for a beginner to do is get involved with a race team/driver or become a member of a sanctioning body for a race season. (see Chapter 12) These organizations break into smaller geographical clubs where everyone gets to know each other more easily. People, while not always willing to except tracksite help, will always be glad to help endoctrinate an individual toward the purchase of a racecar. Be sure these people aren't involved with a deal where they stand to gain financially. That's not a rule set in stone, but a situation to be aware of. Many times these people know of others who are considering the idea of selling their racers. But more importantly, they can get leads on what's available. I've probably learned 25 percent of what I know about racing just by listening to people in "bench racing" discussions. (after I filtered out the BS) It's how I purchased my second racer. The first one was an $800 mistake. It could have been a whole lot worse then that financially. (looking back at that mistake, I'm laughing at myself, . . . yet shuttering at how much more worse it could of been)

The Games People Play

Many 4-wheel race vehicles put on the market do not include engines. If the engine included with a race machine is advertised as competitive, that should be interpreted as . . . competitive for what or who? Competitively priced, competitive on the track . . . or competitive for the sellers convenience? Racing engines don't come with guarantees and strong histories.

As mentioned in Chapter 5, if an engine has an excellent 'win' record, if it's advertised as strong or brand new, a buyer is better off not to take what's claimed at face value. An engine may be new, but that doesn't mean it's strong. Some race shops can just stick a new set of bearing and rings in and call it new. That may be fine for passenger car engines and even some lower classes of racing, but certainly not for the high speed racers. Engines advertised as strong isn't much to get excited about either. Strong is a relative term. Strong, as compared to what . . . a 'street' engine? At the risk of sounding skeptical, . . . it's my intention to be just that, . . . skeptical.

Many of these practices are strictly psychological. Probably something I'd do myself. After all . . . how would I advertise a racecar? "For Sale: A weak-powered, banged-up Lynx "C" Formula Vee; highway-robbery priced at $15,000!?" I hope my point comes across.

Ideally, even an actively honest seller will not insert a detailed classified because it's too expensive. They would rather you call for the details, which sometimes put the burden of costs (long distance phone rates) on the buyer. On the other hand, this helps eliminate "curiosity calls". It might be worth mentioning here, that the caller avoid informing a buyer how far they may be coming from to look at a machine. It puts the seller on notice they can afford to be more rigid in their negotiations.

Despite some things said, a first-time buyer might be better off finding a package deal. That would be a racer with an engine, and possibly spare (suspension) parts. Many times these deals include a trailer and support equipment. It's not that rare. These deals are characteristic of those getting out of racing. Spare engines aren't often advertised, but are used to spice up a deal. If an engine is advertised as quick, that may be partially true. While internal engine components aren't state-of-the-art, the induction system and specially designed cylinder heads may be. This allows it to burn more fuel and breath better at the same time. While that doesn't make the engine reliable, it can be faster. Is that better? Maybe, but not if it blows (breaks) a rod or crank.

Of course, fast and reliable are two engine phenomenons not cheaply balanced, . . . but then we're not talking about a $110,000 Indy car powerplant. With a good, strong, but mostly reliable racing engine, a beginner can learn first things first. That's learning to race, not necessarily learning to build engines, maintain chassis' and at the same time fight the budget. If a beginner wants to include these things, that's certainly okay, but first find out how to run, . . . then walk! (as opposed to the old cliche which goes the opposite way)

10 Ways to Check an Engine

These are the 10 basic ways to determine how a race engine may have been treated. These checks will not always guarantee everything, but at least hidden or obscured problems may be revealed. If a seller isn't willing to allow these checks to be made, then look elsewhere . . . he's hiding something.

1. Start the engine and listen immediately while it's still cold. Any unusual sounds? Are valve tappets quiet? If you can hear them pinging, either the oil circulation is poor or they're way out of adjustment. Either way, this engine hasn't been properly maintained. Also, the oil pump is either worn or the oil has been adulterated with thickening agents. Either way, forget this engine.

Don't be overly concerned with how hard an engine starts. If it's a 'turnover' problem or a poor electrical and ignition system, that may be due to the time it's been dormant. But you have to wonder how long this engine was idle. Don't be too concerned about cylinder compression just yet. Sometimes an engine with a sticky valve is due to oil enhancers acting as glue on the stem of a valve. The engine will backfire and sound generally terrible. After a minute, the valve will free itself and operate normally. If it doesn't, it could be a sign the engine has been sitting too long or a valve spring is broke.

How much does the engine smoke? That is not unusual if the heads were just cleaned. The oil burning off the piston crowns and valve heads takes a few seconds to burn off. If the engine is warm and still smoking heavy, it may be due to high oil pressure, which will lower itself as the oil heats up. If it doesn't stop smoking, the rings are worn, or worse yet, the piston-cylinder wall clearance isn't what it's suppose to be. The rings can be replaced cheaply. But if internal engine tolerances aren't properly met, that's a problem worth walking away from. Actually, only an expert can detect improper tolerances with instruments.

2. Vibration: If an engine is hitting on all cylinders, look for vibration. If you can lay a hand on a perfectly still, operating engine, it's a fair indicator it's balanced, especially if the engine is cold and idling. Sometimes, perfectly balanced engines will vibrate when idling. No problem. It's usually due to a small, correctable ignition problem, (spark plug misfire) or a form of vapor lock. It could also be an inherently high-compression, pis-

ton-stroke to engine-block weight ratio. If an engine still vibrates when it's stoked up to about 2 or 3 times the revolutions it normally idles at, there's an engine out of balance. It may be just missing on a cylinder, which is a small problem; like an unattached or faulty spark plug wire. Some types of ignition distributors intentionally cause rough idling. (why some StockCars sound terrible while idling)

3. Oil pressure is hard to check sometimes. If an engine is mounted within a racecar, an oil gauge should be available and working. If a race machine doesn't have an operating oil gauge, just how much did the driver care about his engine? I'd say not much. 100 percent of all race vehicles, except maybe some Go-Karts and Motorcycles, should have a good quality oil pressure gauge. With an engine shut off, start it and watch how quickly the readout or needle reacts. If it takes more than 2 or 3 seconds of engine ignition to turnover some oil pressure, I would be suspect. On a cold engine, the needle readout should shoot up to at least 25 percent higher than what its normal readout is at high speed on the race course. (due to thick oil when its cooler)

4. Engine compression: (on) Shut down the engine. Watch very closely how quickly it stops. It shouldn't coast to a stop, but stop abruptly within 1 1/2 seconds. It should rotate on its crankshaft back and forth very slightly just before it completely stops. Sometimes this isn't always a good indicator of compression because the engine may be tight until higher temperatures are reached.

5. Engine compression: (off) By far the most practical way to check compression is with a compression gauge. (a leak-down test) Pull a spark plug, screw in the gauge and hand rotate the crankshaft. Get 3 or 4 readings for consistency from each cylinder. If all the readouts on each cylinder indicates equal and consistently high pressure, then the engine has good compression. That doesn't always mean it's a good engine. (it may be still too tight) If the readings are consistently low, more than likely the rings are

worn. If the rings check out okay, then there's a big problem with internal clearances. In contrast, inconsistent pressure at each cylinder usually means the valves are not clean and, therefore, not sealing well. They also may not be closing completely, in which case, the tappets need to be adjusted. Head gaskets may be leaking, but if that is so, it would be very obvious (and louder) with an operating engine.

6. Pull the head(s): Check piston crown and cylinder walls for galling, cracks, scratches or unusual discoloration. A heavily scratched cylinder wall can reduce engine compression. A heavily cracked cylinder means it or the entire block could be junk, unless it can be honed out. But that means changing the size of the piston to fit that newly honed cylinder. But all pistons must be the same size or it throws the entire powerplant out of balance. That means all the cylinders must be honed to the same diameter. In essence, this changes the engine size. That could make it illegal. So one deeply scratched cylinder wall can ruin the block. A burnt piston is replaceable, but one has to wonder two things: what caused it and where did the excess material go.

A burnt piston is usually the result of underrevving or lugging an engine. This burns or cracks a hole in it. Metal burnings or grit contaminates the oil and may scratch bearings and other smooth, delicate, internal engine parts.

7. Pull the oil pan: Check rods for any free vertical play against the crankshaft. If there's any slop, the bearings are worn, there's a loose rod bolt or the crank or rod itself is bad. This can't always be determined on a cold engine. The condition of the bearings is a fair indicator of an engines condition, but not always. The bearings are cheap insurance and are often replaceable.

8. Read the spark plugs: This isn't usually an accurate sign unless a plug is pulled immediately after a race. Many spark plug manufacturers provide a picture chart showing how plugs deteriorate under specific engine conditions.

9. General appearance: You don't have to be a $100,000 a year race mechanic to ascertain, at first glance, whether an engine has been properly cared for or completely neglected. Check how clean the oil is. A concerned racer will always change oil immediately after a weekend of racing. Race oil should never be allowed to get so dirty that it doesn't remain clear. Things such as a dirty and oily block, wires and other accessories aren't quite as important to an engine's potential as much as it indicates how its been cared for.

Some race drivers won't use engine air filters. This is done to gain horsepower. I wouldn't bother looking at an engine mistreated in this manner.

Check the radiator if the engine is water-cooled. It should be in good shape for maximum cooling. If it's dirty, bent, corroded, patched up or not the right size (they can be too large if the thermostat isn't properly functioning) it's a good signal improper temperatures are reached. That can metal-fatigue engine components. Check water and oil pumps, make sure they're in good working order. Don't forget cam components. All these things should be in good shape.

It's worth a few bucks to hire a good mechanic to check these things out. It doesn't have to be a race mechanic. They'll know how an engine was treated with a careful inspection. But the main internal engine clearances (crank, rods, and pistons) should only be checked by accurate instruments at a race shop. But that's expensive, so basically, this depth of checking is for pro levels and those racers wanting very high performance engines. But, these pro teams tear down engines all the time anyway.

10. Heads—Carburetion: A good competitive engine has reworked racing heads and intake systems. This allows better engine breathing. The better it breaths, the more power it produces. Sometimes in the lower ranks of racing, a good set of heads and an induction system can equal the cost for the block. That's how important they are. But check the heads that they are not overworked. Not only may they be illegal, but if too much material is removed from their

chambers, it weakens them. They could crack under the heat and pressure.

Looking Down the Road

After a year or two the amateur racer needs to rebuild a racing engine. Of course at the pro level that is done after every race. But we're not pros, so we can't worry about spending thousands of dollars to gain a few horsepower. Who rebuilds your engine? You, . . . or a professional race mechanic. Even some amateur racing classes don't need high powered engines. Off-road vehicles need more reliability than power. The same with many motorcycle classes.

Who rebuilds your race engine is determined mostly by three things.

1. How competitive is your class? Does it race for a national championship?
2. Are the 'starting fields' filled with about a dozen or more competitors?
3. Are top end speeds over 90-100 mph?

If the answer to all those circumstances is yes, chances are extremely high you'll need engine work done by an experienced race mechanic.

Sometimes, a driver can compete with less than a super engine. But if they're committed to winning, being a 'front pack' competitor or winning a championship, driving talent alone will not guarantee those things. A driver needs to have good racing equipment, and a good start begins underneath the hood. There are many good race engine builders. Some reputable ones build reliable engines. Others are oriented towards getting as much horsepower as possible within specified engine parameters and rules. The difference in results between these types of mechanics may only be 1 or 2 horsepower. But don't look for many builders to admit that.

Most race engines can't put out top horsepower while remaining reliable, . . . at least for the money involved in amateur racing, that's not likely. As mentioned earlier, reliability is sacrificed for power and vice versa. An honest mechanic admits no two perfectly identical engines can put out the same,

exact horsepower. One may show a half or quarter more horsepower on the dynometer. That can be significant. What does a driver do? It depends on his philosophy and money. Hiring an expensive and reputable race mechanic to perform engine work is hopefully advantageous. On the other hand, all that power means nothing if it can't stay together long enough to finish a race. Good drivers go with the horsepower and take careful measures to protect it, but that works only to a point. All drivers are right when they say . . . "there is no such thing as a reliable, low-cost, high speed race engine."

Some drivers build their own race engine. That is great if you know how. Sometimes that can be costly. If you check back, records show consistently top finishers, national champions at both the amateur and professional levels, have their engines built by reputable race shops. These builders know exactly what it takes to build an engine. They don't incorporate some fancy trick-of-the-trade tweaking techniques like some 'fly-by-night' types claim to. Good builders pride themselves on detail. They check, . . . recheck and measure tolerances and distances in tens of thousandths of an inch increments. All work is performed thoroughly, precisely and professionally in immaculately clean facilities. Even the air is clean to prevent dust from settling on internal engine parts. That's fussy, but necessary.

Some self builders can be just as good, but do they have the necessary equipment to test their results or make accurate measurements? Tooling, such as flowbenches and engine dynometers cost thousands of dollars. This equipment is necessary to find that last 1 or 2 horses to put an engine "over the top". The very good self-builder can do as good as the pro on a per se level, but in the long run, the professionals are better. They have access to superior servicing equipment. History backs that up.

Don't Buy Problems. (The Chassis)

About 50 percent of all race chassis' are sold without engines. Sometimes an engine and a possible spare is available for the

213

same chassis. They're sold separately since some feel they can get more money that way. Some used racers may be very competitive for their time. But remember, if a used racer is too old, it's possible the market for their spare parts may be drying up. Thanks to vintage racing, that's been somewhat slowed. Still a serious racer shouldn't purchase an inferior racecar solely for the engine(s). When money is put into that kind of purchase, the engine may not be able to fully utilize itself. That's because a poor chassis can't put all that "paid for" power properly to the ground.

Buying a race car is like buying a home, a lot of thought and money goes into it. What physical characteristics do you check first in a home? The neighborhood? Schools? Shopping centers? No . . . what physical, brick and mortar aspect of the building itself should be checked first, before even considering the purchase. Answer . . . the foundation. It's a beautiful house, . . . brand new . . . it's not built on a nuclear dumping site or Indian graveyard. But is the foundation strong? Make sure it is, otherwise you could be buying a huge headache. The same is true for racecars. If the chassis isn't true and strong, it's junk! Hidden handling problems which are unsolvable is due to a weakened chassis. A bad chassis become very obvious at high speeds.

A bad chassis is like a bad back. Both bears the weight and support of the whole entity. (chassis and body) When they're not right, it's very hard to pinpoint a correction. It's also very expensive to repair, if that's possible. So make sure a racing chassis is thoroughly checked. (all people racing in off-road and some motocross need to be especially aware of a chassis' condition) Check the vehicles log book for racing accidents which hurt the chassis. If a seller can't produce a log book, then you have to be suspicious.

Does the frame have a new paint job? That's cause for even more concern. Something may be hidden. (I personally don't think a race driver would knowingly sell a racecar with a cracked or tweaked chassis to anyone; I do think a nonrace related middle man would) Another thing to watch for on a race chassis is any kind of welding. Any welding on parts of the chassis not designed for it is a definite no-no. I don't trust welds unless their located at joints designed for it.

Buying a poorly supported racecar is more problems and frustration than anyone deserves. That's true at any price, even if the machine is given away free of charge. You can part it out, but don't race on it. Having a chassis fall apart at high speed is extremely dangerous and likely to kill the driver. That's because if it tumbles out of control, in pieces, the built-in safety features (roll cage) may be ineffective.

The Checklist Continues

Even though chassis ailments can't be easily detected, a poor suspension system can be. The connecting points need to be intact, especially if there is any directly on the chassis. (which is usually the case) They can be repaired. Figure on replacing all bushings, rod-end bearings, brakes and shock absorbers. Make sure the original design hasn't been altered outside its functional parameters. Many racers sell spare suspension parts with their cars. If they're not offered, ask for them.

Rust usually isn't a problem with most race cars. But check for it in hidden spots. Deep rust or severe deterioration weakens metal, so look for it at heavy vehicle-support points.

Next, check the vehicles drivetrain. That's not necessarily the engine alone, but also the transmission, driveshaft, rearend, and all housings. (transaxles on rear-engine drive vehicles) If any housing isn't holding oil that's a bad sign because it may be cracked. Therefore, gears may dry up and rust after exposure to the elements. Don't be too concerned about the clutch. It's easy to replace and is subject to normal wear, as opposed to mistreatment and neglect.

Now go ahead and check the engine. I put this last because it's relatively expendable. As established earlier, if a seller claims an engine is new, don't get too excited. So . . . don't expect a super competitive engine. If it was so competitive, an inside buyer would have snapped it up earlier. Matter-of-fact, if any racecar is working well, it'll sell itself by local reputation. Competitors familiar with the car will know its value.

As much as it hurts to say this, I'll admit, it's hard to find a good, fast, inexpensive racecar. But don't be confused with what I really mean. You can buy a cheap race machine that'll cost you more in the long run than what an expensive one would in the first place. Ka-peesh? (Understand?)

That Beautiful Body

The least important determination in buying a competitive race machine is the bodywork. Bodywork is somewhat cosmetic on many racers. Obviously that's not the case for high speed machines. Aerodynamics has played a very important role the past twenty years or so. To the vintage racer, it's very important, even if it's for reasons other than what's necessary. (the looks) But to a sponsor, beauty 'is' skin-deep. They want their name displayed neatly on clean and straight bodywork. More on that in Chapter 9. When looking at race machines don't be too concerned with any bodywork. (nicks and pings) Obviously major damage may signal neglect or hidden problems.

Where Those "Round Things" Meet the Road

Check wheels for cracks, not tires. Tires are so expendable they're not worth checking out very much. The time to check high speed racing tires is right off the track. To those in-the-know, a freshly used racetire tells many things about a vehicles balance and handling. It's no secret a poor suspension setup is usually what determines poor handling characteristics, no matter how new the tires are. If several different setups or attempted corrections doesn't alleviate a problem or if they constantly create other bad handling situations, then the chassis has to be suspect. Many beginners wrongly suspect that the tires are just old. They believe new ones will make the chassis stick to the ground properly. Many times, new ones will

still not work. A poor chassis messes up tires. They must be allowed to roll precisely as they were engineered to.

Anyhow, don't bother with tires when checking out a racer. But wheels are fairly important. Check them for cracks, balance, and wear. Some sellers have a good inventory of spare wheels. These are one of the important aspects to look for in buying a race machine. Some veteran racers may scoff at that. They'll quickly change their tune if a wheel lets go. Usually, wheels are so inherently strong they very seldom fall apart. If they do, it's pure hell.

All these characteristics also apply to vintage racecar buyers. But in most cases, the buyer may insist on having the original wheels, no matter how poor its (then) design was. For the vintage racer, this requirement is understandable.

Now, . . . something about engines. If the serious driver buys a good chassis with a poor engine, they may just as well test that engine at speed. What power do they have to lose? Use it for as long as possible. But don't hurt the block. It doesn't make too much sense going through the lower end of the learning 'curve' on a brand new race engine anyway. That's usually a waste of valuable peak engine life. Get it rebuilt properly after you've seasoned yourself enough. But don't do things that's questionable with a chassis or wheels like you might with an engine. That can be very dangerous.

Back to Basics

Now that you've got a race machine, are you the real serious type of racer or the beginner. (or both) Doesn't matter, racer preparation is the same at all levels, except maybe the work put into an engine. Before putting this racer to speed have it properly prepared or familiarized for yourself. You don't have to in a few cases, but that's a bit chancey. I'd take nothing for granted. Tear it down, inspect it and put it back together. This'll take a lot of (worthwhile) time. Get to know your racecar well. That's especially helpful to the beginner and sometimes a nuisance to the veteran. But do not tear down the trans and internal engine parts. That's for the experts. Don't tear anything down if you can't reassemble it.

How does one know if they can do that? It's common sense, like I'd know not to mess with computer parts on a street car. Don't worry about race engine rules, if you're removing external engine accessories. Putting them back on can't possibly break rules. Screwing around with internal engine workings can. (like the headdeck clearance, as a result of using improper gaskets on the heads) The race shops know these technical things and can reassemble engines. They do it all the time. Leave it to them. It's their business to do things right.

Even though engine builders know the rules, that doesn't mean they offer guarantees on their work, specifically engine work. The best guarantee you'll get is called the 30/30. That would be 30 feet or 30 seconds, whichever comes first. It's not that these people do questionable work, but rather, it's the nature with which the product they service is used. Guaranteed engine work is like on-track racing insurance . . . it basically doesn't exist and is impractical. The risks are high enough that even a good reliable race engine can blow.

Getting Down and Dirty

Tearing down a race machine shouldn't overly intimidate anyone with at least some mechanical ability. Don't get crazy with this. Will you know how to put it back together? Putting coachwork or bodyparts back together is fairly easy. Maybe you can put the suspension back together too. But as forewarned, don't take the internal engine components apart. Of course, if you're mechanically inclined, you may remove the heads, oil pan and induction system. (carburetion and intake manifold) Leave the rest of the motor alone. Do you also know what's very confusing and hard to reassemble? A transmission. Be very careful with them. Leave them to pro mechanics also.

Until you become very familiar with your machine, it's a good practice to have a rough draft or sketch of it. You can make it your-self. That's so everything is put properly back together. Still, bolting parts and components back together isn't as simple as turning down nuts. Proper torque and tolerance must be met. Nuts and bolts tightened too hard strips the threads and weakens the hold. Not enough tightening force is obviously bad also. Either way, a race vehicle's tendency to vibrate or be thrown about at high speed loosens these mechanisms. Proper torque, tolerance and locking devices must be used. (refer back to the appendix on fastening materials) Books are still available on how to do that. But don't be intimidated by it. It's not "rocket science" stuff.

If you insist on reassembling internal race engine components together, you better know what you're doing. I cannot overemphasize that too many times. If you're an automotive mechanic, that doesn't insure you know what you're doing with a highly competitive race engine. Don't be insulted by that statement. The tolerances of a high speed race engine can be as different on a stock, production-make engine as day is to night. Bolting them together is one thing, proper tolerances is another. There's nothing like finding that out at high speed when an engine "grenades." (slang for explode) Leave the internal engine stuff to the racing mechanics.

Actually, nothing can be taken for granted when putting a race vehicle together. Don't go into a job uneducated. If you like mechanics, you won't mind doing what you can. You'll love the learning process. Don't learn the hard way. Read how to do things right. (the appendix will show you where and what to read) There are many good race books on the market. If you have any doubts about your mechanical ability . . . then it's probably justified. An objective home-tinkerer (mechanic) knows for sure what he can do and what he can't do. These people would do it all and would be willing to learn if only those *secrets* were revealed. Those secrets are more myth than anything. The pro just has much better equipment to enhance their work. Doing your own engine work can get expensive if it blows-up.

Are You Rembrandt?

Don't worry what a used racecar's paint looks like. A paint job is expensive and hard to do right, but shouldn't be a factor in purchasing it or not. A paint job doesn't determine a car's speed. Because of that, I taught myself to spray paint. I was fortunate to be given an air compressor. It's pretty substantial the money saved by doing your own painting.

The key to good work is the right equipment, including a temperature controlled painting booth or area. My philosophy is such that formula car body panels are nowhere as much painting as, say, a stock car would be. A bad paint job wouldn't mechanically slow my racer, right? So therefore, I felt it was worth learning. The motorcycle, off-road and kart racers should learn to paint also. Blending is easy with smaller paint jobs. Therefore, the margin for error is low.

Something All Used Racers Need

Somethings aren't practical to do yourself, but these jobs aren't too expensive anyway. Such jobs would include grinding down brake drums and rotors, chrome-plating (can get expensive for vintage racers) and magnafluxing. (a processes to detect metal fatigue) Things you can do is check all bushings, bearings and hosing. All fasteners should be replaced. Quality nuts, bolts and locking devices aren't cheap, but it's cheap insurance against a machine falling apart at high speed.

Fit Like a Glove

How well a driver fits into a racecar usually isn't much of a problem. But it can be a huge problem for a large formula racecar driver. Go-Karts have that problem at times, but its drivers are smaller because most of the time they're younger. Formula cars are low profiled, single seat machines which cannot afford the room for a seat, much less an adjustable one. All a driver really sits on, or actually lies on, is the different metal configurations or, in many cases, a specially shaped and designed fuel cell. This cockpit area is foam padded and stitched down with a leather covering only in the area where a driver's rearend, back and neck lies up against. These cockpits are very restrictive by design because they have to be.

The idea engineered and designed into these racecars are for the lowest possible center of gravity. They're small, narrow, light and usually not heavier than 1600 lbs, with the driver. Some are as light as 900 pounds. That leaves little room to work with and materials to build with. In addition to that, engineered in are such safety features as a protective cage, (which also acts as the chassis) roll bars and a firewall. (driver and engine compartment separation)

A problem with a large person fitting into the formula racer cockpit isn't so much lateral restriction at the upper torso, but their body length relative to the cockpit/chassis length. If a driver's feet are crammed in, he just can't properly react with them, if at all. A good example is myself.

I was 6 foot, 2 inches, and weighed 205 pounds when I bought a Formula Vee. Getting into a formula car is always tough anyway. But once I was in, I found the cockpit area was too narrow at the hips. I had to sit cockeyed. The shoulder area was okay internally, but my shoulders were up too high in the cockpit. Therefore, my helmet wasn't below the main roll bar by two inches as required by rules. The fit was simply miserable. I couldn't concentrate while racing because of it. My feet were so jammed I had to literally pull my legs back and physically keep them there to properly work the peddles. That's tiring on the thighs and also hard on the knees. My knees were rubbing against the top of coachwork and also chafing against the steering bar. If that wasn't bad enough, because the way I was turned in the cockpit, the belts were loosening. I wasn't snugged down tight. That meant there was room for my upper half to bounce and rebound due to the cornering forces. That will physically drain a driver. But the worse thing was I couldn't concentrate on what I was doing, nor could I get proper vehicle feedback because I was not properly snugged down. That's not very reassuring at 100–120 mph.

Those problems aren't the kind a racer should have. There are too many other things to be concerned with in this sport. When you're not fitted in a race car tight and comfortable, it's like playing football without a helmet. You never play your best. So be sure you fit. The formula car prospects need to watch out for this the most. Especially Formula 440 and Formula Vee buyers. If you're taller than 5' 10", and weigh over 180, be especially careful. You're formula car may need special cockpit reconfiguration to properly accept you. Even Indy car drivers have to arrive at the manufacturers request for a special fitting. Those cars' cockpits are built around a drivers specific dimensions. You don't have that luxury when looking at a car. So that's the very first thing to do, . . . even before you check other chassis components.

Beginners, don't let the thrill of hopping into one of these Formula beauties (or any race vehicle) cloud your judgement. It's very, very easy to let your emotions overrule your judgment. If a cockpit doesn't feel tight around your upper torso, that's cheaply correctable. But if the cockpit is too narrow at the hips, actually pushing hard against the hip bones, it'll get ten times more uncomfortable at high speed. If you can't react with your feet in split-second timing, it's dangerous. You should only have to rotate on the heels to place your feet on the various pedals. If you have to lift or pull your legs up or back, even a little, to relocate your feet, it'll slow your reaction and therefore your overall speed. If a dangerous situation quickly arises, the difference of a micro-second could prevent an accident. Believe me, split-seconds count in racing. No seasoned racecar driver will deny that.

8 | Back to School

Speed costs money. The more money available, the quicker you may learn and usually the higher in class you can start at. Sponsorship can play a big part in that, which is covered in the next chapter. Most drivers abhor this part of motorsports. It's a sad fact you'll have to bankroll yourself at least for the first two or three years. It's more than likely most racers will need to do that their entire career. Hopefully a sponsor can help, but too many times, to get that involved means more than just a negotiating skill. Be that as it may, among other things, worrying about sponsorship now is premature. A racing prospect should first test their commitment to racing.

Unless you've hit the lottery big, you had better get rid of that Corvette. Don't they have good resale value? Forget about that vacation at Disneyland. Start saving the bucks! As I suggested in chapter 2, get a second job if you have to. But don't do it if it's going to deprive you of sleep and a family life. Let racing do that, not a job! Of course, there are ways around that family part as previously stated in Chapter 1. No more impulse buying. OK, if you must, make the mortgage payments . . . (Joke) But . . . does your basketball-player son really need those $120 tennis shoes? You know what I'm talking about. You're only buying a 'name' pal! Thirty dollars does the job just as well. Wait a minute! Even as I write this, am I putting the cart before the horse? I've talked about all the commitment it'll take. Now, I'm telling you to do a 180 degree with your lifestyle? You do all that before you step one foot in the cockpit? Shame on me!

Well . . . not really. You must realize what's involved and what your options are before parking yourself in the drivers seat. You wouldn't buy a home sight-unseen and I wouldn't want you to take your first ride without understanding "The Big Picture" concerning motorsports. So before you spend too much money on equipment make darn sure of three things:

1. Do you know for sure racing is what you want to do? (this is almost always answered affirmitively . . . and rightly so)
2. If the answer is yes, what class of racing do you start at? (most prospects know their type of racing; but that ego sometimes gets in the way about what level to start at . . . especially if they have the bucks backing them up)
3. Should you rent or buy your first racer?

How do you determine the answers to these questions? My answer is simple. You don't have to know the answer at this point. It's safe to say, if I had to start racing over again, I'd enroll at a professional driving school and receive more personal and focused instruction, not a sanctioning body school, though you may need one later. Pro schools usually furnish their own racing machines.

Ninety-five percent of these establishments are professional high-performance race-driver schools. Some are street-oriented. They are expensive, but only to the average person who doesn't understand this sport. Actually, they're reasonably priced for what they do. For someone such as myself, who's been racing for years, I can see they're inexpensive. (I hate to use the word "cheap" in motorsports; it doesn't exist) I found out through experience what it takes to learn through the school-of-hard-knocks. It wasn't cheap and it costs time also.

Pro schools are the best way to learn motorsports initially. But you do not have to attend this type of school to fulfill most sanctioning body licensing requirements. There are other ways, depending on the type of motorsport and sanctioning body or association a driver is involved with. Some associations, like SCCA, require a novice to take two of their own schools. A prospect may take that route or do one pro and SCCA school each.

You may rent or use your own racecar in some pro schools or use your own personal 'street' auto. Some people rent race equipment from a personal owner, rather than a rental outfit to attend a race school. You may end up with poor equipment, a situation many pro schools do not want. They know their machines better and therefore can more accurately determine an individuals progress. Some racers arrange their own instruction by hiring a personal instructor. That's good, but can be very expensive. The least expensive way to familiarize yourself with racing (notice I don't necessarily mean learn) is through sanctioning schools, such as SCCA, but they're not always the best way to go.

Some learn through a personal instructor. That personal instructor may be another racer, which isn't necessarily an inferior racer, but an inferior teacher. A great driver doesn't always make a great teacher. You won't hardly ever get pro instruction through a sanctioning school that you'd receive at a pro school. As previously stated, some pro schools will allow you to use your own street vehicle, but use a racer, preferably theirs. It's more expensive, but also more educationally effective. With a real race machine, you'll get more feel for speed. You'll find out better what the meaning of "racing by the seat of your pants" is. Race vehicles are much more responsive and sensitive to the (road) conditions at high speed.

WEIGHING THE PLUSES

The most important thing when starting out racing is to receive good, concise instruction in the best possible race vehicle.

Given a choice of good instruction or good equipment, take the good instruction. To win races you'll need good racing equipment, but first learn to walk, so-to-speak, before you run. You can eventually get good racing equipment, but it isn't as advantageous in the hands of the person not handling it right. You need good instruction to start with. That is something that'll stay with you, whether you've got good or poor equipment. Don't learn the hard way, which is time consuming and even more potentially costly.

Many pro schools use their own racecars, otherwise it's just something else a driver has to worry about. (smashing up his own vehicle) That's still true with racing school equipment, but the schools will be responsible for their own racecars in any accidents not your fault. Therefore they can transfer you to another machine or quickly fix the problem. Either way, it's not distracting and doesn't impede your learning curve or ability.

The pro schools take super care of their equipment and keep them performing equally. In that manner, a student's performance may be consistently measured for progress and compared to other students. They can replace months and maybe years of learning into a 2, 3, 4, or 5 day course. You'll also find out if racing is what you want to be doing or spending all that money on. If you figure out it's not for you, you're out anywhere from 100 to $3,500. But . . . you won't be stuck with a 2000 to $20,000 racer. We already know how tough it is to resell race cars at their true value or for the price you bought it for. That's because even the most uninvolved, nonrace buyers know how they're treated, not to mention how low the market is, since most racecars are not street legal.

Another advantage of a pro school is the matter of a student's own self-judgement. How does a student know their skill or potential? The instructor might. Sometimes racing talent is awfully hard to judge in short time, because of the many variables. But an instructor at a pro school might know what class of racing is best for you. Don't forget, people know what 'type' of racing they like. That's clear! What class within that type is not always so clear. More than likely, money will be a large determining factor in what class or level an individual starts at, no matter how good they are. You can always move up in class later, if so desired. (or if you "hit" the lottery)

CASH? CHECK? PLASTIC?

Some schools start at $100 and go to as high as 3,500 to $5,000. Most are 3-day weekend schools, but they can go to 5 days or through an entire work week. Don't judge them by their costs only. That would be a mistake. Because of some inherently less costly race vehicles, a school for Go-Kart racing is going to be considerably less than for a faster and more sophisticated race-vehicle type school. Schools should be judged by their instructional skill, personnel, organization, equipment and (track) facilities.

I strongly recommend you contact the schools specifically designed and equipped for your type of motorsport. (all address and phone numbers are listed in the back appendix under Racing Schools) They will gladly help you narrow your options. Of course, they'll steer you their way. That's natural. But . . . read between the lines or statements. Do some comparing.

Also, check out George Anderson's book *Racing School Directory* in appendix A in back of this publication. It doesn't go into super detail about each school, but it'll give you an updated idea what each school has, their costs, location(s), types of vehicles used and various packages offered.

9 | Sponsorship

Ah yes, sponsorship. That word has so much in common with the word 'racing', the two words could almost be synonymous. Why? Well, let's debunk a few of the myths about sponsorship.

Myth One (1). When I say the two have much in common, I do not mean they necessarily go hand in hand. The two aren't what they seem. They're both illusionary. Racing is more than hopping in a fast machine and flooring it. Corporations aren't begging to part with their advertizing budgets via raceteams.

Sponsorship isn't something the money moguls seduce a racer with. A fact of the matter is racing needs sponsorship much more than sponsorship needs racing. Some people seem to feel the big sponsors need racing. That's silly! It's just not true. Sponsors have a wide array of fields to promote their goods and services from. They have other mediums such as TV, radio and the printed word at their disposal.

Myth Two (2). Yes, the money coming into racing is more than it used to be. Still, its availability to all racers isn't there. The big dollar, high profile teams do not necessarily get 25 percent support, much less 100 percent from any one sponsor. "Joe Spectator" may assume that the big boys get single, full support all the time, but he'll be assuming wrong. Many of these teams don't come near meeting their costs of racing through just one sponsor.

Myth Three (3). The large, winning, high-profile teams have sponsors knocking down their doors with fistfuls of dollars begging to be spent. Winning races alone will not even guarantee advancement, much less bring in the big money. This is probably the tallest tale of them all. This is similar to the first myth except I'm talking about any one particular big name team as opposed to all the big timers in general.

Myth Four (4). Another myth I need to destroy is how sponsorship bucks get to the raceteams. At the top level of racing, it's usually the sponsor who provides the driver. The sponsor doesn't provide financial help to the team. These drivers pay through their sponsor to ride and/or rent the race machine. The drivers worth to the sponsor is contingent on what he does both in and out of the race machine. Is this driver well known locally, regionally, nationally or worldwide? That and many other factors determine a driver's worth to his sponsor. We'll get into that later on in this chapter.

Those are the main illusions concerning sponsorship which prevail with too many uninformed race fans in this country, if not the world.

Now let's cover an area of which most people do not realize even exists. That would be the kinds of sponsorship available. While going over these, keep in mind I'll be answering or clearing up further details about the myths of sponsorship at the same time. The six kinds are:

A. Corporate
B. Individual (or Patron)
C. Associate
D. Contingency
E. Yourself
F. Uncle Sam

A. CORPORATE SPONSORS

These are the big boys. The "Captains of Industry". The boys you beginners need not waste your time and effort with for now. These guys not only sponsor drivers, some support an entire race or part of a sanctioning body. Example: Winston supports NASCAR (I believe it's more accurately, RJ Reynolds); Pittsburgh Plate and Glass supports CART (PPG IndyCar World Series); and Camel cigarettes helps IMSA in their GT series. (Camel GT) These are a few, but hardly not all. Like I previously mentioned a few lines ago, some companies sponsor the driver and not necessarily the team. Of course, they'll certainly have a 'say' as to which team that driver goes to as much as the team will. But that is not terribly important to us now. That can be confusing and not to our advantage to understand.

For a (driver's) sponsor to subsidize the whole team's budget is pretty much nonexistent. A fortunate team may have 1/2 to 2/3 of their costs paid, but 25 percent is more realistic. At the high levels of racing, corporate sponsored drivers get support contingent on several factors. Examples would be the drivers profile (how well known, etc) and how he actively promotes the sponsors in and outside the race game; how the sponsor utilizes the promotional valve of his driver (and therefore team) at the track itself and away from it also; the expected event(s) attendance figures; and TV, radio and print media coverage.

This can get involved, but we'll leave these things to a professional promotional expert you may hire later on in your career. Don't let this concern you for now. (Yes, you can hire someone to find you sponsorship; more on that in the last part of this chapter)

It may be worth mentioning that these large corporations don't just derive their advertising/promotional budgets for racing from one entity within the company. Many times the money is a compilation of various internal sources. Examples would be their advertising, sales promotion, public relations and employee moral/entertainment departments.

In 1996 it'll probably cost about 6.2 to 6.9 million to run a highly competitive full season with an IndyCar team. The (driver's) sponsors may shell out $400,000 for one race or 6.5 for the entire season. Those (drivers) sponsors may pay out to the team according to various subfactors. The driver may need to finish high, if not win the race. (this is one reason why drivers feel pressure) This is more often not the case, especially for the extremely well known, high profile driver/teams. Still those same big name drivers may be required to appear at various company/employee functions on and off the track, make appearances on TV, radio and ad campaigns. More dollars may be allocated if the team is involved, such as shopping center appearances, tradeshows and automobile show displays.

A team's and/or driver's popularity or success will certainly effect their worth to a particular company. Lesser statured teams will need to work harder. Some team drivers can get by on their previous success, such as AJ Foyt and Richard Petty. Men like those two haven't enjoyed recent success, but they're still popular with the fans. (even though they're both retired as drivers; both have their own teams now) Either way, the bottom line is they must be able to give the sponsor as much success as possible in promoting their goods and services.

These large corporations just simply aren't in racing just to support race drivers, teams and sanctioning bodies. Any fan who thinks these corporations have money to burn, or are just being "nice guys" to the racing world couldn't be more wrong. Real race fans already know this. To the beginner feeling a bit of envy towards the big-name drivers financial support . . . get out of la-la land!!

B. INDIVIDUAL (PATRON)

This was one of the things I was talking about in Chapter One. If you're going to get married you may have to postpone or cancel racing. If you're going to spend eons of time on your knees begging your wife's permission to race, then do it. But she'll only give in if you leave the budget alone. So, you get a second job or . . . this is when you see your buddies wife. That's right, whom ever's loaded. In this case it's your friends wife. No, don't cheat on your 'ol lady. That would really screw up an otherwise clear mind needed for this sport. (also, have you seen what divorces do to peoples pocketbooks?)

No, what I'm talking about is getting the right people involved in this game. Does that sound understated or oversimplified? Granted, it does! But there's a point to be made. There are plenty of ways to get people involved in various activities, in your case, racing. You will need to be a salesman, subtle in your approach and using some imagination. You don't just ask people for money to support something, much less something they may initially find unnecessary. Let's face it, life will go on with or without racing. (although for myself, I don't believe that)

This person you're trying to "woo" needn't be your father-in-law or whatever. It need not be any of your relatives. Nonetheless, I have heard of parents who are contributing quite substantially toward their offsprings racing program. That aside, you need to be at least a friend and/or acquaintance with someone very interested in racing who's moderately or filthy rich. The independently wealthy people tend to be more easily approached since they have more time.

I know most people do not know anyone very wealthy. Personally, I do! Don't think for one minute I'm not cooking up ways to involve this person. What I have working against me is this man is about "third from the top of the corporate ladder". It's a family business worth probably 20 to 25 million and the second man in command is only a few years older than my friend. I will remain subtle in my approach when and if their father decides to retire, which means people will move up. I realize my odds are long, but I'd be ignorant not to give it an All-American effort. If you know such a person, get to work. You have nothing to lose. Remember, this is America, anything can happen here. We've got wealthy people here galore. I'm not just talking about the filthy rich but the well-off too. There's more of 'em out there

than you probably think. Many just don't like to advertise that fact, that's all.

Keep in mind I'm not talking about someone who's wealthy enough to spend 6 million per year on an Indycar ride your very first year in racing. Even if you were lucky enough to find someone that carefree, (and ignorant) USAC or CART never would permit you to race at their level with such inexperience.

If you look hard enough, you will probably know someone 3, 4 or 5 times removed from your acquaintance who is pretty financially set. (100,000 to $250,000/year in earnings; not like Donald Trump) Now I know all this is beginning to sound seedy, but it only sounds that way! There is nothing immoral about befriending such a person. Just make darn sure you get to know this person well if you're lucky enough to meet one. Besides, I'm not saying to actively seek these people out. If you do you'll probably make yourself out to be a golddigger in their opinions. What I am saying, is to take advantage of any opportunity to meet someone of high financial stature. If this happens and you take an instant dislike to them, then move on. At the risk of sounding like Dear Abby, if you can't be a genuine friend to someone, then don't fake it; stay away.

Find out what motivates a wealthy person. Usually, that can be accomplished by figuring out how much ego they've got. That may take a while. But then anything worthwhile always does. If a person is (independently) wealthy, it's a good chance they'll reveal themselves more quickly. Afterall, relatively speaking, people like that have more security and therefore are more outgoing and personable. These kinds of individuals would enjoy racing. This is where you come in. Take them to one of your events. Explain . . . introduce . . . get'em involved. Take him to an event where there will be the most exposure to large crowds and media gatherings. If you don't have that kind of exposure, then you need to attend race events in your kind of racing, but at the higher level. Racing is complicated and that alone may be one factor why this man could fall in love with this sport. (women are complicated—look how men flock to women)

Racing is exciting. It can fill a void with an individual who has it all and is bored stiff. Many times these well-off people take interest in racehorses. You can show them how these same people can get more tangible and quicker results by sponsoring, or at least initially taking an interest in a different kind of horsepower. Whether a person is well-off, filthy rich or just an interested patron, you can show these people ways toward achieving more respect, selfworth and something to feed that ever present ego we all have. Don't laugh, rich people just can't seem to get enough "stroking." (and something we're all guilty of at one time or another) Maybe that's why Bill Cosby helped out Willy T. Ribbs in his IndyCar effort.

A couple of points need to be made now. If that individual is truly interested in racing, he may volunteer some money towards your efforts. Don't point-blank ask for money. You, as a mature person, should know that. If you did, you would reveal an ulterior motive on your part. Sure, you will need to help things along towards that goal. Again, the best way is involving that person. He may become so wrapped up in your endeavor he may want to own your racer. That's great! Understand he may use it as a means to entertain, attract, impress or present to potential clients and/or friends. (or if he's the playboy type . . . to say nothing of how the ladies may think) With this persons help, it's now a team effort you can afford with more financial backing. This also can open more doors for you, such as meeting more potential sponsors. Afterall, wealthy individuals probably have well-off friends down the line. Surprise, you could possibly obtain additional help or crew members by whom they know. You may find an excellent mechanic or engineer, etc, by whom your patron knows. But be sure these people can deliver what they say. Otherwise, it could cost you dearly. Buying expensive equipment on "promises" not delivered by people who say they'll support you is risky.

Suppose your wealthy, potential patron falls for racing like a ton of bricks, but wants to form his own team using another driver. (or himself) Then accept that and help him along. Be sincere. It may benefit you later

on. He may discover that racing's way too consuming for his taste. He may come back to you. He'll appreciate what the race game requires now and may still badly want to participate. Now he may want to participate at the level more easily accessible to him, providing funds to you. Ya never know!

Suppose the potential patron you've been so subtly working with decides racing never was his thing. That's okay. Racing definitely isn't for everyone, especially at the participation level. How many racecar drivers like ballet? You pretty much can't control what you do or don't like. And neither can a person with bundles of money. So move on! People with money who like everything or hate everything could be either overindulged with bliss (no good in the long run) or miserable enough to commit suicide. (real bad) The bottom line is you can't control what a person likes. You can only help them discover things or help them discover themselves.

C. THE ASSOCIATE SPONSOR

This kind of sponsor is much the same as the corporate kind but on a less costly scale. The same corporation that is a primary sponsor on a drag racing team, for example, may be a secondary sponsor on an IndyCar team or another drag racing team. I'm not sure if IndyCar teams are allowed to display on their machines more than one primary sponsor and three associate sponsors. (USAC/CART rules) But judging from their looks, it appears so. That doesn't mean the team may have only a total of four (or whatever) sponsors. It just limits how much a paint job on an IndyCar can be cluttered up with names. But I doubt this is a main reason why some sanctioning bodies limit sponsor-name display on a racecar. For example, USAC and/or CART's reasoning behind their rule to limit sponsorship display is two-fold:

1. Too many names displayed will only water down each sponsors intent. I'm especially sure most sponsors feel likewise. The driver/team needs to also concentrate on

meeting it's obligation to their sponsors. Three associate, one primary or four associate sponsors are enough. The high profile team probably do have more than four sponsors, but only display four on the racer. All sponsors can be displayed on the transporting vehicle and displayed in the companies ad campaigns.

Some sanctioning bodies are concerned about an image created by over-sponsorship. I do not believe a team could be over-sponsored, but I do believe some race teams could corner a market and create an overly unfair financial advantage. That would create a dynasty and negatively effect attendance figures and TV ratings. TV ratings are important to racing. It effects the bottom line.

2. The second reason some sanctioning bodies have a sponsorship package rule is so smaller (associate) sponsors can assess racings impact on their goods/services. These companies (and racing) need to test if corporate sponsorship is feasible in the future to spend in advertising via the sport of racing.

Also these smaller (sponsoring) firms are locally situated near a race event. They can associate themselves with a big time "name" at reduced cost. Racing in general benefits, because without this rule some companies might not get any exposure at all.

D. THE CONTINGENCY SPONSOR

You may say, sure I see all the company names painted on the racers. What about those little stickers that can be seen only when the race machine is standing still? Well, they're not as prevalent in the big-time racing event, but they are in the lower classes. Their elimination in high-profile racing was due to what I just talked about a few seconds ago. (the 1 primary, 3 associates rule)

Contingency sponsors are very necessary and welcome in all racing. They usually involve racing directly because their products are used by the racing fraternity. They post prize money, sometimes to only certain high

profile teams/drivers. It is more individual incentive to do well. Some companies will require you use their products and finish. Some require no use at all but will still pay out to the top four or five positions in a race. Some firms require both.

Some of contingency awards isn't money, but barter, usually racetires, oil, parts and other racing related products/services. A good example is the "big show" held every May in Indianapolis. Many Indy teams receive free tires for the whole month. Some get them free for the race only. When you consider an Indy racetire (not a set) goes for 250 to $300 and might last 80-90 miles, it can add up to big money. This is the exception, not the rule. In the lower classes, if a racer finishes in a predetermined position or higher, with or without using a particular product, contingencies may pay from 25 to $500. There are many variables.

In some racing series, the leader(s) may receive X amount of money, contingent on where they finished in points at seasons end. Products are also given away. Some of these contingency sponsors will pay the better known people, or all the people in a particular race just for qualifying in it. Some pay just to finish. Sometimes the variables are contingent on the product itself. Use their tires, finish as high as possible, win dollars accordingly.

The contingency sponsor can be a beginning racers first jackpot.

E. YOURSELF

In many ways, we've already discussed this in detail. If you're good at racing, lucky and know the right people, you may only have to finance yourself the first few years. It's a sad fact you may do it longer, if not forever. If your goal is to be a professional racer, you should treat your hobby or endeavor as a business. This may entitle you to writeoff many of your expenses. This is where Uncle Sam can help you out.

Basically, this book is partly designed to keep costs down, when you have to sponsor yourself. (by avoiding costly mistakes)

F. UNCLE SAM

This is an entity unto itself. Believe me, everyone in racing who can take full advantage of writeoffs, indeed do. I devote time to this subject in the next chapter. (10)

Do unto others . . .

Now that these six sponsors are covered, I'd like to discuss sponsorship in general. You may get sponsorship, but keeping it is something else. Here today, gone tomorrow. You need to develop an attitude towards sponsorship. Bob Sharp may have put it best when he said he started looking at a "promotion company utilizing racing," rather than "racing needing a promotion." He may be the most astute business man in racing. He knows you need to treat the sponsor(s) as 'you' need to be treated.

Aside from respect, of which I hope I needn't mention, the sponsor is in racing for different reasons than you. You must view racing as the sponsor does. You will need to promote him in as many ways as possible. Are you becoming more successful? Good! Credit your sponsor in interviews and newspaper/magazine articles. (high-profile racers do it all the time) Mention them at speaking engagements and small group seminars. Of course, what I'm talking about is both an individual or a small company sponsor. They're pushing a product or service, so that's what you're racing for, to help promote those things. This is also true with the large corporations and associate sponsors. You need to make an impact to justify the dollars they spend on your race program. Be cooperative but don't be a stooge either. I don't believe that's a problem with overly indulgent sponsors. You will find helping your sponsor in an ad campaign can be fun. You will meet many interesting people through personal endorsements, appearances and promotional gatherings.

If your sponsor begins to realize that racing can't help his company he'll need to withdraw his support. It's nothing against you. It's reality. Understand that it can happen and ask if you can change anything within reason to help prevent that. If not, wish him well, for he can be a good reference for future prospects.

Now that you understand what's involved with racing, you'll need to know where to look and whom to talk to. Where to look depends on where and how often you race. (and who you are) Do you race in front of large crowds, on TV, with radio and media coverage. Large corporate sponsors look for high exposure for their wares. Those are the "big boy" arenas. As a beginner with one or two years experience, don't waste your time and effort with a national promotion campaign. (unless you are a Kennedy) Pursue help with local firms in your area that are automotive oriented. Sporting companies are good prospects. High volume, highly competitive companies are better if you travel far to big events. Examples are companies such as breweries, tobacco and beverage products. They wouldn't reach enough customers at a local level to make racing profitable to them.

It's a good chance your first sponsor will be on an informal basis. The corner station may provide racing fuel. Discounts on parts at the local parts outlet, rooms furnished on your racing trip by ma and dad. Those and contingency awards can add up. You will need to seek them out. Many of your friends and acquaintances may want to go with you to your race to provide free help. I taught high school and sub-taught a bit. Some kids, including even females you'd think couldn't care less about people other than themselves, (know any of those types?) were intrigued by my racing habit. This is one reason why I think a person won't have trouble getting (his) kids to help him. (covered that in chapter two) Anyhow, you'll need to find a company which matches what you can offer. As your exposure increases, money will come relatively easier. That catchword . . . "relatively" means finding money can still seem impossible. (at times) Such factors as the economy, politics and luck can effect cash availability.

When you approach a potential client, the person to talk to is the man who signs the checks. You need to approach him at a time you feel is best and in a private setting. Be formal, don't blurt out to employees asking where the boss is. Phone the owner and set-up an appointment. You will now need to explain how you can be of benefit to him. You'll have to put yourself in his shoes and imagine what he'll need.

To really get the inside dope on approaching sponsors, I would recommend a book from Steve Smith Auto Sports by Pat Bentley. It's called *Stalking The Motorsports Sponsor.* I've read it and I can attest it goes into great detail. It's worth every penny of its $9.95 price tag. Another good book is called *The Great Money Hunt* by Andrew Waite. (see the appendix in back)

Professional promoting companies

A last point I'd like to make is what I consider my most important. After a few years of racing you'll understand how involved racing is. If you want to be good you have to put yourself, time, money and effort into it. You'll want to move up or at least improve your equipment. That'll take bucks. But, unless your dad's loaded, how do you find time or acquire the expertise to find a large sponsor to help you with that?

You've got your job, family and the racing operation to consume your waking hours. Even if you're young and single, you need the expertise. Either way, I'd suggest you hire a Professional Promoting Company to find your sponsor. More than likely you'll frustrate yourself into a straight-jacket going after larger corporation dollars. It's almost a lost cause! If you don't do this for the reason I just mentioned, then do it for the following reasons.

To hire a Professional Promoting Company not only makes sense, it'll save you money in the long run and an awful lot of time. (not to mention frustration) You need to possess some form of profile for these pros to work with. Check with them. You may have some advantage you don't even realize. No, you don't necessarily need the national notoriety of Shirley Muldowny. (a talented female racing personality in drag racing) You'll need to

be established to some extent, be fairly well-known, popular or hot property at some local, regional or national level.

Sometimes people don't realize how much clout they have. Most can't objectively assess themselves. These promotion companies can do that. You'll need to make evident your an 'up-and-comer'. You're moving your way up through the racing fraternity and/or hierarchy. So you will need some racing history and a bit of marketability. Sometimes it's only the latter you'll need, like Bruce Jenner for example. He races. His name alone surely didn't hurt his ability to obtain some finanial help. These professional racing promoters have specially trained people to help you. When you feel you've got yourself into a position of marketability, give'em a call. They'll assess you and eventually decide if they can help you for the time being.

However, if I thought hiring these people could help you from day one, I wouldn't bother with this chapter. Heck, I wouldn't bother with this book. We could all have instant funds to race with in a perfect world. (Ok, . . . back to reality)

Since professional race promoting isn't a highly competitive business, there aren't many around. They may appear expensive. You knew racing wasn't cheap when you entered it, but you entered it anyway! If you could see the possible potential these companies may bring out in you, you may just be crazy not to at least give them a try. At least talk to them and find out what you'll need in reference to the future.

They'll do things you may not know existed. Things you took for granted can work for you. They may be able to take bad things that happen to you, turn them around and get them working for you. They know who to see, when to pursue and how to lure a potential sponsor prospect, among many other things. They can match your needs to a sponsor if you're highly profiled, (well-known) otherwise, they may get sponsors who'll require your unquestioned loyalty. Expect that. Hardly anyone chooses their sponsor. It just doesn't happen. The people with the funds will have the "say." It only makes sense.

As you start your racing endeavor, work

on your profile. In other words, get good. Be personable, cooperative, a sportsman and an asset to racing. Promote yourself and all those involved with you. Don't sell yourself short trying to take yourself to the top by yourself. The money and effort you spent landing the primary and/or associate sponsor will most likely go wasted. It's the most frustrating endeavor you may ever encounter. The time you take trying to land the big bucks would be better spent marketing your other skills. (getting a second job) You then could use that money to hire your promotor. These professional sponsor-finding companies make no guarantees. How can they? They can't even promise long-term help if they do get you some sponsorship in a particularly quick amount of time. Nobody can directly control sponsorship funds except those that have the money. You can bet these promotional companies will try their best for you to obtain these funds. Happy customers keep them in business.

Understand you will need to help them. Count on it! Potential sponsors will want to meet, see, talk and get to know what they are getting for their dollar. Be yourself and show them what they see will be an asset to them.

10 | Taxes and Racing

In starting to race, it's your advantage to at least have a basic understanding how the US Government can help. This is especially so if your goal is to become a professional driver. The racer needs to conduct their racing program in a business-like manner. Even if you decide to remain an amateur, you may have options you're unaware of. Get to know those options. That will give you more criteria with which to make decisions on.

At the pro level, racing could be less expensive for an individual. Remember, I said "could" and emphasize the word "individual." Cheaper pro racing, as opposed to cheaper amateur racing is still expensive. Yet it's worth looking into. You never know.

LOOK BEFORE YOU LEAP

Let me make a point very clear. Any dealings with the IRS calls for caution and more importantly a little help. It's strongly recommended a professional tax consultant, accountant or preparer be employed to handle any tax situations a racer has, especially for a young individual who is just starting out in racing. If you know how to deal with the IRS at an accurate and complicated level, then it is even more financially to you advantage.

Maybe you're already a CPA or a tax man. If not, it's better to hire the services of one. It's even better to hire one that specializes in the racing business. But they may be few and hard to find. They are out there alright, but you'll probably need to do a bit of looking. Call the race shops, talk to the drivers or the people employed in racing associations in your area. They should be able to recommend an individual who is familiar with tax situations in racing. Get several recommendations and narrow it down to who you think is most highly regarded. Get more sources of information through the yellow pages under Motorsports or Racing Associations. You could try talking to each CPA or tax professional in your areas yellow pages, but that's a lengthy chore.

If you can't find a tax preparer which handles racing situations, don't worry. It is not like it's a life and death situation to employ one. I'm sure any tax man will know how to handle a tax return concerning your racing business. But be sure it's someone with a good reputation, preferably older and more experienced and one which will ask you to help him. Helping your tax man is necessary because he'll need to know how to treat specific circumstances, afterall, he can't read minds. If you do not use a tax preparer, it's a very good chance it'll cost you more money in the long run than what it cost to use their services. If you do your own taxes and get just a bit too inventive or imaginative, you could end up with a hefty fine or with free room and board . . . behind bars.

THOSE 'GRAY' AREAS

There are two basic rules or points to follow with taxes in racing. Both are similar. The first point is racecar drivers generally cannot deduct anything in this sport if it's a hobby. It doesn't matter what costs are involved. If you're an amateur racer, you are on your own. There aren't too many exceptions. But one exception might be the following; is your racecar used for the advertising of a business owned by the same racer? (you)

Is it your sole intention to use that advertising to increase your profits? In other words, are you a self-employed business man who can profit directly from racing? You may have a tax advantage. It doesn't matter if racing is your hobby if you're self-employed in a related field or one what can benefit from your own advertising. The problem is, what's related? There are plenty of 'gray' areas in taxes, and racing isn't any different. It's why a professional should be used, the Tax Reform Act didn't simplify anything.

THE IDEA IS TO MAKE MONEY

The second point a racer needs to understand is pretty much an extension of the first one. It's called the "Golden Rule." This implies a businessman makes an organized effort at turning a profit to its maximum. Isn't that the only way in any form of business? Of course it is. Except . . . (of course) . . . racing. Racing just isn't a big profit-making endeavor. This is especially so for any racecar owner whether they are the driver or not, or whether they're an amateur or pro. This doesn't mean you have to run an operation like Roger Penske, Junior Johnson or Don Garlits enterprises. They're big time operations alright, but I doubt their sole purpose is to turn a big profit. This 'Golden Rule' thing means to make a profit or expect to make one. Don't purposely operate racing (or any business) to lose money (except on paper that is) and therefore avoid taxes. Doing that makes racing look like a 'front.' (for covering up something else)

For the amateur racer entering this sport, you have to figure on operating at a loss. But believe me, if you've got a job, whether it's racing related or not, you'll pay taxes no matter how big those losses in racing are. But do keep track of all your racing finances, whether you're treating this sport as a hobby

or not. This will help you to learn the accounting side of racing. You will become familiar with all the variables and options. You'll better understand what to spend money on and how much. You may find those tax considerations later down the road helps determine whether you buy or rent a race machine. (if you want to move up or down in class)

CONFUSION GALORE

Such things as capital investments, lease-back and income average are and should be important to racers and/or racecar owners. Capital investments is the hardware and equipment used in addition to the race machine. A leaseback is similar except you rent some or all of that equipment to someone else. (the owner leasing their racecar and services to a driver) The driver's payments may be deductible if you're following correct business practices. The owner who rents these goods depreciate their initial costs, sets capital investment credits and ends up with paid-off equipment. They can sell that equipment for an additional profit later. (but they have to pay a capital gains tax) Does this sound like mumbo-jumbo? (especially to you younger folks?) It isn't! Take it seriously. When you see the possibilities, you'll want to understand it quickly and take advantage of it. Count on that!

What if you are audited. Do you hold another job? If it's nonrace related and more time consuming than your race business, it'll be up to you to prove racing as one of your legitimate sources of income. That's true only if you write-off any part of your race program. The IRS can and will recognize your program as a 'hobby' business if your profits aren't "up there." Where that is I don't know. Sometimes I think the IRS doesn't know either. It seems to be a judgement call.

A rule of thumb I'd consider in figuring that out would be the following; You spend X amount of hours per year with your nonrace related business or job. You also spend Y amount of hours with your race business. If

X and Y are about the same, it's possible the IRS will expect relatively equal profits from both businesses. I know that's understated and oversimplified, but hopefully, you'll see the thinking pattern. I have a feeling that a race program can get away with a lot less profit (and even a loss) and still be considered a legitimate business. A hobby business can still make a profit to you as a race-car owner and driver. So why lose money in racing to minimize taxes? Why not just minimize your losses.

Whether you call yourself an amateur or professional is merely semantics to the IRS. (unless you like the status of being called a professional) If you write-off portions of your race business or the whole program, be prepared to eventually explain it to the government. So . . . you may just as well gear yourself towards making a profit. That way your business doesn't look like an excuse to avoid taxes. Hopefully, you'll do more racing treating it as a business and . . . hey . . . you may make some money, . . . but don't quit your day job.

TAKING YOUR LUMPS

It used to be a business could lose money an X amount of years. Remember it does happen, even the big automakers lose money. If they can lose money with the huge market they compete in, than certainly racing can too with the tiny market it has. But sometimes the problem is the IRS doesn't consider racing to be in a market. Not too many people are getting rich in racing, but the sport itself does pump its share of the dollars into the economy. The IRS recognizes that and therefore may allow a race program to absorb more losses than some unrelated, more profit-oriented business. If a racer doesn't turn a profit within a certain predetermined number of years, he may have to eliminate the write-offs or pay appropriate taxes.

As a professional race driver relying on racing as a sole source of income, losing money every year in racing, which is easy, doesn't sit well with the IRS. Either way, as an amateur or pro racer (owner or driver) don't figure on showing losses on your tax forms every year. That'll put you in racing as strictly a hobby. In that case, you can write-off absolutely nothing.

It used to be two out of any five consecutive years was all anyone was allowed to write-off a loss on an entire business. The tax laws do change. But then that's just another reason to hire a tax man. The IRS doesn't accept ignorance, so there's no point using that for an excuse to make mistakes figuring your taxes. It's not that the IRS doesn't know mistakes can be made, but rather, they understand human nature for what it is. And that is people will take advantage of any 'gray' area loopholes for their own personal gain. Some taxpayers attitude is "if I'm wrong, let the IRS find me and prove it". (it's a numbers game that the IRS cannot win) The bottom line in a racing business and any business, is to establish your intent to turn a profit. Then strive to do that.

By now you should have an idea how important the IRS and your taxes are to racing. It's another part of this already complicated sport. But what you've read in this chapter doesn't even begin to prepare you to figure out how to figure your taxes. You'll need much more detailed and thorough service from a tax consultant, CPA or a tax preparer. (preferably, one which specializes in racing, if you can find one in your geographical area)

There's a book called *The Racers Tax Guide* which explains in plain english what to expect concerning taxes. (from Steve Smith Autosports) It'll help you understand in more minute detail what to expect when April 15th rolls around. But, I think . . . no . . . I know the best thing to do is make an appointment with a tax person and go talk to them. Tell them what you'll be doing and what you can do to keep the tax bill as low as possible.

11 | Licensing

It would be easy to say the best way to get started in racing is to send for information through the sanctioning bodies and organizations. Well, to a point that's true. They'll tell you the costs involved with licensing and the procedures. Some racing organizations require only a valid state drivers license to race. Others will require an X amount of experience in a level of racing considered by them to be an adequate training ground. In addition to those two extremes, a person may be asked to undergo a thorough physical examination once a year or after a serious racing mishap. It varies in scope between sanctioning organizations from a very regimented ritual to just walking in and saying "I'm ready". You can bet, the more speed involved with a particular kind of racing the more stringent it is to obtain a license. We'll start with the young racers who want to start racing in Go-Karts.

GO-KARTS

As with any racing endeavor you need money, but a lot less in this version of the sport. That is, a whole lot less relative to adults and their bigger, faster race "toys". If a young person is told by their parents they can race karts using their own money, then for 90 percent of school-aged people, it's expensive. It just doesn't immediately start out that way. That's because most kart organizations do not require a formal racing permitt. Some do. In most cases, the organizations will want an individual to have a desire to be competitive, have a knowledge of the rules and regulations and at least an understanding of what it takes to be good. (that way they aren't too slow on the track, which can create dangerous speed differentials between competitors)

The rules and regulations are acquired by writing the kart associations. Many of the Go-Kart tracks around have copies of the regulations for sale. If there isn't a Go-Kart track within a few miles, then many kart affiliated businesses will have them. Look under Karts or Go-Karts in the yellow pages of your phonebook. If you still aren't having any luck locating a kart rule book, two sure-fire ways to get one is to write to the two major karting organizations in the US. The IKF and WKA addresses are listed in the back appendix.

You do not have to be a member of a karting association to get a rules book. (some require membership) Membership in them is about $35 per year for the high-speed Enduro racer. The Enduro Go-Karts reach speeds well over 100 mph. An 8 year old will not be allowed to do that kind of racing in Go-Karts until they're 13 or 14 years old. Even then they'll need a doctors 'Statement of Health For Minors' and a form provided by the WKA and/or IKF signed by both parents.

The two major karting organizations provide racing insurance automatically in their racing events. In addition, they offer members an in-house publication or magazine which help keep members up to date on racing locations and times, new products related to karts, technical articles, race results and classified ads. IKF's (International Karting Federation) magazine is called the Karter

News. WKA's (World Karting Association) magazine is World Karting. For the karting prospects in the western half of the US, it may be better to be under the jurisdiction of the IKF. WKA is based in Ohio and seems to preside primarily in the eastern half of the country.

For those people interested in the pro ranks (over 18 years of age) of karting, check in the back appendix for the address of the PKA. (Professional Kart Association) This is an organization which seems to be continually growing in the US. In Europe, it's much more established and has proven to be very popular. You should check with your organization about the pro-karting schools. Some of them are very sophisticated and high-speed oriented. Others are more based towards entertainment.

For the Sprint and Dirt classes, a driver need only be a member of IKF or WKA. Unlike Enduro, you pay only about $5 less for yearly fees. ($30) Licensing is based on an informal/formal (so-to-speak) observations from track and/or kart officials. A driver would have to mess-up pretty consistently or badly to lose their license. But the high-speed Enduro racers are required to attend a drivers school specifically accredited by the organizations. Once that is done, the drivers first three racing events must be started at the rear of the field regardless of their qualifying speed.

ROADRACING

In the United States there are several licenses you may have for automotive roadracing. One of the most important and hardest to get is from the Federation Internationale De Automobile, which is located in Paris, France. You will need that for most professional racing series. This sanctioning body can get mighty fussy. All applications are judged and granted on an individual basis.

There have been times that they turned down well-established IndyCar drivers for participation in Formula One events. It can be upsetting to more than a few people to think an IndyCar driver isn't capable of han-

dling a Formula One racer. (in the opinion of the FIA) But that's the exception more than the rule. (I suspect politics played a role in cases like that) That aside, there are several categories of FIA licenses. The top level is called a 'Super License'. The rules and requirements seem to change yearly.

For the most part, the general consensus required to obtain a license in Formula One racing is the following; A top-name IMSA GTP, IndyCar or NASCAR driver must finish at least half the races he competes in at the top 3, 4 or 5 positions, with a 'win' thrown in every so often. Well, if that isn't vague enough, if not unfair, what does a good driver do about inferior racing equipment? It seems the FIA attitude is the good teams will seek out the good drivers. They're probably right. If a driver does show potential with poor equipment, it's just a matter of time before they get offered better vehicles.

Of course, all IMSA, CART and NASCAR drivers had to be good to get as far as they did anyhow. But as we've learned earlier in this book, money may have played an important role in how a driver moves up. Because of that, FIA insists these richer drivers prove themselves competitively.

Across the ocean, the Formula 2, 3, 3000 and the Aurora series race drivers are the ones looked at by FIA as the best Formula One prospects to watch for. ACCUS, the Automobile Competition Committee of the US, also helps the FIA in licensing the drivers, but is more concerned with professional racing based mostly in the US.

SCCA NOVICE, REGIONAL, NATIONAL LICENSE

A very important kind of roadracing license recognized throughout the country and much of the world is the one required by the SCCA. If it's not the most numerous of its kind in the world, then it certainly is in the United States.

To obtain an SCCA Regional/National License, first you must join membership with SCCA. It will cost $45.00 per year. (address in appendix) A novice permit or logbook is issued upon request. You enter two racing schools (each about $140) sanctioned by SCCA. They're held throughout the year all over the US. (about 40 to 60 schools per year) After completion of two successful weekend schools, your signed forms are sent to the licensing department of the offices in Englewood, Colorado. But first, you must complete two regional racing events.

Many times these SCCA drivers schools are operated in conjunction with a regional (SCCA) race. You certainly do not have to take two SCCA schools to obtain a license. The completion of an approved private, professional race school will count towards one of the two SCCA schools. Taking two private professional schools will not count towards two SCCA schools. The SCCA will want to see a beginning racer in at least one of their own schools. (unless a pro school will conduct their school with an SCCA driver school; some schools do that) I would strongly recommend taking one professional school, as you surmised from reading Chapter 8.

The SCCA schools are instructed by experienced personnel who race or used to race themselves. Some schools are better than others. Instructors are all experienced racers, although they may not be extremely experienced teachers. Anyway, they'll walk the racecourse with you and then take a ride in a passenger car with groups of 3 or 4 students. They'll show the various racing lines, braking references, high-speed areas, where to take (safer) risks, how and where to apex a corner and the safest places to pass.

Depending on the number of students, the classes are divided equally in numbers per instructor, hopefully no more than 4 students per instructor. These instructors are trained and understand what to look for. What they look for is smoothness, consistency, driver awareness of other competitors and safety. When possible, they will sometimes ride with you. You must spend a certain amount of time on the track depending on your type of race vehicle and the number of other race machines on the racecourse.

The school ends in a couple of practice starts with an entire field of similar cars. Then the last few starts will go a few laps in a sprint-styled type of race. Sometimes a written exam is given. But that seems to be the exception rather then the rule. Very little, if any, classroom time is spent.

If your second school is with the SCCA, you may enter a race if there is one offered for that weekend at the same location. Many times a two-day SCCA school may be operated on a Friday and Saturday or packed entirely on a Saturday with a regional racing event scheduled on a Sunday. This is why I feel it's best to take your pro school first if you are going that route. You can use what you learned at the pro school in the SCCA school then immediately go racing the next day.

After completing a race under novice licensing, you must finish with over 1/2 the laps that the event is scheduled for. You now have one more regional race to complete. When your two regional races as a novice are successfully completed, the chief steward from each race will sign your novice book. Then you send in that book to the SCCA licensing department with $45 and a completed SCCA medical form. (actually, that's usually required before school participation) This form must be signed by your parents (if under 18) and your doctor. In some cases, your doctor, in good conscience, cannot issue or sign a medical form. In that situation, the SCCA will arrange for a doctor specialized in racing physicals to examine you. You then send in the medical form and two passport photo's with proof of age to get your regional license. You should state what you're requesting (a regional license) and when you'll need it by.

You may arrange special speeded-up service by including another 25 to $30. Sometimes the normal process takes longer than it should. The $25 extra will speed up the process. In the speeded-up manner, you can enter an event immediately after you've completed all of the requirements.

Still, using the mails can take well over a week getting the paperwork transferred. If you wish to enter a race before you receive your license, the SCCA will contact the event registrar by phone, at your request, to inform them you're okayed to enter without your license card. (to obtain a National License requires a completion of 4 regional events in one year)

REGIONAL AND NATIONAL LICENSE

To maintain a Regional License on a yearly basis you must do the following:

a. Maintain yearly national SCCA membership at $45 per year. Regional dues are 5 to $15 per year. (depending on the region)
b. Compete in two SCCA driver schools in twelve months or two regional events with no DNF's, (did not finish) or one school and one regional event. No combination school/regional on the same weekend applies. Laps completed in the events must be at least half the laps of the race winner. (in other words, in a 25 lap race, the driver must complete 13 laps and still be running at the finish) Then in addition to the membership dues, the driver also sends an additional $45 for his new competition license and an updated medical exam every two years.

To maintain a National License:

a. Maintain SCCA membership yearly.
b. Complete 4 regional races in one licensing year or 3 national events. (or pro events) No DNF's and over 1/2 of total laps must be completed while still running at the races end. (fees are the same as the Regional renewals)

Some of the requirements may be waived if an SCCA National License holder competes in other FIA or professional events. Other requirements may also be waived if you're an established veteran racecar driver. But you still have to write of any special circumstances you have to an assigned SCCA official appointed specifically for those purposes. That's usually an extra 5 or $10.

IMSA

Another kind of license for roadracing is furnished by IMSA. They recognize experience a prospective competitor gains with another organization. In cases like this, there is no driving or written test. All that's needed to be sent in is the application and a fee of $150.

The successful completion of a recognized private professional drivers school may be one requirement. Another is an SCCA sanctioned school.

You probably will not be able to start as a "raw" rookie in IMSA. It's high-level racing just like any other pro organization. No matter how well a driver is financed they're going to be asked to get more experience. They want about two to four years of high-speed experience with some relatively consistent success. That's vague wording, but what they want is someone who handles machinery which can reach 140-205 mph.

NASCAR

Another roadracing license is available from NASCAR. Many people don't realize they offer several licenses in different divisions of racing. The Grand National License ($95/yr) is only one kind. The Gold Drivers License ($120/yr) entitles NASCAR members to drive in several divisions.

Mechanics are also required to hold a license. NASCAR recognizes prior experience from other license holders in high-speed race sanctioning bodies.

Licensing can be earned through the NASCAR ranks. Their Late Model Sportsman, Modifieds and International Sedan permits are 60 to $70. They also offer a permit in Street Stock, Mini-Stock, Mini-Modified and limited Sportsman for around 40 to $50.

DRAG RACING

In high-speed drag racing, the best way to obtain a license is to attend a drag racing professional school. Otherwise what has to be done is to go to the nearest drag racing facility for more specific requirements. You will still need to have an FAA classed III type physical examination by a sanctioning body-appointed doctor. It's the kind of exam that airplane pilots must undergo.

Then the prospect must arrange a series of tests watched closely by a high ranking official. The testing determines how the driver handles the racer in a series of 3 different dragstrip lengths. They may vary from 50 to 60 feet, an eighth mile and a full quarter mile. Usually a prospect is put through the series twice.

There is also the blind orientation test. What that means is a driver must demonstrate an ability to know where all race vehicle cockpit controls are located without looking. This insures a driver keeps their eyes on the road at all times.

To move up in drag racing, the driver will need to obtain another racing license. This calls for further testing of pretty much the same format or procedure as previously described. The runs in these testings may be cut down in number and must be representative of the performance potential of a race vehicle being used at the time. The race vehicle must meet minimum requirements for weight, lengths, etc.

OFF-ROAD-MICKEY THOMPSON ENTERTAINMENT GROUP (MTEG)

All participants are required to have a valid drivers license in the US, Canada or the country where their legal citizenship is. This organization reserves the right to determine whether an entrant has the required driving or riding ability to compete. Entrants under 21 years old, if considered a minor in their name state or province, must also have a minors release form signed by their parents. Otherwise, a waiver is required for those under 18. Fifteen years old is the minimum age for all racers in this kind of racing.

SCORE/HDRA OFF-ROAD

A competitor does not need a racing license in these kinds of vehicles. Your racer will be closely monitored. The driver will need to have a (street) drivers license in their home state. Although high speeds may be attained in this kind of racing, it can generally be handled without any special schooling or orientation. Also the competition isn't confined to a specific road or racecourse and isn't dangerously close to other vehicles, but rather, more in competition against the terrain itself.

LATE MODEL/STOCKCARS (LOCALLY BASED)

The way to get a license for this kind of racing is generally through the ranks of the Sportsmen classes.

Many short tracks, one-quarter to a half-mile have their own Late Model and Sportsmen series. (or classes) As a support series and training ground for late model stock car racing, those Sportsmen classes are called different names by different tracks. They may be termed such things as Sportsmen, Sportsmen Limited, Mini-Stocks and Street-Stocks. It's usually a matter of semantics, and basically with a few exceptions the racecars are the same. The Late Model classes also vary in a few ways. There are as many minute detailed changes among Late Model StockCars as there is short oval race tracks in the US.

Whatever the case, to get a racing license will require that you contact the people at the track. Almost all of these kinds of tracks are family owned. The operation isn't cluttered by size and therefore someone will tell you exactly who you'll have to see about getting licensed for their particular brand of racing. But in most cases, the (local) track will furnish licensing. Of course, they'll honor competition permitts from other sanctioning bodies simular to their form of racing.

ARS (INDY LIGHT), AIS, INDYCAR

By the time you are qualified to even attempt getting a license for this level of racing, you should already know what you'll have to do. Even some of the fans know how the license is obtained. At Indianapolis for example, the famous driver orientations are held at the Speedway in April and May.

They require a racing prospect to pass a

rigid set of tests. But before they are allowed to attempt that, their credentials had better be up with well established racing series or organizations. It will take quite a racing talent to be even given a chance to take this test. In addition to the Indy 500, these orientations are offered prior to most Indy car races. But to be given a chance you'll need experience in Indy Lights, AIS, Trans-Am, Formula Atlantic or any high speed racing. Drivers with experience in Formula 1, 2, 3, 3000, NASCAR or with IMSA will not have as much difficulty getting their license, but they still must take the test. Sprint car drivers are also good candidates for obtaining a racing license in Indy car driving.

Supervision in the testing of the drivers are held under the sanctioning bodies chief steward and his assignees. (which may or may not be other licensed IndyCar drivers) His judgement whether a prospect is ready is final. It's subject to no protests. Also, all driving prospects must pass a CART, FIA or USAC medical examination not prior to December 1st of the year preceding the race event. Drivers with less than two Indy car starts must file as a 'new driver applicant' for a 500 mile race. The cost of applying for a test is around $500.00.

AMA, WERA, MOTORCYCLES

In the AMA (American Motorcycle Association) a rider must be at least 16 to qualify for a racing card or license. Anyone younger, to the age of 7, is eligible in the youth division. The rules have a tendency to change for licensing. The same is true for fees. Generally, a years membership is $20. A lifetime membership is $250. (associate membership, $125)

A racing license holder must also be a member of their district association. In the AMA Amateur divisions riders shall be classified on the basis of participation and achievement at the district level. The highest classification is A, followed by B, C and Novice. One cannot get a license to race professionally until they're classed as 'A.' Then a medical form is required to be filled out and signed by a licensed examiner. An annual license fee of about $100 is turned in with the medical form.

With WERA, the high-speed roadracing organization, membership is $50. You then must complete a motorcycle roadracing school. A resume or display of another sanctioning body competition license may be accepted as proof of ability. Still, new roadracers will need to complete a written exam so they will know and understand the rules. Then some on-track ability must be demonstrated by the rider. That is done after the rider goes through some formal instruction. If a riders ability passes the school instructors standards, a provisional license will be issued. If a Professional Motorcycle School is attended, the WERA rider school still must be completed. (but for $25 instead of $50) The rider then must race in two regional sprint events with the provisional license. Then upon successful completion of the novice permit a license is earned.

In order to upgrade a Pro license to the Expert class, a rider needs to accomplish one of two requirements, finish in the top ten places for points earned at the national level or in the top 5 places for points accumulated in a riders home region.

12 | Get On The Inside

There are people involved with racing who love it solely for what it is. They're not drivers, mechanics, sponsors or crew members. They love this sport, but they're not quite as crazy as those of us who actually race. Do they only like to watch this sport? Apparently not. There are many who serve this sport in such a manner that without them we couldn't race. I'm not talking about those in the sanctioning body offices who work in racing for a living. Of course, they're important, but I'm referring to volunteers. Where would racing be without them? First, we would be paying out much higher entry fees to cover their pay. The race events would have to be limited in how often they're held.

It takes many individuals to safely organize and run a race event. If you would like to get involved with this part of racing, it's pretty easy. The first thing a person needs to do is get in contact with the sanctioning body in their choice of racing. The SCCA is one of the largest sanctioning bodies in the world. For amateur automobile racing, (closedcourse) they would be the logical place to start. In drag racing, the NHRA can direct you where to go. They'll want you to start at the local track level. The motorcycle sanctioning bodies will also require their volunteers to start in the lower level. It's just common sense. Racing volunteers need to learn procedures like drivers need to learn how they must drive.

First a person must be licensed to volunteer their help. (at least in SCCA they must be) You do not have to join the SCCA if you just want to find out what it's like. The procedure is similar to obtaining a race license.

A volunteer receives a log book. They will then choose their most convenient time to attend a Race Workers School. After that is fulfilled the worker chooses four events with which to volunteer their services. After each weekend of work the Chief Steward signs the log book assigned to the volunteer. After four events (all Regional) the volunteer will have a very good idea whether he or she likes this work. If so, they join the sanctioning body, in this case the SCCA, and apply to a Regional executive for their license. That license will be for one of four areas of work:

1. Flagging and Communications (Observers)
2. Starters, Timing and Scoring
3. Scrutineer (Technical Inspector)
4. Race Control (a through s)

Regional workers with experience may move up to National and Pro events. Their licenses must be upgraded.

1. FLAGGING AND COMMUNICATIONS (OBSERVERS)

These are the largest group. They're stationed at assigned areas around the racecourse. The flaggers warn the drivers of track conditions. Stationed with the flaggers are the Observers who report track conditions to the flagger including any racing accidents or misbehavior. These situations are reported to the race control officials usually by the flagger.

Crash teams, tow vehicles or emergency

crews are ready for service upon word from these people. Observers are usually experienced drivers. They know what to look for before a potential incident happens. Their job is very important. They serve as a form of traffic cop for racers who exhibit certain problems, such as smoke blowing from an engine, loose rubber on a tire, trouble ahead, slippery conditions, etc. Sometimes drivers cannot see things such as that from their race machines. Therefore they will be 'black-flagged' into the pits and/or made aware of a problem.

2. STARTERS, TIMING AND SCORING

The starter is usually the most visible race official on the course, especially to the drivers. With the help of roadcourse workers, he controls the start and finish of a race, practice or qualifying sessions.

The timers and scorers use stop watches and sometimes other instruments to keep track of each racer. They usually are located in an enclosed, elevated tower near the start/finish line. They determine who starts a race and where at on the grid. They determine the finishing order at the end of a race.

Sometimes these volunteers run in short supply. It's not hard work but it's important. I've been to races where race officials practically begged for help in the timing tower. Ideally, race officials want one timer for each racecar on the course. With fields as large as 60 or 70 cars, that can be a problem. A timer may have to score two vehicles in one race. Hopefully, the timer can keep track of two vehicles, if not, then inaccuracies take place and the racer may be credited mistakenly with a higher or lower finish. That can get real sticky to the racers who finished in positions which earned points. (or should have earned points)

3. SCRUTINEER (TECHNICAL INSPECTOR)

Not one race car gets on the racecourse without a prior inspection. The Technical Inspector looks for potential problems or rule infractions. Sometimes these poor souls take a lot of complaints from disgruntled drivers, especially in post race impounding. This takes place for a predetermined number of finishers. Usually in SCCA, the top 4 to 6 finishers are impounded. The racecars may be inspected again for legality. If a competitor files a protest against a certain race car, it is impounded. The scrutineer will closely inspect the vehicle again. Usually that involves pulling the heads off a racecar and checking the piston stroke or clearance, valve size and any such internal components.

A situation which vastly improved about 1987-88 is the way a racecar is inspected. The Technical Inspection rules were changed. A racecar now undergoes an 'Annual Technical Inspection' instead of one before every event. What a relief. No more long lines of racecars with nervous drivers wondering if they're going to make it through inspection quickly enough for the first practice session. This means the number of scrutineers needed isn't what it used to be. But the 'Annual Inspection' is much more detailed. If the racecar is involved with contact on the racecourse, it may have to be reinspected, depending on how heavy the contact was.

4. RACE CONTROL (A THROUGH S)

These officials may be found anywhere on the race course, pits, timing tower or garage areas. Usually they are located in the pit and timing tower areas. There are many different types of officials at this level. You can bet these are the people with the most experience.

a. Chief Steward—The Chief Steward is responsible for the general conduct of the race event. They see that the event is operated according to the general competition rules and supplementary regulations. This person is the highest official at a race. They maintain order, safety, official requests for action, receive protests and act as the final authority in all matters.

b. Assistant Chief Steward (Usually 2 per event)—These people help the Chief Steward if the workload becomes too heavy. They're more safety oriented personnel. They provide the safety crew or teams and help organize information for the track physicians and nurses on each driver and their crew.

c. Chief Starter—Many times there is more than one starter at a race. Some help organize the field at the start of a race so everyone is in the right position. Another may drive the Pace car. The Chief Starter flags the start of a session or race. They may turn those duties over to another starter during the race. Some starters may be located at different areas on the racecourse. They are under supervision of the Chief Steward.

d. Chief Course Marshall—They are in charge of the racetrack. They see to it that the track surface is properly prepped (clean) and maintained. They may be assigned other duties by the Chief Steward, such as: proper location of courseworkers, emergency crews, containment of spectators and assignment of clean-up crews.

e. Chief Flag Marshall—This person is responsible for lining up or recruiting, training and assigning corner marshals, flagmen, workers and sometimes the observers.

f. Chief of Communications—They run and control the communications to all corner stations around the racecourse, pit areas, race control building and to pertinent officials. They also train and assign qualified people to operate and maintain the public address and internal communication systems and equipment.

g. Chief Timer and Scorer—They make sure accurate timing and scoring is kept during an event and done so in accordance with the sanctioning body rules. They must also train, assign, recruit and supervise timing personnel. They furnish the Chief Steward and SOM (Steward of the Meeting) any 'times' or results that they may request. They also maintain records of official times and lap charts for all race vehicles. These official results are compiled and published for the benefit of the news media, spectators and raceteams.

h. Chief/Series Technical & Safety Inspector—This person is in charge of the scrutineers. They also conduct inspections at the Chief Stewards request. They are the final authority on technical safety regulations for the race vehicles at a particular weekend event.

i. SOM—Steward of the Meeting—They enforce compliance with the general competition rules. They act in a sort of judicial capacity and settle administrative disputes, which includes any request for action from the Chief Steward. They impose penalties permitted by the rules and appoint substitutes to replace stewards or officials not able to perform their duties. They may also modify regulations and schedules within an event, if necessary.

j. Chief Race Medical Official—This person is assigned with the Chief Course Marshall for the staffing and equipping of the following personnel: medical personnel, (doctors; which the chief race medical official may be) fire fighters, fire trucks, ambulances and wrecker vehicles. They arrange for hospital dispatching and notification of incoming patients. (and routes for the safest and quickest way to transport personnel to the hospital)

k. Chief Observers—They assign all observers and where their position on the course will be. The Chief Observer may be partially directed by the Chief Steward.

l. (Chief) Grid Marshal(s)—These personnel use qualifying times supplied by the timing and scoring officials to align and position racecars on the false grid before they enter the track. They look for any last second (potential) problems on the racecar or with an individual.

m. (Chief) Course Marshal(s)—These personnel are responsible for final preparation and maintenance of the racecourse and any other related duties assigned by the Chief Steward.

n. (Chief) Pit Marshal(s)—These people are in charge of safety and security for drivers and equipment in the garage and pit areas while racers enter and leave these areas during a race.

o. Paddock Marshal(s)—They assist racing teams in parking the racing equipment. They locate any needed services for individuals unfamiliar with the race circuit and facilities.

p. (Chief) Registrar—The registrar accepts and organizes official entry forms, passes and credentials. They are usually the first person or official the drivers, crew and all race course personnel meet upon arrival at the track.

q. Press Officer—Advises officials on any press information and acts as a liaison with the promoter's press director, if one is assigned. Chief officials shall cooperate with this person on matters of public interest.

r. Judges (Optional)—These people assist any stewards on matters of a particular situation, time or place. They're usually assigned by the SOM or Chief Steward.

s. (Chief) Sound Control Judge—This person monitors racing vehicles sound decibel output in accordance with racing rules and/or the town ordinances within where a race is being held.

WHAT YOU SEE IS WHAT YOU GET

As a competitor, you may or may not be aware of these people, but they make life much easier at a racing event. While they may not be seen, without them, a race would be almost impossible, if not chaotic. Other people, besides the ones just mentioned also help organize and prepare an event. In about all cases these arrangements are made months ahead of time. The roles these personnel take may range from running an office of the sanctioning body to policy making, managing, scheduling and responding to matters that need immediate attention. Without volunteers or hired help, a race event won't happen.

For people interested in becoming one of these volunteers or officials, you need to know some of the top positions will take years to reach. Even the Chief Steward at one race event may not be one at another. He may be the SOM or an assistant steward.

In the case of the SCCA, there are eight geographical divisions in the United States. (other sanctioning bodies have their own geographical borders) Each division has an Executive Steward assigned by the sanctioning body or its board. This person is responsible for many things too impractical to list here. The only thing a person in our position needs to know about this person is that they are the person which trains the steward and assigns the jobs of licensing, scheduling, safety, points keeping and making sure compliance with the GCR (General Competition Rules) is followed by everyone. This person is always anxious to recruit and train new men and women.

I would suggest for those who think they might like getting involved with motorsports as a volunteer, to take it at the level which is more locally oriented. Remember, common sense should tell you that you're not getting paid for this. Don't make it burdensome by traveling too far to offer your services. That will cost you money. (unless that's okay to you)

After the volunteer plows through all the procedures, licensing and various stages of participation, they'll find this sport is a very interesting and fulfilling pastime. Afterall, there are many amateur racers out there paying big dollars out of their own wallets to participate in racing. Despite that, they still think this sport's the greatest thing since the wheel was invented. As a volunteer or an official, paying out all that money for equipment is nonexistent. (thank goodness)

You will find there is a lot of fun at these events. (even though they're serious business) But they're even more fun afterwards. In almost all amateur racing, parties and/or "get-togethers" usually take place after the first day of a weekend event. (especially SCCA regional races) That's when all the "bench-racing" begins. (exaggerated, albeit fun, racing stories)

Appendix A: Racing Books

The following books are what I consider more noteworthy reading. All are of more recent technology type. They don't involve racing history, forecasts, driver profiles or personalities. Books of nontechnical type can be easily found in libraries and bookstores. Also, they can be found under the heading 'Racing Publications' in the appendix. (Appendix B)

My goal in this section is to help you obtain technical information. The books marked (*) will be a bit hard to find. It may take some patience and effort. If you can't find a book, the first people to contact is the publisher. So make an effort to know who the publisher is. It would also help to know the author and the year(s) first and last printing.

AUTOMOTIVE RACERS

Auto Race Pages A 282 page book which is very much the ultimate racing source manual for finding racing manufacturers and race oriented service industries. $21.95, 3500 race businesses. 7745 Herschel Ave, LaJolla, CA 92037 or 1-800-858-4388

Bob Bondurant On High Performance Driving (Steve Smith Autosports) This guy has his own racing school. He knows what he's talking about. For road and oval auto racers.

Crewing: The Answer To There's Nothing To Do And I'm Bored by Grace Smith, 1671 Clovis Avenue, San Jose, CA 95124

Fast Women by Lesley Hazleton, 200 pages, $15.00. Addison-Wesley Publishing. 1992. In most bookstores.

*Formula Car Technology by Howdy Holmes and Don Alexander. This is a very interesting book aimed at formula cars from Formula 440 through the ranks to Indycar and Formula One. They talk about costs, parts, tires, setup, engines, driving, safety and more. May be a hard book to find. Steve Smith Autosports used to sell it. I don't think they do anymore. It's worth hunting very hard for.

*Formula Ford Technical Inspection Guide by Frank Schultheis

*Formula Vee/Super Vee Racing History And Chassis/Engine Prep by Andy Schupack, Tab Books, Inc, Blue Ridge Summit, PA 17214 This may be a hard book to find.

Get Ready-Get Set, Get Sponsored-How To Get The Dollars You Need 200 page guide for seeking sponsors. $29.00. RFT/SC, Box 414, Cuyahoga Falls, OH 44222 (216) 928-3606

SCCA Membership Guide A free manual detailing participation as a driver, worker or official in the SCCA. (800) 255-5550 Ext 78

Mini-Sprint/Micro Sprint Racing Technology (Steve Smith Autosports)

Motorsports Medicine, Lake Hill Press, PO Box 190525, St. Louis, MO 63119-6525 (800) 467-2464 Good book on Physical fitness and nutrition for racers.

National Speedway Directory by LL Yard and AE Brown. This is the yellow pages for all racing tracks in the US and Canada. This book tells where they are, the size and type of racecourse, address of promoters, track location and the sanctioning bodies which use them. Phone numbers are available also. I wouldn't recommend this for any Go-Kart type racing except for the roadracer-classed Go-Karts.

Official Karting Directory And Guide Write to: Kart Marketing Association of America, 26 West 237 Grand Avenue, PO Box 101, Wheaton, IL (708) 653-7368, Fax (708) 653-2637. Everything you need to know about Go-Karts. Manufacturers, shops, clubs, and all the tracks nationwide.

Race Car Fabrication And Preparation by Steve Smith (Steve Smith Autosports) Covers in detail the "goings-on" for a StockCar.

Race Car Vehicle Dynamics by William F. and Douglas L. Milliken. 890 Pages. 400 drawings, diagrams, and photos. $85 and $11.50 S & H. The bible on how race machines operate. To get this book write to: SAE International, 400 Commonwealth Dr, Warrendale, PA 15096-0001.

Racers Guide To Sleeping Around by Barb Gullion, 4354 Sheridan Avenue North, Minneapolis, MN 55412 (612) 529-0362. Listings of 50 tracks with locations, lodges in the area, track layout. Directions and services available.

Racers Travel Guide To North American Tracks by Judy Preston, 128 pages, $12.95. Available through Motorsports International (800) 826-6600

Racing School Directory Everything you need to know about getting started in amateur racing by George Anderson. Publisher: Motorbooks International, Osceola, Wisconsin (612) 439-6001

Racing Engine Preparation by Waddell Wilson (Steve Smith Autosports) This book orient at NASCAR-type StockCars.

Sponsorship And The World Of Motor Racing, Cotter Communications, 6525 Hudspeth Rd, Box 900 Harrisburg, NC 28575 (704) 455-3530 $189.00

Sprint Car Technology (Steve Smith Autosports)

Stalking The Motorsports Sponsor by Pat Bentley

(Steve Smith Autosports) A very good book on what it takes to get financial help in racing.

Tax Guide For Racers by Dave Walker (808) 248-5942

The Complete Kart Guide (Steve Smith Autosports) If you get The Official Karting Directory and Guide, then don't get this. It's basically the same book.

The Great Money Hunt by Andrew Waite A very, very good book. To order: NEXZUS Motorsports Marketing, Inc, PO Box 44990, Phoenix, AZ 85064–4990 (or phone) 1–602–957–7220 This is about a 250–300 page, 8-1/2 x 11 sized, soft cover publication packed with info.

The Racers Complete Reference Guide by Bob Landis (Steve Smith Autosports) When ordering this book, ask when the last year it was updated. If it's not been done within 2 or 3 years, you may find alot of outdated addresses in this book. Otherwise, this book has information concerning where to get anything in all forms or racing. (except motorcycles) It's the yellow pages of the racing world. (don't bother with this book if you have the 282-page Auto Racepages)

The Racers Dictionary by Don Alexander and John Block (Steve Smith Autosports) Good book. You'll learn the "lingo" of race talk and get an in-depth look at terms associated with race vehicle handling, suspensions, dynamics, aerodynamics, tires, car construction, geometry and much more.

The Racers Tax Guide by Steve Smith (Steve Smith Autosports)

Tune To Win by Carrol Smith (Steve Smith Autosports)

OFF-ROAD

Off-Road Racing And Riding by Irwin Stamber. G.P. Putnam's, NY. Found at most out-of-school libraries. Lib. of Cong. #J796.7. This is the most complete book in off road racing I've ever read. A bit old, but the information is very accurate.

MOTORCYCLE RACING & COMPETITION

A Twist Of The Wrist by Keith Code, Acrobat Books. A very good book to read before attending his or anybody's bike racing school. Tells techniques of racing.

How To Win in Motocross by Gary Bailey, HP Books, Tucson, AZ Another good book to read on the techniques of racing.

Motorcycle Racing For Beginners IG Edmonds Holt, Rinehart & Winston. NY. Can be found in most out of school libraries.

Motorcycle Racing In America by James Spense and Gar Brown. Good book on the different types of motorcycle racing. Publisher: J. Phillip O'Har Inc, Chicago, IL. Observed Trail, Tourist Trophy, Hill Climbs, Enduro, Oval, Roadracing, Moto and Desert racing.

DRAG RACING

Drag Racing, Drive To Win by Frank Hawley, Motorbooks International.

Appendix B: Racing Publishers

The following is a list of the major publications and wholesalers/retailers. They may sell other kinds of books, but are still big with racing at all levels. If they no longer have a particular book, ask them where you may look further. If that doesn't work, many race shops can help. Also libraries are one of the best ways to track down a book. By the way, if you are looking for a book that teaches bolt to bolt construction, in super detail on how to build your own race vehicle and high-tech engine, don't waste your time looking. They do not exist anymore than one that explains how to build an atomic bomb.

- Acrobat Books
- Chilton Book Company, Chilton Way, Radnor, PA 19089 (215) 964-4729
- Classic Car Club of America, Box 443, Madison, NJ 07940 (201) 377-1925
- Classic Motorbooks, PO Box 1, Osceola, Wisconsin 54020 (800) 826-6600. These people seem to have every technical, historical and romantic racing book ever heard of.
- Clymer Publications, 12860 Muscatine St, Arleta, CA 91331 (213) 767-7660
- HP Books, PO Box 5367, Tucson, AZ 85703 (602) 888-2150. These people do have some racing books, but not too many on the technical stuff. They do have Design And Development Of The Indy Car. It's interesting. There are plenty of historical development, pictures of Indy cars when they first started around 1910 to the middle 80's. You may want to inquire about their catalog.
- EWA Erie Waiter Assoc./Miniature Cars USA, 369 Springfield Ave, Box 188-30 Berkeley Hts, NJ 07922 (201) 665-7811. Specialists in classic, exotic and racing car models—new or obsolete and books on technical, reference and general works in racing.

- Guinness Publishing LTD, 33 London Rd, Enfield, Middlesex, England Good books on racing stats. (can be found in large libraries)
- Motormedia Limited (Eoin Youngs Catalogs On Racing), PO Box E, Horsley, Surrey, England KT245RL Fax 011-44-483-285257
- Motorsports International Publishing Co, R3 Box 45, Sparta, WI 54656 (608) 269-5591 Racing books and journals.
- Peterson Publishing Company, 6725 Sunset Blvd, Los Angeles, CA 90028 (213) 657-5100
- Pyramid Autosports, Box 905, Chanute, KS 66720 (316) 431-7812. Has a dozen or so books oriented towards front-wheel driving performance, modifications on Camaro's, Firebird's, VW, Mazda, MGB and Mustangs.
- Standard Directory of Advertisers by Arli Goldberg (415) 821-1244. Lists more than 21,000 corporations, contact names, phone numbers and advertising budgets. (an expensive book, $295.00) Good book for locating companies for sponsorship. (large, main libraries have this book in most large cities)
- Steve Smith Autosports, PO Box 11631, Santa Ana, CA 92711. Order line - (714) 639-9741. Publisher of numerous racing books on technology, handling, suspensions, building and prep, engines and driving techniques and all automotive racing. (motorcycles excluded) Send for his catalog. He may charge $2.00 for it. He may not.
- Tab Books, Monterey Ave, Blue Ridge Summit, PA 17214 (717) 794-2191
- Twister Racing Setup Books, 425 West Allen #114, San Dimas, CA 91773 (714) 592-1191. Several books on tuning and setup. Call for a catalog.
- Wards Communications, Inc, 28 West Adams, Detroit, MI 48226 (313) 962-4433
- W.W. Norton & Co, 500 Fifth Ave, New York, NY 10110 (212) 354-5500

Appendix C:
Racing Magazines and Newspapers

The following are nationwide and/or local race oriented magazines. Some are hard to subscribe to unless you're a member of a specific racing club. Anyone outside the interest in a type of racing wouldn't have much cause to subscribe anyway. A good example is the SCCA. The in-house magazine for people of this (50,000) membership is SportsCar. It's automatically mailed out monthly to each member. Most, if not all associations and clubs, even on the local and regional level, have some form of publication. The AMA has American Motorcyclist. Not much use to everyone in auto racing, but very valuable to the motorcycle racer. Listed with most publications is their cover price. They are as much as 50 percent cheaper through subscription. You will note in many of these listings I have a small message what the magazine covers and what associations or type of racing it's aimed at. (if its name does not imply that) These are great sources for finding hard to locate companies or specialists. (if that's not possible through local newspapers and yellow page directories) Most, if not many of these magazines can't be found in libraries or on the shelves of retail outlets. You will have to write or telephone them for special information about their periodicals.

- American Motorcyclist, PO Box 6114, Westerville, OH 43081-6114 (614) 891-2425. Official magazine for the American Motorcyclist Association.
- American Race & Road, HC-31 103-B, Midland, TX 79707
- American Roadracing, 14010 Marquardt Ave, Santa Fe Springs, CA 90670. Monthly $20.00/yr. Motorcycle roadracing oriented.
- Area Auto Racing News, Box 8547, Trenton, NJ 08650
- ATV News, PO Box 1030, Long Beach, CA 90801 (213) 595-4753
- Auto Racers Monthly, Box 21447, Reno, NV 89515. $50.00/yr. A very detailed newspaper aimed at auto racing drivers at pro & amateur level.
- Auto Racing Analysis, Box 98, Sewell, NJ 08080
- Auto Racing Digest, PO Box 3765, Escondido, CA 92025-9687. Every 2 months, $1.30
- Automotive Gazette, Box 38355, Houston, TX 77238
- Auto Racing Memories, Box 12226, St. Petersburg, FL 33740 (Vintage oriented)
- Autosport (Eric Waiter Associates), PO Box 188, Berkeley Heights, NJ 07922-9922 (201) 665-7811, (800) 272-2670 outside NJ. Weekly, $3.90. All kinds of pro races in stock and formula classes.

- Autoweek, 965 East Jefferson Ave, Detroit, MI 48207-9975 Weekly, $1.95. Covers mostly Indy, Formula One and Stockcar racing plus the automotive industry in all countries.
- Autoworld, Dept 74, 701 N.Keyser Ave, Scranton, PA 18508
- Behind The Wheel, Box 10564, New Orleans, LA 70181
- British Car, PO Box 9099, Canoga Park, CA 91309 (818) 710-1234 Vintage car and racing oriented.
- Car & Driver, 2002 Hogback, Ann Arbor, MI 48105
- Cars Illustrated, 299 Market St, Saddlebrook, NJ 07662
- Checkered Flag Racing News, PO Box 454, Watertown, WI 53094
- Circle Track, 6725 Sunset Blvd, PO Box 800, Los Angeles, CA 90099-2035 Monthly, $3.25. Covers mostly Indycars and NASCAR.
- Custom Bike, 4247 E. Lapalma Ave, Anaheim, CA 92807 (714) 996-5111
- Cycle News East, 4190 First Ave, Tucker, GA 30084 (404) 934-7850
- Cycle News West, PO Box 498, Long Beach, CA 90801-7433 (213) 427-7433
- Cycle World, PO Box 51222, Boulder, CO 80321-1222 Monthly, $2.25
- Dirt Bike, PO Box 9502, Mission Hills, CA 91395-9963 Monthly
- Dirt Rider, 6725 Sunset Blvd, Los Angeles, CA 90099-2037 Monthly, $2.25
- Dismantler Digest, 1000 Vermont Ave, NW Suite 1200, Washington, DC 20005 (202) 628-4634
- Drag News, 7215 Garden Grove Blvd, Suite 1A, Garden Grove, CA 92641 (714) 893-1317 $15.00/yr. Monthly
- Drag Racing Magazine, 8490 Sunset Blvd, Los Angeles, CA 90069
- Drag Review, PO Box 3029, Hwy 11E, Bristol, TN 37620 Semi-monthly. The IHRA Publication.
- Drag World, 11030 Granada Lane, Overland Park, KS 66211 (919) 649-9010
- Dusty Times, 5331 Derry Ave, Suite O, Agoura, CA 91301. Monthly, $1.25. Off-Road, mostly 4-wheel vehicles.
- Fastlane Racing News, Box 42853, Fayetteville, NC 28309
- Fastrack, 907 E. Franklin Blvd, Gastoria, NC 28054
- Formula Magazine, 2020-L South Susan, Santa Ana, CA 92704 Monthly, $15.00/yr. A good magazine dealing mostly with Formula car racing.

- FOSA (Formula One Spectators Association), 8033 Sunset Blvd, #60, Los Angeles, CA 90046 (213) 658-5884. $50.00/yr. A fact-filled bulletin for each Formula One race, including qualifications, practice, etc.
- Four Wheel and Off-Road, 8490 Sunset Blvd, Los Angeles, CA 90025 (213) 820-3601
- Four Wheeler Magazine, PO Box 2046, Harlan, IA 51593-2266. Monthly, $2.95
- Gator Racing Photo News, PO Box 2187, Syracuse, NY 13220
- Grassroots Motorsports, PO Drawer A, Daytona, FL 32118 (800) 423-1780 Outside Fl, (800) 858-0095 in FL. About amateur and vintage racing.
- Griggs Publishing Company, PO Box 500, Concord, NC 28026
- Hawkeye Racing News, PO Box 601, Vinton, IA 52349
- Hemmings Motor News, Box 256, Bennington, VT 05201. Oriented at vintage autos and vintage racing.
- Hoosier Racing Newsletter, 616 S. Fuller Dr, Indianapolis, IN 46241
- Hot Rod Magazine, 8490 Sunset Blvd, Los Angeles, CA 90069
- Hot VW's/Dune Buggies, PO Box 2260, Costa Mesa, CA 92626 (714) 966-2560. Monthly. Mostly a street magazine on VW's but also covers VW racing cars at times. (Drags, Formula Vee, mostly Off-Road)
- Indy Car Racing Magazine, 6706 W. Fairfield Ave, PO Box 14395, Milwaukee, WI 53213 (414) 774-6291
- Inside Track Racing News, PO Box 190, Hankinson, ND 58041
- Inside Karting, PO Box 2019, Bushnell, FL 33513
- Kanadian Karting, PO Box 14, Mississauga, Ontario L4W 4X9
- Kart Express, 111 East Main St, Sevierville, TN 37862
- Karter News, 4650 Arrow Hwy, Suite B-4, Montclair, CA 91763. Official publication for the International Karting Federation.
- Kart Sport, 5510 Ashbourne Rd, Arbutus, MD 21227
- Kart Tech, PO Box 488, Star, NC 27356
- Kentucky Racing News, 170 Madison, Danville, KY 40422
- Knoxville Dirt Digest, PO Box 458, Knoxville, IA 50138
- Late Model Digest, Box 69, Marble, NC 28905
- Marc Times Racing News, 5845 Mt. Vernon, Kalamazoo, MI 49002
- Maryland Speed News, 1207 Weymouth, Westminster, MD 21157
- Michigan Checkered Flag Racing News, PO Box 157, Springport, MI 49284
- Mid-American Racing News, PO Box 178, Swanton, OH 43558
- Midgets & Motorsports Illustrated, PO Box 8389, Fresno, CA 93747
- Mid-States Racing News, 638 2nd St, Webster City, IA 50595
- Midwest Automotive News, 2900 W. Peterson, Chicago, IL 60659
- Midwest Racing News, 6646 Fairview, Milwaukee, WI 53213
- Mini-Truck, PO Box 2260, Costa Mesa, CA 92626 (714) 966-2560
- Motocross Action, PO Box 9502, Mission Hills, CA 91395-9963
- Motorcycle Road Racer Illustrated, PO Box 498, Long Beach, CA 90801-0498
- Motorcyclist, PO Box 51352, Boulder, CO 80323-1352 Monthly, $2.95
- Motorsports Magazine, PO Box 8389, Fresno, CA 93747
- Motorsports Marketing News, 1448 Hollywood, Langhorne, PA 19047
- Motorsports Weekly, PO Box 1540, Perry, GA 31069
- Motortrend, 8490 Sunset Blvd, Los Angeles, CA 90069
- NASCAR Newsletter, 1801 International Speedway Blvd, Daytona Beach, FL 32015
- National Dragster, 10639 Riverside Dr, North Hollywood, CA 91602 (213) 877-2751. Weekly Publication of the NHRA.
- National Kart News, 51535 Bittersweet, Granger, IN 46530
- National Motorsports News, PO Box 381998, Duncanville, TX 75138
- National Parts Peddler, PO Box 257, Bridgeport, NY 13030
- National Speedsport News (Kay Publishing Co.), PO Box 608, Ridgewood, NY 07451-0608 (201) 445-7674 $25.00/yr. Covers weekly all types of racing automobiles. Some Drag and Off-Road also.
- Off-Road Action News, 9371 Kramer, Unit G & H, Westminster, CA 92683 (714) 893-0953
- Off-Road American, PO Box 21436, Sarasota, FL 33583 (813) 921-5687
- Off-Road Magazine, 12301 Wilshire Blvd, Los Angeles, CA 90025 (213) 820-3601
- Oklahoma Racer, PO Box 57702, Oklahoma City, OK 73157
- Old Car Weekly, 700 East State Rd, Iola, WI 54990
- On Dirt Magazine, PO Box 6246, Woodland Hills, CA 91365
- On Track, OT Publishing, Inc, PO Box 8509, Fountain Valley, CA 92728-9974 All kinds of pro racing. Every 2 weeks, $2.00.
- Open Wheel, PO Box 513, Mount Morris, IL 61054-7978 Monthly, $1.60 Coverage mostly in Sprint cars.
- Orange Blossom Gazette, 7712 Hoosier Pl, Orlando, FL 32807
- Outdoor Power Equipment, PO Box 2250, Radnor, PA 19080
- Performance Racing Industry, PO Box 9327, South Laguna, Ca 92677
- Performance Racing News, 593 Yonge St, Toronto, Ontario M4Y 1Z4
- Quick Times Racing News, Rt #6, Box 233-T, Lincolnton, NC 28092

- Race Car & Driver, 120 E. 34th St, #7K, New York, NY 10016
- Race Parts Merchandiser, PO Box 12031, Kansas City, KS 66112
- Racer, PO Box 25052, Anaheim, CA 92825-5052 Monthly, cover $3.95. Relatively new magazine which features plenty of color photos and feature articles on high profile pro auto racing.
- Racetime Magazine, 1-800-722-3788
- Raceway News, PO Box 12107, Norfolk, VA 23502
- Racing For Kids, Box 500, Concord, NC 28026
- Racing In The Midwest, 3413 Graceland Ave, Madison, WI 53704
- Racing News, PO Box 668728, Charlotte, NC 28266
- Racing Promotion Monthly, PO Box 277, Chanhassen, MN 55317
- Racing Wheels, PO Box 1555, Vancouver, WA 98668
- Racing's Almost Perfect Magazine, 699 Thomas St, Monroeville, PA 15146
- Road & Track, PO Box 51922, Boulder, CO 80321-1922 Monthly, $2.95. For general street car enthusiasts of sports cars: race reports, road tests, technical features and gauging the future.
- Score International News, 2701 E. Anaheim St, Wilmington, CA 90744 (213) 435-2443 Quarterly in-house publication of the SCORE sanctioning body.
- Southern Motorracing, PO Box 500, Winston-Salem, NC 27102
- Speed Age Magazine, 3615 Victoria Ave, Oxnard, CA 93030
- Speedway Scene, 50 Washington, PO Box 300, North Easton, MA 02356
- Sportscar International, PO Box 1529, Ross, CA 94957 Monthly
- Sportscar Magazine, 9033 E. Easter Place, Englewood, CO 80112 Monthly, $2.95. Official publication of the SCCA. Covers in detail pro and amateur racing (results) in SCCA sanctioned events.
- Sports Illustrated For Kids, 1675 Broadway, Rockefeller Ctr, NY, NY 10019
- Sports Parade, 1720 Washington Blvd, Box 1010, Ogden, UT 84404
- Sprintcar, PO Box 500, Concord, NC 28026
- Stockcar Magazine, PO Box 511, Mount Morris, IL 61054-7982 Monthly, $3.00 Big with NASCAR.
- Stockcar Racing Magazine, PO Box 2218, Alexandria, VA 22301 (703) 836-6106 Monthly, $15.00/yr. Covers racing personalities and technical news in stockcar racing.
- Stopwatcher, 4522 Amherst Lane, Bethesda, MD 20814
- Sunbelt Racing News, PO Box 4849, Huntsville, AL 35815
- Super Stock, PO Box 512, Mount Morris, IL 61054-7980 Monthly, $3.00
- Super Stock And Drag Illustrated, 6728 Eton Ave, Canoga Park, CA 91303
- Texas Racing News, PO Box 101, Abbott, TX 76621
- The Altemate, PO Box 239, Grantville, PA 17028
- The Wheel, PO Box 1203, Pleasanton, CA 94565
- Three & Four Wheel Action, PO Box 9502, Mission Hills, CA 91395-9963 Monthly, $2.75
- Three-Wheeling Magazine, Box 2260, Costa Mesa, CA 92626
- Tri-State Auto Racing News, 567 N. Main St, Greensburg, PA 15601
- Victory Lane Magazine, 2460 Park Blvd, Suite 4, Palo Alto, CA 94306-9826 (415) 321-1411 Monthly, $4.00, Vintage car oriented.
- Vintage Motor Sports, Box 2895, Landland, FL 33806
- Wisconsin Fans For Auto Racing, PO Box 13563, Milwaukee, WI 53213
- World Karting, PO Box 2548, North Canton, OH 44720 (216) 499-0454 Monthly, $23.00/yr. Official magazine for the World Karting Association.

Appendix D:
Racing Schools

- Aintree Racing Drivers School, 1 Fairoak Court, Whitehouse, Runcorn, Cheshire WA7 3DX, United Kingdom, 0928-712877 (Formula oriented)
- Akin-White, 4320 W. Osborne Ave, Tampa, FL 33614-6926 (813) 874-5944 (800) 966-5944 (They use Porsche 944 and 945 Showroom Stock vehicles)
- American Racing School, PO Box 629, Carmel Valley, CA 93924 (800) 722-7223 (Formula oriented)
- American School of Motor Racing Inc, 434 East 56th Ave, Denver, CO 80216 (303) 297-2751 (You can use your own car; also an Indycar program)
- Aspen School Of Auto Racing, Box 6788, Snowmass Village, CO 81615 (800) 554-6960 (Use the SCCA 'Spec Racer')
- Autopian Motorsports Country Club at the Las Vegas Motor Speedway, 4461 W. Flamingo, Suite 168 Las Vegas, Nevada 89103 (702) 644-7223 Wide variety of Formula and Sedan racing programs.
- Bertil Roos Indystyle Race School, Pocono Inter. Raceway, Blakeslee, PA 18610 (800) RACE-NOW (Formula Ford 1600 and 2000 oriented)
- Bill Scott Racing, 1420 Spring Hill Rd, McLean, VA 22101 (703) 893-3992 (For anti-terrorist training driving techniques)
- Bill Tempero's Indy Car School, 1421 Webster, Fort Collins, CO 80524 (303) 484-1990 (Training for AIS Indycar series)
- Billy Pauch Driving School, 611 Hwy 519, Frenchtown, New Jersey 08825, (908) 996-7278 (Asphalt or Dirt Modified oriented)
- Bob Bondurant School Of High Performance Driving, 29355 Arnold Rd, Somona, CA 95476 (800) 446-1444 in CA (800) 336-7223 Outside California. (Formula and GT Stock car oriented)
- Bob Cornish Enterprises, 375 Convention Way, Unit 6, Redwood City, CA 94070 (415) 364-0806 (More individually orient towards any kind of racer)
- Brett Hearn Racing School, PO Box 1175, Vernon, New Jersey 07462 (201) 702-0811 (Dirt Modified oriented)
- Bridgestone Racing School, RR#2, Shannonville, Ontario, Canada K0K 3A0 (613) 969-0334 (Formula and roadcourse GT oriented)
- BSR Driving Training, PO Box 190, Summit Point, West Virginia 25446 (304) 725-6512 (Sedan oriented)
- Buck Baker Driving School, (located) at North Carolina Motor Speedway, Rockingham, NC 28379 (919) 582-2861 (Oval Stockcar oriented)

- California Drag Racing School, PO Box 901690, Palmdale, California 93590-1690 (Mostly Gas Dragster oriented)
- California Superbike School, PO Box 3107, Hollywood, CA 90078 (213) 484-9323
- Carfello Kart Racing School, 23 N. Farview, Paramus, NJ 07652 (201) 845-6333
- Car Guys, 4721 Starkey Road, Suite 212, PO 21275, Roanoke, VA 24018 (703) 772-1517 (Use your own car at this school)
- Carlisle Racing School, 15933 Chandler, E. Lansing, MI 48823 (517) 351-1097 (For Go-Karts)
- Chris Birkbeck International Rally School, Manx Lodge, Low Farm, Brotton, Saltburn, Cleveland Ts12 2QX, United Kingdom Tel-0287-77512
- Circuit Scene LTD., Pembrey Circuit, Pembrey, Dyfed SA16 0H2, Wales, United Kingdom, Tel-0554-891455 (Mostly Formula oriented)
- Cloverleaf Mini-Indy Drivers School, c/o Logic 440 Race Cars, Inc, 30447 Lorain Rd, North Olmsted, OH 44070 (216) 631-1777 (One of the very few schools that use the Formula 440)
- Club 89, 1-3 Friars Lane, Bury St. Edmunds, Suffolk IP33 L00, United Kingdom, Tel-0284-760528 (Use your own racer)
- Competition Engineering, PO Box 1554, Oakwood, GA 30566 (404) 409-1554 (One of the more diverse schools with customized programs in several types of racecars)
- Dale Walkers Holeshot Performance Motorcycle Drag Racing School, 311 Chestnut St, Santa Cruz, CA (408) 427-3625 or 427-0299
- Danny Collins Racing School, 1626 Albion St, Denver, CO 80220 (303) 388-3875 (Formula and Sports-Car oriented)
- Derek Bell Precision Driving School, PO Box 11912, Fort Lauderdale, FL 33339-1912 (305) 561-2881 (Individually oriented using your race machine or car)
- Dirt Track Racing School, (located) at Lincoln Pk Speedway, US Hwy 40, Putnamville, IN 46170 (317) 653-3485 (or Mike Clayton (317) 545-7157) (Sprint-Car oriented)
- 'Do It Your Way' Winged or Non-winged Sprint Car Driving School, Paragon Speedway, Route 1, Box 32, Paragon, Indiana 46166 (317) 537-9326
- Donnie Hansen Motocross Academy, 1418 Plumeria, San Antonia, TX 78232 (512) 494-6019
- Drive It All Ltd., Enstone Business Park, Church Enstone, Oxon OX7 4NP, United Kingdom 0608-

678339 (Rally car oriented, but some Off-road, Quad bikes and 4 wheel-drives)

- Donnie Moran Racing Driving School, 4325 Fawn Drive, Dresden, Ohio 43821 (614) 754-2299 (Late Model Stockcar oriented)
- Drivetech, 12121 Wilshire, Suite 1003, Los Angeles, CA 90025 (800) 678-8864, (310) 826-8864 (Oval and roadcourse racing with Trans-Am racers)
- Driving Dynamics, 25 Bridge Ave, Red Bank, NJ 07701 (201) 870-3222, (800) 225-3479 (More street-oriented for non-high performance driving)
- Elf Winfield-Franan Racing, Inc, 1409 South Wilshire Dr, Minnetonka, MN 55343 (612) 541-1380 (Formula orient and also held in France.
- Fast Company, PO Box 151, Greencastle, IN 46135 (317) 653-2532 (SpecRacer used here)
- Fast Lane Racing School, PO Box 2315, Rosamond, CA 93560 (805) 948-4448 (formerly an off-shoot of Willow Springs International Driving School) Courses in street and competitive driving.
- Fast Track High Performance Driving School, Dept. CT-03, PO Box 160, 5243-B Morehead Rd, Harrisburg, NC 28075-0160 (704) 455-1700 (High speed Oval Stockcar oriented)
- Finish Line Racing School, 3113 South Ridgewood Ave, Edgewater, FL 32141 (904) 427-8522 (Short Oval track Stockcar oriented)
- Florida LEGENDS Driving School, Bill Borden, (904) 257-0414
- Ford Advanced Drivers School, PO Box 35523, Browns Bay, Auckland, New Zealand, (09) 486-4775 (Ford sedan oriented)
- Forest Experience and Rally School, Carno, Montgomeryhire, Wales SY17 5LU Great Britain, 0786-420201
- Frank Hawleys Drag Racing School, PO Box 140369, Gainesville, FL 32614 (904) 373-7223
- Gary Bailey Motocross School, PO Box 130, Axton, VA 24054 (703) 650-3030
- Go 4 It Driving School, 713 Grant Ave, Louisville, CO 80027 (303) 666-4113 (Both bike and car oriented)
- Golden State Kart Racing School, 10019 Genesta Ave, Northridge, CA 91325 (818) 772-6881 (Sprint-type Go-Kart oriented)
- Grand Prix Promotions Performance Driving School, PO Box 507, Mead, CO 80542 (303) 535-4255 (Formula and Sedan Stockcar oriented)
- High Performance Driving School, RR#1, Blackstone, Ontario L0B 1B0 (416) 985-9741 (This growing school uses Corvettes)
- Jean-Paul LUC Winter Driving School, PO Box 774167, Steamboat Springs, CO 80477 (303) 879-6104
- Jim Hall Kart Racing School, 1555-G Morse Ave, Ventura, CA 93003 (805) 654-1329
- Jim Russel Racing School, 1023 Monterey Hwy, Salinas, CA 93908 (408) 372-7223 (One of the biggest and most diverse; several locations; open all year)

- Jimmy Sills School of Open Wheel Racing, 2435 Morrence Dr, Placerville, CA 95667 (916) 622-5493 (Sprint and Midget racer oriented)
- John Watson Performance Driving Centre, JWPDC Rally Centre, Silverstone Circuit, Northants NN12 8TN United Kingdom 0327-857788 (SportCars, Rally and Formula)
- Knockhill Racing Circuit, by Dunfermline, Fife, KY12 9TF Scotland, 0383-622090 (Karts, Rally cars, Formula, Sedan oriented)
- Levolant Racing School, 11958 Lagauchettere East, Montreal, Quebec H1B 2K2 (514) 645-6372 (Canadian school oriented towards Formula racing)
- Lou D Agastino Driver Anatomy 101, 3733 NW 16th Street, Suite B, Lauderhill, FL 33311 (305) 583-1533 (Mechanical oriented for Formula racecars)
- Mid-Ohio School, Truesports Inc., 4355 Davison Road, Hilliard, OH 43026-2491 (614) 876-3354 (Very diversified with several very interesting programs, with 'big-name' instructors)
- Midwestern Council of Sportscar Clubs Drivers School, c/o Ross Fosbender, 1476 S. Winston Dr, Palatine, IL 60067 (708) 359-0204 or 358-8673 (Any racecar may be used by student)
- Mike Baldwin Hi-Performance Riding School, PO Box 3446, Noroton, CT 06820 (203) 656-2107 ("Riding" means motorcycle oriented)
- Mini-Stock Racing School, PO Box 420543, Kissimmee, FL 34742 (407) 933-1820 (Small stock racer, sedan-type oriented)
- Motion Dynamics, Route 16, PO Box 2245, Conway, NH 03818 (603) 447-3543 (Roadcourse oriented)
- Motorcycle Roadracing Association, Inc Riders School, PO Box 4187, Denver, CO 80204 (303) 789-2429 (More of a sanctioning body-styled school)
- Motorquest International Hi-Performance Driving School, 16661 Pine Blvd, Pembroke Pines, FL 33024 (305) 437-2506 or 7 (Go-Karts, Formula and GT oriented)
- Motorsports Training Center Inc, 604 Performance Rd, Rt 3, Mooresville, NC 28115 (704) 664-1784 (Race mechanics and construction oriented)
- Michiana Raceway Park Racing School, 120 Stone Ave, Lake Forest, IL 60045 (708) 234-6357, (800) RACECAR. (Go-Kart school)
- MXK Raceway & Driving School, 800 Bullis Rd, Elma, NY 14059 (716) 674-9494 (Go-Karts)
- NASTRAK (Richard Petty Driving School), 1150 Ivey Cline, Concord, NC 28027 (704) 784-8310 (High-speed oval Winston-cup styled Stock Cars)
- Nissan School of Performance Driving, RR #2, Ameliasburg, Ontario K0K 1A0 (613) 962-5588 (Canadian school designed mostly for sedan-styled roadcourse racers)
- North Motor Sport (not a true school in the traditional sense) Las Vegas Speedway, Las Vegas, NV (310) 866-2334
- Oregon Motorcycle Road Race School, PO Box 6388, Portland, Oregon 97228 (503) 284-7793 (High speed motorcycles)

- Outlaw Driving School, 5411 South Cockrell Hill Rd., Dallas, TX 65236 (214) 331-4664 (Sprint car oriented)
- Paul Smith's Drag Racing School, 800 NE Third, Boynton Beach, FL 33435 (407) 738-0864 (Top Fuel and Funny car oriented)
- Penguin Roadracing School, 223 Franklin St, Mansfield, MA 02048 (508) 339-9645 (For motorcycle racing)
- Performance by Ken Brown, Project Industries, 8549 Lake St, Omaha, NE 68134 (402) 391-3558 (More individually oriented using any racer you provide; or their own Mustangs)
- Performance Driver Association, 75 Madison Ave, Clifton, NJ 07011 (210) 773-4200 (Diversified for street or roadcourse racing, using your machine)
- Performance Driving School 4600-A Middle Dr, Youngstown, OH 44505 (216) 759-1868 (Bring your own racer or use the GTP-styled school race machine)
- Performance Motorsports Kart Racing School, PO Box 12571, Columbus, OH 43212 (614) 294-5020
- Peter Gethin Driving Courses Ltd., Goodwood Motor Circuit, Chichester, West Sussex, PO 18 OPH United Kingdom 0243-778118 (Formula and sedan oriented)
- Phil Price Rally School, 27 Crooked Well, Kingston, Herefordshire HR5 3AF England 0544-230026
- Pitarresi Motorsports Inc, Portland Inter. Raceway, 1940 N. Victory Blvd, Portland, OR 97217 (503) 285-4449 (Sedan-styled Stockcar oriented)
- PM/KZM, 2087 McClaren Lane, Cleveland, OH 44147 (216)-566-5752 (Go-Kart and SpecRacers)
- Pro-Motion Advantage Innovators, 489 Putnam Ave, Cambridge, MA 02139 (617) 547-7459 (Winged and non-winged Sprint cars)
- Race Ready Driving School, PO Box 7, Fortville, IN 46040 (317) 485-4497 (Open wheel Modified oriented)
- Reg Pridmore's Class Motorcycle Safety School, 1495-B Palma Dr, Ventura, CA 93003 (800) 235-7228 (For not so speed oriented prospects)
- Reynard Fiscus Track Rider School, PO Box 3020, Culver City, CA 90231 (800) 729-1819 (For more experienced motorcycle racers)
- Richard Petty Driving Experience, 6022 Victory Lane, Harrisburg, NC 28075 (704) 455-9443 (basically an off-shoot of the NASTRAK school listed earlier)
- Richard Wilson Kart Racing Drivers School, Dunelm, Knox Mill Close, Killinghall, Harrogate, North Yorkshire, HG3 2AG, United Kingdom, 0423-567497 (Sprint Karts)
- Right On Track, Inc., 80 Bond St, Elk Grove Village, IL 60007 (708) 956-4755 (SpecRacer, various SportsCars and Sedan racing oriented)
- Road Atlanta Driver Training Center, 5300 Winder Hwy, Braselton, GA 30517 (404) 967-6143 (Sedan-styled using Nisson 300ZX machines)
- Rod Hall Off-Road Driving School, RHI Motorsports, 340 Western Rd #1, Reno, NV 89506 (702) 786-9922 (For Off-Road racers)
- Roy Hills Drag Racing School, PO Box 70, Marston, NC 28363 (919) 582-3400
- SCCA National Racing School, 14570 E. Fremont Ave, Englewood, CO 80112 (303) 693-2111 (A newer and better form of a sanctioning body school)
- S+G Super Kart Racing School, 36 North Buena Vista, Redlands, CA 92373 (714) 335-2846
- Skip Barber Racing School, Route 7, Canaan, CT 06018 (203) 824-0762; California School (800) 722-RACE (One of the biggest; also Formula oriented; but very diversified)
- Southard School, PO Box 1810, New Smyrna Beach, FL 32170 (904) 428-3307 (Short-track StockCars)
- Speed Zone Racing School, PO Box 3913, Riverside, CA 92519 (909) 686-3069 (For Sprint Go-Kart racers)
- Sportbike Hawaii Riding School, 2646-B Kilihau St, Honolulu, Hawaii 96819 (808) 836-BIKE (Motorcycle oriented)
- Start Racing School, 2721 Forsyth Rd, Suite 466, Winter Park, FL 32792 (407) 678-6531, (800) 243-1310 (For Go-Karts)
- Stephens Racing Inc, 2232 Snogales, Tulsa, OK 74107-2826 (918) 583-1136 (SCCA SpecRacer)
- Team Suzuki Endurance Advanced Riding School, PO Box 964, Guasti, CA 91743 (714) 674-0552 (Motorcycle)
- Team Texas High Performance Driving School, 3700 Ace, Houston, TX 77063 (713) 977-5066 (Winston-cup styled StockCars)
- Terry Ives Driving School, 7707 Ginger Blossom Drive, Citrus Height, CA 95621 (916) 725-6776 (Go-Karts)
- Tom Browns Motor Racing Drivers School, 40 Clydeford Rd., Cambuslang, Glasgow G72 7JF, Scotland, 041-641-2553 (Rally, Formula, Kart racing oriented)
- Tony D Motocross School, 428 W. Maple St, Hazleton, PA 18201 (717) 454-1973
- Track-One, c/o Hot Shoe Racing, PO Box 1321, Watermill, NY 11976)516) 725-0888 (Mostly Formula Ford & Continental oriented)
- West Coast Drag Racing School, PO Box 903085, Paledale, CA 93590 (805) 944-2593, (800) 272-DRAG
- Willow Springs International Driving School, PO Box X, 3500 75th St, West, Rosamond, CA 93560 (805) 256-2471 (Roadcourse racing using the SpecRacer or Toyota Celicas)

Appendix E:
Race Car Rentals

These companies rent various classes of race cars. Practically all of them are formula car oriented. There are also the SportsRacers, such as the SpecRacer and Sports 2000, which are popular vehicles to rent. I am limiting this to the lower or amateur levels of racing. To rent such vehicles as an Indy Car, Formula One or an IMSA GT racer would be completely impractical here. Yes, almost all big-name racecar drivers rent their "rides." Of course it's big money and under circumstances completely different than in the amateur ranks. The big-time renters don't really take just anybody's money and then fit them into their equipment. It's much more complicated than that. Actually, they go out or pursue certain proven, well-established drivers. It's not like a driver hands someone like Roger Penske 5.5 million dollars and says, "There's my money, fit me in for 16 Indy car races this year!" It just doesn't work that way. At the amateur level it is a bit easier to rent rides, but don't necessarily expect to have a "cakewalk" through the process. Those renting out racers will want to know the kind of individual they're dealing with too. There are some exceptions, but the general rule is to display some respect for other peoples equipment. You'll need to get in contact with these companies to find out what they require. Don't forget to shop around, but try to stay as close to home as possible. That will help contain the costs, assuming you race close to home. (within 200 miles) Many of these renters will coach or help you, especially if you're a beginner. This is done, usually, on an informal basis.

This coaching, guiding or whatever you want to call it, is done by the crew provided with the race machine to protect both the renter and the equipment, which also keeps costs in line. Some addresses and all phones are provided with a listing of the type or kind of racing vehicle provided. To find out the 'make' or manufacturer of a particular vehicle rented out by these companies, you will need to contact them. If you're a beginner, I wouldn't be overly concerned about the 'make' of a race vehicle you rent until you've got some races "under your belt." (and a couple of years, or about 10-16 races)

No Go-Kart rentals are listed here. They can be found in the Official Karting Directory and Guide at most libraries or through the KMA. (Appendix A) The listings for Go-Karts is so plentiful, you're much better off checking what's available in your geographical area. You will also find out, most renters are in the racing parts and components business also.

- Abel Motorsports Inc, 1044 Industrial Dr, Unit 5, W. Berlin Industrial Center, Berlin, NJ 08009 (609) 753-0074. Swift FF and Sports 2000.
- Apache Racing, Florida (813) 521-2832. Sports 2000
- BP Racing, North Carolina (704) 697-1717 Formula Ford 1600 & 2000
- Carl Haas Automobile Imports, Inc, 500 Tower Pkwy, Lincolnshire, IL 60029 (708) 634-8200 Reynard FF 1600 & 2000 and other makes of FF. Sports 2000. (same person who rents the Lola Indy Car)
- Compreent Motor Sports, Inc, 123 Inverness Rd, Athens, GA 30606 (404) 543-1797 Rally cars
- Continental Crossle, 9000 Debbie Dr, Westchester, OH 45069 (513) 777-4545 Crossle Formula Ford and Formula Continental.
- Daytona Renoo, Daytona Beach, FL (904) 252-3903 SCCA SpecRacer
- East Anglia Motorsports Ltd, 2921-A Gibbon Rd, Charlotte, NC 28213 (704) 597-5300 or 596-3735 SCCA SpecRacer
- East Coast Racing, Pennsylvania (717) 564-0973 FF1600-2000
- Elite Auto Sport, Illinois (303) 923-2499 SCCA SpecRacer
- Essex Racing Inc, 2350 Industrial Pk Blvd, Cumming, GA 30130 (404) 889-4096 Formula Ford, Vandiemen Formula First, Formula Forward.
- Euro-Motorsports, 20720 Tuck Rd, Farmington Hill, MI 48336 (313) 477-5353 or 476-1463 Swift Formula Ford
- Eurosport Ltd, 1855 W. Union Ave B-3, Englewood, CO 80110 (303) 789-2545 SCCA SpecRacer
- Executive Auto Sport, 247 N. 3rd St, Easton, PA 18042 (215) 559-9232 Swift FF2000 (in Pro Canadian Series, Walter Wolf) Club Ford, Formula Ford 1600, Formula Continental.
- Gee Bee Racing, 1 800-Race GBI, Formula 440
- GRA Motorsports, 14176 Fennbury Dr, Tampa, FL 33625 (813) 264-1391 SCCA SpecRacer
- Hi-Tech Racing, CA (818) 442-7515 Formula Fords
- International Racing Systems, 2203 E. Harrisburg Pike, Middletown, PA 17057 (717) 944-4368 Formula Ford
- Kevin Whitesides Enterprises, Inc, (314) 442-1279 Sports 2000, Formula Ford, Atlantic, Continental and SCCA SpecRacer.
- Koll Motorsports, Huffaker Racing (707) 935-0554 GTP racers

- Levolant Racing, 11958 Rue Lagauchettere Est, Montreal, Quebec H1B 2K2 (514) 645-6372 Crossle Formula Ford
- Lockwood Auto Enterprises, Inc, 127 Chestnut St, Hazelton, PA 18201 (717) 455-6071
- Martin Donney Motorsports, Inc, 800 Morrison Rd, Blacklick, OH 43004 (614) 861-3300, (800) 444-4213 SCCA SpecRacer, Shelby Can-Am
- Martini USA Racing Cars, Illinois (312) 520-9888 Formula Continental
- Midwest Sports Racing Inc, 503 N. Jackson, Papillion, NE 68046 (402) 331-7715 SCCA SpecRacer
- Motion Dynamics, PO Box 2245, Rt 16, Conway, NH 03818 (603) 447-3543 (800) 426-5879 SCCA SpecRacer
- Pacific Race Service, 144 W. Whisman Rd, Unit D, Mountain View, CA 94041 (415) 964-6301 Crossle Formula Ford and Formula Continental.
- PBS Engineering, 11602 Anabel St, Garden Grove, CA 92643 (714) 534-6700 SCCA SpecRacer
- Performance Development & Racing, Colorado (303) 934-5401 Formula Ford, Atlantic and Continental.
- Performance Motor Works, 54 W. Longview Ave, Columbus, OH 43202 (614) 263-6128 SCCA SpecRacer
- Performance Unlimited, 18407 Van Owen St, Unit H, Reseda, CA 91335 (818) 996-7477 SportsRacers, Showroom Stock, Formula's.
- Phillips Motorsports, Oregon (503) 661-0800 ARS, Formula Atlantic, Sports 2000.
- P-One Racing, California (714) 498-7272 Formula Atlantic and Ford, Sports 2000.
- Prather Racing Inc, 37 Sherwood Terrace, Suite 31, Lake Bluff, IL 60044 (708) 234-5241 S2000, FF.
- Prep To Win, 1951 Catanna Ave, Baltimore, MD 21227 (410) 477-6128 SCCA SpecRacer, Formula Vee.
- Pro Formula, California (916) 635-0604 Sports 2000
- Race Spec, Georgia (404) 475-0637 F Production and GT-5.
- Racing Dynamics, California (213) 806-4766 Sports 2000
- RF Racing, Minnesota (612) 831-3201 or 454-2718 Formula Ford

- RIC Racing, New Hampshire (603) 224-9264 Formula Ford
- Royale, USA, Rt 1, Box 520, Niawassee, GA 30546 (404) 896-2446
- Sandy Dells Racing, (619) 758-4510 Formula Atlantic and Ford.
- South Shore, 405-3 Bloomfield D, Berlin, NJ 08009 (609) 751-3633 Swift Formula Ford, S-2000.
- Sports Racing Services, 1205 East New York St, Indianapolis, IN 46202 (317) 636-3883 SCCA SpecRacer
- Sports 2000 Racecars, California (714) 870-1023 S2000
- Speedstar Motorsports, 7999 Hansen, Suite 309, Houston, TX 77061 (713) 941-1025 SCCA SpecRacer
- Texas American Race Team, 1201 East 2nd St, Ft. Worth, TX 76102 (817) 332-1884 SCCA SpecRacer, CSR.
- Texas Sports Racing, 112 Malibu West, Willis, TX 77378 (409) 588-4696 or 856-5872 SCCA SpecRacer
- Three-D Sports Inc, (213) 372-1738 Formula Atlantic
- Toad Hollow Racing, California (415) 229-4294 Showroom Stock B
- TRP, Inc, 1471 Hwy 51 N. Covington, TN 38019 (901) 476-3724 SCCA SpecRacer
- TR Raceservice, California (415) 964-6301 Formula Ford 1600 & 2000.
- Valley Racing Specialist, 5256 Grand Ave, Glendale, AZ 85301 (800) 448-7224 Competition cars & equipment for all levels of racing.
- Vestal Race Cars Ltd, 139 W. Wilson St, Suite 110, Madison, WI 53703 (608) 767-3306 Swift FF & S-2000.
- Weld Motorsports, Orlando, FL (407) 896-8030 Formula Continental and Ford.
- Windstar Racing, Indiana (317) 298-8928 Formula Continental, SCCA SpecRacer.
- Wynnfurst Ltd, Wisconsin (414) 893-0288 S2000, C & D SportsRacers.
- Zephyr Racing, California (707) 935-0525 Formula Continental, Sports 2000.

Appendix F:
Sanctioning Bodies & Associations

These are the main, larger and nationally known racing associations or sanctioning bodies. You may notice one or two familiar associations excluded. This is not a mistake. Some of these organizations have ceased operations. Many of these you probably never heard of, especially the regionally-based ones. There are quite a number of organizations for Off-Road, Go-Karts, Motorcycles and Late Model Stockcar racing at the regional and/or local track level. These small organizations could fill up a small book and cannot be listed here for practical reasons. But most organizations listed here could tell you who and where they are. If not, they can be found by going to a large city library and referring to their collection of city phone directories. To find a small racing organization would only require you to look under the heading of 'Racetrack,' 'Racing Associations' or 'Automobile races.'

This Appendix (F) is subdivided down to the following categories:

a. Large, High-Profile Sanctioning Bodies
b. Regional Auto Associations
c. Motorcycle Associations
d. Off-Road Associations
e. Vintage Associations

To those familiar with the larger well-known sanctioning bodies, like SCCA, the different Pro Series are commercially named. Example, the 'Camel' GTP in IMSA & the 'PPG' (Pittsburgh Plate & Glass) Indycar World Series. Those are the well-established sponsors. But too often, the Pro Series sponsors change (yearly) which creates confusion, especially in the less-profiled Pro classes. Because of this phenomenon, in about 90 percent of the cases, I will refer to specific series by their generic, sanctioning body series name.

LARGE, HIGH-PROFILE SANCTIONING BODIES

- ACCUS (Automobile Competition Committee Of The United States), 1500 Stokie Blvd, Suite 101, Northbrook, IL 60062 (708) 272-0090 An International governing body for most auto racing in the US. It's affiliated with the FISA.
- AIS (American Indycar Series), 1421 Webster Ave, Fort Collins, CO 80524 (303) 484-1990 A yearly 8 to 10 race series for Indycars no older than 10 years.

About 1/2 of the races are on short, 1/2 mile ovals. The other half are on 1 to 2.6 mile roadcourses. Look for this series to grow, including races on larger ovals. (if the IRL flops badly)

- AMA (American Motorcyclist Association), PO Box 6114, Westerville, OH 43081-6114 (614) 891-2425 The largest motorcycle sanctioning body in the United States. They directly sanction professional and amateur motorcycle competition at national and regional levels. (and in conjunction with smaller regional/local associations) Pro events are the 9-10 race schedules of the Superbike, Pro-Twins and the Supersport series, all scheduled at the same weekend and location. AMA sanctions one each of the International FIM World Championship and FIM World Superbike Championship series held in the US. At the amateur level is the Championship Cup Sprint Series (AMA/CCS) of about 20 classes in street-type motorcycles. It composes about 90 events in 11 regions distributed throughout the continental US. They also sanction the following series: 9-10 race National Championship Enduro events; a 17-18 event Camel Pro Series in short dirt track races; a 4 event Daytona Dirt Track Series; a 6-8 race Hare & Hound National Championship Series; a 7-9 event Hare Scrambles National Championship; 6-race National Reliability Trails Championship Series, (this serves as a qualifying series for the US team at the International 6-day Enduro); 1 or 2 events each of ice racing and hillclimbs; a 8-10 event Observed Trials Championship Series; 2 event Grand Prix schedule (combination paved & dirt roadracing in one); and a 25-30 professional Motocross/Supercross schedule. The AMA also sanctions over 100 quadcycle (4 wheel ATV) events.
- ARCA (Automobile Racing Club Of America), PO Box 5217, Toledo, OH 43611 (313) 847-6726 Somewhat affiliated with NASCAR. Main series for stockcars is the Permatex Super Car Series. They race 17-18 races on both short & super speedway tracks, occasionally as a NASCAR support race. They also sanction Midgets, Late Models (Detroit, MI, Toledo, OH area) and 'Figure-8' racing.
- ARS/Indy Lights (American Racing Series), 1395 Wheaton Ave, Suite 700, Troy, MI 48083 (313) 528-3470 Overseen by CART. These cars are almost identical to Indy cars, but are down-powered. These usually run as a support-race at all CART, non-500 mile events. 14-15 events of 75 miles each on large roadcourses.

- ASA (American Speed Association), 202 South Main St, Pendleton, IN 46064 (317) 778-2105 Association for mostly shorttrack high profile stockcars.
- Automobile Club of L'OEST (ACO), Race organizer for the FIA sanctioned World Endurance Race of Lemans 24 hour event.
- Canadian Association of Stockcar Auto Racing, 257 Manitou Dr, Kitchener, Ontario, Canada N2C 1L4 (519) 893-7071 Kind of a NASCAR north of the border.
- CART (Championship Auto Racing Teams), 390 Enterprise Court, Bloomfield Hills, MI 48013 (313) 334-8500 Sanctions the highest-profile racing in the US with 2 or 3 events in Canada. They are beginning to move more races to other countries. Look for a race in South America soon. The 15-18 race schedule is for very sophisticated Formula racers which reach well over 200 mph on large ovals. (about one quarter of their schedule) The other three-quarter are ran on smaller 1-mile ovals and 2-mile roadcourses. These racecars biggest event is the Indianapolis 500, but it is still overseen by USAC. (United States Auto Club) CART also oversees the Indy Lights (ARS) which usually is a support event in non-500 mile races. (a dozen or so races yearly)
- CASC (Canadian Auto Sports Clubs), 693 Petrolia Rd, Downsview, Ontario M3J 2N6 (416) 667-9500 This is one of (if not) the largest sanctioning body in Canada. They are very diversified. Sort of the SCCA of Canada. See the SCCA description later in this appendix and you will have a pretty accurate idea of what amateur classes of racing they sanction. The professional races they sanction isn't quite as diverse as SCCA, but do sanction the 'Walter Wolf' series, a 9-10 race schedule for Formula (Ford) 2000.
- CIK, World governing body for Go-Karts, based in Paris, France.
- CRA (California Racing Association), 1606 Briarvale Ave, Anaheim, CA 92805 (714) 535-8762 Professional series for SprintCars in the western US.
- FCSA (Federation Canadenne Dusport Automobile), French version of CASC. Overseer of all Canadian racing.
- FIA (Federation Internationale De L'Automobile), Paris, France. A voluntary association of auto clubs from about 70 countries to promote automobiles and motorsports internationally. Had more direct sanctioning at prototype styled 'Group C' racing series on a worldwide basis. (called the World Sports Car Championship, which died out in 1992) This series always seems to be unstable. Look for it to rise up again under a different name. FIA also has more direct control over International rally events and most international automobile racing.
- FIM (Federation Internationale Motorcyclist), Geneva, Switzerland. The International organizing body for motorcycles and motorcycle sporting events. More directly sanctions 14-16 event World Championship and Superbike series; 4 events each of Formula One & Endurance motorcycle events.
- FISA (Federation Internationale Du Sport Automobile), 8 Place De La Concorde, 75008 Paris, France Telephone 011-33-1-42-65-99-51 A "leg" of the FIA which is the most race-oriented and somewhat oversees International racing events such as Formula One. (and Indycars to a certain extent, since they now race in Brazil, Canada, Australia and eventually Mexico, if not Britain, sooner or later)
- HDRA (High Desert Racing Association), 12997 Las Vegas Blvd S, Las Vegas, NV 89124 (702) 361-5404 Associated with SCORE, (Short Course Off-Road Enthusiast). They sanction 4 races out of eight in a high-profile desert Off-Road Series in the western US desert. HDRA also sanctions a (couple of) closed, shortcourse Off-Road events. (about 16 classes in HDRA)
- IHRA (International Hot Rod Association), PO Box 3029, Bristol, TN 37625 (615) 764-1165 They sanction 9-12 major Drag racing events, mostly in the eastern half of the US, in 5 pro categories: Top Fuel, Nitro Funnycar, Pro Stock, Alcohol Funnycar and Pro Modified. Also 8 amateur categories: Factory Modified, Top Sportsman, Modified, Quick Rod, Super Rod, Hot Rod, Super Stock and Stock. (amateur categories breakdown to well over 200 classes) IHRA also sanctions a 8-9 Drag Bike series in the following categories: Funny Bike/Top Fuel, Top Fuel/Harley, Pro Competition, Pro Stock and Sportsmen Eliminators. IHRA brackets both auto and motorcycle racing. These people are a bit more amateur racing oriented compared to NHRA.
- IKF (International Kart Federation), 4650 Arroy Hwy, Suite B-4, Montclair, CA 91763 (714) 625-5497 One of the two major Kart sanctioning bodies in the US. Offer classes by weight, engine style and driver age for 11 regions in Canada and the US. The high-speed (up to 140 mph) Enduro category takes place on paved, 2-plus mile roadcourses in 17 classes, for 12 yr and older drivers. Two more categories they sanction is 2-cycle Sprint races on smaller roadcourses (up to 60-70) and 2-cycle Speedway on 1/8 or 1/4 mile ovals. Both have about a dozen classes. The last 2 categories is also the slower 4-cycle and dirt types. Each have about a dozen classes also. IKF is more dominant in the western half of the US.
- IMSA (International Motor Sports Association), PO Box 10709 Tampa, FL 33679-0709 (813) 877-4672 Two championship divisions of Prototype automobiles are sanctioned in a 10-15 race schedule. (Prototypes are somewhat similar to Formula racers, purpose-built for racing and rear engine powered) These are the most sophisticated and fastest of Sportcars. (200 mph range) In addition to GTP & GTP Light are the following support racing divisions racing the same 10-15 race schedule: GTO/GTU are GT cars based on high performance street production vehicles; Supercar for International mid-sized sports sedans; Firehawk endurance street stock category in 3 classes: Grant Sports, Sports and Touring; GTS, for American-built cars with V-6 or V-8

engines; and the Barber-Saab Formula Pro Series, IMSA's only open-wheel racing class. Some of these racers (GTP & GTP Lights) run a lengthy race. (for example, the 24 hrs of Daytona) Up until a few years ago, IMSA was suffering a sort-of 'mid-life' crisis. (as opposed to growing pains) Their main racing classes (GTP, GTO etc) were completely revamped, so to speak. The main classes are now called 'World Sports Car, with further WSC-eligible divisions called GTS-1 and GTS-2

The Supercar series has now been dropped and replaced by the Slick 50 Pro Series for WORLD SPORTS RACERS. (don't confuse this with WORLD SPORTS CARS) These WSR racers are for all intents and purposes, Sports 2000 machines.

- IRL (INDY RACING LEAGUE) 4910 W. 16th Street, Speedway, IN 46224 (317) 247-5151 This is the new 5-race series developed by Indianapolis Motor Speedway president Tony George. Right now it's embroiled in a heated controversy with CART. To make a very long story short and perhaps over-simplified, the idea of this new oval series is to take the outrageous costs out of IndyCar racing. (puts this type of racing back to the drivers foot, not his wallet) What has CART drivers upset is the twenty-three or so Indy 500 positions reserved for IRL (regular) participants. CART drivers feel they are being locked out. Therefore, this year will be the 1st time another IndyCar race will be held at the same time as the Indy 500. It will be called the US 500 and will be held at MIS. (Michigan International Speedway) The better drivers will be there. Whether all this IRL-CART mess will be solved within the next couple of years will depend mostly on which the fans support exclusively. Personally, I think they both can exist together, but I'm not real keen on all those qualifying positions being reserved for IRL regulars. IRL, if you haven't noticed by their address, is located within USAC. (United States Auto Club) Basically, the IRL race machines do not look any different than the CART versions. But, their engines are not as strong and expensive. They will go with stock-block engines of V-8 configuration and race only on ovals. (which I believe IndyCars should race on all the time)
- KIC (Karting Industry Council), 19819 Orchard St, South Bend, IN 46637 (219) 272-0252 A business-end oriented association for finding Go-Kart equipment and accessories. These people do not sanction any racing events.
- MTEG (Mickey Thompson Entertainment Group), PO Box 25168, Anaheim, CA 92825 (714) 938-4100 Sanctions 6 classes of close-course (stadium) off-road events: Sport Truck, Super 1600, Ultrastock, 4-wheel ATV, Superlites and Ultra Cross. All but the Trucks and ATV's are basically Dune-Buggy styled racers. Most events are professional.
- NASCAR (National Association For StockCar Automobile Racing), PO Bin K, Daytona Beach, FL 32015 (904) 253-0611 Largest and most well-known Stock-Car type association in the world. Sanctions a 28-32 race schedule for full length StockCars (Grand Na-

tional) and for smaller powered Stock Cars. (Baby Grand) They are Winston Cup Grand National and Busch Grand National, respectively. NASCAR also sanctions some modified racing and the very popular SuperTruck series.
- NHRA (National Hot Rod Association), PO Box 5555, Glendora, CA 91740-0750 (818) 914-4761 Currently, the largest sanctioning body in the world. Sanctions major pro categories on a 14-18 race schedule throughout the US. Major pro categories are; Top Fuel, (fastest racers in the world) Funny Car, Pro Stock, Pro Stock Motorcycle, Alcohol Dragster, Alcohol Funnycar and Super Gas. The number of amateur categories and classes are similar to IHRA. (see IHRA, further back)
- PKA, (Professional Kart Assn), PO Box 105, Edison, CA 93220
- SCCA (Sportscar Club Of America), 9033 East Easter Place, Englewood, CO 80112 (303) 694-7222 Currently the 2nd largest racing association in the US with 110 local chapters. Six major categories of amateur racing in eight geographical divisions of the US at both the National and Regional levels. (1) Showroom Stock; classes GT, A,B,C. (2) Grant Touring (GT); classes 1 thru 5. (3) Production; classes E through H. (4) Sports Racing; classes Sports 2000, C Sports, D Sports and 'Spec Racer'. (5) Formula; F. Continental (very similar to the now defunct Super Vee), F. Atlantic, Club Ford, F. Ford 1600, F. Ford 2000, (same chassis as Formula Ford 1600 but with 2000 cc motors and wings) Formula Vee and Formula 440. (6) Improved Touring; classes A, B, C, S, and AS. National classed events (about 55-60 per year) race for points for the right to participate in a 8-9 day National Championship event usually held in October at Road Atlanta in Georgia. (now held at the Mid-Ohio Sports Complex near Lexington, Ohio) Regional classed events (about 150-200 per year) race for division points. (no national champion)

SCCA Pro racing includes the following 9 classes: (1) 14-15 race schedule for Trans-Am (popular form of roadcourse stockcar racing similar to the amateur level GT 1) (2) World Challenge, 9-10 race series for high-performance street cars like Corvette, Lotus Esprit, Mazda RX-7. (A,B,C,D-divisions) (3) American Continental, 8-10 race schedules for Formula Ford 2000. (a sort of replacement for the now defunct Super Vee Series) (4) Atlantic Series, (Toyota Atlantic) 13-14 race schedule for a stronger version of a FF2000 similar to Indy Light racecars. (5) Oldsmobile Pro Series, 8-12 race schedule for Sports 2000 racecars. (6) American City Racing League, almost the same as the Oldsmobile Pro Series but uses a smaller engine. (7) Shelby Can-Am, not the original Can-Am. That died years back. This is a newer and less expensive form of it. (8-9 races) (8) Formula Mazda and (9) Barber-Dodge, both very similar to FF2000 or F. Continental. (basically, more commercially supported)

The SCCA also sanctions 2 kinds of Solo racing (on a specified racecourse against the clock) Solo I is the pro level. Solo II is amateurs in 4 categories; (1) Stock classes, 1 thru 7. (2) Street Prepared, 1 thru 4. (3) Prepared, 1 and 2. (4) Modified, 1 and 2. (don't confuse this with circle track modified racecars, such as the ones in NASCAR) Solo also have men and women divisions. An Overall champion is determined in both. SCCA also sanctions Solo for trucks. SCCA also sanctions Rallies of two types, Road and Pro. Road is run on public streets at less than highway speeds. Pro is high-speed, off-public-road, 12 to 16 hour events at both national and divisional levels in 3 classes: Open, Production and Production GT. (similar to SCORE off-road racing, but do not compete in the desert, but rather in forest or parks. Drivers are not allowed to know the course until just before the race) SCCA also sanctions vintage racing in several classes similar to regular SCCA Regional Racing and has sanctioned the FIA US Gran Prix. (Formula One)

- SCORE (Short Course Off-Road Enthusiast), 31125 Via Colinas, #908, Westlake Village, CA 91362 (818) 889-9216 In very close association with HDRA, which sanctions a high-profile series in Off-Road. SCORE sanctions 4 of 8 national races, including the most famous Off-Road event in the world, the BAJA 1000. There are 24 classes; 10 dune-buggy type automobiles, 6 trucks, 6 motorcycles and 2 types of 4-wheel ATV's. SCORE also sanctions 1 or 2 non-series events of closed-course type. (usually at Phoenix International Raceway in Arizona)
- WERA (Western-Eastern Roadracers Association), PO Box 21960 Hilton Head Island, South Carolina 29926 (803) 681-9372 Largest sanctioning body for high-speed roadracing motorcycles in the US. Sanctions series with AMA and other smaller associations of roadracing class. (total over 200 racing events)
- World Karting Association, 10184 Cleveland Ave, NW, Box 2548, Canton, OH 44720 (216) 499-0454 One of the two major sanctioning bodies for Go-Karts. Very similar to IKF. They sanction Enduro (Roadracing) in 17 classes. Also dirt racing: 2 dirt 4-cycle series of 12 classes each and 2 Sprint series of 13 classes each. WKA is more dominant in the eastern half of the US.
- World of Outlaws, 1701 N. Greenville, Suite 1112, Plano, TX 75023 (214) 424-2202 Sanctions a heavy schedule of winged SprintCar racers throughout the US.
- United 4-Wheel Drive Association, 2119 South Birch St, Denver, CO 80222 (303) 753-1464 (United States) Off-Road
- United 4-Wheel Drive Association, Box 2013 Sechelt, BC, Canada V0N 3A0 (604) 885-7438 These two associations publish newspapers for those interested in Off-Road activities. (there are hundreds of Off-Road local clubs; further ahead in this appendix) These 2 United 4-Wheel Drive Organizations are the people to contact if you're interested in forming your own Off-Road events. (Canada)

- USAC (United States Auto Club), 4910 West 16th Street, Speedway, IN 46224 (317) 247-5151 Sanctions racing in the following types: (1) one race, Gold Crown Series, (but it's the biggest single day sporting event in the world) the Indianapolis 500, (for Champ Cars, as sometimes called) (2) Silver Crown Series of about 20 races in the midwestern US for Sprint cars, (3) 2 regions of Midget Car racing (National and Western Series) of 35 to 50 races each per season, (4) Three-Quarter Midgets on a schedule of 28-33 races, almost all held in California, (5) Late Model Stock cars on a very limited schedule, (sometimes only one race per year) (6) Supermodified, only on a special events schedule of one, (like late models) (8) USAC also oversees the special Pikes Pike Hill Climb event held once a year. (no longer sanctions Championship Dirt Car racing; a different and longer form of SprintCar racing) USAC also helps sanction, with the SCCA, the US Formula Ford 2000 series. These FF2000 machines help support high-profile events for NASCAR, CART, IRL, IMSA and TRANS-AM.

REGIONAL AUTO ASSOCIATIONS

The following are smaller and/or regionally based racing organizations, of automotive, closed-course racing. (many work with larger sanctioning bodies)

- ACO (Automobile Club De L'oest Circuit Des "24 Hevres"), 72040 Lemans, Cedex 19, France (Tel. 011-33-43-72-50-25). Works closely with FIA in sanctioning the world famous 24 hours of Lemans Endurance race.
- All Pro Racing Association, PO Box 9099, Prattville, AL 36067 (205) 365-2154
- American City Racing League, PO Box 3420, Sunnyvale, CA 94088 (408) 752-8650. SCCA sanction suborganization for Sports 2000 pro racing.
- American Midget Racing Association, 659 Berry St, Toledo, OH 43605 (419) 241-5754
- American Three-Quarters Midget Racing Association, PO Box 314, Cedar Knoll, NJ 07927 (201) 267-9524
- ARTGO, PO Box 355-D, Libertyville, IL 60048 (312) 362-8833 A stock car series of short track oval racing in the midwest region.
- IIRA (International Ice Racing Association) Six events in January and February in Minnesota and Wisconsin using smaller, relatively unsophisticated stock automobiles. (there are other ice racing associations in Michigan, New York, Alaska and Canada)
- IMCA (International Motor Contest Assn), PO Box 601 Vinton, IA 52349 (319) 372-4713 Modified racing
- IROC (International Race of Champions), 45 Park Rd, Tinton Falls, NJ 07724 (908) 542-4762 This organization is a consolidation of USAC, CART, NASCAR and IMSA for the purposes of staging a 4 to 5 event Late-Model type racing series, (series for-

merly with Camaros) now using Dodge Daytonas, to determine the best driver in the US. (in theory)

- National Midget Racing Association, 6132 McKnight Dr, Lakewood, CA 90713 (213) 867-0414
- Pikes Peak Auto Hill Climb Associate, 135 Manitou Ave, Manitou Springs, CO 80829 (719) 685-4400 Works with USAC in this once-a-year special event.
- Pro Vee Association, DRE, (708) 213-1515. A professional Formula Vee series throughout the midwest of 8-10 races.
- RCCA (Race Car Club of America), 166 Elm St, New Rochelle, NY 10805 (914) 636-9233 An East Coast based Pro Formula Ford 1600 series of 7-8 races.
- SCORE/Canada, 390 Chemin Du Lac, Lery, Quebec, Canada J6N 1A3 (514) 692-6171, 692-8887 Canadian wing of Off-Road racing.
- TAC (Toyota Atlantic Championship), 190-A Skokie Valley Rd, Highland Park, IL 60035 (708) 831-0919 Helps in the SCCA sanctioned Pro Atlantic series for formula car type racing.

MOTORCYCLE ASSOCIATIONS

The following are small regional and/or local motorcycle competition associations throughout the United States and Canada.

- AFM (American Formula Motorbike), PO Box 2088, Menlo Park, CA 94026 (415) 796-7005 7-8 race series for Formula bikes all at Sears Point Raceway in Somona, CA.
- AHRMA (American Historical Racing Motorbike Association), 265 Morris, Morgantown, WV 26505 (304) 291-2253 4 Motorbike Vintage series: 2 race Vintage Trails, 7-8 Roadracing Vintage series, 4 National Class Motocross series; and a 8-11 Regional Motocross series.
- American All-Terrain Vehicle Association, PO Box 1522, Westerville, OH 43081 (614) 891-2491 An organization for off-road motorcycle events very closely associated with the AMA. They are located in the same home base as the AMA, in Westerville, OH.
- AMRA (American Motorcycle Racing Association), (708) 250-0838 10-12 event Harley Davidson Drag Race series held mostly in midwest and northeast US.
- ARRA (American RoadRacers Association), (805) 966-5700 or 256-2471 10-12 1000 cc Gran Prix Motorcycle Roadracing series all held at Willow Springs Raceway in Rosamond, CA.
- ATA (American Trailriders Association), (213) 259-8631 9-11 Observed Trial competition series all held in California.
- Black Jack, (405) 340-7478 9-11 event Enduro series held mostly in Oklahoma, but also in Arkansas.
- BRA (Bakersfield Racing Association), 5001 N. Chester, Bakersfield, CA 93308 (805) 323-7877 Points series in Speedway Motorcycles, Quads and Dune type buggies, in amateur and pro, all held at Bakersfield Raceway in California.

- CMA (Canadian Motocross Association), (416) 363-9035 2 event Supercross series in Toronto and Montreal.
- CRA (612) 332-4070). 5-6 Motorcycle roadracing series all held at Brainerd International Raceway in Minnesota.
- CRC, 37045 Ran Dr, Palmdale, CA 93550 (805) 272-8889. Vintage racing motorcycles.
- Dragbike USA, (315) 735-1661 A 12-14 National Championship Drag racing series held mostly in the southern and western US.
- ECEA (East Coast Enduro Association), 1380 Rt 70, Browns Mills, NJ 08015 (609) 893-7294. 18-20 Event motorcycle Enduro series mostly held in New Jersey and PA.
- FMC, (904) 225-0241 7-9 event Motocross series held mostly in Florida, but also in Georgia.
- FTR, (407) 269-1920 3 events each of Hare Scrambles and Enduro series.
- Golden Crown of Baja, (818) 340-5750 Motorcycle Off-Road Desert series of 4 events held in Mexico.
- Gran Prix De Baja, (818) 340-5750 4 event motorcycle Desert series in Mexico.
- HRRA (Hawaii RoadRacers Association), (808) 836-2453 12-14 event Sprint Roadracing series all held in Hawaii.
- ICE (International Championship Events), PO Box 18233, Tucson, AZ 85731 (602) 299-0206 Ice racing held indoors for motorcycles and ATV's.
- IDBA (International Drag Bike Association), (205) 849-7886 7-9 event Drag series for motorcycles.
- Mid-South, (615) 331-1475 2 event Hare Scrambles series in Tennessee.
- Missouri Hare, (314) 291-7091 11-13 Championship series events in Hare Scrambles in Missouri, except 1 or 2 events held out of state.
- Motocross Northwest Winter Series, (503) 928-4474 8-10 events split between Washington and Oregon.
- MRA (Mountain Racing Association), (303) 789-2429 10-12 Motorcycle Road Racing series all held in Colorado.
- NESC (Northeast Super Cross), (413) 772-0685 25-30 event championship Motocross series mostly held in Massachusetts. (but also Maine, Connecticut)
- NETRA (Northeast Enduro and Trail Riders Associations), (203) 875-5757 12-14 events each of Enduro and Hare Scrambles in New England area. (also a 12-14 Turkey Run series)
- NMA (National Motocross Association), PO Box 46, Norwalk, CA 90650 (213) 868-8112 About 30 classes (half for kids) in Mini and Gran Prix Motocross including Mini and Gran Prix events in Las Vegas, Nevada.
- OCCRA (Oklahoma Cross Country Racing Association), (405) 632-3370 Motorcycle Off-Road series of 7-9 events in Oklahoma.
- OMRRA (Oregon Motorcycle Road Racing Association), (503) 221-1487 4-6 event Road Racing series held at Portland International Raceway in Oregon.

- RMEC (Rocky Mountain Enduro Championship), (307) 742-4136 6-8 events in Enduro held mostly in Colorado.
- SETRA (Southeast Enduro and Trail Riders Association), 2447 Denture Dr, Gainsville, GA 30506 (404) 532-6832 4-5 event Enduro series and 2 events in Hare Scrambles in the deep (coastal area) south.

OFF-ROAD ASSOCIATIONS

The following are regionally or semi-regionally controlled Off-Road and Rally Associations. Some of these associations control smaller local clubs.

- ADRA (American Desert Racing Association), PO Box 34810, Phoenix, AZ 85067 (602) 252-1900
- Alberta 4-Wheel Drive Association, PO Box 65, Station T, Calgary, Alberta T2H 2G7 (403) 252-3027
- All-Terrain Desert Racing Association, 27814 Sycamore Creek, Valencia, CA 91355 (805) 254-2758
- All Terrain Racing Association, PO Box 494, Apple Valley, CA 92307 (619) 247-2527
- American Motor Sports Association, PO Box 5473, Fresno, CA 93755 (209) 439-2114
- American Sand Racing Association, PO Box A, Rancho Cugamonga, CA 91730 (714) 980-3226
- Arizona Desert Racing Association, 1408 East Granada Rd, Phoenix, AZ 85006 (602) 252-1900
- Arizona State Association of 4-Wheel Drive Clubs, 2221 E. Decatur, Mesa, AZ 85203 (602) 962-4175
- Associated Blazers of California, PO Box 1432, Norwalk, CA 90650
- Badgerland VW Club, Inc, 5913 Fond Du Lac Rd, Oshkosh, WI 54901 (414) 688-5509
- Baja Promotions Ltd SA, PO Box 8938, Calabasas, CA 91302 (818) 340-5750
- Bonneville Off-Road Racing Enthusiasts, PO Box 1583, Ogden, UT 84402 (801) 627-2313
- Brush Run Series, PO Box 101, Crandon, WI 54520 (715) 478-2115 or 2688
- California Dept of Parks & Recreation, PO Box 2390, Sacramento, CA 95811 (916) 322-9619
- California Off-Road Vehicle Association, 5518 Colorado Dr, Concord, CA 94521 (415) 672-8278
- California Rally Series, 14550 Dos Palmas, Victorville, CA 92392 (619) 241-4707
- Centerline Racing Series, 3564 Techny Rd, Northbrook, IL 60062 (312) 869-2434
- Champlain Valley Racing Association, PO Box 332, Fair Haven, VT 05743 (802) 265-8618
- Colorado Association of 4-Wheel Drive Clubs, 2395 Wadsworth Blvd, Lakewood, CO 80215 (303) 238-1727
- Colorado Hill Climb Association, PO Box 9735, Colorado Springs, CO 80932
- CORVA (California Off-Road Vehicle Association), 1601 10th St, Sacramento, CA 95814 (800) 237-5436 Not a race association, but rather an organization dedicated to preserving land to insure continued Off-Road racing.

- East Coast 4-Wheel Drive Assn, Inc, 1324 Muhlenberg St, Reading, PA 19602 (215) 374-3468 (C/O Chip Schaich)
- FORDA (Florida Off-Roaders Drivers Assn, Inc), 1717 Marker Road, Polk City, FL 33868 (813) 984-1923 or (305) 823-4487
- Four-Wheel Drive Assn of British Columbia, 12967-107A Ave, Surrey, BC V3T 2G6 (604) 588-2462
- Fudpucker Racing Team, 250 Kennedy, #2, Chula Vista, CA 92011 (619) 427-5759
- Glen Helen OHV Park, PO Box 2937, San Bernardino, CA 92406 (714) 880-1733
- GORRA (Georgia Off-Road Racing Assn), Box 11093 Station A, Atlanta, GA 30310 (404) 927-6432
- Great Lakes 4-Wheel Dr Assn, 915 South Zeeb Rd, Ann Arbor, MI 48103 (313) 665-0358 or 996-9193
- Great Plains Off-Road Racing Assn, 2233 N. 140th Ave, Omaha, NE 68164 (402) 496-9431
- Great Western Points Series, Inc, 12840 Dexter St, Thornton, CO 80241 (303) 452-4013
- High Plains Off-Road Racing Assn, 3503 Hall St, Rapid City, SD 57702 (605) 342-0331
- Indiana Off-Road Assn, 3937 Willow, Hobart, IN 46342 (219) 942-2800
- IOK Four Wheelers, PO Box 36, Cleves, OH 45002
- IRA (Ice Racing Assn of Wisconsin), 370 Linnerude Dr, Sun Prairie, WI 53590 (608) 837-9857
- Larana Desert Racing, PO Box 33, Glendora, CA 91740 (818) 963-9609 or (714) 924-2226
- Michigan Sport Buggy Association, 742 E. Roosevelt Rd, Ashley, MI 48806 (517) 838-4483
- Midwest 4-Wheel Drive Assn, 3318 Howry St, LaCrosse, WI 54601 (608) 783-1187
- Midwest Off-Road Baja Series, 1421 Lee Trevino D-1, El Paso, TX 79936 (915) 594-8266
- Midwest Sand Drags, 9801 East Hwy 80, Odessa, TX 79765 (915) 561-5222
- Montana 4X4 Assn Inc, 215 South 5th, Bozeman, MT 59715 (406) 587-4132
- MORE, 3523 Jim Wright Fwy, Ft. Worth, TX 76114 (817) 625-8841
- M/Tax Enterprises, PO Box 6819, Burbank, CA 91510 (818) 768-2914
- National Assn of Mini-Truck Owners, PO Box 563, Mt. Baldy, CA 91759 (714) 596-5612
- National Mud Bog Assn, PO Box 2364, Glendale, AZ 85311 (602) 842-1405
- Northeast 4-Wheel Dr, Assn, Inc, Box 65, Middlefield, CT 06455
- Ontario Assn of Off-Road Racers, Box 688, Bancroft, Ontario K0L 1C0 (613) 332-3811 or 1610
- Ontario Off-Road, RR #2, Tiverton, Ontario N0G 2T0 (519) 368-7874
- Outlaw Mini Stock Racing Assn, PO Box 204, Palos Verdes Estates, CA 90274 (213) 375-4570 or 719-7036
- Outlaw Racing Association, 330 Orange Show Ln, San Bernardino, CA 92408 (714) 824-3791
- Pacific Northeast 4-Wheel Dr Assn, 946 18th, Longview, WA 98632 (206) 577-0111

- Periscope Productions, PO Box 5652, Orange, CA 92667 (714) 639-3911
- Pro American-Canadian Off-Road Racing, Box 323, Seahurst, WA 98062 (206) 242-1773
- Rocky Mountain Off-Road Racing Assn, 1507 East 5th St, Pueblo, CO (303) 544-6663 or 597-8239
- Sareea Al Jamel 4-Wheel Dr Club, PO Box 526, Indio, CA 92202
- SCAT, Inc, PO Box 277, Morrisonville, NY 12962 (518) 561-3208 or 236-7897
- Short Track Off-Road Enterprises (STORE), 2620 West Washington, W. Bend, WI 53095 (414) 334-3858
- Silver Dust Racing Assn, PO Box 7380, Las Vegas, NV 89125 (702) 459-0317
- SNORE (Southern Nevada Off Road Enthusiasts), PO Box 4394, Las Vegas, NV 89106 (702) 452-4522
- Specialty Equipment Market Assn (SEMA), 11540 E. Slauson Ave, Whittier, CA 90606 (213) 723-3021 or 692-9404
- Superior Off-Road Dr Assn, 7839 W. North Ave, Wauwatosa, WI 53213 (414) 257-0422
- Texas Off-Road Grand Prix, 1606 Lancelot Circle, Grand Prairie, TX 75050 (214) 855-2232
- UORRA (United Off-Road Racing Assn.), PO Box 211, Dunellen, NJ 08812 (201) 752-0299 or 359-2745
- Utah Assn of 4-Wheel Dr. Clubs, Inc, PO Box 20310, Salt Lake City, UT 84120 (801) 250-1302
- VORRA (Valley Off-Road Racing Assn.), 1833 Los Robles Blvd, Sacramento, CA 95838 (916) 925-1702
- Wheel To Wheel, Inc, PO Box 688, Dept 4WOR, Bancroft, Ontario K0L 1C0 (613) 332-1766
- WOR Racing Assn (Western Off-Road), 19125 87A Ave, Surrey, BC V3S 5X7 (604) 576-6256

VINTAGE AUTO ASSOCIATIONS

- ANRA (American Nostalgia Racing Assn), Limited to Top Fuel Dragsters of 60's vintage & 200 in. max wheelbase.
- ASRA (Arizona Sports Racing Assn), 4446 East Shomi St, Phoenix, AZ 85044 (602) 893-3463
- CARE (Classic Automobile Racing Enthusiasts), 3010 SW 14th Pl, Unit 12 & 13, Boynton Beach, FL 33435 (407) 738-6677
- CARS (Classic Auto Racing Society), 1321 Beryl St, #306, Redondo Beach, CA 90277 (213) 374-5783
- CHR (Chicago Historic Races), 825 W. Erie St, Chicago, IL 60622 (312) 829-7065

- CSRG (Classic Sports Racing Group), PO Box 488, Los Altos, CA 94023 (415) 948-2857
- CVAR (Corinthian Vintage Auto Racing), PO Box 232, Addison, TX 75001 (214) 661-9030
- Highlands Classic, PO Box 1652, Highlands, NC 28741
- Historic Sportcar Racing, LTD, PO Box 550372, Atlanta, GA 30355 (813) 931-5642
- HMSA (Historic Motor Sports Association), PO Box 30628, Santa Barbara, CA 93130 (805) 966-9151
- MBHR (Meadow Brooks Historic Races), 4140 S. Lapeer Rd, Pontiac, MI 48057 (313) 373-2500
- MVP (Mountain View Promotions), PO Box 3704, Littleton, CO 80161
- NLRC (Nelson Ledges Road Course), 3709 Valcamp Rd, Warren, OH 44484
- Palm Springs Vintage GP, 330 East Sunny Dunes Rd, Palm Springs, CA 92264 (619) 320-9008
- PVGPA (Pittsburgh Vintage GP Assn), PO Box 2243, Pittsburgh, PA 15230 (412) 3737-8440
- RMVR (Rocky Mountain Vintage Racing), 61 Golden Eagle Ln, Littleton, CO 80127 (303) 933-1207
- SCCA—Vintage, 9033 East Easter Place, Englewood, CO 80112 (303) 694-7222
- SOVREN (Society Of Vintage Racing Enthusiasts), 18820 SE 42nd St, Issaquah, WA 98027 (206) 641-3551
- SVRA (Sportscar Vintage Racing Assn, Inc.), 2725 W. 5th North St, Summerville, SC 29483 (803) 871-3430
- VARA (Vintage Auto Racing Assn), 3426 North Knoll Dr, Los Angeles, CA 90068 (213) 874-9135
- VARAC (Vintage Automobile Racing Assn of Canada), 3300 Yonge St, Suite 202, Toronto, Ontario M4N 2L6
- VMR (Vintage Motorcar Racing), 1800 Market St, #20, San Francisco, CA 94102 (415) 364-8855
- VRCBC (Vintage Racing Club of British Columbia), 5898 Crescent Dr, Delta, BC V4K 2E9 (604) 946-1545
- VSCCA (Vintage Sports Car Club of America), 170 Wetherill Rd, Garder City, NY 11530 (914) 234-6494
- VSCDA (Vintage Sports Car Driver Assn), Box C, 15 W. Burton Place, Chicago, IL 60610 (312) 787-7838
- VSCR (Vintage Sports Car Racing), 8108 115th Lane North, Champlin, MN 55316 (612) 427-9416
- WHRR (Waterford Hills Road Racing), 4770 Waterford Rd, Clarkston, MI 48016 (313) 493-3493
- WMCVG (Walter Mitty Challenge Vintage Group), PO Box 550372, Atlanta, GA 30355 (612) 471-0497

Appendix G: Race services

This section of the entire appendix involved areas which may be put under different headings. But these are more specialized services. There is not a big market for them, such as the insurance companies, who mostly insure race tracks and racing events. Because of these circumstances, it's important to let racers know who these people are and what they offer.

RACE INSURANCE COMPANIES

- Cooper, Love & Jackson, 1804 Hayes St, Nashville, TN 37203 (800) 274-1804 Track insurance, both on and off, including transportation of race cars to a track.
- Heacock Insurance Agency, Lakeland, FL (813) 646-6641 High limits insurance for vintage or historic racing cars.
- Insurance Consultants, Inc, (Lester Seasongood), 1010 Collingwood Dr, St. Louis, MO 63132 (314) 997-7800 On & off track insurance underwriters for Lloyds of London.
- International Racing Insurance Services, Ltd, 10158 116th, Edmonton, Alberta T5K 1V8 (403) 482-5686
- K & K Insurance Agency, Inc, 3015 Bowser Ave, Ft. Wayne, IN (219) 744 4101
- Land Speed Insurors Agency, Inc, 3101 Broadway, Kansas, MO 64111 (816) 756-1600 Mostly covers insurance for track owners.
- National Auto Racing Service, Inc, 3110 First Ave North, St. Petersburg, FL 33733 (813) 822-5354
- Naughton Insurance, PO Box 6192, Providence, RI 02940 SCCA insurer.

GRAPHIC FOR RACE VEHICLES

- Competition Graphics, 31690 W. 12th Rd, Dept SC, Farmington Hills, MI 48334 (800) 872-4614 Send a dollar for their brochure. They do any size, color in logo's, numbers.
- Design Vinyl Lettering and Graphics, 655 N. Berry St, Suite E, Brea, CA 92621 (714) 255-8113
- Drivers Club, 3770 Rosecrant St, San Diego, CA 92110 (619) 293-5630 Send for free catalog. Custom embroidering on racesuits.
- Graphics By Concepts, 24500 Hampton Hill Rd, Novi, MI 48050 (313) 349-8308 Free catalog. They also letter support equipment. (trailers)
- GT Graphics, 2728 S. Lacienega Blvd, Los Angeles, CA (213) 870-5457

- Motorsport Graphics (Automotive Appearance GP), PO Box 720076, Atlanta, GA 30358 (404) 442-8452, (800) 831-9685 24 hr. service. Complex work in screen prints decals, outlines, drop shadows, multi colors in addition to the normal work.
- Mr. Sticker, 18065 Redondo Circle, Huntington Beach, CA 92648 (714) 843-0444 Race car lettering, custom decals, magnetic signs, silk screening, die cutting & numbering.
- Mr. Tape Motorsports Decals, (313) 750-8150 Free catalog.
- Performance Graphics, 3626 E. Bijou St, Colorado Springs, CO 80909 (800) 437-4412, (719) 597-9994 Free brochure. They do metallic, magnetic, even bumper stickers, banner and hats.
- Pro Image Racing Identification, Box 87924, San Diego, CA 92138 (619) 450-1388 Free catalog. Stick on vinyl lettering in various colors & styles in size 1 to 22 inches.
- Pro Places, 58 North Broad St, York, PA 17403 (717) 854-7286 Custom bike numbering & plates.
- Race Car Lettering, 1025 Needham, Modesto, CA 95354 (800) 255-1790 $2.00 for 20 page catalog.
- Sign Tech, 207 Nashville, #C, Huntington Beach, CA 92648 (714) 960-7461 Window sand blast.
- Southern Graphics, 568 Lakeland Plaza, Cummings, GA 30130 (404) 889-2605
- Spahr Graphics, 842 Leyden Lane, Wilmette, IL 60091 (708) 251-7664 $2.00 catalog, refundable with order. Special effects on helmets and cars. Logo's, custom work.
- Springs Protective Fabrics, 615 Washington St, Hoboken, NJ 07030 (800) 433-5422 Explosive color designs for racesuits.
- Superior Signs, 66 E. Village Rd, Monroe, CT 06468 (800) 972-6034
- Troy Lee Designs, 1821 Wild Turkey Circle, Corona, CA 91720 (909) 371-5219 Specialize in custom helmet design. $3.00 for brochure.
- Wally World, (619) 949-1220 Off-Road exotic paint in addition to a full line of car lettering.

RACING TEAM/DRIVER BROKERS

- Apex Sponsorship Services, (216) 797-1463 Professionally prepared driver portfolios, cover letters, marketing packages to promote a racing team in the search for a sponsor.

- Charlie Hayes Action Motorsports, 21213-B Hawthorne Blvd, #5403, Torrance, CA 90509 (310) 568-0073 Call for information package. 35 years experience on coaching individuals and teams in obtaining financial packages from Karts to high-profile pro racing.
- Continental Motorsports, Ltd, Sacramento, CA (916) 920-0073 Helps toward corporate sponsor support. (contact Rick)
- Hot Racing, 3009 Walden Ave, Depew, NY 14043 (716) 683-4997 Send resume or information for help if you're a motorcycle dirt rider looking for sponsorship support.
- International Racing Systems, 2203 East Harrisburg Pike, Middletown, PA 17057 (717) 944-4368 Has a program for learning the business side of racing as a mechanic, bookkeeper, organizational skills. This company may be on the threshold of a new racing concept. A form of time sharing as a way to race more inexpensively. It boils down to several racers purchasing a (new) car and sharing time racing it. (ask for Tom Gearhart)
- NEXZUS Motorsport Marketing, Inc, PO Box 44990, Phoenix, AZ 85064–4990 (602) 957–7220 Represents drivers, teams and sponsors in marketing partnership arrangements through racing. They also put out a monthly newsletter.
- PVB Motorsport, Box 1168-793, Studio City, CA 91604 (818) 508 8661 They buy your racer or broker it to another buyer as a whole or in parts. Basket cases to modern pro vehicles.
- Racetech International, Inc, 6951 Warner Ave, Suite 423, Huntington Beach, CA 92647 A search/recruiting organization for motor racing teams/fraternity.
- RAR Motorsports, 785 Boardman Rd, Aiken, SC 29801 (800) 848-2687, (803) 642-7175 Specialist who research race rental teams for drivers and vice versa. Also works for sponsors and private parties.
- Tesrac Enterprises, Inc, 404 Basinger Rd, Pandora, OH 45877. Occasionally holds seminars for race sponsors and seekers.
- TQ&A Motorsports Marketing (Ted Quackenbush and Associates), (503) 297-8240 Provides a race program with marketing and media help with sponsoring efforts in finding or keeping your current sponsor.

MAINTENANCE SERVICE

These are specialists who do not rent race equipment, but rather maintain, transport, setup and generally oversee your race car and racing operation. (Many racecar rental services will do this also, but the difference here is these following to not rent racers)

- Allen L. Nelson Enterprises, Inc, Roscoe, IL 61073 (815) 633-1100 (Specialist in Formula Ford)
- Formula Car Network, 6308 Frederick Rd, Catonville, MD 21228 (301) 744-9071 or 730-1428 (also buyer & sellers of Formula race cars)

- Lindell Motorsports, 20 E. Chicago Ave, Westmont, IL 60559
- LP Racing, Inc, 7355 S. 50th East, Lebanon, IN 46052 (317) 482-3548

MECHANIC/CREW SCHOOLS

The following 14 race schools have mechanic courses. For address or a brief description of such see appendix D, if not described in this appendix.

1. American School of Motorsports, Indycar oriented.
2. Bridgestone Racing School (Spenard-David Mechanic School) A serious course involving every aspect of automobile racing, from nuts and bolts of technology to total assembly. Meticulous attention to details. Three sessions of 16, 17, & 32 weeks from March to October. (4 to $9,000, furnished apartment included) A good opportunity for young racing enthusiasts who want a career or to work with their own racer. You must be serious and with some mechanical ability.
3. Bill Tempero Indycar School, a two-day course for Indycars.
4. Competition engineering, racer prep, design and development on an individual basis.
5. Finish Line Racing School, 1 or 2 day stockcar mechanics course.
6. Frank Hawleys Drag Racing School, 3-day course designed for the individual to help determine if they'd like a career in this area of racing.
7. Jim Russel Racing School, a career oriented program in maintenance, setup, fabrication, transmission repairs. (1 year long)
8. Levolant Racing School, mechanics school with personal and technical instruction in chassis setup and engine tuning.
9. Lou D'Agastino Drivers Anatomy 101, See appendix D; school for mechanics only.
10. Motorsport Sports Training Center, (appendix D) 11 courses in StockCar and Street Rod.
11. Performance by Ken Brown, (Project Industries) vehicle construction and engineering.
12. Skip Barber, America's only college accredited training school of its kind. Call (800) 422-8867 (Gordon)
13. American Motorcycle Institute, 1445 Sky Trooper Rd, Daytona Beach, FL 32014 (800) 874-0645, (904) 255-0295.
14. International Race System (See this appendix, section on 'Brokers')

OPPORTUNITIES

- 24 Hour Motorsports, 1-900-860-9077, $2.00 first minute, $1.00 each additional minute. Coverage in all auto, formula, motorcycle, drag and off-road racing.
- Daytona Motorcycle Auction & Trade Show, a 4-day event held at the Armory in Daytona, Florida (725 Ballough Rd) during Motorcycle Week. For info con-

tact: Wood & Co, 8735 W. Riverwood Dr, Crystal River, FL 32629 (904) 795-8895

- Formula SAE (Society of Automotive Engineers), 400 Commonwealth Dr, Warrendale, PA 15096-0001 (412) 772-7132 A yearly event held jointly with the SCCA for collegiate engineering students. Rotated among some 36 colleges, participants compete to design, construct and present a prototype racer for production for a target market of formula-styled autocrossers. (solo racing) Strict limitations are avoided to enhance creativity. About 1 year is needed for each team (8-10 members) from each school. Then the prototypes are judged in about 8 categories. (design, maneuverability, fuel economy, endurance, presentation, costs, acceleration and skid-pad performance)
- NHRA Career Opportunities (contact Ken Pyle, Director of Youth), PO Box 5555, Glendora, CA 91740-0750 (818) 914-4761 A series of youth-oriented activities to open dozens of options in drag racing, but not limited to it. The RACE program (Racing And Curriculum Enrichment) links the excitement of auto racing with essential instruction in core subjects, like math, science, social studies, language and vocational education.
- Summers Rent A Ride, 2105 Bonita Ave, Ontario, CA 91762-6709 (714) 986-5986 Not the usual race car rental program, but rather a strictly entertainment venue with a 200 mph Bonneville (Salt Flats) 'Lakester' vehicle. This is serious adult entertainment, and therefore all credentials, safety and medical requirements must be met by both the driver(s) and race equipment. The driver is "oriented" up to the top speed in increment of about 25 mph, starting the first run around 125 mph to the fifth run of over 200. (to 250 mph) Cost: $5,000.00. Optional additional runs available.

VIDEOS

Most videos below are on motorcycle competition. For tapes on auto racing see appendix B. Retail outlets such as Classic Motorbooks, Steve Smith, Twister, Motormedia Limited and Motorsports International have catalogs on auto racing tapes.

- AMA Videos, Dept AM, 1180 Essex Rd, Watkinsville, GA 30677 (800) 462-TAPE Tapes on competitive and street riding. Write for free catalog.
- Bell Motorsport, (800) 669-2355 Video catalog and free cassette on drivers schools, $9.95. Refundable with first order.
- Brazeau Video, 34462 Via Gomez, Capistrano Beach, CA 92624 (714) 493-2160 Custom video of individual racers, in events of off-road and/or motorcycle meets.
- Donnie Hansen Motocross School Tape, 1418 Plumeria, San Antonio, TX 78232 (800) 343-8559 $25.00
- Franam Racing Inc, 1409 S. Wilshire Dr, Minnetonka, MN 55343 (612) 541-9461 30 minute tape on Elf Winfield Racing School, $29.95.
- Gary Bailey, PO Box 130, Axton, VA 24054-0130 (703) 650-3030 Send for order form and small listings on several videos on Historic Motocross events and rider training/instruction tapes.
- Halmar, PO Box 474, Dept F, Lewiston, NY 14092 (416) 356-6865 Free catalog. Roadracing vintage, Motocross.
- The Motorcycle Movie (GR Home Video's), PO Box 341408, Los Angeles, CA 90034 (213) 475-0937 Roadracing, Hillclimbs, Trail Riding, 60's Vintage, Scrambles, Sidecar and more.
- Trackside Photo, Inc, 1507 E. Del Amo Blvd, Carson, CA 90746 (213) 609-1772 Commercial photographs for race events or individual racers, in addition to public relations, promotions, etc. (commercial photographers specializing in sports and racing can be found in most major cities)
- Video Enduro (EVS-Enduro Video Specialists), PO Box 475, Carson City, MI 48811 (616) 956-5127
- Vintage Motorcycle Movies (Earl Mark Productions), 23022 S. Normandie Ave, Torrance, CA 90502 (213) 326-6446 Free catalog.

Appendix H:
Engine Builders

The list below are the well established and well-known engine builders and rebuilders within the inside circles of the racing fraternity. Most private builders of the professional teams aren't listed. They do not work outside the confines of their private contracts or obligations to the race teams. (such as those in IMSA, CART, Formula One and the high-profile ranks of NHRA, SCCA, or motorcycle roadracing) Also many of these builders are in the parts business for engines only or race cars in general.

- AAEN Performance, 1266 N. Sheridan Rd, Kenosha, WI 53140 (414) 552-8981 Formula 440 engines.
- Advanced Design Engineering Co, 1201 Michigan Ave, Columbus, IN 47201 (812) 379-9535 Formula Ford.
- Al Bartz, 15833 Stagg St, Van Nuys, CA 91405 (213) 785-5754 Small block Chevy & Ford engines.
- Al Thomas Engines, 1313 N. Miller St, Unit B, Anaheim, CA 92806 (714) 993-9930
- Armstrong Race Engineering, 2552 Albatross Way, Sacramento, CA 95815 (916) 929-0470 Formula engines.
- Astral Racing Engines, RR 72, Holten St, Danvers, MA 01923 (617) 777-1498
- Autocraft Engines, 1100 Custer Rd, Toledo, OH 43612 (800) 356-6586, outside Ohio (800) 356-1546
- Automotive Development, 501 W. Maple, Unit V, Orange, CA 92668 (714) 633-6672
- Batten Performance, 28884 Highlands Rd, Romulus, MI 48174 (800) 233-1591 Catalog, $3.00. Endurance engines.
- Bayless Racing, Inc, 1488 Nester Rd, Memphis, TN 38116 (401) 346-4622 Fiat engines.
- Bertils Race Engines, Inc, PO Box 438, Antioch, IL 60002 (708) 395-4244 or 5 Small VW and Formula.
- Bettendorf Power, 5901 Firestone, Southgate, CA 90280 (213) 806-3913 Small Fords, Datsun & Toyota.
- Bill Blair Automotive, 788 N. Main St, High Point, NC 27260 (919) 883-7000 Grand National Stock-Cars.
- Bill Scott Racing, 1420 Spring Hill Rd, McLean, VA 22101 (703) 893-3992 (Schrick engine; probably out of business)
- Bley Vintage, 700 Chase, Elk Grove, IL 60007 (708) 437-0671
- Bob Joehnck, 133 W. Figueroa, Santa Barbara, CA (805) 962-1773 Drag racing engines.

- Booth Arons Racing Enterprises, 3861 W. 12 Mile, Berkley, MI 48072 Chevy & AMC drag-oriented.
- Brabham Engines Ralt American, Ltd, 23110 Kashiwa Ct, Torrance, CA 90505 (213) 533-1144 Circle track and roadracing engines.
- Bud Friend Racing Engines, 1825 Roth Ave, Allentown, PA, 18104 (215) 433-3060 Circle track motors.
- Bud Moore, 400 N. Fairview, Spartanburg, SC 29302 (803) 585-8155 Small block Fords for ovals.
- Bunce Engineering (Schrick Engines), 4300 La Palma, Anaheim, CA 92807 (714) 528-4492 Small block engines.
- Carpenter Race Engines, 129-L Gaither Dr, Mt. Laurel, NJ 08054 (800) 677-RACE
- Clem Engines, 10918 Auder Circle, Dallas, TX 75238 (214) 503-8044 Formula Ford and Vee.
- Competition Engineering, 2095 N. Lake Ave, Altadena, CA 91001 (213) 794-8402 VW-Porsche
- Competition Engineering, 68214 Division St, New Paris, IN 46553 (216) 428-2185 Domestic, drag engines.
- Cosworth Engineering, Ltd, 2808 Oregon Ct, Unit 7, Torrance, CA 90503 Well known Indy car engine in its time. Still do some Formula Atlantic work among other engines.
- Cricket Farm Motors, Building 31, Ohio Loop Rd, Greenville, SC 29605 (803) 277-1268 Formula Ford, Vee and Sports 2000.
- Curtis Farley Engines, 1809 Ft. Riley Blvd, Manhattan, KS 66502 (913) 537-4010 One of the best Formula Vee engine builders in the US. Also does Formula Ford 1600, 2000 and Sports 2000.
- Dales Performance, Inc, 1830 Lakeview Terrace, Long Lake, MN 55356 (612) 473-9073 Motorcycles.
- DAVHAR Racing, Rt 2, Box 149-B, Gill, MA 01376 (413) 863-9604
- Deano Dyno-Soars, Inc, 687 N. Main St, Orange, CA 92667 (714) 538-2353 VW engines.
- Dennis Fisher, 9934 Canoga Ave, Chatsworth, CA 91211 Circle track engines.
- Diamond Elkins Engine Service, 3493 10 Mile Rd, Warren, MI 48091 (313) 756-4055 Big & small block drag racing engines.
- Dick Landy Performance, 19743 Bahama St, Northridge, CA 91324 (213) 341-4143 Drag racing engines.
- Dino Fry, 232 Fulton St, Redwood City, CA 90461 (415) 365-8077 Small block Chevies.

- D and J Automotive, 3220 Westwood-Northern Blvd, Cincinnati, OH 45211 (513) 661-8078 Drag oriented towards domestic cars.
- Dolph Van Kesteran Far Performance, 1931 Old Middlefield Way, Mountain View, CA 94040 (415) 968-2976 Datsun
- Donovan Engineering Corp, 2305 Border Ave, Torrance, CA 90501 (213) 320-3772 Aluminum engine blocks; drag oriented. (also used to supply blocks for Indy cars)
- Drake Engineering Corp, 17502 Daimler St, Santa Ana, CA 92705 (714) 540-9530 Builders of Offenhauser race engines. (Powered Indy cars)
- Drino Miller Ent, 942 Sunset Dr, Costa Mesa, CA 92627 (714) 642-3690 Off-Road and specialist in VW.
- East Cost Cycle, 142 Rogers St, Jasper, GA 30143 (404) 692-5681, (800) 225-4923 Motorcycle engines.
- Ed Pink Racing Engines, 14612 Raymer St, Van Nuys, CA 91405 (213) 873-3460 Well known builder of AA/Fuel and Funny Car Dragsters.
- Engine Dynamic Co, 1010 Lakeville Hwy, Petaluma, CA 94952 (707) 763-7519 Motorbikes
- Engine Systems Development, 1315 W. Trenton Ave, Orange, CA 92667 (714) 997-5830 Large & small block Chevy for all kinds of racing.
- Extrude Hone, 8800 Somerset Blvd, Paramont, CA 90723 (213) 531-2976
- Falconer-Dunn Racing Engines, 5728 Bankfield, Culver City, CA 90230 (213) 390-3459 Indy Fords & 500 ci Chevies.
- FAT Performance, 1558 N. Case, Orange, CA 92667 (714) 637-2889 Toyota off-road engines.
- Florida Sports Cars, 4530 NE 6th Ave, Ft. Lauderdale, FL 33334 (305) 491-3939 Formula Ford and small Sports and Formula roadracing engines.
- Fred Opert Racing (Tital & Jaktlund Engines), 266 Rt 59, Monsey, NY 10952 (201) 423-1239 (Probably is out of business now)
- Gale Banks, 929 S. San Gabriel Rd, San Gabriel, CA 91776 (213) 285-3107 Any large domestic race engines.
- Gapp & Roush Performance, 32081 Schoolcraft, Livonia, MI 48150 (313) 425-0640 Small block Ford drag racing engines.
- Gene Berg Enterprises, 1725 N. Lime, Orange, CA 92665 (714) 998-7500 In drag engines.
- George Eickhoff, 11305 Loch Lomond, Los Alamitos, CA 90720 (213) 596-4289 Formula race engines.
- George Foltz, 13926 Leonard, Warren, MI 48089 (313) 772-4626 Big Chevy race engines. (IMSA)
- Hassengren Racing Engines, 815 Gilman St, Berkeley, CA 94710 (415) 525-1164 Formula Atlantic engines.
- Hickman Racing, 6821 Fleur Dr, Des Moines, IA 50321 (515) 285-4332 Motorcycles
- High Performance Service, 123 'C' S. McClay, Santa Ana, CA 92701 (800) 854-3868 Motorbike engines.
- Hoens & Eanes Automotive, 2226 Chamberlain, Richmond, VA (804) 321-6634 Grand National StockCar engines.
- Huffaker Automotive Engineering, Northgate Industrial Pk, 22 Mark Dr, San Rafael, CA 94903 (415) 479-6705 Formula Ford engines.
- Import Auto Electric, Ltd, 7017 S. Tacoma Way, Tacoma WA, 98409 (206) 475-3010 Formula Ford engine and other small block engines.
- Ivey Engines, Inc, 2204-2 NW Birdsdale, Gresham, OR 97030 (503) 667-3616 Good reputation in small block FF and BMW, Datsun, Volvo, etc.
- JC Engines, 318 Rt 434, Shoshola, PA 18458. Trans-Am and SportsCar engines.
- Junior Johnson, Rt 2, Box 86, Ronda, NC 28670 (919) 984-2101 Grand National Stockcar engine builder. (Works for a very limited amount of customers)
- Keith Black, 11120 Scott Ave, S. Gate, CA 90280 (213) 869-1518 Well known Chrysler drag engine builder.
- Ken Automotive Engineering, 15459 Cabrito Rd, Van Nuys, CA (213) 785-5007 or 1548 Drag oriented. Some roadracing engines.
- King Engine Service, 25300 John R Rd, Madison Hts, MI 48071 (313) 543-2393 All kinds of auto racing engine work; prefer Chevy drag.
- Leader Automotive, 1207 Wheaton St, Troy, MI 48084 (313) 689-4737 Late Model Modifieds, Sportsman, Drag engines.
- Louis Unser Engines, 1100 E. Ash Ave, Suite C, Fullerton, CA 92631 (714) 879-8440 Sprint car engines, Off-Road engines.
- Loyning Engine Service, 211-F NE Victory, Gresham, OR 97030 (503) 661-0523 Formula Ford engines.
- Mantapart Performance, 8131 Market St, Youngstown, OH 44507 (216) 783-2800 Formula race engines.
- Marcovicci-Wenz Engineering, 33 Comac Loop, Ronkonkoma, NY 11779 (516) 467-9040 Formula and Vintage engines.
- McLaren Engines, Inc, 32333 W. 7 Mile Rd, Livonia, MI 48152 (313) 477-6240 Used to build Indy engines. Small & large Chevies for Endurance racing.
- Mini Performance, 1100 Custer Rd, Toledo, OH 43612 (419) 476-3711 Off-Road, short track, Midget and VW based. Ford engines.
- Mondello Olds Performance, 1319 West El Segundo Blvd, Gardena, CA 90247 (213) 755-1141 Vintage engine prep.
- Motorsport Research, 1634 Oakton St, Des Plaines, IL 60018 (312) 299-7731 Domestic engines.
- Muzzys Racing & Development, 17216 B-3 Lilac St, Nesperia, CA 92345 (619) 949-5131 Motorbike engines.
- Norm Brown Chevtec Racing, 140 South St, Rochester, MI 48063 (313) 575-4395 Chevy V-8 drag and roadracing engines.
- Paeco Industries, 2400-S Mountain Dr, Birmingham, AL 35226 (205) 823-7278 All kinds of circle and auto roadracing engines.
- Parkey Nall Racing Engines, Charlotte, NC (704) 596-8452 Circle track specialist.

- PBS Engineering, 11602 Anabel, Garden Grove, CA 92643 Specialist on foreign engines.
- PHP Engines, 950 N. Rand Rd, #107, Wauconda, IL 60084 (312) 526-9393 Formula engines.
- PSI, Rt 2, Box 309, Wild Rose, WI 54989 (414) 787-2430 Racing motorcycle engines.
- Quicksilver Race Engines, 1101 Gude Dr, Rockville, MD 20850 (301) 340-2700 Formula Ford and other Formulas.
- Race Engines, 637 Palm St, Unit G, Lahabra, CA 90631 (213) 697-1447 Formula and Sportscars.
- Racetronics, 770 Broadway, Raynham, MA 02767 (617) 824-9074 VW engines for Formula Vee, Mini-Stock and Drag engines.
- Racing Engine Service, 2918 S. Cooper, E-3, Arlington, TX 76015 (817) 468-5418 Motorbike engines.
- Ralph Moody, 1448 Ashley Rd, Charlotte, NC 28208 (704) 394-0363 All kind of engines in amateur, pro and modified, drag engines.
- Ramchargers Racing Engines, Inc, 12480 Allen Rd, Taylor, MI 48180 (313) 287-6010 Drag race oriented.
- Rayburn Automotive, Whiteland, IN 46184 (317) 535-8232 Custom and drag engines.
- Ray Fox Jr Racing Engines, Hwy 49, Harrisburg, NC (704) 455-2014 Grand National Stock Cars.
- RC Engineering, Inc, 1728 Border Ave, Torrance, CA 90501 (213) 320-2277 Toyota engines.
- Reher-Morrison Racing Engines, 1232 W. Arkansas Lane, Arlington, TX 76013 (817) 461-6773 Drag racing engines.
- Richie Ginther, 5716 Camille, Culver City, CA (213) 390-5144 Porsche roadracing engines.
- RW Enterprises, Strasburg Rd 4, Coatesville, PA 19320 (215) 486-0883 Formula and Sportscar engines.
- Sam Gianino Racing Engines, 4812 Leafdale, Royal Oak, MI 48073 (313) 576-0707 Drag engines.
- Shankle Automotive Engineering, 15451 F Cabrito Rd, Van Nuys, CA, 91406 (213) 988-5190 Formula, Trans-Am, IMSA and some foreign engines.
- Sterling Racing Engines, 12104 Ridge Rd, PO Box 374, Jackson, CA 95642 (209) 267-5081 Formula and SportsCar engines.
- Steve Jennings, 1401 E. Borchard, Santa Ana, CA 92705 (714) 547-3717 Formula engines.
- Stimola Race Prep, 57 Birch Hill Rd, Locust Valley, NY 11560 (515) 671-9715 Formula and SportsRacers.
- The Engine Room, 318 A, River St, Santa Cruz, CA 95060 (408) 429-1800 Vintage engines.
- The Machine Works, 42736 Mound Road, Sterling Hts, MI 48310 (313) 739-0808 Vintage engines.
- Tom Rust Racing, 28019 Arnold Dr, Sonoma, CA 95476 (707) 938-4020 Vintage engine rebuilding.
- Traco, 11928 W. Jefferson Blvd, Culver City, CA 90230-6312 (213) 398-3722 All kinds of racing engines including Vintage.
- Traylor Engineering, 1203 Baldwin Rd, Palatine, IL 60067 (312) 358-9616 Drag and SportsCar engines.
- Treuhaft Automotive Specialist, Inc, 730 Monroe Way, Placentia, CA 92670 VW engines, off-road and drag engines.
- Trupp/Kling, 133 Hwy 22, Greenbrook, NJ 08812 Drag engines.
- TSR, 8062 East Rosecrans, Paramont, CA 90723 (213) 531-1619 Bike motors.
- Two-O-Two Racing, 551 Morewood Pkwy, Cleveland, OH 44116 (216) 331-4242 Motocross and DTX engine specialists.
- Varner Racing, 11805 E. Slauson Ave, #B, Santa Fe Springs, CA 90670 (213) 696-9409 2 stroke motorcycle engines.
- Waibel Competition, Rt 5, Box 683, Lakeland, FL 33801 (813) 686-7693 Drag racing engines.
- Waterman Racing Engines, 1939 W. Artesia Blvd, Gardena, CA 90247 (213) 770-0606 Drag engines for Rail/Funny cars.
- West Engine & Machine, 420 Venture St, Escondido, CA 92025 (619) 741-6173 Off-road and VW Porsche engines.
- Wheelsmith Racing, 855 San Anselmo Ave, San Anselmo, CA 94960 (415) 453-0306 Bike engines.
- Wolf Racing Engines, 537 W. Main St, El Cajon, CA 92020 (619) 442-0630 Japanese built race engines.
- Wood Racing, 755 W. 17th St, Unit D, Costa Mesa, CA 92627 (714) 645-0393 Motorcycle engines.
- Zeitler Racing Imports, PO Box 3451, Stamford, CT (203) 323-5660 Formula and SportsCars.

Appendix I:
Construction/Fabricators

The following list are the constructors or importers of vehicles which are purpose-built. Remember, purpose-built means vehicles which are built specifically for racing. That means you will not see generally familiar names in here such as Yamaha, Honda, Chevy, Ford, etc. Those race vehicles are rebuilt, modified or raced after construction off the assembly line. (such as SCCA's Showroom Stock class) All these constructors are small operations. Even the big names in racing construction, such as Lola and March are small, when compared to the 'Big 3.' (Chevy, Ford, Chrysler) Of course, that's because of the market. Some of these constructors are already out of business because, as small as the race car market is, it became too small for some. But these out-of-current constructors still have plenty of their cars still racing. Therefore, it's important to know who and where they were, which may become relevant when it's time to track down hard to find parts. (when your local race parts supply dealer has exhausted their inventory) Kart manufacturers can be found in the 'Karting Directory and Guide.' Racing bikes aren't in here. Their chassis and engines aren't race-built from the ground up. They are more modified on a limited basis. Basically, these builders are Drag, Stock and Off-Road fabricators and US raced Formula and SportsCars. Popular 'makes' which are delivered to the US (importers) are listed. Call these constructors (or fabricators) to locate their assigned representatives/dealers.

- Adams Formula Vee, 5959 Sterling, Howell, MI 48843 (517) 548-5104 (Constructor-dealer)
- All American Racers, 2334 S. Broadway, Santa Ana, CA 92707 (Dan Gurney Shop) Eagle Indy car.
- Autodynamic, Inc, 2 Barnard St, Marblehead, MA 01945 (617) 631-8500 Caldwell FV and F Ford constructor.
- Autofab, 10996 N. Woodside Ave, Santee, CA 92071 (619) 562-1740 Off-road truck modifications.
- Auto Restorations, Inc, 1785 Barnum Ave, Stratford, CT 06497 (203) 377-6745 (Vintage prep)
- Baja Specialties, 741 Rosalie Way, El Cajon, CA 92019 (619) 445-5764 Off-road vehicles.
- Banjo Mathews Performance Center, PO Box 426, Arden, NC 28704 (704) 684-7814 Constructor of Late Models, Sportsmen and Modified racers.
- Bill Stroppe Assoc, Inc, Box 1891, Long Beach, CA 90801 (213) 439-2156 (Anything from NASCAR StockCars to Off-Road)

- Bob Meyer Race Cars, 1445 Pioneer Way, El Cajon, CA 92020 (714) 440-7701 Off-road, drag.
- Bob Sharp Racing, Danbury Rd, Rt 7, Georgetown, CT 06829 (203) 544-9321 GT builder.
- Boyce Engineering, 5622 Northwestern Ave, Chicago, IL 60625 (312) 334-5153 Late model stocks.
- BRD Formula Vee (Buenting Racing & Development), Vallis Motorsports, 2205 Hurricane Rd, RR 2, Welland, Ontario L3B 5N5 (416) 384-0016 (Constructor-dealer)
- Butler Racing, 11813 Major St, Culver City, CA 90230 (213) 391-1785 Drag-Funny cars, Pro Stock.
- California Chassis Engineering, 9821 Owensmouth Ave, Chatsworth, CA 91311 Dragster and modified drag fabricator.
- Campbell Motorsports, PO Box 63, Menominee, MI 49858 (906) 863-5003 (Constructor of 'Laser' Formula Vee)
- Canadian Stockcar Products, Ltd, 37 Creditsone Rd, Box 151, Concord, Ontario (416) 669-2238 Long & short track stock cars.
- Caracar Formula Vee, 4451-2 Sunbeam Rd, Jacksonville, FL 32217 (904) 636-0638 (Constructor)
- Cecil Hicks Race Cars, 3050 Leeman Ferry Rd, SW, Huntsville, AL 35801 (205) 881-3932 Gas powered drag racers.
- Chapman Performance Products, 1505 Burchwood, Des Plaines, IL 60018 (312) 297-1170 Drag builder.
- Cheetah D SportsRacer, (Sunseri/Omni), 260 Cristich Ln, Building A, Campbell, CA 95008 (408) 371-4555 (Constructor-Dealer)
- Chenowth Race Products, Inc, 943 Vernon Way, El Jon, CA 92020 (619) 449-7100 Off-road 'Chenowth' and 'Mini-mag' constructor.
- Chevron Formula Ford and Continental, Winchester, Hampshire, England SO23 7RX. PH: 011-44-962-841084 (Constructor-dealer)
- Chris Smiths' Creative Workshop, 118 NW Park St, Dania, FL 33004 (305) 920-3303 Vintage restoration and fabrication.
- Chrysler Corp Stock Car Program, PO Box 1919-cims, 416-15-05, Detroit, MI 48231 (313) 956-5346 Late Model Stock Car. (Kits)
- Citation Engineering, 1250 S. 950 East, Zionsville, IN 46077 (317) 769-4385 Constructor of 'Centurion' Formula Continental and Formula Ford and 'Citation-Zink' Formula Vee.

- Climax Formula 440 (Motion Tech), 2700 4 Mile Rd, Racine, WI 53402 (414) 639-4044 (Constructor-dealer)
- C & M Off-Road & Truck Center, 8540 Lankershim Blvd, Sun Valley, CA 91352 (818) 504-0306 or 767-0588 Off-road specialists.
- Crossle Formula Ford 1600 & 2000, Holywood, County Down, Northern Ireland PH: 011-44-232-63322 (Constructor)
- Culbert Automotive Engineering, 6580 Federal Blvd, Lemon Grove, CA 92045 (714) 286-2444 (Constructor of Sprint Cars)
- Desert Fabricators, 297 Imperial Ave, Imperial, CA 92251 (VW based, off-road)
- Dick Troutman, 6130 W. Slauson Ave, Culver City, CA 90230 (213) 397-2712
- Don Edmunds Auto Research, 1418 S. Central Pk, Anaheim, CA 92802 (714) 535-8735 Sprint, Midget and SuperModified builder.
- Don Hardy Race Cars, Inc, 202 W. Missouri St, Floydada, TX 72935 (806) 983-2295 Pro Stock drag builder.
- Doren Sports 2000, (Doran Engineering), 7685 Fields Ertel Rd, Cincinnati, OH 45241 (513) 489-8832 (Constructor-dealer)
- Elden Racing Cars, 20 Blue Chalet, Industrial Estate, London Rd, West Kingsdown Seven Oaks, Kent, England TN15 6BQ PH: 011-44-474-853840 (Constructor of 'Elden' Formula Ford 2000/Continental)
- Entropy Racing, 865 Airport Rd, Monterey, CA 93940 (408) 375-5975 Vintage restorers.
- Essex-Tiga Racing, Inc, 2350 Industrial Park Blvd, Cumming, GA 30130 (404) 889-4096 (Constructor-dealer of 'Tiga' Sports 2000 racer)
- Fastech of Jacksonville, Inc, 6933-9 Lillian Rd, Jacksonville, FL 32211 (904) 727-6934 Constructor of 'Fastech' Formula Vee. (Dealer)
- Fiber Tech Engineering, Inc, 10809 Prospect Ave, Santee, CA 92071 (714) 448-0221 (Off-road builder)
- Formula Car Formula Vee (Formula Cars, Inc.), 3113 S. Garland Rd, Garland, TX 75041 (214) 278-9807 (Dealer-constructor of 'Formula Car D-13' Formula Vee)
- Fulmar Competition Services, Unit 24, Roman Way Industrial Estate, Godmanchester, Huntington Cambs, England PE18 8LN PH: 011-44-480-412727 (Constructor of 'Reynard' Formula Ford 1600, 2000, Indy car & FC)
- Funco Race Cars, 8847 9th St, Cucamonga, CA 91730 (714) 981-8743 (Off-road fabricators)
- Garman Fabrication, 1452 E. Third St, Pomona, CA 91766 (714) 620-1242 (Off-road builders)
- Griffith Formula Vee, 1945 E. Aurora Rd, Twinsburg, OH 44087 (216) 425-9462 (Constructor-dealer)
- Hans Rocke Enterprises, Box 1871, Rt 44, Lakeville, CT 06039 (203) 435-0177 (Vintage prep)
- H & H Racecraft, 7838 Burnet, Van Nuys, CA 91405 (213) 781-1900 (Drag racing builder)
- Hickey Enterprises, 1645 Callens Rd, Ventura, CA 93003 (Off-road builder)
- Hi-Tech Tool Co, 9225 Belcher Ave, Downey, CA 90242 (213) 862-5916 (Builder of 'Phoenix' Formula Vee)
- Holman-Moody, Inc, PO Box 27065, Charlotte, NC 28219 (704) 394-4141 (Grand National stockcars)
- House of Buggies, 992 S. Prospect Ave, Santee, CA 92071 (619) 589-6770 (Off-road)
- Howe Racing, Rt 1, Lyle Rd, Beaverton, MI 48612 (517) 435-7080 (Chevy Late Model StockCar builder)
- HRP Motorsport, Inc, 8775 Belding Rd, Rockford, MI 49341 (616) 874-6338 (Builder of 'Zink' Formula 440)
- Hutcherson-Pagan, Inc, Hwy 21, Charlotte, NC (704) 597-1372 (Sportsman Late Model StockCars, Late Models, Grand National StockCar builder)
- JEG's, 751 E. 11th St, Columbus, OH 43211 (614) 294-5454 (Drag racing builder)
- Jim Moulton Racing, 26846 Oak St, Unit G, Canyon Country, CA 91351 (800) 298-1212 (Off-road fabricator)
- Johnny Dawe Racing, Rt 30 & 55, Crown Point, IN 46307 (219) 769-8355 (Midget builder)
- J Penhall Fabrication, 1660 Babcock Bldg E, Costa Mesa, CA (714) 650-3035 (Off-road builder)
- JP Enterprises, 1322-G Virginia, Baldwin Park, CA 91706 (213) 338-8710 (Kit StockCars)
- KBS Engineering, 8296 Fremontia, Suite B, Fontana, CA 92335 (909) 355-4800 (Builder of 'Ramblebee' Formula 440)
- KTR Engineering, Inc, Box 560, Groton, MA 01450 (508) 772-7800 (Vintage restoration)
- Leslies, 416 E. Valley Blvd, Colton, CA 92324 (Off-road fabrication)
- Logghe Stamping Co (Competition Division), 16711 13 Mile Rd, Fraser, MI 48026 (313) 293-2250 (Drag race builder)
- Logic Formula 440, 30447 Lorain Rd, Suite R, North Olmsted, OH 44070 (216) 734-1988 (Dealer & constructor)
- Lola Cars Ltd, Glebe Rd, St. Peters Hill, Huntington, Cambs, England PE18 7DS PH: 011-44-480-451301 (Constructor of 'Lola' Formula Fords, Sports 2000 and Lola Indy racers) Imported by Carl Hass Automotive Imports, 500 Tower Parkway, Lincolnshire, IL 60069 (708) 634-8200
- Lothringer Engineering, 825 N. Glendora Ave, Covina, CA 91723 (818) 915-2212 (Roll cage fabricator)
- Mark Williams Race Car, 4200 Madison St, Denver, CO 80216 (303) 377-1797 (Drag racing builder)
- McCoy Racing, 553 S. 7th St, Modesto, CA 95351 (Grand National, Sportsman, Late Model StockCars)
- Miller Sports 2000 (Pratt & Miller Engineering and Fabrication), 48875 West Rd, Wixom, MI 48393 (313) 344-9930 (Constructor)
- Mirage Chassis, 37925 Sixth St, East, Unit 107, Palmdale, CA 93550 (805) 272-3843 (Off-road builder)
- Mondiale Car Co, Ltd, Balloo Crescent Bangor, Northern Ireland 247-452323 (Manufacturer of 'Mondiale' Formula Ford 1600 & 2000)

- Mueller Fabricators, Inc, 10872 Stanford Ave, Lynwood, CA 90262 (213) 639-6723 (Builder for 'Triumph' Sportcar Racer)
- Mysterian Autoworks, 2890 Vassar No. 12A, Reno, NV 89502 (702) 786-6198 (Constructor for 'Mysterian' Formula Vee)
- New England Classic, 1785 Barnum Ave, Stratford, CT 06497 (203) 377-6746 (Vintage restoration)
- North American Group (International Auto), Tomah, WI 54660 (608) 372-6958 (Vintage restorer of Porsche)
- North American Race Co, 920 E. Arlee Place, Anaheim, CA 92805 (714) 535-4437 or 8 (Chassis fabricator)
- Off-Road Chassis Engineering, 6891 San Diego Dr, Buena Park, CA 90620 (714) 761-9460
- Off-Road Dynamics, 670 Arrow Hwy, Laverne, CA 91750 (714) 592-2271
- Panther Formula Vee, PO Box 8215, Naples, FL 33941 (813) 455-4777 (Constructor-Dealer)
- Paul Peyton Chassis, 3109 Little Rd, Arlington, TX 76016 (817) 429-2001 (Drag car fabricator)
- Pauter Machine Co, 367 Zenith St, Chula Vista, CA 92011 (714) 422-5384 (VW off-road builder)
- Performance Engineering, RD 2, Box 2134, Mohnton, PA 19540 (215) 775-1938 (Constructor-dealer 'Raptor' Formula 440 car)
- Petty Enterprises, Rt #3, Box 621, Randleman, NC 27317 (919) 498-3745 (Constructor Grand National StockCars)
- Phantom Formula 440 (DMD Motorsports), N. 511 Hwy 57, Random Lake, WI 53075 (414) 994-2475 (Constructor-dealer)
- Phil Henry Racing, 15838 Armentia, #22, Van Nuys, CA 91406 (213) 787-2445 (GT racers)
- Photon Formula Vee, 3202 E. Mitchell Dr, Phoenix, AZ 85018 (602) 955-1462 or 254-0024 (Constructor-dealer)
- Piper Engineering, 5 N. 461 Meadowview Lane, St. Charles, IL 60175 (708) 365-5884 (Constructor-Dealer, 'Piper' Formula Ford/FC racer)
- Predator Formula Vee (Crossroads Fabrication), 265 Hillcliff, Waterford, MI 48328 (313) 681-1377 (Constructor)
- Probst, 1121 E. Illinois Hwy, New Lexox, IL 60451 (815) 485-7223 (Off-road)
- Profile Racing, Commerse St, Flemington, NJ 08822 (201) 782-8277 (Circle track, dirt or asphalt race car constructor)
- Protoform Formula Vee, 1140 Ponderosa Dr, Horseheads, NY 14845 (607) 739-7345 (Constructor-dealer)
- Race Car by Behrens, 4072 Crestview Dr, Lake Elsinore, CA 92330 (714) 678-4649 (Off-Road, Drag, Vintage)
- Race Car Division (C&R Enterprises), 3066 River Rd N. Salem, OR 97303 (503) 399-1160 (Midget constructor)
- Race Cars of the Future, 2101 West 2200 South, Salt Lake City, UT 84119-1325 (801) 972-5469 (Constructor of 'Red Devil' Formula 440)
- Race Craft, 677 Elmwood, Troy, MI 48083 (313) 583-9600 (All kinds of racers built)
- Ralt/March Weybridge, Surry, England PH: 011-44-932-54677 (Constructor of Formula Ford, Formula Atlantic, Formula One, Indy car, Super Vee/Formula Continental)
- Ralt American, 23110 Kashiwa Ct, Torrance, CA 90505 (213) 533-1144 (Importer of Ralt and March formula racers)
- Rasmussen Racing, 37607 Vintage Dr, Palmdale, CA 93550 (805) 274-0627 (Off-road truck fabricator)
- Reynard Formula Ford, Formula Atlantic, Indy Car and Sports 2000 (Imported by Carl Haas, see Ralt/March)
- Richard Owens Design & Engineering, Unit 6, Silverstone Circuit, Towcester, Northants, England NN12 8TN PH: 011-44-327-857121 (Constructor of 'Shrike' Sports 2000 racers)
- Roger Beck Auto Racing Development, 4745 Brooks St, Suite E, Montclair, CA 91763 (714) 621-1821 (Sprint car builder)
- Rotary Specialist, Topeka, KS (913) 273-9800 (Constructor of GT-1 thru G-5)
- Royale USA, Sunnyside Rd, Rt 1, Box 520, Hiawassee, GA 30546 (404) 896-2446 (Importer of 'Royale' Formula Ford, S2000)
- Sandmaster, 12945 Sherman Way, N. Holloway, CA 91605 (Off-Road fabricator)
- San Fernando Buggy Center, 1533 Truman St, San Fernando, CA 91340 (213) 361-1615 Off-Road builder.
- SCCA Enterprises, Inc, 14570 E. Fremont Ave, Englewood, CO 80112 (303) 693-2111 (Constructor of 'SpecRacer' and 'Shelby' Can-Am)
- SE-3 Formula 2000/FC, CF Engines, 13200 NW 92 Hwy, Box 20031, Kansas City, MO 64195 (816) 464-2241 (Importer; Racer built by 'Swift-Europe')
- Shannon Sports 2000, Box 422, Rt 83 N, Antioch, IL 60012 (708) 395-5013 (Constructor-dealer)
- Sidewinder Formula 440, 2000 Central Ave, St. Petersburg, FL 33712 (813) 823-5951 (Constructor-dealer)
- Small Car Enterprises, 1001 Arlee Place, Anaheim, CA 92805 (714) 635-3735 (Stocks, circle track racers)
- Speedway Engineering, 2471 Fletcher Dr, Los Angeles, CA (213) 666-9510 (Stockcar fabricator)
- Speedway Motors, 1719 'N' St, Lincoln, NE 68508 (402) 477-4422 (Circle track racecar builder)
- Spirit Formula Continental, 110 N. Las Posas, San Marcos, CA 92069 (619) 471-9210 (Constructor-Dealer)
- Sports Engineering, 14757 Lull St, Van Nuys, CA 91405 (818) 994-7475 (Roll cages for racecars)
- Spyder Motorsports, PO Box 712, Orlando, FL 32802 (407) 843-2111 (Vintage restorer)
- SRD Racecars, 147 Pennsylvania, Malvern, PA 19355 (215) 647-0608 (Drag fabricator)
- StockCar Products, 11904 Burke, Santa Fe Springs, CA 90670 (213) 698-4816 (StockCar builder)
- Stohr Formula Ford, Box 3718, Kent, WA 98032 (Constructor-Dealer)

- Suspensions Unlimited, 1180 Fountain Way, Unit F, Anaheim, CA 92806 (714) 630-3770 or 2681 (Off-Road)
- Swift Europe, Unit 4, Snetterton Circuit, Norwich, Norfolk, England NR16 2XX PH: 011-44-953-878276 (Constructor of 'Swift' Formula Ford 1600 & 2000/FC, Sports 2000, Formula Atlantic & 'SE-3' FF)
- Swift Race Cars, 1027 Calle Trepadora, San Clemente, CA 92676 (714) 492-6608 (US importer)
- Tex Enterprises, Rt 4, Box 348, Asheboro, NC 27203 (919) 625-3943 (StockCars and Modifieds)
- The Buckingham Service, 10944 Grissom, Suite 701-704, Dallas, TX 75229 (214) 247-2654 (Vintage restorer)
- Thomas Speed, Rt 9, Box 21, Dixie Club Rd, Winston-Salem, NC (Grand National StockCar, Sportsmen stocks and Modified builder)
- Tilton Engineering, Inc, 114 Center St, El Segundo, CA 90245 (213) 322-1566 (SportsCar and GT builder)
- Tom Pistone Race Car, 7858 Old Concord Rd, Charlotte, NC 28213 (704) 596-7000 (Grand National StockCars and most circle track racecars)
- Van Diemen International, Chalk Rd., Snetterton, Norwich, England NR16 2JZ PH: 011-44-953-878195 (Formula Forward, First & 'Van Diemen' Formula Ford builder)
- VS Motorsports, 167 Carter Dr, Troy, MI 48098 (313) 332-4456 (Constructor of 'Star' Formula Vee)
- Womer Formula Vee, 4500 Maple Rd, Morningside, MD 20746 (301) 967-3635 (Constructor-dealer)
- Woody Gilmores Race Car Engineering, 12260 1/2 Woodruff, Downey, CA (213) 862-4112 (Drag frame builder)

Glossary

- ACCUS—Automobile Competition Committee of the United States. Branch of FIA. Overseer of US racing.
- Aerodynamics—The science relative to the effects produced by air over and around a body in motion.
- Air Foil—Aerodynamic device commonly called a 'wing' in racing to generate downforce for better traction. (especially in fast turns)
- Altered—A class and style of drag racer requiring the use of a stock autobody, but also permitting the extensive modifications to it.
- Apex—Inside radius of a turn at midpoint.
- Atmospheric—Slang for an engine which is neither super or turbocharged. An engine which has no extra air forced into it by outside means. This type of engine sucks in air created by the low pressure created from an open-valved, downward-stroking piston.
- Autocross—Solo racing. Drivers run against the clock on a twisting, self-made course usually setup on parking lots with rubber pylons as marking barriers.
- Baja—A class of racer in off-road that started out as a VW 'Bug', but is highly modified for racing.
- Bite—Amount of traction on a racetrack or ability of tires to keep from sliding on a surface.
- Blend—The specific mixture of fuel for use in racing. Race fuel may have a blend of nitromethane, methanol and/or alcohol or any combination thereof. Even street fuel has a specific blend, it just doesn't need to have all this extra "kick" that race engine like to have.
- Blown—Failure of an engine internally, sometimes tearing it apart and rendering it permanently damaged. This is also a slang term used by some for an engine which is super or turbocharged. Extra air is forced or "blown" into an engine to create additional power not supplied by an atmospheric engine of the same size.
- Blue Print—To completely rebuild an engine to extreme precision.
- Bore—The diameter or radius of an engine cylinder.
- Break Loose—Slang for the loss of tire traction.
- Break Out—A drag racing term for running a faster Elapsed Time than an individual racers Dialed-In time. Another way to be disqualified during an elimination series. (see "Dial-in" later in glossary)
- Camber—The sideway tilt of a wheel purposely engineered with respect to the vehicle, to enhance turning traction.
- Camshaft—A rotating shaft in an engine with lobes or Cams designed to lift or open valves. These (open) valves feed a combustion chamber fuel and air or allow the escape of spent fuel. An engine may have two camshafts over each bank of cylinders on any configured block. (DOHC-Duel or Double OverHead Cam)
- Can-Am—Canadian-American. A former racecar class coming back, but in a completely different style of chassis and engine.
- Cant Valve Engine—Term used in drag racing in which the engine (or head) valves are angled from the side to provide more room for a Hemi-piston.
- CC—Cubic Centimeters—How engine sizes are communicated in small race engines for piston-cylinder displacement. 1000 cc = one liter.
- Carburetor—A fuel vaporizing apparatus on an engines' induction system sitting atop the intake manifold. In simple terms, fuel in forced through a small hole or nozzle, called a jet, rendering the fuel out of its liquid state. (a fuels' vapor is what actually burns, not the liquid) Spray or aerosol cans, pump nozzles on various products like window cleaners, etc, work by this same principle.
- Chassis—(Pronounced Chassie) The basic frame and/or body of a vehicle minus the engine, drivetrain and suspension.
- Ci—Cubic inch—used in larger engine measurements. 61 Ci's = 1 liter
- Club Racing—Amateur racing. (term used especially in SCCA)
- Compound (tire)—The material used to contruct a tire, or in this case a racing slick. Race slicks are built to perform in a specific way according to their stickiness or bite. The chemical composition of rubber used in tires to determine their softness or hardness. This determines their ability to create adhesion on a road, temperature tolerance, reliability, handling characteristics, safety, etc.
- Compression Ratio—The degree of compression with the fuel/air mixture in the combustion chamber just before detonation by the spark plug. It is the sum of the cubic capacity and the cylinder head space with the piston at TDC. (Top Dead Center) Diesel engines have about a 20:1 compression ratio. Most, if not all racecar engines have less compression. Remember, the more compression created at the TDC of a piston in the combustion chamber, the more power it takes from the other pistons in that same engine to push it up to that point. Ultimately, the power

gained from high compression detonation is slightly and nonexponentially loss. It's sorta like an engine working against itself. (the compression created in a diesel engine is so intense, the heat created by that compression is what detonates the fuel; thus, spark plugs are not needed)

- Coupe—A closed two-door automobile with a body normally designed to be shorter than a sedan. (see "sedan" later on in glossary)

- Crankshaft—This is literally a crank located at the bottom of an engine which is connect to the piston-rods, converting their up and down movement to circular motion. This shaft then transfers that power to the drivetrain and wheels.

- CV joint(s)—Constant velocity joint(s)—Sometimes call a U-joint on a street automobile. These allow a twisting force, in this case a driveshaft, or halfshafts on a rear engine racecar, to be nonstatically angled for accomodating suspension movement between the drive wheels and transmission. (or transaxle on a rear powered racer)

- Dial-In ET—Elapsed Time a drag racer writes on their car with white shoe polish to establish what they feel their machine can run the quarter-mile in after time trials. This is designed to prevent sand-bagging. (holding back peak performance in order to gain an (unfair) advantage later) During bracket racing, if this time is exceeded, the competitor is eliminated, assuming their opponent didn't "break out" by a larger margin.

- Delay Box—Used in drag racing in a limited number of classes. These delay release of a transmission or driveshalf by thousandths of a second to prevent red-lighting at the staging or starting line by dragsters.

- Displacement (engine)—The combined internal size of an engine in CC's, Liters or CI's. The space taken up by an engines cylinders as relative to the stroke of each piston at its BDC. (bottom dead center)

- DOHC—Double OverHead Cam—These two camshafts operates the valves minus the push rods characteristic of the traditionally single and center-mounted cam. This creates slightly more power and better engine reliability.

- Door Slammer—Slang for a type of drag racing machine which must have fully and normally operational doors. (ultimately meaning many of these are usually street legal; this discourages too much aerodynamic body altering and therefore keeps costs in check)

- Double Seater—Slang for a wider cockpit racer such as a StockCar and most street-legal or purpose-built SportsCars and SportRacers.

- Drafting—The use of another vehicles aerodynamics to make cutting through the air easier. The allows the machine cutting through this tunnel of less wind resistance to gain a head of steam (momentum) to pass a racer in front. This works best with Stock and SportCar racers on high speed circuits.

- Dragster—A purpose-built vehicle in drag racing of non-mass production or street type. Sometimes a term used with 'Funny car' dragsters, even though they look production-made.

- Dynometer—A large expensive machine for accurately measuring an engines horsepower output.

- Elimination—A two by two pairing of drag racers that produce one winner at a time at the end of the quarter-mile. This is done in a tournament style eliminator series much like that of the NCAA basketball tournament until only winner is left at the end of an event. The racers are seeded according to their speeds. In a 16-car eliminator series, The 16th slowest racer is paired with the fastest one. The idea is to pair the best two qualifiers in the final run.

- Endurance Racing—Road or Off-Road races of any category or class lasting from usually 3 to 24 hours in length.

- ET—Elapsed Time—The time it takes to cover a pre-determined distance. Usually the quarter mile in drag racing, but sometimes an eighth mile

- F1—Abbreviation for Formula One

- FA—Formula Atlantic. (almost in the same class or level as an Indy Light racer)

- FC—Formula Continental—Almost an identical Formula Ford 2000, but slightly different chassis rules.

- Feedback—The forces felt by a driver at high speed or rough circumstances telling them how a vehicle behaves in high wind, in heavy traffic, and especially in turns.

- FF—Formula Ford—either 1600, an engine no larger then 1600 cc, or 2000, no larger than 2000 cc displacement. Sometimes written as F1600 & F2000, respectively. Also, FF2000 is sometimes called Super Ford.

- Formula—An open wheel, open cockpit and single seat road or oval racing machine built to specific rules for racing.

- Fuel Injection—A system where fuel is delivered more independently, directly and physically closer to each engine cylinder. This enhances engine performance compared to the carbureted system. This is because less fuel is wasted by condensation in fuel injection, unlike that of fuel vapor traveling from a carb to the cylinders. (only fuel vapors burn, not condensed (liguid) fuel)

- Full Floating Axle—A type of suspension which eliminates using a heavy axle like seen on most front engine racers, such as StockCars. This term applies mostly to drag racing. The vehicles rearend uses two halfshafts to power the rear wheels by the front engine drag car.

- Ground Effects—Creation of negative or low air pressure underneath a race vehicle to create downforce at high speed for better tire traction in turns. Simply put, this is accomplished by shaping the bottom floorpan of a racer as an upsidedown airplane wing. This, for the most part, can only be done on formula cars because their floorpans are smooth, even surfaces that are closer to the ground.

- Grand Prix—Formula One racing event. World class high-powered Formula cars. Some motorcycle events also. Sometimes used commercially to promote other racing events.

- GT—Grand Touring. Loosely used by the general public, but a specific type of racecar, some purpose-built, like GTP in IMSA, some modified from production cars. Also used in class category naming. (SCCA, GT-1, GT-2, etc) These racecars at least resemble in one way or another a street or production-looking automobile, whether they are purpose-built for racing or modified from a street-legal version for high speed competition.

- Head(s)—That part of an engine bolted directly on top of the piston-cylinders. This unit contains the valves, which are situated in the combustion chambers. One set of heads (as a one-piece unit) bolts over a bank of cylinders. (usually 4 cylinders, in the case of a V-8 configured engine)

- Hemi—A type of engine used in drag racing which uses dome shaped pistons. This puts the pistons up higher into the heads for greater cylinder pressure at sparkplug detonation, therefore more explosive burning and hense, more engine power.

- Horsepower—Engine power. (The force required to raise 33,000 pounds one foot in one minute is one horsepower)

- Hydroplaning—The racing slick on a high speed vehicle can literally roll on top of a thin film of moisture due to it lack of (deep) grooved treading to channel water away. This dramatically lessens tire contract with the asphalt or cement surface. Given enough water and speed, this can also take place on a good, well grooved tire on your street automobile. (you probably know this from the tire manufactorers advertising; these are not scare tactics, it can happen even with a very good rain tire if you get a bit crazy with your speed)

- Induction System—The units of an engine involved with collecting and mixing the fuel/air formula and delivering it to the cylinders for burning. If that mixture is pressure-enhanced beyond normal atmospheric barometers by a super or turbocharger unit, that unit is also considered to a part of the induction system. (in addition to the air cleaner housing unit, carburetor or fuel injectors, intake manifold and heads)

- IT—Improved Touring. Production-based automotive class in SCCA.

- Liter—Engine displacement measurement equal to 1000 cc's

- Loose—Subjective slang term used to describe oversteer at high speed while turning. Sometimes this is called "coming around". (the back wheels tendency to loose grip and throw themselves out and away from the inside of a turn)

- Marque Class—Classes usually prevalent in Vintage racing which are limited to a very specific year, make and/or model (and even-powered) machine. (obviously, a class had to be relatively popular back in its day to sustain a adequately numbered field for Vintage racing today)

- Methanol—A wood alcohol compound used in racing fuel blends.

- Midget—Open wheel, open and caged cockpit racer using a smaller and less lower slung chassis. Using a smaller engine. (Smaller version of a Sprint car)

- Minimum weight—What a race vehicle must weigh (at least) after a race, usually without the driver or any fluid (fuel) on board, to retain class requirements.

- Modified—A name used informally for a wide variety of race vehicles modified from production-based (street legal) automobiles to racecars. Also a specific class of racer having the use of more free, liberal or open set of rules. These usually appear as a fenderless or open-wheeled, low slung and very powerful stockcar. (actually all nonpurpose-built racecars are modified in the relative sense)

- Monocoque—A frameless chassis. The body and/or subframe combine strength to form one unit. This is also called a stress-skin construction type of vehicle. This also saves the use of materials required to build a (formula) racer with. Therefore, this lightens and strenthens it and makes it quicker.

- Multiclass Racing—More than one class racing at the same time on the same course. This is done mostly in amatear racing and in just about all endurance competition of any level. This helps cut down already long amateur events (which take a full weekend) and indirectly helps contain cost over the long haul in racing. (administrative costs) Matter-a-fact, there aren't too many events that are not multiclass races. About the only ones which are not is the high profile professional events like IndyCar, NASCAR and Formula One.

- National Classes—A class of SCCA amatear racing which compete for points towards the right to compete in a single weeklong race event in mid-october. This event, sort of the "Indy 500" for club or amatear racing, is the national championship for each of the 23—24 (SCCA) classes. This event, called the Valvoline RoadRacing Classic, used to be held at Road Atlanta, but is now held at the Mid-Ohio racecar course. (also, see Regional classes described later in this glossary)

- Nerf Bars—Metal bars used in certain types of racing to protect against incidental vehicle-body damage, but more importantly to prevent dangerous high speed wheel intanglement. These are usually seen on Sprint racers, Midgets, Modifieds and in some cases, Go-Karts and Late Model (shorttrack) Stockcars. (for body protection only)

- Nitro—Nitromethane—A compound/mix of nitroglycerin and wood alcohol used almost exclusively in a limited class of drag racer. (Top Fuelers and Funny Cars)

- Nomex—A brand name and specific material for a fire resistant fabric used in firesuits by racers.

- Normally Aspirated—An engine not turbo or supercharged. One that breaths normally through its induction or air intake system, like most passenger cars. A 'charged' engine has more air literally forced into it creating more power without using more fuel.

- Open (rules)—Rules or a lack thereof. Left to whatever a driver or race car owner feels best suited to their circumstance for the race machine. (also called "free" or "liberal")
- Open Wheel—No fenders or body work over the tires of a race machine.
- Oversteer—Same as Loose. (earlier in glossary)
- Planetary—A type of transmission with a clutch, but no gearing, which supplies a more direct power transfer to the axle and/or wheels. Used mostly in drag racing.
- Power-to-weight ratio—Difference of engine power to vehicle weight. This is how just about all classes of vehicles within a certain type or category of racing is determined. Category of racing is usually determined by style of vehicle, how long it races and on what type of terrain, in addition to weight ratios.
- Production—As it comes from the manufacturer for the general public for use on public roads. (A class in SCCA amateur racing. A smaller version of the Showroom-Stock class)
- Prototype—Specially built vehicle built from scratch, usually for high-speed racing, that does not need to fit any class rules. They are raced for experimental purposes to determine if they have a future in racing both in fan appeal and financial costs. (and sometimes solely for the "entertainment of the masses")
- Pump Fuel—An informal name used by the racing fraternity for street-legal fuel available to the general public for mass consumption.
- Purpose-Built—Built specifically for racing only.
- Purse—Prize money awarded at professional events according to mainly the finishing position. The other factor determining payout is whether one finished the race at all; fastest lap; pole position; most spots gained in position at the conclusion of the race and other small accomplishments. Contingency prizes are usually add-ons, separate from the main purse money, given to those racers who use and display specific company insignias on their machine and/or use their race products. (depending usually on how well they finish the event)
- Push Rod(s)—A set of hollow, oil carrying rods, usually two for each cylinder, depending on the engine and its size, located between a single-camshaft and all the valve tappets. These rods transfers the forces used to actuate the valves via the lobes located on the camshaft.
- Rain Tire—A specifically soft compound, treaded and/or grooved racing tire used in wet conditions on road or streetcoures only. (not on ovals, because the speeds are too high for even special raintires to be any good, gripwise)
- Reaction Time—The time it takes a drag racer to roll forward and unblock the staging beam, without fouling. A perfect reaction time is 1/2 second or 0.500 on a full christmas tree light system, after the first of a series of lights is illuminated. (all the lights,

usually 3, but sometimes 5, take a half second to light up starting from the top to bottom)

- Red Light—A foul in drag racing by leaving too early at the starting line. This disqualifies a competitor in an eliminator series, but not during the time trials, which then can be attempted again.
- Regional Classes—These are all the various classes and categories of amatear racing events which do not compete for points towards a national championship. National racing license holders may compete at the regional level, but regional license holder cannot race in national (sanctioned) events. Competitvely, there basically is no difference between these two types of license holders. National racer simply can afford the further travel and more money it takes to compete for a title. But they must race slightly more often to maintain that status. Regional licence holders do have championships offered in their regions. (all professional licenses require even more participation and maintenance)
- Roadcourse—Unlike an oval, a track incorporating left, right and/or uphill, downhill turns with or without long straights. (Paved or dirt)
- Roll Bar—A single loop, tubular steel structure used in Go-Karts, Formula cars and some open cockpit SportsCars to protect the drivers head from being crushed in the event of a flip or rollover.
- Roll Cage—A more complex structure designed to protect drivers in accidents. (and rollovers) Also adds strength to the chassis, especially stockcar type vehicles. Used in Midget and Sprint cars more for protecting the driver.
- Roll Out—A term used in drag racing based on whether a car is deep or shallow staged at the starting line. Depending on the drivers style, this can be an advantage or a disadvantage.
- RPM—Revolutions-Per-Minute—How fast an engine's crankshaft turns. (About the fastest are Enduro Go-Karts, some as fast as 16,000 RPM's. Maximum for IndyCars are about 14,500; but they're much bigger engines and due to the laws of physics, more likely to blow-up)
- S2000—Sports 2000 abbreviated. (SCCA class)
- Sedan—A type of closed cockpit or non-convertible auto having two or more doors with seats front and rear.
- Single Seater—Usually slang for a formula racecar. Single seaters are alway narrow bodied, purpose-built racers, which can also alude to Midgets, SprintCars, Go-Karts (even though they are not narrow in relation to their low profile chassis) and a few drag racing vehicles.
- Skirts—Formerly used on high-speed, low ground clearance racers such as Indy Cars and Formula One to enhance ground effects. These literally dragged lightly from the racecars sides and to the ground preventing fast moving air under the racer from bleeding out the sides. This create more air movement out the back of the race machines tub and therefore more negative (low) air pressure.

- **Slicks**—A type of racetire minus a grooved tread to channel away water and debris. The rubber is much thinner (to prevent heat buildup) and softer (a special compound rubber) which makes it very sticky on dry asphalt-concrete surfaces, but dangerous on wet surfaces and useless on dirt tracks. Racing slicks don't generally wear thin in shorter races, but rather, lose stickiness after use. (heat cycles) After so many heat cycles, (temperature running up and then cooling after use) the rubber becomes harder and therefore less sticky. This in turn, makes them wear off into those "marbles" seen on racecourses. On slower courses, these marbles are not such a detrimental factor to racecars like they are on high speed ovals. In longer races, such as IndyCar events, rubber will wear off, creating the so-called limited racing line in the deep corners of a high speed turn.

- **Spaceframe**—A chassis constructed of strong square, rectangular and/or round tubing at the bottom of a vehicle, which carries its load in compression. (Body can be separated from the frame, like most older model passenger vehicles and about all trucks) A Monocoque chassis carries loads in shear plane of its entire body/frame. (sort of a 'one-piece' design)

- **SPEC**—Short for Specification. This alludes to very specific regulations as applied to racing. SPEC racing rules are so tight, all racing parts or components must be made from the same kind of materials and, in many cases, by the same company or fabricator. No rules here are left to individual interpretation. The idea of SPEC-styled racing is to make the race vehicles of a particular class perfectly identical. This helps contain costs and puts the race back to the drivers. (and not the manufacturer)

- **Spoiler**—A smaller version of a wing; usually attached directly to the trailing edge of an automobile or stock race car to not necessarily produce downforce, although it definately does, but sometimes, rather, to prevent a low pressure area directly behind the rear windshield area of a stockcar from lightening or lifting it off the ground at high speed.

- **SportsCar**—An especially responsive street car. But in racing, it's an open or closed-cockpit, closed-wheel vehicle which is purpose built or modified for racing. These cockpits are wider than Formula car cockpits. (GT racers are SportsCars, not SportsRacers)

- **Sportsman**—A slower class of Stock Car racer, usually for beginners, allowing few changes to body style. Rules vary widely between different tracks/sanctioning bodies for this type of stock car. (Late Model StockCars are more sophisticated than Sportsmen Stocks)

- **SportsRacer**—Sometimes called SportRacer. (no 'S') A specific class of open-cockpit, closed wheel racecar, which is purpose-built for racing. Sports Cars are mass produced for the general public, then modified for racing. SportRacers are built from the ground up for racing. Racing and the general public uses sportscars terminology pretty loosely. (including myself)

- **Sprint Car**—An open cockpit, open wheeled racer built for short dirt or asphalt ovals. This is among the most powerful closed-course racer in the world. These are larger versions of the Midget racer and a smaller type of Dirt Championship race machine. Sprint cars are also considered among the most dangerous race machines in the world.

- **Staging**—The act of pulling a drag racing vehicle towards the starting line in preparation for a run. Not as simple as it looks due to the possibility of getting close to the line to gain an advantage, but yet fouling and/or red lighting in that process.

- **Stand Alone Race**—One race at one race event. No other support races. There are not very many of these kinds of races held. Not even in the high profile world of professional auto racing like F1, IndyCar and NASCAR. One of the very few "stand-alone" events is the Indianapolis 500, the 24 hours of Lemons and occasionally a NASCAR race.

- **Stock Block**—An engine block with or without the pistons, crank, rods, induction system, heads and pan as it comes from the manufacturer. (usually one not race oriented, but rather, more geared to mass production for the general public) This block cannot be altered in specific ways to gain illegal horsepower. Still, many things can be done to make it a bonified racing powerplant, but the idea is to keep the costs in check.

- **Stock**—Another pretty loosely used term by racing standards. StockCars are anything but stock. The word "Stock" means a quanity of goods kept on hand by a merchant (in this case, one of the Big Three auto makers in this country) for the supply to the auto-buying general public. StockCars hardly ever use unaltered stock products for their machines which are available to the public. Everything is furthur improved. StockCars should be called "HIGHLY-MACHINED-ALTERED-IMPROVED-TECHNOLOGICAL CARS" (. . . naaaaaaa, . . . takes too much time and effort)

- **Stock Silhouette**—Basically, slang used by some race personnel for a class of racer which requires in the rules a racing machine to at least resemble a specific automobile of any manufacturer which is also available to the auto buying public. Obviously, this is mostly possible in Stock & SportsCar classes.

- **Streetcourse**—The same idea as a roadcourse (left, right turns, sometimes even hills) except that it is located in the much more densely populate metropolitan area or cities. They are alway temporary courses set up specifically on city streets (such as Long Beach, Ca) and usually are always much tighter with less runoff space. (also very hard to see the whole course due to the buildings)

- **Stroke**—Two meanings. One is the up or down distance travel by a piston. This distance is effected by the rod length and size of the crankshaft. A longer stroke engine has more low-end (low rpm) horsepower needed for Drag racing and Sprint Cars.

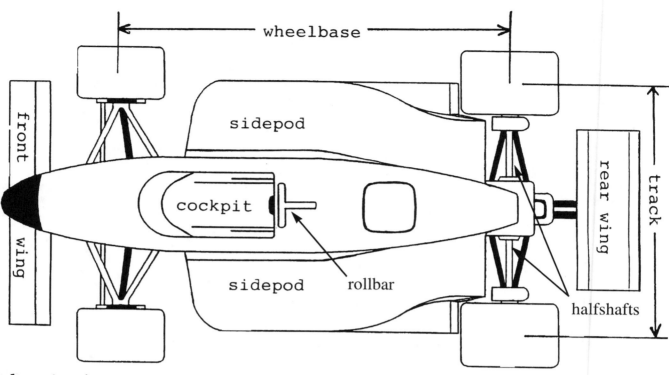

wheelbase

front wing

sidepod

cockpit

rollbar

sidepod

rear wing

track

halfshafts

Indy car top view

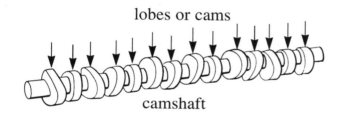

lobes or cams

camshaft

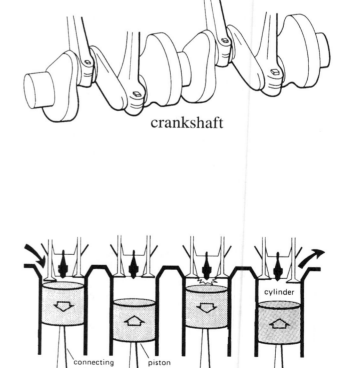

crankshaft

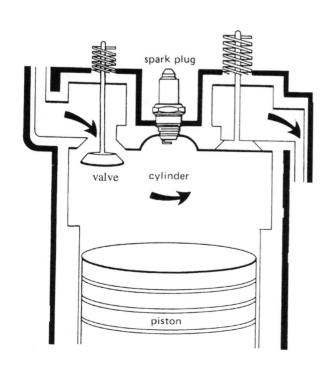

spark plug

valve   cylinder

piston

connecting rod   piston   cylinder

crankshaft

Short-stroke engines reach much higher rpms due to less centrifugal forces and the burning of shorter bursts of fuel. Meaning two; 2 and 4-stroke engines. Smaller 2 stroke engines fire everytime the piston is at TDC. (Top Dead Center) These are hotter and dirtier burning engines because not all spent fuel can be eliminated at each upward stroke of the piston. This also creates less opportunity for high compression in the combustion chamber. (with an open exhaust valve) That means these must be low compression engines since there is no fuel entering the chamber until the piston is completely at TDC or on it way down on the power stroke. 4-stroke engines have a separate cleaning or spent-fuel cycle. That means much more time and low back (or atmospheric) pressure is available for the entrance of the fuel/air mixture, which also can be compressed much greater for more explosive force on the pistons power stroke. That means these type of engines can be much more versatile in the area of (larger) sizes.

- Supercharger—An air pump powered by an engines crankshaft pulley to force more air to the cylinders than what would take place at normal atmospheric pressure. This produces more power. Superchargers produce this extra horsepower instantly, but drain some of the engines power in doing so. So superchargers are much more better for drag racing. (A turbocharger is an air pump powered by the engines 'spent' exhaust gases; see turbocharger later on in glossary) A 'screw' type supercharger is different than the standard type seen on most street cars and racers; it's shaped somewhat like a funnel to create greater pressure for some drag racers.

- Superspeedway—A high-banked, paved track of about a mile or longer. (Short tracks are 5/8 mile or less, and may be banked, flat and/or paved/dirt)

- Support race—one of a few or many races of various classes before the main race. (helps draw spectators in larger numbers)

- Suspension—The system of spring, linkages, shock absorbers, bars, etc, that support a vehicle off the ground and cushions it over various terrain. These are subject to hundreds, maybe thousands of designs on racing and street cars.

- Telemetry—A racecars' devices, usually enhanced by computers, to help a race team or individual determine precisely what the machine is doing or why it's doing something. (even though the driver knows literally by the seat of his/her pants that the racecar isn't performing at the top of its potential, especially when it comes to vehicle handling in high speed turns)

- Track (Tread distance)—The distance between two tires on the same axle (or end of a vehicle) measured from the inside, outside or middle of the tires. This is an important measurement in determining classes and category of race machines. The wider the wheels on one axle or plane are, the better stability and cornering maneauverability a racer has.

- Tire Compound—The chemical composition of rubber that goes to build a tire. (determines its softness or hardness, which determines its adhesion on the road, temperature tolerance, life, handling characteristics, safety, etc.)

- Torque—The twisting force that produces rotation in a metal rod, or for purposes of this book, in an internal combustion engine, at the crankshaft. (via the downward movement of the pistons through their individual cylinders which are attached to the crankshaft by connecting rods)

- Turbocharger—An air pump powered by the powerful thrust of the spent exhaust fumes exiting the heads, which in turn uses that otherwise wasted power sourse to inject extra air into the engines induction system for more horsepower. Unlike the Supercharger, this does not drain any horsepower from the engine to achieve this. On the negative side, the engine needs to reach a certain RPM to create that exhaust thrust to power the turbo. That means turbos will kick in and go to work at RPM's well above idle speed, depending on the type and size of the block.

- Understeer—A condition opposite of loose. A driver feels lack of turning force or responsiveness in a turn at high speed. Car feels like it wants to go straight when turning. (also called "pushing")

- Unibody—Simular to the stress-skin or monocoque construction style. Term used more in nonracing applications. (such as the style of currently contructed production vehicles that use the car body as well as a partial subframe to support the entire automobile)

- Wedge—A type of drag racing engine incorporating a wedged-shaped cylinder-piston setup. This allows for longer valve actuations and therefore more fuel-air entry, resulting in greater power.

- Weight distribution—The difference between the weight on the front set of wheels and the weight on the back set of a 4-wheel racer. (also effects how motorcycles handle. This greatly effects how a race vehicle handles, especially in the curves.

- Wheelbase—A measurement of vehicle size from the center of the wheel hubs in the front portion of the vehicle to the center of the wheels or wheelhubs in the back portion. This is a large determining factor in classing specific race machines. The longer a vehicle is between its front and rear set of wheels, the more stable it is, therefore it is usually able to out maneuver a shorter wheelbased racecar.

- Wing—(See Air Foil)

Index